THE INDIVIDUAL IN THE ECONOMY

THE INDIVIDUAL IN THE ECONOMY

A Textbook of Economic Psychology

STEPHEN E. G. LEA
University of Exeter

ROGER M. TARPY
Bucknell University

PAUL WEBLEY
University of Exeter

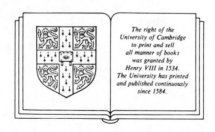

The right of the
University of Cambridge
to print and sell
all manner of books
was granted by
Henry VIII in 1534.
The University has printed
and published continuously
since 1584.

CAMBRIDGE UNIVERSITY PRESS
Cambridge
London   New York   New Rochelle
Melbourne   Sydney

Published by the Press Syndicate of the University of Cambridge
The Pitt Building, Trumpington Street, Cambridge CB2 1RP
32 East 57th Street, New York, NY 10022, USA
10 Stamford Road, Oakleigh, Melbourne 3166, Australia

First published 1987

Printed in the United States of America

Library of Congress Cataloging-in-Publication Data
Lea, S. E. G., 1946–
The individual in the economy.
1. Economics–Psychological aspects. 2. Psychology.
I. Tarpy, Roger M., 1941–   . II. Webley, Paul.
III. Title.
HB74.P8L42 1987 330'.01'9 86-8267

British Library Cataloguing in Publication Data
Lea, Stephen E. G.
The individual in the economy.
1. Economics–Psychological aspects
I. Title II. Tarpy, Roger M.
III. Webley, Paul
330'.01'9 HB74.P8

ISBN 0 521 26872 9 (hard covers)
ISBN 0 521 31701 0 (paperback)

TO OUR CHILDREN –
An account of what we do

CONTENTS

PREFACE

The institutions of education – universities, libraries, learned societies – divide knowledge into convenient packages. This is anatomy; here is physiology; that is chemistry. Sometimes these divisions correspond to real distinctions in the world. Sometimes, however, they do not.

Usually, these institutional divisions do not matter very much. Two academic disciplines may merge and are recognized to do so; the same individual can operate as a zoologically oriented psychologist, among other psychologists, or as a psychologically oriented zoologist, among other zoologists. If an institutional gap is too large, a new discipline may grow up within it. Thus, we have biochemistry between chemistry and biology, or social psychology between sociology and psychology.

In the worst case, however, our institutional divisions may actually create gaps in our knowledge that do not correspond to anything outside ourselves. This book is written in the belief that precisely this kind of artificial divide exists between the academic disciplines of psychology and economics. Economics and psychology both claim to study human behavior, but each rejects the idea that the other could have any insights to offer to it. The present authors, however, do not believe that people cease to be people when they go out to work or to shop, nor do we believe that economic causes have only economic effects on behavior. It should be possible to apply psychological knowledge to understand people's economic behavior, and it should be possible to apply economic knowledge to understand how the economy affects each individual. Those two kinds of understanding are the proper subject matter of economic psychology.

The idea of economic psychology as an interdisciplinary effort is not new; it goes back, at least, to the French social psychologist Gabriel Tarde (1902). Its intellectual roots, however, lie even deeper, in the time when both economics and psychology were studied chiefly by philosophers who moved without hesitation from one sphere of discourse to the other. Even though Tarde was the first to write a book called *Economic Psychology*, he is not the last; a sporadic interest in the joint study of the two disciplines has continued throughout this century. Why, then, has it failed to develop more fully when so many other interdisciplinary areas have flourished?

We believe that the answer lies in the ideology of both psychology and economics. In Western Europe and America, at least, theoretical economics of the twentieth century has had to rid itself of an inappropriate psychology of choice and work toward a highly refined concept of rational behavior. Psychology, on the other hand, in almost all its many schools, has stressed the a-rational determinants of behavior and the limitations of rationality. The stage has been set for headlong collision whenever psychologists and economists have come into contact. Psychologists approaching economics have done so with the idea that they could tell economists how to conduct their own business, indeed, with an attitude of "disciplinary imperialism"; psychology was to provide a new, assured foundation for economic theory. And in recent years, economists seem to have been learning how to carry a similar campaign into the psychological camp.

The time has surely come to try a different approach. This book is not intended to use psychology to reform economics or economics to reform psychology. Rather, our aim is to find what each discipline can contribute to the joint study of problems to which they are both relevant.

What, then, is economic psychology? We do not believe that a person who studies a problem that has both an economic and a psychological dimension is necessarily an economic psychologist. Such a definition would include almost everyone in both disciplines. Nor do we hold that to be an economic psychologist one must be fully expert in both disciplines (or even that you must call yourself an economic psychologist). This definition would leave hardly anyone in the field. An economic psychologist, we believe, is anyone who recognizes that the problem he or she is studying is both an economic and a psychological problem and is prepared to use both economic and psychological methods to investigate it. Economic psychology is the body of knowledge that results from such interdisciplinary investigation. It is economic psychology in this sense, which it tries to report. We hope that many of our readers will discover that they have been economic psychologists for years without realizing it.

The contents of this book reflect our idea of what economic psychology should be. We have tried to cover as many of the areas of academic and applied study to which we can see clear economic and psychological approaches. The one major omission is what might be called "business psychology," that is, the study of human behavior within organizations, and the study of the psychology of financial markets. This omission reflects, perhaps, some bias toward an interest in the ordinary individual living within the economy. Our relative neglect of organizational psychology, however, also results from the fact that it is already a well-organized subdiscipline with an extensive literature of its own.

The structure of the book embodies our view of the way economic psychology should be approached. It is divided into four parts. Part I consists of essential preliminary material. Because we assume that our readers will come to economic psychology from many different directions, we have tried to provide a common foundation of ideas and research methods from both disciplines, and to use these in the rest of the book. The first part also examines, in depth, the key concept of rationality, which is what economics and psychology seem to have in common, and what has most often in the past kept them apart.

Part II contains an examination, from both an economic and a psychological standpoint, of a series of important economic behaviors of individuals. These are work, buying, saving, giving, and gambling. They are chosen partly because of their practical, economic importance, but also because they each pose distinct theoretical questions in both disciplines. The basic idea behind this part of the book is that the behavior of individuals helps determine the behavior of the economy as a whole and that we should therefore make the maximum effort to understand why individuals act as they do in important economic situations.

Part III presents the opposite premise. Here, the ruling idea is that the kind of economy an individual lives in can have an important effect on his or her behavior. This part is less homogeneous in content. Two chapters look at properties of the economy – taxation and money – from a psychological perspective. One considers an economic process, advertising, which is specifically intended to affect individuals. One looks at how children become socialized into life within our modern economy. The remainder examine the psychological effects of certain specialized economic situations, that is, the so-called "primitive" economies of cultures distinct from our own, the economy of depression or expansion in advanced nations and of rapid development in less industrialized ones, and the artificial "token economies" which have been created by psychologists with the aim of changing behavior in clinical or educational settings.

Finally, Part IV considers where this interdisciplinary study has led us. The three chapters can, in a sense, be seen as our conclusions for psychologists, for economists, and for economic psychologists, but we hope that all our readers will be interested by them. We hope that they show that economic psychology can now make progress and can produce results that will be of interest to the wider disciplines from which it springs.

We believe that economic psychology is an idea whose time has come. The last few years have seen the foundation of at least two learned societies and two learned journals devoted to it, indicating that the hallmarks of academic respectability are undoubtedly being conferred. More important is the increasing flow of new ideas into the field, as economists and psychologists from different parts of their own disciplines recognize that they may have something to learn from, and to contribute to, an interdisciplinary approach.

We are well aware that this book will be found to be uneven. All three of us are psychologists by training, and though we have had to learn a great deal of economics to write the book (and have had a good deal of help from friendly economists), we are well aware that economic howlers will remain. Because so few researchers see themselves as economic psychologists, we have had to draw on materials that are highly specialized even within psychology or economics. In trying to make them accessible to an interdisciplinary audience, it would be miraculous if we had not introduced the occasional distortion. And just because economic psychology is reaching the point of takeoff, we have been painfully aware of new ideas being created all around us.

The book has been written partly in England and partly in America and is a truly collaborative effort (the order of authors is alphabetical). We believe that this is one of its strengths. Economic psychology is much better developed in Europe than in America, while other, related disciplines such as consumer science are essentially American institutions. We hope that both European and American readers will be happy to move freely, as we have done, between examples from two continents. At the present stage of its development, economic psychology needs to develop general ideas, and we hope that the international nature of its writing will help this book to escape from the blinders that may be imposed by a single kind of economy. That escape is only relative, of course; readers from Eastern Europe, Japan, or the less industrialized nations will recognize how little we know about the psychology of their rather different economic systems.

Economics is inevitably linked to economic policy, and the writing of this book has brought us rather closer to political issues than most psychologists allow themselves to go. We should make clear that we are not advocating any particular political line, if only because the three of us do not have an agreed political position. On the other hand, we have not drawn back from making points simply because they might bear a political interpretation. Some readers may find the result left of center, particularly in America, since the center of gravity of political thought and the range of political ideas in current use are farther to the left in Europe than in the United States. From other perspectives, particularly European ones, the book may well appear unduly cautious politically, but we hope that it will at least be free of that bias toward right-wing ideas and managerial interests which forms an offensive backdrop to much writing in economics and consumer science.

It may be odd for authors to look forward to their book's being out of date. But if this book succeeds (or, rather, if the process of which it is part succeeds), we hope that, in relatively few years, *The Individual in the Economy* will seem impossibly dated. If economic psychology develops as we believe it now can, there should be so many new ideas in the next decade that much of what we now report will be irrelevant. It should also seem impossible that psychologists and economists should have been so ignorant of each other's concerns as, for all our own interdisciplinary goodwill, we shall have to reveal them to be.

But a necessary part of that process is staking out the ground on which an interdisciplinary study can be built. That is the purpose of this book. Economists and psychologists will find different faults in it, but we hope that this process will help both to see that they do, in spite of history, indeed have common ground.

ACKNOWLEDGMENTS

This book started life in 1982, when the three of us were jointly teaching the economic psychology option course at the University of Exeter. Its first drafts were produced, week by week, as reading for that group of students. We owe a great deal to them and to subsequent classes at both Exeter and Bucknell, who have used, discussed, and criticized successive drafts, sometimes in a very questionable state. They have improved not only our presentation of the material but also the material itself, often by their questions and, not uncommonly, by their own reading and background knowledge. Our first thanks are due to them. We hope they have had as much pleasure following our courses as we have teaching them.

Many colleagues and graduate students have also helped us greatly by reading and criticizing drafts. Particular thanks are due to Edmund Barke, Gonul Hussein, Jon May, Heather Perry, Henry Robben, Jean E. Roberts, and Peter Kresl. Without them, there would be many more errors, omissions, and unclarities than there now are; they are not to be blamed, however, for those that remain.

The secretarial staff in the Exeter Psychology Department, particularly Joan Fitzhenry and Chris Enefer, typed many of the early drafts at tremendous speed, and then witnessed us redoing (and in some cases undoing) their good work as the age of the word processor dawned on our offices. We are very grateful to them for their patience and encouragement, as we are to our colleagues who endured our systematic piracy of departmental computers for other ends.

We would like to thank the members of the Cambridge University Press staff for their expert and gracious help, particularly Louise Calabro Gruendel, Rhona Johnson, and Deslie Lawrence.

Finally, we owe a very considerable debt to Susan Milmoe of Cambridge University Press. She has consistently believed in this book and in our ability to produce it, sometimes despite the evidence, and she has provided the delicate mixture of patience and prodding needed to turn it into a reality.

I

THE ESSENTIAL BACKGROUND

"The thing that most alarms me," wrote Freud when his interests in clinical neurology began to bring him patients whose problems were neurotic rather than neurological, "is the amount of psychology I shall have to learn." Economists approaching economic psychology are likely to sympathize, and psychologists are likely to feel the same about economics. It would be relatively easy to write about economic behavior for psychologists or about the psychological foundations of economics for economists. It is not our intention to do either. This book presents economic psychology as an interdisciplinary enterprise, of interest to economists, to psychologists, and to many others, such as marketing specialists and consumer scientists, who would not readily accept either label.

Part I establishes a background that will enable readers, no matter what direction they start from, to follow the information and argument of the remainder of the book. This background material falls into two divisions.

First, we have to cope with the obvious fact that both economics and psychology are mature academic disciplines that have well-established methods of enquiry and distinct modes of thought. This book would become impossibly congested if we were unable to refer to their results without explaining them at every step. The first three chapters introduce psychology to readers with a more economics-based education (Chapter 1), and economics to those with a more psychological education (Chapters 2 and 3). Economics receives two chapters to psychology's one because, in order to reflect the structure of the rest of the book, we have accepted the conventional economic distinction between microeconomic and macroeconomic issues – questions about the behavior of individual economic agents and about the economy as a whole.

These three introductory chapters do not attempt the ridiculous task of condensing whole text books into single chapters. What we want to do is to give the reader a feeling for the way psychologists and economists go about their business. Although we do introduce some specific ideas that will be used extensively later in the book, each discussion stands by itself, without constant reference back to the introduction. If those of our readers who are economists feel, after reading Chapter 1, that psychology is no longer an unknown and incomprehensible language but one they can pick up as they go along, our introduction will have done its work.

Psychologists may well prefer to pass over Chapter 1, and economists may choose to pass over Chapters 2 and 3. Alternatively, experts in either field may wish to see what positions we are taking up on the many controversial questions they pose. They will find that, so far as possible, we take an eclectic line. We cannot know in advance what kind of psychology will be fruitful when applied to economic behavior. Like any new field, in fact, economic psychology is a potential test case for ideas in both economics and psychology.

Chapter 4 is an introduction of a different sort, concentrating on the methods available for use in economic psychology. The chief evidence that a method is available is the fact that someone has used it. In effect, this chapter is an introductory survey of economic psychology, reviewing the limited range of work done by people who already think of themselves as economic psychologists.

Chapter 5 is yet a different type of introduction, explaining the shape given to the rest of the book. To date, discussion of psychology by economists and of economics by psychologists has generally centered around the key "assumption of rationality" in economic theory. The fundamental axioms of economic theory are statements about the behavior of individuals when confronted with a choice, and it seems obvious to many psychologists that they are inaccurate. In Chapter 5 we attempt to lay this rationality question to rest, if not once and for all, at least for the rest of this book. We give it a fair airing and discuss how it might be resolved. We also show that it cannot be resolved at present and argue that its dominance represents a major obstacle to the progress of economic psychology. This clears the way for the approach we take in the rest of the book, which is to examine how individuals affect the economy and how the economy affects individuals.

INTRODUCTION TO PSYCHOLOGY

Economic psychology is a new field of study, which is emerging at the junction of two well-established academic disciplines. The task of reading about such a topic poses certain problems. For one thing, it would appear that the reader must possess a thorough knowledge of both fields – economics and psychology – before starting. After all, how could a "synthesis" of the two fields be appreciated if knowledge of either is lacking? Fortunately, this is an unrealistic and unnecessary claim. Although some knowledge is essential, the range of relevant concepts from each field is relatively limited. The initial task for the reader is to review those major themes and developments that have been used in the field of economic psychology so that the interplay between the disciplines can be appreciated.

Accordingly, this chapter on psychology and Chapters 2 and 3 on economics are not surveys of their representative fields; they are not introductory textbooks condensed into twenty or thirty pages. Rather, these first three chapters attempt to review a few selected areas of research that bear most directly on the study of economic psychology. Before discussing these topics in detail, however, let us first consider the broader picture, that is, the overall scope of psychological research. This exercise will help us "locate" more easily the special topics that are most relevant to this book.

Most psychologists primarily study behavior, either for its own sake or as a means of inferring the nature of underlying psychological states. But the specific types of behavior studied can vary greatly. Consider these topics: memory for prose, the effects on hunger of drugs injected directly into a rat's brain, the feeding strategies of a spider, the reaction of schizophrenic patients to inkblot pictures, the discrimination between two slightly different tones, the aggression of children after seeing cartoons on television, the behavior of commuters on urban subway trains, the imagery of writers and artists who have undergone a traumatic experience, the size of a food pellet and how it influences the rate at which a laboratory rat will press a lever, the measurement of social moods during national elections, the relationship between expressed attitude and overt behavior, and the effect of experimentally altered areas of a cat's brain on its sexual drive. These examples illustrate the astonishing diversity within the field of psychology. The discipline uses techniques and draws ideas from both microbiology and genetics on the one hand and from sociology and philosophy. Topics range in scale from the reaction of nerve cells to chemical stimulation, to the reaction of whole societies to international conflict, to the meaning of the term *consciousness*.

It is remarkable that scientists whose interests are as diverse as those expressed above should all consider themselves to be in the same discipline. But what unifies much of psychology is generally a shared interest in the study of behavior. There is a strong belief by psychologists at every level that the laws governing behavior are orderly and knowable. That different systems may share in a common set of laws is also an enticing possibility.

Let us be somewhat more specific about the various areas of interest in psychology. If you were to look in the table of contents of most introductory textbooks you would probably discover certain common topics. On one side of psychology are the "biological" areas: physiological psychology, animal learning, and animal behavior. Closer to the "middle" of the discipline would be chapters on human experimental psychology: perception, sensation, human learning, cognitive and attentional processes, and language. A third distinct area would encompass developmental and social psychology. A fourth general area of psychology would be personality and abnormal psychology, including the more practical areas of clinical and community psychology.

Two things should be emphasized. First, the boundaries between these general areas of psychology are not rigid. For example, it is as appropriate for a physiological psychologist to study memory in infants as it would be for a child or developmental psychologist. The techniques, of course, and the type of subject would differ considerably between the two. Second, within a given area of psychology, considerable diversity of techniques are used. For instance, a social psychologist might employ a large-scale survey questionnaire or simply observe the interaction between two individuals on closed-circuit television. Similarly, a cognitive psychologist might use a computer to investigate short-term memory or count the number of adjectives that a person recalls from a passage of prose. In summary, psychology not only covers a broad range of topics, all dealing in some fashion with behavior, but it also has a broad range of methodological approaches within each topic.

What areas in psychology bear most directly on the new topic of economic psychology? All are important to some degree: our personality may be crucial to our economic behavior, our motivation or previous learning may affect how we spend or save, our social context may determine the extent to which we gamble or give, our cognitions and perceptions may influence our susceptibility to advertising, and our biological and genetic state may influence our spending priorities. But not all areas are equally important, and so we have chosen to highlight three in this brief introduction: social psychology, learning and cognition, and the theory of human motivation and personality. Even within those fields, we can only give a highly selective account.

Our selection of these areas reflects our belief about what economic psychology involves. First, we recognize that the economy is a social creation, and that economic behavior, no matter how impersonal it may seem, is always a form of social behavior. Second, we believe that much of economic behavior will be habitual rather than carefully planned, so that we shall need an understanding of how people acquire habits and what the consequences are when they do so. Finally, we agree with Maital (1982) that economic psychology must tackle the "why" questions about economic behavior: Why do people buy what they do, and work at the job they do work at, save, give, or gamble. Because these are questions about motivation, we must call on motivation theory to answer them.

SOCIAL PSYCHOLOGY

Social psychological interpretations of economic behavior will be found throughout this book. For instance, in explaining gift giving, the concepts of norms and social conventions are useful; if we consider bandwagon effects, where people want to buy whatever is being widely bought, we can see that social comparison theories may provide a useful framework.

Clearly, we cannot deal with all the relevant social psychology in this text. Instead, we shall focus on three social psychological concepts that have a broad field of application: attitudes, people's explanations of their own behavior, and the comparisons they make between themselves and other people.

Attitudes and their measurement

Like so many terms in psychology, attitude is a word commonly used in everyday speech, and we all think we have a sense of what it means. It has been surprisingly difficult, however, to devise an adequate formal definition of the term. Many have been proposed (D.T. Campbell 1963), but none is universally approved. A consistent notion running through most of these definitions is that an attitude is a persistent disposition to regard certain objects either favorably or unfavorably. Presumably, if attitudes cause expressive behavior in any direct way (the evidence suggests that they do but only in a limited sense), the implication of this definition is that the "disposition to regard" an object will lead either to a behavioral approach toward or to withdrawal from the object. If this is true, attitudes must lie at the heart of human social and economic behavior. That is, overt behavior involving economic consequences, such as saving, giving, gambling, or buying, must ultimately depend on the person's "disposition to regard" those activities, or objects relevant to those activities, as favorable or unfavorable.

The above definition of attitude is limited to affective or emotional dispositions toward objects. There are other dispositions, however. For instance, attitude is often contrasted with belief. The former is an emotional disposition (to regard an object favorably or unfavorably), while the latter is a cognitive disposition (a thought or association that relates an object to its characteristics). A person might hold the belief that universities are seats of culture and, as a result, have a favorable attitude toward them (assuming that the person values culture). Attitude, then, is a global judgment about the object that normally corresponds to the collective beliefs, the sum of positive and negative bits of information, about the object (see N.H. Anderson 1980).

One of the first, and certainly most important, contributions to the study of attitudes was made by Thurstone (1928), who boldly claimed that "attitudes can be measured" (see Dawes 1972, for a review of attitude measurement). Thurstone's (1931a) method involved devising statements pertaining to an attitude object and then having them rated by a panel of judges on a scale of 1 to 11 (from most unfavorable to most favorable). In the second phase, the twenty-five or so items about which there was most agreement among the judges were selected; the experimenter gave these items to subjects who were asked to indicate which statements they endorsed. The attitude score of the person was based on which items were endorsed. For example, if a person was very favorably disposed toward the attitude object, the mean score, that is, the average scale number, would be high. By contrast, if a person was unfavorably disposed, that person would generally endorse only those statements that had been judged to represent an unfavorable attitude and therefore had been assigned a low scale number.

Thurstone's contribution was a substantial breakthrough in the study of attitudes, but other useful contributions were quick to follow. Likert (1932), for example, suggested a refinement that has proved more popular right up to the present time. Likert scales are used extensively in consumer research and are therefore of great interest to the economic psychologist.

In this procedure, subjects are given a large number of statements regarding an attitude object and are asked to express their agreement with each statement on a 5-point scale: strongly disagree (-2), disagree (-1), undecided (0), agree ($+1$), and strongly agree ($+2$). Correlation coefficients between items are then computed. Only those items that correlate strongly with each other are later selected for presentation to a second group of subjects. Attitude measurement using Likert scales is more precise because the items endorsed by the subjects are scaled in terms of how much they deviate from the "undecided" category. The higher the positive score, the more agreement with, or approval of, the attitude object; the lower the negative number, the more disagreement.

Another very popular way of assessing attitudes is the semantic differential technique suggested by Osgood, Suci, and Tannenbaum (1957). Attitude objects are presented and the subject is asked to rate them on a 1 to 9 scale according to a number of bipolar dimensions: warm–cold, good–bad, strong–weak, and so forth. From these ratings it is possible to assess how favorably disposed the subject is toward the object.

One of the problems with all these techniques is that they may influence how a subject responds. For example, the experimental situation may encourage subjects to answer in a socially desirable way that is inconsistent with their true attitudes. To counteract this problem, indirect methods for attitude assessment have been devised. For instance, Wrightsman (1969) measured attitudes about law and order by observing whether an automobile displayed a sticker endorsing one of the three major U.S. presidential candidates in the 1968 election, each of whom had taken up a different position on the need for tougher law-and-order measures. (It is interesting to note that the cars showing endorsement of the most adamant law-and-order candidate, George Wallace, were those least likely to be displaying the new tax sticker required by state law.) In another study, Milgram, Mann, and Horter (1965) used the technique of "dropping" stamped addressed envelopes in the community. Envelopes with fictitious organizations printed on them, such as "Citizens against gun control," if returned through the mail, were presumed to be from citizens who held a favorable attitude toward the apparent aims of the organization. Unsympathetic citizens would be more likely to ignore the letter, rather than take the time to put it into a mailbox. On the average, then, the more favorable the attitude toward the addressee, the more likely the envelopes would be mailed by their finders.

Other indirect techniques use physiological measurements to assess the attitude toward an object. For example, the pupils of the eye tend to dilate when an observer is looking at something of interest (Atwood & Howell 1971; E.H. Hess, Seltzer, & Shlien 1965; but see Woodmansec 1970). Similarly, Cooper and Pollock (1959) showed that changes in the electrical resistance of the skin – the galvanic skin response (GSR) – vary systematically with the subject's reaction to an attitude object.

Attitudes and behavior

Perhaps the most important issue of all is whether there really is a relationship between a person's attitudes and expressive behavior. The basic assumption has always been that we act in accordance with our attitudes;

our choices at the voting booth, the products we buy, our proclivity to spend or save, indeed all our behaviors are presumed to be determined by some larger internalized disposition labeled attitude. Unless this assumption is true, it is not clear that attitudes (or, perhaps, any other kind of psychological data) have much to contribute to our understanding of economic behavior.

Surprisingly, attitudes and behavior are not always clearly related (see Wicker 1969). The first demonstration of this was by LaPiere (1934), who traveled with two Chinese companions across the United States over a period of two years, staying at 66 hotels and eating in 184 restaurants. Six months later, these same establishments were sent a questionnaire asking whether they would accept Chinese customers. Although LaPiere and his companions had been refused service only once during the actual trip, 92% of respondents claimed that they would not serve Chinese people; the remainder of the establishments said that it would "depend on the circumstances." A similar dissociation between attitudes and behavior has been found for other attitude objects such as prejudice toward blacks (Kutner, Wilkins, & Yarrow 1952) although results have not always been as extreme as in LaPiere's study (see DeFleur & Westie 1958). These and other reports led Wicker (1969) to conclude that behavior is seldom related to attitude, the average correlation coefficient being around .15 across studies.

Recent efforts to resolve this crucial issue have revealed a more positive picture. First, it has been shown that attitudes accurately predict behavior if the experimenter is careful to use multiple behavior measures (Fishbein & Ajzen 1972); there is far less chance of showing a relationship between attitudes and behavior if only a single behavioral index is used. Second, the attitudes and behavior must be at the same level of generality if a relationship is to be found (Ajzen & Fishbein 1977). Very general attitudes, such as "I do not favor nuclear energy," are usually poor predictors of very specific behavioral acts, such as signing a petition against the construction of a nuclear power station. It would be more appropriate, in terms of demonstrating a correspondence between attitude and action, to assess specific attitudes such as "I favor signing petitions against nuclear power" rather than the general ones. When attitudes and behavior are matched in terms of specificity, the relationship between them becomes more apparent: General attitudes can predict broad behavioral measures (e.g., Weigel & Newman 1976), and specific attitudes are highly correlated with specific behavioral acts (e.g., Ajzen & Fishbein 1973; Fishbein & Coombs 1974; Weigel, Vernon, & Tognacci 1974).

Our improved understanding of the theory behind attitude-behavior congruence has had important practical consequences in recent years. Modern political polling techniques have achieved an impressive level of accuracy. Part of the explanation is that most attitude questionnaires now seek to measure specific dispositions that will predict specific behaviors, such as which candidate a person will vote for. In the economic environment, too, marketing specialists have also begun to assess specific attitudes in an effort to predict future purchasing behavior.

We should be somewhat cautious, however, in claiming that attitudes and behavior are highly consistent. Although positive, the correlation between them is nevertheless far from perfect. Obviously a great many other factors beside attitudes influence behavior (Wicker 1969). These include personal factors, such as competing motives or attitudes, verbal-intellectual skills, social abilities, or other personality factors (e.g., Norman 1975). In addition, there will be important situational factors, such as the presence of people, normative prescriptions for proper behavior, alternative behaviors available, or other extraneous events (see Jaspers 1978).

Attitude formation

No one supposes that attitudes are innate. Attitudes must be formed, and having been formed they can be changed. Obviously attitude formation and attitude change are closely related processes, but they have attracted rather different bodies of theory: Attitude formation is usually discussed in terms of learning models, while attitude change is most often considered a process of persuasion.

The first general category of theories suggests that all attitudes are learned according to simple and conventional learning paradigms. Three such paradigms are usually cited: classical conditioning, instrumental conditioning, and modeling. Although all three are discussed in greater detail later in this chapter, let us introduce them briefly here for the purpose of discussing attitude formation.

Classical conditioning deals with the acquisition of meaning by a stimulus. Normally innocuous signals associated with more powerful or meaningful stimuli acquire the ability to elicit a "conditioned reaction" similar in character to the reactions elicited originally by the powerful stimuli. Thus, according to a classical conditioning theory, attitudes are formed toward stimuli as a function of the pleasantness or unpleasantness of the environment in which the attitude objects are experienced. It is certainly easy to establish attitudes toward various innocuous stimuli in the laboratory by pairing them with pleasant or unpleasant consequences (e.g., Staats & Staats 1958); no doubt the process works in real life as well.

According to an instrumental conditioning paradigm, attitudes develop when their expression or rehearsal is followed by a rewarding state of affairs (see Hovland et al. 1953). For example, we may have learned our attitudes toward saving, money, giving, or work because expression of these attitudes was reinforced by the approval and affection of our parents, friends, or teachers.

Finally, attitude formation may be viewed as a social learning process (see Bandura 1972); that is, our attitudes are formed as a result or our imitating the behavior that is "modeled" by others. We may adopt particular attitudes because we have witnessed others expressing or behaving in accordance with those attitudes, especially if we perceive those others to obtain rewards as a result.

All three theories of attitude formation rely on fairly simple, basic learning processes. As we shall see, however, the movement in the modern psychology of learning has been toward more elaborate views of learning and cognition, based on ideas about information-processing systems. This approach has also given rise to a theory of attitude formation (see N.H. Anderson 1971, 1980; Fishbein & Ajzen 1975; W.J. McGuire 1972; Wyer 1974). Like the earlier learning theories, the information-processing approach suggests that discrete experiences of a pleasant or unpleasant nature with an attitude object are fundamental to attitude formation. The information-processing approach differs, however, in emphasizing that many such experiences are integrated or combined to produce a single attitude; that is, a person develops an overall impression or reaction to an attitude object by averaging over, or processing, a number of separate experiences with that object.

The averaging process can be quite complex, necessitating relatively sophisticated explanatory models. One formulation was proposed by Fishbein and Ajzen (1975). The investigators claim that attitudes reflect two sorts of judgments. First, there is an expectancy that the attitude object in fact possesses the attributes it is claimed to have. Second, they assert that an affective value is attached by the person to the object–attribute relationship. The ultimate or overall attitude, then, is a weighted sum of the expectancy times the affective value judgments ($E \times V$).

Let us illustrate this EV model by applying it to gambling behavior. Assume that gambling has three potential attributes. It could (1) be expensive, (2) be a source of income, or (3) bring you into contact with "undesirable" people. First, how strongly do you expect that these outcomes or attributes are true? What probability of occurrence would you attach to them? Such a decision establishes the expectancy portion of the overall judgment. For instance, you might consider a highly probable (.7), b highly improbable (.2), and c only moderately probable (.5).

Second, consider how strongly you feel about these outcomes. What value would you attach to them? This sort of decision establishes the value portion of the judgment. For example, you might not value a (-3), assign a high value to b $(+3)$, and be only mildly negative to c (-1). According to Fishbein and Ajzen, your overall attitude about gambling would be a weighted sum of the $E \times V$ judgments:

$$.7 \times -3 \text{ (for } a) + .2 \times 3 \text{ (for } b) + .5 \times -1 \text{ (for } c) = -2.0$$

This means you will have a relatively strong negative attitude toward that activity despite the fact that you value some aspects of the activity. One attraction of this approach is that it takes into account both the person's cognitions (how likely the attributes or consequences fit the attitude object) as well as the affective value (how important the various object-consequence relationships are to the person).

A rather different explanation for attitude formation was proposed by Bem (1970). He argues that we infer what our attitudes must be from our behavior just as we infer what other people's attitudes are from their behavior. That is, we observe our own behavior in relationship to attitude objects, and only then do we deduce what our internal attitude must be. It is as if one were to say unconsciously, "I save a relatively large proportion of my salary; therefore, I must have the attitude that saving is a good thing." This theory has received some experimental support (e.g., Bem 1965), although other recent evidence does not support it.

Attitude change

Attitude change is crucially important to economic psychology. Both human attitudes and the economic environment are dynamic, changing and interacting with each other over time. For instance, production of a new commodity may reflect the fact that the producers perceive a demand for (i.e., a favorable attitude toward) that item. As a result, subsequent marketing decisions including advertising may well change attitudes toward the product, resulting in a shift in the economic fortunes of the company and associated effects on other sectors of the economy (e.g., employment, savings). In short, attitudes change over time partly as a result of economic conditions; in turn their change creates further adjustments in the economic environment.

The literature in social psychology on attitude change can be divided into two broad categories. The first deals with how persuasion by others results in attitude change; the other deals with how attitudes are changed through self-persuasion. We shall deal with each category in turn.

There is a vast literature on persuasion, and many variables that affect the degree to which a person can change someone else's attitude have been identified. One important class of factors has to do with the person doing the persuading. Variables in this class include the power or status of the communicator. Early research (e.g., Hovland et al. 1953) also pointed to the unsurprising conclusion that credible sources of information are more effective than uncredible sources. Indeed, the source's credibility seems to be more important in changing attitudes than the arguments themselves unless the subject is uncertain about the credibility, in which case the arguments themselves have a larger role (Jaspers 1978). Moreover, the credibility factor is enhanced if the source's motivation is thought not to be externally induced or simply in his or her own interest (Eagly, Wood, & Chaiken 1978). Nevertheless, W.J. McGuire (1969) showed that under some circumstances a source need not be disinterested or unbiased to be persuasive.

Anyone who has ever seen an advertisement in which an attractive woman in a bathing suit extols the virtues of Brand X motor oil will immediately appreciate the finding that the attractiveness of the communicator is a potent persuasive force. But attractiveness and credibility have quite different effects on persuasion. Norman (1976), for example, had subjects listen to a communicator who claimed that they should get less than eight hours of sleep per night. One communicator was an expert but was rated low in attractiveness; another was highly attractive but apparently had no expertise in the subject. The expert source was effective in changing attitudes only when a detailed list of supporting arguments was given, but the attractive source was more effective whether or not supporting arguments were supplied. It would appear that physical attractiveness (Horai, Naccari, & Fatoullah 1974) and other attributes, such as race, color, grooming, dress, and rate of speech (N. Miller, Maruyama, Beaber, & Valone 1976), are powerful agents of attitude change.

Other major factors that affect persuasion by others include the structure or content of the message (see Fishbein & Ajzen 1972; Kiesler & Munson 1975; Leventhal 1970) and the personality of the subject (Hovland & Janis 1959; Hovland, Harvey, & Sherif 1957; E.M. Rogers & Shoemaker 1971). In neither case are the effects simple and direct. For example, one-sided messages are more effective than evenhanded ones, but only for subjects who already believe them (Hovland, Lumsdaine, & Sheffield 1949); high self-esteem may be correlated with understanding the message, but not with being persuaded by it (W.J. McGuire 1969).

The second intensively studied mechanism of attitude change is self-persuasion. This area of research has its origins in the influential work of Heider (1958) and Festinger (1957). The fundamental assumption of their theories is that people strive for cognitive consistency. That is, they are predisposed to organize their attitudes and to adjust their beliefs so that each is consistent with the another. When beliefs or attitudes are inconsistent or dissonant, people are motivated to dispel the dissonance. And they can do so in several ways. For instance, they may attempt to change or leave the environment, so that the two sources of information are no longer in conflict. They may reevaluate the alternatives and convince themselves that such a discrepancy in beliefs doesn't matter. Or, more importantly, they may change an existing attitude to make it more compatible with the reality of their information. It is this third process that interests us here.

Festinger's cognitive dissonance theory offers one widely used model of this process. Literally hundreds of studies have been done on various aspects of this theory (reviewed by Wicklund & Brehm 1976). We shall consider just one example, an experiment by Brehm (1956) that illustrates very clearly one way in which dissonance reduction could influence economic behavior. Women were asked to participate in a market survey. As payment for their participation, they were offered one of eight prizes ranging in value from about $8 to $15. Each subject was asked to rate the prizes for attractiveness and then "to insure that everyone had a chance to get a prize of their choice," they were given a choice between two of them. Some subjects could choose between two items they had already rated as highly attractive; others had to choose between a prize they had rated highly and one they had rated less attractive. After choosing their prize, subjects again rated all the objects. The results showed that when subjects had only one attractive object offered to them (along with the less attractive object), they chose the attractive object and did not change their ratings of the attractiveness of the objects found. When they had to choose between two objects of near equal value, however, the rating of the chosen object increased, whereas the score for the rejected item decreased.

Dissonance theory can easily explain this curious finding. In order to justify their decision, subjects in effect altered their attitude toward these products. Even though the products were equally attractive initially, they deemed the chosen one better in order to reduce the dissonant actions "I like the rejected one as well as the chosen one and yet I didn't choose it." If the rejected item is later claimed to be not so good after all, the person's beliefs are brought into agreement with the action taken. It is certainly easy to see why we tend to rate more expensive items as being of better quality, even if they are not, in fact, better (see Chapter 7).

Before closing this section on attitude change, we should note briefly that other theories have been developed to account for many of these phenomena. The theories of attitude formation mentioned earlier can obviously also serve as theories of attitude change, and Bem's self-perception theory has in fact been important in this role. Other fundamental ideas from modern social psychology, such as role-playing (Janis & King 1954; Janis & Mann 1965), can also be used to help us understand how attitudes may change through self-persuasion. All these theories clearly have implications for how we form and change attitudes relevant to our general economic behavior. The most influential account of self-persuasion, however, arises out of the theory of attribution. This is sufficiently important to merit separate treatment.

Attributions, lay explanations, and locus of control

An abiding concern of social psychology is people's understanding of their social world. What theories do laypeople, as distinct from psychologists, hold about the way the world works? How do these theories guide their behavior? These questions have been answered from a variety of theoretical perspectives; indeed, attitude research provides one kind of answer. But probably the best-known approach is attribution theory.

Attribution theory is concerned with how people make sense of their social world by attributing causes to one thing or another. This theory was proposed by Heider (1958), who maintained that people need to see their social environment as predictable; they therefore predict social events in the same way that they predict physical events, that is, by looking for the necessary and sufficient conditions for events to occur. Most important for Heider was that people perceive behavior as caused. A person may do something because he or she had to (environmental cause) or because he or she wanted to (internal cause). For example, in interviewing for a job that requires extraverted people (e.g., salesman), an interviewer would probably attribute the cause of a candidate's quiet, introverted behavior to the candidate's personality (internal cause) but would be unsure of the cause of extraverted behavior, because the situation requires this.

E.E. Jones and Davis (1965) and Kelley (1967, 1971) elaborated and extended Heider's approach. Kelley discussed two main types of attribution situations: one in which we have information from many observations and another wherein we have just one observation, as in the interview. Let us consider an example of the former situation.

In a certain university department, it was the custom to go for a drink after research seminars. On attending the seminar for the first time, a new arrival in the department noticed that person X did not pay for a subsequent round of drinks. To what should the newcomer attribute X's behavior? Was it that person X was mean (a dispositional attribution), that person X did not like this particular bar (a person × situation attribution), or simply that X had no cash (an accidental circumstance that does not permit any attribution at all)? It is impossible to tell from the single observation. Once the newcomer had seen X behave in the same way after the next three seminars, the newcomer was not surprised when, on further inquiry, three out of four colleagues commented on X's Scottish ancestry. With this information, according to the Kelley model, it would be possible to attribute the cause of the behavior to X.

Kelley identified three attribution rules that we use in this kind of situation: distinctiveness, consensus, and consistency. To attribute the cause to person X, the attribution should be distinct; that is, other people should not give the same impression. The attribution should also have a consensual basis; it should not be attributable to the way in which the observer sees people generally. If meanness is a genuine characteristic of a person, he or she should display mean behavior on a consistent basis. The same rules apply in making an attribution to a type of situation or to an interaction between a situation and an individual.

When only a single observation is available people are forced to rely on *causal schemas* – conceptions, derived from experience, of the way in which two or more factors interact. Two types of causal schemas, involving augmentation and discounting, have been the most researched, although there are potentially a wide variety. Augmentation occurs in situations in which external causes may inhibit the observed behavior. Thus, if the behavior is seen, it heightens the impression that a dispositional cause is present. Discounting means that "the role of a given cause in producing a given effect is discounted if other plausible causes are also present" (Kelley 1971). A good example would be observers' explanations of why a celebrity endorsed a product. There are two obvious causes: The celebrity may indeed use and enjoy the product or be endorsing it for the fee, or both. The role of the product is likely to be discounted unless it is somehow made clear that the endorser is not in it for the money. This prediction from attribution theory is consistent with experimental work on persuasive communication (Eagly et al. 1978).

E.E. Jones and Davis (1965) developed a theory of *correspondent inferences,* that attempts to explain how an observer attributes intent and internal responsibility to another person. A correspondent inference is an inference about another's disposition that "corresponds" to that person's behavior. According to Jones and Davis, the observer first tries to ascertain the actor's knowledge and ability. Was X able to pay? If so, we can reasonably infer intent. To go further and infer a disposition, we need to consider the possible alternative behaviors of the actor. The common effects of all possible behaviors cannot be the reason for the actor's choice of one particular behavior. It is therefore the noncommon effects of the chosen alternative that we pay attention to. Furthermore, we must check the social desirability of an action. If the effects of an action have high social desirability, the action indicates little about the actor. In other words, the fewer distinctive reasons there are for a person's choice, and the more the reasons are widely shared in society, the less informative the behavior.

As we shall see in later chapters, the attribution framework has been applied to a variety of economic phenomena. For example, Smith and Hunt (1978) examined whether advertisements that portray their products as inferior to competing goods in unimportant characteristics are more successful than those that claim to be superior in all characteristics. From the latter, consumers could infer very little because such advertisements are so common. But the former are rare and are likely to give rise to a correspondent inference that the advertiser is honest. Smith and Hunt's results confirmed this prediction.

Although attribution theory was initially concerned with how we understand other people, it has since been applied to our understanding of ourselves. Just as we need to infer the causes of other people's behavior, of wealth, of poverty, and so forth, it is argued that we need to infer the causes of our own behavior. We have already encountered examples of similar reasoning. Bem's (1970) description of how attitudes are formed is a case in point. What is particularly interesting to an economic psychologist is that there seem to be individual differences in self-attribution. Given that a person can learn about the relative contributions of internal and external factors to a particular behavior (in other words, form causal schema), it is reasonable to suppose that an individual will develop generalized expectancies about the relative importance of internal and external factors across situations. Children who are able to control their environment will come to expect success as adults; those who experience failure in affecting their environment will come to expect no control in the future. Thus, people will develop what Rotter (1966) calls "generalized expectancies for internal versus external locus of control of reinforcement." Those with internal locus of control will believe that reinforcement is contingent on their behavior. Those with external locus of control will believe that reinforcement depends on environmental factors over which they have little influence.

Locus of control is relevant to a number of economic behaviors. People high on internal locus of control appear to take greater risks (this is relevant to both gambling and entrepreneurship) in that they bet more following a dice roll than do high externals (Strickland, Lewicki, & Katz 1966). More interestingly, a comparison of workers in two developed and in two less developed countries revealed that the former had a more internal locus of control for success (Reitz & Groff 1974).

Attribution theory dominated social psychology during the 1970s, but recently it has come under increasing criticism. One result is that researchers are now more inclined to refer to lay explanations than to attributions (with the associated emphasis on inferring causes). Furnham (1982a, 1982b, 1983a) carried out a large number of studies of lay theories of economic phenomena such as poverty, wealth, unemployment, and strikes. He noted that explanations for economic behavior fall into three categories: individualistic (e.g., "people are unemployed because they are lazy"), societal (e.g., "people are poor because of government policies"), and fatalistic (e.g., "people are rich because they are lucky"), and that they tend to be coherent. That is, individuals use one kind of explanation for a wide range of economic behaviors. Why this is so can be explained in terms of what Pettigrew (1979) calls the ultimate attribution error. This is the tendency to explain failure in the in-group (the group to which the person belongs) in situational terms but success in individualistic terms, and the converse for the out-group. Thus, British conservative voters explain middle-class poverty in situational ways but working class poverty in individualistic ways.

Social comparison

The final social psychological concept we wish to introduce is that of social comparison. Festinger (1954) suggested that there are two kinds of reality: physical reality and social reality. If you want to know whether a door is locked or a cup is unbreakable you can check directly; you can try the door or attack the cup with a sledgehammer. That is physical reality. But for many aspects of our world there is no direct test; we must rely on others to provide a social reality.

When we doubt our opinions or are uncertain about our behavior we look to others as sources of information. We are engaging in "social comparison" to gain an accurate perception of the world. Imagine that you are participating in a study on reactions to life in the city. You are led to a room and begin to fill in one of the questionnaires that are on the table. After a few minutes, you notice puffs of white smoke coming through the ventilator. What will you do? If you are anything like the original participants in the study, it will depend on whether you had been in the room on your own or with other people (Latane & Darley 1968). Most people who were on their own reported the smoke to the experimenter. Those who were with others generally continued to fill in the questionnaires, even when the smoke had filled the room. What is happening here is that people are using other people's behavior to interpret, or define, an ambiguous situation. If others do not react, the situation is obviously not serious. This may be a particularly dramatic example, but the processes involved are general.

Comparisons with others are not just used to help understand the world. They are also involved in our understanding of ourselves and our judgments of our behavior, and its rewards, in relationship to others. Thibaut and Kelley (1959), for example, in their formulation of an exchange approach to interpersonal relationships, made extensive use of the concepts of *comparison level* and *comparison level of alternatives*. A comparison level is the standard by which a person assesses personal satisfaction with a relationship. It will shift with experience. It is easy to apply this approach to the relationship between a worker and employer, and it may help explain why wages are sticky in a downward direction.

Another approach to social comparisons, also with an obvious relevance to economic issues, is *equity theory*. This theory is concerned with the issue of how people judge what is fair, deserved, or equitable, as well as how such judgments influence behavior. The basic question is how to distribute a limited resource, which might be money, status, companionship, or whatever. One answer is that everyone should get equal shares. But in fact, people seem to prefer to be rewarded equitably rather than equally.

Equity theory states that in a relationship people want to keep their outcomes proportional to their inputs. In other words, each person wants to derive benefits from the relationship which will be proportional to what they put in. Outcomes are rewards minus costs. Thus, we can express the basic equity position as

$$(R_a - C_a)/I_a = (R_b - C_b)/I_b$$

where R is reward, C is cost, and I is input, and subscripts a and b refer to two individuals. There are other versions as well (for a clear description, see Eiser 1980). Equity theory implies that people may see large pay differentials, for example, as perfectly fair, if they believe that the higher paid have greater costs (stress, exposure to criticism) and greater inputs (education, experience) than the lower paid. It is important to bear in mind that according to this theory the values of rewards, costs, and inputs are not held to be determined objectively. What matters is how they are perceived by the people in the relationship.

According to equity theory, being in an inequitable relationship produces tension, whether the inequity is favorable to us or not. Obviously there are numerous ways in which equity can be restored. You can alter your inputs (perhaps by working less hard), distort your cognitions (if you perceive yourself as overpaid you may convince yourself you deserve it), leave the relationship; or alter the other person's inputs or outcomes. If you believe that you pay too much tax, you may indulge in tax evasion, and if you believe you pay too little you may not claim all the allowances you are entitled to. It is the second of these predictions that is counterintuitive. Nonetheless, there is some evidence that overbenefited people do attempt to restore equity. Adams (1963), for example, found that overpaid piece-rate workers would reduce their production rate but would try to improve the quality of the product; overpaid hourly-rate workers would increase their production rate.

Social comparison processes are ubiquitous. We will encounter them in later chapters whenever social aspects of economic behavior are considered. They are at the core of some behaviors – keeping up with the Jones's – but are implicated in many more.

LEARNING AND COGNITION

The second major area of psychology under review in this chapter is learning and cognition. Like social psychology, learning has a vast literature of research and theory, which we cannot treat in any great detail here (see Tarpy 1982 for a more detailed discussion of basic learning). But, as we have already seen in the literature on attitude formation, learning processes are often seen as the most fundamental causes of individual behavior; this applies as much in economic psychology as in any other area. We must give at least a brief introduction to the vocabulary of learning psychology.

The basic proposition implicit in this section is that economic behavior, like most other human behaviors, is learned. We are not born with any fixed habits for, say, buying, saving, or giving, although we may very well have predispositions toward general forms of those behaviors. Rather, we learn about our economic environment, and we learn how to behave appropriately in that environment. Although it is essential to study human economic behavior directly, we should also emphasize that the basic principles of learning involved in such behavior are likely to be the same as those governing other aspects of human behavior. Some of these basic principles have been studied profitably in the animal laboratory; others are unique to humans. In either case, the presupposition is that by studying the learning process in a simplified and controlled situation, we may be able to understand some of the fundamental laws which apply in more complex settings.

Our discussion of attitude formation has in fact served to introduce several major approaches to learning: classical and instrumental conditioning, Bandura's social learning (an example of the more general process of vicarious learning), and the information-processing approach. These, together with the additional area of problem solving, will form the main topics to be discussed in this section.

Stimulus learning

The most elementary type of stimulus learning is classical or Pavlovian conditioning. This involves the acquisition of meaning to a stimulus by virtue of its relationship to another already meaningful stimulus. Let us review the procedures of a typical Pavlovian experiment. Assume that a hungry laboratory rat is placed in a box containing a light and a food cup and is given presentations of the light followed a few seconds later by food. The light has no "meaning" at the beginning of the study; it is a neutral conditioned stimulus (CS). But the food is a biologically powerful unconditioned stimulus (US) that causes the animal to perform reflexive unconditioned reactions (URs) such as salivation, heart rate acceleration, and general locomotion. After repeated presentations of the CS–US sequence, the animal begins to show a conditioned response (CR) to the light itself. That is, the same sort of reflexive behaviors that were originally given to the food are now performed as soon as the light comes on (i.e., well before the food presentation). This indicates that the light has indeed acquired meaning or power; it can now elicit behavioral reactions on its own, whereas it could not do so before conditioning.

Classical conditioning is perhaps the most thoroughly studied of all learning processes. It has been investigated systematically in animal laboratories for nearly a century. The important thing, for our purposes at least, is that although the conditioning process is usually studied in terms of reflexive behaviors, such as salivation or heart rate, stimulus learning can explain the formation of both emotional and cognitive reactions. The fundamental reason that a neutral CS acquires the power to elicit CRs is that it predicts the US presentation; it is the information value of the stimulus that is all important (see Tarpy 1982). Conditional stimuli that are weakly correlated with reward (Rescorla 1967) or CS values that are redundant and uninformative (Kamin, 1969) do not become powerful. This means that stimulus learning ultimately concerns the acquisition of expectancies. Subjects, including humans, learn to expect future events when they are given appropriate signals that in the past were correlated with those events.

The stronger the CS–US correlation, the stronger the conditioned reaction (e.g., Rescorla 1968), and, we assume, the stronger the expectation of the US elicited by the CS. But there are a number of other important principles of conditioning. For example, the more intense the US (Fitzgerald & Teyler 1970) or CS (e.g., Grice 1968) the stronger the conditioned reaction. The argument would be similar in the case of symbols in our world such as attitude objects: Objects that are themselves more salient or those associated (correlated) with very strong emotional stimuli will later produce stronger emotional reactions than will objects that are themselves weak or ones that signal weak events.

It is sometimes thought that this emphasis on strong biologically relevant stimuli makes classical conditioning an inappropriate model for complex human learning. However, this argument is false, for two reasons. First, stimuli do not in fact acquire meaning or power only by being related to biological, or even strong, US values. Research has shown that CSs can acquire meaning when associated with other neutral stimuli. For instance, if a light is continually followed by a tone, the light will acquire the ability to predict the tone. Although behavioral reactions are rarely observed in such an experiment (because both stimuli are weak and therefore do not elicit noticeable behaviors), if the tone were later paired with a US, such that an overt reaction were conditioned to the tone, the light would be able to elicit the reaction as well (even though it had never itself been directly paired with the US). This important phenomenon, called *sensory preconditioning* (see Thompson 1972), illustrates that signals do not necessarily have to predict only powerful biological cues in order to gain strength; stimuli can become meaningful signals even when the events they signal are innocuous. Thus, in the human economic environment, attitude objects can derive meaning when associated with other powerful experiences, with other objects that are already conditioned (see Rescorla 1973), or with relatively innocuous objects.

Second, it could just as plausibly be claimed that the emphasis on important stimuli is one reason why this model is particularly relevant to economic psychology: Economic behavior is often directed toward powerful emotion-producing stimuli for which there is a clear biological need.

Response learning

However important stimulus learning processes may be, they are inevitably unconvincing as a sole model of economic action. To understand why, we must turn to the study of response learning.

Let us begin by reviewing a typical response learning experiment. A hungry rat is placed in the start box of a maze. The door is then raised so that the rat is allowed to run to the goal box to obtain a piece of food. At first, the animal cannot know what response to make, and so it takes quite a while before it eventually finds food in the goal, making many wrong turns along the way. After repeated experience, however, the rat begins to respond as soon as possible, making virtually no errors. It runs to the goal box quickly and efficiently. What has been learned is a voluntary motor reaction involving efficiency of movement as well as knowledge of the correct turns in the maze. Whereas in classical conditioning the subject passively experiences stimulus pairings, in response learning the subject's response is instrumental in producing some outcome. For this reason, this kind of learning is often referred to as instrumental conditioning. An alternative name, operant conditioning, emphasizes the fact that the subject's response operates on the environment.

Our sample experiment is one of the simplest possible, yet it illustrates some important concepts. Most important is the concept of reinforcement. A reinforcer may be defined as a stimulus that changes the probability of a response on which its delivery is contingent: It is a reward that works. Normally, reinforcers are environmental events or conditions, such as food or water, that an organism will naturally seek out or at least never avoid. In everyday terms, they are positive or pleasurable experiences, often fulfilling a definite biological need, just as a food pellet does for a hungry rat. In humans, however, rewards need not always be associated with the reduction of a biological need; more often, in fact, they take the form of money or other material objects, or social interactions such as praise or gratitude (see Skinner 1969, for a more thorough discussion of reinforcement theory).

Negative, or unpleasant, events can also influence behavior. More specifically, behaviors on which aversive events are contingent decline in probability and strength; that is, the administration of punishment after a response has the effect of suppressing the execution of that response. As with positive reward, a punishing event need not be a biological stimulus. The failure of an investment, ridicule or admonition for gambling, and hostile reproaches of all sorts can act as punishers of human behavior.

Let us restate the important principle of reinforcement. By definition, behaviors that produce reinforcement (usually a pleasant state of affairs) or that eliminate punishment (an unpleasant state of affairs) gain in strength and probability. By contrast, behaviors that result in aversive outcomes or behaviors that fail to achieve positive reinforcement are suppressed; the probability of those behaviors is reduced. The application of this principle to economic behavior is straightforward: We learn our economic habits because we have been reinforced by our parents, teachers, bankers, or whomever for behaving as we do. To understand economic behavior then is, in part, to appreciate the theoretical and practical implications of the principle of reinforcement for human behavior in the economic environment.

Few readers will need a psychologist to point out that rewards and punishments can have important effects on human behavior, in economic as in other spheres. However, the detailed research that has been carried out on instrumental conditioning has led to a substantial body of reliable and nontrivial data about the precise ways in which reward affects behavior.

For example, it has been found to be possible to produce elaborate responses by systematic application of reward to small changes in behavior. This process, known as *shaping,* has been used to produce such oddities as pigeons that play table tennis (Skinner 1962) and a porpoise that devises its own tricks (Pryor, Haag, & O'Reilly 1969); more practically, it can be invoked instead of more "rational" mechanisms to account for apparently complex sequences of human behavior, including economic ones.

Other powerful determinants of instrumental behavior include the size of the reward for each response and the delay between response and reward. Both have predictable effects. The larger the reinforcement, the greater the behavioral change, with both positive (Roberts 1969) and aversive (Church, Raymond, & Beauchamp 1967) reinforcers. Rewards that are delivered quickly after a response are more effective than rewards that are delayed (see Tarpy & Sawabini 1974).

The most important contingency variable, however, is the schedule of delivery (see Schoenfeld, 1970). It is obvious that in their natural environments, humans and other animals are not rewarded every time they make a correct response. For example, birds do not find insects under every leaf, foxes do not catch every rabbit they chase, and people do not receive praise every time they behave generously. The list could go on, but the same theme would prevail: Reward is normally meted out intermittently. For reinforcement theorists, the study of just how reward schedules affect behavior has become paramount.

A vast literature using both human and animal subjects has been devoted to exploring the nature of these effects. Experimenters have concentrated on four basic schedules of reward that operate in the following ways. First, rewards may be delivered after a specified number of responses has occurred. Schedules of this sort are called ratio schedules. For instance, a subject might have to execute ten responses for each reward, in which case the schedule would be a fixed ratio (FR) schedules; that is, the number required is fixed from one reward to the next. Alternatively, a subject might be required to make, on the average, ten responses for each reward but the actual number might vary from one time to the next. One time the subject might need to make, say, seven responses, the next time thirteen, but the average over the entire session would be ten. This is called a variable ratio (VR) schedule because the required number of responses is variable.

The two other common basic schedules are called interval schedules. Here, a particular length of time must elapse before the subject's next response will yield a reward. With fixed interval (FI) schedules, the time period is always the same. Alternatively the time period could vary during the session in which case the schedule would be termed a variable interval (VI) schedule.

The effects of these four schedules of reinforcement have been investigated in great detail (e.g., Ferster & Skinner 1957). The details are not important here, but it is worth indicating a few basic properties of the basic schedules to give the flavor of operant conditioning research and to suggest some parallels with economic phenomena.

Ratio schedules produce higher rates than interval schedules, and variable ratios produce higher overall rates than do fixed ratios. Part of the reason is that fixed schedules (whether interval or ratio) tend to generate patterned responding, with a pause after each reinforcement, followed by relatively rapid responding, which in the case of an FI schedule usually accelerates as the time for reinforcement approaches (cf. Caplan, Karpicke, & Rilling 1973). By contrast, variable schedules generate steady rates. The reason may well be that, on a fixed ratio or a fixed interval schedule, the time just after reinforcement is the point during which a further reward will never occur (Dews 1969); adding a cue that makes the passage of time on a fixed interval more apparent increases the differentiation of response rate (Kendall 1972).

The effects of incentive variables, such as the rate or size of reward, are different for different schedules. On fixed ratio schedules, they fall mainly on the postreinforcement pause, while the rate of responding, once it starts, is scarcely affected, even by the size of the ratio itself (Felton & Lyon 1966). On variable intervals, the overall rate is highly sensitive to reward variables; these schedules are very widely used in studies of incentive and motivational effects (e.g., Catania & Reynolds 1968).

While it is hard to find completely unambiguous examples of basic reinforcement schedules in everyday human life, it is easy to recognize one or two plausible analogies. For example, workers who earn their wages on a piece rate, or commission, basis (i.e., so many units of work or items sold for so much money) or consumers who pay a fixed price for a commodity may be said to be rewarded according to a fixed ratio schedule. This analogy is used in animal experiments on work and buying (cf. Chapters 6 and 7). By contrast, the variable ratio schedule, with its high, constant rate of responding, looks like a good model for some types of human gambling behavior (see Chapter 10).

These four basic schedules do not exhaust the possible contingencies between response and reward. Recent research has focused particularly on the effects of combining two or more schedules of reinforcement; these compound schedules may well lead to more interesting models of economic situations than the simple textbook schedules we have discussed so far. Compound schedules seem to have systematic effects on behavior. For example, when two schedules are available either simultaneously or in rapid succession, a high rate of reinforcement on one tends to diminish the rate of response on the other, a phenomenon known as contrast. One special case of this effect arises if two variable interval schedules are arranged for different responses that are simultaneously available. It is then found that animal subjects distribute their responses between the two schedules in roughly the same proportion as the reinforcers (Herrnstein 1961). This rule, known as the *matching law,* has been investigated in great detail (e.g., Baum 1974, 1979) because it offers an instrumental conditioning account of choice. The idea that choice is lawfully determined is important to every branch of psychology; it is obviously particularly relevant to economic behavior.

Although many of the fundamental experiments on instrumental conditioning have been carried out on animals, we have emphasized the notion that human behavior, too, is subject to the effects of reinforcement and that the schedule of reward helps determine the actual rate and pattern of behavior. This belief is confirmed in the vast literature on behavior modification, which is the name given to the systematic use of instrumental conditioning in clinical, educational, and other applied settings. The underlying notion is simple: Maladaptive or inappropriate behaviors are never reinforced (sometimes they are even punished), whereas appropriate responses are rewarded openly and immediately by the attendant. In an impressive proportion of cases, the person's behavior changes in accordance with the reinforcement schedules. So for example, maladjusted youngsters who threw temper fits at the least frustration (they were quite unable to participate in a normal school setting) were "cured" of this by their teacher. The simple technique was to ignore all crying behavior but to give attention and warm approval when they behaved constructively (Hart, Allen, Buell, Harris, & Wolf 1964). Within a short period of time, these children adjusted to their surroundings and began to have a productive and satisfying relationship with their peers. Behavior modification helped them through a difficult period when the "normal" rewards, sufficient for the other children, were, for some reason, ineffective.

Behavior modification has also been used to treat people who were severely schizophrenic. Meichenbaum (1969), for example, ignored schizophrenic patients when they talked "crazy" (e.g., when they said things like "the green Martians are after me") but showed interest and approval when they uttered sane and intelligible remarks. Other clinicians (see Ayllon & Houghton 1962; Ayllon & Michael 1959) have used these techniques successfully to reinforce cooperative social behavior in schizophrenics who were otherwise totally withdrawn and unreachable.

Because of the powerful effects of schedules of reinforcement in laboratory studies and in clinical work, it has been suggested that they are the fundamental determinants of all behavior at all times. This is much too simple a view, as we shall see. But there is no reason to suppose that instrumental conditioning works only in the animal laboratory or the schizophrenic ward. We live in a world full of reinforcers and punishers. Our behavior is constantly being modified by friends, parents, and teachers. Most of the reinforcers are subtle. We hardly notice them, at least consciously. Indeed, if the reinforcer in a situation becomes too salient, human behavior may come to be controlled by very different principles from those involved in animals' adjustment to schedules of reinforcement (Lowe 1979, discussed under the heading Problem Solving). But the economic environment is full of reinforcers of which we are only vaguely aware. We should expect them to have a powerful effect on our social, intellectual, and economic behavior.

Vicarious learning

The two conditioning models discussed so far have been investigated in enormous detail by psychologists, but they do not provide a complete description of how humans learn or behave. Other processes are important too, one of which is "vicarious learning," mentioned earlier in the discussion of attitude change. Modeling, imitation learning, and social learning are common alternative names for vicarious learning.

The conditioning paradigms largely depend on the actual presence of a reinforcing event that "operates" directly on the subject. This is a potential shortcoming in an analysis of human behavior, because much of our everyday behavior stems from imitating the behavior of others. Arguably, what makes human behavior distinctive is the cumulative nature of our culture, which depends on our ability to profit from others' experience, either through observing it directly or through the medium of spoken or written language. Some have argued that we imitate others because we are reinforced with approval for doing so (e.g., N.E. Miller & Dollard 1941); this is the familiar social learning theory. But there is evidence that people will perform new responses after merely observing the successful behavior of others (Bandura, Ross, & Ross 1963). Under some conditions at least, modeling or imitation can be even more powerful than direct reinforcement in changing behavior (see Marlatt 1970).

The concept of imitation or modeling has direct implications for an analysis of economic behavior. People may save part of their income not because they are merely reinforced for doing so as suggested earlier, but also because they may observe others saving. Another example would involve buying habits: We observe the items that other people buy and, in turn, imitate their behavior by purchasing the items ourselves. This is one possible origin for the bandwagon effect in consumer demand (Leibenstein 1950).

Problem solving

Classical and instrumental conditioning are processes that were first studied systematically in animals. Even vicarious learning is widespread in the animal kingdom, although it has received less attention from animal investigators. But there is one form of learning that we cannot study conveniently except in humans. We refer to the change in behaviors brought about when we describe our situation to ourselves in abstract symbols, manipulate those symbols, and come up with a new description of the situation to which we then respond. The symbols involved might be words, pictures, numbers, algebraic formulas, or musical notes. We may manipulate them entirely "in our head," by writing them down, by consulting with other people, or by entering them into a computer. In any case, the process can be referred to as reasoning or problem solving.

This is the kind of learning with which economists are most likely to feel at home, because it seems likely to lead to what they would call rational behavior. We shall see later that this expectation may be misplaced (Chapter 5), but there is no doubt that problem solving is very important in economic behavior. Unfortunately, it is the hardest type of learning to generalize about, perhaps because it can involve the very limits of human intellectual capacity. Some of the processes involved in problem solving have been the concern of the important modern school of cognitive psychology; we now have a great deal of systematic knowledge and theory about the working of human pattern recognition, attention, and memory (e.g., Neisser 1967).

Generalizations about the actual phenomena of problem solving and reasoning are harder to come by. There are some, however, that may have importance for economic behavior. For instance, De Groot (1966) found that experts in a given field (in this case, chess) are able to organize their memories in quite different ways from nonexperts. Nisbett and Wilson (1977) showed that when people have made a choice without any apparent problem solving, they will sometimes offer a spurious problem-solving account of their behavior. Maier (1931) found that people are often unaware of the cues from the environment that provide the solution to a problem; an example of this kind of dissociation with an economic problem was given by Broadbent and Aston (1978). Wason and Shapiro (1971) demonstrated that people could solve a reasoning problem much more easily when it was presented in an everyday guise than when it was given in an abstract "laboratory" form.

When people construe a situation as involving a problem to be solved, they may well become disengaged, as it were, from the schedules of reinforcement that determine habitual responding (Skinner 1969; Lowe 1979). At this level, there is clearly a conflict between the analysis of behavior as *rational* (i.e. thought through in advance), or as *a-rational* (determined by automatic nonconscious processes, such as conditioning). Most of the recent psychology of human learning has regarded the rational approach as by far the more important and conditioning as at most a marginal influence (e.g., Howe 1980). Clearly, we are reversing this order of importance here. The reasons for this will be more apparent if we place problem solving within a wider context.

The information-processing approach

In modern cognitive psychology, in fact, the study of problem solving is just one part of a much more general approach to the understanding of behavior. This is the information-processing approach, which draws heavily on the analogy between human and machine intelligence. Cognition is viewed as a process in which information is received from the environment, transformed, stored and computed upon within the mind, and transmitted as speech or behavior. During the past twenty years, the information-processing approach has pervaded every aspect of psychology.

The psychology of economic behavior is no exception. For example, most recent treatments of consumer behavior (e.g., Howard & Sheth 1969; Engel & Blackwell 1982) make heavy use of elaborate diagrams in which the consumer is seen as a complex system made up of many interacting subsystems, each of which is open to an information-processing analysis. The model is attractive as well as fashionable; it provides a convenient means of organizing a great deal of knowledge about consumers. Why, then, are we standing back from it and from the general apparatus of modern cognitive psychology in this book? There are two reasons.

First, the cognitive approach is essentially cognitive. Its superiority over more traditional models of learning seems to us to have been more clearly demonstrated for questions about what people know than for questions about what people do. In our view, it is questions about motivation and action that seem to us most important in economic psychology.

Second, the emphasis in modern cognitive psychology has been on just those processes that are most different from simple conditioning. It is undeniable that simple conditioning cannot account for all human learning, as was once quite seriously supposed. But the reaction to this extreme position has gone too far. The current emphases in cognitive psychology neglect the possibility that classical and instrumental conditioning, vicarious learning, and problem solving may all occur together in any given situation. No doubt, a behavior is occasionally created through, or controlled by, the action of one process to the exclusion of the others, but it would be very surprising if this were always or even usually the case. We may perform a response because of an attitude we have, because we have been reinforced for doing so, and because we are imitating others. All these processes can be active at the same time, as indeed can others.

In the specific case of economic behavior, the cognitive dimension in causality is quite likely to be well captured by a conventional economic account. It is the additional factors that are most likely to give us new information. Economic psychologists (e.g., Katona 1975; Reynaud 1981) have therefore rightly been concerned with the circumstances that make one process more or less important than another.

MOTIVATION AND PERSONALITY

In our discussions of social psychology and of learning, it will have become obvious that some kinds of stimuli, objects, and events are more significant than others. People hold attitudes and beliefs about questions that are important to them. The simple models of learning depend on the existence of special classes of stimuli (unconditioned stimuli or reinforcers). Part of our unhappiness with the prevailing cognitive or information-processing approach to learning is its inability to grapple with the question of the value of particular events. The concept of value is crucial to economics and therefore (because it is also a psychological concept) to economic psychology.

Within psychology, the study of what things are important to people is the province of the theory of motivation. The third section of this introduction to psychology therefore deals with motivational issues. As it happens, motivation theories often involve assumptions about the structure of personality, so we shall also be giving a brief introduction to some of the most prominent views in the psychology of personality, including the problem of measuring individual differences of personality.

Psychologists have studied motivation for decades, but they have reached little agreement about its laws. Part of the problem has been the diversity of research paradigms they have used: Physiological psychologists study the biochemistry of hunger and thirst, learning theorists try to discover what all reinforcers have in common, social psychologists study the condition under which subjects attempt to eliminate conflicting beliefs, and Freudian psychoanalysts study the unconscious conflicts that may drive people to drink or gamble excessively. All of them claim to be studying motivation, and in a sense they are all correct. But they clearly disagree about the level on which motivation operates and the techniques by which it can be studied – which may be physiological, psychodynamic, social, or any combination.

Nonetheless, motivation does have a central meaning for psychologists. Specifically, it refers to the energy or impetus for behavior, the underlying force that impels an organism into action, and the way that force is directed toward specific objects. The following sections briefly discuss three motivational theories, all of which have been used in the analysis of economic behavior (see Beck 1978; Bolles 1975; Weiner 1980).

Activation and drive theory

One of the oldest and most widely cited theories of motivation suggests that basic drives are important to behavior. In particular, drive combines with knowledge or habit to produce overt responding. Note how similar this type of theory is to the expectancy × value (EV) model considered earlier in the section on attitudes. The main argument is that organisms have evolved with an inherent tendency to fulfill various biological needs, and drive is the psychological mechanism by which physiological needs are translated into behavior. That is, physiological needs give rise to a drive state (the psychological counterpart to need), in turn goading the organism into action so that it can fulfill the need. Consider this example: If an animal were deprived of food, causing a biological need, its corresponding drive state would activate the animal's behavioral tendencies. It would become active, search for food, and ultimately perform whatever behavior is required to secure the food and eliminate the need.

Drive theory of this sort was first systematized by Hull (1943). Although the details of Hull's theory are not important here, an overview is appropriate. According to Hull, drive is a psychological state created by need; the stronger the need, the stronger the drive. Drive moreover is an undifferentiated or general state; it is not specific to any given need but rather is a generalized state to which various sources of need contributed. So, for example, if a person has general anxiety in addition to laboratory-induced fear, the behavioral reaction is larger, because of greater general drive, than if that person has only one of those sources of motivation (K.W. Spence 1958).

Hull's theory emphasized that drive is a psychological state dependent on biological needs. It is tempting to think that it must therefore be instinctual. However, a great deal of research has demonstrated that drive can also be learned; it does not have to arise out of any biological deficit (see D'Amato 1974). For example, if one were to present a tone followed by a shock to a laboratory animal (recall this is the classical conditioning technique), the animal would eventually exhibit fear of the tone and would learn various responses to turn the tone off, even in the absence of shock (Miller 1951). In other words, the tone induces a motivational state of fear that in turn energizes behavior.

Learned motivation, moreover, is not limited to aversive stimuli. If a tone is paired with the presentation of food, an incentive drive is formed (see Osborne 1978). Such incentive motivations energize behavior like a primary drive, but they do so by enticing the animal toward a particular goal object rather than by goading it aimlessly, as Hull claimed for hunger. A primary drive pushes or goads the animal into action, but incentive stimuli, those paired with reward, entice the animal by creating a craving for the reward. Either way, behavior is set into action (see Cravens & Renner 1969).

Much of drive theory has emphasized that drives reflect a deviation from the normal condition of the animal; they are something the animal normally wishes to reduce. But there is another perspective that is important to our understanding of motivated states. Many theorists have noted that organisms are motivated to maintain an optimal level of activation, not just reduce drive to its lowest value. In fact, if an organism's level of activation falls below a certain point, stimulation will be sought, not avoided (see Berlyne 1960; Eisenberger 1972; Fiske & Maddi 1960; Kish 1966). Investigators have shown, for example, that increased drive is, under some conditions, reinforcing (see, e.g., Kish 1955; Fowler 1967; G.T. Taylor 1974; Montgomery 1954; Butler 1953). Animals will perform certain behaviors in order to increase their level of activation. In summary, drive induction as well as reduction can be reinforcing, depending on the base level of activation. This fact has led to some important and interesting theories about human economic behavior (see the discussion of Scitovsky's theory in Chapter 19).

Maslow's theory of self-actualization

Drive theory makes good intuitive sense. All of us can readily understand and accept the notion that organisms of all sorts are motivated to reduce biological deficits. The counterpart to that argument, the notion that organisms also seek out stimulation when their activation level falls too low, makes sense as well. But drive theory clearly gives a simple undifferentiated view of human motivation, and it is all too likely that it fails to capture some of the subtleties of individual feeling. In particular, there may be "higher" goals or motives that are especially pertinent to humans that do not operate in the same way as the simple biological factors stressed by Hull. Abraham Maslow (1943) put forward a theory which tries to capture these more sophisticated features of human motivation. Since his theory has been widely applied to behaviors of economic importance, we shall describe it in some detail.

The basic tenet of Maslow's theory is that humans strive to actualize, or realize, their individual potentials, that is, to grow and enhance the self. According to Maslow, the proposition that people attempt to grow and fulfill their highest potential is not debatable, but axiomatic. They fulfill this potential according to a hierarchy of needs. The first level of needs is the physiological level: hunger, thirst, sexual fulfillment, fatigue, illness, and so forth. This is not very different from drive-reduction theory. People are motivated to satisfy these basic physiological needs first. Beyond that basic level, however, are what Maslow calls the higher human needs.

The second level, in particular, represents the need for safety. These deficiencies (insecurity, yearning, fear, sense of loss) are fulfilled by the person achieving security, comfort, calm, and balance.

The third level is labeled love. Here, the condition of deficiency is being self-conscious or feeling unwanted, worthless or empty, lonely, or isolated. People are motivated to reduce these deficiencies and achieve a sense of wholeness, warmth, and strength. They accomplish this primarily by experiencing acceptance in a love relationship.

The fourth level of need in Maslow's scheme is esteem. We all have the need for confidence and a sense of mastery and self-regard. Without these we feel incompetent, negative, and inferior.

Finally, the highest level of motivation is the fifth category, self-actualization. The deficiencies experienced at this level are feelings of alienation, notions that life has no meaning, and boredom. To become self-actualized, that is, to eliminate even this level of need, is to have a healthy curiosity, to experience creativity and insight, and to work at something that is pleasurable and that embodies high values.

Maslow believes that these higher needs are more human than the base needs (see also Schultz, 1976). They cannot appear until more basic needs have been satisfied. They tend to appear later in life, and they often require particular external conditions for their fulfillment (e.g., economic security). Failure to gratify these needs results in dysfunction (Arkes & Garske 1977), whereas fulfillment remedies the dysfunction. As lower needs are fulfilled, higher needs can be addressed.

Whereas Hull was trying to construct a theory of motivation that would be open to experimental test, preferably with animal subjects, at every step, Maslow's aim was to try to capture the full range of motivation recognized within society, even if the resulting theory would inevitably remain at a speculative level. As a result, it is difficult to point to experiments that confirm that higher needs are, indeed, inherent in the human condition, much less that they form such a hierarchy. Maslow himself tended merely to demonstrate his system by considering or analyzing very exceptional people who were unusually intelligent or creative. But this provides a somewhat distorted view. While it may be true that those people have fulfilled the lower needs and are motivated to achieve full self-actualization, they do not necessarily represent the average person. Were we to consider humans who are not so exceptional, we might very well come to a different conclusion about the hierarchy of needs. It is an interesting, and open, question as to whether exceptional or average people are more important to the behavior of the economy they live in.

It is not really important to prove Maslow's scheme. It is sufficient to note that many people do act as though they have this hierarchy of needs. It is perhaps in the area of economic behavior that the striving to fulfill these needs is most evident: Vast sums of money are spent to provide security and comfort, to relieve loneliness and isolation, to gain confidence and self-respect, and to relieve boredom. If for no other reason, Maslow's theory deserves to be taken seriously. We shall return to it in Chapter 19 when we consider the implications of economic behavior for psychology in general.

Psychodynamic theory

Perhaps the best known psychologist of all is Sigmund Freud, the founder of psychoanalysis. Nonpsychologists are often surprised to discover that Freud's theories are not universally accepted in psychology, primarily because they are said to be untestable and therefore unscientific. Nevertheless, Freud has provided us with a view of humankind that is compelling and often useful. Because psychoanalytic theory has been used to account for various economic phenomena, including societies' reaction to and use of money, we shall introduce it briefly here (see B. Weiner 1980, for more details). Freudian theory is a good example of a theory of motivation that grows out of a theory of the structure of personality.

Freud began his work during the late nineteenth century, at a time when the main subject matter of psychology was consciousness (see Boring 1957). One of his earliest and most important contributions was the idea that overt human behavior reflects another kind of psychological reality, namely, the unconscious. In particular, the human personality, including its motivational forces, exists in both the conscious and unconscious domains; according to Freud, it was the unconscious that plays the major role. The problem is that we cannot know our unconscious side in the same direct way as our consciousness. For Freud, something is not unconscious if it is, like an inactive memory, simply not in consciousness at the present time. Freud called ideas or motives that could be called to mind when required *preconscious*. He reserved the term *unconscious* for materials that are inaccessible to ordinary consciousness, at least without help such as might be provided in psychoanalytic therapy. This inaccessibility necessarily means that Freud's theory must be largely speculative and cannot be based on direct observation, although that does not mean it is completely inaccessible to empirical test (see Kline 1981).

Freud believed that the unconscious level of our personality contains several kinds of psychic energy that are the sources of motivation and impetus for our behavior. He considered psychic energy to be instinctual in nature and to be derived from the basic all-important life-and-death instincts. To Freud, the life instinct consisted of forces primarily for sexual reproduction, while the death instinct showed itself primarily in the repetitive-compulsive patterns of behavior that were performed despite the fact that they brought pain and suffering to the person.

The psychic energy (instincts) constitute the motivational component of Freud's theory. Despite the superficial differences, the stress on a limited number of sources of energy makes Freud's ideas recognizably similar to the type of drive theory we have already considered (cf. Hinde 1960). But Freud viewed the instincts as operating within a hypothetical personality system, and it is this system that is Freud's most widely recognized and distinctive contribution to psychological thought. It also leads to important implications for economic motivation.

Freud's personality system involves a three-part division of the personality. The first major division is the Id. This is the primitive reservoir of instinctual energy, which is regulated by the pleasure principle (the hedonistic notion of seeking pleasure and avoiding pain). Freud called the Id a "cauldron of seething excitement." It is unbounded sexual energy. The Ego, the second part of the personality, is a controlling force for the Id. The Ego develops after early childhood and is governed by the reality principle. It observes and tests reality; it remembers and monitors the world. The Ego is our rational self; it checks the unbridled energy of the Id and permits us to behave appropriately in a social context. The third part is the Superego. This develops from the Ego; that is, through the contacts with the outside world, certain perceived patterns become internalized. These patterns reflect values and moral judgments from our parents and from society in general. In short, the Superego strives for perfection; it is our moral sense, guiding the rational behavior of the Ego by providing it with moral direction.

In summary, the picture drawn by Freud is of a person motivated by primitive energies and instincts while at the same time governed and checked by rational and moral forces. The tension created by the clash of these mechanisms leads to various dynamic behavioral processes, such as identification, displacement, sublimation, repression, and defense. These processes describe how conflict and tension between parts of the personality are resolved. When the resolution is not satisfactory, neuroses and other deleterious conditions can arise.

Is Freudian theory relevant to the study of economic behavior? The answer would appear to be a qualified "yes." First, the theory represents a world view or perspective on humankind that has a certain intuitive validity to it. People do seem to be driven by unconscious and instinctual tendencies. Furthermore, psychoanalytic thought is clearly opposed to the rationalist psychology that pervades economic theory. According to Freud, realistic and rational processes only account for a part of behavior, and perhaps not the most significant part. The theory seems to account for a range of general economic behaviors much as Maslow's theory does. For example, we spend a good deal of time and money behaving in a way that Freud can predict given the premise that our personalities are configured as he claims. Finally, Freud's theory seems especially useful when considering abnormal or excessive economic behaviors. That is, highly inappropriate or deviant actions, such as excessive gambling, compulsive buying, and inordinate allegience to authority, may be more easily understood from Freud's perspective than from many others.

The psychometric approach to personality

Freudian theory is by no means the only approach to personality, however. Another very influential view can be described as *trait theory*. According to this theory, there are a limited number of characteristics (or traits, or factors, or dimensions) of personality, along which individuals differ. If the key dimensions can be discovered, and individuals located on them, the differences between them can be understood and their differences of behavior predicted. Widely used personality dimensions include extraversion/introversion, stability/neurosis, and psychoticism/normality. Eysenck (1977) claimed that these three dimensions account for almost all the variations between people in systematic personality testing. Individuals with different values on some personality dimensions can be expected to have different patterns of motivation. For example, an extreme extravert, someone whose personality is directed toward other people and external events, will presumably show far more social and sociable motivation than an extreme introvert, literally, someone who is turned in upon himself or herself.

In contrast to Freudian theory, which was originally derived from the detailed clinical observation of a few abnormal individuals, the psychometric approach to personality involves giving relatively simple tests to large numbers of people, and subjecting the results to elaborate mathematical analysis. The trait approach is not irrelevant to clinical questions, however. If we take the three personality dimensions propounded by Eysenck, for example, we can see that all have their origins in clinical distinctions. Extraversion and introversion were first defined by Jung (1921/1971) to describe types he encountered in therapeutic analysis. Neuroticism means a tendency toward the less serious mental disorders, such as phobias, hysteria, and anxiety states, while psychoticism is a tendency toward the severe disorders such as manic depression and schizophrenia. Most psychometricians would argue that these dimensions are nowadays to be defined in terms of the measurement operations and personality tests that demonstrate them, but they would nonetheless agree that individuals who have extreme values on them are unlikely to be in a state of mental health. For example, Eysenck and Eysenck (1976) associate each of the common neurotic disorders with particular extreme combinations of the extraversion/introversion, neuroticism/stability, and psychoticism/normality dimensions.

The psychometric measurement of personality is an attractive idea for an economic psychologist. People show very different kinds of economic behavior; they also live in very different economic environments. It is reasonable to guess that these will be produced by, or will produce, different personality types, which in turn will be associated with different kinds of economic motivation. We shall therefore meet many different kinds of personality measurement in this book.

CONCLUSION

Our discussion of personality measurement brings this chapter full circle, as it involves many of the same techniques that are used in attitude measurement with which we began our discussion of social psychology. That circularity is symbolic. There is no logical beginning, and no logical end, to a discussion of psychology. In fact, even a circle is too simple a symbol. Many connections could have been made in this chapter, but we have had to omit them. For example, attribution theory can be linked to the theory of classical conditioning (e.g., Alloy & Tabachnik 1984). It can also be related to a theory of motivation that will become important later in this book (e.g., Chapter 6), in which motivational forces are divided into those intrinsic to the individual or extrinsically applied.

Psychology is thus not a subject with a few well-established basic principles, from which the rest of its ideas can be derived. Rather, it is a closely woven web of interrelated concepts and empirical results. We shall discover a very different situation as we now turn to a brief introduction to some key ideas in economics.

2

INTRODUCTION TO MICROECONOMICS

Our aim in this chapter is to introduce the fundamental ideas of micro-economics that will be used later in the book. It is not our intent to try to produce a substitute for a good textbook or a summary of one. Rather, we hope to convey the essence of the microeconomic approach and thereby to introduce some of the analytical tools in the economist's work-box. Microeconomics has a great deal to say about many of the topics covered in Part II of this book. However, the economist's approach to these topics is characteristically very different from that of the psychologist, and it is with this distinctive approach that we begin.

ECONOMIST'S APPROACH

General characteristics

Faced with an interesting economic behavior, an economist will typically consider a range of explanations involving mainly economic variables, such as income, costs, and prices. The first step is usually the construction of a model of the behavior in question. The model makes a number of simplifying assumptions, and variables are dealt with one at a time. So, for example, if modeling the purchase of houses, the effect of income and distance from work will be considered independently. The model of the relationship between income and house purchase may be accurate, "other things remaining equal." The behavior of *units* of the economy will be described by assumptions, postulates, or axioms. (The terminology differs between economists.) The units may be individuals but may equally be idealized households, firms, or central authorities. An interesting characteristic of the economist's approach is not just that assumptions are made about the unit's behavior but that these assumptions are of a particular kind. Generally it is postulated that units will behave in the best possible (most rational) way. Thus, in the elementary theory of the firm, the latter maximizes profits; in the elementary theory of demand, households maximize utility – the satisfaction they derive from consuming goods and services. The model is built up from these assumptions; it predicts the behavior of large groups of individuals. Note that economic models do not usually predict the behavior of individuals. Rather, they depend on the "law" of large numbers to predict average behavior. This is quite deliberate. Modern microeconomics is not the study of individual units as units but the study of systems in the economy.

We can briefly illustrate this approach if we consider gifts and giving, an area of interest to economists, psychologists, and anthropologists. This is what Alchian and Allen (1969, p. 166) had to say:

The economics . . . of gifts may seem contradictory. If . . . people seek to increase their own utility, how then can they give gifts? Are these acts to be set aside from economics as unexplainable behavior? Not at all. The postulates of economic theory do not say that man is concerned only about his own situation . . . If other people are miserable, he may himself feel a lower level of utility.

These workers go on to deduce that, all things equal, as a giver's wealth decreases relative to the recipient's, the former's willingness to give will decrease.

The example illustrates a number of features of the economists' approach. Income, a standard and powerful economic variable, is used to predict the average behavior of individuals in the economy. It is assumed that people are maximizing utility in their behavior and that utility is not narrowly defined. The analysis considers, moreover, who gains what from a gift, the waste from the receiver's point of view, and the transfer of specific resources and general purchasing power.

This brings us to the central concern of economics: How does the availability of resources interact with behavior? Economics deals with this issue mainly through the concept of choice. The concern then really becomes how an economy or an individual chooses to allocate scarce resources. Three basic kinds of decisions have to be made: *what* goods or services should be produced and consumed, *how* should they be produced, and *who* shall consume them. It is obviously possible for a central authority to make these decisions; modern economies clearly differ in the degree to which a central authority is involved. Most of these decisions are not taken by governments; they are taken by the business community influenced by the decisions of individuals. Producers and consumers communicate through the market and the communication they have is a monetary one, that is, via the price mechanism.

The price mechanism

The price mechanism is essentially an automatic signaling device which coordinates the actions of buyers and sellers. The price of a good or service indicates whether too little or too much of it is being produced and consumed. We can illustrate this by reference to the market for strawberries. Growers of strawberries may offer them for sale at a price that covers costs plus a small profit. The quantity buyers wish to purchase at this price may not be the same as the amount the growers have for sale. In this case, the price is too high or too low, and it will tend to move up or down to establish an equality between the amount growers want to sell and the amount buyers want to purchase. (How this happens will be discussed in the section, Theory of Price.) The price mechanism, then, tends to equate supply and demand.

This seems straightforward, although this is clearly a very idealized example. But the notion of the price mechanism is a very powerful one, occupying a central position in microeconomics because it is assumed that price operates to make the what, how, and who decisions that the economy must make. The price mechanism operates not only in commodity markets but throughout the economy: in the money market (the rate of interest is, in effect, the price of money), in the factors of production market (e.g., the price of labor, land), and in international transactions. Thus, the price mechanism serves to allocate scarce resources of all types. To see how this works, we need to consider the elementary theory of price in more detail.

THEORY OF PRICE

This section describes the theory of price. We shall first consider demand from the point of view of the individual buyers and then sum over individuals to derive the overall market demand for a good. We shall then do the same for individual suppliers and, by considering them together, examine the working of the price mechanism. Finally, we shall reexamine individual demand.

Theory of demand

The amount of a good that an individual wishes to purchase may depend on a number of factors: the person's liking for the good, how much of it is already owned, income, price, the price of other similar goods, and so forth. Of greatest interest is the relationship between the price of a good and the quantity demanded, that is, the amount an individual would be prepared to purchase at a given price. This relationship can be examined assuming that the other determining factors do not change. Table 2.1 represents the present authors' effective demand for strawberries in one week in June at various prices. RMT is a strawberry freak, PW has a liking for them, and SEGL buys them as a treat for his tortoise. If we make the unreal assumption that we are the only buyers of strawberries, we can derive the total market demand curve simply by adding together our individual demand schedules. Such a curve is usually represented

Table 2.1 *Imaginary demand schedule for strawberries.*[a,b]

Price (cents)	X	Y	Z	All consumers
80	0	0	0	0
70	0	1	0	1
60	0	1	0	1
50	0	2	0	2
40	0	2	2	4
30	0	4	4	8
20	1	5	5	11
10	2	9	6	17

[a]Quantities demanded per week (in pints).
[b]X, Y, and Z represent three different consumers.

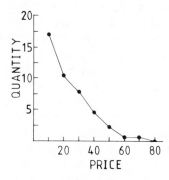

2.1. Market demand for strawberries (in pints) as a function of price (in pence) derived from data in Table 2.1 plotted according to psychological conventions.

graphically as in Figure 2.1. (Note that all these figures are plotted according to the convention in psychology, with price on the horizontal axis.)

All four of these demand schedules – the real individual ones and the hypothetical market one – are downward sloping. This is true of nearly all demand curves (for examples, see Lea 1978) and indicates that more of a good is demanded when its price is lower. Why should this be so? The standard explanation is that the added satisfaction or utility that an individual gains from additional units of a good, whether strawberries or televisions, tends to decline as the individual acquires more of it. This principle of diminishing marginal utility states simply that the marginal utility attached to an additional unit of a good diminishes as more and more of the good is acquired.

Other factors are also important in affecting the amount of a good that an individual wishes to purchase. In general, as income rises, we might expect an increase in the quantity demanded of a good. Goods that fit this expectation are called normal goods; those that do not are called inferior goods. For these, a rise in income above a particular level leads to a drop in the quantity demanded; this is true of margarine and potatoes in some countries. The price of other goods may also be important. If a reduction in the price of one good leads to a fall in demand for another, the goods are considered substitutes. Butter and margarine and rail and bus travel are good examples. Alternatively, a price fall for one good may lead to an increase in demand for another. In this case the goods are complements. This relationship will hold for goods that tend to be consumed together, such as videorecorders and videotapes.

Theory of supply

The amount of a good that an individual or firm wishes to supply will, like demand, depend on a number of factors, including the cost of production, the price of the good, and the prices of other goods. Other things being equal, the higher the price of a good, the more profitable it will be to produce it. Because we assume, in the simplest case, that firms try to maximize profits, we can draw a supply schedule, similar to our demand schedule, that relates price and the amount a producer is willing to supply (see Table 2.2). In this example, the two producers differ in the number of acres of land under cultivation but little else. Again we can derive the total market supply curve by adding the individual supply curves. This gives us a curve as shown in Figure 2.2. Unlike the demand curves, these supply curves slope upward. This is related to the costs of production. For a producer to offer additional amounts of good for sale, it is clear that the price must cover at least the cost of producing them. If we assume that the cost of the additional amount of the good (marginal cost) increases as output increases, then there is some justification for the upward slope of the supply curve. To get more strawberries to market, for instance, one might have to buy expensive antibird devices or take more care and time when picking the fruit.

Factors other than the price of the good will also be important determinants of supply. For instance, if the prices of other goods that an individual firm supplies go up, there may be a tendency to switch production into these alternative areas. If raspberry prices go up, Growmore and Grewsome may well increase the acreage they devote to this fruit and thereby produce fewer strawberries. Changes in the state of technology may also be important; for example, the use of cheap insecticides and nylon netting can dramatically increase strawberry production. Finally changes in the prices of factors of production – land, labor, and machinery – will also affect supply. If strawberry production is, for example,

Table 2.2 *Imaginary supply schedule for strawberries*[a]

Price (cents)	Growmore	Grewsome	All producers
80	24	11	35
70	20	10	30
60	16	9	25
50	12	8	20
40	8	6	14
30	4	4	8
20	3	1	4
10	0	0	0

[a]Quantities supplied per week (in pints).

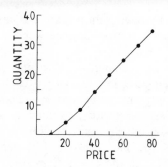

2.2. Market supply for strawberries (in pints) as a function of price (in pence) derived from data in Table 2.2.

labor intensive and the average real wages increase, then strawberry growers may switch to growing fruit that uses less labor.

Working of the price mechanism

Having independently derived the relationship between price and quantity demanded and price and quantity supplied we are now in a position to combine them on the same graph. Figure 2.3 shows that supply and demand are equal only when the price is thirty cents. It is at this price that the market is described as being in equilibrium. If the price were higher than this, say forty cents, there would be an excess of supply over demand: Consumers would only want to buy four pints but fourteen would be on offer. Sellers would compete with one another to unload their stocks by reducing their price to a more favorable level. Conversely, were the price only twenty cents, there would be an excess of demand over supply and consumers would compete with each other for the limited

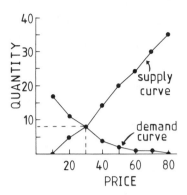

2.3. Quantity of strawberries purchased as a function of price.

supply of strawberries by paying more and thus forcing the price up. At the equilibrium price, the competition between suppliers and between consumers is resolved.

What happens if there is a change in the conditions of supply (e.g., the strawberry crop is decimated by slugs) or a change in taste? This will obviously shift the supply and demand curves and alter the equilibrium price. The four simplest cases are described in Figure 2.4. If people suddenly dislike strawberries for one reason or another, the demand curve will shift downward, that is, less will be demanded at each price. This will cause a decrease in the equilibrium price and the amount sold (see Fig. 2.4). Similarly, a decrease in supply will alter the equilibrium price as well; in this case, price will increase and the amount sold will decrease (see Fig. 2.4).

This very simple analysis depends on the assumption that supply curves slope upward and demand curves downward. Obviously a supply curve could be horizontal in the short term. This would imply that a producer had a fixed quantity to dispose of and would sell it for whatever price it would bring. A farmer who has just gathered a crop of strawberries might well be in this position, since the product will rot if it is not sold quickly. In this case, a change in demand would produce no change in the amount sold, but it would cause a relatively large drop in equilibrium price. This illustrates the importance of the responsiveness of demand or supply to changes in price.

Elasticity

The responsiveness of demand to changes in price is assessed by examining the proportionate change in quantity demanded relative to the proportionate change in price, that is, change in quantity/quantity divided by the change in price/price. In our earlier example, a ten-cent fall in the price of

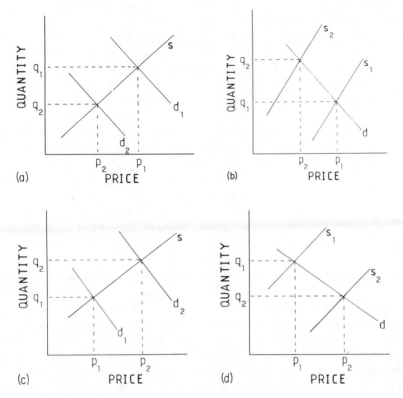

2.4. The effects of changes in supply and demand on the quantity purchased and price of a commodity. (a) A decrease in demand leads to a fall in price and quantity. (b) An increase in supply leads to a fall in price and an increase in quantity purchased. (c) An increase in demand leads to an increase in price and quantity. (d) A decrease in supply leads to an increase in price and a decrease in quantity purchased.

strawberries, from fifty cents to forty cents would bring about a two-pint rise in quantity demanded, from two pints to four pints. Here, the elasticity of demand is 2/2 divided by 10/50 = 5 – arc elasticity. Strictly speaking, elasticity is defined at each point on a curve, that is, point elasticity, and not between two points in the curve. If elasticity is greater than one, demand is said to be elastic, as in the above example. Here demand is responsive to changes in price. On the other hand, if elasticity is less than one, demand is inelastic; that is, demand is insensitive to changes in price. This would be true for a good if a 10% price fall led to only a 5% increase in quantity demanded. There is obviously another type of elasticity – unit elasticity – where demand falls by 1% when the price rises by 1%. Clearly, total expenditure on a good for which the demand is of unit elasiticity is the same, whatever the price. For goods with an elastic demand, however, total expenditure increases as price falls; for goods with an inelastic demand, total expenditure decreases as price falls.

The elasticity of supply is defined in a similar way. It is a ratio of the proportionate change in quantity supplied relative to the proportionate change in price. Again, if the ratio is less than one, supply is inelastic; if it is greater than one, supply is elastic. The farmer who has just gathered the strawberry crop and who now must dispose of it has an inelastic supply curve.

The example of the strawberry farmer illustrates the importance of time. In the short term, the farmer has an inelastic supply curve; the strawberry crop must be sold, whatever the price. In the long run, however, the farmer will not be prepared to sell strawberries at low prices; other crops would be planted instead. So the long-term supply curve is more elastic. A similar effect may occur with demand. If people habitually buy a particular good, they may continue to do so in the short term despite an increase in its price. In the long term they may adjust their habits as they find acceptable substitutes.

It is reasonable to ask what determines elasticity. For demand curves, we can explore this question by identifying two effects produced by a change in price. These are the *substitution effect* and the *income effect.*

The substitution effect occurs when people buy a good the price of which has dropped instead of another good whose price has remained the same. For instance, if the price of butter fell, consumers would substitute butter for margarine. By contrast, the income effect occurs when a decrease in prices, leading to a rise in real income, causes us to buy more. This may be trivial in most cases, but in some quite substantial. Changes in mortgage interest rates, or rent, for example, which take up a large part of our budgets, will significantly alter our real income. For the average British housebuyer, a 2% drop in mortgage interest rates leads to an approximately 5% rise in real income. Such an increase obviously means that we have more to spend; some of this extra income may be used to buy the good where price has fallen, in this case by buying a bigger house.

The responsiveness of demand to changes in price, that is, the elasticity of demand, will depend on the size of both the substitution and the income effects. The more close substitutes a good has (e.g., cabbage, Brussels sprouts, spinach), the more elastic demand for it will be. Variations in the income effect also occur but are less important. If a good is an inferior one (i.e., consumption of it falls as income rises), the income effect will lessen the substitution effect. If a good is a normal one, the income effect will reinforce it.

The most important determinant of elasticity for supply curves is the way in which costs alter when output changes. If costs per unit increase greatly when output rises, supply will be inelastic; that is, a large proportionate change in price will bring about only a small increase in quantity supplied. If unit costs barely increase, if at all, as output rises, supply will be elastic other things being equal.

The concept of elasticity can also be used to measure the response of quantity demanded (or supplied) to changes in other important factors, such as income or prices of other goods. Cross-price elasticity, for example, is a measure of the responsiveness of quantity demanded of one good to changes in the price of another. If goods are substitutes for each other, the cross-price elasticity will be positive; a price increase for one will lead to an increase in demand for the other. If goods are complements, such as bread and butter, the cross-price elasticity will be negative; a price increase for one will lead to a decrease in demand for the other. The income elasticity of demand indicates whether goods are normal or inferior. Normal goods have a positive income elasticity (consumption increases with income), inferior goods negative income elasticity (consumption falls as income rises).

The importance of elasticity can be illustrated if we consider the effect of a sales tax on the price and sales of a good. If a tax is imposed and sellers must pay this to the government, they will no longer be prepared to offer the same quantities at the same prices. They will add the tax to their costs, and this will shift the supply curve to the right (see Fig. 2.5). The effect of this depends on the elasticity of the demand curve. Only with a perfectly inelastic demand does a tax have the effect of increasing the price by the full amount of the tax and of leaving sales (and the revenue of the sellers) unchanged (Fig. 2.5c shows that buyers will always purchase the same quantity whatever the price). In general, a tax will raise the price paid by buyers and reduce the price received by sellers, although in each case by less than the amount of the tax.

We can see that the effects of changes in supply and demand, whether brought about by taxation, changes in taste, or whatever, will depend on the elasticity of the supply and demand curves. These, in turn, depend on the prices of other goods, the relationship between income and demand, and so on. On the basis of this type of analysis, we can begin to see how all the interdependent sections of the economy can be built up. Through the price mechanism, which maintains equilibrium, scarce resources in the economy are allocated. But all this depends on the assumptions underlying demand and supply curves. In the case of demand, these assumptions consist of assertions about individual behavior. Let us examine these assumptions in more detail.

Theory of demand revisited

Most demand curves are downward sloping, as we explained in terms of the principle of diminishing marginal utility. This principle, however, is either no more than a label for the phenomenon we are trying to explain,

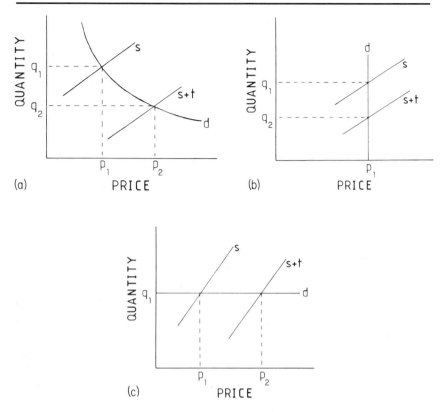

2.5. The effect of a tax on price and quantity purchased. (a) with unit elasticity of demand, (b) with perfectly elastic demand, (c) with perfectly inelastic demand.

or an untestable assertion about subjective states of mind. Understandably enough, economists have attempted to put demand theory on a firmer basis. This includes assumptions or axioms about peoples' preferences.

The first assumption is that every individual has consistent transitive and well-defined preferences. This means that, given a choice between various collections of goods (sometimes called commodity bundles) A, B, and C, a person prefers either A to B or B to A or is indifferent to them. These preferences are stable over time (consistent) and are such that if A is preferred to B and B to C, then A is preferred to C (transitive). Furthermore, it is assumed that every individual prefers to have more rather than less of a good. (If a person prefers less of something, like rubbish, it is a "bad.") This *axiom of greed* implies that if collection A includes more of all goods than does B, a person will prefer A; even if A includes more of one good and no less of another, that person will still prefer A.

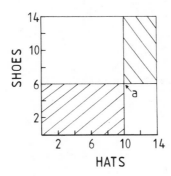

2.6. Collections of shoes and hats.

To illustrate how demand theory can be built up from these assumptions we will use a concrete example of collections of two goods, hats and shoes. Each point in Figure 2.6 represents a combination of a number of hats and a number of pairs of shoes. Point A, for example, represents six pairs of shoes and ten hats. From the assumptions made above, we can deduce that A will be preferred to any collection represented in the lower shaded area and that any combination of shoes and hats in the upper shaded area will be preferred to A. We cannot make any deductions about whether A will be preferred to combinations in the unshaded areas; it depends on the particular individual's taste. If we offer an individual a choice between combinations in the unshaded area and A, we will find that some are preferred to A, others are not preferred relative to A, and still others for which the individual is indifferent. Nine pairs of shoes and four hats, for instance, may give the individual identical satisfaction to six hats and six pairs of shoes and so there is no preference one way or the other. If we find all the combinations that give equal satisfaction, we can plot an indifference curve (sometimes known as a constant utility or iso-utility curve). Thurstone (1931b) did this by presenting a respondent with a series of combinations of hats and pairs of shoes and asking for a judgment as to whether each combination was preferred to a standard. It was assumed that the two combinations would cost the same and that the articles were freely chosen by the respondent. Thurstone's results are plotted in Figure 2.7.

Any point to the right of this curve shows combinations of hats and pairs of shoes that would be preferred to those actually on the curve; similarly, points to the left show combinations that would not be preferred. For the individual depicted, four hats and eighteen pairs of shoes is preferable to eight hats and eight pairs of shoes. Obviously, we can plot a series of such indifference curves, which will give us an indifference

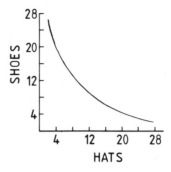

2.7. An indifference curve (after Thurstone 1931).

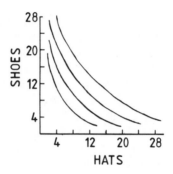

2.8. An indifference map showing a family of indifference curves for hats and pairs of shoes (after Thurstone 1931).

map for the individual. Figure 2.8 shows four indifference curves that Thurstone obtained from his subject.

This indifference map describes the verbally expressed preferences of the particular individual who participated in Thurstone's experiment; it does not tell us what combination of hats and shoes the person would actually buy. Figure 2.8 also illustrates that there is a diminishing marginal rate of substitution between hats and shoes. This is equivalent to the idea of diminishing marginal utility. This idea suggests that the less of a good an individual has, the more unwilling the person will be to give up a unit of that good to obtain an additional unit of a second good. This accounts for the convex shape of indifference curves.

To examine what this person would actually do, unfortunately we need to use an imaginary example. An indifference map indicates an individual's tastes. On the same graph, we can indicate what possibilities are available. This is done by drawing in a budget line, which shows the

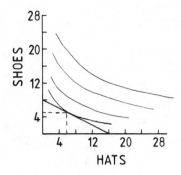

2.9. An individual in equilibrium: income = \$160, hats = \$10, shoes = \$20.

combinations of two goods that are just obtainable given the individual's income and the prices of the two goods. Figure 2.9 adds a budget line to our indifference map, assuming that the individual has an income of \$160 and hats cost \$10 and shoes \$20 per pair. The person could spend the entire income on sixteen hats, or spend it all on eight shoes or buy some combination of hats and shoes that falls along the budget line. How many shoes and hats will actually be bought? Assuming that the person wants to maximize utility, the combination of hats and shoes will be that which is on the highest indifference curve. This cannot be one that is cut by the budget line; it must be the one that just touches the budget line, that is, where an indifference curve is at a tangent to the budget line. In our example, the person would buy six hats and five pairs of shoes because it is at this point that utility is maximized – the slope of the indifference curve equals the slope of the budget line. What this means is that the individual adjusts to prices by choosing a combination of two goods in such a way that the subjective relative evaluation of them corresponds with the objective relative evaluation. Put another way, this ensures that the utility obtained for each dollar spent is the same for all purchases. The subjective relative evaluation is shown on the indifference curve and indicates how many shoes the person would willingly give up to get an additional hat. The objective relative evaluation (prices) is shown on the budget line and indicates how many shoes the individual would have to give up to get another hat.

Indifference maps can be used to examine what happens when an individual's income or the price of a good changes. A change in income involves a shift in the budget line, outward if income rises and inward if it falls. For each income, there is an ideal point at which utility is maximized; that is, the point at which the budget line is at a tangent to an indifference curve. If we connect these ideal points we derive an income-

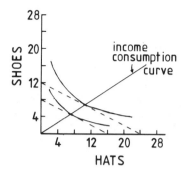

2.10. The effect of a change in income on quantity of hats and shoes.

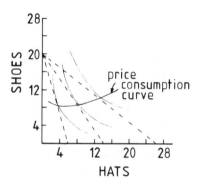

2.11. The effect of a change in price on quantity of hats and shoes.

consumption curve, which shows how the consumption of hats and shoes changes as income increases (see Fig. 2.10).

A change in the relative prices of the two goods alters the slope of the budget line. If the price of hats increases, the slope of the budget line becomes steeper; that is, if all income is devoted to hats, fewer can be bought if the price has increased. For each price of hats (the price of shoes remaining unchanged), there is again an ideal point at which utility is maximized. If those points are connected, we derive a price-consumption curve (see Fig. 2.11).

Obviously a price–consumption curve plotted on an indifference map can be used to derive an individual demand curve. We can illustrate this with a different example: quantities of tobacco on one axis and the value of all other goods consumed on the second axis. Figure 2.12 assumes that the individual has an income of $5,000 per year. The price–consumption curve is in the upper part of the diagram because whatever the price of tobacco, the individual does not spend much income on it (in fact 10 pounds of tobacco per year is purchased for $25 per pound, i.e., $250, or

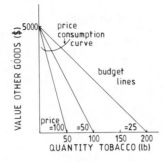

2.12. Price–consumption curve for tobacco.

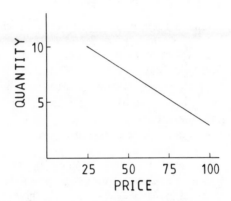

2.13. An individual's demand curve for tobacco.

5% of the total income). If we transfer the information from the indifference map to a conventional demand curve we derive a fairly inelastic demand for tobacco (Fig. 2.13) – at $25 per pound the arc elasticity is 1/5.

This hypothetical demand curve for tobacco slopes downward, the normal case. Does this have to be true given the axioms we started with? The answer is "no." A demand curve could slope upward but only under rather special conditions, the so-called Giffen case. Because these conditions are of some psychological interest (see Chapter 7), we shall consider them here.

Earlier, we distinguished between the substitution effect of a price change and the income effect. These can be analyzed more precisely using indifference curves. Figure 2.14 illustrates this in the case of a drop in the price of tobacco. Such a fall increases the amount of tobacco bought from A to C but also increases the amount of alcohol bought from D to E. Recall that the income effect occurs when a fall in the price of a good enables an individual to buy more of all goods; that is, it increases the real income. We can analytically remove this income effect by keep-

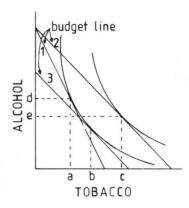

2.14. The income and substitution effect of a fall in the price.

ing the individual on the original indifference curve. We draw a new budget line (3) parallel to budget line 2, so that the relative prices of alcohol and tobacco are the same at a tangent to the original indifference curve. The increase in the consumption of tobacco from A to B is the substitution effect. The substitution effect always involves an increase in quantity demanded when price falls because indifference curves slope downward.

The increase in the amount of tobacco bought, from A to C, can therefore be analyzed into a substitution effect (the result of the change in relative prices, from A to B) and an income effect (the result of the change in real income, from B to C). The result of the change of price of any good can be analyzed in this way. This means that we can state precisely the conditions under which a demand curve will slope upward, namely, only when an increase in income leads to a reduction in consumption sufficient to outweigh the substitution effect. So a normal good must have a downward-sloping demand curve; an inferior good may have an upward-sloping demand curve, depending on the relative strengths of the income and substitution effects. We would expect that, for most goods, demand curves would slope downward.

This traditional approach to demand theory assumes that goods are desired for themselves rather than for the various attributes they possess. A more realistic approach views each good as a bundle of attributes or characteristics. For example, a hat yields protection from the weather as well as decoration. We do not desire hats per se; what we want is to look decorative and be warm and dry. This characteristics approach was first stated formally by Lancaster (1966b) and, as we shall be making considerable use of this approach later in the book (see Chapters 6, 7, 12, and 18) we shall consider it briefly here.

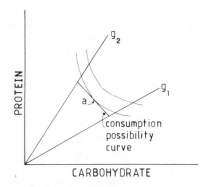

2.15. Consumption possibilities for protein and carbohydrate given relative price and income (see text for explanation).

The demand for characteristics

Different hats provide protection and decoration in different proportions and at different costs. A balaclava provides a lot of warmth but, given current fashions, it is not too decorative. A tassle ski hat is quite warm and also reasonably decorative, and Ascot or top hats are simply decorative. The new theory of demand for characteristics can provide an account of how demand for such groups of similar goods is related. The traditional theory cannot.

Let us consider another example, shown in Figure 2.15. Imagine that we want to examine demand for a group of goods that have only two relevant characteristics, A (carbohydrates) and B (protein). The quantity of characteristics obtained is directly proportional to the amount of the good consumed. Suppose that there are initially only two goods, G_1 and G_2. In each kilogram, G_1 has 80 grams of protein and 500 grams of carbohydrates; G_2 has 160 grams of protein and 250 grams of carbohydrate. If an individual has a budget of $1.50 and both goods cost 50 cents per kilogram, 3 kilograms of either good or some combination of them could be bought. If the person buys only G_1, 1.5 kilograms of carbohydrate and 240 grams of protein is obtained. If the person buys only G_2, 750 grams of carbohydrate and 480 grams of protein is acquired. Obviously by spending part of the $1.50 on G_1 and part on G_2, the individual can obtain the combinations of characteristics represented in the consumption possibility line. If the person had more money this line would move outward from the origin. If the relative prices of the goods changed its slope would shift.

Previously we drew indifference curves as though an individual was indifferent between combinations of various goods. But in this approach a

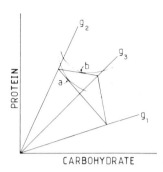

2.16. Consumption possibilities for protein and carbohydrate given relative price of three goods (see text for explanation).

person's preferences are for characteristics rather than the goods themselves. If we draw indifference curves between combinations of characteristics, we can infer that the preferred combination is at A, where the consumption possibility line is at a tangent to an indifference curve.

If a third good is introduced (see Fig. 2.16) that yields protein and carbohydrate but in different proportions from either G_1 or G_2, its place in the system depends on its price. Suppose that in each kilogram of G_3 there are 80 grams of protein and 250 grams of carbohydrate. This looks like a worse good than either G_1 or G_2. But if the price is low enough, say thirty cents per kilogram, its presence extends the consumption possibility line. The individual will choose some point along this line, in this case point B. If the price of G_3 increases up to 33.33 cents per kilogram the consumption possibility line would be the same as in Figure 2.15; the combination of 360 grams of protein and 1,125 grams of carbohydrate could be obtained either by spending one-half of the budget on each of G_1 and G_2 or by spending all of it on G_3. In this case, the individual would choose point A and would spend 50 cents on G_2 (yielding 160 grams of protein and 250 grams of carbohydrate) and $1 on G_3 (yielding 240 grams of protein and 750 grams of carbohydrate). If the price of G_3 increased any more, none would be bought; instead, the individual would spend $1 on G_2 (yielding 320 grams of protein and 500 grams of carbohydrate) and fifty cents on G_3 (yielding 80 grams of protein and 500 grams of carbohydrate). This type of behavior is common: A comparatively small increase in price is enough to make an individual cease buying a product. Despite a preference for Dolchelatte, if its price goes higher than $4 per pound one may switch to another blue-veined cheese, such as Stilton or Mycella. This behavior is not explained by traditional demand theory, but the characteristic approach deals with it well.

Using this model, Lancaster was able to make several valuable distinctions. One was between primitive and sophisticated consumption technologies, in which characteristics outnumber goods in the former, or vice versa in the latter. In a primitive consumption technology, the consumer may have to accept more of one characteristic than would otherwise be desirable in order to get enough of another, because not enough combinations of characteristics are on sale as goods. For example, when buying an automobile, one may have to put up with more ostentation than desired in order to get a large enough family car, given the primitive state of our car-consumption technology.

A second distinction Lancaster makes is that between personal and efficiency substitution. In the face of limited income, all goods are potential substitutes. One may have to sacrifice visits to the cinema in order to pay the rent, even though both commodities concerned share virtually no characteristics. Lancaster calls this behavior *personal substitution*. But if one spends $200 per year on novels instead of buying a television, that behavior is *efficiency substitution* – one is obtaining the same characteristics (entertainment, ideas) at a lower cost.

THE EVIDENCE

We have devoted considerable space in this chapter to theories of price and demand. Given that the reader may have some doubts about the axioms on which the theory of demand is based (see Chapter 5), it is reasonable to ask how accurate these theories are. Here we will give only a brief consideration of a few selected predictions of these theories; a more detailed account of relevant empirical work can be found in later chapters. It should be borne in mind, however, that these elementary theories describe markets in which there is perfect competition; in the case of a monopoly or oligopoly, in which a few firms dominate the market, predictions may be rather different. Let us follow the order in which various predictions were introduced in the section on the theory of price.

Shape of demand curves

We asserted earlier that for most goods demand curves should slope downward. Lea (1978) reviewed a large number of studies of demand curves from a variety of sources including econometric studies (based on a combination of observations and techniques of statistical estimation), interviews with consumers, experimental manipulations of prices in shops, token economies, and studies of laboratory animals. Out of forty-seven studies, only two contained upward-sloping demand curves (Hirshleifer, 1980). Given the many different methods used in these studies, this evidence strongly supports demand theory.

Effects of changes of supply and demand

The simple predictions of elementary price theory were diagrammatically presented in the section, Theory of Price. To recapitulate, a decrease in demand leads to a reduction in price and a drop in the quantity bought, whereas an increase in demand leads to an increase in price and in the quantity bought. A decrease in supply leads to an increase in price and a drop in the quantity bought, while an increase in supply leads to a fall in price and a subsequent increase in the quantity bought. Clearly, the precise effects depend on the elasticity of the supply and demand curves. If demand is perfectly inelastic, for example, changes in supply do not alter the quantity purchased, although the price does change.

Unfortunately, when we come to examine the evidence for these simple predictions, we come across the identification problem. At its simplest, the problem is that econometric data consist of a set of price–quantity points gathered over time. From these points alone it is difficult to tell whether demand, supply, or both have changed. When we have additional information, however, the identification problem can be overcome. For example, in December 1966 the Roman Catholic Church altered its rule requiring Catholics to abstain from eating meat on Friday. Instead of applying throughout the year, the rule was to be in effect only during Lent. This change would obviously shift the demand curve for fish, at least in regions with a large Catholic population. Bell (1968) studied the impact of this decrease in demand in New England by comparing prices for fish before and after the change in the rule. He found that for all seven species of fish considered, the price dropped just as price theory would predict.

Let us now consider changes in supply. In agricultural markets at least, it is often easy to identify changes in supply, because farmers harvest bumper crops one year and suffer a crop failure the next. Suits (1970) gives the example of the U.S. apple market. When 4.9 billion pounds of apples were marketed in 1960, the price was 4.84 cents per pound. In 1961 farmers obtained a better crop: 5.63 billion pounds were marketed and the price dropped (as price theory would predict) to 4.15 cents per pound. Such examples are typical and suggest that, for certain markets at least, the predictions of price theory are supported.

Elasticities

Earlier we made some predictions about elasticity, the responsiveness of demand or supply to changes in price. First, elasticity should be greater in the long run than in the short run. Second, the more substitutes available for a given good, the more elastic demand for it will be. Both predictions hold up. Suits (1970) summarized data on elasticities of demand in the

United States. For two-thirds of the goods, short-term demand is more inelastic than long-term demand. For example, the estimated elasticity of demand for airline travel in the short term is extremely inelastic – .06 – but in the longer term it is fairly elastic – 2.4. Lea's (1978) review of demand curves from a wide range of sources also shows that the more specific the good is in use or style and the more alternatives it has, the higher its demand elasticity (see Chapter 7).

Indifference curves

From the fundamental axioms of demand theory, we can deduce that indifference curves should have a negative slope and that they should not intersect. From the concept of diminishing marginal utility, we can infer that these curves should be convex. What evidence is there that these assertions about indifference curves are true?

In general, economists have shown little interest in the empirical determination of indifference curves. The handful of studies that have been carried out have considered a rather limited subset of the universe of goods (eggs and bacon, money and pens, leisure days at a state park, and days at a swimming pool), so the results must be treated with caution. Nonetheless, the empirically derived indifference curves, although they look nothing like the beautiful textbook examples, generally display the properties they are supposed to have. MacCrimmon and Toda's (1969) study of indifference curves for money and pens is a good example. None of the curves for any one of their seven subjects intersected, and all had a negative slope. Only isolated instances of nonconvexity were found, although the degree of convexity was not great and many curves had long linear segments.

MacCrimmon and Toda (1969) obtained their curves in the laboratory using an extended training period and rewarding subjects for recording their preferences accurately. By contrast, Dunn (1978) and Sinden (1974) obtained real-world indifference curves. For example, Dunn investigated indifference curves for income and leisure using an interview technique and, after combining curves for selected groups, validated his findings against data on actual behavior. Groups who were less willing to work overtime had more sharply bending indifference curves, as one would expect.

THE ROLE OF MICROECONOMIC THEORY

Microeconomic theory has been traditionally concerned with explaining the exchange and production of goods such as butter, wine, and land. The theory described in this chapter can be extended to explain how much time people will spend working. Work is seen solely as an instrumental activity. Workers trade their leisure for goods because by giving up leisure (i.e., by working) they obtain money that they can spend on goods. The question is, how much will they work? This can be examined in the same way as choices of combinations of goods or combinations of characteristics. Indifference curves connecting combinations of leisure and income can be drawn. An individual ends up choosing that combination of income and leisure that produces a wage–rate line at a tangent to an indifference curve (see Chapter 6 for a more detailed discussion).

In recent years, however, the economic approach to behavior has been extended even further. It has been applied to social interaction (through the work of the exchange theorists such as Homans 1961), to criminal behavior (Ehrlich 1982), to the behavior of rats (Kagel, Battalio, Rachlin, & Green 1981; Lea 1981), to behavior within the family (Becker 1976a), and to a wide range of other behaviors. Psychologists and other non-economists already have a nodding acquaintance with economic explanations of behavior of interest to them. Our hope is that this chapter will have deepened the acquaintance. Many of the issues raised will be dealt with in more detail in later chapters, but one important point should be emphasized here. The causal sequence in microeconomic theory flows from the individual to the economy: Group decisions and actions are seen as the result of individual actions and decisions, and the workings of the economy are seen as aggregations of the behavior of the individuals. Thus, the workings of many separate markets are responsible for the general equilibrium and the allocation of all of a society's scarce resources. This makes the concept of price extremely powerful.

Microeconomics and the workings of the price mechanism represent only one side of economics, albeit the most obviously relevant to psychologists. The other side of economics is macroeconomics, which is concerned with the functioning of the economy as a whole. It is to this side of economics, and to the possibility of causal sequences flowing from the economy to the individual, that we now turn our attention.

3

INTRODUCTION TO
MACROECONOMICS

In contrast to the single introductory psychology chapter, we devote two introductions to economics. This is because economic theory falls naturally into two parts. First we have the theory of the behavior of the individual components of the economy – individual people, households, and firms – the subject matter of microeconomics (see Chapter 2). But we also have the theory of the entire economy – the subject matter of macroeconomics. The purpose of this chapter is to introduce the noneconomist to the major concepts of macroeconomics.

THE ECONOMY AS A WHOLE

Individual economic agents and their actions make up the economy and its behavior in much the same way – or perhaps as a generalization of the same principle – as individual people and their actions make up society and its behavior. Perhaps it would have been sensible to include an introduction to the theory of society as a whole, parallel to this one, following our introduction to the theory of individual behavior in Chapter 1. But whereas microeconomics and macroeconomics form complementary halves of a single discipline and share a common core of concepts, methods, and vocabulary, an introduction to "macropsychology" would, in fact, have been an introduction to sociology, which is a quite different discipline from psychology, with its own distinct history and ways of thought.

WHY MACROECONOMICS?

Macroeconomics might be thought to have a lesser part to play in economic psychology than occurs in microeconomics. After all, Chapter 2 was largely concerned with the behavior of individuals about which psychological theories could be devised. These theories would complement the economic theories that are more usually applied to individual behavior. Moreover, if the economy as a whole has its own distinct laws and principles, that would seem rather remote from individual behavior. Shouldn't psychologists therefore be content to leave macroeconomics to the economists, while concentrating on those areas that seem to be more relevant, namely micro-economics? The answer is "no" for several reasons.

First, in discussing macroeconomic problems, economists frequently make assertions about individual behavior. A famous example is Keynes's (1936, p. 96) description of a particular macroeconomic assumption (about the proportion of the income generated in a community which will be saved) as, "The fundamental psychological law, upon which we are entitled to depend with great confidence both *a priori* from our knowledge of human nature and from the detailed facts of experience." Two leading economic psychologists, Katona (e.g., 1975, pp. 67–72) and Reynaud (e.g., 1954, p. 90), have both tried to show that this remark is actually wrong at the psychological level (see Chapter 8). Similarly, in a discussion of another classic macroeconomic question, that of taxation and the distribution of incomes, Cairncross (1973, p. 587) argues that increasing levels of taxation on high incomes will, after a certain point, reduce the incentive for highly paid individuals either to work or save, with disadvantageous macroeconomic effects. Again we shall see (Chapters 6 and 11) that this assumption is questioned by recent data about individual behavior.

Second, what the layperson – and most psychologists are laypeople in this context – thinks of as economics is largely macroeconomics. Government economic policy, the determinants of levels of inflation and unemployment, the problems of the balance of payments, and the relative levels of currencies – these "stock-in-trade" of the media treatment of economics represent macroeconomic questions. An interdisciplinary approach to economic psychology must therefore make contact with this common, if dim, background knowledge.

Finally, the most important point is that to leave the macroeconomic level out would be to ignore at least half the purpose of this book. It is within the economy as a whole that individuals live. If there are distinct macroeconomic laws, they must in some sense govern the behavior of the individuals who make up the economy. Such effects of the economy on individual behavior are, at least in our view, an essential part of economic psychology, as important as the effects of individuals on the economy. Indeed, the two kinds of causal interaction form complementary halves, neither of which makes sense without the other.

MACROECONOMIC QUESTIONS

Obviously, this chapter cannot provide a complete introduction to macroeconomics. As Chapters 1 and 2 did for their subjects, this chapter aims to provide a general feel for what macroeconomics is about as well as enough information for the reader to recognize a macroeconomic problem when he or she sees one. Another aim is to let the macroeconomically educated reader know what positions we are taking on the many contentious issues within the subject, although as before we shall do our best to remain neutral.

We have already said that macroeconomics is the study of "the economy as a whole." What does that mean? What is the whole economy? In principle, it ought to mean a system small enough that every part of it (i.e., every individual and every firm) is linked by a chain of economic transactions to every other part of it and large enough that no part of it is linked by economic transactions with any entity outside it. Conventionally, it tends to mean the economy of a nation state.

This is only an approximation to "the whole economy." The only economy that could ever conform precisely to the definition of the whole economy is the economy of the entire planet Earth. But nations can form useful approximations to the whole economy to the extent that by far most individuals within them have vastly more economic transactions with other entities within them than they do with entities outside them. Although a number of other political or geographical entities, both larger and smaller than the nation state, would also conform to this definition, there are three advantages to considering the nation state as a macroeconomic unit. First, nations generally use a single currency that is not used outside their frontiers (money is a macroeconomic question in itself, intimately interwoven with many others). Second, many macroeconomic questions are closely related to questions of economic policy, and the nation is the primary focus of policy formation. Finally, macroeconomic data are commonly available at the national level. It should not be surprising, therefore, that questions in macroeconomics usually refer to the economies of nations.

The best way to promote a feel for a subject is to consider the questions it tries to answer, as these, in effect, set the agenda for the entire discipline. The following list discusses some of the characteristic questions posed about national economies. Largely borrowed from Cairncross (1973), this list is neither exhaustive nor uncontroversial either, as some questions might belong to microeconomics or macroeconomics, depending on one's theoretical standpoint.

1. *What kind of economy are we dealing with?* Most conventional economic theory, especially microeconomic theory, works in terms of an idealized *market economy.* The prices of goods, the quantities produced, the identity of the producers and consumers, and the incomes of all concerned are assumed to result from the free interplay of individuals' utility functions, working through the interaction of the supply and demand functions they determine. In political writing, this state of affairs is often referred to as *capitalism.* By contrast, much Marxist or other socialist writing on economics envisages an idealized *command economy,* in which the prices and

quantities of goods produced, and so forth, are determined by a central authority (the state) which aims to produce the greatest efficiency and the greatest good of all concerned. Economic anthropology tells us of the existence of communities in which the goods produced are determined by tradition, without any obvious effect either of economic exchange or of central direction (e.g., the Laotian villagers described by Halpern, 1964, p. 99). In real economies tradition, command forces, and market forces all have some role; but it is important to establish their relative significance and their particular spheres of influence.

2. *What proportion of economic effort occurs in the economy?* This apparently paradoxical question refers to the fact that in any society a substantial amount of activity goes on without any money changing hands, even though in other circumstances the identical activity, or an obvious substitute for it, would involve a financial transaction. For example, there are two ways of obtaining bread: You can bake it yourself, or you can buy the factory-made product. Both individual and industrial bread makers must pay money for flour, yeast, salt, and other ingredients and for the energy to heat their ovens. Both add value in converting those constituents into bread. If you make your own bread, your household can enjoy the added value without any money being paid to anyone, but if you wish to enjoy whatever value is added by the industrial process, you must pay money to do so. Even though there is a considerable difference between the type of effort you exert in your kitchen and the kind of work done in the bread factory, it is still surprising to discover that, according to the conventional macroeconomics of developed nations, the second is economic behavior and the first is not. If you switch from home-produced bread to the factory product, you actually contribute to the economic growth of the nation.

This is not entirely an anomaly, for what is done for money is subject to economic pressures in a rather more obvious way (both to the participants and to the theoretician) than what is done for oneself or for pleasure. Also, the psychology of financially motivated behavior may be different from that of activities performed "for their own sake" (cf. Chapter 6). But in the discussion either of primitive economies (cf. Chapter 15), where strictly economic exchange may be weakly developed, or of economies in rapid transition (cf. Chapter 16), the question of how much and what kind of activity "goes through the market" is crucial. Even within developed economies, at most two-thirds of potentially economic activity goes through the market in any way. Scitovsky (1976, chapter 5) discusses this question in detail, and Becker (1976) has argued for the extension of economic analysis to activities not generally thought of as proper subjects for economic exchange, such as decisions about family size. It is always possible to impute an economic price to goods and services supplied by individuals to themselves or to others without charge. One case in which this is regularly done is in the calculation of national income statistics: owner-occupiers are taken to derive income, as landlords, from the ownership of their homes, the imputed income being the rent they are considered to pay themselves as tenants (Maurice, 1968, p. 106). In the main, however, economists only take note of what happens in the economy, narrowly defined; that qualification is implicitly added to all the other macroeconomic questions listed.

3. *What goods and services will be produced?* Microeconomics tells us how variations in the quantities of individual commodities coming to the market will affect the prices individual consumers will pay for them, in turn affecting the quantities that will be brought to market in future. The macroeconomic study of resource allocation attempts to integrate or aggregate this microeconomic understanding in order to explain the quantities of goods that will be produced in the entire economy, recognizing that the purchasers of one kind of commodity will be the suppliers of another. In its purest form, resource allocation theory would assume that only market forces had any effect on any of these quantities, so it would only apply to a perfectly competitive market economy. The theory, however, can be extended to deal with central direction and monopoly power of various kinds.

4. *How will income be distributed within the economy?* The question about income distribution has two rather different senses within macroeconomics. On the one hand, the total income within the economy is distributed among different kinds of income recognized by economists, namely wages, rent, and profits. This is important from the point of view of theoretical understanding. On the other hand, income is distributed among the different entities within the economy, namely persons, firms, and public authorities, and within each sector among the individuals making up that sector. The most important question from a psychological point of view concerns the distribution of income among individual people.

5. *What is the level of activity within the economy?* What do economists consider the heart of macroeconomics, and what do many laypeople consider the whole of economics? What are the factors that determine whether an economy is growing, stagnating, or declining? What determines the level of unemployment in a country? What causes booms and slumps? These questions have preoccupied some of the best-known names in economics, such as Keynes's noted work, *The General Theory of Employment, Interest and Money* (1936). They are also the focus of a great deal of the economic policy of modern governments. At least until

around 1970, it was widely believed that the sustained low levels of unemployment combined with moderate economic growth of the post-1945 period were a unique triumph of the application of economic theory (Keynesian, as it happens) to economic policy. Although this view is now out of fashion, various schools of macroeconomics would agree that a government's policies toward public expenditure, levels of taxation, levels of interest, and the supply of money in the economy have very definite effects on the levels of economic activity. We shall look at some of the competing theories in a little more detail later in this chapter.

6. *What is inflation?* Apart from unemployment, inflation is probably the most talked-about economic problem of our time. It has been repeatedly argued, by politicians as well as economists, that inflation and unemployment are in some sense two sides of the same coin, although theorists differ as to what the coin in question might be. Because the value of a currency is, in effect, just the inverse of the average price within the economy, inflation is unmistakably a macroeconomic problem. It has been studied by economists at least since John Locke (1691/1777) and Adam Smith (1789/1908, book I, chapter V). We shall look at some of the competing views below.

7. *What is welfare?* An entire branch of economics is devoted to questions about the ways in which the economic satisfaction of all the individuals within an economy, or some particular groups of them, can be best ensured. This is referred to as *welfare economics*. Welfare is partly a microquestion, but clearly many of the macroquestions we have already raised have welfare implications – income distribution and level of activity are obvious examples.

8. *What is international economics?* We saw above that national economies are not perfect subjects for macroeconomic analysis in the sense that they are not *closed systems*. *International economics* is the response to that imperfection. International economics is the study of the adjustments that have to be made to the macroeconomics of single nations in order to take into account their existence in a web of other nations and of international trade in general. It deals with questions such as the relative values of national currencies as well as the volume of exports and imports.

There is a certain amount of psychology in international economics. Speculation in currencies, which can have a major effect on a country's economic fate, would certainly be a rewarding subject for psychological study, and media campaigns exhorting us to "Buy American" or "Back Britain" suggest that someone, somewhere, thinks that individual psychology affects international trade. The different extent to which imports penetrate apparently similar markets in different countries may be related to individual attitudes. For example, a much lower proportion of British people buy cars built in their own country than is the case in other European countries with major car industries (Sinclair 1983). It is easy to see how this might be related to well-known British attitudes toward home industries. We shall say relatively little about the international dimension in this book. To a first approximation, it can often be ignored when studying national macroeconomics. More generally, international trade tends to involve individual behavior less directly than do many other economic phenomena.

METHODS OF MACROECONOMICS

The role of data

Comparing Chapters 1 and 2 we can see that microeconomics is a much more theory-driven discipline than is psychology. It would not be uncommon to find a textbook of microeconomics that did not contain a single observed datum although it might contain references to facts as "self-evident" or "matters of common observation." Despite the sophisticated theorizing it has inspired and the intense theoretical disputes it has witnessed, macroeconomics is a rather more empirically oriented subject.

This is partly attributable to the application of macroeconomics to economic policy. Microeconomics can be applied by governments in such questions as taxation levels, rationing, and rent control. But the major users of microeconomic concepts are particular firms working within particular contexts. The data generated in connection with such applications are generally not published (in a effort to preserve commercial secrecy), and the effects of the policies they help determine are difficult to disentangle from the many factors operating on an individual firm's financial health. By contrast, macroeconomic concepts are applied to the determination of public policy. The data they call for are collected by public agencies and are generally published. Because they apply to the whole national economy, they have an air of the universal, although national economies are just as likely to be "blown off course" by outside factors as any business. Furthermore, considerable theoretical work within economics has gone into determining the right way to present national accounts, while the corresponding problems at the microeconomic level are the subject of the well-demarcated applied disciplines of accountancy and bookkeeping.

Macroeconomic debate thus takes place in the context of readily available data about the levels of various kinds of economic activity, the distribution of income and the value of money for many years in the past. Of course, there are grave difficulties in making comparisons between years, given constant changes in the value of money and the technology of production. But solutions to those problems can be proposed; indeed, the refinement of such solutions has been part of the history of macroeconomics. The data also tend to be by-products of various other government activities such as tax gathering, and they are of varying quality; usually the older, and the less developed the country, and the older the data, the worse, but the quality of the data also varies in any one country and year. Knowing how much reliance to place on what data is part of the art of being a macroeconomist.

It is worth making a few remarks about the kinds of national economic statistics that are readily available, if only because we shall need to refer to some of them later in this book. (Cairncross 1973, Appendix to Chapter 25, provides an excellent summary of the United Kingdom conventions.) The first step is to provide a breakdown of national income, expenditure, and output, each of which must add up to the same figure as we shall see. Income is broken down into income from employment and income from property (which includes interest payments); the sum of these two (with minor adjustments) is called the gross domestic product (GNP). Adding property income received from abroad, and subtracting payments of property income to foreigners, gives the gross national product (GNP), probably the most commonly cited measure of national economic performance. Expenditure is broken down into expenditure by individuals, expenditure by public authorities, and net expenditure by firms (the increase in the value of stocks held and work in progress over the time period concerned); after allowing for imports and exports, and making some technical adjustments, the sum is again the GNP. Output can be broken down according to the industry producing it, and must add up to GDP. Other national accounts break down saving according to its source (individuals, firms, public authorities), investment according to its nature (additions to the stock of capital goods, increases in the values of stocks, investment abroad), persons', companies', and government income according to their sources, and international transactions. It should be clear why macroeconomic discussion is under the discipline of regular interaction with data.

The cornerstones of theory

Later in this chapter, we shall briefly explore some typical macroeconomic theories, and find that they disagree sharply about the causation of macroeconomic phenomena, and the policies that should be adopted to control them. There are some points, however, about which all theories must agree. The kind of national economic statistics we have just been discussing are often referred to as the "national accounts," and they are subject to the overriding constraint of all accounts: The books must balance. There are a series of "accounting relationships" between different elements of the accounts which, though logical necessities, provide a strong framework within which macroeconomic theories must operate. They are usefully expressed in the following simple equations (we have used the nomenclature conventional in economics):

$$Y = O = D \tag{3.1}$$

$$Y = C + S \tag{3.2}$$

$$O = C + I \tag{3.3}$$

$$S = I \tag{3.4}$$

In words, Equation 3.1 asserts that national income Y, national output O, and national expenditure D must all be equal. Whatever money is received by one person must be spent by another, and must be spent on something. Equation 3.2 asserts that national income equals the total consumption in the economy C plus the total saving in the economy S. All the money obtained in the economy is either spent on current consumption or saved to pay for future consumption. Equation 3.3 asserts that output equals consumption plus investment I. Whatever is produced in the economy is either consumed immediately or used to provide for future consumption, i.e., invested. Equation 3.4, which can be deduced from the other equations, asserts that total saving and total investment are equal.

At one level, these assertions are obvious tautologies. At another, they are immediately open to question. Surely if one gives away some earned money, then don't Y and D become unequal? Surely if one saves by hoarding coins in an old sock, then money is not invested, and so don't S and I become unequal? Some of these questions arise from a failure to understand the macro nature of the equations. If one gives away income, one must give it to someone else; even if that person gives it away in turn, and so on, sooner or later the money must be spent on something that has been produced, bringing O and D back into line with Y. Some of the questions are real enough, but are answered by the way the terms are defined. For example, either money received as a gift is not counted with a person's income for national accounting purposes, or else giving must be counted as a kind of expenditure, and the recipient must be counted as producing a commodity, presumably the service of gratitude. Some of them can be answered once a firmer grasp on macroeconomic phenomena is gained. For example, when people save in old stocks, investment does indeed occur, although in an involuntary form because shopkeepers find that they have actually invested in increased stocks, because of the goods that remain unbought on their shelves.

Income, output, expenditure, consumption, investment, and saving, as defined in these specialized ways, may not be the operative variables in determining behavior, either of individuals or of the economy. For example, Katona (e.g., 1975, Chapter 15) argues that repayment of loans and purchase of durable goods, which for the purposes of national accounting are both varieties of saving, are viewed by most individuals as kinds of spending, and function accordingly in determining their behavior (we shall discuss this further in Chapter 8). At the individual level, the deviations between theoretical and operative categories may be large enough to be very important, but at the macroeconomic level, they are probably small enough to be ignored; and in some cases there are good arguments that the theoretical categories actually are the operative categories in any case.

A second general constraint on macroeconomic theorizing is the existence of a number of well-known and apparently reliable empirical relationships between macroeconomic quantities. One of the best known, although recently less reliable, is the curve first identified by Fisher (1926) and Phillips (1958), showing that the level of inflation in a given economy is inversely correlated with the level of unemployment, rising more sharply as unemployment approaches zero. Another is the tendency for the proportion of income saved to be roughly constant from year to year (Kuznets 1946). A third is the tendency for the distribution of incomes in the economy to follow, roughly but not exactly, the lognormal form (Lydall 1968; see also Chapter 3). More controversial are the various suggestions that fluctuations in the national output are cyclic, either with the short period of the "business cycle" that preoccupied earlier generations of macroeconomists (e.g., Jevons 1871) or with the "Kondratiev long wave" which is now coming back into fashion (Van Duijn 1983). None of these relationships is immutable, but any macroeconomic theory that deals with the relevant area must at least be consistent with them and ideally should explain why they are so often found.

Models of the national economy

The accounting relationships and the known empirical regularities are sufficient to place quite powerful constraints on macroeconomic theorizing. Such theorizing can take three forms. First (logically and historically), we have essentially verbal argument. At a second stage, those arguments are recast into mathematical forms of greater or less sophistication, so that the consequences of different hypotheses and parameters can be explored analytically. Most recently, however, much more elaborate theorizing has been carried out by means of "computer models" which simulate the national economy (or sectors of it), or the world economy. The type of macroeconomic hypothesis that goes into such models may not be very sophisticated, but the models incorporate a great deal of data about the structure of the national economy, and assumptions about the ways in which different sectors will respond to different kinds of economic change. These assumptions are not arbitrary – they are based on previous performance, and in some cases they can be varied to test the robustness of the model's predictions. However, to simulate the entire economy involves more assumptions than could ever be varied systematically. Even the structural data are approximate and have to be interpreted in various ways before they can be entered into the model. There can thus be no definitive model of the national economy. For the U.S., for example, Naylor (1971, p. 142) lists three major models – the "Brookings," "Wharton," and Office of Business Economics models – and there is at least one other influential example, that due to Fair (1974–6). For the United Kingdom, there are at least five influential models, to which Holden, Peel and Thompson (1982) give an excellent introduction.

Once such a model has been constructed, it can be used to test predictions about the effects on the real economy of various kinds of economic change, whether produced by policy or by outside circumstances. The results of such "experiments" will depend partly on the theoretical assumptions that have contributed to the model. But if the experiments are well devised, their results will depend more strongly on the empirical data, which also form part of the model. If several models all agree on a prediction, we can have reasonable confidence that it is right.

As with all theories, the test of these different models will ultimately be their ability to predict and explain new data as history makes them available. The models are constantly being improved as inadequacies are detected. One possibility is that they will all evolve toward a common form, which will then be, in a sense, a complete macroeconomic theory of the economy in question. Unfortunately, it will probably not be a theory that will easily be expressed or communicated, except to another computer. This book can give no account even of the current generation of models. We can expect, however, that in due course it will become increasingly possible for "outside" researchers to mount experiments on the more sophisticated models, just as an outsider can use someone else's theory to generate predictions. Although the models are large and complex, versions of them are beginning to be available even for desktop computers, and these are already being applied to test ideas about economic psychology (Maital 1984).

THREE MACROECONOMIC PROBLEMS

In order to introduce some of the major theories that have been current in macroeconomics, we are now going to consider three basic problems in the macroeconomic areas; we shall also review what different theories have had to say about them. The three problems, chosen because of their importance for individual behavior and as objects of economic policy, are the level of output in the economy, inflation, and the distribution of income among individuals. Clearly, these are not independent problems. The measures that one political party advocates to improve sluggish output are condemned by another as causes of inflation. The second party's chosen measures are in turn proclaimed to create an unjust distribution of income. However, they do show rather different kinds of macroeconomic theorizing in rather different lights, so it is convenient to consider them separately here.

Level of activity

We saw above that income, output, and expenditure must all, at the macroeconomic level, be equal; any of them could be taken as a measure of "level of activity." Usually we talk about output in this context, since this is held to be the measure of the extent to which the economy is "doing its job." Economics is about coping in the face of scarcity of resources; output is what makes resources less scarce.

The level of output of an economy depends primarily on the natural resources of the country, the state of technological knowledge, the skills of the population, and the level of economic development of the whole. Only the last of these is really considered as part of macroeconomics, although occasionally the others are as well. In any case, we are not concerned with the theory of development here, but rather with the level of activity observed with given resources.

The "classical" theory of the nineteenth- and early twentieth-century economists led to the conclusion that in the long run a purely market economy, with perfect competition between firms for markets and for labor, and between individuals for goods and jobs, would tend toward "general equilibrium." In this state, all the resources of the economy would be fully employed in the sense that any unemployment would be either "frictional" (a temporary consequence of the time taken to move from one job to another) or "voluntary" (the result of workers refusing jobs because it was more unpleasant to do them than to suffer the absence of a wage). This state of "full employment" would not maximize output, as more could always be produced if the voluntarily unemployed would enter work, but it would maximize the total satisfaction of all the individuals in the economy, since only those who would become less satisfied by taking work would not have a job. General equilibrium theory therefore predicted a specifiable optimum level of economic activity.

In practice, it was obvious that the general level of activity varied considerably from year to year. The "business cycle" from boom to slump and back to boom was a particularly noticeable feature of nineteenth-century economic life (Schumpeter 1939). There is no logical incompatibility between the existence of an equilibrium and the existence of variations around it, so it was perfectly possible to construct a theory of variations in unemployment within the general equilibrium framework (e.g., Pigou 1933). But the depth and severity of the reduction in output in the Great Depression of the 1930s created a climate of acceptance for a quite different sort of theory.

The central proposition of Keynes's (1936) famous book, *The General Theory of Employment, Interest and Money,* was that the whole framework of general equilibrium theory was wrong. Keynes argued that there was no unique equilibrium toward which the economy must tend, or around which it would oscillate. Equilibrium could be reached at almost any level of economic activity, and most of these would involve substantial numbers of people in "involuntary" unemployment. That is, there would be people who would be happy to take jobs at real rates of pay less than those currently in force but for whom no jobs would be available. Economic recession, and the mass involuntary unemployment that goes with it, was the most salient fact of economic life during the 1930s. Keynes here was responding to the constraint by data which we have identified as one of the major characteristics of macroeconomic theory. But he also made use of the other constraint, the accounting relationships described above. Because his theory is essentially simple, it is worth setting it out briefly.

Keynes (1936, chapter 10) starts by supposing that the proportion of any increment of income which people will spend is roughly constant (it is usually referred to as the "marginal propensity to consume"). He also uses the accounting relationship by which total saving and investment must always be the same. He then considers what will happen if investment is suddenly increased by a certain amount. By definition, this will involve the production of goods that are not immediately sold and consumed. For example it might take the form of a government program of public works to improve the "infrastructure" of the economy. The workers employed in such a program will have to be paid; in order to preserve the accounting relationships, this will inevitably bring about changes elsewhere in the economic system until an amount of extra saving corresponding to the extra investment has been produced. Because the proportion of income that is saved is roughly constant, and less than one, this rise in saving can only occur by way of a greater rise in national income. For example, if people typically spend nine-tenths of their income (average propensity to consume = 0.9), a given rise in investment will produce a rise in national income (and hence, by another accounting relationship, in national output) ten times as great. Thus the government, by investing money it has not raised in taxes, can stimulate the level of activity in the economy. This is usually referred to as a "reflationary" policy.

The required rise in national income will come partly from the incomes of those employed in the original investment program, but mainly from the incomes of additional people, who will have to be employed, in order to produce the extra goods which the original new employees will consume; if the marginal propensity to consume is 0.9, the additional employment will have to be nine times as great as that produced by the original investment. The factor by which the additional employment, indirectly generated by an investment, exceeds its direct effect is called the "multiplier."

As Keynes noted, an investment program of this sort will be accompanied by a fall in the real value (i.e., purchasing power) of wages, because fewer consumption goods will be produced per worker than before. The workers employed in the investment program will produce none; and the additional workers taken on elsewhere in the economy will produce less per head than those who were previously employed, because of "diminishing returns"; that is, additional resources devoted to any industrial process tend to be used with decreasing efficiency. In other words, Keynesian "demand management" is inherently inflationary, a fact to which we shall return below.

In Keynes's analysis the cause of unemployment is therefore deficiency of demand. The economy can be stable at any level of output; the accounting relationships will see to it that corresponding levels of consumption, saving, and investment are established. Keynes is quite clear about the theoretical price required for this result: He has to abandon the classical assumption that the real value of wages will be just such as to offset the unpleasantness of working compared with not working. For if this assumption holds, the fall in real wages due to diminishing returns, mentioned in the last paragraph, would cause workers to leave their jobs, until the same level of unemployment was reached as before the attempted intervention. Keynes (1936 pp. 8 ff. and 272 ff.) argued that, as long as there was no accompanying fall in money income, this would not happen. He supported his argument partly by an appeal to experience, and partly by arguing that there is in fact no causal relation between the level of money wages and the level of real incomes, so that there is no mechanism by which the classical assumption could become true.

As Keynes recognized, his entire argument only holds if the money for the new investment comes from new saving (implying, with a constant propensity to consume, new income) rather than from redirection of existing saving, which would cause reduced investment elsewhere in the economy. Furthermore, in a national economy in which we allow for the existence of foreign trade, the mechanism by which the new saving is to be produced will fail if a substantial proportion of the incomes of those employed on the investment program is spent on imported goods. It has been the consistent experience of British economic planners during the past two decades, for example, that attempts to stimulate employment by government spending fail partly because British people spend a high proportion of extra income on imported goods.

From the famous wartime "Employment Policy" White Paper (Command Paper 6527, 1944) onward, the United Kingdom government adopted "the maintenance of a high and stable level of employment" as a major policy target, and Keynesian "demand management" as the means of achieving it. Other governments were not slow to follow, and a comparison of unemployment levels for the decades before and after World War II suggested to many that the policy was spectacularly successful (e.g., Robinson 1964, chapter 4). For ideological reasons, the United States was the slowest of the major capitalist economies to follow this road, but by 1970, President Nixon could say, "I am now a Keynesian" (quoted by Samuelson 1976, p. 205). By the late sixties, however, serious doubts about the Keynesian analysis were beginning to be felt. Unemployment was creeping obstinately upward, and inflation had begun to be worryingly high and persistent. The subsequent decline in the prestige of Keynes's ideas owes probably less to these empirical problems, than to the rise of an alternative general theory. This was the position which has become known as "monetarism," and is particularly associated with Milton Friedman and other economists of the "Chicago school."

In many respects, monetarism involves a reversion to the classical ideas which Keynes discarded, a fact that emerges very clearly in its treatment of unemployment. Monetarist theorists (e.g., Friedman 1977) argue that, in any given economy, there is a unique "natural" level of employment, which is a function of such variables as the mobility of the workforce, the value of unemployment benefits, and so forth. In a perfectly competitive economy, the natural level of employment would be the "full employment" of the classical theory, and most (although not all) deviations from perfect competition will tend to decrease employment from this level. Any attempt to raise employment above its natural level by Keynesian demand management may be effective in the immediate short run, but in the longer term it will inevitably lead to a return to the natural level, combined with a fall in the value of money, that is, inflation. If the government is to have any effect on the level of unemployment, it must therefore avoid Keynesian measures and move instead to weaken or dismantle those institutions that distort competition in the labor market, such as Social Security for the unemployed, business monopolies and cartels, licensing arrangements for the practice of professions, and trades unions, particularly when they succeed in imposing a "closed shop" (Friedman 1962). In practice, monetarist theory has been espoused by right-wing governments that have been happier to move against unions than firms and professions, but that is not an essential part of the theory.

Friedman (e.g., 1977) develops this theory by way of a discussion of the expectations of workers in the face of the possibility of inflation. In effect, his analysis restores the assumption that Keynes abandoned, that employees' behavior will be governed by real rather than money income. It is not surprising that he reaches essentially the same conclusions as Pigou (1933) and other classical theorists.

It would be inappropriate at this stage to try to assess these competing theories, but we should point to one level at which they agree. Both Keynes and Friedman can only see full employment in a context in which a positive amount of national income is spent on investment. Because of the ways in which the terms of the accounting relationships are defined, replacement of existing capital goods, without improvement, does not count as investment. If productive capacity is simply allowed to wear out as it is used, that constitutes negative investment; the "wearing out," or rather the replacement and repair it makes necessary, is a form of consumption. Thus, in the long term, both monetarist and Keynesian prescriptions for full employment are prescriptions for increased productive capacity, and so for economic growth. Economic theory thus unanimously declares that economic growth is desirable, and throughout the history of the industrialized nations, the policies of their governments have consistently endorsed this view.

Noneconomist writers, and a few economists, have frequently challenged this unanimity. From Meadowes et al. (1972) on, there have been a series of claims that in the long term, economic growth cannot be sustained because of the demands it makes on the finite, exhaustible resources of the planet. This is not the place to take up that controversy, but we should be wary of automatically assuming that growth is either a desirable goal or even an acceptable by-product of economic policy. We have already seen that GNP, which is the Y of the accounting relations, fails to include many of the ways in which individuals help one another live and enjoy life, and does include some activities that are clearly negative in some sense. From a psychological point of view, therefore, economic growth cannot simply be equated with progress.

Inflation

Inflation, as everyone knows, is a general increase in all prices and wages, so that the "real value" of money, the quantity of goods and services that it will buy, declines. Macroeconomic theorists disagree sharply about the origins of inflation, and about its importance.

Keynes (1936, p. 296) recognized that inflation was an inevitable consequence of the type of demand management he proposed. The kind of government-sponsored investment program he described would not produce as many salable goods per head as the kinds of employment already in existence in the economy. More workers would be receiving the same money wage than before; with more money per person available to buy fewer goods per person, the real value of wages must fall, and the way this happens is by means of a rise in prices. Keynes makes very clear (pp. 8 ff.) that his entire analysis depends on the assumption that, although this will happen, it will not cause workers to abandon their jobs (although a fall in the money value of wages might). Furthermore, the additional workers who will be brought into employment by the "multiplier" effect of the original investment will, in general, be producing salable goods; thus, as long as the multiplier is large, the inflationary effects of demand management will be small. In other words, the general expansion of the economy brought about through demand management will bring enough benefits for everyone for inflation to be regarded as a harmless side effect.

The monetarist theorists arrive at a very different conclusion. As in many other cases, their account of inflation is essentially a return to a classical analysis, in this case the quantity theory of money, which has been a part of economic thought at least since Locke (1691/1777). This theory considers how P, the overall level of prices (conceived of as the price per unit of output, i.e., as the price of a kind of hybrid commodity representing everything produced in the economy) will be determined by M, the quantity of money circulating in the economy, V, the speed at which it circulates, measured in the number of transactions per year in which each unit of money is involved, and T, the total volume of transactions per year. We then have an accounting relationship, attributable to Fisher (1911, pp. 24–54), whereby

$$P = MV/T \tag{3.5}$$

If V and T are taken as fixed, it follows that any increase of M must increase P. But attempts at Keynesian demand management precisely have the effect of increasing M *without increasing T* in proportion: The government pays wages to workers who are not adding to the national output (or who are adding relatively little to it), so there are no extra goods to form the subject of extra transactions. The inevitable consequence is an increase in P, the overall level of prices, or, in a word, inflation. According to the monetarists, governments can and should prevent inflation, by following policies which control M, the quantity of money in circulation. By the end of the 1960s, there had begun to be a steady and apparently unstoppable rise in the moderate inflation that had accompanied postwar Keynesian economic policies in the advanced economies of Western Europe and North America. A theory that offered to explain inflation, and to provide policies that could contain it, had obvious attractions.

Monetarist policies are not just different from Keynesian policies – they are radically opposed to them. Steps that tend to reduce the money supply, such as upward manipulation of exchange rates and reduction of public sector employment and wages are "deflationary"; they tend to reduce the effective demand in the economy. The dispute between Keynesian and monetarist economists has therefore been sharp and politically charged. But, as so often occurs in a theoretical dispute, the difference between the theorists is as much one of emphasis as of fact. Keynes recognized the quantity theory of money as an accounting relationship. His argument was that government investment would increase national output as well as the quantity of money in circulation (by substantial amounts, because of the multiplier), so that the inflationary effect of demand management would not be serious; T, the total of annual transactions, would be effectively constant only if the economy were in theoretical full-employment equilibrium, so that a fall in real wages would cause people to stop producing. In opposition to this theoretical analysis, the monetarists have pointed to the empirical fact of the failure, in recent years, of demand management to produce any worthwhile expansion of the economy without producing unacceptable levels of inflation at the same time or, worse, instead.

Attempts to resolve the argument have not been very successful. Part of the problem is that although M, the quantity of money in the economy, is well defined in theory, in practice there are many different possible definitions. It is not clear which definition we should use, either as social scientists trying to test the quantity theory or as social engineers trying to prevent inflation by "controlling the money supply." There is an easy definition of M as the quantity of cash circulating in the economy plus the amounts held by individuals and firms on current account at banks (referred to by the Bank of England as $M1$). But a policy which depended on controlling $M1$ would be doomed because there are too many other things which can be used as money. For instance, individuals can use building society deposits, and firms can use various kinds of bonds. A range of successively more encompassing definitions of money have been devised (e.g., $M2$, $M3$) for the purposes of reporting and controlling money supply, but any of them can be circumvented if controlled. The more encompassing the definition, the greater the risk that controls on money supply will turn into controls of other kinds of economic activity, and so distort or reduce national output. In practice, this tends to take place in rather abstruse ways inside the banking industry, but we can illustrate the point by imagining a more domestic example: If the supply of cash were so severely restricted that individuals took to using pins in transactions, the pin supply would have to be controlled, with consequent inefficiencies in the dressmaking industry. Individuals are in fact adept at finding new and different kinds of money, and firms and financial institutions have much greater sophistication with which to do so (see the discussion in Chapter 12).

Another problem in deciding whether Keynesian policy has really failed is the effect of international trade. In Britain at least consumers have a very high tendency to spend increments of income on imported goods. Under these conditions, Keynes's own theory predicts that demand management will be both ineffective and inflationary. It is not surprising that the remaining Keynesian theorists nowadays call for demand management to be accompanied by import controls (e.g., Godley & May 1977).

Both analyses of inflation seem to ignore what, to anyone who attends to the media, must seem to be its most obvious cause: In the face of rising prices (which may be caused by external factors such as an increase in the price of imported goods), workers demand, and frequently get, wage increases. This increases costs and causes firms to increase prices. But this kind of process can be seen as merely the mechanism by which the fundamental processes outlined above take effect. Admittedly, the different institutions of different countries mean that the same amount of "cost push" may produce different inflationary effects. From a monetarist point of view, this can in fact be seen as another demonstration that the Keynesian analysis fails. When the cost of living rises, so reducing the real value of wages, workers indeed do not react (as classical theory demands) by leaving their jobs. But they do react by threatening to do so, at least temporarily. For example, they enter into wage negotiations, and the threat of a strike is implicit in all wage bargaining. By exacting a higher money wage, they prevent the Keynesian expansion of output following from an increase in investment. If the trades unions' power as monopoly sellers of labor did not exist, this would be impossible.

Income distribution

The final problem we shall consider here is that of income distribution. As we mentioned earlier, this phrase has two meanings within economics. The first refers to the distribution of the national income between the different "factors of production." By the factors of production, economists mean the three different kinds of resources that must be brought together in any productive activity: land, capital (machinery and equipment of all sorts), and labor. Obviously, different kinds of production require these resources in different proportions. Subsistence agriculture requires quite a lot of land, a great deal of labor, and not much capital. A highly automated microelectronics factory uses relatively little land, very little labor, and huge amounts of capital. Obviously, too, each factor exists in many different forms. Land on Manhattan Island has different possible productive uses from land in the Adirondack Mountains. A computer and a lathe make different kinds of production possible. And different types of people are needed to dig for coal and to audit accounts.

In any modern economy, very different kinds of production will coexist. The entrepreneur who wants to run a particular kind of firm will have

to bring the right kinds of the three factors together in the right proportions. But the price required for each will depend, in part at least, on the
other possible uses for the relevant varieties of each factor. Whether the
person can pay that price will depend on the demand for the kinds of
goods to be produced. Thus there are many possible, and profitable, uses
for land in Manhattan, so it commands a high price. The entrepreneur
who proposed to use it for growing turnips would not be able to proceed,
because the proceeds from turnip sales would not cover the cost of production. The only way to make a profit in Manhattan is to use large
amounts of either labor or capital or both, so as to extract a very large
amount of production from each unit of expensive land.

The effect is that the greater the supply of any factor, the lower its
share in the national income, for two interlocking reasons. First, if land
(for example) is very scarce, so that for each piece of land many potential
uses are in competition, the price that must be paid for the use of land
will be high. Second, because the price is high, land will be used very
efficiently. Both mechanisms combine to ensure that land will take a high
share of the proceeds of production, that is, of the national income. But if
land is freely available, the suppliers of labor and of capital goods will
take a higher share.

Our main interest, however, is in the second sense of "distribution of
income." That is the question of the distribution of income between
different kinds of each factor. The most interesting case is the distribution
of income to different kinds of wage earners. This is not quite the same as
the distribution of income across all the individuals in an economy, because the highest individual incomes are always derived from capital or
land (Pen 1971, pp. 54–6), but it comes close to it.

In general, workers who possess a scarce skill for which there are
many profitable uses can expect to command relatively high wages. Both
conditions are needed. For example, there are many profitable uses of
the ability to read, but the skill is so widely distributed that it confers
little bargaining power; on the other hand, a deep knowledge of ancient
Icelandic is rare but has few profitable uses, so that professors of Old
Norse are unable to demand very high salaries. Within any economy,
the overall pattern of skills and potential uses for them will presumably
affect the extent to which different wage earners tend to obtain different
incomes.

Empirically, it has been found that the distribution of incomes between
individuals in an economy tends to have a positive skew (Lydall 1968).
That is to say, if we plot the number of people having a certain income as
a function of that income, we see that most people have rather less than
the average income, and that there is a long "tail" of a small number of
people with very much higher incomes. If the graph is plotted with income transformed onto a logarithmic scale, it comes nearer to the famil-

iar bell-shaped gaussian or "normal" distribution, although there is still something of a "tail" covering the top 10–20% of incomes. These tend to have the shape of an exponential distribution function, a fact sometimes referred to as *Pareto's law*.

Although the form of the distribution tends to be the same in all economies, its spread and skew can vary. Spread, or dispersion, measures the extent of income variation in the economy; skew measures the extent to which income is concentrated in the hands of the richest. There are a variety of measures of each of these, none of them wholly satisfactory (Lydall 1968, chapters 2 and 3; Pen 1971, chapter VI), but by looking at the income distributions for two economies, it is not difficult to see which is the more egalitarian.

It is the small number of very high incomes that have the strongest effect on income inequality. Because these high incomes tend to be derived from capital and land, the inequality of personal incomes in an economy tends to be a function of income distribution in the first sense, rather than of the distribution of incomes between wage earners in different occupations. The latter, noted in Chapter 6, is relatively constant between economies in any case (Phelps Brown 1977, chapter 2), although the proportions of people in different occupations will vary as a function of a country's level of economic development. But there are two further, essentially macroeconomic, factors that affect income distribution. One is the level and form of taxation, the other the level and nature of "transfer payments," the technical term covering Social Security benefits.

Taxation can be divided into "direct" and "indirect" taxes. Indirect taxes are levied on commodities, so their effect is felt when people spend. Direct taxes are levied on income or wealth, so their effect is felt when people earn or save. Either sort of tax can be "regressive," "neutral," or "progressive." These are not political evaluations (although they are often confused with them) but definitional distinctions. A progressive tax is one that falls more heavily, in proportional terms, on individuals of higher income; a neutral tax is one whose effect is independent of income; and a regressive tax takes a higher proportion of lower incomes. It is obvious how a direct tax can be made progressive (like income tax in most European countries) or regressive (like National Insurance contributions in the United Kingdom). Less obviously, the same is true of indirect taxes. In England, stamp duty is payable on the sale of houses at a percentage rate that rises sharply as a function of sale price; since purchasing expensive houses is correlated with high income, this is a progressive tax. Equally, a flat-rate tax on cigarettes is regressive; the number of cigarettes even an addict can smoke per day is limited, so the proportion of income spent on cigarettes tends to be higher for poorer people.

Progressive taxes tend to reduce the inequality of income within an economy, even if the government does nothing with the money it collects.

Such taxes, however, are usually combined with two other steps that also tend to redistribute income so as to produce greater equality. The first affects money income, the second real income. Money income is affected whenever there are support payments to those of low income. Unemployment benefit is an obvious example, but the child benefit payments which are made, regardless of income, to mothers in the United Kingdom are also redistributive, as families with children below wage-earning age must always tend to have less income per head than childless individuals or couples.

Other kinds of government activity have redistributive effects by changing real income. Any kind of state provision that is available without charge raises everyone's real income by a roughly constant amount, while the taxes that pay for it are likely to be either neutral or progressive. This is true of the classic "public goods," which (according to economic theory) the state must provide, since no one can make a profit from them, because their use cannot be restricted to those who pay for them (lighthouses and defence forces are the classic examples). It is more obviously true of "welfare state" provisions such as universal free education or medical attention.

Redistribution, whether through taxation or through the provision of benefits, will not be without macroeconomic effects. In theory, at least, a more equal distribution of income should reduce (1) the incentives to entrepreneurs to set up new productive enterprises, since the very high incomes that can only be obtained in this way will be subject to punitive taxation; (2) the incentive to enter the workforce, so reducing the efficiency of the economy and encouraging inflation; and (3) the real value of money by making available a pattern of commodities which is not what people would freely choose, thereby reinforcing both tendencies 1 and 2. In practice (as discussed in Chapters 6, 9, and 14), it has been hard to demonstrate any of these effects, and people have clear preferences for more egalitarian social arrangements. But these are data at the micro level, and it has not yet been possible to bring them to bear very effectively on the formulation either of macroeconomic theory or of economic policy.

RATIONAL EXPECTATIONS

Our discussion of three macroeconomic problems has made repeated reference to Keynesian and Monetarist theories, which are certainly still the public face of macroeconomics. But recent developments have been transforming macroeconomics through what has been called "the rational expectations revolution" (Begg 1982).

The central idea of rational expectations is extraordinarily simple. It is that people use currently available and relevant information to forecast the likely future value of economic variables (such as the rate of inflation) and that they do not make systematic errors in making these forecasts. They may well make mistakes, but they will learn from them so that predictable errors will be eliminated. This sounds very reasonable, but it may not be obvious that people's expectations are important to macro-economic theory.

The importance of expectations in macroeconomics

To demonstrate this, we shall take as an example the consumption function, which we shall study in some detail in Chapter 8. This function relates consumption C to income Y. In its simplest form, this function asserts that current consumption depends only on current income; thus we can write

$$C = f(Y) \tag{3.6}$$

Any realistic version has to add the influence of wealth W, *changing the equation to:*

$$C = f(Y, W) \tag{3.7}$$

More sophisticated theories supply additional explanatory variables. An important example is Friedman's *permanent income hypothesis*. According to this influential theory, current consumption is a function of permanent income, which is an average of current income and expected future income. We can see that expectations (in this case of future income) must be of major importance in this theory.

Other examples confirm the crucial importance of expectations. Consider inflation. It is clear that people's expectations about future inflation will alter behavior that is causally related to it. Wage negotiators, for instance, will attempt to strike bargains with their employers that take into account expected future rates of inflation. Borrowers and lenders of money will similarly need to make allowances for inflation in fixing rates of interest. Or, to take a topical example, dealers in foreign exchange markets must make forecasts about the future price of oil, the likely levels of American interest rates, and so on.

Models of expectation formation

Given that expectations are important, how has their formation been modeled in the past? There are two main alternatives: static expectations and adaptive expectations. Static expectations deals with the problem by assuming that the economy is in equilibrium and therefore that expected future values of economic variables are equivalent to current values. The growth rate in future is assumed to be the same as the growth rate today.

This may seem rather absurd but, if the static expectations view is re-stated such that current real values will be maintained in the future, it becomes more tenable. Comparative price ratios generally change rather slowly. Nevertheless, we know that the economy does suffer unexpected shocks (like the change in oil prices in 1973), and that the rational indi-vidual will not assume prices will continue as before but take into ac-count, say, OPEC announcements in forming his expectations.

The adaptive expectations thesis looks intuitively more appealing. It maintains that individuals' expectations will change in the light of their experience. Basically it assumes that people use their past forecasting errors to revise their current expectations. For example, in the case of price estimation, this can be expressed formally by the equation

Expected price $(t + 1)$ = expected price (t) + k [*actual price (t)* −
expected price (t)]

with k taking a value between 0 and 1. Thus if one believed that the price of a dollar this year was going to be equivalent to 80 English pence and it was actually 1 pound, with a k value of 0.8 one would expect the price next year to be 96 pence. During periods in which prices were stable, k would probably be low; if they were volatile, k would be close to 1. Obviously the influence of past expectations gets less as time goes on, and with high values of k, they have little effect.

Although the adaptive expectations ideas may appear plausible, putting it into formal terms shows that it is actually a rather odd theory of expectation formation. It implies that systematic trends in economic pa-rameters will always lead to systematic errors in expectations. For ex-ample, during periods of accelerating inflation, it implies that people's expectations of inflation always lag behind actual inflation, which does not seem to be the case. Furthermore, it assumes that people ignore announcements of future changes, professional forecasts, and so on.

The rational expectation formation model

Because adaptive expectations were unsatisfactory, economists turned to an alternative model: rational expectations. The central idea was intro-duced earlier. It is assumed that individuals do not rely solely on past experience, but use current information, and process this optimally. People do not use all possible information; some will be costly to acquire. It also does not mean that all the information used is analyzed thor-oughly. [As Shaw (1984) says, "most economic agents do not possess elaborate home computers upon which they perform nightly simulations of that economy."] But it does mean that individuals will not make sys-tematic errors. If a person ignores OPEC announcements in forming an expectation of oil prices on the spot market, that person will learn from experience and pay attention to them in the future. What this implies is that people will gradually learn to anticipate macroeconomic policy changes and, more important, change their behavior as a result. Thus if a finance minister announces an increase in the money supply, in the hope that interest rates will fall, the minister may be disappointed. Those lending money will have learned that a money supply increase is likely to lead to inflation, and so to secure the same real return on their capital they need to increase the interest rate. Similarly, those borrowing money will anticipate the future inflation and happily pay the higher nominal interest. The end result of the minister's action is therefore higher inflation and higher interest rates.

Most people have a very limited understanding of economics and so may not know what to expect following government announcements. But, at least according to rational expectations theory, the media do a good job of reporting the consensus of economic opinion, and this is presumably what most people rely on. Firms, trade unions, and other important economic agents certainly do use highly qualified professional advisors, so organizations within the economy may be acting as rational expectations theory predicts even though individuals do not.

We cannot do justice to the full implications of the rational expectations approach (good introductions are Shaw 1984, Begg 1982, and Parkin & Bade 1982), but it seems worthwhile to sketch out how a rational expectations model adds to our understanding of one of the macroeconomic problems considered above, namely what determines the level of activity within the economy. Recall that, in Keynes's analysis, the cause of unemployment is deficiency of demand, whereas for the monetarists there is a natural rate of unemployment determined by supply side factors, such as the existence of minimum wage laws. The rational expectations approach can be seen as an extension of monetarism. Because the policies a government will follow to regulate demand are predictable, in time they will be perfectly anticipated and lose their effect. The authorities will no longer be able to generate the systematic expectational error that produces changes in demand, and so Keynesian policies become ineffective. The policy implications of this are fairly clear. First, policy should aim at minimizing erratic variations in those economic variables that are under the control of the government. For example, the government might follow a publicly announced rule which related the money supply to the growth of the economy. Second, if nominal values of economic variables can be controled they should be. Stabilizing inflation would thus be a good thing, since it would minimize expectational error. And changes in supply side factors are the only possible sources of enduring change in the level of activity.

The rational expectations approach provides a challenge to economic psychologists. Expectation formation is obviously a psychological process, and the description of it given by rational expectations theorists should have aroused some skepticism among most psychologists. But, as we shall see in Chapter 5, it is all too easy to criticize the rationality assumptions of economists. What is needed is the construction of superior theories that can be incorporated into economic theory. It has yet to be demonstrated that this can be done in the case of the formation of expectation.

THE STATE AND THE ECONOMY

Even in this brief discussion of macroeconomics, it has been impossible to avoid repeated mentions of "the government" or "the state." That is understandable. All macroeconomic theorists assign an important role to central government. It is common to think of Keynesian macroeconomics as particularly "interventionist," since it requires government to intervene by spending money which (in a certain sense) it has not got in order to support new investment. But monetarism also requires major government intervention. Current "monetarist" economic policies have involved government action in an attempt to control the money supply. A thoroughgoing monetarism would involve the breakup of business and trades union monopolies, and this would require very energetic government action indeed. Businesspeople do not form cartels and monopolies, and workers do not form trades unions out of perversity or even original sin. They do so because their profits and incomes and conditions of work can thereby be improved; it is the natural thing to do according to the precepts of economics.

The classical economists recommended a government policy of laissez faire, on the grounds that in the long run the greatest good of the community would be produced by allowing everyone to act in his or her self-interest. In the long run, all monopolies and cartels (including trades unions) will be broken up. But this ignores two crucial facts. First, economic agents may use political power to negate the economic process. Second, even if any given monopoly is indeed destined to break up, new monopolies will tend to form, so that at any given time, the economy will generally contain a number of monopolistic agents – just as a pocket generally contains some money, even though any given coin is destined to be spent.

In practice, even avowedly monetarist governments have taken only mild action against trades unions and none against business. This is not because they do not understand monetarist theory but because governments do not exist in the abstract. They have aims of their own as well as limitations that are of the essence of their position. No government has limitless power. Most monetarist governments have been to the right politically, and their supporters, both those who provide voting support within legislatures and those who provide financial support outside them, would not tolerate strong action that was seen as "antibusiness." A left-wing government that took strong action against monopolies would find itself subverted in a variety of ways by financial institutions; a right-wing government that took strong action against trades unions would create intolerable levels of social disruption. In a democracy, any policy must be seen as advantageous by at least a large minority of the population, or else it will have to be abandoned well in advance of the next election. Dictatorships have more freedom of action, but it is never total. Most dictators are beholden to the armed forces whose commanders are usually linked by personal or party ties to large holders of land, wealth, or industrial authority. And even dictators may be unable to institute economic policies against the wishes of the majority, as was demonstrated by the events in Poland in 1970 and 1980, when the government tried to impose major rises in the price of food and was overthrown by the consequent riots.

During recent years, some attempt has been made to develop an economic theory of the influences to which government is subject (for an introduction, see Tullock 1976). As a crude example of the kind of argument involved, consider a proposal to introduce a universal free health service, to be paid for by a neutral tax, into an economy in which all health expenditure has previously been met by personal insurance. Let us further suppose that the total amount of health care available is to be kept constant, in both price and quantity (which might well be impossible in practice). Any system that supports a universal benefit out of a neutral tax tends to redistribute real income toward the poorer members of a community. All those with less than the mean income will therefore be better off under the new scheme. Since the distribution of incomes is skewed, as we saw above, most people have incomes below the mean. It is therefore to be expected that a majority of electors will vote for the proposal to set up the health service.

The resulting distribution of health care between individuals will not be the same as it would have been had matters been left to the market, because the distribution of voting power is different from that of purchasing power. Analyses of referenda have shown that this kind of process does occur: People of below average incomes are more inclined to vote for redistributive measures, which cost them less in taxes and benefit them more than they do the rich; the better off are more inclined to vote for environmental protection, which benefits them in terms of their leisure interests (e.g., Deacon & Shapiro 1975; Frey & Kohn 1970; Noam 1981).

Economically motivated voting of this kind is sometimes described as a distortion of the market: "Majority voting . . . will tend to result in an overinvestment in the public sector when the investment projects . . . are financed from differential taxation" (Buchanan and Tullock 1962, p. 169). But "distortion" and "overinvestment" are clearly both evaluatively biased terms; they assume that the distribution of resources which will be arrived at by the free play of market forces is in some sense the "correct" one, and there is no convincing argument for this. Even if it were true, as classical theory suggests, that purely selfish economic action in a purely competitive economy guaranteed the greatest economic benefit for all (most famously expressed by Adam Smith's, 1789/1908, book IV, chapter 2, reference to the "invisible hand"), this gives no grounds for preferring votes counted in terms of dollars to votes counted in terms of heads. One could just as reasonably say that the market distorts the democratic process as that democracy distorts the market. The central point is not to bewail the situation, but to recognize it: Governments, especially democratic governments, will not always be able to act in such a way as to maximize either economic output, or "welfare," in the sense in which it is used by economists, or even fairness. According to the kind of theory described here, a democratic government will be constrained to extract excessive taxes from any well-defined minority group. Friedman (1962) argues that the usual progressive income tax is an example of just this process, the minority group in question being the rich. Even if that extreme analysis is rejected, it remains true that the theory of economic policy is not economic alone; it is also political.

In practice votes are not determined by quite such narrow self-interests as the "economic theory of democracy" suggests. This is partly because of party allegiances and the nature of elections. People vote for packages of attitudes and policies that may include some that are quite disadvantageous to them. At least some people will vote for measures they see as socially desirable, even if they recognize the personal costs. For example, in the 1983 U.K. General Election, large numbers of unemployed people voted for monetarism. Economic theory is by no means irrelevant to this process, albeit in a distorted way, it finds its way into the mass media (Mosley 1982). People have clearly identifiable views about the causation of macroeconomic phenomena, and these are correlated with their voting behavior (Furnham 1982). At first glance, the government (even more so, if we call it "the state") seems the most macro of macroeconomic phenomena, and thoroughly remote from the influence of individual behavior. Maturer reflection suggests that, on the contrary, governments are more exposed to individual influence than are most other economic agents. They are open to economic influence (if they raise taxes too high, they will lose revenue in the same way as a firm that raises its prices excessively) and to political influence at the same time. If a macroeconomic theory assigns a role to government that is inconsistent with these influences, the theory is doomed to find no application in policy.

4

METHODS FOR ECONOMIC
PSYCHOLOGY

As an interdisciplinary subject, economic psychology has a wide range of methods to draw on. At this early stage in the development of the subject, it would be rash for us to try to say which is the most appropriate. Rather, because very few readers are likely to be familiar with all the techniques that underlie the empirical work to be discussed, this chapter reviews as many of the approaches as possible, explaining the advantages and disadvantages of each. And since it is impossible to talk about methods without citing examples of their use, this chapter also serves to extend the introductory material of the previous chapters.

It would be possible to organize a chapter on methodology along disciplinary lines, discussing first psychological methods and then economic ones. It seems more appropriate, however, to use principles of categorization that cut across disciplinary boundaries. The most obvious distinction is between macro and micro approaches. On this basis, we can categorize methods of investigation according to the effective unit of study, which may be an individual person, the entire economy, or something in between. Within these broad groupings, there are additional distinctions to be made. Some methods make substantial use of conceptual analysis, others rely on a purely empirical approach. Some attempt to control and manipulate situations, others rely on observation of spontaneous variations. Some aim for direct observations of behavior; others accept people's verbal reports of what they expect or tend to do. Each of these variations has its own characteristic problems and advantages.

Although it is too soon to say which of these approaches holds the most promise for the future of economic psychology, one thing does seem clear: None of them is likely to be sufficient on its own.

THE STUDY OF INDIVIDUAL ECONOMIC BEHAVIOR

The conceptual, micro approach: rationality

The simplest way of investigating economic psychology is, undoubtedly, to consider the traditional "rationality" question of theoretical microeconomics, that is, to ask how a well-informed person maximizes either objective value or subjective utility. For example, if someone received an unexpected legacy equal to a month's income, would the person increase expected lifetime pleasure most by spending it now or by saving it for later retirement? With reasonable assumptions about the relative importance the person might attach to present and future pleasure, an economic theorist could provide an answer to such a question. This technique, of finding the behavior that maximizes utility, was discussed in connection with the axioms of demand theory and their consequences in Chapter 2.

Many psychologists have argued that the task of economic psychology is, in fact, to disabuse economists of the idea that it is reasonable to assume that people will maximize utility. We shall argue at length in Chapter 5, however, that such an approach to economic psychology is actually sterile and that excessive attention to the rationality question is likely to impede progress. But there is no doubt that rationality considerations have some part to play in economic psychology. They form the core of one kind of economic theorizing, and so they are likely to be relevant to our discussions. In both economics and psychology, these considerations have been used to provide hypotheses for investigation at a more empirical level, for example in the study of saving or gambling.

The individual in the experiment: the laboratory approach

Once we begin to look for a more empirically oriented approach, the obvious candidate is experimentation. The techniques have mostly been developed by psychologists, although they have been used by economists too (for a survey, see Naylor 1972). The approach is basically simple. The experimenter identifies some manipulation that can be made in the laboratory but, in theory at least, engages the same behavioral patterns, or underlying mental mechanisms, as an economically important manipulation. Put another way, we construct a laboratory model of an economic phenomenon and then expose subjects (either different subjects, or the same subjects at different times) to different conditions which vary by virtue of the manipulation in question. The variations in behavior are the result.

In economic psychology, one must always ask whether the model of the economic process under study is valid. The answer may not be obvious. Aronson and Carlsmith (1968) draw a useful distinction between "mundane realism," which exists when the experimental situation seems to resemble the real world, and "experimental realism," in which the experiment evokes the same processes as the real-world situation it is trying to model. It is obvious that mundane realism will usually help ensure experimental realism, but it is not always sufficient, and may not always be necessary. In some recent experiments on gambling, for instance, a casino situation was reproduced in an apparently convincing manner, yet the behavioral and autonomic responses of habitual gamblers to a blackjack game were very different from what the same individuals showed in the real-life situation (Anderson & Brown 1984). Here mundane realism failed to guarantee experimental realism. Conversely, a number of recent experiments (surveyed by Lea 1981) have used animal subjects to mimic human consumers or workers. This seems quite removed from the real-life situation, yet at the level of observed behavior the model is quite convincing. For example, rats react to increases in the price of food in much the same way as people, making substantial increases in the amount of work they do rather than reducing the amount they eat. Despite their lack of mundane realism, the animal experiments may be strong on experimental realism. Human volunteers can usually only be tested in an experimental situation for an hour or two at a time, whereas rats or pigeons can be made to live in it indefinitely, and so may behave in the same way as real consumers and workers do in the real economy.

A major problem with all experimentation in social science is that the experiment itself is a social situation (Orne 1962). Either the experimenter's behavior, or the way the experiment is described, might tend to elicit certain kinds of reactions from the subjects. It has frequently been argued that experimenters' expectancies, in fact, influence the results obtained. This claim has been contested (e.g., Barber & Silver 1968), and it may be impossible to say whether the claim is justified; nevertheless it is important to consider how such an expectancy effect might come about.

One possible mechanism is through what Orne called "demand characteristics." These arise when subjects are able to guess the aim of the experiment, and then feel pressured to behave in ways that will help achieve it. Although the evidence for demand characteristics is actually quite weak (Weber & Cook 1972), it has become conventional to try to design experiments to avoid them. The rationality framework of economic thought seems likely to create particularly strong normative pressure on individuals to behave (or, rather, to be seen to behave) in particular ways in economic contexts. Thus, unless experiments in economic psychology are carefully designed, their results may reflect a person's understanding of economics rather than the economic behavior that would be displayed in a real situation.

A second problem with experimental research is that it is often difficult to obtain large or representative samples. Notoriously, most psychological knowledge applies to North American college students fulfilling course requirements. In some branches of psychology this does not matter, but students make a very unsatisfactory sample for many economic studies. Whether we consider overt current economic behavior, or the motivational and cognitive tendencies that may underlie it, students are likely to differ sharply from the general population. This is not to say that experiments with students are useless, but rather that they will always require careful interpretation.

The great advantage of a well-designed experiment is that it can isolate the variables of specific interest and study them with the assurance that any effects seen do not result from extraneous factors that happen to covary. No other method at our disposal will reliably meet this condition, so experimental work is always likely to be useful in the empirical support of any general argument. Suppose, for example, that we want to know whether people use price as an indicator of quality. In an experiment, we can attach different prices to identical samples of a product, say, beer, and demonstrate that people will indeed rate the more "expensive" sample as slightly better, at least if no additional information is available (e.g., Jacoby, Olson, & Haddock 1971). If we try instead to rely on spontaneously occurring price variations, we are likely to find that they are always associated with variations in the quality of the product or in the source of supply.

A few particular kinds of experimental research are of special interest in the present book. One type is represented by the formal studies of choice. These experiments attempt to abstract the essence of the choices made by individuals in the economy, and to describe these choices in noneconomic contexts. For example, in a study of the principles underlying gambling behavior, Tversky (1967) asked subjects to report the lowest prices at which they would sell the opportunity to bet on a "wheel of fortune" game. The pointer on this gambling device could land at one of ten positions, different numbers of which were colored black or white. The numbers of black and white dots, and the payoffs for them (in money, cigarettes, or candy), were varied systematically. Tversky was able to discover subjective transformations of objective probability and value that rendered the observed behavior consistent with expected value theory (which is one of the many variants of the rationality approach). Wherever the rationality question can be deployed (and that means in almost every field of economic behavior), it is usually possible to devise formal choice experiments that test whether choice is indeed rational. It is not certain, however, whether experiments such as those will always be illuminating.

A second kind of experiment to which we shall often appeal is the study of laboratory animals working under schedules of reinforcement. There are three reasons why we find these useful. First, as we saw in Chapter 1, the whole Skinnerian approach to psychology emphasizes the importance of the consequences of instrumental responses. This makes it highly congenial to an economic approach. It also means that many existing experiments are relevant to economic behavior. For example, Fantino (1967) showed that pigeons preferred a situation in which the cost of food was variable to one where it was fixed even though the average cost was the same (this finding is relevant to the topic of gambling). Ainslie (1974) showed that pigeons preferred a small amount of food, delivered immediately, to a larger amount delivered after a small delay; he also showed how this preference could be reversed (relevant to saving). A number of experiments have shown that animals will increase their rate of working rather than decrease their rate of eating when the cost of food increases (relevant to demand theory).

Second, animal experiments are relatively free of the problems of demand characteristics. Of course, an experiment on a rat, pigeon, or monkey can never give definitive information about human behavior. But it may be very useful either in suggesting explanations to be tested in other ways, or in controlling for the social and economic properties of other methods of investigation.

Finally, it is often possible to test variables over a much greater range in an animal experiment than in a more conventional one. In one of the experiments on the cost of food, Collier, Hirsch, and Hamlin (1972) varied cost by a factor of more than 200, a situation only likely to occur in rare and disturbed circumstances in ordinary life.

Opinions, attitudes, behavior predictions, and lay explanations

If large and representative samples are needed, they are much more likely to be available if we ask people to respond to a questionnaire instead of asking them to take part in a formal experiment. The simplest approach involves merely asking people to express their views on specific issues, either about the world at large or about their own behavior or expected behavior. In the economic context, questions might concern the progress of the economy, whether particular objects are suitable as gifts, or the individual's own plans for purchases in the coming days or months. In this sort of research, the person's answers are treated as directly usable data. The proper design of the questions is crucial, since there are several well-known biases that tend to influence people's responses to questionnaire items. For instance, most people tend to answer "yes" more often than "no" (e.g., Messick 1967) and to give the answer they believe will show them in the best light in the interviewer's eyes – the social desirability effect (Edwards 1957, 1967).

Well-designed questionnaires can minimize these problems, but they can never eliminate them entirely. To do that, we have to use the more sophisticated approach of formal attitude scaling. Here subjects are asked numerous questions about a single topic; multivariate analysis (e.g., factor analysis) of the agreement between the various answers is used to investigate whether the questionnaire is assessing one or many underlying psychological processes and whether it is capable of assessing them consistently (reliability analysis). Correlations with other kinds of measurements can then be used to determine what exactly the questionnaire measures (validity analysis). These psychometric techniques are used all too rarely in economic survey research; their systematic application would probably do much to reduce the number of apparently conflicting results which occur when we simply ask people what they think or typically do.

In some cases, however, such psychometric sophistication is less important. Often we are interested in very simple behavioral data, such as whether a person has made a certain kind of purchase within a certain recent time period. If our questions are posed with sufficient clarity and tact to ensure an honest answer, we shall very likely get reliable data. In some other cases, the possible biases are actually part of the data. For instance, if we ask someone whether he or she expects to buy a car in the next twelve months, the element of "self-presentation" in the answer may not be an artifact but may be a crucially important part of what we are trying to measure; it may be part of how that individual communicates to others and thus contributes to a general climate of consumer optimism or pessimism.

During recent years, there has been a surge of interest in a special kind of opinion data called "lay explanations" of economic phenomena. These are explanations given by representative or specially selected individuals for what happens in the economy. Feagin (1972) found that most of an American sample believed that poverty was caused by intrinsic characteristics of the people affected, rather than by the properties of society or by accident. Such data are clearly interesting in themselves, especially when they can be correlated with other variables (e.g., Furnham 1982, has shown that, in a British sample, Conservative voters were especially likely to attribute poverty to properties of individuals rather than of society). But we must beware of the implicit assumption that peoples' explanations of economic phenomena will play a causal role in their economic behavior. Like any other kind of opinion or attitudinal data, lay explanations may be causes of, caused by, or independent of behavior; only systematic investigation will tell us which. Lay explanations are also subject to the usual unreliabilities and biases of opinion data. Despite their current popularity, therefore, they do not yet have as much to offer to economic psychology as more conventional survey data.

There are a number of well-known examples of survey research in economic psychology. Adam (1958) instituted a method of investigating demand for particular products in which a sample of people are asked whether they would buy the product at a certain price ranging above and below the current price. This technique has been refined and expanded by Gabor and his colleagues (e.g., Gabor & Granger 1966); they call it the "buy–response" method. The observed function relating the proportion of people who say they would buy is called a buy–response curve. Typically, the function passes through a maximum at a price somewhat less than the current one, and falls off sharply to either side (e.g., Gabor

1977; see also Chapter 12). Another example is the attempts by Bruce, Gilmore, Mason, and Mayhew (1983) to discover what design of one-pound coin would be regarded as most valuable by the British public before the coin was issued. Such an attempt was needed because of the common public suspicion of new forms of money; a similar phenomenon had earlier led to the virtual withdrawal of the one dollar coin introduced in the United States in 1979.

Perhaps the best known of all economic psychologists, George Katona, made survey research the core of his approach to the subject. His major achievement was the development of the Index of Consumer Sentiment, a measuring device constructed from extensive interviews with representative samples of consumers across the United States. Katona aimed to produce a quantitative index of people's confidence in the economy from essentially qualitative information. The respondents in his surveys were asked, for example, whether they thought that economic prospects, or some particular feature of them, would get better, stay the same, or get worse in the forthcoming period; they were not required to put any figures on the likelihood of the change. Considerable psychometric work has been done (e.g., Adams 1964) in constructing a reliable index from these expressions of attitudes, and although by modern psychometric standards it is far from being a perfect instrument (for a critique, see Didow, Perreault, & Williamson, 1983), there is no doubt that consumer confidence as measured in this way is well correlated with the subsequent performance of the economy. If people in general are optimistic about the economy, expansion tends to follow three to nine months later (e.g., Katona 1975, chapter 6).

By far the largest application of survey research in economic psychology, however, comes in commercial market research. Some of this is closely linked to scientific investigation. For example, Gabor has turned the buy–response method into a successful commercial market research technique, and at the same time made commercial results (with confidentiality suitably protected) available for academic discussion (e.g., Gabor 1977; Lea 1978, fig. 5). Other kinds of commercial investigation are of little or no scientific interest (e.g., the "panel discussions" that pass as "qualitative research" in the advertising industry: cf. Chapter 13). In general, commercial market research can not afford the time for the complex procedures needed to establish a reliable and valid attitude scale; it is much more likely to take the form of opinion polling (and we have seen that this is a weak technique). On the other hand, the samples used by commercial market researchers are often larger and better constructed than often obtained for purely scientific purposes. It is unfortunate that so little commercial market research appears in a form where it could influence theory construction; this is, in fact, part of a very general problem to which we shall return later in this chapter.

Field observation and experimentation

Instead of bringing people into the laboratory to set up models of their economic behavior, or asking them questions about their behavior in the abstract, we can follow them into the real world and either observe their real economic behavior as it occurs or manipulate the economic conditions they face there. The former process merges into the study of the economy as a whole, which we shall take up in the second major section of this chapter. The second, usually known as field experimentation, deserves some discussion here. In effect, it forms a bridge between the "micro" and "macro" approaches. Often, we are not working with identified individual subjects, so it is not a truly micro approach; by contrast, the typical field experiment takes place on a small scale relative to the entire economy in which it is, as it were, embedded, so it is not a macro approach either.

Examples of field observation in economic psychology can be found among the studies, made by consumer scientists, of the variables which affect sales of consumer goods, especially in what Engel and Blackwell (1982) call "low-involvement purchase decisions." For example, Engel and Blackwell describe a number of "traffic-pattern" investigations, which involve tracing the routes taken by consumers through supermarkets. Field observation gradually turns into field experimentation when the variables thought to be important are actually manipulated, as, for instance, when Frank and Massy (1970) offered the same goods at different shelf heights at different times, and found that for most goods (but not large or heavy items) purchase was most likely when the display was at eye level. A less trivial example of field experimentation in economic psychology would be the studies of the effects on sales of different prices for the same goods. Bennett and Wilkinson (1974) priced M&M candy at prices ranging from 31 cents to 71 cents per half-pound at different times in the same discount store. They observed that sales increased dramatically when the price was below its usual level (51 cents), although the effects of increases above that level were unsystematic. Much empirical work on advertising can also be thought of as field experimentation. For example, Raj (1982) investigated the effect of increased advertising of one brand on sales in a market dominated by two brands, A and B. He found that while increased advertising of brand A increased the quantity of brand A bought by those already loyal to it, it did not decrease purchases of other brands. Conversely, those loyal to brand B bought less brand B as a result of increased advertising of brand A, but did not actually buy more of brand A.

Evidently, much work of this kind is done for practical, commercial reasons rather than for scientific purposes. Some modern commercial practices produce very large amounts of field observation data as a by-product. For example, credit card and store account transactions are generally handled by computer, and, in principle, could be monitored and sampled on a very wide scale. At the commercial level, field experimentation becomes what is called "test marketing," that is, the placing of a new commodity, or a new advertising campaign, in some small part of the total market (usually a well-defined geographical area) to see how it will sell. As such, the sales of individual products are rarely of scientific interest, but test marketing may involve manipulation of variables that do have general implications.

Thus economic psychology can certainly make use of commercial data, and a considerable number of potentially useful data have been collected. Unfortunately, however, really interesting results are likely to remain the property of the firm or market research organization that obtains them. This is one facet of a very general methodological problem which faces us in economic psychology. Our subject matter is not "neutral"; our subjects have all kinds of direct interests in the results we obtain. This creates a constant danger that data will be distorted, or hidden, to suit someone's financial interest. Since this problem flows from precisely that property of our subject that makes it interesting, namely its relevance to "real life," it cannot be circumvented, but we must always be aware of it.

Another category of "real-life" investigations that can be regarded as field experiments in economic psychology involves the various attempts to change the nature of working life. Some of these have been on a grand scale (e.g., the reforms of wage rates that followed the Russian and Chinese communist revolutions – see Phelps Brown 1977, pp. 38–54) and so fall under the heading of macro economic experiments. But there have been many smaller-scale projects, from Robert Owen's nineteenth-century model community at New Lanark in Scotland, to the socialist kibbutzim in Israel, some of which still flourish today. These form "laboratories" in which various aspects of the work relationship can be investigated and, although the people involved in them are obviously not a representative sample, the patterns of joining and leaving such communities are in themselves interesting data.

Some of the theorists who have set up such communities derived their ideas from explicitly psychological sources. Perhaps the most interesting from our point of view are those theorists who have started with the Skinnerian, or "operant," psychology viewpoint (see Chapter 1) and have gone on to create communities governed by explicit contingencies of reward and punishment. A few of these have been typical "Utopian communities" in the sense that their inhabitants have chosen that particular way of life (e.g., Feallock & Miller 1976). Far more, however, have involved involuntary subjects, since a major application of Skinnerian psychology has been the construction of "token economies" for therapeutic purposes (see Chapter 17).

The principle of a token economy is that each subject is rewarded with tangible but inherently worthless tokens (e.g., plastic chips) for certain activities that are desirable in the context of that individual's therapeutic program. The tokens can subsequently be exchanged for any of a wide variety of backup reinforcers, ranging from cups of tea, to a pass to leave the ward, to an interview with the chaplain. The "token wage" for any activity, and the "token price" for any commodity, can be varied separately for an individual, and such variations are, in fact, made frequently for therapeutic purposes. Token economies therefore offer substantial opportunities for the investigation of the economic behavior of individuals. Although the subject population will often be an unusual one, the data need not be. For instance, Winkler (1971) observed an orderly small decline in consumption of cups of tea when their price was doubled from one to two tokens; this is precisely the result we would expect on the basis of other studies of price variation (Lea 1978).

INVESTIGATING THE ENTIRE ECONOMY

Although we began the previous section with a consideration of the methods for studying the behavior of individuals within the economy, the macro level was seen to be relevant as well. This section follows the reverse course: We shall begin with a consideration of the methods used to study the economy as a whole, but shall also consider data which are relevant to the study of individuals.

The national accounts

The most obvious source of data on the entire economy are the "national accounts" or census. Most countries collect and publish official statistics of the economic situation, and there is an agreed standard (United Nations 1968) for what statistics should be reported and the manner in which they should be presented. In many cases, the statistical series are accompanied by handbooks that clarify exactly how the data are collected, as well as what errors are likely to enter into them (e.g., for the United Kingdom, see Copeman 1981; for greater detail, see Maurice 1968). National accounts statistics rarely answer questions posed by economic psychologists directly, but they often do provide valuable information concerning the differences in macroeconomic variables between times in one country (for longitudinal studies), or between countries at one time (for cross-sectional studies). For example, we might wish to investigate the relationship between unemployment and mental health by correlating national unemployment levels with mental hospital admissions either longitudinally or cross-sectionally. The national accounts (or the additional tables which usually accompany them) would be the appropriate source for the economic portion of our data.

The existence of a U.N. standard does not mean that all national statistics are collected or presented in a standard or even comparable way. Most are derived as by-products of the taxation system, which varies between countries according to their ideologies and traditions. Furthermore, not all national statistics are to be relied upon. Some nations are more secretive about their economic performance than others, and nations as well as individuals may indulge in "self-presentation." International organizations publish statistical series (e.g., the U.N. Statistical Yearbook) in which such gaps and distortions are to some extent commented on and corrected. These can be very useful sources for comparative investigations since the data are likely to be, as nearly as can be managed, on comparable bases.

National surveys

Most advanced nations have organized national surveys that complement and extend the information provided by the national accounts. For example, in Britain there are the Family Expenditure Survey (FES), the General Household Survey, and others; in America, the National Census Bureau publishes a number of volumes in this area, including the General Social and Economic Characteristics Index.

Econometrics

The study of the national accounts obviously represents the most macro possible level of analysis. Scarcely less aggregated is the statistical study of the movements of prices, and other economic variables, within the entire economy. This is the business of econometrics.

In the simplest possible econometric study, the price of a particular commodity (potatoes, for example) is recorded week by week or year by year, along with the quantities bought and sold. Quantity can then be plotted against price to yield a simple *own-price demand curve* (see Chapter 2). When this kind of study was first attempted, the results were puzzling. For example, quantities purchased were found to increase with increasing price. The problem is that the conditions of supply, the prices of other commodities, and consumers' incomes will all change at the same time as the variables we are primarily interested in (Working 1927). A variety of statistical techniques are now available to take all these factors into account at once (e.g., see Johnston 1972; for a simple introduction, see Surrey 1974). The nature of the data, and of the analytic techniques required to make sense of them, usually prevent us from plotting a demand curve comparable to the theoretical demand curves described in Chapter 2. Instead, we obtain equations for the best-fitting line of a given form, or estimates of key parameters such as elasticity of demand. Although such estimates usually apply to the totality of consumers in a market, they can be useful in tackling questions in economic psychology (seee Chapter 7).

Macroeconomic modeling

In one sense, of course, this kind of econometric study is concerned with microeconomics rather than macroeconomics, since it looks at a single commodity rather than the economy as a whole. The commodity in question may be more or less "aggregated," varying from a particular brand of a single product, to large classes such as "all food" or "all clothing." Some ways of taking into account the movements of prices of related products, however, begin to look like models of the entire economy. To take an historically important example, the *linear expenditure model* proposed by Stone (1954) investigated the sales and prices of every commodity on the market, although to do so the model had to aggregate them fairly broadly. Econometric techniques can in fact be applied to completely macro quantities like GNP or the level of unemployment. The modern way to do this is to build up a large quantity of statistical data, together with econometric treatments of them, into a computer model of the economy. Such models were described briefly in Chapter 3, where we noted that they are now relatively available to the academic community and that economic psychologists are already beginning to use them to investigate psychological hypotheses about the functioning of the economy as a whole. One example is Maital's (1984) demonstration that there are some conditions under which employees and employers might be expected to collaborate to reduce unemployment and inflation simultaneously.

Economic experiments

It might be thought that the only way of investigating the economy as a whole is through passive observation. But it is also possible to intervene experimentally. In one sense, whenever a government establishes a new economic policy (or even applies an old one in a new situation), it is making an experimental test of some economic theory. The problem with such "natural experiments" is that there is often no proper control group, though sometimes a comparison with other countries will provide one. For example, opposition politicians claimed that the experiment with (relatively) strict monetarism of the British government of 1979–83 led to levels of unemployment in Britain that were roughly twice those of comparable nations (the relevant international statistics, International Labour Organization, 1983, table 9, do not confirm this conclusion). But even such controlled natural experiments do not happen either by accident or in isolation, and it could easily be that there was more in common between the governments of Europe in the early eighties than political rhetoric suggested. In a true experiment, this possibility would be eliminated (as far as it ever can be) by assigning countries to distinct policies, by a random process.

In a few cases, such experiments with economic policy have been attempted. The best-known example is the "New Jersey income maintenance experiment." This was carried out to investigate the effects of replacing a complex of social security benefits by a single system of "negative income tax" designed to maintain everyone's income above the poverty line while eliminating the constraints on individual choice, disincentives to work, and indignities of means-tested benefits often delivered in kind. A large sample of the poorer inhabitants of the State of New Jersey were absorbed into the experimental benefit system. However, since the existing benefits were statutory rights, people had to volunteer for the experiment, and by no means everyone did. The results were analyzed in great detail in terms of the cost of the experimental system, and its effects on such variables as the incomes of welfare recipients and their tendency to take up work if it was available (see Kershaw & Fair 1976; Watts & Rees 1977). There have been a number of other experiments of this sort since that time. But there are obvious problems. It is unlikely that any legislature would sanction an experiment involving a really important economic policy, since it would necessarily involve making some people in a country subject to different laws from those governing the remainder. On a smaller scale, however, experimentation is now an established part of the administrative scene. Just as companies test-market new products in localized markets, so the economic bureaucracy tries out new procedures (methods of making welfare payments, for example) in local areas before introducing them on a large scale.

Token economies

Nation states are not the only organizations that possess an economy. Any group of people who are economically isolated are likely to develop their own system of trading. The cigarette economies of prisons are famous examples; those that developed in prisoner of war camps during World War II have been described in the economic literature (Clarke 1946; Einzig 1945). These smaller economies are much more attractive targets for experimentation than are whole nations. As it happens, psychologists have actually created a number of types of "miniature economy," usually for purposes that have nothing to do with economic psychology. The commonest is the "token economy."

The token economy is based on the "operant" approach to psychology pioneered by B. F. Skinner. As we saw in Chapter 1, the Skinnerian approach focuses on the environmental consequences of responses as defined by their effects on the environment. These techniques have been applied in many different types of settings – educational, industrial, clinical, and penal. One problem with operant programs in applied settings is that the need for immediacy severely limits the range of reinforcers that can be used. It is frequently clumsy to interrupt some ongoing behavior in order to deliver a conventional reward such as food or punishment. Ayllon and Azrin (1965, 1968) attempted to overcome this problem by using "token reinforcement." It is known that, even for rats or chimpanzees, direct reward by, say, food, can be replaced with a tangible token that is later "cashed in" for food. Ayllon and Azrin used metal tokens as rewards for severely institutionalized schizophrenic women who were being retaught the basics of self-care and social functioning. The tokens were exchangeable for a very wide range of "backup" reinforcers, many of the exchanges taking place in a ward shop. As Ayllon and Azrin recognized, this was obviously the beginning of an economy in miniature, and for the title of the book in which they described the system, they coined the phrase "the token economy." Later researchers have extended the analogy in a number of directions, both in bringing economic theory to aid in managing token economies (e.g., Winkler 1971), and in advocating and carrying out explicit economic experiments within token economies (e.g., Kagel & Winkler 1972). In fact, there have even been a few experimental economies established purely for the purpose of economic experiment (e.g., Miles, Congreve, Gibbins, Marshman, Devenyi, & Hicks, 1974). Clearly, both microeconomic and macroeconomic questions can be posed in this type of setting, but it is probably as models of entire economies that the token systems offer the greatest advantages over other approaches. We shall make considerable use of data from token economies in this book, and in Chapter 17 we shall survey their properties and problems in detail.

The comparative approach

If we wish to investigate the economy as a whole, one of the simplest strategies is to look at the differences between countries that organize their economies in different ways. We can also look at those that differ in other economically relevant ways, for example, in the availability of raw materials, or in their apparent economic success.

At an anecdotal level, such international comparisons are the stock in trade of economic commentators, both amateur and professional. Adam Smith (1776/1908) was fond of praising the economic dynamism of North America, and, at the present time, financial journalism frequently revolves around comparisons between the economies of the traditionally developed west and the rapidly expanding countries of East Asia. Comparisons may also be made between the developed countries of the North and the less developed ones of the South or between the (broadly) capitalist economies of the West and the (broadly) socialist ones of the East. We shall make a certain amount of use of such comparisons in this book (especially in Chapter 16, where we consider the process of economic development). On the whole, however, these comparisons are difficult to interpret. The economic condition of a particular country at a particular time is the product of a long and usually complex history, as well as of the factors currently operating.

There is a slightly different sense, however, in which the comparative method should always provide a necessary check on our thinking. It is all too easy to produce hypotheses and generalizations about economic behavior which are true or even plausible only about behavior in our own economy at the present time. Consideration of whether our ideas would be equally valid for, say, Japan, the People's Republic of China, or India, is likely to be worthwhile but often likely to be disconcerting.

A second kind of comparison involves the investigation of the economies of so-called primitive peoples. Primitive here means only that the people are not, or have not been, in touch with the common, Euro-American-based culture of the rest of the world. The study of such "primitive economies" is the province of economic anthropologists. Their findings are of great interest in the study of the economy as a whole, because a primitive economy often constitutes a natural experiment. It may, for example, lack certain institutions that we take for granted in our own economic arrangements (e.g., there are many cultures in the world that have no money system); or it may be organized on principles that would simply never occur to us as possible from an examination of our own economy. Among the Kuikuru people of Brazil, work activities are coordinated through the ownership of ceremonies that govern them; the only way to initiate a given activity is to organize a feast for the owner of the corresponding ceremony (Dole & Carneiro 1958). It would be hard to reconcile this with many theories of the motivation for work. Yet truly general principles of economic psychology ought to apply just as well to such a primitive economy as to a "modern" one.

The study of international and cross-cultural differences is not the only way of using the comparative method, however. To a psychologist, "comparative" tends to imply comparisons between species, and we have already referred to the uses we can make of nonhuman animals. It is also possible to make comparisons between different sorts of people within an economy. We may, for instance, use the existing variations in wealth and income to see how these variables affect economic behavior. Econometricians routinely find that buying of some goods increases sharply with increasing income, while buying of others falls either relatively or even absolutely. And there are special groups (children, perhaps) within the economy who are either affected by it in particular ways, or relatively insulated from it. The comparative approach, therefore, is not so much one method as a family of methods, different members of which are likely to be appropriate to different problems.

CONCLUSION

We have now surveyed quite a range of different methods of investigating economic behavior. It would be premature to try to decide which is the most useful. Indeed, the problem is not one of trying to find the right method to answer each particular question—we need to use as many methods as possible on every question. This is in accord with our general approach to economic psychology. If we are to develop a truly interdisciplinary approach, we must consider economic behavior from as many perspectives as possible. Our aim should not be to decide whether "the psychological theory" or "the economic theory" is correct. Rather, we should try to produce an account in which economic and psychological approaches have complementary roles. At times, different methods of investigation will tend to produce contradictory answers. In the long run, though, it should be possible to produce an integrated account of economic behavior within which all methods of investigation illuminate a common reality.

5

IS HUMAN BEHAVIOR RATIONAL?

Now that we have assembled some basic concepts and some methods of investigation from both economics and psychology, it should not be hard to see why the history of economic psychology has centered around a single issue: rationality. Almost all economic theory, and almost every empirical economic investigation, seems to be fundamentally based on the idea that human behavior is rational, in the sense that it can be understood by asking how a well-informed individual would act to secure his or her best advantage. By contrast, almost every approach to psychology implies that something other than rationality determines behavior. For learning theorists, it is schedules of reinforcement; for Freudians, unconscious motivations; for developmentalists, the individual's stage of cognitive development; for social psychologists, the current social context and the way the individual represents it; even cognitive psychologists argue that the individual's particular information processing machinery will constrain his or her performance.

Throughout its history, most of those interested in economic psychology have been preoccupied with the conflict between these points of view. In this chapter, we shall take three classic situations in which the question of rational behavior has been discussed and investigated experimentally. We shall indeed find, in each case, that psychological experiments demonstrate that the principles of rationality, on which economic theory is founded, are untrue. But we shall argue that the implications of these experiments for real economic behavior are hopelessly unclear and that the framework of rationality theory can always be retained by making additional assumptions. In consequence, we shall argue that economic psychology's preoccupation with the rationality question has been fundamentally sterile.

The aim of this chapter, therefore, is to complete our introduction to economic psychology by considering rationality. Once this issue is put aside, we can proceed to pose three questions we believe are far more important (indeed, they give the rest of the book its shape). How does individual behavior influence what happens in the economy? How does the economy influence individual behavior? How do these two processes interact?

How has the rationality question been posed? Chapter 2 introduced the way in which economics uses the concept of rationality, using the example of the theory of consumer demand. In deducing the effects of price changes on quantities of goods purchased, we identified the objective constraints faced by the consumer (prices determined by others, and limited income), the consumer's objective (to maximize utility). In a simple way, we then used mathematics to find out what behavior would best achieve the stated objective under the given constraints. This strategy is used repeatedly in economic analysis. As a way of predicting human behavior, however, it obviously suffers from one potentially fatal flaw: It assumes that people will, in fact, behave in the way that maximizes utility. Most laymen believe that this cannot be right; and many psychologists have said that they know it is not right. As an initial assumption, rationality seems to impute far too much wisdom and forethought to very fallible human beings. It would appear that the role of psychology ought to be to correct the economists' false assumptions, and so make possible a corrected economics.

Rationality, maximizing, and optimizing

There is, however, an important semantic issue involved here. In ordinary language, "rationality" has two senses. We describe someone's behavior as "rational" if what the person does seems sensible under the circumstances. But we also use "rational" to describe how someone decides what to do: We call people rational if they work out the probable consequences of different courses of action, and consciously choose the action whose outcome they most like. In the first sense, "rational" is a description of behavior; in the second sense, it is a description of the mechanism underlying behavior.

What economists assume is that people are rational in the first sense. Of course, it is because people (unlike other animals) are capable of being rational in the second sense that the economists' assumption of rationality in the first sense is so plausible. But it is important to recognize that the two kinds of rationality are quite independent. Even if you spend a great deal of time thinking about some problem, your final behavior may well be "irrational," if you are unaware of relevant circumstances, misinformed, or if you make a mistake in your reasoning or calculation. Similarly, some "lower" animals are presumably quite incapable of "thinking ahead," yet an animal may distribute its time between different sources of food in such a precise way that the maximum possible food intake is achieved. In many environments such "rational" behavior can be explained in terms of very simple learning or perceptual mechanisms that involve no conscious forethought or choosing at all. In other words, behavior may be rational in the first sense (i.e., be sensible) without being rational in the second sense (i.e., consciously reasoned through), and vice versa.

To avoid confusing the two senses of rationality, scientists often eliminate terms like "rational behavior" or "rationality" altogether from their discussion. Instead, they talk about "maximizing." This word makes it clear that they are referring merely to the behavior that maximizes some good outcome, not to a mechanism (e.g., thinking, choice) that produces the behavior. But the term maximization also suggests that "rational behavior" needs further specification; in particular, we need to know what it is that certain behaviors maximize, that is, what the *maximand* is. It makes a big difference whether we assume that people will maximize objective economic benefits or whether we suppose instead that they will maximize some subjective quantity (usually called "utility") whose relationship to objective quantities of goods is unknown.

Another word, often used interchangeably with *maximizing*, is *optimizing*. *Optimizing* means "doing the best thing possible," whereas the word *maximizing* implies that, in addition, some measurable quantity is being maximized. In many real economic situations, however, we are concerned with tradeoffs between different kinds of benefit that are hard to measure on a common scale. As a result, there simply is no obvious maximand. In such situations, many authors prefer to talk about optimizing rather than maximizing, although this is more a convention than a hard-and-fast rule.

Even the simplest real economic situations tend to be too complicated for one to specify an obvious maximand. In a world of many different goods, we cannot merely say that we maximize our input of goods. Are three apples and an orange more valuable than three oranges and an apple? There is no way to know. We can address this problem by assuming that apples and oranges both contribute (perhaps unequally) to utility and that people maximize utility (see Chapter 2). But this solution seems less appropriate in other cases. For example, maximizing your intake of apples, given a limited amount of money to spend on them, involves finding the supplier of the cheapest apples. It may cost time and money both to find out where the cheapest source of supply is and to travel to the source once it has been identified. While some of these costs may be easily quantified, others probably will not be. Sometimes we just ignore these costs and talk about maximizing. Other times, when we make a serious effort to identify and analyze the costs, we prefer to describe rational behavior as optimizing rather than maximizing.

To summarize, in economic psychology the "assumption of rationality" means the assumption that people behave in such a way as to maximize some (subjective) function of all the costs and advantages operating in a situation. It does not involve any assumption about the way people come to behave in such an optimal way, and so there is no objection to talking about rational behavior even in a rat or a pigeon. In other words, *rational* and *irrational* and *maximizing* and *optimizing* describe behavior, not mechanisms.

To discover what rational behavior consists of in any given situation, we must take two steps. First, we must identify the function to be maximized or optimized. Second, we must ask what pattern of behavior would produce the maximum value of this function. This second question may well be hard to answer, but it is at least clear cut. We have in fact already seen the process at work, in Chapter 2, when we looked at the microeconomic theory of demand.

Alternatives to rationality

Once we have discovered what rational behavior consists of in a given situation, it is quite often easy to test experimentally whether or not people do behave rationally. But that is not a very interesting issue in itself. For one thing, it is all too easy to find excuses that explain any apparent lapse from rationality. If we are going to make any real progress on this question, we need to have some alternatives to rationality ready to hand. Then, if we find that one of these alternatives consistently gives a better account of behavior, we will be in a strong position to reject the original assumption of rationality.

Four alternatives to rationality need to be discussed. The first is the notion that behavior is completely random. As a full account, this will always be an explanation of last resort because it is not really an explanation at all; behavior cannot be explained if it occurs randomly. However, any practical description of behavior (including descriptions involving rationality) usually permits some random element, that is, the "unexplained variance," in the observed behavior.

Second, the various kinds of learning mechanisms mentioned in Chapter 1 can be used to generate hypotheses about how people will behave in simple economic situations. For example, operant psychology can readily be used to explain how hard people will work, or what they will buy (Skinner 1953, chapter 23). Often we say that "habit" has a role in economic psychology. It is not only learning psychologists who have brought forward "habit" models of economic behavior. Marketing scientists have used them too in analyzing consumers' purchases of different brands of a single product (e.g., Ehrenberg 1972, pp. 6 and 259).

The third position is rather different and has been advocated by some less psychologically inclined opponents of the rationality assumption. These authorities (e.g., Simon 1955) do not predict that behavior will be optimal in the usual sense. Rather, they retain the idea that the mechanism underlying and producing behavior is rational forethought and argue that the forethought will stop when some "good enough" behavior has been found. In other words, nobody goes on thinking forever in the hope of finding the best possible solution; they stop when a "satisfactory" solution is achieved. Simon (1957) called this sort of behavior *satisficing*, finding a satisfactory behavior without bothering about whether there is one even better. Katona (e.g., 1975, p. 210) called it the problem-solving approach, whereby forethought stops and action begins as soon as a solution has been found to the problem at hand.

Finally, some economic psychologists have seen the dispute between rational and irrational, maximizing and satisficing, habit and problem solving, as a sterile argument that must somehow be bypassed if economic psychology is to make any progress. There are two versions of this point of view. The more radical is well expressed by Rachlin (1980), who argues that any behavior maximizes some function or other and therefore that the task for economists, psychologists, or economic psychologists is simply to discover this maximand.

Less radically, but perhaps more realistically, both rational and irrational behavior may fit into some overarching schema. For example, Katona (e.g., 1975, pp. 210–26) argued that people use more or less rational forethought, and hence behave more or less rationally, depending on the importance of the decision to be taken. Reynaud (e.g., 1981, p. 162) agrees but adds that different people are capable of different degrees of rationality as a function of the different quantities of mental energy at their disposal. These quantities in turn depend on such factors as the person's intelligence and education as well as on the other competing demands on the limited mental resources.

Assessing rationality

The offer to integrate rational and irrational behavior has considerable appeal, but it is not necessary unless human economic behavior is indeed irrational, at least some of the time. The next three sections of this chapter discuss three classic test cases for the rationality of behavior.

Let us briefly preview these areas, all of which are fundamental to our understanding of economic behavior. The first area, consumer demand theory, involves an investigation of the so-called axioms of microeconomics, often called the theory of riskless choice. Demand theory was introduced as informally as possible in Chapter 2; here we reduce it to a few mathematically essential statements about choice, and consider what psychological evidence there is that supports their accuracy as generalizations about human behavior. The second area, choice involving risk, is one where psychologists as well as economists have used the assumption of rationality. There is a substantial experimental literature investigating the usefulness of this idea. The third area, often referred to as the study of intertemporal choice, is one that has been considered by many different sorts of social scientists who have had little interaction, at least until recently.

In these three areas, the rationality analysis has been applied directly to a particular class of economic behavior, that is, the theory of riskless choice to buying behavior, choice under risk to gambling, and intertemporal choice to saving. This chapter does not consider the results of these applications and the economic data that bear on them. Instead, we shall look at the most direct possible tests of the principles that are supposed to guide rational behavior in each situation.

HOMO ECONOMICUS

The microeconomic theory of demand involves choices between options that are certainly available to the consumer if only he or she will pay the price. This is why it is sometimes called the field of riskless choice. The reason there is a choice problem, even in the absence of risk, is that both the goods on offer and the consumer's wants are infinite, while the consumer's resources are limited.

For formal purposes, economists often reduce the basic ideas of the theory of demand to a set of "axioms." These axioms are abstract, formal statements about behavior, which are just sufficient to generate the theory mathematically. There is now general agreement among economists about what those axioms should be, although there is a large number of distinct but logically equivalent ways of stating them. In mock zoological spirit, the person who obeys, perfectly, the axioms of microeconomic theory is often referred to as *Homo economicus* – Economic Man. The implication of the name is obvious: Economic Man is a distinct species from Homo sapiens. Real people are not expected to obey the theory.

Maximizing ordinal utility

Is this implication correct, though – is Economic Man really different from "real people?" Simple microeconomic theory, as we explained it in Chapter 2, does not seem very restrictive; in fact, it is difficult to believe it could ever be shown to be wrong. It remains highly plausible if we express the theory in the usual, slightly more abstract form. According to this version of the theory, all it requires is that people maximize a quantity called utility, which is a function of the qualities of the various goods consumed. The nature of that function is deliberately left very open. The only essential point is that, of two collections of goods ("commodity bundles"), the one that is preferred has the higher utility. Hence, in getting what he or she most prefers, a consumer inevitably maximizes ordinal utility ("ordinal," meaning that only the ranking of utilities can be determined by direct observations of behavior, not actual numerical values). We might suspect that psychologists could add something to this account, for example, by showing how utility is related to quantities of goods, but it is difficult to conceive of experiments that could challenge the foundations of the theory.

Axioms of demand theory

Theoretical economists have examined the foundations of the theory of demand in great detail; in particular, they have discovered the essential properties that must be true of individual choices if there is to be any utility function that they maximize. These essential properties are referred to as the axioms of demand theory. Surprisingly, some of these axioms have rather strong and testable psychological content. In this section of the chapter, we shall consider whether they are consistent with psychological experiments on riskless choice. First, we shall state the axioms in relatively formal terms (using the version of demand theory given by Simmons 1974). In what follows, A, B, and C are arbitrary commodity bundles – "shopping baskets" filled with goods.

Axiom of completeness: For any two bundles A and B, the consumer either prefers A to B, or prefers B to A, or is indifferent between them.

Axiom of greed: If A contains more of one good than B, and at least as much as B of all other goods, A will be preferred to B.

Axiom of transitivity: If A is preferred to B, and B is preferred to C, then A will be preferred to C.

Axiom of convexity: If B is a mixture made by taking $x\%$ of A with $y\%$ of C, where $x + y = 100$, then neither A nor C will be preferred to B (but B may well be preferred to either A or C or both).

Axiom of continuity: This is impossible to state nonmathematically, but the underlying idea is that similar commodity bundles will be close to each other in the preference ordering, and that between any two bundles there will always be other bundles that are similar to both. Not all ways of ordering have this property. Consider the alphabetic ordering of words ("lexicographic" ordering): "Amber" and "umber" are very similar words, as similar as two distinct words can be, differing only in one letter, but they are far apart in the dictionary, separated by many words that are very different from either of them.

All these axioms seem to say something straightforward about human preferences; it is easy to think of experiments that would be direct tests of them. We shall not work through all of them systematically, since most discussion has focused on the axioms of greed and transitivity, but it will be useful to consider one problem that is raised by the axiom of completeness.

Stochastic preference and the axiom of completeness

This axiom appears innocuous, but it implies that preferences will be consistent, that is, if one apple is preferred to one orange today, the same will be true tomorrow. Common observation suggests that this is untrue and that preferences are actually variable. Technically, we can accommodate this finding by saying that people show "probabilistic" or "stochastic" rather than "absolute" preferences. But such a claim can cause serious problems of analysis, as discussed below in connection with transitivity. Furthermore, there are some situations where preferences are not just random but predictably inconsistent (e.g., it is possible to reverse people's preferences between two gambles in a controlled way that completely violates the completeness axiom, see Grether & Plott 1979).

Objections to greed: generosity and satiation

Is it really correct to assume, as the second axiom seems to require, that people are insatiably greedy? Critics of economics have focused on this axiom, claiming that it gives an obviously false (and furthermore unduly pessimistic) picture of human nature.

In the first place, we know that individuals often expend their scarce resources for the benefit of others rather than themselves. Giving is, in fact, such an important kind of economic behavior that we devote an entire chapter to the subject later in this book. We do not have to go into detail, however, to see that the everyday fact of giving might bring that axiom into disrepute. It is possible, however, to define utility in such a way that "benefit to others" contributes to a person's own utility. The conventional axioms of demand theory will then work perfectly well for the purchase of gifts, donations to charity, and so forth. Furthermore, although the total of giving is large, as a proportion of all economic behavior it is really quite insignificant, so that even if redefining utility is considered somehow unsatisfactory, the violation of the greed axiom is so slight that it is unlikely to affect the normal working of theories based on it.

Even if people can be treated as being entirely self-centered, it does not follow that they are *insatiably* greedy; the possibility of having too much of a good leads immediately to the greed axiom either being violated or becoming useless for purposes of prediction. The psychological evidence against insatiability is actually quite strong and general. For example, Premack (1965, 1971) argued that, contrary to previous ideas, there is no fixed list of stimuli or activities that can act as rewards or punishers. Any response might act as a reward for any other response, provided that the first was the more probable of the two when both were freely available.

Premack's early demonstrations of this phenomenon were made with rats; later, the principle was applied to human behavior, for example in token economies (cf. Chapter 17).

A simple demonstration of the Premack principle involved giving rats access to water and to a running wheel. Under conditions in which the rat had not drunk for a few hours, water functioned as a reward for running. But under conditions in which the "brakes" on the wheel had been locked for some time (in essence, the animal had been deprived of exercise), releasing the brakes and allowing the animal to run functioned as a reward for drinking; that is, it caused the subject to drink well in excess of "natural" levels. Conversely, making a less probable response follow a more probable one served as a punishment; that is, if a thirsty rat had to run in a wheel after every drink, drinking was somewhat suppressed.

Similar reversals of reward and punishment relations can be produced without manipulating an animal's motivational state. Mazur (1975), for example, found that rats spent about 2.5 times as much time drinking as they spent running in a wheel when both activities were freely available. If they were required now to spend three seconds running for every one second drinking, the rats ran more but drank less than normally; that is, drinking rewarded running, but running punished drinking. If, however, Mazur made the subjects spend nine seconds drinking for every one second of running, then running decreased and drinking increased; that is, running rewarded drinking and drinking punished running. The point is that both running and drinking were "goods" in that either could function as a reward up to a certain point; after that, either of them could become a "bad."

These experiments point to a general conclusion: Organisms have "ideal" distributions of their time between different activities. If they are deprived of one activity, they will work to get its rate back to the ideal ("baseline") level, but equally, if they are forced to engage in one activity at more than the baseline rate, they choose to suffer losses of another activity, again in order to get back to or close to baseline. Scitovsky (1985) has discussed economic phenomena in humans that mirror this effect very closely.

Economists describe this kind of situation in terms of the existence of "bliss points" of consumption. A bliss point is simply a condition from which any change is for the worse. Figure 5.1 shows the kind of indifference curve analysis that is needed to account for Mazur's rat data. But now consider what would happen if we tried to develop the usual microeconomic demand theory from indifference curves like these, in the same way as we did in Chapter 2, using more conventional indifference curves. It is obvious that it would not work. The evidence is that the axiom of greed must be rejected, because real people, unlike *Homo economicus*, are not insatiable.

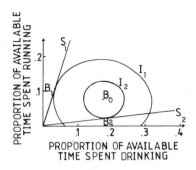

PROPORTION OF AVAILABLE
TIME SPENT DRINKING

5.1. Indifference curve analysis of data obtained by Mazur (1975) using rats. With no contingencies in force, behavior is at point B0 (1 wheel turn/min; 2.5 licks/min). Under reward schedule S1, three times as much running as drinking must occur, and behavior settles at point B1, tangent to indifference curve I1. Under schedule S2, drinking and running must be in proportion 9:1, and behavior settles at B2, tangent to I2. The three observed behavior points cannot be explained without postulating closed indifference curves.

Transitivity of preference

Transitivity looks like an easy area for direct experimental enquiry. The principle at issue is easily stated: Given three goods (or combinations of goods) A, B, and C, any individual who prefers A to B and B to C should also prefer A to C. All we have to do to test this idea is to present a subject with pairwise combinations of some set of commodity bundles, say $A \cdots Z$, and look for any "circular triads." A circular triad occurs when, for instance, L is presented with M and L is preferred; M is presented with N and M is preferred; and L and N are presented but N is preferred (see Figure 5.2).

Some early experiments on transitivity followed this procedure exactly. For example, May (1954) asked 62 students to make pairwise choices between three hypothetical marriage partners; 17 chose intransitively. This kind of paper-and-pencil experiment is never very convincing as a model of real economic behavior. Moreover, there is a problem when a simple experiment of this sort finds a small number of intransitivities. The number of pairwise presentations possible, given a set of n alternatives, is $n(n-1)/2$. This number rapidly gets very large indeed (with 10 alternatives, there are 45 possible pairings; with 20 there are 190; with 30 there are 435). If all these choices are given, and a few intransitivities are observed, it is tempting to suggest that they are attributable to some random factor superimposed on an underlying transitive process. The only way to find out is to present at least some of the choices more than once, so as to find out how stable preferences are, and this makes the experiment even more cumbersome than it would be anyway. We already

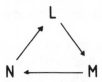

5.2. A circular "triad" of preferences. The arrow indicates direction of preference, so that L is preferred to M, M to N, and N to L. Circular triads violate the axiom of transitivity in demand theory.

know that subjects frequently are not perfectly consistent in their choices; in the terms used earlier, preference is stochastic rather than absolute. Stochastic preferences create two problems for experimental tests of transitivity. First, how do we decide whether we have observed more intransitivities than we can explain in terms of the known inconsistency of choice? Second, how do we even define transitivity when preferences are stochastic? Several investigators have considered these questions (e.g., Davis 1958; Papandreou 1957; Tversky & Russo 1969).

Davis asked male undergraduates to choose between potential marriage partners on the basis of verbal descriptions, for example, between a "pretty, average charm, well-to-do" woman and a "plain, very charming, wealthy" woman. All possible pairwise choices between nine such descriptions were recorded twice, with one week elapsing between the two tests. Davis found that 22.8% of all choices were reversed on the second test; that is, preferences were moderately stochastic. It is therefore not obvious how we can even state the requirement of transitivity, let alone test it. Perhaps the simplest definition would be what Coombs (1964) called "weak stochastic transitivity." It requires that if A is chosen over B more often than not, and B is chosen over C more often than not, then A should be chosen over C more often than not also. But even this simple idea leads us into further problems. If, like Davis, we give each choice only twice, how can we possibly estimate the probability that a given subject prefers A (pretty, average charm, well-to-do) to B (plain, very charming, wealthy)? All we know is that one description was preferred to the other twice, once, or not at all.

Remarkable mathematical virtuosity has been shown in efforts at solving this problem. They have not produced any clear evidence that people choose intransitively. Papandreou (1957) concluded that the proportion of intransitivities he observed, in choices between bundles of tickets for different kinds of entertainment, was acceptably low (i.e., intransitivities could reasonably be explained in terms of the observed stochasticity of choice). Davis came to the same conclusion in his work on choices between hypothetical marriage partners, and between gambles which varied in both stakes and odds. Other investigators have offered people choices between hypothetical gambles of much the same sort, and have concluded that the great majority of people choose transitively when stochastic preference is allowed for.

A rather different conclusion emerges from the work of Tversky (1969), however, who considered whether there were conditions that would reliably produce intransitive choice. Tversky claims that such conditions are readily found. Like May (1954), his key point is that objects should be "multifaceted;" that is, that they should have many different independent properties and that people should tend to make their choices in a number of stages, using first one characteristic, then another. This is obviously a plausible way of approaching the problem of choosing between the gambles used by Davis and the hypothetical marriage partners used by May and by Davis. If this kind of object does tend to produce intransitive choice, the implications for demand theory are distinctly alarming. Time and time again in this book, we are going to return to the idea (mentioned in Chapter 2), that consumers respond to goods as bundles of characteristics that appeal to different needs. Tversky's approach to choice is obviously highly compatible with this idea, a fact that was already obvious to May (1954). If Tversky is right, intransitivity is likely to be ubiquitous.

But the artificiality of the choices offered in most experiments on transitivity has made it all too easy to dismiss them as irrelevant to real economic behavior. Much more convincing experiments on transitivity have been done with animals, using an instrumental conditioning technique, devised by Autor (1969), known as "concurrent chain schedules of reinforcement." In this procedure, there is an initial phase in which the subject has two responses available. The reward for either of them, however, is neither food nor any other primary reward, but access to a "terminal" phase in which responding on one of the two keys (the last one pecked in the initial phase) does lead to food reward according to some specified schedule of reinforcement. The relative rate of the two responses in the initial phase gives a measure of the subject's preference between the two different schedules available in the terminal phase. Using this technique, the same few outcomes can be presented over and over again, so that accurate measurements of choice probability can be made. The results of such experiments are consistent and clear: Preference is nearly always intransitive when the schedules offered in the terminal phase differ in kind as well as in simple quantitative parameters such as a delay in the delivery of food (Navarick & Fantino 1972, 1974).

These experiments have the usual advantages and the usual difficulties of animal research. On the positive side, the objects of the choices are of real importance to the subjects, and the conditions can be presented over and over again so as to get stable results. By contrast, we cannot be sure what the results mean for humans. Clearly what we need is some experimental work with human subjects that has the same merits as the animal work.

It is not easy to summarize the empirical literature on transitivity. Direct tests like Davis's or Papandreou's seem to find no more intransitivity than expected given that human choice is nearly always stochastic. On the other hand, Tversky claims to be able to produce intransitivity more or less at will, under conditions that we expect to be ubiquitous in real economic choice. And animal studies show that where we can study choice in great detail, transitivity is glaringly lacking. We reached a rather similar point in our discussions of the axiom of greed. There clearly are conditions under which it is violated, but it is less clear how relevant they are to everyday economic behavior. Does all this mean that human behavior under riskless conditions will be irrational? The answer still is not clear. As we turn to other fields in which the rationality assumption is deployed, we shall find that this lack of real clarity is by no means uncommon.

RISKY CHOICE: CLASSICAL DECISION THEORY

Rationality in the face of risk

The theory of riskless choice applies to a world where, if you choose three oranges over two apples, you know that you will actually receive three oranges. One of the objections to *Homo economicus* is that the real world is not remotely like that. Even in the simplest choice, say to spend 20 cents on a bar of chocolate, there is some risk: The chocolate might turn out to be unpleasantly stale, you might suffer a heart attack between handing over your money and receiving the goods, and so forth. Many real economic choices involve more obvious risks. If I am planning a visit to Europe next month, should I buy foreign currency now, when $1 will buy 2.80 deutsch marks (DM), or should I wait until the day before I go, when the dollar may have risen to 3.20 DM – or fallen to 2.40? Can I risk buying a new washing machine on an installment plan when there is talk of my company closing next month, so I would not be able to keep up the repayments? In fact, all real economic behavior involves making choices between actions, all of which involve some degree of uncertainty.

To solve this kind of problem, we need some means of taking into account the chance that the benefit will really be obtained (or the penalty really incurred) when we estimate the value (or cost) of any object. The rational way of doing this has been obvious at least since Bernoulli (1738/1954), and he asserts it was known long before him. If we are not sure that we are going to obtain some good, then its effective value (usually called its expected value) is simply its value to us if we do obtain it, multiplied by the probability that we obtain it.

The simplest example is the purchase of a lottery ticket. Suppose that a million tickets are sold and that there is only one prize, of $100,000. How much is each ticket worth? Clearly, its expected value is $0.10 – the value of the prize, multiplied by the probability (one in a million) of winning it. A rational person would buy such a ticket if it cost less than ten cents and would refuse to buy it if it cost more.

The lottery example is simple because only one of the two possible outcomes (winning or losing) has any value. Most risky options involve two or more possible outcomes, each of which has some cost or value associated with it. In this case, we find the expected value of the entire option by adding up the expected values of all the possible outcomes. As an example, let us go back to the currency exchange problem mentioned above.

Suppose I have $500 to exchange into marks. If I exchange at today's rate, I will obtain 1,400 DM with certainty, so the expected value of this option is just 1,400 DM. The expected value of waiting to exchange depends on the probabilities that the exchange rate will rise or fall. Suppose I estimate that there is a 20% chance that the rate will rise to 3.30 DM/$, a 50% chance that it will not change, and a 30% chance that it will fall to 2.40 DM/$ (obviously this is simplifying the problem considerably!). The total expected value of waiting is then

$$1,650 \text{ DM} \times 20\% + 1,400 \text{ DM} \times 50\% + 1,200 \text{ DM} \times 30\%$$

which equals 1,390 DM. This is less than the expected value of exchanging immediately (1,400 DM), so the rational tourist will not wait to buy his or her marks.

There are three problems with expected value analysis. First, real situations will be much more complicated than these simple examples. Lotteries have a great range of prizes, not just one, and currency rates may move to an indefinite number of different levels, not just to three. Second, the probabilities involved may be very difficult. However complicated this may make the arithmetic, it does not make the situation more complicated in principle. More fundamentally, the probabilities involved may not be known or even knowable. How could I calculate the probability that the deutsch mark will rise or fall against the dollar? It is not an outcome like the fall of a die, where the mathematics of the situation allow probabilities to be determined exactly.

The biggest problem, however, is that people clearly do not behave in accordance with the expected value principle. If no one bought a lottery ticket unless its expected value exceeded its price, lotteries would cease to exist (lottery organizers make their money from the difference between total ticket sales and the cost of the prizes). Obviously, not just lotteries, but all commercial gambling, relies on consumers' willingness to buy bets whose expected values are less than their price.

Very similarly, the cost of an insurance policy is always less than its expected value. Suppose you have a video recorder worth $250, and it costs $25 to insure it for a year against theft. If the probability of the recorder being stolen is one-twentieth, the expected value of the insurance policy is only $12.50; yet everyone who buys insurance must be doing so under these kinds of conditions, or insurers would go out of business. Can it really be irrational to do so? Most people regard it as not only rational but prudent and responsible to insure their property.

There are three basic ways in which expected value theory can be adjusted in order to cope with this fundamental problem. They are discussed in the next three sections.

Bernoulli and utility

The first systematic discussion of why people should take out insurance, even though the insurer makes a profit, was given in a classic paper by Bernoulli (1738/1954) on whether merchants sending ships on the dangerous waters between Amsterdam and St. Petersburg should insure their contents. Bernoulli understood that taking out insurance usually violates the expected value principle, but he argued that it could nonetheless be rational. He proposed that this is because the utility (or subjective value) of wealth does not simply increase with the amount of money you have. Instead, each extra ducat (or dollar or pound) you own adds a little less to your feeling of well-being than the previous ducat did (this is called the principle of diminishing marginal utility). According to Bernoulli, a rational choice is one that maximizes not expected value but expected utility, and the decision to insure might well accomplish this.

For example, how would Bernoulli explain why you insure your video recorder? Suppose you have savings of $1,000, out of which you would have to pay the insurance premium or replace the recorder if it were stolen while uninsured. Then if the recorder were stolen, your wealth would fall to $750. Paying the insurance premium only reduces your wealth to $975. Bernoulli argues that the relationship between utility and wealth must be like the graph in Figure 5.3. In this graph, the drop from $1,000 to $750 corresponds to a loss of 135 units of utility (or *utiles*), while the drop from $1000 to $975 only corresponds to a drop of 3.5 utiles. With a 1:20 chance of theft, the expected utility of the insurance is therefore 6.75 utiles, which is more than the cost in utiles of the premium. It is therefore rational to insure.

Clearly Bernoulli's idea is completely consistent with our general characterization of economic rationality, as implying the maximization of utility. Can it be submitted to experimental test? There are several problems. Obviously, before we can carry out a direct test, we need to know the exact form of the utility function. In Figure 5.3, we simply assumed a

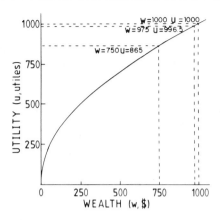

5.3. Hypothetical relation between utility and wealth, with the figures for a video recorder insurance examples added. Utility is scaled so that wealth of $1,000 has a utility of 1,000 utiles. A loss of $250 leaves wealth at $750, which has a utility of 865 utiles, a loss of 135 utiles. Paying an insurance premium of $25 leaves wealth at 996.5 utiles, a loss of only 3.5 utiles. Thus if the probability of theft in a given year is one-twentieth, the expected utility of insurance (−3.5 utiles) is greater than that of not insuring (−135/20 = −6.75 utiles).

form (actually a square root curve, one of Bernoulli's suggestions), which we knew would make the behavior in the example under consideration seem rational. Clearly, this is unsatisfactory. A scientific theory that can be made to fit all facts just by choosing the right form for an unknown function is no theory at all. And economists have never been able to agree what shape the utility function ought to have. At one time (e.g., Marshall 1920/1949) it was generally thought that the principle of diminishing marginal utility must hold, that is, that the slope of the utility function should become less and less steep as wealth becomes greater and greater, but it is now known that demand theory can be constructed without making this assumption (Hicks & Allen 1934; Samuelson 1938), because the convexity axiom serves instead, and says nothing about utility functions at all.

At first sight, the unknown form of the utility function appears to pose a first-rate opportunity for psychology to test Bernoulli's utility maximizing hypothesis indirectly, and, in doing so, to "rescue" economics. Utility functions are, preeminently, properties of individuals, and so surely psychologists could find out the form of the utility function once and for all. If this could be done, it would enable demand theory (and much else besides, including the theory of risky choice) to be built on surer, more empirical foundations. In particular, it seems obvious that psychologists could discover the shape of the utility function by finding out precisely what risks people will take, and how these vary as a function of the costs and probabilities involved. One should then be able either to construct the correct utility function, which is consistent with all these data, or to discover that no single function will do the job, in which case we can regard Bernoulli's expected utility theory as disproved. Here, surely, psychologists have a splendid research program for testing the general economic assumption that people act so as to maximize utility.

A few experiments of this sort have been carried out (for an early example see Mosteller & Nogee 1951), but they quickly ran aground on the second basic problem associated with the Bernoulli approach. There is an alternative way of thinking about decisions under risk that is just as powerful in explaining deviations from the expected value principle. This alternative does not require us to replace objectively specified costs and benefits with subjective utilities at all.

Subjective probability

This alternative approach is straightforward. Once again we consider the hypothetical video recorder-insurance problem. In the expected utility analysis, the probability of theft was supposed to be accurate and objective. This may well be true for the insurance company since they have observed, over the years, that one out of every twenty video recorders insured with them gets stolen. You, however, have to rely on their estimate of the probability that your recorder will get stolen, an event that may be influenced by many factors other than the objective (actuarial) figures available. For instance, you may know that there have been numerous break-ins on your block, or you may feel that you are a particularly unlucky person where theft is concerned; or you may even have dreamed about your video equipment being stolen. In any case, you will be working with "subjective probabilities" or "expectations," and these will tend to differ from objective probabilities.

The differences may be idiosyncratic (like some of those suggested above), or systematic. Suppose, for example, that people always overestimate the probabilities of rare events such as a theft. This tendency would clearly raise the subjectively expected cost of failing to insure, because a large contribution from the rare event of loss would be involved. The subjective probability analysis has great applicability to the decision to engage in gambling. If people overestimate the probability of rare events, the subjectively expected value of lottery tickets and other bets would be inflated relative to their prices. By contrast, Bernoulli points out that his negatively accelerated utility function cannot explain why people bet; in fact, the kind of utility function shown in Figure 5.3 makes even a fair, noncommercial bet irrational for both players (Bernoulli describes this fact as "Nature's admonition to avoid the dice altogether"). Furthermore, it is highly plausible to suppose that gamblers always overestimate the probability that they are going to win, perhaps because of some personality trait, because they believe they have privileged information, or perhaps because they have, by chance or conspiracy, won more often in the past than the odds suggest they should.

We now have two possible ways of accounting for violations of the expected value principle in risky choices. Which should we use? Unfortunately there is no obvious way of deciding between them. Subjective value taken with objective probability will explain almost exactly the same range of phenomena as objective value taken with subjective probability. In fact Preston and Baratta (1948) carried out an experiment to measure subjective probability that was logically identical to Mosteller and Nogee's experiment to measure utility. Admittedly, under Bernoulli's expected utility hypothesis, different utility functions are required to explain the behavior of gamblers and people who buy insurance, and this is a bad sign. But exactly parallel problems can occur with subjectively expected value theory. There is an obvious symmetry between the two theories, and both seem likely to have very similar explanatory power; each allows us one arbitrary function which we can adjust to make the theory fit any given set of data.

Subjectively expected utility

No one has ever gone to much trouble to discover which of these two hypotheses is the better, however. The reason is simple: There seems to be no good reason why value and probability should not both be subjective quantities, so that both should be transformed before we work out the equivalent of an expected value. What we get in this case is a model in which subjectively expected utility (usually abbreviated as SEU) determines choice (Edwards 1955). In order to predict what action a person will take, using the SEU model, we first have to find out how utility is related to objective value. Next we have to find out how subjective probability is related to objective probability. Finally we have to go through all the usual processes of expected value theory to calculate the SEU values for the different possible actions.

This sounds like a formidable undertaking, and it is. Two approaches have been proposed. The first is to find some way of measuring utility and subjective probability outside the choice situation. Stevens (1959) and Galanter (1962) suggested the boldest and simplest way of doing this. They asked people to assign numbers to the subjective probabilities and subjective values of outcomes, drawing on the techniques Stevens (1957) had developed for the direct measurement of subjective quantities like the brightness of a light. The procedure involved asking people questions like, "How probable do you find it that the sun will not rise tomorrow?," or "How much money do I have to give you to make you twice as happy as a gift of $10 would make you?" (not their exact wording). Astonishingly, people can and do give consistent answers to such questions. This procedure is regularly used almost exactly in research on attitudes, using the Fishbein expectancy-value theory introduced in Chapter 1. In fact, as readers should now be able to recognize, Fishbein's theory is simply a version of SEU theory and represents one of the most successful intrusions of economic thinking into the mainstream of social psychology. In the attitude context, the expectancy-value approach has proved fruitful, although it has never yielded any consistent set of utility of subjective probability functions that we could take away and use regardless of context. Among those directly interested in decision under risk for its own sake, however, the Stevens–Galanter approach has never been regarded as more than a curiosity.

Much more attention has been given to a second way of trying to use the SEU model. This involves taking a series of choices between uncertain outcomes and extracting a set of utility and subjective probability functions that must underlie them. With sufficient mathematical ingenuity, this can be done; the original accounts of the solution are given by Ramsey (1928) and Davidson, Suppes, and Siegel (1957), although a later version by Tversky (1967) is much easier to understand. Even Tversky's version, however, is much too complex for us to consider here. Nor do we need to. Although Tversky did succeed in producing some utility and subjective probability functions, his approach has not proved a fruitful one. The experiments it demands are long and tedious, and the analytic procedures are worse. There have been a few other attempts to use Tversky's techniques and many applications of the more general model underlying it, that is, the "fundamental conjoint measurement" procedure proposed by Luce and Tukey (1964) which can also be applied to produce utility functions from experiments on riskless choice. Neither the SEU model nor fundamental conjoint measurement failed in experimental tests. But they have conspicuously failed to produce consistent utility or subjective probability functions that would apply across situations, or even across subjects within a single situation. It is obviously essential that such subjective functions should vary according to individual circumstances. But no one has ever been able to suggest any consistent pattern they follow, a much more damaging result. Perhaps the SEU approach has not had a fair trial. But so far it has been more of a spur to mathematical ingenuity than a systematic account of apparently irrational behavior under uncertainty.

Yet the SEU model is undoubtedly where we logically must arrive if we take the expected value approach to choice under risk. Not surprisingly, therefore, dissatisfaction with it has caused people to turn to quite different accounts of such choices, which simply make no reference to rationality. We shall look at some of these alternatives when we discuss gambling behavior in Chapter 10.

The many facets of risky choice

As if we did not already have enough theories, there is yet a further way in which we might explain why decisions under risk regularly violate the expected value principle. Let us return once again to the video recorder-insurance problem. Perhaps all the costs and probabilities to be used should be the real, objective costs and probabilities, as the expected value principle dictates; it could still be that there is some factor we have left out of the account. Perhaps what is really important to you is that you would feel horribly foolish if your video recorder was stolen while it was uninsured. In other words, to the financial loss you have to add some loss of self-esteem (cf. Friedman and Savage 1952). Similarly, in the case of gambling, it may be that the mild uncertainty involved is pleasant or exciting in and of itself and that this added value outweighs the admitted expected financial loss.

This kind of proposal seems to be open for psychological investigation, but not much relevant research has been done. Some work has been done on *variance preferences* or *utility for gambling* (e.g., Edwards 1954b), but no clear message has yet emerged from it.

It is important to realize that it might not be possible or necessary to quantify this added value in monetary terms. Rather, we should view any risky option as a commodity bundle in itself, containing a variety of distinct sources of utility. Choice between such bundles might then be tackled using the standard theory of riskless choice or by a variant of the "characteristics" theory of Lancaster (1966). The development of such a theory is beyond the scope of this book; here, all we can do is to suggest that it serves as a focus in future research.

Is behavior under uncertainty irrational?

In this chapter our primary concern is not risky choice as such (that topic is taken up in greater detail in Chapter 10), but rather the implications behavior under risk has for the general notion that human behavior is rational. What conclusions can we draw?

First, the simple use of the expected value principle, on its own, is insufficient. Second, it seems that applying subjective transformations to the factors in risky choice does not lead to any coherent or consistent result. As Fjellman (1976) puts it, "the decision theory literature has not been very useful so far in helping us understand natural decision-making." At best, therefore, risky choice offers no empirical support for rationality as a general description of human behavior. Economists' typical dependence on the expected value theory therefore rests on unsupported assumptions about individual behavior. On the other hand, there is no conclusive evidence *against* the more elaborate rational theories, such as the SEU theory. Once again, we find that we cannot resolve the "rationality question."

Most of the choices we have considered so far have been essentially timeless. Should you buy three apples or two oranges now? Should you insure your video recorder now or decide not to insure it minimally now? Many real economic choices take a different form: Should you spend money on cigarettes now, or save it to spend on a holiday next summer? Should you spend all your income now or invest some of it to raise your income in a retirement you may never reach? These choices between outcomes that occur at different times are called intertemporal choices.

Time and economics

Conventional economic demand theory says nothing about intertemporal choice; it does not even say which I should choose if I were faced with a choice between, say, 1 pound of jam delivered today, and the identical 1 pound of jam delivered tomorrow. To be sure, the expected value principle predicts that I will choose jam today, because there is a finite, if small, chance that a heart attack or a nuclear attack will prevent me from enjoying jam tomorrow. But this is not enough. Koopmans (1960) pointed out that to give any coherent account of most intertemporal choices, we need to make an assumption in addition to the conventional axioms of demand theory. In effect, we need to add a new axiom, the axiom of *time preference proper*. This axiom asserts that, if two outcomes differ only in the time of delivery (certainty of delivery therefore also being equated), the sooner outcome will be preferred. Koopmans also argues that any attempt to construct an economics based on reversed time preference quickly runs into a mathematical quagmire, as well as being contrary to obvious facts (this depends on special assumptions).

Although time preference is rarely included in elementary treatments of microeconomics, it is very important in economic psychology. Economists have certainly neither ignored it nor been slow to offer explanations of it. Interestingly, those explanations are often couched in psychological terms. Some of the most important economic decisions involve intertemporal choices. When someone decides to save money rather than spend it immediately, that decision has two important effects. First, it reduces the total demand for goods in the economy, and thereby reduces the demand for labor to manufacture goods. Second, if the money saved is invested, either by lending it to an individual or firm or by depositing it in a bank that is thereby able to increase its lending, the action increases the supply of money available for borrowing, which may in turn affect the rate of interest that borrowers must pay. The rate of interest also affects the tendency to save (invest) rather than spend. Both effects have great potential significance to the behavior of the economy at large.

A little reflection shows that our theoretical rational human, *Homo economicus,* will be influenced by at least four factors in making any intertemporal choice:

1. *The probability of receiving the commodity bundle chosen:* Objectively, the further into the future something is to be delivered, the lower the probability of receiving it, either because the recipient might die in the meantime or because something else might go wrong. *Homo economicus* should use the probabilities of death and default to calculate the expected value of the bundles on offer.
2. *The interest rates available:* Given a choice between $100 now and $105 in one year's time, it is better to take $100 now (assuming no chance of death or default), whenever interest of greater than 5% can be obtained. For if the interest rate is, say, 6%, and one takes $100 now and deposits it in a bank, in a year's time one can withdraw $106, clearly a better strategy than simply accepting $105 in a year's time.
3. *The likely movement of prices of the commodities concerned:* In the case of money, this means the rate of inflation. If, by next year, $6 will be needed to buy what $5 will buy today, then $5 now is to be preferred to $5.50 next year, even if interest rates are zero and there is no chance of death or default.
4. *Time preference proper:* Taking account of inflation (or price changes), interest rates, and the probability that something will go wrong, is called "discounting" to obtain the "present value" of a future outcome. Only if present values are exactly equal does time preference proper have to be invoked to predict what choice will be made.

Experiments on delay of gratification

Intertemporal choice has been studied extensively by psychologists. The commonest paradigm is the so-called delay of gratification experiment, in which subjects are faced with a choice between a small, immediate reward, and a larger one delayed by some fixed or variable time (typically between a day and a week). With the usual parameters, at least some subjects choose the small immediate reward; this is referred to as "failure to delay gratification." It is usually considered a suboptimal behavior in some sense, although not perhaps in strictly economic terms. In agreement with the idea that failure to delay gratification is an inferior form of behavior, it has been shown that young children are less likely to delay gratification than older children (Mischel & Metzner 1962); psychotics are less likely to do so than are normal controls (Shybut 1968); and animals such as pigeons (Ainslie 1974; Rachlin & Green 1972) or rats (Logan 1965) are particularly prone to choose small immediate rewards, even if a reward of twice the size is available just a few seconds later.

Because many of these studies have been comparative, that is, concerned with showing the emergence of delayed gratification with increasing age, intelligence, or education, they have left unsettled the question of whether normal, adult, human subjects show delay of gratification. Obviously this is a question that is crucial to a comparison between psychological data and economic theory in this area. In an effort to fill this gap, Lea (unpublished data summarized in Lea 1978) showed people two envelopes and asked them to imagine that one contained a check for 5 pounds, dated for the day of the experiment and the other contained a check for 10 pounds, dated for some time in the future. The subjects were then asked how far into the future the second check would have to be dated in order for them to prefer to have the 5 pounds now rather than the 10 pounds later. The median answer was around two months. This would be rational only if the rates of interest obtainable, or inflation expected, were on the order of 5,000% (or the probability of death or default was alarmingly high). More elaborate experiments of this general sort have been done by Turchi (1980), and although he did not obtain quite such inordinate implied interest rates, his results still show that normal adults certainly do not delay gratification to a rational extent.

The entire delay of gratification literature, in fact, suggests a far greater preference for immediacy than any economic theory could justify. Ainslie (1975) brought together most of the available psychological, sociological, and economic data and theory relating to time preference, and has shown that most of the economists who have considered intertemporal choice (e.g., Boehm-Bawerk 1891; Fisher 1930) have been aware of this "excessive" preference for immediacy and have made attempts to explain it. Ainslie also considers a series of explanations which can be derived from psychological theories involved with learning and incentive. He, and others such as Herrnstein (1970), have shown that theories of choice derived from animal experiments on instrumental conditioning can predict failure to delay gratification.

The most important of these theories is Herrnstein's (1970) *quantitative law of effect*. This law offers a general quantitative formulation of the relation between rates of reinforcement and rates of response, with both being expressed as frequencies (numbers of events per unit time). Herrnstein suggests that the rate P at which a response will be performed is given by the equation

$$P = kR/R + R_0 \tag{5.1}$$

where R is the rate of reinforcement of the response in question, the quantity R_0 is the rate of reinforcement of other simultaneously available responses, and k is a constant. The accuracy and generality of Herrn-stein's equation, and principles (such as the "matching law:" Herrnstein, 1961) that can be derived from it, are matters of current controversy in operant psychology (compare, for example, Herrnstein & Vaughan 1980 with Staddon, 1980). But the equation certainly does an excellent job of predicting failure to delay gratification. Ainslie (1975) showed that it also makes a number of other interesting predictions in this area, such as the occurrence of what has become known as "commitment" responding. If a pigeon is offered a choice between two seconds' access to grain at once, or four seconds' access after a few seconds' delay, it will choose the small but immediate reward. However, if, 30 seconds before this choice is to be offered, the bird has the opportunity to commit itself in advance to the larger, delayed reward, it will take this opportunity. Advance commit-ment is, of course, rational. And while rationality theory offers no expla-nation of the switch from irrational to rational performance, the matching law does. Here we have the first signs of a systematic challenge to ration-ality from a competing account of choice.

Subjective discount rates

There is an alternative way of explaining people's irrational preference for immediate rewards. Just as we replaced objective values and prob-abilities by subjective transformations of them in analyzing choice under risk, so we might suppose that there is a subjective discounting function that is not identical to the objective function dictated by objective rates of death, interest, and inflation. Presumably the subjective discount rate would be related in some systematic way to these factors and also to factors such as age and intelligence that are known to affect the capacity to delay gratification.

Unfortunately this hypothesis is insufficient. Ainslie (1975), for in-stance, showed that it could not explain the occurrence of commitment responding in intertemporal choices, at least if we think (as economists generally do) that even subjective discounting ought to take place by an ordinary compound interest process. Under such discounting, if one op-tion is preferred to another at any point in time, it will still be preferred at any more remote time; there can be no crossover of the sort that makes us put our alarm clock on the window sill, out of reach from the bed, in the evening, even though in the morning we would choose, if it were in reach, to turn it off quickly and have five minutes' extra sleep now rather than be at the office promptly.

The best-known subjective discount rate hypothesis is the one advanced by Friedman (1957). This hypothesis forms part of an elaborate theory of the choice to spend or save, known as the "permanent income hypothe-sis." The basic idea is that people have an (adjustable) conception of what their income, in the long term, is likely to be. Saving is adjusted to maintain income at this "permanent" level despite fluctuations in actual income due to "transitory" effects. But in Friedman's theory, future consumption is discounted according to a subjective discount rate rather than any "rational" rate. The permanent income hypothesis has been applied quite widely, and with some success (see Chapter 8). The interesting point is that the size of the subjective discount rate is quite large (even though the rates that have to be postulated to explain actual spending and saving behavior do not approach the thousands of percent per annum implied by delayed gratification experiments). Specifically, Friedman (1963) suggested rates of about 30% for economies in which inflation and interest rates were in low single figures. Qualitatively, these data (derived from large-scale panel interview studies or in some cases from econometric studies of entire economies) support the conclusion that there is more preference for immediacy than rationality predicts.

Rationality and intertemporal choice

In the case of rationality and intertemporal choice, we have at last a fairly clear result: The assumption of rationality is definitely inadequate. Furthermore, the obvious minor modification, of allowing a subjective discounting rate to replace the objective one, despite its success in some contexts, fails to predict a clear and replicable phenomenon, namely the occurrence of commitment responding. Our conclusion must be that we should look for some alternative way of discussing this kind of economic choice. The law of effect and other ideas derived from animal learning theory have been suggested, but as yet they have not been tested in any real economic context.

RATIONAL BEHAVIOR AND ECONOMIC BEHAVIOR

In all three areas we have examined (riskless choice, choice under uncertainty, and intertemporal choice), we have seen that, in an analysis of real human choice behavior, the rationality assumption is at best unproven, generally unhelpful, and sometimes clearly false. We could add many other situations to these three, for example the tendency to commit further resources to a failed course of action (see Staw 1976), or the kind of situation studied by Teger (1980) in which short-term "rational" behavior leads people into long-term disasters, such as bidding $20 in an auction for a one-dollar bill. What should we conclude about the theoretical underpinnings of economics? Do psychological data indeed show that economists have been barking up an overidealized tree for 150 years? Should economic psychology consist of an attempt to rebuild economic theory on empirically acceptable choice axioms?

We believe this conclusion would be as premature as it would be pretentious, impertinent, and silly. The three sections that follow explain why it is reasonable for economists to continue to use the rationality assumption.

Pragmatic defense of rationality

Many economists (e.g., Friedman 1935) have been willing to concede the psychologist's objections to the choice axioms, but argue that they are irrelevant. What matters, they argue, is whether the detailed economic predictions worked out from rationality theory turn out to be correct. If they do, on the average at least (and Friedman argues that this is, in fact, the case), then rationality as an economic hypothesis is justified, even if at another level of discourse (the level of psychological experiments) it is known to be false. "Justified" here means that it is legitimate to use the hypothesis to make new economic predictions. The analogy with the ideal gas laws of elementary physics is much overworked in this context: Just as physicists make assumptions about molecules that are known to be absurd (even novice physicists know that molecules are not smooth, perfectly elastic spheres) but are good enough to predict the behavior of real gases, so economists may make assumptions about individuals that are known to be false but are good enough to predict the behavior of the economy as a whole.

The argument has some force, although it would be more convincing if the economists' ability to predict and control economic phenomena approached the physicists' ability to predict and control the behavior of volumes of gas. Furthermore, false assumptions are tricky tools. Constant effort is required to make sure that their implications are kept out of the range where their falsehood matters (cf. Stewart 1979, chapter 6). By itself, then, this pragmatic defense of rationality would seem to be insufficient.

Flexibility of the class of rational behavior

Rachlin (1980) has advanced a much subtler reason why economic psychologists should not spend their time exposing failures of rationality. He argues that any behavior that is consistent (and thus amenable to scientific inquiry) is capable of being described as rational. Thus an economic psychologist interested in the irrational side of economic behavior would find this field of study constantly absorbed into mainstream economics.

We have already seen two examples of this process at work. In the case of choice under uncertainty, the expected value principle, which is the relevant variant of rationality, clearly fails. But the SEU theory that replaces it is ordinarily seen as a version of rationality, even though this obviously requires a redefinition of the nature of *Homo economicus*. Similarly, a person who complied with Friedman's permanent income hypothesis would probably be viewed by economists as behaving rationally, even if his subjective discounting rate was much greater than the objectively "rational" rate.

Even clearer examples exist in other branches of economic psychology. For example, the rational behavior toward money is apparently to get rid of it as fast as possible, since by definition it is used only in exchange for goods (see Chapter 12). In practice, however, people choose to hold money balances of various sorts. This does not lead to an abandonment of economic theory. What is done is to include money balances as a new kind of commodity within the standard framework of the theory (and we begin to hear about the demand for money, the supply of money, and so forth). Similarly, the rational theory of saving explains saving in terms of the potential it creates for future consumption (the permanent income hypothesis, which we met above, is just one version of this general idea). All such theories run into difficulties (Johnson 1971). Accordingly, Clower and Johnson (1968) devised a theory in which wealth appears as a good independent of its role in allowing future consumption. People can then be supposed to maximize a utility that is a function of both consumption and wealth, and the standard apparatus of optimizing theory is in action once again.

Rachlin therefore argues that psychologists should not spend their time on the impossible task of trying to disprove maximization; rather, they should throw themselves wholeheartedly into the task of finding the maximand, the quantity being optimized in any given situation. As strategic advice, this may well be sound. However, it is possible to imagine simple laws of choice that might be discoverable at the level of individual behavior but that would give rise to very awkward maximands. Equally, there seems to be more that we might say about the mechanism of economic behavior than can be expressed just by stating the maximand.

Approximate maximization

Finally, there are mathematical reasons why behavior might be quite different from the optimal form predicted by strict rationality, and yet its results might be very little different from those of rational behavior. Mathematically, at the point where any function passes through a maximum, it is changing rather slowly, more slowly than anywhere else in fact. Thus quite wide variations in behavior will produce rather little deviation from the optimal outcome. This means that the range of behaviors that would be acceptable approximations to the optimum is likely to be quite wide.

THE UNIMPORTANCE OF RATIONALITY

Clearly, we cannot conclude that the rationality assumption is indefensible. What we can conclude, is that the concept neither exhausts nor implies everything that can be known about the behavior of the individual in the economy. The next part of this book contains a series of chapters about various kinds of individual economic behavior. In all these cases, both rationality and deviations from rationality have a part to play in describing behavior; in no case is rationality the beginning and end of the discussion.

Let us return briefly to Rachlin's (1980) view of rationality. Recall that he argues that any consistent behavior can be described as maximizing something. Although this would seem to make the whole question about rationality futile, it really does not. Rather Rachlin's argument shifts the focus of our interest. Instead of asking *whether* something is being maximized, we need to ask *what* is being maximized. According to Rachlin, this is likely to be a more fruitful question.

Maximands, goods, reinforcers, and fitness

Rachlin's argument has close parallels to several others in biological and social science. Consider, for example, the problem of defining "goods" in economics. A "good" or "commodity" is anything that can be traded. Taken strictly, this definition threatens to short-circuit all discussion of the greed axiom, even at a psychological level. Once a consumer is sated with a good, it ceases to be a good (and may become a "bad"); the greed axiom is necessarily confirmed. The only effective challenge to the axiom, then, is to advance a rival assumption which makes the existence of satiation a central tenet. This is why we introduced the Premack principle into our discussion of greed earlier in this chapter.

A second parallel to the maximization problem comes from psychology. Much effort was spent on defining rewards and discussing whether rewards were necessary for learning, until Skinner (1938, p. 62) short-circuited the problem by defining reinforcers as stimuli that, presented after a response, increased the future probability of that response. This definition shifts the focus of discussion from the necessity of reinforcement to other more tractable questions: Are there any stimuli that have the property Skinner specifies and, if there are, what other properties do they share?

Yet another parallel can be drawn from evolutionary biology, where we encounter the concept of "fitness." Nowadays, an animal's fitness is defined in terms of the number of fertile descendants it leaves. Such a definition eliminates any discussion of one apparently fundamental tenet of Darwinian theory, for it eliminates any possible doubt as to whether or not it is the fittest that survive. They survive by definition. But this act of definition then leaves us free to discuss, in a coherent way, the true core of Darwin's theory, that is, the proposal that it is the survival of the fittest that is the origin of species (cf. Lea 1984, chapter 1). It also leaves us free to ask what contributes to fitness.

In all these cases, progress was made possible by sidestepping what appears to be a central question. In this book, we attempt to use the same strategy to make progress in economic psychology.

Is human economic behavior rational?

We agree with Rachlin that this question must somehow be evaded. Asking "rational or not rational" can sometimes be a useful approach to economic behavior, but as an overall and all-pervading question, it is sterile. Furthermore, trying to find a set of nonrational axioms, or modifications of rationality, does not seem to be a very promising approach either. In this chapter we have seen how it has been tried and has encountered problems, e.g., in demand theory, in the theory of risky choice, and to a lesser extent in the theory of intertemporal choice.

Why does the rationality question turn out to be sterile? Looking back over this chapter, we can see that it constrains economic psychology in a number of ways. First, it tends to establish an economics (rational) versus psychology (irrational or a-rational) dichotomy. This is not helpful, for our aim is to establish an interdisciplinary synthesis, not to emphasize the divisions between the disciplines. We are trying to use psychology and economics to enrich each other, not to advocate either as supplanting the other. Second, concentration on the rationality question compels us to adopt a "theory-first" economic psychology, in which the data we choose to examine are dictated by their relevance to the rationality question. Psychology is an empirical science, and accordingly it has a respect for data, and for the importance of constructing the theories the data compel us to use rather than those that are merely elegant or intellectually interesting. This data-driven approach is something psychology has to offer to economics, and it would be foolish to throw it away.

Finally, and in partial agreement with Rachlin, we believe that one of the most important and illuminating things economic psychology can do is to ask what the ends of economic behavior are. If behavior is rational, we want to ask what it is maximizing. This, as we shall see in later chapters, is a question about human needs. Economic activity accounts for a major proportion of people's time and effort, and a psychological analysis of that activity ought to be a fertile source of information about human motivation. Therefore, we shall find ourselves attaching less and less importance to the question of rationality and concentration more on the content of economic behavior.

But if we are not to organize our discussion around the rationality question, what structure can we give it? As we shall see at the end of this volume (Chapter 20), this is really a question about the paradigm within which economic psychology is to be studied. The structure of this book reflects our view about the paradigm that should replace economic psychology's current preoccupation with the rationality question. We take the view that there are two kinds of question about the interaction between the individual and the economy. First, we can ask how individuals' economic behaviors affect the behavior of the economy; second, we can ask how the economy acts upon individuals. At the extreme, the dialogue between these two kinds of questions turns into a clash between political philosophies: Is it the needs of consumers that determine how the economy runs? Or does the economy determine what consumers experience as needs? In practice, we expect to find that economic structure and individual need are bound up together in an interacting system. The remainder of this book is devoted to a systematic study of that system.

II

THE ECONOMIC BEHAVIOR OF INDIVIDUALS

Everything that happens in the economy happens as a result of the behavior of some individual. Sometimes that person will be only the agent of a vast organization, with well-established rules and conventions, but even then those rules may be obeyed either with conviction, or reluctantly, or not at all. More usually, however, people act on their own initiative, and it is the multitude of those individual initiatives that makes up the behavior of the economy. Indeed, the ideal world of microeconomic theory is one in which the consumer is sovereign: The entire course of economic affairs is dictated by the motivations and preferences of individuals as they buy the commodities offered for sale and use or sell their labor time to help produce them. If we are to understand the economy, we must understand the economic behavior of the individuals within it.

From the individual point of view, also, economic behavior is of major importance; indeed, we spend a substantial proportion of our waking lives engaged in it. The most time-consuming activity, of course, is work and, although many groups within the population are not employed, most are still affected by the world of work. Either they are preparing for it, like many students, or they are actively seeking it, like most unemployed people and some nonemployed groups such as housewives, or their income depends on a past working life, like most retired people.

Economic theory does provide a picture of individual economic behaviors, but economists would be the first to agree that it is an abstract and oversimplified picture and that little attempt is made to fill in the details by considering how theory relates to the available data. Psychologists have largely ignored the economic aspect of life. This section tries to take what information is available from both psychology and economics, and weave it into a coherent, empirically based picture of what people do in their major economic activities.

We have not considered every single economic or economically relevant kind of behavior. The first two chapters in the part selected themselves: They deal with work and buying. These are two kinds of economic behavior that virtually everyone engages in and that take up substantial time and effort for many people. They also constitute the major flow of exchange within the economy: Households exchange their labor for money, and they exchange the money they earn for the goods and services that their and others' labor produces. It is possible to envisage an economy without most other kinds of economic behavior, but without the exchange of productive labor for commodities it would scarcely be an economy at all.

The remaining three chapters deal with kinds of economic behavior which are, in different ways, theoretically challenging. We saw at the end of Part I that saving, the subject of Chapter 8, poses problems for the analysis of economic behavior in terms of rationality. It is also one of the areas in which there is a strong background of relevant psychological research (most of it done without any serious thought of application to economic questions) and in which psychological processes have been invoked to explain the behavior of the economy at large. Giving, the subject of Chapter 9, also poses problems for a simple-minded rationality approach; it is also an area in which we have the benefit of much preexisting psychological work. As an area of specifically economic psychological interest, however, it is relatively new. By contrast, gambling, dealt with in Chapter 10, is a traditional area of cooperation between economics and psychology. We saw in Chapter 5 that it too is problematic from a rationality point of view, but psychologists have been ready to work within an optimal decision framework, which economists have also been interested in a more theoretically neutral approach.

Although both work and buying are mainly the province of economists, there are major groups of psychologists taking an interest with them. Whole textbooks are regularly produced to cover the areas of industrial and consumer psychology. Economics, too, has well-developed specialisms in labor economics and (to a lesser extent) consumer economics; because of the central importance of these areas, the literature on them is vast. Although they are the longest (and probably the most difficult) in the book, Chapters 6 and 7 do not try to summarize these entire literatures. Rather, they pick up the major points of theory and the major empirical generalizations, so as to set these important topics into their proper place in the general framework of economic psychology. In the remaining chapters of this part, we have a little more room to maneuver and to test out the different kinds of approach, so as to see which is the most fruitful.

The result of this part of the book, we hope, will be a new way of looking at individual economic behavior. The way people act within the economy cannot, we believe, be described properly, let alone predicted, by a few abstract statements about preferences. By contrast, it is not a morass of disconnected facts – it is lawful in its own terms. Both economic theory and psychological theory can make predictive generalizations that will help us to understand behavior.

6

WORK

Work is crucial to economic psychology. From an economic point of view, work (in the form of employment) makes up one half of the major cycle of money and resources between firms and households: Household members provide labor to firms by working and in return receive money, which they use to buy commodities and services from firms. From a psychological point of view, work is part of the chain of instrumental activities that is central to human economic behavior: Individuals' work is rewarded with money, and money makes possible the instrumental activity of buying. Generally speaking, work is a large and important category of human behavior. In the modern economy, employed people spend roughly one-fourth of their lives at their jobs, and many people who are not formally employed (students and housewives, for example) spend similar amounts of time working, often according to the rhythm set by the world of paid work.

Both economics and psychology have branches wholly devoted to the study of work. For several reasons, this chapter does not attempt to summarize everything that is known about labor economics or about industrial, occupational, and organizational psychology. For one thing, the literature is too voluminous to be summarized in a single chapter. Such a summary would, in any event, be unnecessary, since excellent textbooks in all these areas are available (e.g., Bellante & Jackson 1979; Ehrenberg & Smith 1982; Gilmer & Deci 1977; Helfgott 1974; Katz and Kahn 1978; Kline 1975). More important, however, the emphasis of much of the existing literature is not quite suited to our needs because it is slanted too heavily toward firms rather than toward individuals. It would not be hard to find academic articles discussing how a firm can secure the maximum work from its employees for the least pay, but it would be much harder to find one discussing how an employee could secure the maximum pay for the least work. Yet the two questions seem to be of equal economic and psychological validity, if not moral status.

Instead of trying to condense all the literature into this chapter, we shall concentrate on a few questions about work that bear on central issues within both economics and psychology and that are also of obvious importance to firms as well as individuals. The most central of these questions, and the one around which almost all others turn, is, quite simply: Why do people work? An economist might ask what the incentive is for working, while a psychologist might be more inclined to ask what the motivation is, but these are fundamentally the same question.

This issue is not a simple one. There are many different ways of asking it and many ways of answering it. The first two sections of this chapter therefore, try to identify the different kinds of questions and answers that are brought together when we ask why people work.

DIFFERENT WAYS OF ASKING WHY PEOPLE WORK

There are two distinct ways in which we can categorize the questions about why people work. The question can obviously be posed at different levels of generality: Why do people work at all, why do they do the kinds of work they do (and not others), and why do they work for as many hours as they do (and not for more, or fewer), and so forth? At a slightly deeper level, we find that there are different senses of "Why?" Do we mean to ask what actually prompts people to go to work, or are we asking what benefits they derive from working?

The level of generality

The distinctions to be drawn under this heading are fairly obvious, and we do not need to dwell on them at length. We shall find that substantial bodies of theory and data are devoted to all three of the questions identified above: Why work at all? Why do one particular job? Why work a given number of hours? But another very important question is what determines the quality of the work a person does. Although all these questions interact to some extent, we should not be surprised if their answers are apparently contradictory. For example, a person who would rather take almost any job than do without money, might choose a relatively low-paid job because the work involved was satisfying.

Part of the reason why it is helpful to divide our investigation in this way is that the different questions listed here correspond to distinct real and important human choices. People have to take decisions about whether to work, what job to take, and so on.

The causes and functions of work

The second kind of distinction we can draw is more subtle. It is between the factors that tend to make people work and the effects that work has on them. One of the reasons it is so hard to decide why people work is that these two kinds of questions are frequently confused. But they are different kinds of questions, and they need to be investigated by looking at different kinds of data.

To find out whether something causes work, we would, ideally, remove that factor and see whether the individual concerned continues working. For example, Morse and Weiss (1955) asked 401 employed men whether they would continue to work even if they "unexpectedly inherited enough money to retire at the same level of comfort." Perhaps surprisingly, 80% of subjects replied that they would go on working, suggesting that the need for pay is not a particularly important reason for work.

To find out whether something is a function of work, on the other hand, we would, ideally, remove the opportunity for work, and see what ill effects people suffer. For example, in a recent questionnaire study, Kelvin (1982) interviewed people who had been thrown into long-term unemployment by the recent recession in the United Kingdom. He found that those who had been out of work for a substantial period complained most vociferously of the shortage of money.

Neither of these kinds of ideal investigation is easily carried out in practice. Many of the factors proposed as causes of work are not open to experimental manipulation; the benefits proposed as functions of work are so important that individuals, and society, find other ways of providing them when work is not available. The two studies cited as examples above illustrate the problems: Morse and Weiss were driven to asking hypothetical questions rather than carrying out a real experiment, and Kelvin's respondents were all receiving quite substantial social security payments. Nonetheless, it is clear that at least some information was obtained on both questions.

The examples cited were also chosen to illustrate a second important point. It is entirely possible for the causes and functions of work to conflict. Morse and Weiss's data suggest that the need for money is not the most important cause of work, but Kelvin's data suggest that the provision of money may be one of its most important functions. We shall be led to qualify both these conclusions when we look at the data in more detail later in this chapter, but it is essential to recognize that there is no conflict between them. What makes someone take up a particular kind of job (or, indeed, a kind of unpaid work) may be quite unrelated to the advantages he or she ultimately derives from it.

Finally, both causal and functional questions can be asked at all levels of generality. Someone may become a farmer because that is what the person's father did previously, but the person may nonetheless derive personal enjoyment and social benefits from farming. Similarly, a person may work overtime only because it is necessary to retain an otherwise desirable job yet may nonetheless enjoy the extra income it produces.

A CLASSIFICATION OF REASONS FOR WORKING

We now turn to consider the kinds of answers we can give to the question why people work. We shall describe the reasons for working as instrumental, enjoyment, self-fulfillment, or social. We are not advancing these as theories of work but rather are introducing them as a rough classification of possible kinds of theory. Any complete theory of work behavior is likely to incorporate elements of more than one of them.

It is fairly obvious that any one of these kinds of answers can be given to any of the kinds of questions stated earlier. It is also obvious that different kinds of answers may be appropriate for different sorts of questions. We could have an instrumental theory of the functions of different types of jobs at the same time as a social theory of the determinants of hours worked. This is one reason why, as we begin to look at the theoretical and empirical literature on work, we shall find that it includes quite a number of apparently contradictory theoretical positions, all well defended by both logic and data.

Instrumentality

The most obvious reason for working is that work is an instrumental activity. This applies both to employment and to unpaid work. According to this account, people take employment to obtain pay, and they do unpaid work, such as housework, because the results of the work are directly useful to them.

This argument seems almost too obvious to be worth much discussion. But it needs to be stated explicitly, partly because we shall see that it is not the whole story and partly because the perspective it represents means different things to economists and psychologists. Economists would consider how the individual would maximize personal utility given two possible sources of benefit (consumption paid for by earned income, and leisure obtained by not working). Psychologists might consider how rewards contingent on the execution of work behaviors act on or strengthen those behaviors.

The conflict between these two points of view is one form of the long-running argument about the suitability of rationality as an explanation of economic behavior. In Chapter 5 we concluded that this question ought not to dominate our thinking; this conclusion obviously extends to the topic of work motivation. In particular, it would be a mistake to suppose that an economic ("rationality") analysis of work could only take account of pay; job satisfaction, for example, can certainly be considered as an additional source of utility. It would be appropriate to reject a "rational" theory of working only if the detailed action of reward factors on work behavior is better accounted for by, say, operant principles.*

---

*Furthermore, the opposition between pecuniary and other accounts of work motivation becomes much less when we remember the important distinction between *marginal* and *average* conditions (cf. Chapter 2). Pay may determine whether people will do an *extra* hour's work, while other factors determine what job they work at.

Work as enjoyment

Diametrically opposed to the instrumentality theory is the view that at least some work is done "for its own sake," namely, because the activity is inherently enjoyable. Superficially, many kinds of employment seem to satisfy this definition. The supply of people wanting to become actors, football players, stable hands, veterinarians, and perhaps even university instructors does not seem to be related in any obvious way to the level of earnings of the average member of those professions. Moreover, both current practitioners and aspiring entrants to these job areas would almost certainly claim that it is the work, not the pay, that they are seeking (examples are to be found in the interviews reported by Terkel 1974).

But if work can be enjoyable, what do we mean by work? The reason the instrumental account seems so obvious is that we use "work" to describe those activities we would not do unless there were some extrinsic reward. In the case of employment, it is fairly straightforward to ask whether someone enjoys his or her job. But in the case of unpaid work, the problem is not as clear. For example, if we define work in terms of muscular or intellectual effort, competing in sports and puzzles would be classified as work. But does this conclusion really fit with our intuitions? Probably not.

In addition to this logical problem, there is an interesting psychological dilemma in attempting to describe work as enjoyable. Many theorists have suggested that, in various ways, people's expressed attitudes will tend to adjust themselves to be consistent with their behavior (see the discussion of cognitive dissonance theory in Chapter 1). It follows that people may say that they enjoy their work simply because not to enjoy it would be inconsistent with the fact that they engage in it. There are other complications as well. Payment may undermine both expressed and felt enjoyment of an activity, making it difficult to assess the role that enjoyment plays for the average worker (see the discussion of the overjustification effect and Deci's intrinsic motivation theory). Clearly, if we want to describe work as being enjoyable, we must be prepared to specify exactly what we mean by both work and enjoyment.

Work as self-fulfillment

Superficially, the suggestion that people work in order to find self-fulfillment seems just to be a subset of the idea that work is enjoyable. Logically and psychologically, however, there is an important difference, and a self-fulfillment hypothesis may be substantially more tractable, simply because it makes stronger assertions. The basic premise is that people seek to engage in work that most fully uses their abilities and interests. There may even be a fundamental human motivation to be "fully employed" in this way. From the point of view of maximizing efficiency, society too has an interest in seeing that its members' talents are as fully employed as possible, as Reynaud (1981, p. 175) discusses. Unfortunately, the pattern of interests and skills demanded by firms may not always correspond to what households want to offer. If the primary motivation for work is the desire for self-fulfillment, we should therefore expect to find substantial frustration with existing employment even among those who have jobs.

Work as a social institution

All the motivations for working discussed so far have focused on the needs of the individual or on the household with whom the person shares both income and frustrations. But working is an act of powerful social significance, and there are a variety of ways in which social motivations affect work.

First, there may be a social pressure to "go out to work" and a social stigma attached to not working. Even in times of high unemployment, when virtually no one can get a job without depriving someone else of it, the unemployed are likely to suffer disapproval as much as sympathy (see, for example, Furnham 1982, 1983; Williams 1983). Although such social pressure works to the advantage of employers, since it may induce people to take jobs at a lower pay rate than they otherwise would, the pressure comes as much from the working classes as from other strata of society.

But for most people work fulfills much more positive social needs than mere avoidance of stigma. As Morse and Weiss (1955) discussed, the working environment provides many people with their primary social group outside the family. Work ties a person to society. For those whose family life is deficient or unsatisfactory, work may even provide the major source of social interaction. Obviously, much of this depends on the nature of the work being done and on the management regime. Managers and foremen may well be inclined to view employees' socializing with a jaundiced eye, yet the efficient operation of a complex organization is likely to depend greatly on good personal relationships between the individuals involved. A classic demonstration of this was the disastrous effect on productivity in British coal mines of the introduction of a labor system that disrupted the miner's traditional working groups and interactions (see Trist & Bamforth 1951).

The social function of work for the individual is not limited to the actual place of employment. One of the most obvious effects of a job (or nonjob for that matter) is to provide a social context. Asked to describe themselves in a variety of different ways, people mention their occupation at a very early stage, often first (Banister & Fransella 1983). We believe we know something about a person when we have heard that he or she is a doctor, or a truck driver, or "just a housewife." Clearly, social status is part of this; people have very well-defined views about the status of a great variety of occupations (for an international survey of data on this point see Hodge, Treiman, & Rossi 1976). But it is not just a matter of status. To work as a nurse or a probation officer, for example, is to pronounce oneself as holding certain kinds of values; to be a soldier or a police officer is to say something rather different.

The relative importance of the reasons for working

We have listed four reasons for working (extrinsic reward, intrinsic enjoyment, self-fulfillment, and social contact). Obviously these are fairly crude categories, and others could be proposed. But can we get any feel for how important these different categories or factors are in motivating people to work? A partial answer comes from the study by Morse and Weiss (1955). Recall that 20% of employed men said they would not go on working if they received a large legacy; presumably work is largely a necessary means for obtaining money for those men rather than a source of enjoyment, although the attractiveness of other nonwork activities (golf?) may have influenced their decision. The remaining 80% claimed that they would continue to work. Of these, 32% said they would continue to work in order to "keep occupied"; 36% gave negative reasons such as "warding off boredom or loneliness"; 14% claimed that a person would feel "lost" without work. Interestingly, only 9% of these men reported that they would continue working because they "enjoyed the work."

These results seem to suggest that a person's committment to work is far greater than his or her committment to a particular job. Working, in general, is valued because it integrates the person into society, and because activity is preferred to inactivity, even though a given job may or may not provide satisfaction or enjoyment.

There are at least three other points, however, that we must bear in mind. First, the reasons for working may differ according to the various subsets of the population. For example, Morse and Weiss found that "middle-class" workers emphasized an interest in their job more than did "working-class" people. The former valued a chance to accomplish goals in their work, whereas the latter more often said that they worked merely to earn money or to occupy their time. Similarly, Friedman and Havighurst (1954) found the meaning of work to vary among different people in terms of the importance of the work (e.g., as a way of maintaining a certain standard of living, or of achieving self-respect, friends, self-expression) as well as the affective reaction that the work had on them. Second, the various reasons for working may all apply to some degree for any given individual. Indeed, few would deny that "good" jobs are precisely those that enable a person to achieve several goals at once, including adequate pay, social contacts, and the opportunity for advancement or self-expression. Finally, as we saw at the beginning of this section, there are many different ways of posing the question, "Why do people work?," and different kinds of answers may be appropriate to each of them.

GENERAL THEORIES OF WORK MOTIVATION

Having briefly surveyed the possible kinds of explanation we can give for work behavior, we now consider the detailed theories which have been developed. Inevitably, we shall find that they do not fit into the neat categories we established in the last two sections. By keeping these distinctions clearly in mind, however, we should be able to see whether the theories really do conflict or whether they might be complementary accounts that could be brought together in an integrated theory of work behavior.

There are four categories of theory. The first is the economists' theory of the labor–leisure choice. The remaining three have been introduced by psychologists and invoke three distinct psychological concepts to account for work: need, cognition, and reinforcement. Each has a variety of specific formulations. In some ways, the psychological theories can be seen as specifying either deviations from the economic theory, or mechanisms by which it will act. It is therefore convenient to start with economic theory.

Economic theory of the labor–leisure choice

The classic economic theory treats work as wholly instrumental and supposes that all a person's activities can be divided into two classes: leisure and consumption. Since the total time available is limited, the longer a person works, the less time that person has for leisure activities. But consumption costs money, and money is obtained only by working: the longer a person works, the more that person can afford consumption. This relationship is represented in Figure 6.1. The graph defines a space whose coordinates are consumption and leisure. The two oblique lines show the combinations of consumption and leisure that can be achieved under two different wage rates.

Just as in the theory of consumer demand (see Chapter 2) there is a system of indifference curves that connect combinations of consumption and leisure between which the individual has no preference. A few of these are added to the diagram in Figure 6.2. The rational person will choose that combination of consumption and leisure whereby the current

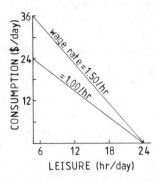

6.1. The labor-consumption diagram, showing how fixed hourly wate rates make possible a range of combinations of consumption and leisure.

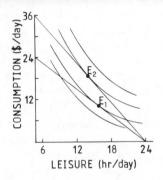

6.2. The labor-consumption diagram with indifference curves added. The rational worker will choose combination E1 (13 hours leisure and $11 worth of consumption) at a wage rate of $1/hour, and combination E2 (14 hours leisure and $15 worth of consumption at a wage rate of $1.50/hour).

wage–rate line is tangent to an indifference curve (E1 in the figure for wages of $1 per hour, E2 for wages of $1.50 per hour). As the figure suggests, the most likely outcome is that a rise in wages will lead to an increase in both consumption and leisure, but obviously there could be systems of indifference curves in which rising wages lead to decreased leisure and greatly increased consumption, or even to decreased consumption and greatly increased leisure. From the various points of equilibrium under different wage rates (e.g., E1, E2) we can extract a graph plotting labor supply (hours worked) as a function of wages. Economists generally call this relationship the labor–supply curve, with wages on the vertical axis. Thus, a situation like that depicted in Figure 6.2, where a decrease in labor supply follows from an increase in wages, is called a backward-bending labor supply curve.

In reality, the wage–rate line facing individual is rarely straight as in Figure 6.1. Modern societies provide some social security benefits even to those who choose to do no work; thus, at zero hours of work, some consumption is possible. When an individual becomes employed, these benefits are lost, so a small amount of work may bring little or no increase in consumption. After that point, consumption will increase linearly with work done for some time, until overtime rates become payable, at which point the effective wage rate will rise. If income becomes large enough, higher rates of taxation may be encountered, so that the effective rate becomes less. Thus the wage–rate line facing any real individual may contain numerous bends (Brown 1980, chapter 2). This does not change the principles of the analysis described above, but it does complicate any attempt to apply it empirically so as to discover the nature of the labor supply curve.

The economic theory of the labor–leisure choice can be seen to be a fairly typical utility-maximizing theory. It assumes that the economic subject is a rational utility maximizer. Its predictions in this simple form are quite weak; that is, almost any shape of labor supply curve would satisfy the theory. The main use of such a theory is in fact to predict what happens when extra factors are included, so that the wage–rate line becomes nonlinear or is shifted in various ways. The theory provides a framework under which the effects of such manipulations can be predicted, given the basic idea that individuals seek to maximize the utility they obtain from leisure and consumption combined. Later in this chapter we shall see some attempts to test such predictions.

In the simple form in which we have presented it here, the microeconomic theory of the labor–leisure choice clearly focuses on the instrumental reasons for working, and on hours worked rather than other possible issues concerning work. Neither of these limitations, however, is inherent in the theory. If work is enjoyable in itself, that could easily be represented in the theory by a shifting of the system of indifference curves away from the "leisure" axis, corresponding to a reduced valuation on leisure relative to nonleisure (i.e., work). If more than one kind of job is available, the indifference space can be expanded to three dimensions in order to represent preferences between different sources of income. Such extensions are, indeed, occasionally made (e.g., Ehrenberg & Smith 1982, pp. 170–1).

Need theories

But however we elaborate the economic theory of work behavior, basically the theory takes a particular approach to the question of work motivation: It sees motivation in terms of the satisfaction (utility) that can be anticipated as deriving from it. In other words, motivation is out of the future; subjects are pulled toward work behavior by incentives to be realized after it has been performed. This is by no means the only possible approach to motivation. Psychologists have been more inclined to look to the past as the source of motivation. What drives, presses, or needs has past experience established in the subject, and how do these forces push this person into work behavior? Any approach that asks this sort of question can be classified as a "need theory."

In Chapter 1, we introduced Maslow's (1954/1970) hierarchical theory of human needs, which has been widely applied to the problem of work motivation. Maslow conceived of five levels of need, arranged in a hierarchy in such a way that higher needs only affect behavior when all the so-called lower needs have been met. The lowest level of need embodies the physiological needs for food, water, warmth, sex, and so on. Directly above that are the "safety" needs the goal of which is the provision of a secure and safe environment. At the third level are needs for love and affection, to belong to a social group, and to be accepted by one's peers. The fourth level contains the needs for social status and the esteem of others as well as to receive recognition and attention. Finally comes the highest need level, the need for self-actualization. This is a more sophisticated form of what we earlier called "self-fulfillment"; it is the need for a person to develop his or her fullest potential as an individual.

Maslow conceived of the dynamic forces of behavior as being deprivation and gratification. Deprivation, or dissatisfaction with respect to a particular need, leads to dominance of that need; the person's behavior is entirely devoted to satisfying that need. Once satisfied, or gratified, however, the need recedes in importance and the next highest level of need is stimulated or activated. Thus, beginning with the lowest level, the entire process involves deprivation leading to dominance, gratification, and activation of the next level.

As applied to work motivation, Maslow's theory asserts that, at the very least, people will work to provide for their physiological and safety needs. This is tantamount to an instrumental account of work; that is, people work because work is instrumental in securing the "basic necessities" of life. If, for whatever reason, the basic needs are met, then social motivations become important. That is, people will work for social companionship or to obtain a position of esteem in society. Finally, if these social needs are also satisfied, people may work purely for the sake of developing the full potential of their personalities.

Clearly, Maslow's theory can provide an integrated account of a variety of different reasons for working and can be applied to a variety of questions about work behavior. It is not surprising, therefore, that it has received a great deal of attention. Unfortunately, much of Maslow's work has been criticized (e.g., see Wahba & Bridwell 1973, for review), especially recently by those who have applied the theory empirically to the specific question of work motivation (e.g., Hall & Nougaim 1968).

Both the key concepts of Maslow's theory have encountered empirical difficulties. First, few researchers have found any support for five distinct levels of need. In one study by Alderfer (1969), some evidence was found for a two- or three-tier system (roughly corresponding to "lower" physiological and "higher" social needs), but there were no grounds for proposing anything more complex; further evidence of this sort is given by Centers (1948), Friedlander (1963), Mitchell & Mowdgill (1976), and Schaffer (1953).

Doubt has also been cast on Maslow's idea that the gratification of one need stimulates or activates the next-highest category. The clearest and most direct tests of this notion have failed to support the theory (e.g., Hall & Nougaim 1968; Lawler & Suttle 1972). Researchers writing at a more general level, however, have continued to find it useful. For instance, some have claimed that in a wealthy consumer society the "effective" motivation to fulfill "higher-level" needs is a result of the fact that more basic needs are routinely met; in less developed economies this would presumably not be true (Inglehart 1979). Other researchers see the transition from one level to another as due to affluence or better education (e.g., Argyris 1964; Galbraith 1975, p. 249 ff; Reynaud 1981).

Although a very popular explanation of work motivation Maslow's theory has little in the way of empirical support. But we should not be too quick to dismiss the theory altogether. First, the research is not entirely conclusive; most of it used a correlational approach which is largely unsuited for testing causal models of this sort. Second, Maslow's unit of analysis was the individual, whereas the research has focused on groups. Third, the measurement problem in this sort of research is so involved that one is never sure that an adequate test of these ideas has been achieved. For example, how does one measure unambiguously whether a person works for the purpose of achieving self-esteem? Quite simply, the construction of a measuring instrument that translates such a motive adequately into a quantifiable response is difficult. Finally, even some of Maslow's critics want to retain at least the general concept of levels of need (Wahba & Bridwell 1973). Although self-actualization may be a problematic concept, research certainly has supported the idea that two (or perhaps three) distinct groups of needs play a role in the modern workplace (see Morse & Weiss 1955).

A second type of need theory stems from the classic work of Murray (1938). Murray asserted that people had manifest needs such as the need for achievement, nurturance, autonomy, power, understanding, aggression, and so forth. These needs are learned, and they are usually triggered by an environmental cue. Psychologically, needs refer to a "force . . . in the brain region, a force which organized perceptions . . . and action in such a way as to transform in a certain direction an existing, unsatisfactory situation" (Murray 1938, p. 123). Thus, needs provide a direction to behavior as well as an energy which impels the person toward the need object. Murray's approach has been systematically applied to economic behavior by McClelland (1961), who suggested that the needs for achievement played a crucial role in motivating entrepreneurial behavior and, in turn, promoting economic development (for a more detailed discussion, see Chapter 16).

Murray's system is in some ways superior to Maslow's. For instance, the needs (personality traits) are more highly specified. It would therefore seem that a worker's ambition could be related to that person's need for achievement (Murray) more easily than to an ambiguous need for "self-actualization" (Maslow). Research has confirmed exactly that point: Performance in many situations is, indeed, strongly correlated to achievement need (Steers 1975; see also Chapter 18). In addition, Murray's system seems more flexible. The needs are not hierarchical and people can have many of the two dozen or so needs at the same time.

The inherent problem with Murray's approach, however, is that it provides useful labels (e.g., a person who works long hours can be said to have a high need for achievement) but little else. A learned personality trait such as need for achievement is not really a suitable explanation for behavior because it is entirely post hoc; it reveals neither the conditions under which the need will be expressed nor the dynamics of the need–environment interaction. And so while Murray's system may be a useful descriptive device, it does little to advance our understanding of specific issues related to work behavior.

More specific predictions can be found in a further need theory, specifically developed to deal with issues related to work. This is the hygiene–motivator theory of Herzberg, Mausner, and Snyderman (1959). Somewhat like Maslow, Herzberg and co-workers proposed that there are two kinds of human need, hygiene needs and motivator needs. Hygiene needs are for such things as pay and recognition. If they are not met, dissatisfaction is experienced, but they cannot provide positive satisfaction. That is only found through motivators such as achievement, responsibility, and the exercise of skill. Unlike Maslow, Herzberg and co-workers specifically deny the possibility of progressing from one kind of need to the other. They argue that hygiene needs are essentially insatiable, so that if positive satisfaction is to be found in a job, both kinds of needs must be met simultaneously.

A final need theory, also specifically developed to handle questions related to work motivation, is Jahoda's (1979) theory of the "latent functions of employment." It is unlike other need theories in that, instead of focusing on the needs which press a person into working (thus concentrating on the causes of work), it considers what needs work actually fulfills (thus concentrating, as its name suggests, on the functions of work). Jahoda accepts that pay and the working conditions provide an account of the primary causes or "manifest functions" of work behavior but argues that in addition (and in a way which the worker may not be able to verbalize) work has at least five latent functions: It provides time structure, a regular sharing of experiences and contacts, links to goals and purposes that transcend the individual, personal status, and sheer activity.

Jahoda's theory of manifest and latent functions has been popular in recent accounts of the psychology of unemployment, and it is easy to see why. It provides a systematic account of the kinds of psychological difficulty an unemployed person is likely to encounter. Nonetheless, in its present form, it is open to many of the same criticisms as Murray's theory. It is too flexible; it says nothing about the relative importance of the different functions of work, or the time course with which deprivation of work will make them apparent. These are deficiencies that could be remedied by further theoretical work and, as the most recent of the need theories we have described, Jahoda's is the most likely to be developed further in the near future.

Reinforcement theories

We now consider the third type of theory, the reinforcement theories. In some ways, these approaches are intermediate between economic theory and need theory. Like economic theory, they see work motivation coming essentially from the future benefits which work behavior will produce. But they do not rely on anticipation as the mechanism by which the future affects current behavior; rather, they specify how a history of past benefits, or reinforcement, modifies behavior so that (if the world does not change) future benefits will be secured.

The first reinforcement theory we shall consider is the direct application of behavior modification principles to the work situation (thus it is based on the laws of instrumental conditioning – see Hamner 1974; Luthans & Kreitner 1975; and see also Chapter 1). Behavior modification claims to provide procedures by which human performance can be shaped and altered. At the heart of behavior modification is the concept of reinforcement contingency: The rate of performance will increase when valued outcomes (reinforcers) are made contingent on the performance. It makes no difference to the theory what the person needs or expects. It is sufficient merely to establish the reinforcement contingency in order to affect a behavioral change.

The application of this approach to the issue of work is quite straightforward. The argument is that people perform certain work-related acts that are subject to reinforcement (or punishment and extinction) contingencies. For instance, people choose the type of job they work at, they perform at a certain rate, and with a certain degree of effectiveness. When a particular behavior results in a reward (there is a reinforcement contingency between, say, payment and work efficiency), performance improves.

In short, learning theorists such as Skinner assert that all behavior is shaped and sustained through the action of contingent reinforcement; work-related behaviors are simply special examples of this more universal phenomenon (and probably useful examples at that since the receipt of pay for work completed, particularly on a piecework basis, would seem to be a particularly graphic case of contingent reinforcement).

Behavior modification procedures are now widely used in industry as well as in clinical and educational settings. Consequently, the literature in psychology is full of reports about improvements in productivity, satisfaction, and so forth. Nevertheless, behavior modification has not met with universal approval, either as a theory of work behavior (e.g., Deci 1972, claims that it ignores the role of intrinsic rewards – see below), or as an ethically acceptable approach to work management (e.g., Kelman 1965, argues that behavior modification may severely restrict a worker's freedom of choice).

A second type of reinforcement theory is the social learning theory of Bandura (1977; see also Chapter 1). Whereas need theory attributes work solely to the person (internal motives), and behavior modification theory explains work in terms of the action of the environment (contingent reinforcement), social learning theory emphasizes both the person and the environment. That is, the individual (who has cognitions, perceptions, and so forth) and the environment (which provides reinforcement) combine to affect performance. It is not sufficient to say merely that a person works because he or she is reinforced; one needs to take the person's cognitions, attitudes, or emotions into account as well. For example, a person learns work performance through copying the behavior of others as a consequence of the reinforcers they are perceived to obtain, not simply through a series of discrete trial-and-error experiences (see Flanders 1968). Moreover, cognitive processes appear to mediate behavior; feelings, images, thoughts, and so forth affect the way we experience and perceive reinforcers and thus the way we perform (see Meichenbaum 1977).

A number of managers have begun to use social learning theory in the workplace. Some of the strategies have been directed at changing the environmental stimuli which set the occasion for rewarded behavior, while others have manipulated the consequences of behavior (e.g., Luthans & Davis 1979). Although a great deal of research is still required before we can fully accept social learning theory as an explanation of work motivation, it is certainly true that the theory broadens the general approach taken by the behavior-modification position.

Cognitive theories

A very different kind of psychology is involved in the last category of theory, the cognitive approach to work motivation. Cognitive theories generally assume that people engage in conscious "thinking" processes;

they reason, they perceive the consequences of their behavior, and they try to produce the best outcomes they can. Obviously, the economic theory is a cognitive theory in this sense: Like the economic theory, cognitive theories see anticipated future benefit as the source of work motivation. In another sense, however, cognitive theories differ sharply from the economic approach. Rather than attempting to specify the best possible decisions, they attempt to specify the processes by which work-related decisions are made. They are set in the context of known limitations on human information processing, rather than abstract utility maximization.

The most important theory in this category, perhaps the most influential of all current psychologically based theories of work motivation, is the expectancy/valence theory. It was originally conceived by Peak (1955) but was developed more fully by Vroom (1964). Fundamental to this theory, and in contrast to need theories, is the notion of instrumentality. An activity, such as work, may be instrumental in securing a valued outcome; if it is, the activity is performed. Thus, it is the instrumentality of work that is central to the behavior rather than an internal need or motive to work per se. If the work is not instrumental in securing the reward, then the behavior is not performed. This simple prediction is quite different from one derived from a need theory, which would predict that the behavior would be performed regardless of the instrumental outcome, provided that a need was present. The theory also differs from the economists' approach, in that it takes no account of the benefits to be obtained by not working at all.

The other major elements in Vroom's theory are valence and expectancy. Valence describes the attracting strength of the reward object, that is, the value of the reward (higher values producing a greater attractive force). Expectancy is the person's estimate of the likelihood of the relationship between the work activity and the reward; the expectancy component is stronger when the probability of the desired outcome, as a consequence of the action, is perceived to be higher.

The specific way in which the components are formally related involves two equations. First, the valence of outcome j (the attractiveness of that particular outcome) is a function of the valence times instrumentality summed over all the alternative outcomes. In symbols, the equation is as follows:

$$V_j = f \sum_1^N V_k I_{jk} \qquad (6.1)$$

where f is a constant, V_j is the valence of outcome j; I_{jk} is the perceived instrumentality for achieving j with outcome k; V_k is the valence of outcome k; and N is the number of outcomes. Instrumentality, according to Vroom, varies from -1 (the outcome k never leads to the attainment of outcome j) to $+1$ (outcome k is perceived as always leading to outcome *j).* The classic situation to which this equation has been applied is workers' satisfaction (e.g. see Graen, 1969). Satisfaction with a job (outcome *j*) is related to how instrumental that job is at achieving certain other outcomes such as salary (outcome *k*) and the valence or attractiveness of those outcomes (V_k).

The second equation involved in the theory deals with a person's motivation to perform. According to Vroom, the force acting on a person is the sum of products of the valences of the outcome and the strength of the expectancies that the behavior will result in the outcome. Specifically,

$$F_i = \sum_1^N E_{ij} V_j \qquad (6.2)$$

where F_i is the motivational force to perform act *j*; E_{jk} is the expectancy that act *j* will be followed by outcome *k*; V_j is the valence of outcome *j*; and *N* is the number of outcomes. This equation has been used to predict the choice of occupation, duration of work, and effort. For example, it has been shown that the stronger the attractiveness of a certain outcome, and the more a person believes that his or her job is instrumental in achieving the outcome, the stronger that person will be motivated to perform the work behavior (see Holmstrom & Beach 1973; Sheard 1970; Wanours 1972).

Overall, the expectancy/valence theory seems to have provided reasonably satisfactory answers to several of our questions about work. The theory has been successful in predicting job effort in the United States (Galbraith & Cummings 1967; Porter & Lawler 1968) and Japan (cross-cultural studies by Matsui, Kagawa, Nagamatsu, & Ohtsuka 1977) as well as job satisfaction and job choice. But many problems must still be resolved before we can have ultimate confidence in this theory (see Landy & Trumbo 1980; Mitchell 1974, for critical reviews). The major problem is that, so far, tests of the theory have been a good deal less specific than the theory itself. As Mitchell (1974) pointed out: "While it is relatively clear that expectancies, instrumentalities, and valences are significantly related to their various criteria, we really know very little about just how the relationship occurs. Our empirical tests are inaccurate representations of the overall theory. Our measures do not reflect the underlying theoretical components" (p. 1074).

A second cognitive theory or work motivation stems from the work on equity theory in social psychology (see Adams & Freedman 1976; Campbell & Pritchard 1976; Goodman & Friedman 1971). It has been especially useful in accounting for work effort and workers' reactions to pay rates.

An equitable relationship between a "person" (or *P*) and an "other" (or *O*) is said to exist when the ratio of outcomes to inputs for *P* equals the ratio of outcomes and inputs for *O:*

$$\frac{O_p}{I_p} = \frac{O_o}{I_o} \tag{6.3}$$

Whenever these ratios are not equal, an inequity is said to exist. That is, with an inequitable relationship P is benefitting more (or less) than O relative to the effort or investment each is making. If P works twice as hard as O, then P should receive twice the pay in order for P to perceive that the relationship is equitable. If P does not receive twice the pay, and thus perceives inequity, then P is motivated to restore equity. Person P can do this by altering the input (e.g., work less hard) or the outcome (obtain a raise in salary), distort the facts so that the relationship appears to be more equitable, or try to change O's input and/or outcome.

It is clear how equity theory can be applied to work motivation, especially the issue of job performance: A person will adjust his or her efforts in order to achieve and maintain equity with their fellow workers. A number of studies have confirmed just this point. For example, Goodman and Friedman (1968), Lawler (1968b), and others showed that experimental subjects who are "overpaid" for performing a task actually were more productive than were control subjects paid the "normal" amount. This theory is, however, less suited for addressing other questions such as job choice.

Although equity theory has been successful in accounting for such issues as job performance, research interest in the theory has nevertheless declined in recent years, for two main reasons. First, confidence in equity theory has waned among social psychologists generally. Second, most investigators now believe that equity theory can be incorporated into expectancy/valence theory (e.g., see Lawler 1968a, 1973). That is, the two cognitive approaches to work motivation are no longer seen as being in conflict. Equity theory, however, may yet prove to be a unique and powerful means of investigating certain neglected issues such as how employees and employers deliberately change equity relationships by manipulating inputs and outcomes in order to exact more pay or greater productivity (see Adams & Freedman 1976).

Status of the theories

We have now surveyed a considerable range of theories about work motivation. It should be clear that different theories are adapted for different kinds of questions, and are, therefore, likely to provide different kinds of answers. Vroom's expectancy/valence theory seems to provide a satisfying causal account of the quality of an individual's work; Jahoda's theory of latent functions to explain the kinds of problems people experience when they lose their jobs.

Nonetheless, the ultimate test of any theory is its ability to predict the data. We have already hinted that several popular theories are in danger of failing this test, either because they are in conflict with available data, because they are too flexible ever to be falsified (and so cannot make any useful predictions), or because their proponents have not carried out the necessary empirical tests. The remainder of this chapter is devoted to a more detailed study of the data available on the four key issues we identified earlier. Why do people work at all? Why do they choose particular jobs? What determines the hours of work? What determines the time and quality of work? Although we shall be trying to specify the implications of each kind of data for the theories we have reviewed, in many cases theory and data are not easily harnessed to each other. We shall therefore concentrate on providing an overview of the available data rather than focusing too narrowly on the relatively few studies that are illuminating at the theoretical level.

WORKING AND NOT WORKING

Work virtually dominates the lives of those who are employed. However, these people only account for about one-half the population. The remainder, made up of children, students, housewives, the unemployed, and the retired, lie outside the network of social, financial, and motivational relationships that paid work establishes. Some are outside it from choice, others by no choice of their own. What makes some people choose not to work? And what are the effects of exclusion from the world of work, whether it is voluntary or enforced?

These questions are clearly of major importance at the present time, when unemployment is at high levels in most of the world's advanced economies. Despite some recent improvement in the U.S. situation, the proportion of the population out of employment is still high by historical standards. The steady rise in the age at which students leave education and the fall in the retirement age mask the irreversible effects of technological and social change to some extent. This means that fewer people are needed to produce the same quantity of goods and that more people are available to produce them (because more women see themselves as part of the workforce). Governments try to manipulate the boundaries of the workforce in order to make unemployment figures look more palatable. Some of the resulting measures may well be desirable social reforms, but they leave unchanged the number of people out of employment. An important question in the economic psychology of work is whether they also leave the psychological condition of people unchanged.

The "work ethic" and the factory mode of production

The distinction between work and nonwork is almost entirely an artefact of the dominance of the employment scene by factory employment. Where the "domestic" mode of production dominates; that is, most people work as subsistence farmers or as self-employed craftspeople (Sahlins 1974, chapters 2 and 3), children's play merges smoothly into work, and no one ever completely retires. Much the same is true in the early stages of capitalist development, when most employment is in cottage industries. Modern concern with the problems of unemployment and leisure can make this kind of arrangement sound idyllic, but the reality was often brutal. In the Industrial Revolution, the worst excesses in the exploitation of child labor occurred in cottage industries (Marx, 1867/1977, vol. 1, chapter 13, section 8d).

The crucial step in the separation of the worlds of home and work is the gathering of employees into factories. Weber (1904/1976) argued that the rise of factory work coincided with the rise of a "Protestant work ethic," the idea that work, meaning employed work, is good in and of itself and that it is somehow shameful to obtain income other than by working. This principle is often cited (e.g., McClelland 1961) as an explanation of the drive for a better life through work that characterized so many people in northern Europe and North America in the nineteenth century, surviving to some extent today. Other uses of this protean concept include explaining the difficulty of adjusting to a new technological situation, in which individuals can enjoy greater leisure than in the recent past (e.g., Scitovsky 1976, chapters 10 and 11; Williams 1983), and even the preference of rats for food obtained by instrumental responding relative to food delivered unconditionally (see Osborne 1977).

There have been numerous attempts to produce psychometric tests which would measure the extent to which individuals hold the work ethic, such a measure would make it possible to determine how the ethic relates to work behavior. For example, Feather (1982) found that unemployed young men had lower scores than a comparable employed sample on the Protestant Ethic scale developed by Mirels and Garrett 1971), although there was no such effect for women. Furnham and Lewis (1986, chapter 8) discuss many further examples of this kind of research. But in our view, the whole concept of the work ethic will not stand up to inspection as a direct cause of individuals' work behavior. As Kelvin and Jarrett (1985) point out, it has never been applied in criticism of the idle rich, only of the idle poor; it might better be called a "wealth ethic." We have already seen that there are many powerful motivations for working, and we see no need to add this speculative morality to them. There may be some kind of "employment ethic"; that is, if someone is prepared to pay for an activity, that activity itself, or the person who performs it, is socially "valid." But this too seems doubtful; the evidence, if anything, favors an opposite process (see the overjustification effect below).

Alternative sources of income

The most obvious reason for working is instrumental. Work is the chief source of income. Most, but not all, general theories of work motivation predict that if a person has a source of income that is independent of work, his or her motivation to work will be reduced. Do the data support this prediction?

Before we can answer this question, we need to distinguish two cases. In the first, employment will as usual bring in some income in proportion to the time committed to it, but the individual has an additional income that accrues regardless of work. In this case, theoretical predictions are equivocal. For example, according to a microeconomic analysis, the individual might work more or less in the presence of the unearned income, depending on the shape of his or her indifference contors. The second case is more severe. Not only does the individual have some income whether the person works or not, but working makes no difference to that income. In this case, only nonpecuniary motivations can lead to any work being done at all.

Two groups within society are obvious sources of data on this question. The first consists of those whose own wealth, or whose family's wealth, provides them with a "private income." To the best of our knowledge, there have been no systematic studies of such groups. Anecdote and history provide some evidence, however. On the one hand, the idleness and dissipation of the nobilities of France and Russia, before their respective revolutions, are notorious. On the other hand, the great scientific achievements of the seventeenth to nineteenth centuries were largely made by people who could have lived comfortably on their incomes from land without doing any work at all. The folklore of modern capitalist societies contains its own quota both of wealthy people who spend their time in foolishness, and of business executives whose virtually incalculable incomes are exceeded only by their determination to continue working well past the age of retirement. These observations suggest that the need for income is indeed a very important motivation for entering employment, and normally a dominant one. When it is removed, the effects of the remaining motivations can be seen in a greatly exaggerated form. But the data from this source are so weak that in themselves they do not justify any firm conclusion.

The second group whose behavior is relevant here is those who are eligible for social security payments if they do not work. Because such payments are commonly "means-tested," that is, reduced in proportion to any earned income, a substantial minority of people face a situation in which the amount of money they receive is very little changed by any work they do. This is because the only jobs available to them yield very little more income than is available from means-tested social security benefits; in extreme cases, people may actually lose income by taking a job, a situation known as the "poverty trap."

There is ample historical and comparative evidence that the availability of unemployment benefits and other social security payments does affect the probability that people will take jobs. The levels of pay and conditions of work which were common in the British Industrial Revolution (Marx 1867/1974, vol. 1, chapters 8 and 13), and remain common in many Third World countries (e.g., see Banks, DeWitt, Carlip, & Overstreet 1981), are simply not acceptable in modern economies. In terms of the labor–leisure choice analysis, the evidence is that this kind of work will only be done when the alternative is zero consumption, that is, starvation. In terms of a needs theory such as Maslow's, the evidence is that only physiological need will drive people into such work.

More detailed evidence on this point come from the series of "economic experiments" that have been carried out in the United States, mostly involving the replacement of all taxes and benefits with a single "negative income tax," which ensures both a decent minimum income and removes the danger of a poverty trap, by ensuring that any employment a person takes leads to a clear increase in his or her income. As we saw in Chapter 4, there are problems with these experiments, but their data are still important. The earliest and most extensively documented of these studies took place in New Jersey between 1968 and 1972 (see Kershaw & Fair 1976; Peckman & Timpane 1975; Watts & Rees 1977b). It was found that increases in either the guaranteed minimum income or the effective marginal tax rate (the proportion of additional income which the person was allowed to keep) led only to a small, and generally statistically insignificant, decrease in the number of people seeking employment. The only substantial effect was on the proportion of working wives in intact nuclear families.

In contrast to our anecdotes of the idle rich, these results suggest that though the need for income is an effective motivation for work, it is by no means a dominant one under modern conditions. Absolute poverty may make it dominant; and perhaps a very large income from nonwork sources makes possible such attractive modes of consumption that the noninstrumental reasons for working fade into insignificance. But for most people in present-day conditions, the motivation to work is not a simple instrumental one. There is nothing in this conclusion to disturb any of the general theories of work motivation we discussed earlier, but it is clear that the economic analysis of the labor–leisure choice will, as we predicted, need to be extended to take account of nonpecuniary motivations.

Redundancy and unemployment

The previous section was very largely concerned with the causes of work. When we turn to studies of the effects that redundancy, and unemployment in the longer term, have on the individual, we are clearly concerned with the functions of work. Our knowledge in this area, although increasing sharply in recent years, is still scanty.

Some studies are largely empirical. For example, Warr (1983) reviews a number of studies by himself and his colleagues, showing that unemployment causes a decline in mental health for most people, taking the form of increased anxiety, decreased life satisfaction, inability to concentrate, depression, and general listlessness. These effects are accentuated by a high personal commitment to employment, middle age, longer unemployment, and by being psychologically vulnerable for other reasons, such as poverty or physical illness.

More theoretically oriented studies have mostly been organized around one of two frameworks. The first is the "loss" model. It has long been recognized (e.g., Holmes & Rahe 1967) that loss of a job is a "stressful life event" that can induce both psychological and physical illness. It is thus classed with such obviously psychoactive events as marriage, bereavement, or divorce, though also with events of less obvious psychological content such as moving house. A number of investigations (surveyed by Hayes & Nutman 1981, chapter 2) have reported that the sequence of experiences of people suddenly losing a job parallel those of people suffering other loss experiences. The unemployed commonly report stages of response, in which they first seek out all chances for reemployment, but later become prey to despair or depression. This is reminiscent of the sequence in other loss situations (as reported, for example, by Bowlby 1980, pp. 85 ff.).

But what is the mechanism of this effect? The various consistency theories of attitude change (see Chapter 1) would lead us to expect that when work was hard to get, people who had none would change their attitude to it, treating it as less and less important to them. The consequence is likely to be that the longer someone is unemployed, the less likely he or she will be to find employment or keep it when found. There are other reasons for thinking the same thing, and these provide the rationale for "work experience programs," "youth-training schemes," and the like. It remains to be seen whether these programs will be effective given that, according to our casual observations, they tend not to be seen by society at large as constituting "work" in the full sense; their clients, however, may feel differently (Breakwell, Collie, Harrison, & Propper 1984).

The second organizing scheme that has been popular in recent studies of unemployment is Jahoda's (1979) list of the "latent functions" of work, which was outlined briefly above. This has been used, for example, by Hayes and Nutman (1981). Studies using this scheme are potentially valuable sources of information about the relative importance of different motivations for work. In contrast to the investigations of the effects of income level on the probability of taking work when it is available, studies of unemployment suggest that the provision of money may be a very important function of work. What the unemployed complain about most bitterly is their relative poverty (Kelvin 1982). We know much less about the psychological effects of sudden reductions of income; until we do, we shall not be able to differentiate the direct effects of loss of work from these indirect effects.

Retirement

One possible way of disentangling these two kinds of effect is to look at other situations in which people cease to work. Retirement, for example, has been claimed to be one of the major crises of adult life. In the Holmes and Rahe (1967) scale of stressful life events, it ranks tenth, scoring 45 on a scale on which "death of spouse" rates 100, and "fired from job" rates 47.

Much has been written about the problems of adapting to the new conditions retirement imposes (e.g., Friedman & Havighurst 1954; Parker 1982). The problems most frequently mentioned sound remarkably like those ascribed to unemployment: depression (Spence 1968), general listlessness, and a fall in life satisfaction (Parker 1982). The last of these is particularly associated with cases in which there is no satisfactory pension cover, but otherwise the mediating variables are also similar to those found with unemployment; in particular, those who retire because of ill health are the most at risk psychologically.

Many people are financially comfortably when they retire, the decline in income being offset by substantial declines in outgoings. The problems that are often precipitated by retirement are therefore a powerful tribute to the nonpecuniary motivations for working, although we must remember that, given the modern nuclear family, retirement is likely to coincide with a sharp decline in nonwork responsibilities. Unlike unemployment, retirement is not associated with any stigma, yet the loss of social interaction, and of the status conferred by a job have been claimed to induce severe problems (Parker 1980).

Unpaid work

Just as retirement allows us to study the effects of loss of job without loss of income, so there are situations in which people work without pay. Children, students, homemakers (usually housewives), and voluntary workers are all able to divide their lives into "working time" and "leisure time," but they receive no income as a direct result of their work. In some cases, as in much current voluntary work, the work is undertaken as a conscious substitute for a job, in the explicit hope of obtaining the nonpecuniary benefits which the individual perceives work to provide. Kelvin (1980) argued that "do-it-yourself" activities will have an increasingly important role to play in the psychology of a future leisure-oriented society. In other situations, unpaid work is enforced and often resented. Schoolwork is an example. There is remarkably little systematic research on the psychology of most of these categories of unpaid workers. This gap in our knowledge is particularly unfortunate because everyday experience suggests that these kinds of work can indeed fulfill many of the nonpecuniary functions of employment we identified earlier and that they are satisfying to the extent that they do so.

Some psychological work has been done on housewives and on the reasons why women who might choose to live on their husbands' incomes nonetheless seek employment. We saw earlier that, in the New Jersey income-maintenance experiments, improved benefit payments led to a sharp decrease in the proportion of working wives. The experimental sample included many poor families with young children. It would seem clear that, at this level at least, financial necessity is a major motivation for working outside the home. In more representative samples in both the United States and West Germany, housework has been reported to provide less self-esteem, social support, and time structure than employment. Housewives seem to have poorer physical and mental health than comparable employed women (Heinemann, Roehrig, & Stadie 1980; Nathanson 1980). It is reasonable to suggest that, where there are young children to enforce time structure and (in many societies) frequent social contact inside and outside the home, the role of homemaker may be an acceptable substitute for employment if the family's economic condition allows. Once that stage in family life is past, however, the nonpecuniary needs satisfied by a job are not really met by housework.

THE CHOICE OF A JOB

There is a very large psychological literature both on the choice of jobs by individuals, and the choice of individuals to fill jobs. We cannot attempt to summarize it here (see Kline 1975). However, several points are relevant to the general questions being considered in this chapter.

Job choice and the reasons for working

First, how do the reasons for working we listed above affect the choice of a job? Among essentially similar jobs, especially at low levels of skill, there is no doubt that rates of pay are important, as would be expected on an economic analysis (and almost any other general theory). For example, in an early token economy study, Kagel, Battalio, Winkler, and Fisher (1977) varied the number of token reinforcers given for particular behaviors or groups of behaviors, and observed that, on the average, increased wages for a behavior increased the labor supplied to it.

On the other hand, there are clearly some jobs to which recruitment cannot depend purely on rates of pay. Most people who become ministers of religion, for example, could obtain much more highly paid work elsewhere; their choice of a job is said to depend on a "vocation," in our terms on their enjoyment or self-fulfillment they find in their work. In the terms of labor economics, this kind of job has a very high "psychic wage," and its money wage is correspondingly low.

Conversely, jobs that are very unpleasant may be expected to have relatively high money wages. A direct study of this process has been carried out by Lucas (1977), who investigated the typical earnings in 295 different categories of jobs, and regressed them against a number of characteristics of the individuals who did them (age, sex, race, educational level) and of the jobs themselves (repetitiveness, supervisory function, pleasantness of the work, sedentary nature, and so forth). Obviously, all these characteristics are highly correlated but, by using census records, Lucas was able to get enough data to estimate their independent effects. He showed that, whatever the levels of other variables, repetitive work and harsh physical conditions both led to higher rates of pay by a factor of from 12 to 57% for the least-educated (hence worst paid), and from 7 to 29% for the best-educated workers. Also relevant to this point is the unwillingness of modern workers to take on some of the work that has been done at other times or in other places. Really unpleasant jobs must be compensated with sufficient pay, or they will not be taken. Unless the work is of great economic value, this often means that it will not be done at all under modern conditions.

Skill, training, and investment in human capital

Clearly, not all people are able to choose all jobs. Different jobs call for different characteristics in the people who do them (e.g., muscular strength, intellectual ability, social facility, and various kinds of previous experience and training). If we try to aggregate the labor–leisure choice analysis to give a picture of overall supply and demand for different kinds of labor, we shall therefore find that the supply curves for different kinds of labor are different. Different kinds of work have different rates of pay, quite apart from the need to compensate workers for unpleasant aspects of some jobs.

Other things equal, a type of work that requires a scarce characteristic will be relatively highly paid. The demand for different kinds of work also varies, so a scarce ability is not necessarily a great advantage in the labor market. But the individual who has any skill has a wider potential range of jobs available and is therefore likely to end up better paid. Perhaps this explains why Lucas found that men (and not women) doing jobs with a supervisory component were 16–25% better paid than those doing otherwise comparable jobs: The ability to organize other people effectively is certainly scarce, though many people would affirm that it is not always present in those whose jobs demand it.

Because many of the characteristics that are in demand have a psychological component, we can have a psychological theory of the variations between individuals' incomes. For example, Lydall (1968, chapter 4) shows how the approximately log-normal distribution of earnings could be derived from a normal (gaussian) distribution of inherent abilities, interacting multiplicatively with a skewed distribution of parental socio-economic status and hence of educational and other opportunities.

The most interesting kinds of ability that affect the range of jobs an individual can take are, in fact, those that can be acquired by committing time or money to education or training. As economists at least since Adam Smith (1776/1908, book 1, chapter 10) have pointed out, the differential pay for such skills ought, in the long run, to be equivalent to the costs of acquiring them. From this point of view, the training of an individual is an "investment in human capital" (Schultz 1961), that is, a cost incurred now in order to secure a return at a later time. Both individuals and institutions have to take decisions about such investment. Individuals have to choose whether to take relatively low-paid work now or to defer entering work while they train for better-paid work later. Firms and governments must choose whether to encourage various kinds of education and training in the hope of having a more highly skilled work force in the future. It is possible to provide an economic analysis of this intertemporal choice, along the lines sketched out in Chapter 5. Much work has been done by labor economists on the macroeconomic effects of such decisions, and there have also been a few studies of individuals. For example, Koch (1972) found that the number of undergraduates changing into a major course in a large U.S. university was strongly correlated with the expected lifetime earning of a person graduating with that major.

TIME SPENT WORKING

Given that an individual is working, and in a particular job, an obvious further question to ask is how long that individual spends working, each day, week, or year. Other things equal, we would expect the time spent at work to vary with the strength of the motivation to work, so the question provides a strong test of theories about work motivation.

In one sense, however, other things can never be equal. The greater the satisfaction derived from an hour of work, the fewer hours need to be done to achieve a fixed total of satisfaction. This argument applies most obviously to the instrumental reason for working. In the formal development of the economic theory of the labor–leisure choice, it quickly becomes apparent that it is impossible to predict whether an increase in the wage rate will lead to more or fewer hours being worked. While this decreases the theoretical interest in time spent working, it increases the practical importance of obtaining some data on the question, since we have no clear theoretical expectations to guide us.

Economic data on hours of work

The most obvious empirical fact about the labor–leisure choice is that most people cannot attain all the combinations of leisure and consumption implied in Figures 6.1 and 6.2. Many of us, much of the time, have only two choices: to work 40 hours a week (or whatever is conventional) or not to work at all. This limits the data available from the real economy.

However, there are sources of data on variations in hours worked by those actually in employment. A much cited example is the study of changes in hours worked over fairly long periods of time. Data reviewed by, among others, Scitovsky (1976, pp. 93 ff.) show that the hours worked by most kinds of employees have decreased considerably over the past hundred years. This is usually interpreted to mean that a considerable proportion of the increase in real income made possible by technology has been taken in the form of leisure rather than consumption. Scitovsky also shows that the hours worked by "professional" employees such as higher civil servants, university teachers, and doctors have tended to increase. This is particularly striking in that these groups commonly receive no overtime payment, so that their increased work cannot be taken as an attempt to maintain differentials (which have also tended to decrease in the long term). Scitovsky argues that the greater potential for self-fulfillment in professional work means that it has increasingly been found more satisfying than consumption; it is certainly clear that something more than an instrumental effect is involved here.

A second source of economic data on hours of work is the empirical study of rates of taxation. Changes in the rates or structure of taxes can have a marked effect on the effective wage rate an individual faces. This is especially true if we include social security benefits, and the means tests applied to them, as part of the tax system. Two groups in the population are particularly vulnerable to such changes in taxation. The first are the relatively wealthy. Higher incomes are frequently subject to more severe rates of tax (85% was the top rate in Britain until 1979), and a small change in tax rates such as these, or in the income levels to which they apply, can produce dramatic changes in posttax income. It is notorious that people who are liable to such rates often have the means to defend themselves by a combination of tax evasion and avoidance. However, this is much less true of the other group strongly affected by changes in taxation. These are the relatively poor, and, in particular, those who are receiving social security payments and are therefore vulnerable to the "poverty trap" described earlier in this chapter.

Politicians of the right commonly assert that these very high marginal tax rates must discourage people at both ends of the income scale from being productive, but we have already seen that, even under a purely instrumental theory of work, this need not be so. A lower effective wage rate may produce more, not fewer, hours worked, depending on the form of the labor/consumption indifference curves.

As regards high income earners, Brown (1980, chapter 4) reviews data from a number of surveys in which high income earners were asked whether high marginal taxation had a disincentive effect on them. Between 10% and 15% did report such an effect, but as many reported the opposite incentive effect. Brown cautions that the sample is biased in that those most discouraged by high taxation presumably never achieve a high income any way, but there seems to be little evidence here for a strong disincentive effect. Furthermore, Brown and Levin (1974) reported very similar results from a survey of the hours of overtime worked by weekly paid employees in Britain, who had a tax rate of about 33% rather than the 40-to 85% applied to high earners.

More objective data give a slightly different result. In the New Jersey income-maintenance experiments, discussed in connection with the decision to work, the hours worked by husbands who took employment did decline when the effective tax rate was more severe, at least among whites; increases in the guaranteed minimum income had a similar effect (Watts & Horner 1977). Among working wives, there was also some effect of the guarantee level, although the tax rate was apparently unimportant (Cain, Nicholson, Mallar, & Wooldridge 1977). Econometric studies also suggest that tax rates may have some disincentive effects. Brown (1980, chapters 4 and 6) discusses several studies of the hours worked by people who were free to work overtime. The best results indicate that the substitution effect of an increase in pay (the tendency to work more because work now yields relatively more satisfaction) is several times larger than the income effect (the tendency to work less because real income is now higher, so that as much or more satisfaction as before can be obtained with less work). Under these conditions, high tax rates would have a strongly disincentive effect.

Further data come from investigations of the practice of "moonlighting" (taking a second job when already employed). Moonlighting is much more common among those whose regular work involves a four-day week rather than the conventional five days, even when the total hours of (regular) work, and the income from it, are the same (Poor 1970). This may reflect the greater opportunity for moonlighting given by a free "working" day, or even good organization of regular employment by determined and energetic moonlighters. But it may also reflect the social pressure to be working during the conventionally defined working week.

Although there clearly are inconsistencies to be resolved within these economic data, a reasonably coherent picture does emerge in agreement with what we have learned from considering whether people will work at all and what jobs they will choose. The obvious economic variables (rates of pay, rates of tax) do affect the hours that people will work, but they are not overwhelmingly important. Convention, and perhaps social pressure, are probably the strongest determinants. Above a certain level, hours of work may even increase where there is no immediate money incentive at all, a phenomenon most readily explained by saying that much high-paid work is actively enjoyable.

Token economy studies

An environment in which almost everything an individual does is liable to be paid for in tokens and in which all behavior and all token payments are carefully recorded is obviously an ideal setting in which to investigate what determines hours spent working. Futhermore, the question is of critical importance to those using token economies, since the behaviors for which tokens are paid are precisely those which the therapists or rehabilitators are trying to encourage.

An early study of this problem was reported in a paper by Kagel and co-workers (1977), which we have already mentioned in connection with job choice. Kagel and colleagues lowered the token prices for all rewards within their token economy (thereby sharply increasing real wages) and observed a decline in the total of token-earning behaviors by the highest token earners but a small increase by low earners. A statutory minimum of facilities were available to the patients regardless of tokens, so that Kagel and co-workers' system mimicked a modern, social security economy rather than one in the early throes of industrialization. In contrast to the economic data we have just considered, their results suggest that an increase in the marginal tax rate might well have a net incentive effect in a modern economy. No explanation for this inconsistency is yet forthcoming.

Laboratory studies of animals

Skinner (1953) suggested that two of the basic schedules of reinforcement used in operant conditioning experiments were analogous to the simplest arrangements for paying workers (see Chapter 1 for a discussion of schedules of reward). The fixed ratio (FR) schedule in which a reward is given for every nth response is like piecework. The fixed interval (FI) scheduled in which a reward is given for the first response after time t is like a weekly or monthy wage. The direct application of results obtained from experiments using animals on such schedules (as proposed, for example, by Aldis 1961) is surely foolish, but animal experiments can have their uses. For example, Battalio, Kagel, and Green (1977) applied the classic economic labor–leisure choice analysis to the results of a number of experiments on fixed-ratio schedules in which rats and pigeons "worked" by pressing levers or pecking keys for rewards of food. The usual result of such experiments is that, faced with increasing FR schedules (falling wages), animals spend more time working, but not quite enough to maintain their "income" of food rewards. However at sufficiently low "wages," work output may fall or even cease altogether. Lea (1978) summarizes a large number of other studies that lead to a similar conclusion, though he construes them in terms of demand for food rather than supply of work. This implies that, in general, the income effect of a wage increase (or tax decrease) will outweigh the substitution effect, as Kagel and co-workers found in the token economy.

Animals' work output is also reduced by the availability of alternative source of "income." For example, Lea and Tarpy (1986) studied hamsters who, unlike other species, greatly reduced their work output when the "wage rate" fell, because they were able to live from food they had previously hoarded, or reduce the amount they transferred to their hoards. Battalio and co-workers (1977) neatly combined these two effects in order to show that the predictions of the "revealed preference" (Samuelson, 1938) approach to the labor–leisure choice held for animal "workers." They reduced the "wage rate" paid to rats working for food reward but gave enough "free" food (independent of lever pressing) for the rats to be able to reach the same level of consumption as they had before by doing the same amount of work. All the animals reduced their work output (hence their income of food).

The value of these experiments is that they show what behavior may be like in the extreme, that is, when the alternative to work might indeed be starvation. Under these conditions, it appears that rats will do whatever work is needed to maintain a minimum (necessary?) food income, virtually so long as that is biologically possible. Reductions in the wage rate only serve to increase the output of work. That finding is in sharp contrast with the way people behave in a modern economy, but it is not inconsistent with historical data noted previously. Later in this book we shall consider in more detail just what "economic development" might mean but, on the basis of these results, a useful definition of a developed economy might be one that has progressed far enough for people to be unwilling to behave like rats.

The "overjustification effect"

We have suggested that incentive effects do not fully account for the total hours people work. We now discuss a body of research that shows that reward may in fact destroy the effective motivation to work. Such a finding has important implications for the reinforcement theories discussed earlier.

This research has its origins in the use of behavior modification techniques (see Chapter 1) in educational settings. Although some spectacular successes have been claimed, projects of this sort sometimes fail for no obvious reason. Levine and Fasnacht (1974) concentrated attention on one particular type of failure. They noted that activities that had been explicitly rewarded and that had been shown to increase in frequency while rewards were being given declined not only to, but beyond, baseline levels when rewards were removed. There was nothing shocking about a decline to baseline; an economist would predict it and so would a behavior modifier. But a decline below baseline suggests some unexpected process. A variety of explanations have been offered, one of which (by Lepper, Greene, & Nisbett 1973) gave the phenomenon its common name: the "overjustification effect." Using attribution theory (see Chapter 1), Lepper and associates argue that a reward gives subjects too good an "explanation" for the rewarded behavior; since the behavior can be justified merely in terms of the reward received, subjects need not tell themselves that they enjoyed performing it. Therefore, when reward ceases, the subject has no reason to continue the behavior. In a less cognitive style, but to very similar effect, Deci (1971) argued that the "intrinsic motivation" to perform the rewarded act would be diminished by providing extrinsic incentives.

These ideas are clearly important to the notion that work is enjoyable or self-fulfilling, since they suggest that the instrumental motivation for work will tend to corrupt and eliminate all other reasons for working. Behavior modifiers have suggested that the decline in performance after rewards are removed can easily be understood in terms of operant concepts like contrast (e.g., Feingold & Mahoney 1975), and that the concept of "overjustification" lacks explanatory power (Scott 1976). Furthermore, although the overjustification effect has been observed under a variety of conditions, it is not completely reliable (for a recent survey see Lepper & Greene 1978, chapter 6), and at least some of the original evidence given by Levine and Fasnacht (1974) was not very compelling (e.g., some of it described only the ordinary and predictable decline to, rather than beneath, baseline following cessation of reward).

Nonetheless, the concept of overjustification has been useful to many investigators. For example, Schwartz, Schuldenfrei, and Lacey (1978) appeal to it as part of a general argument that incentive principles are relevant only to a debased, factory kind of work because it is almost axiomatic that no one would do these jobs except for pay. Moreover, in a society inured to factory work, to give pay for any activity is to bring it down to that level. Payment for work implies an exact numerical assessment of the worth of both the work and the worker, the kind of assessment polite people avoid making, or at least communicating, where friends, neighbors, and relations are concerned. Payment implies a certain political relationship between payer and paid. In terms of interpersonal politics, therefore, there is every reason to predict something like the overjustification effect. Whatever its mechanism, it presumably operates during reward as well as after it, so that rewarding someone for performing an act may, paradoxically, tend to reduce the time the person spends doing it. Normally the straightforward "incentive" effect of reward dominates (i.e., reward causes an increase in performance); if it did not, employment would not be an important social fact. But it is important to realize that incentive need not be the only effect of reward.

QUALITY OF WORK

Finally, given that someone has a particular job, what determines the quality of the work? This aspect of work can be looked at from two points of view. The worker asks "how pleasant is the work experience?," while the employer asks "How good is the work being done?" These questions are only first approximations and they do not address the important issues of what we mean by "pleasant" and "good." Nevertheless, it would be convenient to review the question of the quality of work under the two headings they imply – job satisfaction and productivity – relating to the different and probably conflicting interests of worker and employer. But the two themes are intricately intertwined, in both theory and practice. On the one hand, the best way for employees to enhance their satisfaction may be to increase their productivity, hence their pay; on the other, the best way for employers to raise productivity may be to enhance the workers' job satisfaction.

Taylor and Tavistock

These two extreme points of view are seen most clearly in the historical development of studies of work quality. The first systematic framework to be suggested was that of "scientific management" (Taylor 1912/1947), which centered around time and motion study. Simply stated, workers were once considered simply as physical devices to be trained to operate in the most efficient way possible and to be rewarded on a piece rate basis. At the opposite extreme were the ideas of the "human relations" school (e.g., Mayo 1933), stimulated by a famous series of experiments carried out at the Hawthorne factory of the Western Electric Company. According to this approach, the crucial requirement was to treat workers well to ensure both job satisfaction and highest performance. The Hawthorne experiments seemed to show that no matter what environmental change was made in a group's working environment, it always improved the quality of work, a phenomenon that has given psychology the phrase "Hawthorne effect." The reasons for the improvement, it was believed, were that management showed an interest in the workers' welfare and that the workers had an opportunity for social relationships in their employment.

Oddly enough, the data from the Hawthorne experiments provide little evidence of a Hawthorne effect (McCullough 1983), and a series of subsequent research reports have found correlations between productivity and job satisfaction that were low or nonexistent (e.g., Brayfield & Crockett 1955; Vroom 1954). This meant that productivity and satisfaction were controlled by different factors. It is perhaps not surprising that more recent theorists (described as revisionists by Bennis 1961) have proposed a compromise between the two extreme positions. But any such theory runs the risk of being able to describe anything but predict nothing. A more interesting approach for economic psychologists is to try to specify the conditions under which workers can maximize their job satisfaction by helping to boost productivity, or managers can boost productivity by helping the workers achieve greater job statisfaction. This leads naturally to consideration of the determinants of efficiency of work.

Maier and efficiency

Many recent views on work quality derive from a formula put forward by Maier (1946/1970). He suggested that working efficiency could be predicted by a simple equation:

$$\text{Efficiency} = \text{skill} \times \text{motivation} - \text{fatigue} \qquad (6.4)$$

Psychologists will recognize this formula as an application of Hull's (1943) basic performance equation, derived from laboratory studies of animal learning:

$$E = H \times D - I \qquad (6.5)$$

where E is the effective reaction potential, H is the habit strength, D is drive, and I is inhibition. The problem for Maier is that Hull's approach to motivation is now largely discredited. Furthermore, Maier's equation is much too simple; it begs many of the really interesting questions, such as the origins of motivation and fatigue. It does, however, take a usefully clear position on the interaction between job satisfaction and productivity. According to this view, the worker's attitude toward his or her job will be just one of several sources of motivation, all of which will combine to determine the worker's efficiency.

There are two major problems with this kind of formula, however. The first is that it treats "efficiency" as a global variable. From the beginning of studies of job satisfaction, it was clear that the benefits that accrue to a firm from a contented workforce are indirect. Higher job satisfaction tends to lead to lower absenteeism (at least for manual workers – Metzner & Mann 1953), labor turnover (Brayfield & Crockett 1955), and so forth. Direct evidence of changes in productivity is harder to document though one would think that the changes must follow from these general improvements.

The second problem with Maier's approach is that the "productivity" of labor is a very confusing statistic. Output per-person per-hour is much more influenced by the quantity and quality of machinery employed than by anything the workers themselves do. In many jobs, productivity automatically rises and falls with the volume of trade, since the number of people employed cannot vary strictly in proportion to how much there is for them to do. If these factors are independent of motivation and fatigue factors, then equations like Maier's are potentially usable, though attempts to assess the factors will be difficult. But if volume of trade and the capital employed covary with these psychological variables, the psychological factors in productivity are likely to be very hard to discover.

Vroom's expectancy theory of work motivation

Earlier, we briefly described the influential theory of work motivation put forward by Vroom (1964). Recall that he claimed that a person's satisfaction with his or her job could be predicted from the following equation:

$$\text{Motivational force} = f_i \sum E_{ij} V_j \qquad (6.6)$$

where E_{ij} is the subject's expectancy that activity i will lead to outcome j; V_j is the subject's valuation of outcome j; and f_i is an arbitrary monotonic function.

As we explained earlier, Vroom's equation is a kind of rationality approach; in fact, it is one version of subjectively expected utility (*SEU*) theory. The person choosing a job (or choosing to remain in one) is treated as someone taking a risky decision between alternative sources of satisfaction. In Chapter 5, we criticized the *SEU* theory as a means of predicting decisions (see also Chapter 9). Is there any reason to expect that the theory is more satisfactory when applied to employment decisions?

The short answer is "no" (see Behling & Starke, 1973 for a thorough discussion of this point). Vroom's model, however, tends to be applied to the issue of work in a slightly different way from the classic applications of *SEU* theory. The intermediate terms (expectancies, utilities of individual outcomes) are frequently assessed by direct questions to the subjects (e.g., Starke & Behling 1975), and the general effort is toward data collection rather than mathematical virtuosity. The results of investigations are correspondingly more useful even when they do not support the model in detail.

Work as a social situation

As we have already seen, for almost all employees, work is a social situation; it may be the prime place for meeting friends and acquaintances. For at least some people, interpersonal relationships are not only an incidental consequence of work but the essence of the work they do. This applies particularly to those who deal with the public and to anyone whose primary task is supervision. But almost all employees must interact, at least to some extent, with other people who are at different levels of authority as well as at their own level.

The consequences of these social relationships for the quality and productivity of work have been investigated extensively in the literature on organizational psychology and on management. Most of this work is beyond the scope of this book. However, two points that have received much attention are the nature of the authority structure within a firm, and the style of supervision. Organizations may be strictly hierarchical, or they may involve more or less independent "departments" whose members need acknowledge authority only within their own section. Similarly, a hierarchy may have either many levels, or relatively few, and the extent to which workers can influence decisions taken further up the hierarchy varies greatly in different organizations.

The merits of these different systems have been argued at considerable length (for summaries see Argyle 1972, chapter 8; Reynaud 1981, chapter 5). The most obvious conclusions are that the social environment is one of the most important properties of a workplace, from the point of view of both of the worker's happiness and the plant's efficiency, and that there is no single "best" way of organizing it. What is good for efficiency may not be good for the contentment of the workers, and vice versa. What is efficient and pleasant in one social and industrial context may not be either in another place or time.

WHY DO PEOPLE WORK?

Why, then, do people work? We started this chapter by suggesting four kinds of reason: external reward, intrinsic enjoyment, self-fulfillment, and social contact. The data assure us that all four play an important role in work and in employment as we understand it in present-day society. We have also been able to get some idea of their relative importance, although we have seen that in fact that varies according to circumstances; for example, income may be overwhelmingly important when there is no other source but quite irrelevant when a person has a private income.

From the point of view of general theories, however, the position is less satisfactory. We have used an economic analysis but have consistently had to point out that it needs to be developed to include nonpecuniary work motivations. Although this clearly can be done in principle, it has not been done in practice. None of the other general theories has been shown to be useful on a more than qualitative level. That is partly because none has been applied in detail to the data that are available. This is one function of the present book.

What is clear is that no simple theory is sufficient at this time. There are different kinds of work, and each kind seems to provide several different kinds of satisfaction. Any comprehensive theory in the future will need to handle this essentially multivariate situation. Perhaps the best strategy will be to look at economic psychology more generally, discover what kinds of theory are useful in analyzing other kinds of economic behavior, and return to the analysis of work with the advantage of that knowledge.

7

BUYING

Like work, buying is critical to economic psychology. From the economic point of view, it forms the second half of the circulation system between households and firms by which households receive money from firms in return for their members' labor, and use it to obtain goods and services from firms. From the psychological point of view, buying again complements working; it is the second part in the chain of instrumental behaviors by which individuals obtain the goods and services that psychologists regard as the goals or reinforcers that maintain economic behavior. Finally, the commercial importance of buying means that it has been studied extensively by consumer and marketing scientists, and their work provides a rich source of empirical information.

Consumer scientists have also done a great deal of theoretical work on buying behavior, and a number of integrative models of the buying process have been produced (e.g., Howard & Sheth 1969; Nicosia 1966; Engel, Kollat, & Blackwell 1972). These are elaborate structures incorporating all the possible social and psychological processes that may be involved in different kinds of purchase. All of them are based, more or less closely, on an information-processing approach to individual psychology. They are sometimes referred to as theories, but in a sense they are not theories at all, since any data whatsoever would be consistent with them. Rather, they are frameworks within which data about buying can be organized.

Models of this kind are too detailed for the purposes of this chapter, and we shall use a much simpler approach. We shall describe the purchase of any commodity as the culmination of a series of choices. The buyer must choose to (1) buy that commodity at all, (2) visit a particular shopping area or center, (3) enter a particular shop, and (4) buy a particular quantity. Obviously, this is an idealized scheme. We should not necessarily think that the buyer consciously makes each choice. Indeed, at the level of the mechanisms controlling behavior, there may be no real decision whatsoever at any particular stage (Olshavsky & Granbois 1979–80). In our analyses, we may talk in purely behavioristic terms, in which case all we would mean by "choice" is that one thing is done rather than another; the conscious experiences involved would not enter into our theories. But at each of the stages we have listed, there is a choice in the sense that alternative courses of action are open. The exact sequence of choices may not be followed in every case; for example, the process might be aborted at any stage or someone might buy something in a shop without having had any prior intention to do so (this is called impulse buying). Consumer scientists have also stressed that there are important processes that occur after purchase. To take an obvious example, the consumer's satisfaction with what he or she has bought will affect the likelihood both of a repeat purchase and of a complaint. Repeat buying (e.g., Ehrenberg 1972) and complaining (e.g., Gronhaug & Zaltman 1981; Folkes 1983–84; Gilly & Gelb 1981–82) have both been investigated extensively in recent years.

THE DECISION TO BUY

In one sense, the choice of whether to buy a commodity is really an extreme case of the choice of how much of it to buy; not buying is opting for zero quantity. This is the way microeconomic theory treats the decision to buy; for some goods and services, notably small items for current consumption, it would seem to be the best approach. But for larger or more expensive items, particularly those of which a household would normally own only one, it may be better to focus attention on the decision to purchase as the origin of subsequent buying behavior. The goods that most clearly fit this specification are the so-called "consumer durables" (e.g., cars, washing machines, and television sets). People's decisions about whether to buy such things have attracted much attention from economic psychologists and consumer scientists. Naturally, those who sell consumer durables are also vitally interested in the question.

Needs and durables purchase

First, why does someone decide to buy a particular commodity? The obvious answer is because he or she needs it. But this is inadequate for a number of reasons. First, the word "need" may be too strong for many real economic decisions. One needs food and housing, but is it reasonable to say that one needs an automatic washing machine with built-in warm-air drying capability? Might it not be more accurate to say that what one needs is a way to keep clothes clean? And a person could meet that need just as well by hand-washing, persuading a spouse to take on the chore, using a laundry, or joining the armed forces.

Second, even if it is reasonable to say that one needs a washing machine, can a person really say that he or she needs, for instance, a single washer-drier unit rather than separate units for each function? Or, even more implausibly, a Hoover automatic washer-drier rather than the equivalent machine made by Hotpoint or General Electric? Surely not.

Third, even if one does need a washing machine, the need may have existed for a long time. To talk about need obscures the real question, which is why a person should decide to buy a washing machine now rather than last year or next year. In some cases the answer to that will be obvious and compatible with an explanation in terms of needs (e.g., perhaps the person always has had a washing machine and, when the current one has broken, a new one is needed now). But still the question remains: Why does one replace it rather than getting it repaired? Certainly not all replacements are due to breakdowns. Juster (1964) showed that attitudinal variables, such as whether the time seems "right" for making major purchases, predict total durables purchased at least as well as the amount of stock currently owned and identified as needing replacement.

Let us grant, though, that some replacement purchases may be in a different class from first-time purchases (advertisers certainly treat the two cases differently). For first-time purchases there is the additional issue concerning why one selects an item to begin with. A person may have some degree of need for many different items, so why does he or she decide to buy, say, a home computer this month (or this year) rather than a microwave oven or a video recorder? It is not obvious how a "needs" theory approaches this question.

Finally, the word "need" may suggest too utilitarian an approach to buying. Holbrook and Hirschman (1982–3) argue that we must also take into account fantasy, feelings, and fun if we are to make a complete analysis of consumer behavior.

In summary, to say that we buy things because we need them seems to be an insufficient explanation, at least at the present stage of our knowledge. That is not to say that need and buying are unrelated; in fact, one of the main themes of this chapter is that a study of buying behavior is one of the best available ways of finding out about human needs. After all, it is through goods bought in the market that many needs are satisfied. However, we lack a ready-made theory of needs that will explain what we know about buying. Therefore, we shall emphasize an empirical approach and consider the available data on buying behavior. At a later stage, an interpretation in terms of needs may become possible.

Market penetration and diffusion models

The first set of data we shall consider shows that, at least for some consumer durables, the decision to buy is influenced by social pressures. The way in which new goods spread through the economy can be predicted and described by means of mathematical models similar to those used in the study of how diseases spread through a population. Robertson (1971) surveys such theories of innovation in detail; an influential recent application to consumer behavior is that of Midgeley (1976–7). This "epidemiological" approach is an example of the study of what is currently called "cultural evolution" – the idea that words, ideas, fashions, and many other social and psychological phenomena spread through a population of human brains in more or less the same way that genes spread through a population of chromosomes (Pulliam & Dunford 1981).

But we cannot think of the population of consumers as an undifferentiated mass. In terms of a diffusion model, we have to recognize that demographic factors (e.g., age, social class, domicile) will have a profound effect on whether an individual consumer comes in contact with a new product (i.e., is in a position to acquire the need for it) and also on whether that contact will affect behavior. These factors provide a possible explanation for a very well known phenomenon in the purchase of new products. Stoetzel, Sauerwein, and Vulpian (1954), and hundreds of others since, have demonstrated that there is a kind of "life cycle" of products. For example, an innovation may be bought at first by the young, the wealthy, town dwellers, and the upwardly mobile individuals, and only later by others. Stoetzel and co-workers studied the extent to which wristwatches had replaced pocket watches in France. They found that, among other things, wristwatches were more common, by factors of 1.5 to 3, in the wealthiest than the poorest classes, among city dwellers than among country dwellers, and among those under age 35 than among those over age 65.

The precise characteristics of innovators vary with the product field (Robertson 1971; Rogers 1975–6), and the rate of adoption of innovations has increased within the past few decades (Olshavsky 1979–80). Personal experience with the digital watch example suggests that the product life-cycle concept is only a first approximation; at times, the "smart" and innovative thing to do has been to go against the trend and replace a digital watch with an "ordinary" one, or even with a pocket watch (see the discussion of the counter-Veblen effect).

Thus innovation, diffusion, and adoption are complex processes (Midgeley & Dowling 1977–8). Nonetheless, the systematic spread of innovations presumably does reflect two simple psychological processes. First, as we have already indicated, a consumer cannot buy something he or she does not know about. As we shall see in Chapter 13, knowledge about products that is derived from friends or neighbors is taken much more seriously than knowledge derived from media advertising. Second, pressures for group conformity and social emulation are no doubt operating. These are topics where social psychology has contributed a considerable range of both theory and experimental data (see Suls & Miller 1977). Unfortunately, few if any of the empirical studies in this area have dealt with the real economic behaviors involved in "keeping up with the Jones's," despite the fact that this phenomenon is taken for granted in everyday speech.

Assuming that these variations across segments of society will always exist, it is useful to talk about the "penetration" of a commodity, that is, the proportion of households that own a television, video recorder, home computer, and so forth. Obviously, penetration statistics are of interest to marketers, who want to know whether to direct their attacks at a "replacement market" or at first-time buyers. But they also have some psychological significance. In 1953 (i.e., at an early stage of the post-World War II explosion in consumer goods ownership) Cramer (1962) found that the relative penetrations of various goods in the United Kingdom were as follows: 10.5% for refrigerators, 17.0% for television sets, and 12.5% for washing machines. These data tell us something about the relative importance of different needs. For example, they suggest that, at that time, entertainment was more important to consumers that minimizing labor. Although this is not a radical conclusion in everyday terms, it is enough to give severe problems to several much-vaunted theories of need, such as Maslow's (1970) hierarchical theory (introduced in Chapter 1).

The motivational significance of penetration statistics should be enhanced when they can be extended to show what combinations of goods are particularly common, and the typical order of acquisition of goods. A number of studies have reported that both of these tend to be consistent and fairly stable (e.g., Paroush 1965; Pyatt 1964; Clarke & Soutar 1981–2; Kasulis, Lusch, & Stafford 1979–80). Kasulis et al. specifically link them to the relative utilities of goods. It should be possible to use combination and order or purchase data to shed light on more subtle needs. However, we must not be naive in interpreting the data. Some goods, for example, are rarely acquired early in a family's life cycle because they are traditionally supplied in rented accommodation, and in many cases the acquisition order is effectively determined by the (much more easily obtained) penetration level (Dixon, Lusch, & Wilkie 1982–3). Using a survey technique that avoided this problem, Patterson (1983) has obtained preliminary data that suggest that there is also a stable order of disacquisition of durable goods when people are becoming poorer because of prolonged unemployment. This order too should reflect the pattern of people's needs.

Consumer confidence and durables purchasing

Within the field of economic psychology, the factor in durables purchasing that has received most attention has been general consumer confidence. Katona (e.g., 1960, 1975) has stressed this point in particular. Because there are many potential purchases that might be made at any given time, none of them forced on the consumer by immediate physical need, there is a much greater margin of discretion for the consumer in durables purchase than in the purchase of, say, food, clothing, or housing. Katona makes much use of the concept of "discretionary income," that is, what remains to the consumer after financial commitments have been met and the essential needs of life bought. Discretionary income may be spent in a variety of ways, or it may be saved (see Chapter 8). But it is particularly important as the source of money for most durables purchases, whether they are paid for immediately or by installments. Katona argued that what consumers do with their discretionary income depends crucially on how they feel about their own economic prospects and the state of the economy as a whole. In 1946 Katona began collecting data on consumers' attitudes toward their personal and national economic situation and prospects. (Strictly speaking, what Katona collected were data on beliefs rather than attitudes as such, but within this field the term "attitudes" is used more commonly; see Chapter 1.) Katona's sample surveys have been continued ever since by the Survey Research Center of the University of Michigan, and similar data have also been collected in several European countries. Although these surveys of consumer attitudes have involved quite complex and sophisticated interviews, most attention has been given to the simplest measurements in which consumers are asked questions such as: "Do you feel that your personal financial position has improved, gotten worse, or stayed the same during the past year?", "Do you feel that this is a good year in which to buy a new car, or not a good year?", or "Do you expect the state of the economy to improve/stay the same/get worse during the coming year?"

These questions are fairly crude, but Katona claims that they are nonetheless of considerable practical importance, because the total of all consumers' discretionary incomes represents a considerable proportion of the gross national product of a modern economy. Thus, if consumers decide to spend heavily one year, that will have a significant macroeconomic effect; it will be substantially reflationary. Equally, if all consumers decide to save, the effect will be a substantial deflation. Consumers' decisions are likely to depend on their attitudes and expectations about the progress of the economy, and these will vary between individuals and between times. Although macroeconomists such as Keynes (1936, pp. 95 ff.) argue that, on the average, these varying expectations will tend to cancel each other out, Katona's data suggest that in any one year, there will be consistent trends in attitudes across all the consumers in an economy. The Index of Consumer Sentiment is a quantitative summary of survey data. Katona claims that it is significantly correlated with economic trends manifesting themselves a few months later and gives information that cannot be obtained from conventional economic indicators. For example, in 1946, most economic data suggested that the U.S. economy was about to enter a recession. Attitude data, however, suggested the reverse: Consumers claimed to be ready to spend heavily. As it turned out, a considerable consumer-led boom did occur.

It is not seriously disputed that attitude data can predict the behavior of the economy. But Katona's second claim, that attitudes tell us something that cannot usually be deduced from economic data, has been more controversial. Recent data suggest that attitudes, in fact, add nothing to more conventional predictors of economic trends, examples such as the one given above notwithstanding (Hymans 1970; Shapiro 1972; Vanden Abeele 1983). This implies that consumers' beliefs, insofar as they are measured by the Index of Consumer Sentiment (not a perfect instrument: Didow, Perreault, & Williamson 1983–4), and insofar as they affect purchasing, are effectively determined by economic variables we can measure in simple statistical ways and are no more than "intervening variables" in an economic analysis. For particular goods attitude data may still be the best available predictors of sales (as Wetzel & Hoffer 1982–3, argue for the U.S. car market). And it is not hard to see that the year 1946, so crucial to the development of Katona's thought, could well have been a more general exception, given that the recent end of the war provided an overwhelming noneconomic reason for consumer optimism.

In any case, from the point of view of a study of buying, it is the correlation of the index with the subsequent state of the economy that is most interesting. That correlation demonstrates an influence of the overall and personal economic mood on the decision to make inherently postponable purchases. It also shows that this effect is large enough to be measurable at the macroeconomic level. These arguments hold whether or not the index can itself be predicted from the previous and current state of the economy.

Buying intentions and buying behavior

Consumer surveys often include questions like, "Do you intend to buy a new car this year?" Juster (1964) has shown that people's answers to such "intentional" questions predict their subsequent behavior quite well. For some years, in fact, U.S. federal agencies collected intention data for use in economic forecasting, although this practice has now been dropped (McNeil 1974–5).

Across product fields, Juster also found a number of consistent regularities in the relation between predicted and actual buying. For example, the higher the proportion of people who predict that they will buy, the lower the proportion of predicted buyers who actually do buy. Within any particular product field, Ehrenberg (1966) claimed that we can express the relationship between intentions and behavior in a more detailed mathematical form. Using market research data on purchases of cheap, immediate-consumption commodities, he argued that the relation between *B*, the proportion of people who will actually buy a commodity in a given time period, and *I*, the proportion who will claim in advance that they intend to buy in that period, reliably takes the form:

$$B = k\sqrt{I} \qquad (7.1)$$

where *k* is a constant for any given time period and product field. Obviously, *k* may also vary with the time between the expression of intention and the opportunity to buy. If Ehrenberg's "law" turns out to be reliable, it will in fact give us a useful way of talking about such variations.

Ehrenberg claims that there are two reliable exceptions to this law. For new products or brands, he finds that *B*, the proportion of people who buy, is higher than the law predicts. And for dying products or brands, he finds that *B* is lower than predicted. Both these exceptions imply that trends in buying behavior tend to run ahead of trends in intentions to buy. To put it more generally, behavior seems to change before measured attitudes change. This is consistent with the behavioristic theory of attitude proposed by Bem (1972; see Chapter 1). It would be very interesting to know whether Ehrenberg's law, and the systematic exceptions to it, would apply to more expensive, durable goods as well as to the essential but trivial purchases for which it was originally proposed. As we shall discuss below, Katona and others have suggested that larger purchases involve more cognitive, decision-making processes than regular purchases of consumables. If Katona is correct, we might expect attitude change to be a cause rather than a consequence of behavioral change for durables purchase. So far as we know, the data required to test this prediction are not available.

Habitual buying

At least for small regular purchases, the evidence we have discussed so far points to a behavioristic account of the decision to buy. Katona (1953) makes this fact the cornerstone of his argument that traditional economics, with its dependence on the assumption of rationality, is radically incomplete. To some extent, Katona's argument depends on a confusion between rationality as description and rationality as mechanism (see Chapter 5); furthermore, we are holding by our decision, made in that chapter, not to approach every problem in economic psychology by asking whether observed behavior is rational. But it is still important to explore what we know about the role of habit in buying.

Two lines of evidence support the importance of habit in buying behavior. First, there have been a number of attempts (e.g., Lilien 1973–4; Massy, Montgomery, & Morrison 1970; Srinivasan & Kesavan 1976–7) to apply learning theories, particularly mathematical ones, to individual purchasing behavior. Insofar as such attempts succeed, they give evidence that habit is a useful construct in an analysis of purchasing. But their success has been rather limited; the theories are more impressive as displays of mathematical virtuosity than as stimulants to the collection of real data. Furthermore, they are usually concerned with the decision about which brand of a product to purchase (a matter we deal with later in this chapter) rather than with the decision to purchase a given product in the first place.

Better evidence for the importance of habit in buying comes from survey data. Houthakker and Taylor (1970) applied learning theory to data on buying and ownership of 65 commodity groups. Their model included a parameter which would be negative if purchasing was restrained by accumulated stock of the commodity, and positive if it was habitual. For 46 of the commodities, habit seemed to dominate the "inventory" effect. Sexauer (1977) pointed out that these conclusions would depend on the accounting period chosen, but on an analysis of purchases of 16 commodity groups, he found that even with short accounting periods, habit was important in some cases.

A priori, it is difficult to see how habit could play much of a role in the majority of purchase decisions. Except for a few goods that are discarded, used or not, without much sense of waste (newspapers are an obvious example), or services that require minimal or no effort to consume (insurance, perhaps), purchasing by habit without regard for subsequent use would soon result in overflowing cupboards. Surely this would quickly bring about some reassessment of behavior. According to this view, what matters is not that a person habitually buys, say, chocolate, but rather that he or she habitually eats it.

For many purposes, of course, we do not need to distinguish between consumption and purchase. Nonetheless, habitual consumption is an interesting phenomenon with obvious implications for the nature of human motivations. Buying for habitual consumption is clearly an instrumental behavior, but is its apparent reinforcer (the product bought) a primary unconditional reinforcer or something that has itself been learned either by the subversion of simple biological drives or by some process of social influence? And to what extent is the economy and the way it makes goods available responsible in either case? These are major questions to which there are no easy answers (see Chapter 18).

The existence of habitual consumption does not, however, rule out the possibility that truly habitual buying also occurs. There is anecdotal evidence, at least, to suggest that it does. We know of parents who go on buying what their teenage sons and daughters used to consume long after the latter have left home and gone to college; here, at least, the overflowing store cupboards occur but do not seem to check the behavior. Furthermore, it is not unknown for goods to be consumed simply because they have been bought ("since we have this, we might as well eat it").

Such behavior could protect habitual purchasing more or less indefinitely. After all, in many households purchasing and consuming are done by different individuals and may therefore be relatively independent. Both habitual consumption and habitual buying are areas that need psychological investigation.

Conclusions on the decision to buy

This section on the decision of whether or not to buy a product has yielded a number of reasonably trustworthy generalizations. Patterns of buying are not random. There are systematic trends, both in the order in which a single individual acquires different goods, and in the order in which different individuals acquire particular goods. Furthermore, purchases are related in orderly ways both to people's expressed feelings and beliefs about the economy at large and to their expressed intentions to buy particular commodities. There is some evidence that these verbal expressions may be driven by habitual purchasing or habitual consumption or by statistically observable economic trends (these two possibilities could be two ways of looking at essentially the same tendency). But neither possibility undermines the orderliness of purchasing behavior or of its relationship to verbal statements. All of this encourages us to believe that buying is related to stable, comprehensible, and relatively universal psychological phenomena. In order to gain further information about what those phenomena might be, we turn to the next decision in the chain of events leading to purchase: the choice of a place to shop.

SHOPPING

Not all buying involves shopping. In the first place, important processes take place between the decision to buy and the point where the consumer makes the purchase. Second, some buying is done elsewhere than in shops, either between individuals directly, or by mail order. Before we turn to look at shopping itself, we shall look briefly at each of these areas.

Prepurchase processes

Much attention has been given to processes by which consumers acquire information about products before embarking on a purchase. Under the prevailing cognitive model of consumer behavior, this is referred to as the stage of "information search." In more prosaic terms, it consists of being exposed to advertising and to independent evaluations such as those offered by consumer associations, evaluations derived from "shopping around" and from consulting friends and acquaintances. It has attracted attention for two reasons. First, there is an interesting theory as to how much of it consumers should do (the "economics of information" approach pioneered by Stigler 1961). Second, it is obviously the stage at which consumers are most susceptible to influence by marketers. There have been many empirical studies of consumers' information acquisition, both in the laboratory and in the field (see Newman 1977, for a review).

There is no doubt that, in laboratory simulations of buying, consumers do engage in information search, that the amount of it they show is lawfully related to the variables one would expect to be important (e.g., time pressure, see Moore & Lehmann 1980–1), and that the information acquired is used (e.g., Sheluga, Jaccard, & Jacoby 1979–80). It is not so clear that these laboratory studies reflect what happens in *real* purchases. Olshavsky and Granbois (1979–80) reject the whole information processing model as a description of actual purchasing behavior, and there are some data on their side. For example, Furse, Punj, and Stewart (1983–4) found that prepurchase behavior varied greatly between different types of new car buyers, while McEwen (1977–8) found that use of objective ratings of different brands was concentrated among a minority of relatively well-educated, middle-class consumers, whether the ratings were available through subscription to consumerist organizations or via a toll-free telephone number. Furthermore, in a study of women's shoe purchasing, Newman and Lockeman (1976–7) found that the commonly used survey methods of assessing information search were inaccurate when compared with direct observation. Perhaps, however, these studies have used too simple an approach to the economics of information. Shugan (1980–1) uses Stigler's approach to show why something not unlike Olshavsky and Granbois's account of nonrational consumer behavior might actually be rational, given the cost in time and effort of thinking through to an ultimately optimal decision.

Direct buying and selling

Many economic psychologists and economic anthropologists would argue that gifts are a primitive form of trade. From this point of view, we should have to include the whole gift exchange system within direct buying and selling, and this amounts to perhaps 5% of consumers' economic activity (see Chapter 9). Even if we exclude gifts, a substantial amount of direct trade remains, both between individuals and between individuals and mail order firms. The significance of both these kinds of trading is shown by the success of newspapers which contain nothing but personal and mail order advertisements. In many U.S. towns and cities such newspapers are distributed free, while in Britain there are two long-established highly successful papers (*Exchange and Mart* and *Dalton's Weekly*) which both have very healthy national, paying circulations. This form of trading

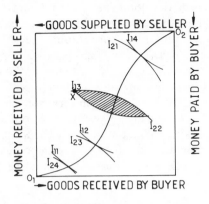

7.1. The Edgeworth box diagram for describing bargaining. I_{11}, I_{12}, I_{13}, and I_{14} are indifference curves for the seller: They join price–quantity combinations between which the seller is indifferent. I_{21}, I_{22}, I_{23}, and I_{24} are indifference curves for the buyer: They join price–quantity combinations between which the buyer is indifferent. Any point such as X, where indifference curves for the two parties cross, is unstable; points within the shaded area are on indifference curves further from the origin (O_1 for the seller, O_2 for the buyer) for both parties, so represent a gain in utility for both. Points such as Y are stable: Neither party can gain utility without the other losing. These are points where the two parties' indifference curves are tangents to each other. The wavy line $O_1 - O_2$, the contract curve, joins all such points. (Modified from Lancaster 1974, which explains this in more detail.)

seems likely to increase as various kinds of computer database are brought to bear on it.

Despite the collapse of some traditional operators in the mail order market (e.g., Arsenal in France), many successful new retail firms of the past decade or two have made mail order an essential part of their business (e.g., Habitat and Mothercare in the United Kingdom). Little attention has been paid to this form of trade, however, either by economists, psychologists, or consumer scientists. There has been more interest in direct trade between individuals, mainly because it raises the possibility of bargaining. This is a topic that has been studied in considerable depth.

Economists have given much attention to the rational resolution of bargaining situations, perhaps because the mathematics of the question are complex but ultimately elegant. The simplest analytical tool is the two-person "Edgeworth box" illustrated in Figure 7.1. The opposite corners, O_1 and O_2, represent the maximum attainable utilities for two bargainers in the situation. The bargain is struck on some point on the "contract curve" $O_1 - O_2$, along which the two sets of indifference curves meet each other at tangents (for a full yet clear explanation, see Lancaster 1974, pp. 249–53).

An interesting recent development is the attempt to submit the pure economic theory of bargaining behavior to experimental study. V.L. Smith and colleagues (e.g., Smith 1976) carried out a series of experiments inspired by the classic Edgeworth box approach. Not surprisingly, they find that real people do not bargain according to the textbooks, though economists are not easy to persuade that this matters (e.g., Cross 1980; Stafford 1980). Social psychologists have also been very interested in the bargaining situation (e.g., Miller & Crandall 1980), and there have been serious attempts to bring this experimental literature to bear on the real economic bargaining in wage negotiation. But the buying context has been largely ignored, and obviously deserves more attention in the future.

Choice of a shopping area

Despite the importance of direct trading, the great majority of purchases are made in shops or stores of one sort or another. Shopping involves the next two stages of the decision chain laid out at the beginning of the chapter: choosing an area or center in which to shop and choosing a shop to enter. Sometimes these two decisions will not be separated. A decision to use a highly specialized shop may force a decision to visit the only shopping center where it is to be found. Conversely, for rural consumers, a decision to shop in the nearby village rather than traveling to town may entail a decision to enter the one and only village store. Taking a world-wide view, most of consumers may well be in this latter situation. But the majority of studies are of urban, Western shopping, where consumers do have a choice as to where they can shop.

The obvious factors that should influence the attractiveness of a shopping center are its size and its distance (or, more precisely, the travel time to it). The actual tendency to visit any given shopping area will presumably also depend on what competing attractions there are in the vicinity. These are precisely the factors that influence the gravitational effect physical objects have on one another, so it is therefore no surprise that several "gravitational" models of shopping have been developed, asserting that the "pull" of a shopping center will be a direct function of its size and an inverse function of the travel time to it. Some of these models have been quite successful (e.g., Brunner & Mason 1970; Huff 1962; and Hubbard 1978–9, provide a useful review). The most interesting thing about them, however, is how closely they resemble models of quite different kinds of choice. Huff's model, for example, which deals reasonably well with data on the relative attractiveness of two centers for consumers setting out to buy upholstery or furniture, is very similar in its mathematical form to Herrnstein's (1961, 1970) matching law, which was developed to deal with pigeons' choices between schedules of reinforcement in Skinner boxes (see Chapter 5; see also Graft, Lea, & Whitworth 1977).

Clearly, the replacement of distance by travel time is essential if gravitational models are not to be disrupted by geographical eccentricities. For example, Cox and Cooke (1970) report a case in which travel times gave reasonably good predictions of choices between shopping centers, but crude distances did not (the study area, around Cleveland, Ohio, included Lake Erie). But the social and psychological environment also distorts any simple gravitational pattern. MacKay and Olshavsky (1975–6) argue for the use of subjective ("cognitive") maps, not objective ones, to estimate distances, but there are also more directly predictable distortions. An example is "Brennan's Law" of retail patronage: People are far more likely to travel toward the center of a town to shop than around its periphery or away from the center, even when the kind of shop they are wanting on their current trip is readily available in any direction (Brennan 1948; Lee 1962). The law has no clear explanation in terms of rationality, but it would be an obvious consequence of habit formation. The town center, with its greater range of shops, is likely to be the dominant and therefore the most frequently reinforced destination for shopping trips, so that a person will tend to direct trips there out of habit even when it is not the objectively preferable destination. Similarly, Dickinson (1982–3) argues that people will develop habits of normal (nonshopping) travel that take them past shops that offer good value.

Choice of a shop

Simple rationality considerations would suggest that, once the items to be bought are known and an area or center for shopping has been chosen, the choice of which shop to enter should be made on the basis of a simple function of prices and travel costs (if any). More sophisticated rationality techniques use ideas about the different costs of time to people in different economic circumstances (Becker 1965) and the cost of obtaining details of current prices (the "economics of information": Much of the literature we considered above under prepurchase processes is concerned with choice between shops). These approaches would predict individual and class differences in shop choice; that is, wealthier and busier people would pay (by tolerating higher prices) to use more convenient shops. Neither prediction is borne out as regards shop choice, even though higher-income consumers do buy different goods, as we shall see later in this chapter.

In fact, it seems that shop choice is a function of habits and social factors as much as "economic" variables. A study by Reynaud and his collaborators (reported by Reynaud 1981, chapter 7) showed that prices for identical merchandise varied greatly between nearby shops in each of several European cities. Reynaud points out that, had the consumers been simply "rational," the more expensive retailers could not have survived, since everyone would have deserted them in favor of cheaper competitors. In this study there was no obvious or consistent relationship between the socioeconomic nature of the neighborhood and the prices in force there. But in other studies, shops in poor areas have been found to charge more for lower-quality goods, particularly through the provision of more expensive credit arrangements (Andreasen 1975; Caplovitz 1967; Frank, Massy, & Lodahl 1969 provide some conflicting data).

Consumers are often unable to recall the exact price of goods they have bought in a shop they have just left (e.g., Brown 1971; Gabor & Granger 1961), so it would be no surprise if small price variations escaped buyers' notice. The range of prices reported by Reynaud is considerably greater than can be accounted for in this way, however. Nor can the economics of information be called to the rescue. Goldman (1977–8), in a careful study of where Jerusalem housewives did their shopping for furniture, clothing, and shoes, found class and income differences, but these were more in the nature of subcultural variations in opinions and knowledge as to where the best value was to be had than a reflection of the greater cost of "shopping around" to a higher-income consumer. With more frequently purchased, but still relatively expensive items (meat products), however, Goldman (1977) did find that lower-income consumers were more knowledgeable about the prices available in different kinds of retail outlets. This is what one might expect from the economics of information, since a person whose earning capacity is lower loses less by spending time shopping around.

But further evidence against the economics of information approach comes from a study by Goldman and Johansson (1978–9). They studied the gasoline-buying behavior of a panel of 500 families. Although there was considerable variation in the amount of search carried out, and more extended search did lead to a lower average price, the amount of search was not correlated with any measure of the cost of time (e.g., income, wife's employment status) or the value of information (e.g., quantity purchased) to the household.

Other studies support the idea that social class differences affect shop choice, over and above any effect of the income differences with which they are obviously correlated. Large department store chains have (and cultivate) "images," to the extent that poor people declare that they would not feel "comfortable" shopping in the most up-market stores even if they have not actually tried those stores (e.g., Wingate 1958; Dornoff & Tatham 1972). In other words, habits and attitudes play a large role in shop choice (in the light of the data on attitudes and buying discussed above, we may suspect that attitudes will include some after-the-fact rationalizations of habits).

From the consumer's point of view, it may well be good strategy for habit to govern shop choice. People buy a wide range of immediate consumption goods, and, especially in times of continuing inflation, it is not practicable to remember the prices of all of them. Perhaps it is better simply to return to a shop at which the total cost of a previous shopping expedition, consciously or subconsciously, seemed "reasonable," rather than spending a great deal of time trying to compare advertized prices or flitting from shop to shop to get each item at the lowest possible price. Naturally such dependence on habit is readily exploited by marketers, so as a permanent strategy it is certainly shortsighted. Nonetheless "store loyalty" probably plays a major role in choice of shops (e.g., Goldman 1977–8).

Behavior in shops

Substantial research efforts have been devoted to studying the behavior of people in shops, particularly supermarkets. The questions posed usually have obvious practical implications; for example, What is the effect of point-of-sale advertising? What is the effect of the layout of goods on the shelves on purchasing? What induces "impulse buying," by which we mean any purchase that was not intended when the customer entered the shop? The commercial importance of these questions is sufficient to explain the attention that has been given to them. It also makes one suspect that the generally low quality of published research results in this area may not be an accurate guide to what has been acheived.

The published results are occasionally interesting; for example, overweight consumers are more likely to impulse-buy food items in response to samples (Steinberg & Yalch 1978), but mostly they are obvious or even trivial. Goods tend to be bought more when displayed at eye level (although floor level is better for very heavy items, for example, a 54-ounce pack of fruit juice) or for sweets bought mainly on the promptings of children (Colonial Study 1964). Often the results are not consistent from one product to another or from one supermarket to another. For example, Engel, Kollat, and Blackwell (1972, p. 479) could not draw any general conclusion from a series of five well-controlled experiments on the relationship between sales and the number of rows of a product exposed on the supermarket shelves. Yet the possibilities of research on behavior in shops are genuinely interesting. The stylized spatial layout of most supermarkets makes them an obvious arena for studying the way people respond to and use space; Sommer and Aitkens (1982–3) showed that recall of the location of goods in supermarkets was usually best for the peripheral aisles. The way the goods are laid out is also of considerable psychological interest. Moles (1972) considers the layout of an idealized "Universal Store" in which every possible object would be offered for sale, and uses this as a metaphor for our understanding and categorization of objects generally. Clearly, real store layouts must reflect both assumptions and data about the way in which people categorize objects.

Such categorization is part of the problem of "semantic memory," which has recently been a very active field of psychological research (e.g., Collins & Quillian 1969; Rosch & Mervis 1975).

Most fundamentally, the array of goods on sale in a supermarket is a realization of the economist's idealized consumer's choice: an almost infinite range of commodity bundles simultaneously available, subject only to a budget constraint. It is disappointing that the published data on behavior in shops provide little help in making a detailed test of choice theories.

Another kind of behavior that occurs in shops is bargaining. This has attracted considerable theoretical and empirical interest. It might be thought that bargaining had disappeared from modern life except for transactions between individuals, but this is far from true. In industrial buying, it is probably sound policy for a firm to assume that there is no such thing as a list price (cf. Radke 1972). Industrial buying strategies are outside the scope of this book, although they have been discussed by economic psychologists and marketing scientists (e.g., Reynaud 1981, chapter 5; Wilson 1977). But for relatively large items, there is the potential for some haggling even in the consumer sector. Car sales, for example, frequently involve substantial discounts, sometimes given under polite disguises (unrealistic part exchange deals, allowances for not making a part exchange, "free" optional items, and so forth). These have to be bargained for. Although the dealer usually has the advantage in such bargaining (Crafton & Hoffer 1980–1), it remains an important component of the price-fixing process (Pennington 1968). Bargaining has been investigated in the field by Cialdini, Bickman, and Cacioppo (1979), who demonstrated that a tough initial stance by a car purchaser led to a better price being offered by the salesman. Rejecting the price offered for car A led to a final offer on car B that was roughly $150 lower than in the control conditions, where there was no initial bargaining or an acceptance of the price offered on car A.

Conclusions from shop-choice studies

The study of shopping reinforces the conclusions we drew from our consideration of what people buy. An analysis of shopping behavior seems to involve a mixture of two psychological themes: social processes, such as the class images formed and encouraged by stores, and basic choice theories, such as gravitational attraction or Brennan's law. We find the same mixture persisting as we consider the quantities of goods that are bought.

QUANTITY OF GOODS BOUGHT

The theory relating the quantity of a commodity that will be bought to its own price, to prices of other goods, and to the consumers' incomes, is, of course, the classic business of microeconomics in general and the theory of demand in particular (see Chapter 2). The area, however, is one that also lends itself to empirical study within psychology. Comparisons between different kinds of theory and different kinds of data in this area have, in fact, been relatively numerous in economic psychology. A number of detailed and technical reviews are available (e.g., Allison 1979, 1981; Hursh 1980; Kagel, Battalio, Rachlin, & Green 1980; Lea 1978, 1981), all supporting the conclusion that there are many points of contact between the microeconomic approach and experimental work in psychology.

In discussing these data, we need to recall some basic concepts from Chapter 2. Demand curves (functions relating quantity purchased to price) and Engel curves (functions relating quantity purchased to income) will obviously be useful in describing empirical data relating to the quantities of goods purchased. We must also bear in mind the difference between income-compensated and uncompensated demand curve: In the former case, the consumer's income is adjusted to allow for the "income effect" of a price change, that is, the change in the consumer's real income resulting from a change in prices. For descriptive purposes, we shall make use of the own-price and cross-price elasticities of demand, so it is worth repeating the definition of elasticity here. For any function y of a variable x, elasticity is defined as

$$\text{elasticity } \eta = \frac{d_{y/y}}{d_{x/x}} \qquad (7.2)$$

Because elasticity is dimensionless, it is independent of all units of measurement; thus it is useful for comparing data involving different commodities and different currencies. The slopes of curves plotted on log-log coordinates (i.e., with the scales of both axes transformed by logarithmic functions) equal their elasticity.

A final key concept is substitutability, that is, the extent to which one commodity will take the place of another that has become unavailable or expensive. In Chapter 2, we introduced Lancaster's distinction between efficiency and personal substitution, which takes into account the fact that different goods may contain overlapping sets of characteristics. We shall see that substitutability is readily investigated by psychological methods.

In its pure form, the microeconomic theory of demand makes remarkably few predictions. All it says for certain is that income-compensated demand curves will be downward sloping (i.e., will have negative elasticity). This section is not designed to test this prediction, or to test the theory as a whole. What the theory gives us, however, is a vocabulary with which we can discuss the empirical effects of price on demand.

Empirical study of demand

Given the wealth of data on demand, it is surprising that most economics textbooks, with a few exceptions (e.g., Dorfman 1978; Hirshleifer 1984; Lancaster 1974), contain only hypothetical demand curves that bear little

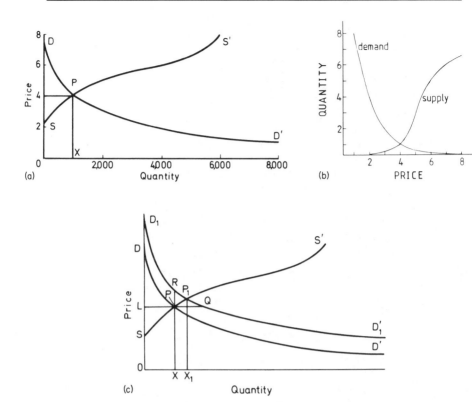

7.2. Textbook demand curves. The curve in (a) is based on the plausible-looking "demand-schedule" shown in (b). Note the smooth, flowing curve, and the assumption that a change in conditions will lead to a simple increase in demand at all prices (c). Note that these curves are plotted according to economists' conventions, with quantity treated as the independent variable. (Based on Cairncross, 1973, diagrams 14.1 and 14.2 and table 14.1.)

resemblance to the real thing. Figure 7.2 shows a sample of such "textbook" demand curves. By way of contrast, we shall now consider five different techniques for obtaining real demand curves, and the data they produce.

1. *Experimental manipulations of prices of individual commodities in shops.* Studies of this sort have usually been carried out by consumer or marketing scientists. Doyle and Gidengil (1977) provide a caustic summary, pointing out that there has been very little improvement in technique since the exploratory studies of Whitman (1942), and that the experiments usually stop just at the point of demonstrating the viability of the technique, rather than going on to provide data that are interesting in

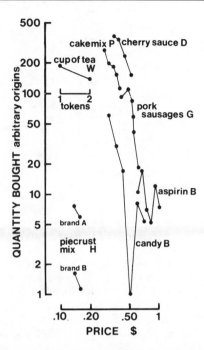

7.3. Demand functions from retailing experiments, collected by Lea (1978). The curves are appropriately positioned on the price axis but placed arbitrarily on the quantity axis, with the two curves for piecrust mix in the correct relative positions.

their own right. Figure 7.3 shows some of the more usable data from such studies, plotted in the form of own-price demand curves. The erratic nature of some of the data, and the miscellaneous collection of commodities involved, lend weight to Doyle and Gidengil's opinion. Nonetheless, these data are by no means useless, as we shall see below.

2. *Statistical studies of the effects of naturally occurring price changes, usually on the quantities bought in an entire economy.* This is the business of econometrics – empirical quantitative economics. Some economic psychologists such as Reynaud (see Albou 1982) have regarded econometrics as a quagmire from which we should keep the greatest possible distance. In our view, however, econometrics is our best single source of data, because econometric studies have obtained exhaustive sets of demand curves for whole sectors of the economy (e.g., Schultz 1938; Stone 1954b).

In using econometric data, however, it must be understood that the studies are, essentially and irrevocably, statistical. The primary data are "spontaneous" variations in prices and quantities purchased, which are produced by outside forces that ought, if possible, to be identified, but may remain inscrutable. In order to derive demand curves from these

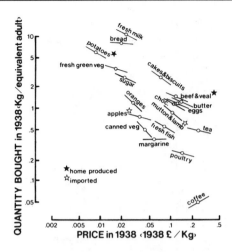

7.4. Demand data for several types of food in the United Kingdom between 1920 and 1938, as obtained by Stone (1954b). The points show mean price and consumption in 1938, and the lines drawn through them show the elasticity of demand for the whole period. (From Lea 1978.)

data, a functional form is chosen; the best-fitting demand curve of that particular type is then found by regression techniques, often quite complex ones. It follows that econometric demand curves build in a considerable structure of assumptions, and that they are susceptible to biases from sampling methods and from statistical procedures. But this does not prevent them from yielding useful information, especially when we have a body of data produced by essentially uniform methods. In such cases, demand curves for different commodites can be compared and generalizations sought.

There are two ways in which we can derive demand curves from market data. The first is the "single equation" technique, in which a demand curve for a single commodity or commodity group is fitted to data on its own price and those of other commodities, which are thought, on a priori or empirical grounds, to interact with it in the market. The second is to fit a "demand system," in which demand for all the commodities in the economy is fitted to the vector composed of all their prices. This better technique obviously requires much more elaborate computation, and the commodities have to be grouped into a fairly small number of categories. The technique, however, does have the advantage that theoretically necessary relationships (e.g., that the total spent on all commodities must equal the total of consumers' incomes) can be used to constrain the solutions found. Each technique is useful for different purposes, but it is easier to present the results of single-equation analyses. By way of example, Figure 7.4 shows a collection of data on the demand for food, from Stone's study of the U.K. economy during the period 1920–38.

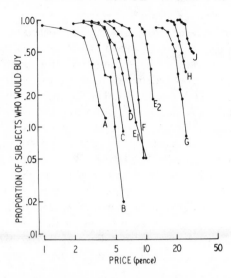

7.5. Buy–response curves for ten food commodities, obtained by the method of Gabor and Granger (1966). (From Lea 1978.)

3. *Studies of individual consumers.* These can take a number of forms. Gabor and his colleagues have strongly advocated the simple method of asking representative samples of consumers what they believe they would do in the face of hypothetical price changes (e.g., Gabor, Granger, & Sowter 1970). Although this method lacks face validity, and we may question the absolute accuracy of the demand curves it produces, this "buy-response" technique does seem to produce quite good relative or comparative data as shown by the fact that Gabor has made it the basis of a successful market research firm. Figure 7.5 shows demand curves derived from some of this firm's commercially commissioned studies. Sowter, Gabor, and Granger (1971) have used data like these to suggest a functional form to which demand curves might be fitted (this is discussed in more detail later in the present chapter). The validity of the "buy-response" method should not be taken for granted, however. Pitts, Willenborg, and Sherrell (1981–2) asked a panel of households to report their car ownership and mileages over a period during which gasoline prices were varying markedly. Buy-response measures of price sensitivity were also taken. Pitts et al. found no differences in measured price sensitivity between households which did, or did not, reduce either their annual mileage or the size of the engine.

4. *Experimental manipulations of prices in artificial or experimental economies, such as hospital token economies:* Token economy studies can allow good experimental control in a setting where the whole economy is open

to study. In the first experiments, prices of single commodities were manipulated. For example, Winkler (1971) increased the price of a cup of tea in a hospital token economy from one to two tokens and observed a 26% drop in the number of cups consumed; not surprisingly, this basic commodity showed inelastic demand. Rather more surprisingly, Hayden, Osborne, Hall, and Hall (1974) doubled the price of cigarettes, and observed a more than 50% decline in cigarettes purchased, indicating elastic demand for a commodity that in every other kind of study responds inelastically to price changes. Subsequent token economy studies have become more sophisticated. They have looked at entire bundles of goods bought in order to see how purchasing responds to changes in the price(s) of one or more of them (e.g., Battalio, Kagel, Winkler, Fisher, Basmann, & Krasner 1973). Because of their mathematical sophistication, the results of these studies are not easy to summarize, except to say that in general the predictions of economic demand theory have been upheld. Given the rather weak nature of those predictions, however, this is not surprising.

5. *Studies of laboratory animals.* Large quantities of data are available from experiments where animals lived in operant conditioning apparatus (Skinner boxes) and had to obtain all their food, or some other commodity, by pressing levers, etc., on fixed-ratio schedules of reinforcement. It will be recalled from Chapter 1 that, on a fixed-ratio schedule, an animal must "earn" each reward by making a fixed number of responses. If the fixed ratio is varied, the amount of work the subject has to do to gain each unit of food varies correspondingly. In effect, a change in the ratio changes the price of food. If the amount of food eaten is recorded, we can plot a demand curve (most of these data were gathered by psychologists with no thought of economics in their minds, however). Several collections of such data have been published (e.g., Allison 1981; Hogan & Roper 1978; Hursh 1980; Lea 1978). Figure 7.6 reproduces one of these collections.

In addition to these experiments, a few psychologists have made deliberate studies of economic questions. An early topic was the effect on demand of the availability and price of substitutes. Figure 7.7 shows data from experiments by Kagel, Battalio, Rachlin, Green, Basmann, and Klemm (1975) and Kagel, Battalio, Rachlin, and Green (1981) (as reported by Kagel, Battalio, Green, & Rachlin 1980), and by Lea and Roper (1977). All these experiments used rats and showed that the better and cheaper the available substitutes, the more elastic the demand for foodstuffs.

Recent work has become even more sophisticated. Figure 7.8 shows data from Kagel, Battalio, Rachlin, and Green (1981), which indicate that income-compensation (changing the consumer's income after a price change so that he or she can still buy the same combination of goods as

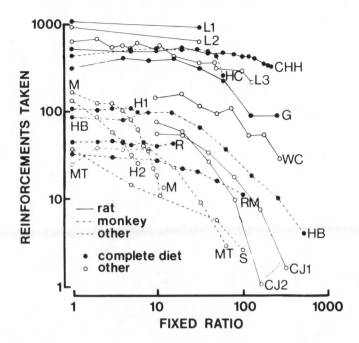

7.6. Demand curves from psychological experiments on animals. (Compiled by Lea 1978.)

before) makes demand curves more elastic. This is precisely in accordance with the predictions of demand theory. Hursh and Natelson (1981) used the difference in rats' elasticity of demand for food rewards and reward by direct electrical stimulation of the brain as evidence that the two rewards were not equivalent.

There are obvious problems of face validity in using rats or pigeons as a source of data on demand. But not all the objections raised against such studies are valid. Often the objections depend on confusion about the meaning of rationality (see Chapter 5 as well as Lea 1981). And there are some compensating advantages of using nonhuman animals in research. First, in contrast to many laboratory experiments using human subjects, the "consumers" are engaged in real-life (one might even say life-or-death) choices. Second, prices can be varied over very large ranges; factors of 1,000 or more are perfectly practicable.

7.7. Effects of substitutes on elasticity of demand. (a) Mean demand curves for six rats working for food, with no substitute (*EC*), a different kind of food (*S*), or another source of the same food (*MD*) available. (From Lea & Roper 1977.) (b) Four individual demand curves for rats in different two-choice situations. (From Kagel et al. 1980; note that price is plotted as a function of quantity.) In both cases, the availability of closer substitutes leads to more elastic demand.

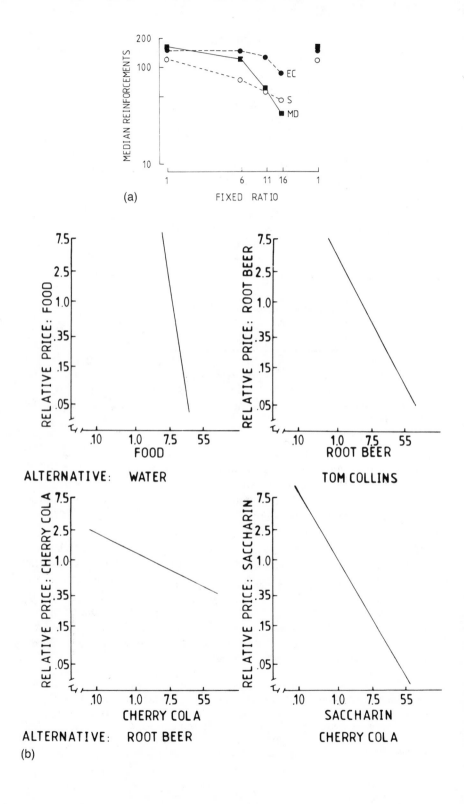

(a)

(b)

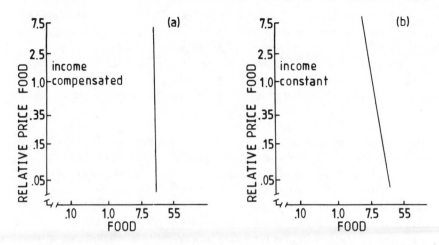

7.8. Effect of income compensation on demand curves. Both curves show the effect of a change in the price of food on the amount of it that a single rat (a different rat for each curve) ate. (a) The price change was "income compensated," that is, the total number of responses the rat was allowed to make per day was adjusted so that exactly the same amounts of food and water (the alternative commodity, whose price was not changed) could be purchased as before the change in the price of food. (b) The total number of responses allowed was unchanged. Income compensation leads to a more elastic demand. (Note that quantity is plotted as the independent variable, so that steeper slope implies lower elasticity. (From Kagel et al. 1980.)

Effects of price on demand: empirical generalizations

As a survey of Figures 7.2–7.7 shows, the results of these various research tecniques are by no means identical. Nonetheless, they fit into a number of coherent patterns.

1. *The "Giffen case."* As we noted in Chapter 2, economic demand theory does allow for a demand curve to be upward sloping (consumption rising with price increases), if the commodity concerned is essential and takes up a large proportion of consumers' resources. Empirically, this so-called Giffen case seems to be rare or nonexistent. The data we show do include very few cases of positive own-price elasticity of demand (e.g., for coffee in Stone's data, shown in Fig. 7.3). It must be said, however, that econometric techniques often demand auxiliary assumptions before demand curves can be fitted. If the effect of income on demand is removed statistically, presumably no Giffen cases would be reported, because they can arise only from the summation of the income and substitution effects of a price change (cf. Chapter 2). Also, econometricians sometimes specifically reject analyses that yield negative own-price elasticities of demand, using this

as a filtering device to help choose among equally plausible sets of assumptions. Thus the absence of Giffen cases could be, in part at least, artifactual. Claims for the existence of Giffen cases do occur, however. For example, Bardhan (1969) observed that in Indian peasant communities aggregate demand for food grains increased with price, and argued that this is a Giffen phenomenon resulting from the fact that the consumers are also suppliers.

2. *Specificity increases elasticity (across techniques).* Studies that look at more specific commodities show much more elastic demand than studies that consider more generally defined products. This is what we should expect from the results of experiments on making substitutes available (see Fig. 7.5). Thus the interview techniques, and consumer behavior experiments in shops (Figs. 7.1 and 7.4) often give elasticities in the range −5 to −10; animal studies and econometric surveys more often find elasticities in the range 0 to −2. It is easy to understand this. A change in the price of a given brand of chocolate bar in a given shop is readily avoided by substituting another brand or another shop; a change in the "price" (in lever presses) of a rat's only source of food, or a change in the price of potatoes throughout a nation's economy, offers much less scope for substitution.

3. *Specificity and elasticity (within a technique).* Within a single research technique, the effect of product specificity on elasticity of demand is less obvious. For example, in Stone's data shown in Figure 7.3, demand for "all food" is no less elastic than demand for many individual foods. It can be shown mathematically that the elasticity of demand for a generic commodity is a function of the own-price elasiticities of all the goods in the set, together with all the cross-price elasticities between them. The general empirical trend implies that, within the groups into which we commonly draw commodities, there are complementary goods that provide negative cross-price elasticities, balancing the positive ones contributed by substitutes.

4. *Elasticity of demand varies with price.* Wherever measurement technique allows them to appear, changes in elasticity of demand for a given commodity, as a function of changes in price, are common. In particular, demand tends to become more elastic as prices increase. An extreme case of this is where elasticity becomes positive at very low prices, i.e., demand falls off when price is below a certain level. This has been demonstrated only in interview studies (e.g., Adam 1958; Gabor & Granger 1966), although analogous phenomena exist in some animal experiments done for noneconomic purposes (e.g., Mazur 1975). In interview studies, positive elasticity is usually attributed to the "price-quality effect." This effect has been demonstrated experimentally. When consumers are asked to make judgments of quality, consumers will often report as better the

one of two identical samples that bears the higher price tag (Leavitt 1954), at least for some groups of consumers (Etgar & Malhotra 1981–2), or where all other indices of quality are lacking (Jacoby, Olson, & Haddock 1971).

5. *Cross-price elasticities.* Between closely related commodities, cross-price elasticities are commonly high, and, as noted above, may be positive or negative. They are difficult to summarize graphically, which is why we have not shown any examples. One important point to note is that they are not necessarily symmetrical. Thus, in most countries, changes in the price of beer do not greatly affect demand for wine (which is both more expensive and of higher status), while wine prices do affect consumption of beer. Econometric studies using systems of demand equations which have to aggregate commodities into quite broad groups have commonly found quite substantial cross-price elasticities even between these groups.

Effects of price on demand: theory

The quantity and quality of data available on the effects of price on demand suggest that this is a good area for testing theories about the origins of economic behavior. Clearly, most of the generalizations reported above are consistent with the microeconomic theory based on rationality. But, as we have seen, that theory predicts little except that own-price demand curves will generally be downward sloping, and we have found more consistency in the data than that simple fact (e.g., the consistencies in the range of elasticities found with particular techniques, the general absence of Giffen cases). Can we find any alternative or extended theory of demand that could account for these data more fully? There are at least five approaches that deserve serious consideration. Three derive from psychological studies of noneconomic choices, and the other two from econometric research. Let us consider these approaches in turn.

1. *Herrnstein's matching law:* The psychological theory of choice with most empirical support, at least within its chosen sphere of application, is probably the matching law proposed by Herrnstein (1961, 1970; see also Chapters 1 and 5). Recall that Herrnstein studied pigeons who were exposed to two concurrently available reinforcement schedules and found that the ratio of response rates on the two schedules was approximately equal to (i.e., it matched) the ratio of the observed (not programmed) rates at which food rewards were delivered. Using symbols, the matching law is expressed as:

$$\frac{b_1}{b_2} = \frac{r_1}{r_2} \qquad\qquad (7.3)$$

where b_1 and b_2 are rates of behavior and r_1 and r_2 are observed rates of reinforcement (it is important to remember that all these rates are taken per unit time rather than per response). This simple matching law has been extended in a number of directions by different authors. Herrnstein (1970) himself suggested that it could be derived from a more fundamental relation between response rate and reinforcement rate for any single instrumental response:

$$b_i = \frac{kr_i}{(r_0 + r_i + \Sigma_j r_j)} \qquad (7.4)$$

where k and r_0 are empirically determined constants. To apply Equation 7.4 to buying behavior, we have to suppose that r_i, the observed reinforcement rate, corresponds to the rate of purchasing some commodity, and b_i, the instrumental response rate, corresponds to the rate of spending money on it, so that its price, p_i, is given by b_i/r_i. These assumptions are natural ones, and we have already, in effect, made use of them in plotting Figure 7.5 as demand curves derived from animal data. But with these assumptions, we can show that Equation 7.3 makes one definitely wrong prediction. If only one commodity is available, the quantity $(\Sigma_j r_j)$ will be zero. In this case, simple algebra shows that the demand curve should follow the equation:

$$q = \frac{k}{p - r_0} \qquad (7.5)$$

This implies an own-price elasticity of demand, η, given by

$$\eta = \frac{-k}{k - pr_0} \qquad (7.6)$$

With this equation, η can never be more than -1; that is, demand must always be elastic. A glance at Figures 7.2–7.7 shows that this is wrong. Many of the data in those figures came from procedures whereby the assumption of a single source of a reinforcer was, to a good approximation, true.

Other authorities have extended the simple matching law (Eq. 7.3) in different ways. Rachlin, Kagel, and Battalio (1981) noted that the matching law had been developed to deal with choices between different sources of a single reinforcer, whereas real economic choices are usually between different goods that are rarely perfect substitutes. Rachlin and co-workers tried to deal with variations in substitutability by using a variant of the matching law suggested by Baum (1974), according to which

$$\frac{b_1}{b_2} = a\left(\frac{r_1}{r_2}\right)^s \qquad (7.7)$$

where a and s are constants. As Rachlin et al. showed, the gross facts of substitutability can be handled by allowing the exponent s to take different values. If $s = 1$, the two reinforcers are perfect substitutes and we have simple matching; if $s = 0$, demand for the goods will be completely independent; and if $b < 0$, the goods will be complements – increasing the price of one will decrease demand for the alternative. There are two problems with this interesting and stimulating suggestion. In the first place, it is not easy to derive equations for demand curves or elasticities from it. Second, it treats substitutabilities as completely symmetrical. As we have already mentioned, this is not consistent with the data. The price of wine affects demand for beer but not vice versa, and so forth. The model used by Rachlin and co-workers cannot accommodate such asymmetries.

3. *Allison's conservation principle:* A second psychological model has been developed precisely to deal with the kind of data plotted in Figure 7.6. Allison (1976, 1979, 1983) proposes a so-called conservation model, according to which (retaining the same symbols as in the previous paragraph):

$$b + Ar = K \tag{7.8}$$

where A and K are two new constants. Allison's idea is that both the instrumental response and the reinforcer contribute something, in different proportions as measured by the constant A, to some underlying quantity (we might suggest utility), and that the subject responds in such a way as to keep this quantity constant. This may seem like an odd suggestion in the economic context, where b signifies the rate of spending money, but it makes good sense in its original field of application, which was to explain experiments in which b and r were the rates of two behaviors, both potentially valuable to the organism (e.g., Mazur 1975; Premack 1965, 1971). Oddly based or not, the conservation model makes quite accurate predictions for economic data (Allison 1979, 1981). Substituting the definition of price ($p = b/r$) into Equation 7.8, we obtain the following equation for a demand curve:

$$r = \frac{k}{(p + A)} \tag{7.9}$$

This equation predicts an elasticity of demand that is zero at some very low price and steadily becomes more negative as price increases, which agrees very well with the data shown in Figures 7.2–7.8. However, no matter how high price becomes, Equation 7.8 can never predict an elasticity of less than -1; that is, it does not allow for strongly elastic demand. Although this is a fair description of the animal demand curves of Figure 7.5, it fails when applied to the consumer behavior or econometric data (Figs. 7.2 and 7.3). What is wrong with Allison's model is that it does not allow for the possibility that the underlying, that is, the conserved, quantity can be obtained from more than one source. That is no problem in the animal experiments where no alternatives were available, but it is critically important in the real economy. Exactly how the model should be extended to take this possibility into account is still under discussion (Allison 1983; Lea 1981, 1983). Allison's model, therefore, is promising but not yet satisfactory.

3. *The law of comparative judgment:* Herrnstein's matching law is one variant of a very general approach to the psychological study of individual choice; that is, Luce's (1959) choice axiom. Mathematical psychologists (e.g., Laming 1973) regard the choice axiom as one of two possible broad approaches to the study of preference. The alternative, first discussed in detail by Thurstone (1927), is the *Law of Comparative Judgement.* Thurstone supposed that any object would give rise to an inherently variable psychological effect. If the objects are goods, or rewards, their effects should be measured on a scale of utility. Usually, the utility effect of a preferable object, or a larger amount of a good, or a cheaper price, will be greater than that of a less preferable object, a smaller amount, or a higher price. But because psychological effects are always variable, Thurstone argues that choice will always be somewhat stochastic.

Sowter, Gabor, and Granger (1971) used Thurstone's principle to derive a theoretical equation for demand in the situation in which two closely similar brands are available at different prices. Their demand equation is awkward to state algebraically, since it involves inverse normal distribution functions, so let us simply consider some of its qualitative predictions. First, it is able to deal with the fact that demand sometimes declines when prices are very low (the price–quality effect). Second, it provides the theoretical basis for the buy–response method, by which the interview demand curves plotted in Figure 7.4 were obtained. It is thus certainly a fruitful concept. Lea and Roper (1977) claimed that the equation did not fit their data from an experiment on rats' choices between sugar and mixed diet, but theirs is the only experimental test of the model and it is not an adequate basis for dismissing it. The most significant criticism of this model is, in fact, the lack of general application. And it is not obvious how the model can be brought to bear on, for example, the econometric data of Figure 7.3.

4. *Econometric models: the single equation approach.* All econometric work involves the selection of a functional form to fit to the data. The forms used for fitting the demand for single commodities are relatively simple to describe, although they are usually chosen for their statistical convenience (and their relatively good fit to the data) rather than on any theoretical grounds. The simplest is the log–log model, according to which, using the symbols above, with the addition of Y to represent income:

$$r_i = cy^y p_i^{a_i} p_j^{a_j} p_k^{a_k} \ldots \tag{7.10}$$

By taking logarithms, this can be written in a more convenient form:

$$\log r_l = \log c + y \log y + a_i \log p_i + a_j \log p_j + a_k \log p_k \quad (7.11)$$

It has the very useful property that the constants a_i, a_j, and so forth are the own-price and cross-price elasticities of demand. This property is also the equation's weakness, since, as we have already seen, elasticities often are not constant. The alternative log-linear form is often used, therefore, according to which the logarithm of demand is a linear function of prices and incomes.

5. *Econometric analysis: demand systems*. The more recent econometric approaches, in which an attempt is made to model the entire system of interacting demands within the economy, have a stronger theoretical content. The first model of this kind was developed by Stone (1954a) and is commonly referred to as the Stone-Rowe linear expenditure system. More recent developments include the Rotterdam model of Theil (1965), the translog model proposed by Christensen, Jorgenson, and Lau (1975), and the Almost Ideal Demand System of Deaton and Muellbauer (1980a, 1980b). The details of these systems, and the differences between them, are beyond the scope of this book, but it is worth noting some of the theoretical assumptions which they either incorporate or allow to be tested. These include a separation of demand for a commodity into a "subsistence level intake," unaffected by prices, and additional intake; the "adding-up" assumption, that all demands taken together will use up all income; homogeneity, which implies that if all prices change in the same proportion, the pattern of demand will be unchanged; and symmetry, which implies that the effects of the prices of any two goods on demand for each other will be the same. We have already seen that symmetry is sometimes violated; Deaton and Muellbauer (1980a) also argue that, where the analysis does not assume that homogeneity holds, the data consistently contradict it.

Effects of income on demand

Economic theory expects demand to be a function of income as well as prices. Almost all data confirm this prediction. Recall that the function relating the quantity of a good purchased to income is called its Engel curve. Such curves can be obtained from expenditure surveys and from econometric data; in fact, as we saw above, any econometric study of price effects must include a study of income effects to avoid confounding. Engel curves have also been obtained from token economies and animal experiments.

All sources of data confirm that demand does vary with income, and all have yielded many examples of normal goods (for which consumption increases with income), and a few of inferior goods (consumption falls as income rises). Normal goods include both necessities (on which expenditure as a proportion of income falls as income rises) and luxuries (proportional expenditure rises with income). The property of being normal or superior, or a necessity or a luxury, is relative to particular times and circumstances. For example, econometric data obtained by Kilby (1965) show that bread, which is an inferior good in Europe and North America, is a normal good in West Africa, where it is an expensive, status-conferring substitute for local staples such as millet. In a token economy, Winkler (1971) demonstrated that a decreasing proportion of income was spent on meals as token income rose, while an increasing proportion was spent on cigarettes; meals functioned as necessities, cigarettes as luxuries.

The theory of the economics of information, which we discussed above in connection wi h prepurchase commodities and shop choice, makes clear predictions about what kinds of goods should be particularly susceptible to income changes. The higher a person's income, the greater the cost of his or her time, and so the greater the value of time-saving goods. Survey studies have shown that higher-income consumers do buy more of goods such as disposable diapers and meals outside the home (Nickols & Fox 1983–4; Strober & Weinberg 1977–8; Weinberg & Winer 1983–4). Unfortunately, these studies have repeatedly failed to confirm two other predictions of the economics of information: There is no evidence that time-saving goods are more income-elastic than other comparable goods or that they are disproportionately bought by households that are time-poor because both husband and wife are employed.

Social effects on demand

From time to time, psychologically or sociologically oriented economists have suggested that factors other than prices or incomes might affect demand, or that these factors might affect buying in quite a-rational ways. The most famous proposal is Veblen's (1899/1979). Veblen held that there is a general tendency for "conspicuous consumption," wherein wealthy individuals buy expensive goods just because they are expensive, in order to display their wealth. Leibenstein (1950) showed that conspicuous consumption could play havoc with the conventional analysis of demand. He proposed two additional social effects: the "bandwagon" effect, in which consumers want to buy whatever is being widely bought, and its opposite, the "snob" effect. These have, if anything, more disastrous implications for microeconomic theory and econometric practice than the Veblen effect. Lea (1980) completed the picture by proposing a "counter-Veblen" effect in which consumers bought cheaper items than they needed in order to avoid ostentation, or, as Brooks (1981) suggests, because "the most effective status-seeking style is to make a mockery of status seeking"; conspicuous nonconsumption, perhaps.

Although there has been a little more theoretical work on these social effects on demand (e.g., Kalman 1968), almost no empirical work has been done. Mason (1981), in a recent survey of conspicuous consumption, relied almost entirely on the same kinds of nonexperimental (although highly plausible) analyses of history, society, and behavior that Veblen himself used. The social meanings of consumption have been discussed (e.g., Solomon, 1983–4), and it has been shown empirically that goods serve as reliable indices of status. The distinctions involved are learned quite early in life (by age 12: Belk, Bahn, & Mayer 1982–3), although they may not be stable over time (Felson 1976). This is an obvious field for further investigation by economic psychologists. The one well-researched phenomenon that does comply with Veblen's analysis is the price-quality effect. In addition, Lea (1980) produced some very preliminary data suggesting a counter-Veblen effect in rats, and Verhallen (1982) recently described an effect of scarcity on demand that may point the way to a parallel empirical analysis of bandwagon and snob effects.

Bandwagon and Veblen effects offer one way of talking about one of the most obvious social effects on demand, namely fashion. Alternatively, one could use Lancaster's "characteristics" analysis, in which case being "in fashion" would be a characteristic that any commodity may possess, to a greater or less extent. Admittedly, fashion is a characteristic that is defined socially rather than physically; Lancaster (e.g., 1971, p. 7) argues that the characteristics must be kept objective. We shall return to this problem at the end of this chapter.

GOODS, PRODUCTS, BRANDS, AND CHARACTERISTICS

In our discussions so far, we have sometimes talked about general classes of goods (like "food") and sometimes about highly specific commodities (say, a box of a particular brand of breakfast cereal). We now need to be more precise about these different levels of description. In doing so, we shall find that we can move toward a discussion of the question that opened this chapter: Why do people buy what they do buy?

Goods, products, and brands

The "goods" of the economics textbook are broad, conceptually defined categories: buns or butter, cars or carrots, guns or gutters, watermelons or water supplies. With the exception of a few fresh foods, these are not what consumers buy. Rather, we buy commercially defined products: a 1-pound bag of Bird's Eye frozen peas, an 8.2-cubic-foot Hotpoint refrigerator with automatic defrost, etc. Somewhere between the abstract "goods" and the actual "brands" come the ideas of the "product" (frozen peas, automatic washing machines, family sedan cars) and the "product field" (convenience vegetables, kitchen durables, cars).

What differentiates these different levels of discourse is, clearly, the expected potentials for substitution between them. The distinctions are important to marketers because the potential for substitution creates the potential for competition. The distinctions are important to consumers, too, because the lack of potential substitutes means that we are confronted with monopoly power. But is the potential for substitution in fact translated into behavior? And can we discover any laws to describe the ways in which consumers respond to the substitutabilities of commodities? If we can answer these questions, we shall come close to an explanation of why people choose to buy one set of goods over another.

Brand uniqueness and brand loyalty

An obvious strategy for a marketer is to try to get consumers to think of an item as being not merely one brand of a more generally defined product, but a product in itself, with its own unique attributes. A variety of vaguely psychological techniques have been proposed for achieving this. The most discussed is giving the brand a distinct image, or, through advertizing or packaging, getting the brand name known. There is a clear and predictable relation between consumers' awareness of brands and the sales achieved (Muraz 1977; but see Ehrenberg 1972, for a contradictory view). Of course, the direction of causality here is uncertain. However, in laboratory buying simulations, Jacoby, Szybillo, and Busato-Schach (1976–7) found that consumers did less prepurchase information acquisition when brand names were available, and Bettman and Park (1980–1) showed that consumers with the most knowledge of a product field (microwave ovens) made most use of brand names. Clearly a successfully promoted brand name will be used by consumers.

The creation of brand names is clearly an attempt to influence consumers' judgment and behavior. It will succeed insofar as consumers use the brand names to organize the complex of information that constitutes a product field. This may or may not be in the consumer's interest. On the one hand, it may involve mere image creation in a product field where all the brands are effectively identical; it is hard to see how this can benefit the consumer. Alternatively, the brand may be made truly different (e.g., by technological advance). This is more likely to serve the consumer's interests, though even technological innovation may not create a better product, since some innovations are of low or zero value and merely obstruct useful standardization. However, the consumers' interests may coincide with the marketer's at a more subtle level: If the good in question has a predominantly social function, and snob effects are paramount, then functionless uniqueness may be just what the consumer needs (cf. Douglas & Isherwood 1979, chapter 5).

In the normal case, however, a clash of interests is inevitable. Who tends to win? Superficially, the marketers seem to be well ahead. Brand names increasingly pervade everyday speech (Friedman 1982). Everyone knows that "the Rolls" or "the Cadillac" means something different from just "the car." On the other hand, one of the most striking phenomena in contemporary retailing has been the spread of "own-brand" goods in supermarket chains, and in chains of independent retailers organized into purchasing groups. These, however, may involve no more than the substitution of a store image and store loyalty for a brand image and brand loyalty. Some of the stores concerned advertise heavily and include details of own-brand goods in the advertisements. Consumers do seem to have clear images of own-brand goods, and even of the so-called "generic" or "unbranded" goods that are beginning to replace own-brands at the bottom of the price (and quality) scale (McGoldrick 1982). But the popularity of own-brands does seem to be a clear setback for the purveyors of brand images in the strict sense.

More systematic data on the artificial uniqueness of goods come from studies of "brand loyalty," the alleged tendency of consumers to buy the same brand over and over again despite opportunities to try competitors. Attempts have been made to relate brand loyalty to the consumer's shopping pattern (Carman 1970), the market structure for the product (Farley 1964a, 1964b), and the socioeconomic, demographic, and personality characteristics of the purchaser (Frank et al. 1969). This has been a fertile field for the application of considerably complex mathematical models, often based on learning theories or other established psychological principles (e.g., Ehrenberg 1972; Herniter & Magee 1961; Kuehn 1961). Ehrenberg argues from his analyses that purchasing pattern in fact is a function only of the penetration of the commodity and the frequency with which it is bought. This implies that brand loyalty as such is not a quantitatively important process, except insofar as habitual buying may tend to inhibit consumers from trying new brands. What this suggests is not that marketers are succeeding in inducing artificial uniqueness but rather that habit has an important role in buying and that brand names merely trigger an habitual response.

Substitution and characteristics

Brand names and brand images are obstructions to substitution, benign if they correspond to real and useful differences between commodities, manipulative if they do not. But we still have not considered, beyond the intuitive level, what makes one commodity a good or a bad substitute for another. Practical marketing obviously requires an excellent sense for what will compete with what, but it offers no theoretical analysis. Psychology has nothing to offer either, except the extension of the matching law proposed by Rachlin et al. (1980), which is deficient because it forces all substitutabilities to be symmetrical. At least the outlines of an answer can be found, however, in economic theory, in the form of the characteristics analysis of demand suggested by Lancaster (1966), and introduced briefly in Chapter 2.

The essence of Lancaster's position is that goods, as such, are not what is demanded; instead, he sees goods as bundles of characteristics, and the characteristics, rather than the goods they constitute, as the source of consumers' utility. These ideas are not unique to Lancaster. Within economic theory, Adelman and Griliches (1961) used similar ideas in an analysis of the concept of the quality of goods. Rosen (1974) has extended them to a consideration of the production as well as the consumption of goods and, as noted earlier, there are close parallels to Lancaster's ideas in the notion of a utility tree (see Gorman 1959, 1968). Within psychology, the Fishbein multiattribute approach to attitudes (see Chapter 1) similarly leads to a consideration of the characteristics of commodities. All these approaches have been used to some extent in both theoretical and empirical analyses of buying behavior.

Consider first the idea of a "utility tree." The idea here is that, presumably because consumers first tend to budget in fairly broad categories (e.g., housing, food, transport), and only subsequently to allocate money to specific goods available within those areas, there should tend to be hierarchies of cross-price elasticities of demand. Only the most closely related products should influence one another's prices at all strongly. More important, if the price of a commodity on one "branch" of the utility tree changes, the effects of that change on demand for goods on another branch should be homogeneous; all should be affected in the same way. Explicit tests of this model are few and, as we saw in our discussion of econometric demand systems, demand is sometimes significantly affected by the prices of quite unrelated goods (e.g., Deacon & Muellbauer 1980a). Nonetheless, utility tree ideas are effectively used in all single-equation econometrics, whenever the decision is made as to what other commodity prices should be examined as potential influences on demand for the commodity under study. Very similar ideas have been used in a quite different way by Fraser and Bradford (1983–4). They argued that purchases of nonsubstitutable items should be sequentially independent of one another, and showed how this principle could be used to construct a hierarchy of substitutabilities for the coffee products market from panel data.

Second, consider the distinctions Lancaster makes between "primitive" and "sophisticated" consumption technologies (where, respectively, characteristics outnumber goods, and vice versa), and between "efficiency" and "personal" substitution. These can be used to shed light on the status of brands. The progression from abstract "goods" through "product fields" and "products" to "brands" is one of increasing numbers of characteristics in common, and increasing tendency to efficiency substitution. The progression also shows that the marketer's struggle to make a given brand unique may serve the consumer's interest after all, provided that the efforts tend to make additional combinations of characteristics available. Presumably the marketer's best interests will be served by trying to make a brand unique since, if we accept the optimistic view (e.g., Reynaud 1981, pp. 147–9), the only sustainable marketing policy is ultimately the maximization of consumers' utility.

Lancaster's model itself has been subjected to empirical test using econometric data (e.g., Lancaster 1971, chapter 10). Lancaster (1971, p. 7) argues that, for practical reasons, characteristics must be objective, physical attributes, not inherently subjective properties such as "beauty." To an economic psychologist, it seems clear that characteristics need to be related in some way to the underlying needs they serve. Some theoretical work has been done on the relationship between characteristics and needs (e.g., Douglas & Isherwood 1979, pp. 110 ff.; Lea 1981b). In some cases, it may be possible to make progress by thinking in terms of objective characteristics, to which different people attach different utilities according to their tastes, as Lancaster proposes. In other cases, the characteristics themselves will have to be viewed as subjective.

The potential of a characteristics analysis has been recognized in a number of ways. Ladd and Zober (1977–8) and Agarwhal and Ratchford (1980–1) have attempted to find ways of getting from psychological data on characteristics and their importance to individuals to market data on demand for goods, and the latter authors have shown how their model can be used in an analysis of the automobile market (although they also show that its predictions for individual preferences are weak relative to more direct methods). Morgan, Metzen, and Johnson (1979–80) used a characteristics approach in an analysis of state purchasing agents' demand for breakfast cereals. This investigation is particularly interesting in that the data suggested a pattern of characteristics that was not what the authors had expected. They found that purchasers behaved as though all vitamins and minerals contributed to a single characteristic.

More detailed information about characteristics has been obtained from experimental studies. Sheluga et al. (1979–80) produced an intriguing integration of a multiattribute approach with the economics of information. In a simulated buying situation in which information about pocket cameras was under the experimenters' control, they found that subjects obtained more information about characteristics for which they had the highest valuation. And they used this information efficiently, even though the resulting choices were, in general, not those which would have been made by a fully informed consumer who set the same valuations on the characteristics. Lea (1983), looking for a situation in which objective characteristics could be specified with some certainty, investigated rats' choices between different foodstuffs. He found that they were best accounted for by a model in which the rats minimized the differences from their ideal intakes of several underlying characteristics, not of the foodstuffs themselves. For the rat, therefore, foods are not foods; they are valued for the characteristics they contain.

This chapter on buying has now come full circle. We started with the question, "Why do people buy what they do?" We found that the answer "People buy what they need" has some merit but is obviously incomplete because it does not deal with the details of buying behavior. Lancaster's model suggests a rather fuller answer: "People buy what they do because those goods contain characteristics that correspond to their needs." In searching for a more adequate analysis of buying behavior, we thus find something that relates in an obvious way to an analysis of needs.

The data discussed in this chapter show that characteristics will often be social rather than physical and that they may be subjective rather than objective. The relationships among characteristics, needs, and goods may be transitory and socially defined. But Lancaster's analysis fits at least the data at hand, and prompts further investigation. It will be interesting to see whether, as economic psychology develops, those further investigations will transform that qualitative fit into quantitative confirmation that a characteristics analysis is the best way to look at buying behavior.

8

SAVING

Whatever income is not spent is, by definition, saved. A chapter on saving, therefore, naturally follows one on buying. Although the ways in which we save are relatively few compared with the ways in which we spend, from the economic point of view more kinds of behavior count as saving than the layman would suppose. There is remarkably little direct psychological work on saving, but there are a number of psychological theories that may be brought to bear on it. Furthermore, some of the leading economic theories of saving behavior are couched in apparently psychological terms. It is therefore not surprising that economic psychologists have taken considerable interest in saving; in particular, it was one of the major concerns of George Katona, probably the best-known economic psychologist to date.

THE NATURE AND DEFINITION OF SAVING

At one level, the definition of saving is straightforward. Income must be either spent or saved; in symbols, we have the equation

$$Y = C + S \tag{8.1}$$

which holds either for an individual or for an entire economy. When we attempt to analyze this issue in more detail, however, we encounter a number of problems.

The accounting period

Even to talk about saving requires that we specify, at least implicitly, a time period. If a person saves 10% of his or her income from January to July and then spends it all on an expensive holiday, a good deal of saving has been done on a monthly accounting period, but none at all on an annual basis.

Once the time period is specified, we can consider the decision to save really as a decision to defer consumption to a future time period. While saving increases the resources available for future consumption possible, it does not ensure that all those resources will be consumed. At present, it is an open question whether future consumption is the effective motivation for saving.

Furthermore, the amount of consumption postponed during one time period may not equal the amount of consumption made possible in the future. Usually, savings earn interest, but they may shrink, perhaps because they have to be held in a perishable form or perhaps because the saver has to pay someone to look after them. Such shrinkage can be represented by a negative interest rate. Finally, savings may remain constant or even increase, in monetary value yet lose part of their real value (their power to purchase consumption goods) because of inflation. Shrinkage due to inflation happens whenever interest rates are less than the rate of inflation; the money interest rate minus the inflation rate is usually referred to as the real interest rate.

The propensity to save

Obviously, those with larger incomes have the possibility of saving more. For comparative purposes, it is often useful to work with the propensity to save or saving ratio, the proportion of income that is saved (in symbols, S/Y). Its complement, C/Y, is called the propensity to consume. A related statistic is the marginal propensity to save (or to consume), the proportion of any increase in income which will be saved (or spent). Like the basic equation $Y = C + S$, these propensities are meaningful either for an individual or for an entire economy. Both the propensity to save and the marginal propensity to save have the advantage that they are independent of money units. They are therefore particularly useful in comparing saving between countries with different currencies, or between time periods when there is inflation.

Macroeconomic versus behavioral definitions of saving

Most individuals, if willing, could say how much money they save. However, it is likely that they would leave out of account a number of behaviors that from a macroeconomic point of view, are considered saving (although economists also differ among themselves about what should count as saving – cf. Darby 1975). In effect, the individual's definition of saving differs from the economist's (Katona 1975, pp. 229 ff.; Olander & Seipel 1970, pp. 19–23). Since it is laymen, rather than economists, who do most of the saving, this difference in definitions may be quite important, especially if a person's concept of what saving is has some effect on how and how much he or she saves.

By our simple definition, saving is any use of income that does not involve immediate consumption. It follows that certain kinds of behavior count as saving; such as putting money in teapots, old socks, the pockets of spare jackets, under mattresses (often called hoarding to distinguish it from all other forms of saving); placing money in bank accounts, interest-bearing or otherwise; purchasing securities (e.g., national savings bonds, stocks, shares); using money to buy goods or services required for a business (e.g., stock for a shop, rent for office premises); lending money to other individuals; contributing to pension schemes, whether privately arranged, organized by an employer, or state-run; and purchasing durable goods, that is, goods that will last longer than the current accounting period; and repaying loans. For individuals, the most important instances of this last kind of saving are payments for house mortgages or for goods bought on installment plans (hire purchase). Note, however, that the interest charges that are usually a part of such repayments are not a form of saving, but payment for a service for current consumption, that is, the continued use of the borrowed money.

Most people would recognize the first three behaviors as examples of saving but would be doubtful about the rest, particularly about the last two (durables purchase and repayment of loans). To the layman, both seem more like spending than saving. The issue here is not whether the economic definition or the lay definition is right or wrong; rather, which definition is relevant to the different kinds of question we may want to ask about saving. When we consider the macroeconomic consequences of saving, we clearly need to consider saving macroeconomically defined. By contrast, the factors that enhance individuals' saving may act only on the types of behavior that individuals recognize as saving, thus compelling us to consider savings in a different light. This fact has important consequences for economic policy. A policy designed to stimulate saving, for example, might be a success in terms of the behaviors individuals construe as saving, but a failure overall.

Contractual, discretionary, and involuntary saving

Even within the category of behaviors that everyone could agree are saving, there are clearly different kinds of behavior. Merely having money left over in a checking account at the end of the month is something quite different from deliberately putting a fixed sum into a savings account (perhaps even taking out a contract to do so) month after month, as soon as the wage or salary is received. Making a one-time decision to buy a valuable antique piece of furniture instead of a cheaper, more utilitarian item is different again; at a psychological level, the status of such a decision may differ depending on whether the aim is to acquire a beautiful and interesting object or to have a hedge against inflation.

Katona (e.g., 1975, pp. 230–2) draws a distinction between discretionary and contractual saving. Discretionary saving involves an active decision to save (or at least not to spend) during the current accounting period. Contractual saving involves a decision having been made previously, for example, to enter a pension plan that requires regular payments.

Another useful distinction is between voluntary and involuntary saving. Involuntary saving occurs when there is no explicit decision to save, past or present. It often arises from institutional arrangements. For example, a past or present decision to buy life insurance may involve saving of which a person is quite unaware, since a common technique in selling combined life insurance/investment plans is to stress the insurance element (usually small and cheap) rather than the investment element (large and expensive). A second cause of involuntary saving is inflation (cf. Jump 1980; Siegel 1979). In inflationary times, interest rates tend to rise. Most of the interest is simply compensation for the attrition of capital caused by inflation so that the real rate of interest is much lower than the money rate, and may even be negative. If savings is reckoned in money terms, however, it will appear to rise, as long as savers do not draw out the imputed interest.

From a macroeconomic point of view, it may not matter much whether saving is discretionary or contractual, voluntary or involuntary; from the point of view of psychological causation, it obviously matters a great deal. However, the psychology of saving may well have important macroeconomic effects. For example, discretionary saving is likely to be much more volatile than contractual saving, and much more likely to be affected by shifts in economic policy or in the overall performance of the economy.

THRIFT, IMPATIENCE, AND THE PSEUDOMORALITY OF SAVING

Many issues in economic psychology come close to being moral questions, such as the work ethic and the whole idea of rational behavior. In the case of saving, moralizing has been rampant. In English, the very word "save" brings to economics strong positive evaluative connotations from its other uses, where it is linked to words like "safety" and "savior." Is the moral view of saving a mere accident of this etymological fact, or is it a more substantial phenomenon?

The perceived morality of thrift

Moralists as well as moralizers have certainly perceived saving as a virtue. Aesop's fable allows the frugal ant, who spent the summer storing food, to turn from her door the feckless grasshopper, who sang all summer and now, in winter, is starving; La Fontaine (1668–79/1974) placed this fable first in his collection. Samuel Smiles (1875) devoted a book to thrift and explains why in its preface: "Thrift is the basis of Self-Help, and the foundation of much that is excellent in Character" (p. v). Keynes (1936, p. 362), who wanted to argue that saving could be economically damaging, complained of the "opprobrium of two centuries of moralists and economists" that descended on Mandeville (1714–29/1924) when he expounded the heretical doctrine that thrift was evil, since it caused unemployment. Modern economists putting forward Keynesian views sometimes use the phrase "the paradox of thrift," clearly expecting that thrift will normally be regarded as virtuous.

But do people in fact take this view? There is little doubt that they do, at least within Western society. Keynes reports that Mandeville's book was convicted as a nuisance by the grand jury of Middlesex in 1723. Wallberg (1963, reported by Olander & Seipel 1970, p. 63) found that 76.1% of a representative Swedish sample thought that the majority of households ought to save some of their earnings; only 7.6% thought the opposite. Katona (1975, p. 235) notes that, year by year, people plan to save more than they actually do. Interviews with children make it clear that they believe that saving is a good thing to do, and that parents encourage them in this belief (see Chapter 14). Critics of advertising complain that they tempt people to spend (see Chapter 13); they do not argue that bank advertising tempts people to save; indeed, the phrase sounds like a contradiction in terms.

In other cultures different values can be found. As noted in Chapter 9, there are societies where prestige and power depend on consumption, and the most wasteful forms of consumption at that. Even our society holds values that conflict with thrift. Veblen (1899/1979) argued that conspicuous consumption always confers status; and it is clear that saving at the expense of giving is not regarded as virtuous (see Chapter 7). Scrooge was not intended to be admired, and "the man with no hands" (who will not buy his round) is reviled in any English pub.

On the whole, thrift clearly is seen as a virtue. Why should this be? The answer is by no means obvious, for it does not link directly to the major currents of moral thought in Western society. The only direct connection is through utilitarianism (e.g., J. S. Mill 1891, book 1, chapter 11, paragraph 2, describes the "desire of accumulation" as a "moral attribute"), but that has always been an academic rather than a popular view of morality. At times government propaganda has tried to make a virtue of thrift, because of the macroeconomic consequences of saving. To some extent, saving is the logical consequence of abstaining from luxury, which has traditionally been seen as a vice, so that thrift has become associated with the ascetic and puritanical current of moral thought (although the consistent puritan would presumably give away what he did not spend, rather than saving it). The quotation from Samuel Smiles, above, suggests a second reason why thrift is seen as virtuous: It enables a person to be independent, which, until the development of modern social security, meant being independent of private charity. In part this idea suggests that thrift is one of those "convenient" social virtues, propagated by the charitable to reduce the calls on their resources. However, in a society in which men were the major breadwinners and there was neither social security nor insurance to provide for widows and orphans, a thrifty provision for dependents could properly be seen as a virtue.

We are no longer puritans, and to a greater or lesser extent we live in modern welfare states. Why is thrift still seen as a virtue? One possible answer is a Marxist one. Private saving is a necessary part of the working of a capitalist society that shapes its morality to suit its ends. Katona's work hints at a second answer. Saving is something that we find hard to do, although we can see advantages in doing it. Most such situations involve moral questions, and the common way of coping with them is to invent moral precepts to constrain our behavior. Perhaps saving is seen as moral just because it is difficult. We now turn to examine the nature of that difficulty.

The problem of deferring gratification

As we have already seen, saving makes possible future consumption, one obvious motivation for saving behavior. Insofar as it is the operative motivation, the choice between saving and spending is, in fact, a choice between consumption now and consumption later. Most economic and psychological analyses of saving have considered it within this framework of intertemporal choice.

Much economic analysis has naturally concentrated on determining how the rational person would distribute his income between current and future consumption. This is a nontrivial problem. It has always been obvious, however, that people save less than is rational, whatever the criterion of rationality. This "impatience" has caught the attention of philosophers (e.g., Locke 1690/1961, book 1, chapter 21, paragraph 63) and economists (e.g., Fisher 1930) and has dominated psychological investigation. In experimental situations, people, especially some categories of people, seem quite unable to choose to save rather than spend.

We introduced some of the psychological experiments and theories involved in intertemporal choice in Chapter 5. The literature has been reviewed in detail by Gorin (1985, chapters 6 and 7). The basic fact, from which all the rest of the research follows, is that when children (or animals, or, in a few experiments, adults) are given a choice between a reward that is available immediately and a larger reward that is available only with some delay, they tend to choose the small, immediate reward (Mischel 1958). This is referred to as "failure to delay gratification."

Preference for an immediate reward over an identical one delivered after a delay, is not, in itself, irrational. Koopmans (1960) argued that the existence of some time preference is close to being a consequence of the normal economic concept of rational man. A number of factors make current consumption objectively more attractive than saving – the possibility of death, the risk of inflation, the risk of default on future payments, and so forth (see Fisher 1930; Ainslie 1975) – so that it might be rational to prefer an immediate reward to a slightly larger delayed one. But the extent of the observed failure to delay gratification seems to defy all rational analysis, at least for certain subjects and certain ways of doing the experiment. Pigeons prefer two seconds' immediate access to grain to four seconds' access (yielding twice as much grain deferred by even four seconds) (Rachlin & Green 1972); normal, adult, humans say that they would prefer 5 pounds now, rather than 10 pounds in two months' time, a preference that could be rational only if the inflation rate were several thousand percent (unpublished data described by Lea 1978).

Failure to delay gratification has been studied in a variety of experimental paradigms. The simplest involves giving the subject a direct choice between two real, visible outcomes; this was the technique of the earliest studies (e.g., Mischel 1958, 1961a, 1961b, 1961c; Mischel & Metzner 1962). Later experiments used a technique of self-imposed delay, in which subjects could choose to take a (usually visible) reward at any time, but the longer they waited, the greater the chance of securing the larger reward (e.g., Mischel & Ebbesen 1970; Mischel, Ebbesen, & Zeiss 1972; Toner & Smith 1977; Miller, Weinstein, & Karniol 1978). More recent experiments have involved replacing the real object by some kind of representation (e.g., Mischel & Moore 1973, 1980; Moore, Mischel, & Zeiss 1976; Nisan 1974), putting the presentation of the objects or their representation under the subject's own control (e.g., Yates & Mischel 1979) or simply asking the subject to imagine the choice, rather than offering it directly (e.g., Mischel & Mischel 1983).

These variations in procedure do produce somewhat different results. For example, preschool children will wait far longer for a reward that is not visibly present than for one that is (Mischel & Ebbesen 1970), although this effect can be reversed if the subjects are instructed to think about the rewards (Mischel et al. 1972). However, the general result remains the same: Children (by far the commonest subjects) find it very difficult to defer taking a reward, even for a few minutes. The capacity to delay gratification does improve with age but remains weak even in adults, in the few experiments in which they have been tested systematically. If failure to delay gratification on this scale were completely general, we should be living in a no-saving economy. This is contrary to the facts; children commonly show very high propensities to save out of their very slender money resources (see Chapter 14).

How do we combat our impulsiveness? In general terms, the most effective strategy is to avoid or escape from the temptation to take the immediate reward. Rachlin and Green (1972) devised a procedure that enabled pigeons to do this. During one phase of the procedure, they were offered the direct choice described above, between two seconds' immediate access to grain, and four seconds' access delayed by four seconds. Ten seconds before this choice was offered, the pigeons could peck a key that denied them access to the immediate reward on the next trial. The pigeons learned to make this commitment response and so managed to obtain the larger reward after all. From an early age, children are able to describe strategies that have similar effects, such as hiding visible rewards or thinking about irrelevant activities (Mischel & Mischel 1983). Psychologists refer to such behaviors as techniques for "self-control."

Delayed gratification experiments are not a perfect analogy to economic saving behavior. Most saving depends on the assumption that the opportunity to go on saving will be available, repeatedly, in the future. Furthermore, saving often involves giving up resources which we already have in our hands (perhaps literally), rather than abstaining from collecting small rewards now. Nonetheless, the analogy is clearly close. Formally, both are examples of intertemporal choice, and much everyday behavior concerned with saving can be regarded as commitment responding, in the sense in which that occurs in delayed gratification experiments. Saving institutions, from piggy banks to bank accounts, obviously serve to protect the individual's savings from others. But their most important function is probably to protect savings from the saver by imposing time, effort, and inconvenience between a decision to spend and any possibility of realizing it.

The measurement of impatience

The universal difficulty of delaying gratification shows that consumption now will always be preferred to consumption later, other things being equal. This tendency is referred to as "time preference" or "impatience." Theories of saving have to find some way to take it into account, preferably quantitatively.

An obvious way of doing so is to assume that future consumption is devalued by a constant factor for each time period between the present and the moment of consumption. There is thus a subjective process of "discounting the future" to add to the similar more objective discounting processes needed to allow for the possibility of death, the rate of inflation, and the rate of interest that could be earned on assets now owned.

In his permanent income hypothesis of saving behavior, which we shall discuss in more detail later in this chapter, Friedman (1957) suggested that both the objective and the subjective factors leading to preference for present consumption could be summarized in a "subjective discounting rate" which should be applied to future consumption in order to make it comparable with current consumption. From time series of income and consumption, he suggested that its value might be as high as 33%. Holbrook (1967) argued that the value may be as high as 50%, while Darby (1974) proposes that 10% would be more consistent with data now available (as well as intrinsically more plausible). Similar constructs turn up in many theories (e.g., the quantity rho in the generalization of Friedman's theory proposed by Blinder 1975).

All such theories encounter problems, however. For example, a constant discount rate cannot explain why preference for immediate reward can be reversed by adding a constant to both the delays (Ainslie 1975). Yet this is the basis for all commitment responding, whether habitual or deliberate. Borch (1978) points out that a constant discount rate would predict that people should choose pensions which get smaller as years after retirement pass by, and this is clearly contrary to the facts. Ainslie suggests that an effective way of discounting future consumption, consistent with experimental work on animals, would be to divide its value by the time until it will be realized. This suggestion has the merit of simplicity, but it has yet to be tested in a wider context. Another way of looking at impatience quantitatively, without assuming a constant discount rate, is to use the elasticity of substitution between present and future consumption. This has been included in some theoretical developments (e.g., Evans 1983), but reliable estimates of its value have not been produced.

Our discussion of delayed gratification and impatience has illustrated how hard it is to talk about saving in nonevaluative terms. "Self-control" and "temptation" are unmistakably moral concepts. But at least since Keynes (1936) it has been part of the common stock of economic ideas that, whatever the merits of saving for a household, it may not be good for the economy as a whole. At the level of macroeconomics, morality tends to boil down to pragmatism. We need to ask, therefore, what effects saving has on the economy.

MACROECONOMIC CONSEQUENCES OF SAVING

All schools of macroeconomics (cf. Chapter 3) regard saving as being of practical importance in determining the fate of the national economy. The encouragement (or even enforcement) of saving is therefore frequently an element in economic policy. This explains, at least in part, the interest that economic psychologists have taken in the matter.

Inflation, deflation, and the money supply

The most obvious macroeconomic effect of saving is its influence on the money supply, the total amount of money in circulation. As noted in Chapter 3, the concept of the money supply is, unfortunately, not well defined. According to some definitions, when a consumer chooses to save rather than spend, the money supply is reduced. It follows that if restraining the money supply is a goal of economic policy, encouraging saving will also be a goal.

In the past decade, restraint of the money supply has been part of the monetarist doctrine of political economy. This doctrine asserts that money supply causally determines other important economic phenomena, such as the rates of unemployment and inflation. The success of monetarist policies is open to debate, but it cannot be doubted that monetarist doctrine contains at least some truth. Whether or not normal fluctuations in inflation and other such effects are caused by changes in the money supply, sufficiently drastic increases or decreases in money supply certainly have some causal effect. It follows that no government, whatever its attitude toward monetarist dogma, can be indifferent to money supply. And under conditions in which restraint is appropriate, governments may seek to encourage saving.

The classic condition in which control of the money supply becomes important is war. Wars tend to be inflationary. Soldiers, munitions workers, and everyone else involved in the military effort must be paid. In the words of a World War II source (with the evocative title, "The Consumer goes to War"):

"We cannot spend all this income without serious effect, for the goods that many of us are paid to make do not go back onto the market for us to buy . . . the combined incomes of the people making war goods and the people making civilian supplies will buy more than the amount of civilian goods – unless prices rise to fantastic heights . . . The first way to fight inflation is to keep the 'money with no place to go' from being spent. This is the purpose of drastic taxes, war-bond sales campaigns, and proposals for forced savings. (Ware 1942, pp. 33–6)

During World War II, all the governments involved used a good deal of propaganda to encourage saving. Saving was portrayed as a patriotic duty, a way in which civilians could strike a blow against the enemy. In the United Kingdom, saving was enforced. Extra taxes were levied with the promise to repay after the war was over. These were called "postwar credits" and the sum of money involved was, in the end, so large that it was not considered possible to repay them all until 25 years after the end of the war, much to the bitterness of those who held them. A similar procedure has recently been initiated in the German Federal Republic as part of a monetarist government's attempts to cope with peacetime inflation.

Anyone can see that "Buy War Bonds!" is a powerful appeal. But World War II also brought attempts to harness psychology to find further ways of encouraging saving. Katona's first foray into economic psychology was the result of one such attempt: "War without inflation" (Katona 1942) is the outcome of his wartime work for the U.S. government.

Saving, investment, and capital formation

Whenever a consumer saves instead of spends, the supply of money being spent on consumption goods is reduced. The money saved, however, does not disappear. According to the "accounting relationships" of macroeconomics (see Chapter 3), it is an inevitable consequence that the money saved is invested. Saving and investment are different kinds of economic behavior, though unfortunately they are often confused (especially in advertisements for savings institutions). Mathematically, however, they must add up to the same totals within an economy. In some cases this identity is obvious, in others it is quite surprising.

By definition, investment is adding to the stock of productive assets in an economy. Purchasing a machine that will be used to make consumer goods is an obvious investment. Buying stocks that will be sold in the future at a profit is another obvious kind of investment. Less obviously, obtaining an education that will enable a person to secure a higher salary at a later date, is also a kind of investment – sometimes called "investment in human capital." The accumulation of productive assets in an economy is commonly referred to as "capital formation."

Capital formation thus depends on saving. Because it is a cumulative process, the effects of changes in people's saving behavior can be quite substantial. Feldstein (1974) estimated that changes in saving following the introduction of social security in 1937 have reduced the capital engaged in the U.S. economy by $2 trillion. Feldstein's deductions about individual behavior are almost certainly wrong, but there can be no dispute about the scale of their possible consequences.

In a pure subsistence economy, saving and investment are done by the same people; they are one and the same thing. Seed not ground for flour today (saving) is sown to produce crops next season (investment). The same processes do sometimes occur in a modern economy. Large corporations, in fact, behave rather like humans in a primitive society: Most of their investment is financed out of retained profits (Galbraith 1972, chapter 4). What is more typical under modern conditions, though, is that saving and investment are done by different people. Sometimes the relation between savers and investors is obvious. The dominant source of borrowed money for people buying houses comes from Savings and Loan organizations in the United States and Building Societies in the United Kingdom. Saving in these institutions is largely done by middle-aged houseowners. This is often referred to confusingly as "investment," but in fact the corresponding investment is being made by younger people who borrow from the institutions in order to buy houses. Sometimes saving and investment are linked in less obvious ways. For instance, if consumers save half their incomes under their mattresses, the goods they might have bought but did not, pile up in the shops, and retailers find they have unintentionally invested through the stockpiling of merchandise. Clearly, this kind of investment may not be very productive (Oommen 1961; Steurle 1983).

Given that saving and investment are being done by different people, it is possible that one group's desire to save could be out of balance with another group's desire to invest. In the case of house purchases, mismatches of this sort, leading to "mortgage famines" or "mortgage gluts," have been a recurring news story for decades. Even under this kind of mismatching condition, however, saving must still equal investment. Crudely put, what happens when there is an imbalance between intended saving and intended investment is that involuntary investment displaces investment that people actually want to make, sometimes with disastrous financial or economic consequences. Economists have studied this problem in considerable detail, for it is at the heart of some of the major current disputes about macroeconomics and its implications for economic policy (see Chapter 3).

The details of the theoretical relationships between saving and investment are beyond the scope of this book, but one point needs to be noted: In order to make any theoretical progress, it is necessary to make assumptions about the relationship between income and the propensity to save. This relationship is clearly open to psychological investigation and has attracted great interest within economic psychology. It is the subject matter of many of the theories of saving to which we shall now turn.

THEORIES OF SAVING

Why do people save? Until we have an answer to this question, it is difficult to construct a coherent economic theory of saving; that is, unless we know the goal of a behavior, it is impossible to specify the optimal means of achieving it. One way to test a theory about the motivation for saving is to figure out the optimal behavior that the theory predicts, and then see whether real behavior approximates it. A considerable number of possible motivations for saving have been suggested, by economists, psychologists, and economic psychologists. Here, we have tried to group them according to the kind of answer they give to the basic question of why people save. Accordingly, each of the following sections deals with several theories, and in some cases they are superficially very different. We do not spell out the predictions from each theory in great detail, nor do we assess the evidence for and against each of them. Those questions will be dealt with later in this chapter, when we consider the factors that affect saving behavior.

Income and saving

The first group of theories says more about the factors affecting saving than about the motivation to save. However, it is convenient to consider them here since more motivational theories were subsequently formulated partly in response to the empirical failure of these ideas.

These early theories asserted that the fundamental determinant of saving behavior is the consumer's income. Keynes (1936, p. 96) advanced, as a "psychological law, upon which we are entitled to depend with great confidence," the proposition that the proportion of income that a person saves will be constant regardless of how income changes. This means that the propensity to save (and hence the propensity of consume) will be independent of income. This is sometimes called the *absolute income hypothesis* of saving.

Perhaps because of the apparent appeal to psychology from such an eminent economist (who probably did not mean it very seriously), economic psychologists have been very interested in the accuracy of this "law." The absolute income hypothesis, however, cannot account for all the econometric data, quite apart from any problems it may have with the results of psychological investigations (but see below for further discussion). The function relating consumption to income is called the consumption function, and the marginal propensity to consume is simply its slope. Keynes's "law" implies that the consumption function will be a straight line through the origin, and Kuznets (1942) found that this was true of the U.S. economy for the period 1870–1938. However, the United States (and also the United Kingdom) turns out to be exceptional in this respect. In most other countries, time series data show the propensity to save increasing with national income (Kuznets 1966, pp. 234–243). Furthermore, a much larger increase in savings ratio with income is found in cross-sectional studies, which investigate the effects on saving of differences in income within an economy (e.g., Bean 1946).

This disparity between longitudinal and cross-sectional data on the consumption function has been a major spur to theorizing about saving. An early attempt to resolve it was the Relative Income Hypothesis of Brady and Friedman (1947) and Duesenberry (1949). Using ideas derived from anthropology and psychology, Duesenberry argued that consumption will always depend on consumers' relative incomes, that is, their incomes as a proportion of the average income in what they perceive as their community. Preferences are thus interdependent, not independent, as assumed by classical economic theory. Duesenberry supported this argument by showing that individual consumers' propensities to save were determined by their position within the income distribution of their own local or racial group, rather than their absolute incomes (the cross-cultural implications of Duesenberry's work are discussed further in Chapter 15). He showed that the effect of such a social comparison process would be for consumption to increase when income increases, but not fall when income falls. This leads to a constant average propensity to save as the average income in an economy changes but allows for high-income earners to have a lower propensity to consume than low-income people at each point in time (the observed cross-sectional result). However, like the absolute income hypothesis, the relative income hypothesis gives no insight into *why* people save, and it has not been particularly influential.

Saving for future consumption

The most obvious reason for saving today is to be able to consume tomorrow. As already noted, saving necessarily involves the possibility of deferred consumption, but that might be an incidental by-product rather than the primary purpose of the behavior. There are many examples of behaviors that give rise to deferred consumption, but are not included by consumers among their saving, at least on the conscious level. For example, the purchase of a washing machine obtains laundry services spreading over several years, and the purchase of a season bus ticket obtains transport services that are gradually consumed over the next weeks or months. Both purchases would be saving by the macroeconomic definition, but few consumers would naturally consider either to be saving or see deferred consumption as their goal. They are simply ways of achieving particular consumption goals more cheaply or more conveniently.

Nonetheless, several theories imply that deferred consumption is the essential and deliberate goal of saving. Among them are the most influential economic (rationality) approaches. This is not surprising – if the purpose of saving is future consumption, an intertemporal choice framework is obviously relevant. In the simplest case, there is a choice between consumption today and consumption tomorrow (i.e., spending or saving). With more sophistication, the argument can be cast in terms of alternative "consumption streams," that is, patterns of consumption over a series of future years, each associated with a pattern of saving and dissaving designed to support it. In either case, the rational person's problem is to choose the pattern of behavior that has the greatest current utility.

We have already introduced the factors that ought to influence the present value of a consumption stream: the probability of actually obtaining future consumption, interest and inflation rates, and time preference proper. We have also reviewed the evidence, which suggests that, at least in laboratory experiments on delayed gratification, people are a lot less likely to save than rationality considerations predict. A theory that asserts that people save to make future consumption possible therefore also has to explain why they do not save as much as they might. Although these theories have typically been put forward by economists, most of them contain explicit psychological assumptions, recognized as such by their authors.

We can divide the future-consumption theories of saving into those that deal with certain and those that deal with uncertain contingencies. The simplest kind of certain future contingency is the desire to buy something which is beyond current resources. This leads to "saving up." Few individuals regard this as an important motivation for saving (Katona 1975, p. 235), yet much saving effectively has this function, since one-third of all savings account holders draw on their accounts to fund major purchases each year (Mueller & Lean 1967). But such drawings are rapidly replenished, creating a pattern of irregularly alternating saving and dissaving (Katona 1959).

According to the macroeconomic definition of saving, repayments on items bought on credit also constitute "saving up." This is a very common behavior. During the early 1970s, up to one-half of all U.S. households had some installment debt (Katona 1975, p. 272). Another variant of saving up is to acquire a *masse de manoeuvre* for financial operations (Keynes 1936, p. 108). Saving up, in one form or another, is thus very widespread, but it has not excited much theoretical interest.

Most theoretical interest in saving for known future consumption has concentrated on those forms of saving that aim to combat the predictable variations in income within a consumer's lifetime. Harrod (1948, chapter 2) called this "hump saving." Its purpose is to produce a level stream of consumption from an income which peaks in midlife. The idea was developed further by Modigliani and Brumberg (1954), who called it the *life-cycle hypothesis*. It has become one of the foundations of the modern economic theory of saving. According to this theory, saving at any stage of a person's life cycle can be estimated from his or her current income and wealth, expectation of future income, and life expectancy, by finding the stream of consumption over the remaining years of life that will maximize total utility. In any particular year, differences between required and actual income are taken up by saving (or supplied by borrowing).

The consumption plan which will be predicted by the life-cycle hypothesis obviously depends on the institutions of the economy. Samuelson (1958) worked out the solution for an economy that had neither money nor durable goods, but this is only of theoretical interest. More practical questions include the availability of insurance and annuities, although these are not needed in a world of total certainty.

A closely related theory, which deals with a less certain future, is Friedman's (1957) *permanent income hypothesis*. Friedman argues that people have an idea of their "underlying" income and plan to consume a fixed portion of that money in each accounting period. Actual income and consumption will normally vary from these "permanent" values, the differences being called "transitory" income and consumption. Saving results from the difference between permanent plus transitory income and permanent plus transitory consumption; thus it acts as a buffer against uncertainties of income and consumption. In its simple form, the permanent income hypothesis makes one straightforward prediction: The elasticities of saving with respect to income and wealth should add to one, since (in simple terms) income and wealth are treated as alternative sources of a fixed value of current consumption.

Income is not the only uncertain quantity in the economic world. Another commonly cited purpose of saving is to cope with unpredictable demands for expenditure (e.g., unexpected medical bills, or house repairs). On this view, savings represent an emergency fund (it is sometimes called the "rainy day" theory), and the amounts people save are expected to be partially determined by their preferences for or against risk (e.g., Hahn 1970). Yet another kind of uncertainty is the uncertainty of life expectancy; taking this into account greatly complicated the life-cycle hypothesis (see Yaari 1965).

The different kinds of future-consumption theories of saving are obviously not incompatible. Indeed, many modern treatments (e.g., Blinder 1975) regard the life cycle and permanent income hypotheses as parts of a single framework, within which detailed theories are to be worked out. Nonetheless, different forms of future consumption theory do make different predictions about some aspects of saving behavior. "Smoothing" theories, such as Friedman's or Modigliani and Brumberg's, seem to imply that windfall income will be spent rather than saved, since permanent or planned income is more often below or around current income than above it. By contrast, "saving up" seems to predict the opposite: A windfall makes it likely that the current saving target will be reached or exceeded, making it possible for the planned purchase to be made, or at any rate for the bulk of the windfall to be spent.

Saving for interest

An obvious motivation for saving is the interest earned by savings. One of Keynes's (1936) most radical departures from received wisdom was to argue that interest was unimportant as a motivation for saving. The effect of interest on saving behavior is still hotly disputed. But even if interest as such is not an important motivation for saving behavior, it needs to be taken into account in theories of other kinds. For example, under the life-cycle hypothesis, the higher the real rate of interest, the lower the level of savings needed to ensure a given level of future consumption.

Saving to bequeath

Marshall (1920/1949, p. 189) argued that the chief motive for saving was to establish wealth to bequeath to one's heirs. In a society in which power, status, and the quality of life depend greatly on inherited wealth and in which this fact is generally perceived and accepted, the desire to bequeath may be a very powerful motive. In most modern societies, however, conditions (or at least perceptions) are quite otherwise, and it would be surprising if bequest were a powerful motive. It is, in fact, rarely reported (by fewer than 3% of respondents, according to Katona 1975, p. 235), although it does seem to increase in importance with increasing wealth (Guthrie 1963) and income (Barlow, Brazer, & Morgan 1966, p. 32; Menchik & David 1983), and Munnell (1976) found that a high proportion of people *wish* to bequeath. Menchik and David in fact suggest that legacies are a luxury good, with an income elasticity around 2.5.

Marshall's chief argument for the importance of the bequest motive was his impression that the elderly tend to retain (and often add to) very substantial savings. We shall see later that subsequent empirical studies have confirmed this trend. The bequest motive can be included in a life-cycle approach, as noted previously, although effects of doing so may not be trivial (Barro 1974; Evans 1983).

Saving as a goal in itself

Keynes (1936, p. 108) gives, as the very last in his long list of possible motivations to save, the satisfaction of "the instinct of pure miserliness." This is one form of the simplest hypothesis of all about saving behavior, that either the behavior of saving, or the possession of a certain amount of savings, is a goal in and of itself. In other words, saving may be a primary motivation not requiring any other explanation. A few individuals will acknowledge that their saving behavior is habitual (Barlow et al. 1966, p. 32), but more commonly, the idea of saving as a goal in itself is disguised.

The simplest form of this "saving drive" idea is biological. Many species of animals are known to hoard food and the conditions that tend to elicit the behavior have been studied in considerable detail, particularly in rodents (see the review by Lanier, Estep, & Dewsbury 1974). Hamsters, for example, are spectacular food hoarders. Lanier et al. report that, in the wild, one hamster weighing perhaps 100 grams was found to have more than 25 kilograms of grain in its nest. Moreover, hamsters that have been deprived of food for a day hoard increased quantities of food when it again becomes available, while eating no more than normal (Lea & Tarpy 1986). A few animal species hoard nonfood objects, the best-known examples being jackdaws, magpies, and pack rats. Perhaps humans are similar to those species: Our homes, with their vast collections of objects of one sort or another (cf. Moles 1972), and our financial savings, could then be seen as the result of a primary biological drive or instinct.

The evidence in favor of this biological theory of saving is not impressive. The outstanding hoarders in the animal kingdom are not very similar to humans, either in phylogenetic or in ecological terms (Naumov & Lobachev 1975). They are also distant from us in both nutritional and social ecology. They eat a relatively restricted range of foods (mostly seeds), and are apparently solitary. Two species of birds which have recently been shown to be adapted to hoarding by having excellent memories for cache sites (marsh tits: Shettleworth and Krebs 1982; nutcrackers: Balda 1982) are both solitary, territory-holders specializing in eating seeds and nuts. Rats, though rodents, are relatively similar to humans ecologically (they are social omnivores); they hoard only in the face of food deprivation (Morgan, Stellar, & Johnson 1943) or the threat of predation (Roeder, Chetcuti, & Will 1980).

In short, saving as a straightforward primary biological drive seems implausible. Nonetheless, three other theories still in current use seem to assert essentially the same thing. The oldest and most discussed derives from Freud's psychoanalytic theory of the origin of money (discussed in more detail in Chapter 12). According to Freud, the interest in money derives from a childish interest in feces, in turn derived from early childhood anal eroticism. Saving is then seen as a developmental descendant of anal retention. Given other Freudian assumptions, this theory leads to the idea that saving should vary according to personality type, those personalities associated by Freud with high anality (e.g., male homosexuals or obsessionals) being the most likely to do a lot of saving. Although this idea has at least some credibility among analytically oriented psychotherapists (cf. Bornemann 1976), the evidence in its favor is weak.

In Kline's (1981) comprehensive survey of empirical data relating to Freudian psychology, saving is not even mentioned, although Kline (1967) did include a number of items relating to saving in his psychometric test of the anal character, and these items correlated well with the rest of the scale. Fisher and Greenberg (1977), who also surveyed empirical evidence relating to psychoanalysis, only mention three studies involving saving. Of these, two give some support to a connection between anality and parsimony and one gives no support. Noblin (1962) found that psychiatric patients regarded as highly anal were better motivated by pennies than gumballs, whereas the reverse was true for patients regarded as oral, and Rosenwald (1972) found that college students rated as anally oriented were less likely than others to risk winnings from an experimentally arranged gamble on a second wager. By contrast, Rapaport (1955) found no correlation between anality and concern with money as demonstrated by a projective technique, the Thematic Apperception Test, devised by Morgan and Murray (1935).

Katona's (1975, pp. 230–2) discussion of discretionary and contractual saving seems quite different from either a biological or a psychoanalytic theory about a saving drive, but it leads to the identical conclusion, that saving must be considered as a goal in itself. Katona concludes that discretionary saving is very similar to discretionary spending, and occurs in response to the same or similar attitudinal variables. The reason, according to Katona, is that an adequate "reserve" in the form of savings is a kind of consumer good, much like a car or a television. People view it as one of the things they will acquire as they secure their economic position.

Katona's idea of a savings target as a consumer good is perhaps the most plausible version of the "savings drive" theory that we have considered so far, if only because it is shorn of excess psychological content. An even balder version of the theory has been put forward by Clower and Johnson (1968). These investigators propose that wealth (i.e., accumulated savings) should be treated as an autonomous source of utility. The common rationality approaches to saving, such as the life cycle hypothesis, regard wealth as valuable (i.e., as yielding utility) only insofar as it is convertible into consumption in some future time period. Clower and Johnson drop this assumption, supposing instead that consumers maximize a utility function which increases both with consumption during the year and with wealth remaining at the end of it. They then pose a standard utility-maximization argument, making it clear that theirs is a "last-ditch" rationality theory. It is not clear that the life-cycle hypothesis says anything very different once the zero-bequest assumption is dropped, as it is in many modern uses of it (e.g., Blinder 1975).

Yet another form of the savings drive hypothesis derives from the literature on token economies. Winkler (1973) investigated the means by which savings affected the behavior of patients in a token economy. He found that the level of savings had a direct effect which could not be explained by the way it, in turn, affected the flow of primary reinforcers (i.e., consumption). Token-earning behavior seemed to be a function of the ratio of current savings to income. Winkler (1972) argued that patients were trying to maintain their savings within a "critical range." In one sense, this is a specialized form of Clower and Johnson's theory. In another sense, it echoes some of the data on the effects of inflation on savings targets.

We have not exhausted all the possible motivations for saving behavior, but we have given enough information to indicate that there is no set of conflicting theories, but rather a set of distinct motivations, all of which might be operating. The problem is therefore to assess the importance of each kind of saving motivation. In order to do this, we need to review the factors that have been found to have an effect on saving behavior.

FACTORS THAT AFFECT SAVING

In this section we shall briefly review the factors known to affect whether, how, or how much people save. Some of them have been mentioned in connection with one or other of the theories discussed above.

Income

The consumption function, discussed earlier in this chapter, summarizes what we know about the variation of saving with income. Across the entire economy, there is no doubt that saving increases with income, whether we obtain our data from longitudinal studies (e.g., Kuznets 1942; Koskela & Viren 1983a) or by cross section (e.g., Bean 1946; Goldsmith 1955) – although Modigliani (1970) found that the savings ratios in different countries were not correlated with national income per head. Cross-sectional studies also show that the propensity to save (though not the marginal propensity to save, except perhaps at the highest income levels) increases with income. These results hold not just for national economies but in token economies as well (Winkler 1980). Almost every econometric study of saving includes income as an explanatory variable in its regression equations and finds that it accounts for significant amounts of variation.

However, these general tendencies conceal important individual and year-to-year differences. Some of them are revealed in responses to sample surveys of the sort favored by Katona. According to Katona (1975, pp. 237 ff.), people with higher income are indeed much more likely to save, and save more, than poorer people. But high-income individuals are just as likely to dissave (i.e., to have less in savings at the end of a year than at the beginning) as anyone else. Even on average incomes, saving is highly variable from year to year, and most American households dissave one year out of every three or four.

Given these data, what can we conclude from the constant propensity to save shown in longitudinal studies? In part, it reflects an average tendency that conceals the year-to-year variations in individual behavior. It may also reflect the difficulty of making comparisons across time periods in which the value of money and the range of goods to spend it on has changed dramatically. The "income" axis on longitudinal consumption functions is very closely correlated with time, and is thus an axis of social and economic change as well as of income.

So far we have only considered how the gross level of income affects the tendency to save. But the source of income also has an effect. Friedman's (1957) permanent income hypothesis makes the surprising prediction that the propensity to save "windfall" income, gains that were unanticipated and that are not likely to be repeated, will be essentially zero (because windfalls are pure "transitory income"). Early attempts to test this prediction (e.g., Bodkin 1959; Jones 1960) suggested that, in fact, windfalls were almost always spent. Data more consistent with the permanent income hypothesis were not long in appearing (Kreinin 1961; Reid 1962), and the issue has been debated at some length.

The balance of the evidence now seems to favor what Bird and Bodkin (1973) call the loose form of Friedman's hypothesis: The marginal propensity to consume windfalls is greater than zero but less than the marginal propensity to consume permanent income. The early contradictions are at least partly explained by two other interesting trends. First, the consumption function for windfalls has a positive intercept and a slope less than one, so that small windfalls are spent and large ones are saved (Doenges 1966; Landsberger 1966). Second, the data are more nearly consistent with Friedman's views if durables purchases are, as Friedman suggested, counted as saving (Laumas 1969; Laumas & Mohabbat 1972; Hayashi 1982 – a common behavior on receiving a windfall seems to be to make a major purchase that will bring benefits for some years to come).

An unexpected loss of income, such as is caused by a temporary tax surcharge, is a kind of negative windfall.

Springer (1968) points out that according to the permanent income hypothesis, such one-time surcharges should be ineffective at reducing consumption, since people would use up savings to maintain spending at the level of their permanent income. Springer confirms this prediction for the surcharge imposed in the United States in 1968; there was a sharp drop both in financial savings, and none in consumer spending. Less happily for the theory, there was no drop in consumer purchases of durable goods either. The effects of windfall drops in income are therefore not a perfect mirror image of the effects of windfall gains.

The direction of more permanent changes of income is also important. Katona (1975, p. 242) argues that increases in income will lead to increased discretionary saving, and Koskela and Viren (1983a), in a crossnational econometric study, found that unanticipated increases in the average levels of real income in an economy led to increases in savings ratios. All these asymmetric effects offer some support to the "ratchet effect" predicted by Duesenberry's relative income hypothesis of saving.

Wealth

Wealth is simply accumulated savings. Most theories of saving predict that the greater an individual's wealth, the lower will be his or her propensity to add to it (recall that the propensity to save is the ratio of saving to income, so that even with a lower propensity to save the wealthy, who tend to have high incomes, may well save much larger amounts of money than those with no reserves). Among the formal rationality theories, only that of Clower and Johnson (1968) allows for the possibility that, above a certain level, wealth may create an incentive for still further saving because it produces a worthwhile income from interest.

Most econometric studies of saving include wealth among the explanatory variables, and find that it has an effect on the proportion of income saved. Of course, wealth is strongly correlated with income, but econometricians disentangle the two by multiple regression techniques. It is important to recognize that there are different possible definitions of wealth. In particular, much depends on whether future entitlements to pensions or social security payments are included. Intuitively, it seems best to treat them separately, and again this can be done by multiple regression. When this is done, nonpension wealth is still found to affect saving behavior. For example, Boyle and Murray (1979) and Feldstein (1974, 1982) found that wealth had a negative effect on saving in Canada and the United States respectively (in both these studies, the effects of income were controlled statistically, but private pensions counted as wealth and contributions to them counted as saving).

Using survey data, Katona (1975, pp. 247–51) confirms that those with more savings are more likely to add to them than those with few or none, but they are also more likely to make substantial dissavings. In other words, those with most savings were the most active, both in adding to them and in using them. These differences could not be explained by differences in income.

Pension plans and social security

One particular form of wealth is membership in a pension plan (either private or state controlled) which can be relied on to furnish an income in the future. If, as the life cycle hypothesis supposes, the goal of saving is to provide for future consumption, it is obvious that membership in a pension plan or the provision of social security should substantially reduce other forms of saving. Also, since pension provision constitutes a form of wealth, any other theory that supposes that wealth discourages saving should make the same prediction. Economists have therefore been gloomy about the effects that the spread of such schemes would have on saving behavior (e.g., Friedman 1957, p. 123), hence on capital formation within the economy.

Nonpension wealth tends to decrease saving. This suggests that pension plans will have a similar effect. The actual state of affairs has been the subject of furious controversy. Two independent, and quite different, early investigations (Cagan 1965; Katona 1965) found that pension scheme members saved slightly more than nonmembers. Cagan suggested that this is because pension plans draw people's attention to the question of retirement income, and hence to the necessity to save. Katona adds that the pension may bring an acceptable retirement income within one's grasp, and so make further saving for old age sensible.

More recent studies, largely inspired by the life cycle hypothesis, have found contrary results. Munnell (1976) found that both membership of private pension plans and expectations of social security benefits had a depressing effect on consumer saving. Furthermore, in reanalyzing Cagan's original data in more detail, Munnell found that they were consistent with the trends she had found. In a time-series study using U.S. data from before and after World War II, Feldstein (1974) found that social security wealth greatly reduced personal saving. Hemming and Harvey (1983) refer to a time-series study of U.K. data by Threadgold, which found that membership of private pension schemes reduced other saving.

However, these results have not gone unchallenged. Leimer and Lesnoy (1982) traced a computing error in the work of Feldstein (1974), and although the depressing effect of social security on saving was still present when the error was removed, the effect was no longer statistically significant (Feldstein 1982). Using U.K. cross-sectional survey data, Green (1981) reported a positive effect of pension contributions on other saving. Hemming and Harvey (1981) found a similar result, again in U.K. cross-sectional data, but it was not robust. If contributions level was supplemented by indicators of anticipated pension quality, the effect disappeared, although it did not go into reverse as predicted by theory.

Although private pension contributions and social security entitlements are likely to have similar effects on individual behavior (since both are highly illiquid but relatively secure forms of wealth), they are likely to have very different macroeconomic consequences. Private pension plans are usually "funded"; that is, contributions are collected and invested through financial institutions. Social security is normally "pay-as-you-go"; claims are met out of current contributions. From the point of view of capital formation, therefore, the replacement of private pensions by social security reduces the productive assets in an economy (e.g., Feldstein 1974).

Of course, whatever theory predicts, it will not necessarily be true that the introduction of social security will reduce private saving. That was part of the burden of the argument summarized above. There is some evidence (Daly 1983) that social security contributions do reduce the amount people save in funded pension plans. But it has been argued (e.g., Burkhauser & Turner 1982) that adequate provision for old age, in whatever form, will reduce the age of retirement, and thereby increase the amount of hump saving. In a cross-national time-series study, Koskela and Viren (1983a) found that the proportion of people working past the age of 65 was indeed negatively correlated with social security benefits.

The rate of interest

Another hotly contested issue has been the effects of interest rates on saving. Here, theoretical predictions are less clear. On the one hand, high interest rates increase the reward for saving, while on the other, they mean that any particular saving target can be achieved with less saving. In the terms introduced in Chapter 2, an increase in interest rates has both a substitution effect (the increased reward) and an income effect (the increased ease of reaching a given target) on saving.

It is not surprising that predictions about the effects of interest rates tend to emerge from detailed developments of particular theories. In practice, there seems to be a correlation between theories about interest and theories about pension wealth. Those authorities who argue that pension plans reduce other saving also tend to argue that high interest will increase it. In some cases (e.g., Powell 1960) this link can be attributed to ideological persuasion, but in others (e.g., Boskin 1978; Summers 1981) it seems to emerge from the mathematical development of the theories, and the constraints imposed on them by other aspects of existing data. For example, Summers (1981) attempted to substitute into his life-cycle model plausible values for variables such as the rate of population growth and the elasticity of substitution between past and future consumption. Summers found that the result was always a high interest elasticity of saving (i.e., a given rise of interest rates produced a large increase in saving).

By contrast, Weber (1970) developed a life-cycle model in which the income effect of high interest rates exceeded their substitution effect, so that the net effect was for high interest to discourage saving. Evans (1983) criticized Boskin and Summers for ignoring the uncertainty of the human lifespan, and found that when this was taken into account, any conditions which gave high long-run interest elasticities would also produce huge effects of interest rate changes, which are contrary to experience. He also found that if the bequest motive was introduced, the life-cycle hypothesis predicted much lower interest elasticities of saving than Boskin and Summers had suggested.

Most direct empirical studies find low, or even negative elasticities. For example, using an uncertain-lifetime life-cycle hypothesis with U.S. time-series data of 1952–80, Friend and Hasbrouck (1983) found a positive but small effect on saving of the expected real rate of return. Boyle and Murray (1979) found no significant effect of interest rates on Canadian saving, again in a time-series study. Giovanni (1983) found zero or negative effects of interest on saving in time-series studies of a number of developing countries, and Juster and Taylor (1975) found a significant negative effect using U.S. data. Weber (1975), who took into account wealth attributable to the ownership of consumer durables, also found that higher interest rates depressed saving; he argued that this arose because people postponed durables purchases in the hope of lower interest rates (for installment plan payments) in the future.

With so much confusion at the theoretical and econometric level, it is interesting to extend the data base by looking at attitude surveys and experimental studies. Katona (1975, p. 244) argues, from survey data, that interest rates affect the kinds of savings people hold, but not the amount. An experiment by Northrop (1978) attempted to increase children's saving by quite substantial interest payments, but only managed to rearrange the temporal pattern of their saving. In a token economy in which saving of money was rewarded with points, Phillips, Phillips, Fixsen, and Wolf (1971) were able to induce saving by reward but again found that the time distribution was more sensitive than the amount.

These psychological data suggest that the amounts of money normally paid as interest may be too small, and too remote, relative to the amounts saved, to have much effect on individual behavior. That conclusion is, of course, consistent with the literature on preference for delayed gratification: If choice was governed by the relative amounts of the currently available and postponed consumption, no one would save at all. The kinds of self-controlling strategies that enable people to save despite this impatience are unlikely to be sensitive to interest rate variations.

Inflation

Another factor that, to a simple rationality analysis, ought to affect saving, is inflation. The higher the rate of inflation, the less future consumption can be achieved by foregoing a given amount of current consumption. High inflation should therefore lead to reduced saving.

Attitude surveys suggest the exact opposite. It has repeatedly been found that inflation increases people's determination to save (Katona 1975, pp. 144–6), usually at the expense of spending on durable goods (which counts as saving from an economic standpoint, but is not seen as saving by consumers). Some econometric data have shown a similar trend. For instance, Boyle and Murray (1979) found that higher inflation led to higher saving in Canada; Juster and Taylor (1975) found a similar though slight effect in the United States; and Koskela and Viren's (1983a) cross-national time-series investigation found that unanticipated inflation led to higher savings ratios. By contrast, Branson and Klevorick (1969) found some effect of money prices (as against real prices) on consumption, so that a "money illusion" led to increased spending under inflation. This result is not necessarily at variance with those cited above, since much depends on whether wages or prices are moving faster, or have been moving for longer.

A number of explanations have been put forward for the positive effect of inflation on saving. In survey responses, people include inflation among the signs of bad economic conditions (Katona 1975, pp. 139–43). Saving tends to increase in prolonged bad times, and the effect of inflation is consistent with this (as we shall see). Another obvious factor is that, if the goal of saving is to make a particular amount of real consumption possible in the future, the inflation-induced decline in the real value of money wealth makes it necessary to save more (Mundell 1963).

Some economists have suggested that extra saving under inflation is accidental. Deaton (1977) claims that, in times of unanticipated inflation, inflationary price rises in particular goods are misinterpreted as increases in relative prices. Consumers therefore buy less than they intend, intending to reallocate their income to goods that have not suffered relative price rises but, since there are no such goods, they end up making involuntary additions to their savings instead. A different account of accidental saving under inflation has been suggested by Jump (1980) and Siegel (1979). They argue that only the real interest on savings deposits is available for spending; that part of the money interest that merely compensates for inflation is effectively ignored. However, standard statistics include any interest added to savings and not drawn out as new saving; saving is thus "overmeasured." Davidson and MacKinnon (1983) investigated both these possibilities, and found that the effect of the inflation-compensation portion of interest rates on measured saving was much higher than that of "unanticipated" inflation (measured by the increase in inflation since the previous time period). They therefore concluded that the Siegel and Jump hypothesis was the best explanation of increased saving during inflation.

The state of the economy

Prevailing general economic conditions affect people's incomes and wealth, and so they are bound to affect saving indirectly. According to Katona (1975, pp. 239–43) economic conditions also have a number of direct effects. Some of these enhance saving, and some depress it, making it impossible to make general predictions. But Katona does predict that when people perceive that times have been hard and are likely to continue to be hard, they will tend to save more.

From a psychological point of view the general trend toward saving in bad times is interesting. It suggests that saving should be seen as a defensive behavior, perhaps mediated by "safety" needs as described in Maslow's (1970) need hierarchy scheme (see Chapter 1). Durables purchase, on the other hand, is often thought of as a way of striving after social status, a higher kind of need in Maslow's terms. It is entirely consistent with Maslow's theory that people should come under the control of lower needs when under threat.

There are, however, other ways of looking at the same phenomena. If we recognized durables purchasing as a kind of saving, we also need to recognize that it is a very illiquid kind, in the accounting sense. Resale values of durable goods tend to be low, and the resale market is poorly organized except for cars. Shifting from durables purchase to bank deposits in times of economic difficulty can therefore be seen as a sensible move from illiquid to liquid forms of saving, rather than a reduction in saving as such. In agreement with this analysis, one econometric study that takes account of wealth due to durables ownership finds little effect of general economic conditions or inflation (Weber 1975). We can be fairly sure that few consumers would represent their actions in this way. This simply represents another case in which people do the right (or more or less rational) thing for the wrong reason.

Age

According to the life cycle hypothesis, age should have a crucial effect on saving. Before they reach peak income, people should borrow rather than save; in their middle years they should repay these borrowings and save to provide an income after retirement; and in retirement, they should consistently dissave. However, many of the factors already discussed, such as income, also vary with life cycle, so it not easy to determine whether age has a direct effect on saving.

Empirically, however, there is no doubt that saving does vary with age and that the variation does not take the form that the life-cycle hypothesis predicts. Middle-aged people save more than either retired people or those in their twenties, but at least part of this effect can readily be explained in terms of income and institutional factors. For example, many younger people will be living in rented accommodation rather than paying off loans on their housing (which counts as saving), or else they will be in the early stages of paying off a house mortgage when the payments made will be almost purely interest and so do not count as saving.

Most notably, many retired people either do not dissave, or even continue to save beyond any conceivable need in their own lifetimes. For example, Mirer (1979) found that after controlling for educational level (to take into account the fact that poorer people may die younger), mean net wealth was positively correlated with age in the postretirement population. This effect was nonsignificant and slight ($20 per year of age) but, as Mirer points out, it was obtained despite the fact that people retiring more recently have greater wealth at retirement, because of inflation and institutional changes. In a very careful survey based on census and probate records, Menchik and David (1983) found that average bequests increase with age, implying that wealth accumulation continues after retirement.

The two main possible accounts of this surprising phenomenon are an increased interest in bequeathing with age, and increased risk aversion with age. In survey data Projector and Weiss (1966) found that only 4% of respondents aged over 65 mentioned bequest as a motive for saving. The important factors, according to this sample, were provision for old age (not all those over 65 years of age regard themselves as old) and provision for emergencies, both of which can be brought under the heading of "risk avoidance." Davies (1981) found that, when the usual simplifying assumptions were replaced with observed data on survival probabilities and real incomes after retirement, slow or negative dissaving was in fact consistent with a zero bequest life cycle model. On the other hand, as we saw above, there is some evidence in favor of the bequest motive, at least for higher-income or higher-wealth individuals. What is quite clear is that the simple life cycle model, of saving in the middle years, dissaving in retirement, and zero utility for bequests is inadequate.

Simple predictions from psychological data are equally inadequate to explain how saving behavior varies with age. From the experiments on delayed gratification, we should expect children to save very little until the age of 8 or 9, and then to show a gradually increasing ability to save. In fact, young children save much of their pocket money (see Chapter 14). The disjunction between laboratory results and everyday experience in this area is striking, and deserves further attention.

Other personal characteristics

Despite the Freudian theory and a certain amount of popular belief and literary tradition consistent with it (consider Dickens's Scrooge), there is no firm evidence to link saving with particular personality types. Olander and Seipel (1971, pp. 77–86) review a number of attempts to find a relation between saving and a variety of dimensions of personality, for example the need for achievement (e.g., Morgan 1964). Although they do list some positive results, no very consistent pattern emerges.

The experimental literature has revealed a number of trends in the ability to delay gratification, but the jump from these experiments to observed saving behavior is too great in the case of the effects of age. The same is true of some of the other variables. For example, severely mentally ill people are very poor at choosing a larger delayed reward in experiments (e.g., Shybut 1968), but the amount of saving that is done within token economies on mental hospital wards (see Winkler 1981) is sufficient to discredit any idea that the mentally ill simply cannot save.

Some of the earliest experimental work on delayed gratification revealed differences between sociocultural groups (Mischel 1958), and recent work has found differences between socioeconomic classes (Freire, Gorman, & Wessman 1980). Class, race, and religion have been linked to differences in saving behavior by sociologists and psychologists from Weber (1904/1976) to McClelland (1961). The ambitious middle class groups, often from racial or religious minorities, are seen as providing the entrepreneurial thrust within society, and hence to include the major accumulators of wealth. In this case, laboratory and societal results seem to converge. As we shall see in Chapter 16, the Weber–McClelland approach has come under empirical attack in recent years, although there is certainly evidence that social factors influence saving. For example, Martineau (1958) found that when asked the question, "What would you do if you were given $1,000 tomorrow?," higher-class respondents were much more likely to say that they would save the money. Similarly, Lluch, Powell, and Williams (1977, chapter 10) find that the marginal propensity to save is much higher among farmers than in other households, both urban and rural.

Social class is obviously highly correlated with income and wealth which have strong effects of saving. These directly financial variables, however, do not exhaust the meaning of class, which also involves a complex of attitudes, habits, and experiences many of which are potentially relevant to saving. In a path analytic study of the factors affecting saving behavior, Lindqvist (1981) found that educational level, a good proxy for class, had quite a strong effect on saving behavior via attitudes and expectations, as well as its effect via its relation to household income.

Attitudes and expectations figure strongly in survey studies of economic behavior, and these have included several investigations of saving. People are asked questions about their view of their own and the nation's recent economic performance and future economic prospects. Katona (1975, pp. 242–3) argues that subjective notions about the permanence of income increases or decreases will affect the propensity to save, though he admits that the evidence is fragmentary.

CONCLUSION: WHY DO PEOPLE SAVE?

Saving is an area of economic behavior in which economists have made a specific appeal to psychology – and sometimes even to psychologists – for explaining underlying trends. It is also an area in which there is a reasonable amount of relevant research, drawing most from sources of data that we mentioned in Chapter 4. Yet this chapter has not altogether succeeded in bringing data to bear upon theory. For once we cannot blame the pervading rationality assumption. It is plain that humans are irrationally impatient in intertemporal choices, so that any theory of saving has to explain why people save as little as they do.

No doubt, part of the problem is that saving is a compound activity, subserving many different motivations. None of the motives for saving mentioned in this chapter was completely implausible. As so often, we find ourselves trying to understand the relative importance of all the different factors concerned rather than deciding that one of them is crucial and the rest irrelevant. The only way to do this is to build a strong data base; in practice, the data available are frustratingly contradictory. The psychological evidence, taken on its own, would suggest that saving is virtually impossible. We need to know what processes go on in the real world to overcome the excessive impatience detected in the laboratory. The econometric and survey data frequently give directly opposite answers to apparently identical questions. We need more, and more varied studies, so that we can detect the pattern underlying different kinds of results.

At the level of theory, the framework of rational intertemporal choice, provided by the life-cycle hypothesis, has proved fruitful. But its simple forms are clearly too simple. We need to take account of the effects of uncertainty, of the desire to bequeath, and of the varying extents to which behaviors, all constituting saving at the macroeconomic level, are perceived as saving by the potential savers.

In terms of both theoretical and empirical work, these are achievable goals, at least in the medium term. The study of saving should be a fruitful area of economic psychology in the next few years.

9

GIVING

This chapter contrasts with Chapters 7 and 8 in at least two different ways. First, the topics of work and buying contained a rich literature from both economics and psychology. Giving has not been studied in as much detail in either discipline. Second, we found many ways in which psychological ideas have been applied to what are usually seen as economic phenomena in the areas of work and buying. Giving, on the other hand, has usually been thought of as a psychological phenomenon, although we shall find that economic ideas have been brought to bear on it.

THE NATURE AND EXTENT OF GIVING BEHAVIOR

Gifts only comprise a few percent of the average person's monetary income. But in absolute terms, annual giving in most Western societies represents a very large amount of money (Collard 1978). In this chapter, we shall use "giving" in the widest possible sense, encompassing not only gifts that one typically gives to relatives and friends, but also other forms of altruistic behavior such as donations to charities, volunteer work for nonprofit organizations such as youth clubs and hospitals, and even voting for welfare payments to the poor. What these situations have in common is the fact that someone involved behaves in a way that benefits other people at his or her own expense. We call this altruistic behavior.

In economic terms, altruism can be defined as a concern for someone else's economic bundle of goods in addition to one's own bundle of goods (Collard 1978). On the surface at least, altruism seems to be central to our society. Quite apart from the individual behaviors mentioned above, the welfare state of the twentieth century is based on the altruistic notion that the economic condition of all people is the business of society in general. The key problem in any account of giving is to interpret this altruistic behavior.

There are three kinds of interpretation we can give. We can attempt to trace some economic benefit to the giver, so that the giving behavior is seen as only superficially altruistic. We can argue that the economic loss involved in giving is outweighed by some other kind of gain, perhaps psychological, so that the giving behavior is seen as altruistic at the economic level but selfish at another level. Or we can accept that there is such a thing as "genuine" altruism, in which the welfare of another individual, or other people in general, is capable of motivating human behavior. It should not be assumed that these three kinds of account can be separated.

The interpretation of altruism is particularly crucial for economic psychology. In the first place, all gifts are economic transactions in some sense. Second, it has often been claimed that Economic Man, the hypothetical subject of economic study, is fundamentally and absolutely selfish. On this view, economics is the "dismal science" which denies that altruism is part of "human nature."

AXIOM OF GREED

Collard (1978) begins his excellent book on economics and altruism in the following way:

My thesis in this book is that human beings are not entirely selfish, even in their economic dealings. It may seem strange to a layman, or even to his fellow social scientists, that the economist could consider such an assumption to be in any way remarkable or controversial. Yet it is the case that self-interested "economic man" dominates the textbooks. Indeed rationality and self-interest are taken as one and the same thing. (p. 3)

A few pages later, Collard elaborates on this point:

Practically the whole of [neoclassical] economic theory is built upon self-interested individuals maximizing utility and firms maximizing profits or minimizing loss. It is an assumption not likely to be abandoned or even modified. (p. 6)

Modern economic theory, in other words, is based upon the axiom of greed (see also Chapter 2). Indeed, the dominant view of mankind is embodied in the term *Homo economicus*. In Chapter 5, we discussed how this view depicts Rational Man as a maximizer of utility. However, we now confront a further apparent implication of this rationality principle: If humans are designed to maximize personal utility, to be rational, then it seems that they can have little room for altruism. It is not that Economic Man is a dark and sinister monster whose intentions are to harm others; spite is as irrational as selfishness (Wilson 1975). Rather, Economic Man is supremely indifferent to the plight of others; Economic Man is totally self-serving; what happens to others is of little concern.

The self-serving nature of Economic Man is given expression in the axiom of greed, which, as we saw in Chapter 2, is one of the cornerstones of microeconomic theory. It is stated more formally as follows: If one bundle of goods labeled A contains more of one good than another bundle of goods labeled B but has the same amount of all the other goods, bundle A will always be preferred to bundle B. In other words, humans always crave more than they currently have.

The basic problem of interpreting altruistic behavior can now be restated: Clearly, humans often do act selfishly, but altruism also seems to occur. How is altruism to be reconciled with the axiom of greed? In the next two sections of this chapter we look first at the biology of altruism, and then at the social psychology of altruism, examining in turn the suggestions that human nature is basically altruistic, or that there are psychological gains which offset the economic costs of altruism. Finally, in the last section of this chapter, we return to the question of the economics of giving behavior.

THE BIOLOGY OF ALTRUISM

Recent developments in evolutionary theory have led to a new understanding of what it means to talk about "human nature." As it happens, the explanation of altruistic behavior has been of crucial importance in these developments. The biology of altruism has thus received a great deal of attention; this section attempts to give a very brief review of the main conclusions.

The theory of evolution by natural selection

We begin with a review of the theory of natural selection. The ideas involved are probably familiar to most readers, but the subtlety and power of the overall theory are less widely understood. Obviously, we cannot describe it in detail here; more thorough discussions are given by Lea (1984), Maynard Smith (1966), Simpson (1951), and others.

The raw material of the theory consists of the following four facts. First, many more animals are born into the world than survive to maturity. This is a matter of common observation. Not all organisms survive their youth; many die before they become fully reproductive adults. Second, not all organisms of the same species are identical. The differences between two individuals of the same species are not always dramatic or even apparent to the human observer, but variation does occur. Third, some of these variations are heritable. Finally, some genetically based variations are better than others; that is, some of the variation is to the advantage of the individual in securing resources and some of it is disadvantageous.

Given these four facts, the theory of natural selection seems so obvious that it is almost a tautology. Clearly, organisms with genetic mutations that permit them to be slightly more successful than they would be otherwise, on the average, tend to survive and pass their mutant gene onto their offspring. Organisms with slight disadvantages, on the average, do not survive to reproductive age. It is this process that is called natural selection, and no one can doubt that it must occur; the only possible point of theoretical dispute is whether it is indeed, as Darwin asserted, the origin of species, including the human species. We shall assume, along with almost every modern biologist that human beings are indeed the products of evolution, so that evolutionary arguments can validly be used in accounting for human behavior.

Although variations between individuals often involve differences in physical attributes, they also may involve changes in behavioral potential. Let us pursue this idea a bit further. Genes program the construction of the body in which the genes reside. For example, they determine eye color, hair color, height, number of toes, and the millions of other physical characteristics that make up an individual. Genes are also responsible for programming the development of the brain. And residing in the brain are neurochemical structures that serve as substrates of behavioral potentials. Behavior is dependent on these potentials. Animals with different brains have different behavioral potentials; they differ in terms of the memories they can develop, the physical responses their brains permit, their sensory capacities, their learning capacities, and so forth. On one level of analysis, then, behavior is loosely determined by the general behavioral potentials that are programmed by the brain. These in turn are programmed by the genes. In this sense, genes help determine behavior because they direct the development of neural structures in the brain which, more directly, help determine behavior. All of this is not to ignore the enormous role played by the environment. Humans, and many other higher organisms, are not mechanical prewired creatures. Although we have potentials for behavior within our nervous system, those potentials are fulfilled and realized only within the context of our environment.

Nonetheless, the obvious conclusion from evolutionary theory is that individuals must act in a self-interested manner if they are to survive. Individuals who are born with a slight advantage over their conspecifics, on the average, will survive to maturity, but they do so only by "competing" with their conspecifics. The competition need not be direct, as in an actual fight, but competition is nevertheless present. It is obvious that the theory of natural selection portrays organisms in general in the same light that the theory of Economic Man portrays humans. In both cases the individual functions in his or her own self-interest at the expense of others.

The evolution of altruism

The picture described above leaves little room for altruism. Yet altruistic acts on the part of many species have long been known. In the biological sense, an altruistic act occurs when one organism behaves in a way such that the survival of another organism is enhanced at the expense of that animal's own chance for survival. For example, bees will sting intruders in order to protect the hive. In some cases, the stinger is attached to the internal organs of the bee such that when the stinger is deposited into the intruder the entire insides of the bee are extracted, resulting in the bee's death. In a sense, the bee commits suicide in order to save the hive.

Another example involves small birds, many of which give alarm calls when a predator comes near. The call has the effect of alerting other members of the flock so that they can fly to safety. It also has the effect of isolating the alarm call giver and thus of attracting the attention of the predator to that individual. Alarm calls are therefore altruistic in the sense that the giver of the call is at great personal risk when alerting other members of the flock.

Consider an example. The English lapwing gets its name from the following impressive example of altruistic behavior, also shown by many other ground-nesting birds that have to contend with predators such as foxes. If a female lapwing is sitting on her eggs and an intruder approaches, she will scurry from the nest flapping one wing on the ground in the manner of a badly wounded bird. As the predator pursues the "wounded" animal, it is led increasingly away from the nest itself. When the distance is sufficiently great, the "wounded" bird simply flies away and returns to her chicks, leaving the predator stranded at some distance from the nest and in doubt of its location. According to a naive view of natural selection, all these examples of altruism are paradoxical, because animals are "deliberately" putting themselves at risk and therefore jeopardizing their chances of surviving. The "rational" animal, just like Economic Man, should surely never risk its chances for survival by acting in such a selfless way.

One of the major advances of evolutionary theory in recent years has been the consideration of "altruism" within the context of natural selection. This has been at the center of the approach known as "sociobiology" (Barash 1979; Trivers 1971; Wilson 1975, 1978). The sociobiological argument is that altruistic acts occur because, although they do indeed jeopardize the individuals that perform them, they favor the survival of genes that are shared between those individuals and those that benefit from the altruism.

It is easy to see that some individuals have genes in common. Every individual is related to its parents; in most sexually reproducing animals an offspring shares half its genes with each parent. In addition, individuals share genes with their siblings (because both are related to the parents) and, decreasingly, with other kin (through common ancestors). The subtle part of the theory comes when we consider the consequence of an individual being altruistic. If the altruistic acts are directed toward relatives, or kin, then the chances for survival of the commonly shared genes increases despite the fact that the altruistic individual is put at risk. By definition, altruism jeopardizes the individual but enhances the survival chances of another individual; when the two individuals share genes, the altruistic act may paradoxically enhance the survival of the shared genes. Now, if one of these is a gene for altruism, we have a mechanism whereby natural selection can result in the evolution of altruistic behavior.

The simplest example of altruism is parental care. Parenting involves the sacrifice of resources and time. But it is easy to see how it is explained within sociobiological theory: The parents' self-sacrificial behavior results in an increase in the probability of their offspring's survival, hence an increase in the probability of survival of any genes contained in both the parent and offspring. In a sense, then, altruism on the individual level is selfishness on the genetic level (Dawkins 1976). Such "kin altruism" need not be limited to close relatives, but it is most likely to occur in animals that show intensive parental care and that live in large social groups of related individuals. Both are characteristics of the human species.

Kin altruism is not the only possible way in which altruistic behavior could be produced by natural selection. Trivers (1971) proposed a further mechanism, called "reciprocal altruism" to explain the evolution of altruistic acts between strangers, and even between members of different species, provided the possibility of enforcing reciprocity is assumed. The kinds of animal in which reciprocal altruism is most likely to evolve are long-lived social animals of relatively high intelligence and, in particular, those with a capacity to recognize and remember other individuals. These too are characteristics of humans.

Altruism, then, is rather likely to be produced in the human species by natural selection operating at the genetic level. It might also evolve through cultural traditions. Dawkins (1976) suggested that cultural units, such as ideas, catch phrases, habits, ways of making tools, and clothes are self-replicating units that are passed via word of mouth from one generation to the next and are maintained through imitation (see also Pulliam & Dunford 1980). One such cultural unit could be the belief in and practice of altruism. It is certainly true that, for thousands of years, religious traditions and other social institutions have advocated altruism. Perhaps this is part of the reason why our modern welfare state is based on altruistic values.

It should be stressed that, although sociobiological theory can thus explain why some altruistic behavior occurs, it still predicts that the majority of behavior will be directly self-serving. Nonetheless, we can conclude from the biology of altruism that altruistic acts may be expected to occur at the individual level (although they may perhaps be selfish on the genetic level). Moreover, sociobiological data suggest that this limited kind of altruism is, in fact, an important and pervasive phenomenon among social species. Biology, therefore, would appear to challenge the concept of Economic Man. Perhaps we are not naturally the self-serving creatures that traditional economics would have us be.

As a biological phenomenon, altruism does indeed exist. It is therefore reasonable to suppose that some altruistic behavior occurs for no other reason than that another individual benefits. But is it true that at least some altruistic behavior, although it causes an economic loss, affords the person who does it a psychological gain? To answer this question, we turn to social psychology, and in particular to research and theory concerned with helping behavior.

In 1964, a woman named Kitty Genovese was brutally murdered on a street corner in New York City. Thirty-eight neighbors witnessed this event, yet not one of them called the police or gave assistance (Rosenthal 1964). This callous and inhuman behavior is in stark contrast to the wealth of evidence that in other situations people are helping and caring. The case of Kitty Genovese is not necessarily typical of "human nature." But what went wrong? Why was it that no help was rendered? At the time of this incident, social psychologists knew very little about helping behavior, but the Kitty Genovese murder prompted them to investigate this question. As a result, a great deal of information has been uncovered concerning helping behavior specifically and altruism in general (Wispe 1978; Rushton 1980; Rushton & Sorrentino 1981). This area of research is often referred to as the study of "prosocial behavior," and one of its main aims has been to identify the factors that dispose people to behave altruistically or prosocially.

Factors affecting helping behavior

Darley and Latane (1970) argued that one of the important variables affecting altruistic behavior is the cost of helping. The general notion is that helping is inversely related to the cost or the degree to which it intrudes on the helper's personal life. For example, Darley and Latane (1970) asked New York passersby for the time, for directions, for change of a quarter, or for the person's name; the proportions of people complying with the request were 85%, 85%, 73%, and 29%, respectively.

Another study was conducted by Piliavin, Rodin, and Piliavin (1969). These experimenters investigated helping behavior by feigning collapse while traveling on the New York City subway system. In some cases, the experimenter smelled of alcohol; in other cases, he appeared to be an invalid. Both white and black experimenters were used in these studies. The results showed that helping behavior was more commonly offered to the "invalid" traveler than to the "drunken" traveler. Men helped more than women and help came from the same race more when the traveler appeared drunk. If blood dripped from the traveler's mouth, helping behavior was significantly reduced (Piliavan & Piliavan 1972). Similarly, if the traveler was scarred with a rather noticeable birthmark, helping behavior was reduced (Piliavin, Piliavin, & Rodin 1975). All these studies suggest that helping behavior is inversely related to the degree of intrusion or the cost involved. There is, in addition, the implication that helping behavior is drastically reduced if some future entanglement is suggested (many fewer people agreed to provide their name than the time or directions) or if there are immediate complications (e.g., the alcoholic might become sick or aggressive).

A second major factor that influences altruism is the number of bystanders. The more bystanders there are, the less help is offered. Three processes seem to be involved in this: audience inhibition, social influence, and diffusion of responsibility. The presence of others can inhibit helping if a person is worried that his or her actions will be seen and may be evaluated negatively. Helping will also be inhibited if the situation is ambiguous. In this case we look to other people to help define the situation. If people in a group look calm, then an emergency may be wrongly perceived as nothing serious. Finally, helping may be reduced because in a group the responsibility for helping is diffused; any single person is less likely to feel responsible when there are many others present.

In Darley and Latane's (1968) important demonstration of the effect of group size on helping, a positive relationship was obtained between the time it took to report an accident and the size of the group. A "confederate" of the experimenters (i.e., a person who worked in collaboration with the experimenters to stage a fictitious incident and thereby allow the experimenter to examine the subsequent behavior of the subject) feigned an epileptic seizure. The accident was reported within about 52 seconds by all subjects when they were alone. However, when the subject thought that a third person was present (known via an intercom connection), only 85% of the subjects reported the accident and the time taken was about 93 seconds. When four others were thought to be present, only 66% of the subjects reported the accident after about 166 seconds.

Other research has considered the definition of the situation. In one important study, Ross and Braband (1973) tested subjects in the presence of a normal or blind confederate. The subject was ostensibly being "interviewed" when an accident occurred (a workman in a nearby room screamed for help). It is important to note that the confederates were instructed not to react to the accident. The results showed that 64% of the subjects reacted to the screams when they were alone. By contrast, only 28% reacted when they were with the blind confederate and 35% when they were with the normally sighted confederate. These results emphasize the importance of the information that the reactions of others provides. Only the presence of the normally sighted confederate should produce diffusion of responsibility, since such a person could not reasonably be expected to help. The person's failure to react defines the situation as nonserious and so leads to less helping.

These and other experiments (Clark & Word 1972) suggest that the inverse relationship between helping behavior and the number of bystanders is partly caused by the ambiguity of the situation. People are uncertain about what behavior is appropriate during an emergency. They use reactions of others to gauge what behavior is expected of them. All three processes, however – audience inhibition, social influence, and diffusion of responsibility – are involved in decreasing the likelihood of helping in groups; the effects of each are independent and additive (Latane, Nida, & Wilson 1981).

The third major variable affecting the degree of altruism is the type of plea rendered. Dorris (1972) conducted a study in which the experimenter visited various coin dealers offering coins for sale (the experimenter claimed the coins were a gift and that he knew nothing about their value). In a neutral condition the average amount offered by the dealers was $8.72. However, when the experimenter explicitly mentioned that he needed the money in order to buy textbooks for college, the coin dealers, on the average, offered $13.73 for the same coins. Apparently, helping behavior is more readily offered if justifications are given or if the subject appeals to the person's sense of moral justice.

A fourth factor is the environment. It is not surprising to find that large differences in helping behavior have been found between city dwellers and those who live in smaller towns (Korte 1980). City dwellers are less trusting (Milgram 1970) and they are less likely to help others (Amato 1983). In particular, they are less likely to let someone make an important telephone call, to return an overpayment, or to return a "dropped" envelope (Korte & Kerr 1975). Takooshian, Haber, and Lucido (1977) found that 46% of the city dwellers were likely to help children call their parents, while 72% of town dwellers were likely to render the same service. These experiments demonstrate that the atmosphere or environment is extremely powerful in nurturing altruism. In the town environment, where relationships are more personal, helping behavior is more likely to occur. By contrast, in large towns (those with populations over 20,000) and cities, where people are less likely to know each other personally and therefore less likely to rely on each other, helping behavior is relatively low (Amato 1983).

Mood, too, influences the degree to which a person will exhibit altruistic behavior. Much of the work has been done by Isen and colleagues. The general finding is that if a person is in a good mood, he or she is more likely to donate money (Isen 1970) or help in an experiment (Isen

& Levin 1972). In one study by Isen, Clark, and Schwartz (1976), one experimenter gave a free sample of stationery to various households. Subsequently a second experimenter called at the house and asked whether the person would make an important telephone call for them (they claimed that they had no more money left). Having received the free sample increased the frequency of calling. In another field experiment, people leaving a cinema were asked to donate to a charity. Those who had seen a sad film made fewer donations than those who had seen a happy one (Underwood, Berensen, Berenson, Cheng, Wilson, Kulik, Moore, Wenzel, & Cobbleigh 1978).

Learning to be altruistic

According to Rushton (1980), socialization includes two kinds of learning that have a major effect on later altruism. First, we have to learn the capacity for empathy. Empathy exists when one person shares the feelings of another person. It is generally believed that empathy is learned early in life and that humans may even be genetically predisposed toward it; certainly its presence can be demonstrated at a very early age. For example, Sagi and Hoffman (1976) played various sounds to babies. These workers found that the babies began to cry when they heard the cry of others. Empathy is easily demonstrated in adults. Stotland (1969) measured heart rate and galvanic skin response (GSR) while subjects watched confederates undergo a painful experience. The result was an elevation in heart rate and GSR levels. Similarly, Krebs (1975) found that subjects would react physically in the same way as the confederates. However, the reaction was more pronounced when the subjects perceived the confederates as being similar to themselves; when viewing confederates deemed different, empathy was much less.

It would appear obvious that empathy should predispose people to altruistic behavior. Several studies have demonstrated that empathy and helping behavior are highly correlated. Coke, Batson, and McDavis (1978) asked subjects to concentrate on the plight of accident victims (the scenario was delivered over a radio set) or, simply, on the "techniques" of the radio broadcast. All subjects received a harmless placebo pill, but half of them were told it would cause physiological arousal while the other half of the subjects were told that the pill would produce relaxation. Later they measured the helping behavior of the subjects. It was found that those subjects who focused on the plight of the victim generally helped more than those who did not (i.e., than those who focused on the techniques of the broadcast). Presumably the helpers had experienced "empathetic arousal" from hearing the distress. However, the pattern of helping varied according to the perceived cause of arousal. That is, when arousal was attributed to the pill, helping went down. But when the subjects could not explain their arousal at hearing the distress in terms of the action of the pill, the helping behavior was very high. In other words, when arousal (empathy) was attributed to the pill or when they were not empathetic to begin with (those that focused on the broadcast technique), helping was rather low. But when arousal was not thought to be caused by the pill, empathy and helping were high.

Socialization does not only involve learning general tendencies like empathy. We also learn highly specific norms for appropriate prosocial behaviors. Norms are a standard by which we judge events and then register approval or disapproval. According to Rushton (1980) three norms are relevant to prosocial behavior. One is the norm for social responsibility, that is, a stipulation that one is obliged to help others. This norm is influenced by a number of factors. For example, Berkowitz and Daniels (1963, 1964) showed that a person is more likely to be helpful to another person if that other person is dependent on the helper. Second, helping behavior increases if a person believes that he or she has violated the social norm for responsibility. This has been demonstrated in two contexts. Freedman, Wallington, and Bless (1967) had a confederate tell a subject in private about the details of a forthcoming experiment. The experimenter then entered the room and asked the subject if he or she knew about the experiment (and claimed that innocence was required or else the experiment would be ruined). Most of the subjects lied and said that they didn't know about the details. Then all the subjects were given a test and asked to volunteer for a second experiment. Those who had been induced to lie were more likely to volunteer; that is, they were more likely to try to make up for their lying by volunteering.

A similar effect is found when subjects believe that they have hurt other people. Carlsmith and Gross (1969), for example, had students complete a "learning task" where they were instructed to give either a buzz or a shock to a confederate. Later the subjects were asked to volunteer to help the experimenter in another study. Only 25% of the "buzz" students volunteered, whereas 75% of the students who had given shocks volunteered. In other experiments, subjects who merely witnessed someone inflicting harm upon a confederate were more likely to engage in helping behavior (Cialdini, Darby, & Vincent 1973). All these examples show the restoration of the social responsibility norm. When we violate these norms we feel guilty and are therefore more likely to rectify our lapse by giving helping behavior.

A second standard we learn is the norm for equity (see Chapter 1). We all have a sense of what is fair and equitable, and we behave in ways that maintain balance and equity. When something happens to upset equity, we behave in such a way as to restore it. We saw in Chapter 6 how this process might influence working behavior; an additional example may be seen in an experiment conducted by Adams and Jacobsen (1964). These investigators hired subjects to be proofreaders. Some were told they were unqualified but were being paid at the same rate as qualified subjects; according to our social norms, this is not an equitable situation. Other subjects were told that they were unqualified and therefore were being paid less than qualified subjects. A third group of subjects was told that they were qualified and therefore were being paid at the rate appropriate to qualified proofreaders. The results showed that the first group, the overpaid group, found more proofreading errors in the text than the other two groups. The authors reasoned that these subjects had redressed the inequity by working harder at the task.

An experiment by Miller and Smith (1977) showed the consequences of such results for our understanding of altruistic behavior. They used the same technique (over-, under-, or correctly paying subjects for a task), and then measured sharing behavior. The overpaid subjects gave more to groups of children who had not been paid or who had lost their pay, than either of the other types of subjects. The message here seems to be quite straightforward: We give or share or help when we believe that we are in a more favorable position than the recipients; if we believe that we are unfairly less well off than the recipients, then altruism is exceedingly weak.

The concept of deservedness is fundamental to the issue of giving and altruism. It appears that most people want to believe that they live in a world in which people get what they deserve or, rather, deserve what they get (Lerner 1970). A number of authors have suggested mathematical relationships describing equitable relations (Lerner 1974; Adams 1963, 1965; Anderson 1976); we mentioned these briefly in Chapter 6. For the purposes of this chapter, these formulations are not important. But the general concept of deservedness is important because it suggests that altruism is guided by a sense of a "just" world. People will not help others, and will not give to others, if they believe that the donation would imbalance the equitable relationship currently in effect. Conversely, people will give to others in order to redress an imbalance in equity.

The third and final norm affecting prosocial behavior is the norm of reciprocity. In one sense, this is simply a special case of equity in that helping behaviors, gifts, or acts of altruism are expected to be returned in one form or another. That gifts imply a need to return gifts is easily observed in primitive societies (e.g., Levi-Strauss 1965; Mauss 1954) although we are perhaps less willing to admit it of our own society. But research has confirmed that people in Western societies also have a strong norm for helping those who have helped them in the past (Bar-Tal 1976; Goranson & Berkowitz 1966). As we saw earlier in this chapter, reciprocal altruism might well be a biological tendency in the human species, as well as a norm of particular cultures.

Mechanisms for learning altruism

If we learn empathy and norms for appropriate behavior, and if these underlie our altruistic acts, one way to understand giving behavior is to find out how we learn these behavioral potentials. Rushton (1980) argues that an important role is played by the kinds of simple learning that we discussed in Chapter 1, classical conditioning, instrumental learning, and observational learning. Let us briefly review the evidence.

Classical conditioning has been used to explain the formation and change of attitudes. People like stimuli associated with reward and dislike stimuli associated with punishers (see Byrne 1971). For this reason, the recipient of an altruistic act may develop a high regard for the person who behaved altruistically and, in turn, perform similar acts of altruism to the person or others in the future. Similarly, instrumental conditioning may play a role in the sense that altruistic behavior may increase when it is followed by reward of some kind. An example of this was shown by Allen, Hart, Buell, Harris, and Wolf (1964). They described how a child in a nursery school, who normally isolated herself from the other children, gradually learned to share and participate with the others after receiving the teacher's approval for doing so. In another study, Fisher (1963) rewarded marble-sharing behavior in children and found that it increased with training. In general, then, altruism seems to be susceptible to physical rewards (like candy) or social approval (see Midlarsky, Bryan, & Brickman 1973).

Finally, children and others learn to behave altruistically by observing others behave in such a manner (Bandura & Kupers 1964). For example, a number of experimenters (Grusec 1971, 1972; Grusec & Skubiski 1970; Rushton 1975) have shown that children imitate generosity: When they see adults being generous by donating tokens to a charity, they too become generous. Adults are also influenced by observing generous-behaving models (Schachter & Hall 1952; Rosenbaum 1956). In one experiment, Bryan and Test (1967) found that only 17 out of every 1,000 cars passing a particular point on a highway stopped to help a stranded motorist with a flat tire. However, if, one-quarter of a mile before the stranded car, the motorist saw a man helping a woman with a flat tire, 29 out of 1,000 stopped to help. The implication is obvious: People serve as models for other people; if the models behave generously, so do those who are observing. The characteristics of the model make a difference too; for example, well-dressed models are more effective than poorly dressed models (Lefkowitz, Blake, & Mouton 1955).

The psychological compensations for altruism

Some of the evidence we have reviewed suggests that there are psychological processes, operating during socialization, which will tend to accentuate any natural human tendency toward altruism. But we have also seen evidence that the economic costs of altruism may sometimes be offset by psychological gains. This is seen at its starkest in the instrumental conditioning of sharing, for example, but also occurs in more subtle ways. Empathy is an example. If I share someone's feelings, then giving that person pleasure brings me pleasure, too. Conformity to norms presumably also brings comfort, as does the restoration of the feeling that people are getting what they deserve from the world.

The clearest evidence from social psychology, however, is that psychological costs can inhibit altruism. This phenomenon is seen very obviously in the literature on helping behavior. It lends further support to the idea that altruistic behavior can, in some cases at least, be interpreted as the result of a balance of benefits and costs to the altruistic individual, some of them "economic" and some of them "psychological."

EXCHANGE AND ASSURANCE MODELS

From the previous two sections we have concluded that the good of another individual may be a direct motive for economic behavior, and that economic cost may be offset by psychological gain. It is not our purpose to try to decide which of these explanations best accounts for altruism in humans. Probably both are important, and the goal for future research will be to decide how far each operates in any given situation. What matters for the moment, however, is that there is good reason to expect humans to be altruistic and that humans indeed are altruistic, to some extent at least. How can we reconcile this with the axiom of greed? The purpose of the next section is to review two models which attempt to bring altruism into the mainstream of economic theory, rather as sociobiology aimed to bring it into the mainstream of evolutionary theory.

Exchange model

A theory of exchange has been developed in the context of welfare economics by a number of authors (e.g., Mansfield 1975) and has been extended to a study of altruistic economics (by Collard 1978). This model illustrates how it is possible for one person to yield a certain amount of goods to another person and still remain at some kind of optimal economic level.

The exchange model relies on the use of the Edgeworth box, which we introduced briefly in Chapter 7 in connection with bargaining behavior. There we used it to determine the equilibrium at which two bargainers

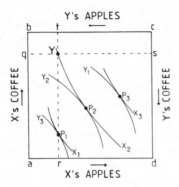

9.1. Edgeworth box illustrating indifference curves for two individuals. Exchanges of goods may take place, and an equilibrium may be reached. See text for details.

should agree to trade. Here we shall use it to describe the processes by which they can reach equilibrium, and the consequences of showing a limited kind of altruism within those processes.

The Edgeworth box is illustrated again in Figure 9.1. Let us assume that we have two people called person X and person Y and that they are isolated on a desert island with a certain amount of two commodities, say, coffee and apples. The vertical axis represents coffee and the horizontal axis represents apples. The amount possessed by person X is measured from the bottom left corner of the box, while person Y's possessions are measured from the upper right-hand corner of the box diagram. Any point in the box corresponds to a possible distribution of the goods on the island between the two people. Thus, at the point marked ψ, person X possesses $A-Q$ amount of coffee and $A-R$ amount of apples, while Y possesses $C-S$ amount of coffee and $C-T$ amount of apples. Obviously the amount of coffee owned by person X is equal to the total amount of coffee minus the amount owned by person Y; similarly, the amount of apples owned by Y is equal to the total amount minus the apples owned by X.

Suppose that these two people begin their stay on the desert island at point ψ. Is this allocation of commodities optimal, that is, the best possible? Or would it be fairer to say that one person should have more of one (or both) commodities than is currently the case? It may be possible, for example, to reach what economists call a Pareto equilibrium. This equilibrium is named after the nineteenth-century Italian economist Vilfredo Pareto, who proposed one criterion by which any proposed change in any economic system may be judged. According to Pareto, the change will be an improvement if it harms no one and improves the lot of at least one person. Using the Edgeworth Box, we can analyze whether any exchange of goods would be an improvement by Pareto's criterion. When no change could achieve such an improvement, we say that the system has reached a Pareto equilibrium. In such a situation, no act of giving could make the recipient better off without making the giver worse off.

Clearly, giving which produces a Pareto improvement is hardly giving at all in our definition. Nonetheless, it is interesting to consider its consequences. To do this we have to consider the indifference curves shown in Figure 9.1 (see Chapter 2 for a discussion of indifference curves). Recall that in any two-dimensional consumption space there exists an infinite number of indifference curves (none of which intersect), which depict the various points at which combinations of commodities are equivalently desirable. Lines X1 , X2, and X3 are three such indifference curves for person X. Person X is indifferent between the stated amount of coffee and apples at one point on X1 as that person is between the amount at any other point on X1. Recall also from Chapter 2 that the further the indifference curve is from the origin (the point of zero consumption of either commodity), the better. Higher indifference curves are more desirable because they involve an absolute larger number of items. Thus X2 is more desirable for person X than X1, although every point on X2 is equilavent to every other point on X2 in terms of the person's preference.

Now consider person Y, who has indifference curves Y1, Y2, and Y3. Note that these curves are concave downward because person Y's ownership between the two commodities originates in the upper right-hand corner of the box diagram. Again, each point on Y1 is equivalent to every other point on Y1; each point on Y2 is equivalent to all other points on Y2. For person Y, however, existing on Y2 is preferable to Y1, since it involves a greater total amount of coffee and apples (it is a higher indifference curve).

Point ψ falls on the indifference curves X2 and Y1. It is clear that there could be some exchange of apples and coffee which would harm no one and benefit at least one person. In particular, person Y could give up a certain number of apples for a certain amount of coffee by changing to point P3 (but remaining on indifference curve Y1). This bundle would be equivalent to the bundle of goods at point ψ because the two points lie on the same indifference curve. However, consider what happens to person X when this exchange takes place. Person X now has jumped from indifference curve X2 to curve X3. Such a jump, because it represents a greater absolute amount of goods, is an improvement in person X's welfare.

The reverse would occur were person X to exchange commodities. That person could sacrifice coffee for apples and go from point ψ to point P2. The new amount would be equivalently desirable because it would still be on the same indifference curve. If this exchange were to take place, however, then person Y benefits because Y now is on indifference curve Y2 rather than Y1.

Either of these two alternative courses of action requires one person to be wholly altruistic in the sense that all the benefit of the exchange accrues to the other person (although the altruist is not worse off). How-

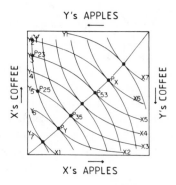

Y's APPLES

X's COFFEE

Y's COFFEE

X's APPLES

9.2. Edgeworth box illustrating indifference curves and trade options. See text for details.

ever, any decision about the exchange of commodities that lies on the line P2–P3 represents some degree of altruism and correspondingly some improvement in the overall welfare of the two people. If X is altruistic first, allowing a movement to P2, it would be open to Y to be altruistic as well, moving to P4 and permitting X to change from curve X2 to X3. Here no further change can be made without violating the Pareto equilibrium criterion. The two persons are at contract point where their two indifference curves are tangential (because it is there that the marginal rate of substitution will be equal).

This process of alternating acts of weak altruism looks more like trade than serious altruism. The Edgeworth box was in fact developed to deal with barter, not giving. But if the two people were engaged in trade without regard for each other's welfare, their behavior and their aims would be rather different. Consider Figure 9.2, which shows a larger number of indifference curves for two individuals. If the starting point is again ψ, a realistic trading objective for X would be to try to reach Px where X would be substantially better off, and Y would be no worse off. Person Y, on the other hand, would try to reach Py. Let us now change our notation to make the example clearer. Points ψ, Px, and Py now are called P22, P62, and P26 respectively. It should be clear that if X makes what we called an altruistic trade by moving to P25, the best final equilibrium point one could hope for would be P35. If X's first move only is to P23, the best equilibrium point might end up to be at P53. It is obvious, therefore, that in the long run each individual will be best served by making a series of very small exchanges, even though in the short run neither of them loses by larger exchanges. This example illustrates the weakness of the Pareto criterion: any point on the line Px and Py would be better for the two persons than ψ, and it would be stable; but we cannot say what point would be equitable. The example also illustrates another point: Altruism depends on a time scale. Usually we think of behavior which is apparently altruistic in the short term turning out to be advantageous to the performer in the long term. Here we have a case where behavior that costs the individual nothing in the short term turns out to be altruistic in the long term.

Collard's model does not require us to modify the axiom of greed. Neither participant was required to value the other's welfare to the extent of giving up anything of his or her own. In practice, any process that fitted this formal structure would work much better given a sense of altruism, a positive caring for the other person's welfare. But it is important that such weak altruistic tendencies can produce apparently unselfish behavior.

Game theory

Rather similar conclusions follow from a second approach to the study of nonselfish economics, using the prisoner's dilemma game. This well-known game is based on the following imaginary scenario. Two prisoners, awaiting trial, are held separately without being able to communicate. Each is told that a confession will result in a very light sentence but a very severe sentence for the other person. If neither informs, both sentences will be moderate. If both prisoners inform on each other, they both will receive a moderately severe sentence. Since the prisoners have to make their decisions independently, the dilemma is whether to trust the other person. If they do trust the other person not to inform, it is in the person's interest also not to inform. However, if they do not trust the other person, then clearly a different strategy is involved: They must inform to avoid taking all the blame.

There are two basic strategies to the prisoner's dilemma. The first is cooperation C, and the second is competition or defection D. Normally, the development of cooperative behavior between two people is studied in the laboratory by varying the payoff matrix in a prisoner's dilemma "game." Here, each person is awarded points according to the strategy that the person takes relative to the strategy that the other person takes. The surprising thing about this game is that cooperation is normally very low (subjects give C responses only about 30% of the time). If one of the players cooperates on 100% of the trials, a subject is more likely to make a C response too. Conversely, if the other person is seen as powerful, then an exploitation strategy is adopted (see Oskamp 1971 for a review of strategy variables). Not surprisingly, being able to discuss strategies (Scodel et al., 1959) or to pass notes (Voissem & Sistrunk 1971) increases cooperative behavior. Even telling subjects to be concerned with cooperation affects their tendency to cooperate (Deutsch 1958). In addition, cooperation in the prisoner's dilemma game depends on the way a subject approaches the game, that is, on the person's intentions and the intentions that that person attributes to the partner (see Eiser 1978, 1980).

Although the prisoner's dilemma game leads to a selfish strategy under normal conditions, it is clear that the cooperative outcome is better for the two players considered on the whole. Can one improve the outcome? Obviously, if both players show the strongest possible form of altruism, a concern for the other's welfare and disregard for their own, the result will be the cooperative solution, which is best for both of them. But are there conditions where weaker forms of altruism will suffice? The answer to this question is a qualified "yes" (Collard 1978). What one needs is a way of making cooperation by both players a more tempting alternative than a mixed strategy.

According to Collard, the way to do this is to convert the prisoner's dilemma game into what Collard calls an assurance game. An assurance game is one in which each player has some assurance that the other player will cooperate. The way to make this conversion is to assume that each player attaches a weight v to the other person's payoff. The overall value to any given player, then, is that player's own payoff, plus the other's payoff multiplied by v. How big does v have to be before a prisoner's dilemma game is converted into an assurance game? To answer that question we have to introduce another term: π. π is the probability of cooperation; when $\pi = 0$ no assurance of cooperation is given, as π approaches 1.0, the probability of cooperation, that is, the assurance, increases. As Collard has shown, the cooperative strategy, the altruistic strategy, will be played by either player if $v > 1/2(1-\pi/2)$. This formula indicates that if assurance for cooperation is very high (say, $\pi = 1.0$) then only a small regard for the other person's payoff is required ($v = 1/4$). If, however, no assurance for cooperation is given ($\pi = 0$), then cooperative strategies will be adopted only when $v >$ so that each player gives the other's welfare over half the weighting they give to their own. Although this falls well short of total altruism, even a limited altruistic tendency may ensure altruistic behavior.

In summary, cooperative behavior will be each individual's best strategy either if the other person's payoff is treated as valuable to some degree, or if there is some assurance that cooperation will ensue. The more assurance for cooperation, the less wholly unselfish behavior is required (see also Becker 1976).*

---

*But just how is such a competitive situation converted into an assurance game? How could an altruistic regard for another's welfare come into being in a culture when the D, or selfish, strategy is clearly the "safest" (confessing never results in the heaviest penalty and may just produce the lightest sentence)? If a selfish strategy were safest, wouldn't it also be stable in the culture and wouldn't it be impossible for a cooperative strategy ever to become established? According to Axelrod and Hamilton (1981), the answer to this latter question is "no." Whereas the D response is admittedly the "better" and more stable strategy, a tit-for-tat response *can* be established in a culture, and, once in existence, can rapidly lead to a new and stable response strategy. We shall not cover Axelrod and Hamilton's work on the evolution of cooperation in any detail because it really lies outside the scope of this book. But briefly, they argue that any single act of altruism, committed by a "mutant" in the culture (whose general strategy is all D), will gain a foothold largely because the mutant's reaction can be recognized and valued by kin. Once committed, this act of generosity will elicit a tit-for-tat reaction and

Both exchange analysis and game theory offer us economic analyses of altruistic behavior. They give us two frameworks within which we can reconcile the axiom of greed and either a straightforward human tendency toward altruism (innate or acquired) or a psychological compensation for economic altruism. In the exchange analysis, all we had to suppose was that if an individual's welfare was not affected one way or the other by an action, then outcomes that promote another individual's welfare will be preferred. This involves, in effect, supplementing the axioms of demand theory. In analyzing the prisoner's dilemma, we had to allow that the other's welfare is taken into account along with one's own (though possibly with a lesser weighting). This amounts to saying that other individuals' welfare can be a source of utility, and it in no way contradicts the axiom of greed; it simply extends the range of "goods" to include the good of other people. Perhaps the axiom of greed should be renamed, but need not be replaced.

GIVING BEHAVIOR IN THE ECONOMY

In this final section, we consider the nature of gifts and various examples of charity which confirm that human altruism is visible at the economic level. We shall also discuss several factors that affect charity. The examples we use, plus others discussed by Collard (1978), strongly suggest that it is appropriate to abandon the notion that all economic behavior can be understood in terms of self-interest.

Gifts between individuals

Individuals give one another many types of gifts. Moles (1972) suggests that they can be categorized into four groups. The first is gift as payment. Here there is a sense of reciprocity; although there is no official charge, there is the tacit agreement that the gift is given for some service rendered. The second category of gifts is the ritual present. In contemporary Western cultures, birthdays, Christmas, and anniversaries provide the occasion for such gifts. In other cultures, gifts may be an important part of other rituals, such as puberty or circumcision rites, childbirth, marriage or funeral ceremonies, and trade agreements (Mauss 1954). The value of these ritual gifts, of course, is dependent upon the type of occasion. Weddings are more important than engagements and so the value of wedding gifts is usually much greater than engagement gifts. Value is determined also by the strength of the sociometric bond between giver and recipient, the overall socioeconomic level of the two, and the relative

spread throughout the culture, becoming stable and impervious to D responses. In summary then, societies *can* evolve response styles or strategies that convert what would otherwise be competitive situations into cooperative ventures. On the level of the individual or society, altruistic strategies may indeed develop.

dominance–submissive relationship between them (e.g., Moles 1972). The third type of gift is the spontaneous, or symbolic, gift. Here, objects of near-equal value are exchanged by two people. Although neither is better off than before, the gifts have served to symbolize an exchange between the parties. This exchange generates what Moles calls "surplus value," a term indicating that gifts may involve a variety of things beyond their monetary value: empathy, dominance, payment, and so forth. Finally, Moles suggests that business gifts constitute the fourth category. There is an elaborate code governing these gifts. They must not be "too" personal; they must be valuable but not "too" valuable, small but not "too" small, and they must constantly remind the receiver of the donor.

One of the important themes developed by anthropologists who have studied giving in primitive societies is the notion that gifts imply a responsibility for repayment. Mauss (1954), for example, suggests that such a policy of exchange is fundamental to societies that "have not yet reached the stage of pure individual contract, the money market . . . fixed price, and weighed and coined money." (Mauss 1954, p. 45). The ancient tradition of giving or sacrificing to primitive gods reflects this morality.

The principle of reciprocity is not, however, confined to primitive cultures. Mauss suggests that all of us have a need to reciprocate; unrepaid gifts debase the receiver. What this means is that the gift transmits obligations and meanings beyond its monetary value (Schwartz 1967). In addition, gifts communicate the donor's notion of what the recipient needs; they make the receiver subordinate or inferior; they may be designed to display the wealth or magnanimity of the giver; and they can even be cynical and unfriendly. In short,

Goods are not only economic commodities but vehicles and instruments of another order: influence, power, sympathy, status, emotion; and the skillful game of exchange consists of a complex totality of maneuvers, conscious or unconscious, in order to gain security and to fortify one's self against risks incurred through alliances and rivalry. (Levi-Strauss 1965, p. 76)

A second important theme in the study of giving between individuals is the existence of norms regarding who may give what to whom. Certain types of gifts are inappropriate in certain types of relationship. It is not "appropriate," Moles (1972) argues, to give a corset to your boss's wife, or lipstick to a (male) engineering employee; perhaps for slightly more subtle reasons, young adults regard money as an unsuitable present for their mothers (Webley, Lea, & Portalska 1983).

Charitable giving

Despite the importance of giving between individuals in our society, and despite the evidence above, that it can be investigated systematically, rather little is known about it at an empirical level. More studies have been made of giving to charities, however. This kind of giving is particularly interesting, since in most cases the principle of reciprocity must either be in abeyance or be operating very indirectly.

Numerous examples of charitable giving in our society could be discussed. Here, we discuss two that show particularly well how altruism can be consistent with overall economic well-being. The first example is the action of the Labour Party in Great Britain. The October 1974 Labour election manifesto called for wage restraint by the trade unions. This so-called social contract required each union to moderate their wage bargaining so that the pressures on inflation would ease and the less well-off members of society, for example the pensioners, would benefit. Insofar as inflation is a social evil, the union members would also benefit but experience at the time suggested that this was not sufficient to cause the moderation of wage demands. The manifesto was a direct plea for altruistic behavior, and it was supported by the majority of unions; the Labour Party in fact won the election (although it got only 39% of the votes).

Collard (1978) analyzed this example and developed a model to explain how such altruistic behavior could, in the long run, benefit the union members. Collard suggests that if the unions as a whole valued the pensioners' welfare with a weight of $1 - r/(1 - r)(1 - N3)$, where r is the rate of inflation divided by the rate of wage increase, and $N3$ is the number of pensioners divided by the number of unionists, a cooperative strategy would have a higher payoff than a competitive strategy (see Collard for the mathematical proof of this claim). In other words, if members collectively valued the well-being of the poor people in the society, even to a small degree, then a cooperative response benefits all.

It should be noted that agreements of this sort have occurred from time to time under various governments. The particular agreement cited above eventually collapsed for a variety of reasons. Nonetheless, this and other examples illustrate that altruism does play a role in important economic decisions and when it does so, economic gains may be realized by all.

The second example is blood donation. In the United Kingdom, blood banks are stocked entirely with donated blood whereas in the United States blood was generally purchased, at least until recently (Johnson 1982). According to Titmuss (1970), the quantity and quality of blood supplied in the United Kingdom far exceeded that in the United States. Moreover, the United States, because of its near disastrous blood program, had, on occasion, attempted to purchase blood from Third World countries. This practice produced many unfortunate consequences such as children selling blood without their parents' consent, poor people literally dying through excessive donations, and people selling diseased blood.

Why did voluntary donations produce better results than commercial programs? According to Titmuss (1970), blood donations reflect a purely altruistic motive: "In terms of a free gift of blood to strangers, there is no formal contract, no legal bond, no situation of power, domination, con-

10

GAMBLING

havior involves choice. To do one thing involves giving up the
unity to do another. Rats that run down one arm of a maze cannot
vn the other; consumers who spend all their income on beer cannot
e rent. Even in the most constrained situations, there is always the
of whether to make a response or to withold it. Rats in a Skinner
ay press the lever or not; consumers faced with a limited range of
on sale may buy them or choose to keep their money in their
ts. If there is no choice whatsoever, that is, if a particular behavior
occur, then its occurrence is no longer of interest to either psychol-
r economics; it becomes a matter of physics (perhaps the best ex-
is the behavior of a person who has fallen off a cliff!).
choices we have studied so far – the choices to work, buy and
– all lead to fairly certain outcomes. As a first approximation at
working will produce a known wage, buying will result in the pos-
on of known goods, and saving will lead to a nest egg of predictable
In this chapter, we consider the strategies that govern choices whose
omes are *un*predictable.
ne language of choice is more pervasive in economics than in psychol-
In economic psychology, it is important to recognize that it can be
l in two ways. We can talk about a person "choosing," meaning that
or she consciously considers the different possible kinds of behavior,
ghs their benefits and costs, takes into account the risks involved, and
kes a deliberate decision to do one thing rather than another. Alterna-
ly, we can talk about choice in an *as if* fashion; that is, we can try to
cribe behavior in terms of strategies that the person is following as if
or she were consciously aware of the strategy, without asking whether
deliberate mental process is, in fact, involved.
n the case of risky choices, we have far more data on behavior than we
ve on conscious processes. But since risky choice is particularly inter-
ing to many theorists involved in both economics and psychology,
ich of the theory we shall need to discuss has been cast in the language
"decisions" and "strategies." In this chapter it is particularly important
remember that when we talk about "choice," "decision," or "strat-

straint or compulsion, no sense of shame or guilt, no gratitude imperative, no need for penitance, no money and no guarantee of or wish for a
reward or a return gift. They are acts of free will; of the exercise of
choice; of conscience without shame" (p. 89). In short, people feel a
sense of duty to give blood because they see transfusions as part of the
essential life support system in a society and individual citizens as the sole
source of this precious resource.

Titmuss also suggests a grander theme: If a society discards a voluntary
system of blood donation, there will be unfavorable effects throughout
society. "It is likely that a decline in the spirit of altruism in one sphere of
human activity will be accompanied by similar changes in attitudes, motives, and relationships elsewhere" (p. 198). Many people have been
skeptical of this aspect of Titmuss' analysis, and obviously we cannot
resolve this important dispute here. But Collard (1978) provides some
evidence in support of Titmuss' thesis. The introduction of payment in a
previous gift-based system reduces the amount of blood given voluntarily.
In addition, there seems to be a permanently reduced willingness to give
in communities where payment has been introduced. This is reminiscent
of the effect of paying people for tasks which they previously performed
"for their own sake," which, as we saw in Chapter 6, may serve to reduce
intrinsic motivation.

The picture of blood donation offered by Titmuss and Collard has not
gone undisputed. A recent analysis by Johnson (1982) takes a very different view. Johnson disputes Titmuss' claims that purchased blood was
unhealthy, in short supply, or was sold for selfish reasons. First, Johnson
notes that blood is a private, not a public, good; it is not consumable by
everyone. Indeed, it is no different, in principle, from the services of
physicians, which are sold (although in many societies they are not sold
on an open market). Second, he argues that the problem of serum hepati-
tis is a legal, not a moral, issue. Johnson sees no reason to doubt that
offenders could be dealt with by the courts, in the same way as other
purveyors of harmful products are treated. Third, Johnson points out
that, even during the period when the purchase of blood in the United
States was at its peak, supplies of plasma were ample. In fact, U.S.
pharmaceutical firms provided blood not only for U.S. citizens but for
half the consumers in the Western world (Johnson 1982, p. 103). Fourth,
the exchange of money does not necessarily mean that the donor is selfish; the money may pay for legitimate costs such as travel, babysitting,
and so forth. Conversely, the absence of a payment does not necessarily
mean that the gift is based wholly on a sense of altruism. "Volunteers"
may be donating because they get time off from work, or they may simply
be complying to pressure from their peers. Finally, Johnson argues that a
system in which both parties benefit, that is, one person receives blood
and the other money, is a more equitable and ethical system than one in

which only one person benefits. Indeed, the benefit to the paid donor is often considerable given that they are usually from the lower-income groups, such as college students and unemployed people.

We cannot attempt to resolve the conflict between Titmuss and Johnson here. To some extent, it depends on legitimate and unresolvable differences in values, to some extent the data are in dispute, and to some extent on untested speculation, that is, that moving to payment for blood would diminish altruism throughout society (Titmuss), or that the sale of infected blood can be effectively controlled by the courts (Johnson). We should, however, point out that psychological gains (for instance, from group conformity) do not stop behavior being altruistic at the economic level. Failure to recognize this crucial distinction would make any analysis of the economic psychology of giving impossible.

Factors affecting charitable giving

Let us now consider several factors that may have an influence on giving behavior. Some investigators have considered that atruism is a stable personality trait (e.g., Cattell & Horowitz 1952). As with other personality traits, it is difficult to know for certain whether people are inherently altruistic, at least from a paper-and-pencil test. But other more promising approaches have been taken. Sawyer (1965), for example, developed an altruism "scale" which is presumed to reflect both the person's traits and his or her situation. He used the following notation: p stands for the welfare of the person and o for the welfare of another. A cooperative strategy would attempt to maximize $p + o$. The opposite strategy would be to maximize $p - o$; Sawyer calls this the "competitive" strategy, but in more modern (sociobiological) terms it would be described as spiteful. Finally, there is the individualist strategy, in which the welfare of others is irrelevant, and the person simply attempts to maximize p. For any individual, the total welfare of a two-person group can be written as $p + ao$, where a is an altruism score varying from -1 to $+1$. If $a = -1$ then the formula represents the spiteful strategy; if $a = +1$ then it equals cooperative strategy. Saywer tried to assess the strength of a from the person directly. This was done by having the person rank his or her preference for various outcomes for him or herself and a colleague. If the subject gave high ratings to outcomes that benefited others, then a would be positive. The more of these responses given, the higher the a score.

Sawyer's technique has been found to be useful in some settings. Experiments in which various groups of people gave ratings showed that groups of college students differentiated (i.e., demonstrated different degrees of altruism) among friends, strangers, and antagonists. Women were more altruistic than men. Social worker trainees achieved higher a scores than members of any other group; they were concerned about the welfare of other people regardless of whether those people were strangers

or antagonists. Finally, business students maximi[...] more than any other group; they behaved most co[...] fore received the lowest a scores. In summary, th[...] suggest that altruism may be a measurable and end[...]

A second factor that has been shown to be [...] whether or not the society is under some stress. [...] theories stipulate that disasters should lead to highe[...] (because the demand for those necessities increas[...] fixed or reduced). Douty (1972) analyzed this pheno[...] opposite. Charity appears to flourish during times [...] what Douty terms the "disaster syndrome." In a d[...] organizes itself in a different manner from ordinary[...] the stress places a greater premium on interfamily d[...] eration. In addition, firms may well wish to pror[...] workers in these firms are part of the immediate soci[...] affected by the disaster just as much as the comm[...] therefore do not raise prices.

Finally, the amount of philanthropy shown by an [...] hold increases with income and decreases with the [...] modities. Charity, in fact, is much like most other kir[...] diture (e.g., Schwartz 1970). Collard (1978) has analy[...] in greater detail. He proposes that the proportion of [...] by an individual should be predicted by the equatio[...] $v)(1/r)$, where r is the proportion of the person's inco[...] receiver), and v is the the power or regard that the [...] receiver's utility. It is possible to substitute numbers [...] and make predictions about giving behavior. These pre[...] kably accurate. The mathematical relationship, moreov[...] general patterns: The wealthier the person is in relatio[...] the more the donor gives away; the more altruistic the [...] donated. Interestingly, the model also predicts that a [...] money to someone else who is actually wealthier provi[...] son's sense of altruism is sufficiently high. This may e[...] charismatic religious leaders are so wealthy; their follow[...] welfare below that of their leader's. The formula is re[...] include the case in which tax concessions reduce the cost[...] the recipient benefits by more than the donor gives up. [...]

This chapter has shown that, notwithstanding the axiom [...] ent economic psychology of giving can be developed. B[...] psychology give us reasons to suppose that people will so[...] altruistically, either because that it is in their nature or nu[...] because there are psychological gains from giving. Econc[...] vides us with the concepts to analyze this giving behavior sys[...] economic data confirm that it does occur. Human beha[...] largely self-interested, but it does allow room for at least[...]

egy," we usually mean only that people are behaving *as if* they were deliberately using such-and-such a strategy to make such-and-such a choice, not that they have consciously worked the strategy out. This is obviously how we must proceed if we want to make use of the substantial body of data on animal behavior in risky situations, but it is also a useful technique where human behavior is concerned because it enables us to pose separately the question of whether conscious choices and behavior are in harmony. In at least some kinds of risky decision, we shall see that they are not.

Very many choices have to be made with some degree of uncertainty about their outcomes, and this includes many of the choices we make about economic behavior. However, there is one type of behavior that is inseparable from risk and that is specifically economic: gambling. It has been extensively studied, both at the theoretical and the empirical level by economists, sociologists, and psychologists. This chapter therefore serves both as a study of an important economic behavior and as an introduction to the more general topic of risky choice.

DEFINITION OF GAMBLING

In everyday terms, no one is in much doubt what gambling is. It is a well-established social phenomenon. Although there are cultures in which it is apparently unknown (see Chapter 15), gambling seems to have been part of Western civilization from its very beginnings. It was noted in the earliest recorded histories. Dice and gaming boards have been found in prehistoric ruins dating back nearly 3,800 years; and Queen Elizabeth I of England initiated the first English lottery in 1566 in order to raise capital for repairing harbors (Cohen 1964). In modern times, gambling has grown to be a socially accepted business involving vast sums of money. In Britain alone, the turnover (i.e., money wagered and won) was around 800 million pounds in 1962 and 3,530 million in 1976 (Cornish 1978); these were, respectively, 3.1% and 3.2% of GNP. These figures are not surprising given that there are 13,865 offtrack betting licenses and 1,775 authorized bingo clubs. Surveys have shown that as much as 37% of the British population, 16 years or over, made bets on soccer games in 1976; 12% regularly placed bets on horses.

Herman (1976) among others has noted that it is far easier to identify examples of gambling than it is to devise a formal definition. In common speech, we use it to mean simply taking a risk, and nearly everything we do involves a risk of some sort. For instance, we say we are taking a gamble when we scale a cliff or go hang gliding; we gamble that a friend will be home when we try to phone; we gamble that a savings-and-loan institution will not go bankrupt when we deposit our money. In short, gambling has come to mean no more than the potential loss of something valuable. But for a systematic discussion, we need to restrict the field somewhat. The following conditions seem to us to separate gambling, in the strict sense, from mere risk taking.

First, gambling is a social activity. It involves an exchange of money (or something of value) in which the winner gains at the expense of the loser. Second, the exchange is contingent on a future event, the outcome of which is unknown, and in practice determined at least partly by chance. Finally, the risk is an unnecessary one; losses could be avoided simply by not taking part in the gamble (Devereaux 1968).

Although these are all necessary conditions for risk-taking behavior to be considered as gambling, we shall need to consider some choice situations that do not meet all of them when trying to understand gambling behavior. Furthermore, as we have already said, gambling is a social institution, and whether an activity is considered gambling may depend on whether people merely judge it to be. This social definition may affect behavior, as the following example shows. Strickland and Grote (1967) allowed people to play a modified "fruit machine" containing three wheels that the subject could stop independently. The three wheels bore different proportions of winning symbols and, as in the commercial fruit machine, all of them had to show a "win" in order for the subject to win the "game." People generally chose to stop the wheel with the most winning symbols on it first. But R. L. Reid (personal communication) asked people to solve a similar problem, with the identical structure of gains, losses, and probabilities, except it involved a busy secretary trying to organize a meeting between three people, one of whom is less likely to be available than the others. His subjects preferred the strategy of consulting the busiest person first. This behavior is equivalent to stopping the fruit machine wheel with the lowest number of winning symbols.

NORMAL AND EXCESSIVE GAMBLING

Most gambling is what we might term "normal" gambling. This involves the occasional punter who plays bingo, bets on a horse, or buys a lottery ticket. Participation in this kind of behavior is so extensive as to make it an integral part of our everyday lives. Nonetheless, it has always attracted a certain amount of moral disapproval.

Some moral systems hold that it is wrong in principle to benefit from avoidable chance events, and on this view gambling is inevitably objectionable. Others, however, take a more pragmatic view, and object that gambling, in any guise, inevitably leads to cultural degeneracy in general and financial and moral ruin in particular. This argument is open to empirical investigation, and in practice there is very little evidence for it. For example, there is no evidence that normal gambling causes interference with work habits, more divorces, or a higher incidence of loan default (Cornish 1978). Gambling as such is clearly not a moral danger to most individuals, because most people have no difficulty in controlling their impulses for gambling; they gamble only to the extent that the size of their income permits, just as they buy or save within the limits of their incomes.

Nonetheless, gambling clearly does have a darker side. It has long been realized that gambling can be excessive, and it has often been argued that people can become addicted to gambling. The Russian novelist Dostoevsky, himself an excessive gambler, wrote a novel in which the protagonist was a compulsive bettor:

Again I staked the whole of my gold, with eight hundred gulden in notes, and lost. Then madness seemed to come upon me, and seizing my last two thousand florins, I staked them upon twelve of the first numbers – wholly by chance, and at random, and without any sort of reckoning" (Dostoevsky 1866/1915, p. 270).

Dostoevsky's account provides a rich poetic insight into the personality and behavior of an excessive gambler; recent surveys have helped to elaborate the picture, and put it onto a sounder, if more prosaic, empirical footing.

Although the percentage of excessive gamblers is quite small – just under 1% of the adult population (Dickerson 1984), their behavior is fairly predictable. One study (see Cornish 1978) estimated that more than 79,000 people in Britain either bet whenever there is an opportunity, stay at the betting shop for more than two hours, or bet until the end of the racing program. Using these criteria to identify those "at risk," it was found that, indeed, 53% of this group had gambling debts, 75% spent more than they had "intended," and 45% regularly lost all money they had with them. Further analysis indicated that excessive gamblers, defined as above, seem to suffer from their behavior in other ways too: Compared with normal punters, they exhibit greater social isolation, and more often there is a pronounced degeneration in their work and family life. This is not surprising given Dickerson's (1984) estimate that they may spend between 15 and 30 hours per week gambling.

Moran (1970) studied fifty individual cases of excessive gambling and established five separate categories of patients. The *subculture* type gambled excessively because others in their social environment gambled heavily; to avoid the habit was to cast oneself as an outsider. These patients were characterized by their unique environment and, perhaps, by their relative inability to take an independent course of action. The gambling of *neurotic* gamblers, on the other hand, was related to stress or emotional difficulties, and they saw gambling as a means of relief from their problems. Third, some patients were categorized *impulsive* types, for whom gambling was associated with a sense of loss of control. Much like Alexis, the hero in Dostoevsky's novel, the "madness" that possesses them controls their betting. It is this variety of pathology that produces the most serious disturbance in the social and economic functioning of the person. Finally, excessive gamblers may fall into the *psychopathic* or *symptomatic* categories, where gambling is viewed as only part of a global disturbance occasionally stemming from a primary psychotic disorder.

The characterizations of excessive gamblers by Moran and others are not without their problems. For one thing, it is not always clear whether gambling is the cause of the problem or the effect. The existence of gamblers of the neurotic variety, who rely on gambling for relief from stress, suggests that the behavior is a result of other causal factors. On the other hand, the fact that impulse gamblers seem to "lose control" suggests that gambling is the source of their problem. The issue remains unresolved and seems likely to be unresolvable in general, since excessive gambling may be the cause of the problems for some individuals but the effect for others.

Excessive gambling is commonly labeled as "compulsive," implying a parallel to other patterns of behavior involving addictions, as well as to the kinds of excessive behavior seen in obsessional psychiatric disorder. Herman (1976) has argued that the parallel to other addictions is misleading, since there is little evidence to suggest a dependence on or tolerance for gambling as is found with, for example, drug addictions. By contrast, Dickerson (1984) defends the notion that gambling is an addictivelike phenomenon, citing as evidence loss of control, escalation of stake size, and "cold turkey" experiences (tremulousness, headaches, nightmares, etc.) following sudden cessation of gambling (e.g., Wray & Dickerson 1981). Obviously, excessive gambling does not involve the same potential for physiological dependence as addictive drugs, and the issue of whether it can properly be labeled an addiction will probably not be resolved until the nature of addiction in general is better understood.

Gambling seems to differ from many other economic phenomena in that we are unusually aware of its excessive forms. However, saving is done by misers, food-buying by compulsive eaters, and work by workaholics (see Ehrenberg & Smith 1982), and yet these pathological cases have not dominated our discussion of work, buying, or saving. Therefore, in this chapter, we shall be more concerned normal than pathological risk taking, although we must recognize that much of the research stems from a desire to understand and help the minority of excessive gamblers. We must also recognize that the extent of normal gambling in our economy may not be "normal" in any absolute sense; when we look at the way in which the economy affects individual behavior (see Part III), we may want to ask whether all (actual or conceivable) economic systems would give rise to quite as much gambling as we now take for granted. And, even though in the great majority of cases, normal gambling clearly does not lead to excessive gambling, it is equally clear that all excessive gamblers are likely to have started as normal gamblers.

FACTORS INFLUENCING GAMBLING BEHAVIOR

In this section we review five important factors which contribute to gambling behavior in our society. Further evidence comes from cross-cultural studies, since gambling is not as widespread in some other societies as in our own; these investigations are reviewed in Chapter 15.

Economic and sociological factors

The factor stressed by many theorists is the economic (or socioeconomic) situation of the gambler. Quite simply, gambling is seen by most people as an economic venture, one in which the potential payoff is highly attractive (economically) relative to the cost. This is particularly true of people in the lower socioeconomic strata and of betting opportunities such as lotteries, where the cost is very small and the potential winnings are very large. It has been shown that people in the lower socioeconomic levels gamble more than those in the higher strata. They also engage in different forms of gambling. Furnham (1984) reports that the less well educated indulge in bingo, dog racing, and slot machines whereas the better educated bet on horse races. Interestingly, these low-status people report greater dissatisfaction with their jobs and a stronger belief that winning, say, the lottery is the economic solution they require (Cornish 1978). This generalization, however, may only hold for some forms of gambling, specifically the football pools where the discrepancy between losses and potential gains is enormous. In this respect it is interesting that in Furnham's survey those with the highest income gambled the least on lotteries and the football pools and most on premium bonds. In short, gambling is viewed by many purely in economic terms; it offers a chance, however slender, of economic mobility to those who have no other means of transforming their circumstances. The vast majority simply have no legal way to procure a fortune, no matter how hard they work or how intelligent they are. Against this background, lotteries with small costs and high winnings may well seem a sensible alternative (see Rubner 1966).

Situational factors

It is not surprising to learn that situational factors play a vital part in a person's desire to gamble. Placing bets has never been easier. The betting shop is a familiar sight in most Western countries and casino owners have gone to considerable lengths, including provision of free buses to customers in order to encourage patronage (Cornish 1978).

One of the most thoroughly investigated situational determinants is the marketing effort of the gambling industry. Hess and Diller (1969) visited casinos in Las Vegas and observed a number of the tactics designed to encourage gambling. For example, there were clear appeals to a person's rational/economic motives: Winning Keno tickets were posted, and bells clanged when someone won at a slot machine. All were designed to convince the customer that winning was a normal, even frequent, occurrence – and therefore that gambling was economically viable. Other policies appealed to a person's sense of recreation ("go where the fun and action is"), prestige (extravagant surroundings, complementary meals), or even aggression (customers were urged to "beat" the house or to "go against" the cards).

A different sort of situational factor, the effect of group pressure, has been investigated at casinos by Blascovich and co-workers (1976) and at racetracks by Knox and Safford (1976) and McCauley et al. (1973). In the study by McCauley et al., punters were approached shortly after leaving the betting window at the racetrack and told they would receive a free $2 ticket if they would meet two other punters (who had been similarly approached) and agree on a horse. Control subjects were asked to make the decision by themselves. Sixteen of the 22 groups made a more cautious bet (e.g., chose the "favorite") than they had done on their own shortly before being approached by the experimenter. Apparently, the influence of the group was to shift the decision to a safer option. By contrast, 13 of the 22 people in the "alone" condition made the same bet as before; their choice was neither more nor less risky. Groups may therefore exert an influence on the gambling decisions of many punters and, as noted before, they can be strong enough to cause excessive participation. While the influence may be toward a more conservative choice, as in the study by McCauley and colleagues, a shift toward a more risky outcome has also been observed (Blascovich et al. 1976).

An important aspect of the situation is whether or not it is a "real" (as distinct from laboratory) gambling context. Anderson and Brown (1984) showed that both the autonomic responses and the gambling behavior of habitual gamblers took different forms in a casino and in a (reasonably realistic) laboratory simulation. This result obviously has important, as well as worrying, implications for many of the investigations we are discussing in this chapter, since it casts some doubt on the entire laboratory technique (cf. Chapter 4).

Learning

It would seem plausible for learning or experience to affect gambling behavior, particularly the willingness to continue gambling. A number of studies have confirmed this point. Phillips (1972) gave stake money to a group of gamblers and a group of nongamblers and asked them to play a "new" game of chance. Each subject could vary the odds in this game. Phillips found that inexperienced subjects chose unrealistically high odds such as 1,000 to 1, whereas all but one of the experienced gamblers chose more favorable odds. Clearly, the gamblers had "learned" through experience to interpret the odds of a bet.

It is not surprising that experience with gambling helps a punter to bet more wisely. It also affects whether or not a person will gamble at all. In the study by Strickland and Grote (1967), mentioned at the beginning of this chapter, gamblers were observed while playing a slot machine. Each was required to play at least 100 times as part of the study. The authors were interested to see if the order of winning symbols, as they appeared sequentially on the three spinning drums, affected the subjects' willingness to play. The results showed that subjects who saw more winning symbols on the drums that stopped spinning first or second were more likely to continue to play beyond the required 100-trial limit, even though the probability of an overall win was the same in all conditions. Those who saw more winning symbols on the last-to-stop drum (when losing symbols had, in many cases, already appeared on the other two drums) played significantly fewer extra games.

One explanation for this finding comes from traditional learning research. It is well known that the sooner a reward is delivered, the stronger the response (Tarpy & Sawabini 1974). Delayed rewards lead to lower rates of behavior. There seems little doubt that the winning symbol is a reward for playing the machine. If this is the case, then it makes good sense for the strength of the response, measured by the willingness to play beyond the first 100 games, to be lower when the winning symbol is consistently in the third position. This effect, that responses closest to the onset of reward are the most strongly reinforced, would also predict that, for regular gamblers, late bets should increase and earlier bets decay. Regular roulette players commonly wait until the ball is released before placing their bets (Oldman 1974), and in betting shops high-frequency gamblers place their bets later than low-frequency gamblers (Dickerson 1979).

Because gambling involves chance outcomes, different individuals making the same choices may have quite different consequential experiences. It has often been suggested that excessive gamblers may have become "trapped" by runs of luck early, or at crucial points, in their gambling careers. Greenberg and Weiner (1966) investigated this "reinforcement history hypothesis" experimentally. Subjects engaged in a gambling game in which the payoffs and the probabilities were rigged. Half of them won a large amount of money, the others a small amount. Some of the people in the "large" winning group were permitted to win many times relative to the number of losses, some had an equal number of wins and losses, and the remaining lost more times than they won. The same was true for the "small" amount subjects: Some won more times than they lost, some had equal wins and losses, and some lost more times that they won. After this phase of the study was completed, all participants were tested for their preference for risk; that is, pairs of bets were offered and the subjects had to choose which bet they preferred. The authors discovered that the amount of previous winnings did not affect preferences. Those who had won a lot of money, on the average, behaved just like those who had won a small amount. Previous percentage wins, however, did affect preferences. In particular, subjects who had won as many times as they had lost became more conservative in their choice of bet, whereas those that had a high win–lose ratio and those with a low win–lose ratio became relatively more risky in their choices. The authors reasoned that the successful subjects behaved as if their former good luck would continue in the future; by contrast, the least successful subjects appeared to behave recklessly, as if they were trying to compensate for a run of bad luck. The controls became more cautious because of their inability to win consistently.

Factors influencing evaluation of probabilities

The results of Greenberg and Weiner's study discussed above are best explained in terms of a change in the subject's perception of the probability of winning. Some researchers have suggested that when experience with gambling affects future gambling behavior, it does so via such a change in attitude and perception (Slovic 1964). Research certainly has confirmed that people have large biases in judging the likelihood of some kinds of outcomes. For instance, Cohen (1964, 1975) found that most people prefer to draw from a pile of 100 cards with 10 winners than from a pile of 10 cards with 1 winner; the objective probability of winning is the same, but the typical perception is that the probabilities are unequal. It would appear that the larger number of possible wins caused the subjects to be biased toward the first option. However, when the draw is from the same two piles (100 or 10 cards), this time containing 90 and 9 winners, respectively, the subjects choose the latter option. Here, they seem to be unduly influenced by the number of losing cards.

Cohen discussed another finding which is apparently irrational. People prefer to choose once from a pile of 100 cards containing 10 winners than to draw from each of two piles of 50 cards each containing 5 winners. Again, the fact that the first option contains a larger absolute number of winning cards seems to affect the subject's confidence of winning.

The general problem of estimating the probability of uncertain events was discussed in an important paper by Tversky and Kahneman (1974). Probability is a subjective judgment, similar to the judgment of the distance of an object. Furthermore, it cannot be measured directly, only estimated by reference to past experience or assumptions about the nature of the situation. And just as our judgment of distance can be distorted (e.g., blurred objects are usually judged to be further away than they actually are and the distance of clearly visible objects is usually underestimated) so can our judgment of the likelihood of an event be biased. According to Tversky and Kahneman, people normally use three techniques for assessing the probability of events and each of these has serious sources of error. First, we use the representativeness of an event as a guide. If we notice that a particular race horse had previously won on a wet track, and that the race we are about to watch will take place on a wet track, we are likely to judge that this particular horse has an unusually good chance of winning. The problem is that we tend to ignore prior probabilities and sample size. In reality, the horse may have a miserable overall record, notwithstanding a win or two on a wet track. Indeed, the horse may even have a poor record on wet tracks, but, given that it had won, we may think that this race fits the same pattern.

The second heuristic for judging probabilities is based on how available the event is in recent memory. We tend to think of outcomes as being highly probable if an example of the outcome can be brought to mind easily. Here the trouble is that we are susceptible to forgetting. The context of the event may adversely affect our memory retrieval process, and some events may be highly salient and yet improbable. We may vividly remember once seeing a pink Rolls Royce; this does not mean that such cars are numerous (i.e., that there is a high probability of seeing another one in the future), but we tend to overestimate the chances nonetheless.

Finally, we judge the probability of future events in terms of anchor points. That is, we find an instance appropriately similar to the one in question, and then somehow adjust our estimation of the probability in light of the probability of our anchor point. The problem is that we tend to stay near the anchor point; that is, we usually underestimate the difference between the anchor and the new instance. For example, Tversky and Kahneman (1974) asked subjects to estimate the percentage of countries in the United Nations that were located in Africa. As a "starting point," one group was given the figure 10%, whereas the other group was give 65%. The final estimates were 25% and 45%, respectively. Clearly, the initial anchor point influenced the final judgment. Interestingly, the same effect was observed even when the anchor points had been selected by the subjects' own spinning of a roulette wheel.

These ideas suggest that all of us, gamblers or not, are prone to commit errors of judgment when estimating the probability of uncertain outcomes. Gambling behavior will be affected to the extent that we overestimate or underestimate our chances of winning. The type of influence, for example, whether we are more or less persistent in our gambling, will depend on the type of error in judgment we have made.

The perception of skill factors

Finally, several interesting results suggest that any perception that skill is involved in a task dramatically alters gambling behavior. For example, subjects who are asked to wager on the throw of dice show greater restraint (i.e., they bet less money and report that they are less confident that they will win) if they are forced to wager after the dice have already been thrown (Strickland, Lewicki, & Katz 1966). Presumably they believe that being permitted to throw the dice themselves, that is, to exercise their "skill," will have some effect on the outcome.

A study by Langer (1975) showed similar anomalies. Langer's subjects bet more when cutting cards against a "nervous" competitor than against a "confident" competitor or when they were given the choice of several lottery tickets as opposed to having the seller "assign" a ticket. The results suggest that we suffer from an "illusion of control"; that is, we do not always distinguish correctly between purely chance and skill events. Roulette players, for example, clearly see their game as skillful; they consider where to put their chips and offer explanations (generally based on the behavior of the wheel-spinner) of why they failed (Oldman 1974). Certain other factors, such as familiarity of the task, the nature of the competition, or the degree of personal involvement influence the belief that skill is a controlling force. It is not surprising to learn, therefore, that casino owners use every opportunity to induce the illusion of control, from challenging the customer to "beat the house" to encouraging each dice player to execute dice-throwing "rituals."

Part of the explanation of this phenomenon may be that gamblers evaluate outcomes in a biased manner, accepting wins at face value but explaining away losses, often mentally tranforming them into "near wins." This produces overoptimistic assessments of skill and of the chances for future success. Gilovich (1983) demonstrated this effect with students who bet on football games. They discussed losses more than wins but also discounted them. Interestingly, if a fluke that had occurred in a game was made salient by an interviewer, this had a greater impact on those respondents whose team had lost. It restored their faith, and altered their estimations of success in future games.

Another important factor may be the inherent tendency for humans to ascribe control for events either to themselves or to the environment, the "locus of control" variable introduced by Rotter (1966). As we explained in Chapter 1, Rotter suggested that people can be categorized as having primarily an internal locus of control in which case they believe that events occur because of their own doing, or an external locus of control, where they believe that things happen because the environment causes them to happen. This concept is obviously likely to be useful in the analysis of gambling behavior, where chance and skill factors become confused. Schneider (1968) showed that people who score high on the internal control scale tend to prefer skill activities, such as volley ball, as compared to chance activities, such as roulette, though this relationship was true only for males. In the Strickland et al. study (1966), high internal subjects took greater risk, i.e., they bet more following a dice roll than external control subjects. It appears therefore that the proclivity to engage in certain forms of gambling would depend on the person's assessment of control, that is, of the involvement of skill factors. Obviously, locus of control is only one of many personality factors which may affect gambling; others are discussed later in this chapter.

DECISION MODELS OF RISK TAKING

Decisions involving risk are one of the key areas for investigating the idea that people's behavior is rational, in the special sense that it maximizes utility (see Chapter 5). It is not immediately obvious how a rational person should choose between two actions, each of which brings a different return, with different probabilities. Under plausible assumptions, however, it is possible to make clear predictions using decision theory, although some of those predictions seem to be directly inconsistent with laboratory experiments and everyday behavior. Not surprisingly, a substantial literature on decision models of risk taking has developed (see, e.g., Edwards et al. 1965; Rapoport & Wallsten 1972). Much of this literature has been concerned with gambling.

Decision theories, in fact, provide one way of explaining gambling behavior. By attempting to find the rule which predicts which of two risky actions a person will take, they can, at least potentially, predict whether that person will gamble. Once specified, the rule may also point to a more general, conceptual account of the occurrence of gambling.

From expected value to subjectively expected utility

The first notion that was proposed as an account of risk taking behavior was the expected value *EV* model, clearly stated by Bernoulli (1738/1954). The *EV* model claimed that people attempt to maximize the expected value of their options. "Expected value" here has a straightforward mathematical sense, that of the value of the outcome (expressed in monetary terms) multiplied by the probability that it will be obtained. So, for a simple gamble where there is one outcome for winning and another for losing,

$$EV = P_w V_w + P_l V_l \tag{10.1}$$

where P is the probability of the outcome, V is the money value, and w and l are subscripts indicating whether the outcome is a win or loss.

Consider this simple example. A fair coin is tossed; if it lands heads you win $3, if it lands tails you lose $1, that is; you gain $-1 (losses have negative value). The probabilities of heads and tails obviously both equal one-half. The expected value of this bet is therefore

$$EV = (1/2 \times \$3) + (1/2 \times \$-1) = \$1 \qquad (10.2)$$

Stated in words, you could expect (on the average) to gain $1 if you were offered such a bet; on any given trial, you might win $3 or you might lose $1, but over a long series of trials you would win $1 per trial. Now consider this bet. A fair die is tossed. If it shows a 3 you win $18, otherwise you lose $3. Which bet, the coin or the die, would you prefer to play? Obviously the coin toss, since the average amount you could expect to win on the die would be 50 cents, as against $1 for the coin toss.

The *EV* model is simple and appealing, and it has been claimed that it describes gambling behavior satisfactorily. Munson (1962) set up a booth at several neighborhood carnivals and offered the public an opportunity to play a game of chance, specifically guessing the number of heads that would occur in a toss of 10 coins. In one condition the *EV* values were equal for all outcomes; in another condition they were different. Munson found people to be influenced by expected value; they placed many more bets on the higher *EV* choices even though they were not prompted to do so.

As we saw in Chapter 5, however, there are severe problems with the *EV* model, which have been known at least since Bernoulli. Because bookmakers and other gambling professionals make a profit, the expected values of most commercially available gambles are negative, which means they should never be preferred to the simple alternative of not gambling (Bernoulli calls this "nature's warning against the dice"; the same applies to many other decisions involving risk, e.g., the taking out of insurance). And laboratory research has confirmed that choices between gambles are poorly described in terms of maximization of *EV* (see, e.g., Lichtenstein, Slovic, & Zink 1969; Pruitt 1962).

Furthermore, the expected value model seems to be too simple on theoretical grounds. We normally describe rational behavior as tending to maximize utility. Utility is subjective value, not objective value, and it seems obvious that it cannot be directly measured in monetary units. For example, one dollar is "worth" far more to a poor person than to a wealthy person. That is, the utility of $1 is greater if you only have a few dollars than if you are rich. To apply this kind of insight in the risk-taking situation, it is useful to imagine a quantitative scale of utility (Edwards 1954). For example, one dollar may represent 10 utiles (an arbitrary unit of utility) to a poor person but only 1 utile to a rich one, so that the same monetary value has actually 10 times the personal value or utility for the poor person.

We can then state an expected utility *EU* model of risk-taking behavior, according to which people choose the action of greatest expected utility, as

$$EU = P_w U_w + P_l U_l \tag{10.3}$$

where U_w and U_l are the utilities due to winning and losing. If we are to use this model to predict and understand risk-taking behavior, we need to be able to assess utility. How can this be done? There are really two ways. First, one could present subjects with various commodities and then compute indifference curves (Edwards 1954). Recall from Chapter 2 that an indifference curve indicates what combinations of the two items are equally preferable. For example, one could determine how many tennis balls would be sacrificed for (i.e., would be worth or equally preferable to) one additional pair of opera glasses. While this technique is, in principle, a perfectly valid way of assessing utility, in practice it is cumbersome and thus relatively little used. The second approach, direct estimation, is far simpler. One can determine utilities merely by asking people to rate the utility of an object (e.g., Galanter 1962). From these ratings one can then calculate the *EU* value of a gamble for that person.

Unfortunately the *EU* model suffers from nearly the same shortcomings as the *EV* model. As Bernoulli pointed out, if commercial gambles have negative *EV*, then they will certainly have negative *EU*. That is, since winners will be (by a small amount) richer than losers, the utility of winnings to winners will be less than the utility of losings to losers, so the *EU* model cannot account for the prevalence of gambling. And, just as personal utility is not always the same as monetary value, so perceived probability is not always the same as actual probability. Reconsider for a moment the previous sections in this chapter on "factors influencing evaluation of probabilities" and "perception of skill factors." The most basic message in those sections was that people are poor at judging the real likelihood of uncertain outcomes. Yet both the *EV* and the *EU* models include the objective probabilities of winning and losing. Clearly, we ought to revise them to make probability assessment, as well as value, subjective. The result is the subjective expected utility model *SEU* of Edwards (1954), which is stated as follows:

$$SEU = SP_w U_w + SP_l U_l \tag{10.4}$$

where *SP* is the subjective probability of an outcome.

It might appear that the *SEU* model offers a powerful account of decision-making under risk, but there are two severe problems. First, the model includes two sets of subjective quantities, utilities and subjective probabilities. How are they to be measured? It would be possible to use the direct estimation technique, mentioned for utilities, but more attention has been given to mathematically sophisticated techniques for deriving scales from people's choices between gambles, in experiments that also test the applicability of the *SEU* model (Ramsey 1931; Davidson, Suppes, & Siegel 1957; Tversky 1967). Although the techniques are elegant and could work, in principle, the results obtained from them have been disappointing. Consistent scales of utility and subjective probability have not emerged.

Furthermore, at least one underlying assumption of the model has been shown to be violated. Just as rational choice between commodity bundles must be transitive (see Chapter 5), so the *SEU* model, which is a variety of rationality theory, requires that choices between gambles must be transitive; that is, if bet A is preferred to B, and B is preferred to C (preferences being based on differences in *SEU*), bet A should also be preferred to bet C. Tversky (1969) found that when subjects were offered choices between gambles in an experiment they often chose intransitively. This suggests that gambling behavior is not governed or described by the *SEU* decision model.

The above criticism does not mean that choices under risk are "irrational." The *SEU* model may fail because it does not identify the crucial *sources* of utility in gambling behavior. For example, Coombs and Pruitt (1960) claimed that the variability of possible outcomes, not just the average *EU*, influenced the choice of bets. In other words, gambles are chosen because they produce a pleasurable degree of uncertainty, although subjects may also prefer higher *EU* choices. This intuitively plausible suggestion has not been supported in subsequent laboratory studies (Lichtenstein 1965; Slovic & Lichtenstein 1968), but it does show how concentration on the *EV/SEU* family of models may represent too narrow a view of gambling behavior.

Conversely, many theorists have claimed that the *SEU* model is altogether too broad, that it accounts for risk-taking behavior so easily that it has become an empty hypothesis. How could anyone not wish to maximize their (subjectively assessed) chances of gaining in (subjective) utility? The model is so "subjective" that nearly anything would satisfy it. We have seen that there are data which are inconsistent with the *SEU* model, but the suspicion remains that it could cover very many situations without giving us much information. The *SEU* model is only likely to be helpful if the same utility functions, and the same principles for deriving subjective from objective probabilities, work consistently across situations and across subjects. That may be true for some kinds of gambling behavior and not for others. As Rapoport and Wallsten (1972) put it: "The basic experimental question should not be whether to accept or to reject *SEU* theory as a whole, but rather to systematically discover the conditions under which it is or is not valid" (p. 141).

Information-processing models

It is far easier to reject an influential theory of behavior if there is a reasonable alternative available. In the case of decision making, the alternative to *SEU* models are models based on the concept of information processing.

One such model, called the additivity model, was formulated by Lichtenstein and Slovic (Lichtenstein & Slovic 1971; Slovic & Lichtenstein 1968). They asked subjects to choose between bets, but to express their choice in two different ways. First, they indicated which bet they preferred, and second, they indicated how much money they would be willing to pay in order to be able to play the bet. The *SEU* model assumes that the two measures would agree with each other, since all that is important to the model is the *SEU,* which does not, or should not, change as a function of the measure. However, for some combinations of bets, Lichtenstein and Slovic (1971) found that 73% of the people preferred bet A to B, but bid more for the chance to play B than they did to play A. The authors argued that this inconsistency was due to the fact that the different tasks forced subjects to process the bets in different ways. Merely expressing a preference requires a simple, global comparison of the two bets. Bidding to play a bet, however, involves calculating the maximum bid that would be sensible (namely the amount to be won) and then adjusting downward, depending on a variety of factors the most important of which is the probability of winning. The conclusion was that gambling represents a multidimensional stimulus to a person. The decision to gamble and the choice of the bet are governed by an information processing system that is sensitive to probabilities and payoffs in a rather complex way. People have "importance beliefs" (Payne 1973); that is, they pay more attention to some dimensions of a decision than to others because they believe that those dimensions have a special importance to the outcome. These beliefs combine with strategies. For example, a subject might view the probability of the bet as more important than the payoff (an importance belief), and this notion might then combine with a particular strategy such as minimizing losses.

There are a number of other information-processing models of decision making (Payne & Braunstein 1971), which suggest that decision making involves assessment or processing of multiple levels and types of information; it is not governed by a simple and invariant *SEU* strategy. Current thinking therefore favors these newer information-processing models because they better encompass the complexity of the decision-making task. As models of human reasoning they appear to be more accurate than the older *SEU* formulation; therefore, they seem to provide a better assessment of the psychological substrates to economic behavior, in general, and gambling, in particular.

THEORIES OF GAMBLING

In a limited sense, the decision models discussed above are theories of gambling. But they are purely descriptive theories: They make no attempt to identify the underlying psychological "causes" of the decision strategy. The *SEU* model, for example, proposes that people maximize *SEU;* to discover that they do indeed maximize *SEU* is all that the hypothesis demands. It is thus part of a simple, Economic Man approach to economic psychology, in which investigations stop once it has been shown that behavior is consistent with a mathematical description of what the optimal behavior should be. Information approaches to decision making are rather similar. They imply that people come as close to the optimal behavior as their limited cognitive powers permit.

As in other areas of economic behavior, we find this an unsatisfactory approach to the study of gambling. As a paradigm for research, it is likely to lead to concentration on those kinds of behavior for which no "rational" explanation has yet been found. A more balanced approach would want to know what sources of utility contribute to the decision to gamble, and what circumstances, that is, psychological states or environmental conditions, make people behave in accordance with the *SEU,* or information-processing, models. In order to provide this broader perspective, we now turn to a discussion of several psychological theories of gambling.

Psychodynamic theory

Several psychodynamic theories of gambling have emerged. These deal primarily with compulsive gambling. Freud was one of the first psychologists to discuss gambling, in his essay on Dostoevsky (Freud 1928/1961). Both the life and writings of the great Russian writer contained strong symbols of self-destruction. The source of the problem according to Freudian theory was as follows: Young boys have a love–hate relationship with their father, love because of paternal care and kindness and hate because of a sense of rivalry for the mother's affections. This is the much discussed Freudian oedipal complex. The resentment and hostility directed toward the father is, in fact, a desire to kill him. This, in turn, leads to guilt and fear of castration. Gambling is a way to punish oneself for the guilt. The self-recrimination stemming from the repression of the oedipal complex are sources of psychic struggle the expression of which is excessive gambling.

The psychodynamic approach to compulsive gambling was extended in a somewhat different direction by Bergler (1958; see also Greenson 1947; Lindner 1950). Unlike Freud, who stressed the importance of the oedipal complex, Bergler argues that gambling revives the childish fantasies of grandeur; gambling is a latent rebellion or an aggression against logic, intelligence, moderation, and morality. Since these qualities were instilled and represented by the parents, gambling is seen as a denial of parental authority, a neurotic aggression against parental logic and moraltiy. In short, a gambler is one who denies the reality principle because no one, not even the parents who symbolize logic and intelligence, can predict the winning number in roulette.

The second aspect of Bergler's theory is that the gambler has a neurotic and unconscious wish actually to lose money despite the overt concern for winning. The cause for this seemingly paradoxical wish is guilt, stemming from the aggression described above. That is, by losing the gambler pays a penalty for his aggression. And the penalty is, according to Bergler, essential for the gambler's psychic equilibrium.

In summary, the psychodynamic theories emphasize that the motivation for gambling is an unconscious wish for self-punishment. It is difficult to substantiate such a claim empirically (see Chapter 1), but there is no doubt that a small percentage of compulsive gamblers do indeed behave in a self-destructive fashion. For them at least the psychodynamic theories provide a useful language and perspective.

Personality theories

One assumption of the psychodynamic theories is that the proclivity for gambling on an excessive level is an integral part of the gambler's personality. It is possible to expand this assumption further to cover more than compulsive gamblers. In particular, one could ask whether gambling behavior per se is related in some fundamental way to certain personality traits.

It is intriguing to speculate that there might be a "gambling personality," a cluster of traits that invariably marks a person as a habitual, or even compulsive, risk taker. Unfortunately, the data are not very promising. Some theorists have constructed personality profiles for gamblers (e.g., Morehead 1950), but these are highly subjective. Other researchers have administered a battery of personality tests and have failed outright to show any organization in the data (Weinstein 1969). Kusyszyn and Rutter (1978), for example, studied the personalities of race-goers whose gambling ranged from never to frequent and found no relationship between amount of gambling and personality. Still other investigators have shown minimally positive results. The experiments on locus of control discussed previously are good examples of these latter efforts.

In one study, Cameron and Myers (1966) administered to their subjects the Edwards Personality Preference test, an inventory test that measures some 15 variables of personality. Subjects were also given a choice of outcomes based on the spin of a roulette wheel. For instance, a subject was offered the choice between winning $2 if the wheel stopped on 2 but losing $3 if it did not. The main finding was that subjects differed in terms of the conservatism of the bet. Those who had scored high on the exhibition, aggression, and dominance scales preferred a more risky bet with a high payoff. By contrast, subjects who were high on the autonomy and endurance scales preferred bets with a high probability of winning despite a low payoff.

Another attempt to relate risk-taking behavior to personality structure was made by Atkinson (1957), whose interest was in the relationship between risk and what is called need for achievement and fear of failure. Need for achievement (n Ach) and fear of failure are motives that influence the degree to which we strive toward some particular goal, high need achievers being those people who strive the hardest. Often these enduring personality traits are assessed via a projective test called the Thematic Apperception Test (TAT). Pictures, somewhat ambiguous in character, are given to the subject who then proceeds to "tell a story" that is depicted by the picture. The stories are later scored for achievement imagery. For instance, one picture is of a young boy looking at a violin. High n Ach subjects often remark that the boy is contemplating how hard he must work to become a world-famous violinist; low n Ach subjects do not mention such ambitious strivings.

According to Atkinson's theory, a person is motivated to perform on a task according to that person's achievement motivation, the expectancy of succeeding at the task, and the attractiveness or incentive value of a success. In more formal terms

$$\text{Behavior} = M \times P_s \times I_s \tag{10.5}$$

where M, P_s, and I_s are motive, probability of success, and incentive, respectively. Achieving less probable goals is assumed to be more attractive than achieving easily reached goals; thus, $I_s = (1 - P_s)$. This means that for any given level of need for achievement above zero, the behavior tendency will be maximum when the probability of success is 0.5. In other words, Atkinson predicts that people with a high need for achievement will prefer risks that have a probability of succeeding of 0.5 more than they will prefer other types of risks. In contrast, people who predominately fear failure, the opposite motive, will tend to chose risks with a very high probability of success (because they fear failure) or a very low probability (because they cannot be blamed for failing with such poor odds).

A number of studies have verified that risk taking is, indeed, related to need for achievement. Atkinson, Bastioni, Earl, and Litwin (1960), for example, measured the need achievement of their subjects using a special perceptual test called the French Test of Insight. Then they had them play a shuffleboard game. Those subjects who scored highest on the need achievement test chose to shoot from a distance that resulted in their winning 50% of the time. That is, they preferred a risky behavior with a 0.5 probability of succeeding. Subjects who were low on n Ach shot from very close or very far as predicted. In a second phase of the study, subjects were given pairs of imaginary bets and asked to state a preference. Again, high need for achievement people preferred bets with success probabilities near 0.5.

In summary, the evidence relating personality traits to risk taking is only moderately convincing. The reason that more compelling relationships have not been found is probably the same reason that personality traits do not correlate well with other behaviors: Behavioral causality is complex and multidimensional, and the personality variables, such as self-esteem, are simply too global to serve as a single "cause." Need for achievement does seem to predict certain behavioral outcomes (e.g., preference for risk), but we are certainly unable to make very specific predictions about actual gambling behavior using n Ach as the guide.

Reinforcement theory

Psychodynamic and personality theories of gambling direct attention away from its economic nature. But it is more plausible to assume that what keeps people gambling is the possibility of financial reward; an idea that comes to the fore when we consider reinforcement theories of gambling. As we discussed in Chapter 1, the essence of a reinforcement theory is the idea that behaviors tend to become strengthened when they are followed by reinforcement. As applied to gambling, when reinforcement (e.g., money) is contingent on the execution of a certain response (say, betting), the response will increase in strength. The degree to which it increases and is sustained depends on the details of the contingency.

First, let us consider what the reinforcement may actually be in the gambling situation (Saunders 1979). Money won from gambling is most obviously a reward; while every player loses in the long run, this certainly is not true of all bettors in the short run, especially in situations in which the probability of winning is reasonably favorable. And we know, furthermore, that early success at gambling may have a strong effect on the persistence of the gambler (Greenberg & Weiner 1966).

Another potential reinforcer is activation (see Chapter 1), i.e., the "thrill" of gambling. The gambling situation certainly offers an opportunity for such activation. To quote Dostoevsky's hero again: "fear casts its spell over me . . . for with horror I had realized that I must win, and that upon that stake there depended all my life. 'Rouge' called the croupier. I drew a long breath, and hot shivers went coursing over my body" (p. 270). It would be ridiculous to suggest that the casual lottery punter feels emotion of such intensity, but some lower level of arousal might still be present and it might be playing a role in the punter's behavior.

In laboratory work, the most impressive demonstrations of control over behavior by reinforcement come from systematic research on schedules of reinforcement. Recall from Chapter 1 that reinforcement is usually delivered to the subject after a certain number of responses has been executed (ratio schedules) or after one response has been made after a particular period of time has elapsed – the interval schedule. The rate and pattern of behavior depend strongly on what type of schedule is used, and on the severity of the schedule. For instance, ratio schedules induce a much higher rate of responding than interval schedules.

Many common gambling situations have features in common with schedules of reinforcement. The parallel between slot machines and variable ratio schedules is particularly obvious. Formally, both arrange probabilistic reward, and in practice, both seem to induce very high and perhaps "irrational" rates of behavior. The analogy has some experimental support. When humans are rewarded with money for playing slot machines, their behavior is very much like that of an experimental rat or pigeon who is rewarded with food for operating the Skinner box (e.g., Davidson 1974; Orlando & Bijou 1960; Yukl, Wexley, & Seymore 1972; see Bijou & Baer 1966).

As noted in Chapter 1, much of the fundamental research on schedules of reinforcement has used animal subjects, and it is an open question how far this can be applied to human behavior. Some experimenters have found that schedules produce much the same rates, pauses in responding, and so forth, in human as in animal behavior. For example, Matthews, Shimoff, and Catania (1977) rewarded university students with money for pressing a telegraph key. One student responded on a ratio schedule while another on an interval schedule. The data were virtually indistinguishable from data using pigeon subjects. And when the reinforcement schedule is changed, the human performance showed the appropriate adjustments (see also Laties & Weiss 1963; Weiner 1964).

On the other hand, other experimenters have found no parallel at all between human and animal behavior on schedules of reinforcement (e.g., Lowe 1979; Schmitt 1974). For example, Lowe provides an analysis of performance on *FI* and *FR* schedules. In both cases, the behavioral patterns shown by rats and pigeons (e.g., the "scalloping" effect on *FI* schedules) is not found in the human data. Humans tend to respond steadily throughout the *FI* interval at either a high (e.g., DeCasper & Zeiler 1972) or low (e.g., Weiner 1969) rate. Moreover, humans do not have the same degree of sensitivity to changes in schedule parameters shown by rats; wide variations in the *FI* value do not produce comparable changes in behavior (Leander, Lippman, & Meyer 1968).

These data are important because they indicate that humans and rats differ in the way they respond to reinforcement schedules. The differences may be entirely "explainable." For instance, the "cost" of the response (Weiner 1962), previous exposure to reinforcement schedules (DeCasper & Zeiler 1972), and verbal instructions (Kaufman, Baron, & Kopp 1966) have been shown to be among the factors which contribute to the differences. However, the differences may also be more fundamental; the very fact that humans are verbal creatures, that they can provide instructions or rules to themselves, suggest that their behavior may be affected by schedules in a qualitatively different way from that of rats and pigeons. Support for the crucial role of language in human behavior under schedules comes from further work by Lowe and colleagues. Lowe, Beasty, and Bentall (1983) found that children too young to have functioning language did behave like pigeons on interval schedules; and Lowe, Harzem, and Bagshaw (1978) found that adults also behaved like pigeons on a task which was not seen as a problem to be solved (i.e., key pressing to obtain the time until the next reward was due).

The implication is that human behavior will only be determined by schedules of reinforcement when people are not trying to "solve" the problem posed by the schedule. We must therefore not expect schedules to account for the complex systems used by roulette or blackjack players, as an example. But the repetitive, apparently mindless, playing of a simple slot machine may well yield to an analysis in terms of the schedules in operation. So many aspects of a gambler's behavior are less central than the actual placing of a bet, yet may have a substantial influence on the amount of gambling that gets done. For instance, Dickerson (1979) draws attention to the way the regular sequence of races may act as an interval schedule and thereby entrain a sequence of behaviors that tends to keep regular gamblers in a betting shop for the entire day and thus set them on the path toward excessive gambling.

Apart from rate and pattern of responding, learning theorists have been particularly concerned with the effects of schedules of reinforcement on the persistence of behavior. This is particularly important in connection with gambling, where we have the problem of explaining why people go on gambling in the face of what must be, on the average, consistent losses. In both humans and other species, there is an extremely well-documented relationship between the reinforcement schedule and later persistence of behavior. Reward schedules in which the payoff occurs only intermittently (precisely the schedules which seem to resemble gambling situations) produce greater persistence after reward is discontinued altogether than schedules that program reward very frequently (Bijou 1957; but see Keppel, Zavortink, & Shiff 1967). This is called the partial reinforcement extinction effect (PREE), which provides one possible explanation for persistence in gambling. Indeed, many laboratory investigations of PREE have used simulations of gambling for experimental purposes.

In one series of experiments, Lewis and Duncan (1957, 1958) permitted university students to play a slot machine that was programmed to present reward on 0, 11, 33, 67, or 100% of the plays. Except for the 0 condition, the smaller the percentage of reward, the greater the persistence later when reward was discontinued. What this suggests is that it is the rarity of success at gambling that induces the gambler to return to the game, not the profitable run of good luck. And the higher the payoff, the more this relationship between percentage of payoff and persistence is inflated (e.g., Ratliff & Ratliff 1971); that is, infrequent, but large, winners are likely to be the most persistent gamblers of all.

Why do people and animals endure nonreward for longer following intermittent reward than following continuous reward? This question has been the subject of a vast number of studies (see Tarpy 1982, for a survey), and there is no simple answer. Generally, though, it is believed that responding on nonreinforced trials is strengthened because reward is eventually forthcoming (Capaldi 1966). Persistence, in some sense, eventually pays off. Thus in gambling, continued betting until a run of bad luck is over is eventually rewarded. Patience on the part of the loser is sustained. The winnings paradoxically strengthen (reinforce) the placement of losing bets.

Amsel (e.g., 1967) has suggested that an important factor in this process is frustration. This idea has particular appeal when we apply the PREE to gambling. Failing to win when one is striving for and expecting a reward, results in a sense of frustration. Normally this is an aversive state which subjects will attempt to terminate or avoid (e.g., Daly 1970). But when the subject eventually gets a payoff, the frustration is dissipated and the response which led to the dissipation is strengthened. In other words, the dissipation of the frustration, not to mention the receipt of the reward itself, is enormously reinforcing. Repeated experiences of this sort produces a person who not only can sustain the gambling behavior in the face of a loss, but one who actually enjoys it; patience during a streak of bad luck is more than compensated for by a subsequent win. Amsel's frustration theory was originally developed to account for animal behavior, but it is also compatible with the special properties of human instrumental responding. Eventual reinforcement for tolerating losses may establish a "rule" that the individual covertly rehearses when gambling. And it is well established that persistence in behavior may occur because a person is insensitive to changes in the schedule of reinforcement, preferring to "obey" a now-inappropriate rule (e.g., Lowe 1979).

CONCLUSIONS

We have dwelt at some length on the learning theory approach to gambling behavior for two reasons. First, it does provide a good account of some kinds of gambling. Second, it concentrates on the obvious economic properties of gambling (the costs, rewards, and probabilities involved) but is still able to provide a uniform account for "rational" gambling (where the expected value of betting is higher than that of not betting), and "irrational" gambling (where the reverse is true). This is an important advantage given our aim of escaping from the straitjacket of the "rationality question" (cf. Chapter 5).

Nonetheless, reinforcement theory is not a complete account of gambling behavior. For example, it can only provide a speculative explanation of why some people apparently become addicted to the activity while others do not. Many who obtain occasional reinforcement from their gambling experience but never become compulsive gamblers. Therefore, other perspectives focusing on the early environment of the person, or even their unconscious motives, would appear to be essential for a complete explanation of the behavior. In addition, the psychological processes (e.g., judgmental heuristics), which predispose people to distort their judgments and to attribute a skill factor to outcomes where no skill is involved, also seem to be exceptionally valuable concepts.

No single theory will account for all the different kinds of gambling behavior, and it is fairly clear that the relevance of different kinds of theory will depend quite strongly both on the situation and on the person doing the gambling. Reinforcement theory may be appropriate for slot machines, cognitive analysis may be needed where people have a wide choice of different bets, and a psychodynamic approach may be useful in helping explain excessive gambling. A clear implication is that the next phase of research on the economic psychology of gambling will have to concentrate on the kinds of gambling behavior in which people engage spontaneously. We now have at our disposal a wide range of general principles, which have been studied in considerable detail in artificial laboratory situations. We know that direct application of these to everyday situations is unlikely to be successful. We need to establish which principles are of greatest use in which situations.

III

HOW THE ECONOMY AFFECTS
INDIVIDUAL BEHAVIOR

Part II of this book centered on the idea that the behavior of individuals determines the behavior of the entire economy. In different ways, that proposition is likely to be accepted readily enough both by economists and by psychologists. For psychologists, the behavior of individuals is the central point of interest, so that it is natural to see it as a major causative factor in any social process. For economists, individual choice is, in principle at least, the core of theory. While the two disciplines might disagree about the way in which individual behavior is relevant, or the detail in which it needs to be studied, both should be able to understand the direction of our argument in Part II.

In this part, we are going to turn that argument on its head, and consider how the economy in turn has a causative influence on individuals' behavior. This is a much less obviously acceptable idea. Its extreme form is the "vulgar Marxist" position that the nature of the economy in which individuals live, and their position within it, totally determine their mental life and behavior. We do not have to go to those extremes, however, to recognize that the economy is an influential social fact in many aspects of our behavior. Most simply, many kinds of economic behavior cannot be performed unless we live in the right kind of economy. Only slightly less simply, socioeconomic status is a pervasive variable in most kinds of social psychology. And few economists are totally apolitical; most would argue that the difference between a traditional economy, a capitalist economy, and a socialist economy will have quite wide-ranging effects on the ways in which people think and behave.

The economy can affect individuals in a variety of different ways, at different levels. The chapters in Part III are therefore not very homogeneous. The first three, on taxation, money, and advertising, look at fairly specific institutions within the modern economy. Advertising, at least, is directly intended to influence individual behavior; and money has been very widely believed to do so, for a very long time ("The love of money is the root of all evil," alleged St. Paul). In all three cases, we need to consider both the small-scale, direct effects on the details of behavior as well as the much more general effects on the whole style of individuals' life, which may (or may not) result from living in an economy in which those particular institutions exist, and take the particular forms that we are familiar with.

The economy in which we currently live is not an absolute, eternal fact. It is a particular historical situation that has developed over time from probably simpler, and certainly different, situations. Similarly, each individual economic agent has behind him or her a history of development. The next two chapters, therefore, consider how the development of societies and individuals influences economic behavior. This is partly a matter of asking how, through a developmental and historical process, we come to have the economic behavior we do. Thus we look at the "economic socialization" of children – how they adapt to the economy in which they find themselves growing up – and the transformation of isolated "primitive economies" when they come into contact with the pervasive, worldwide, "modern economy." But it is also an opportunity to look at the causative effects of the economy more directly. Primitive economies are different from one another and from the modern economy. Children of different ages live in quite distinct economies of their own. By looking at the different kinds of behavior shown in these different economic situations, we can try to come to some comparative conclusions about the effective economic causes of individual behaviors.

The same logic is at work in Chapter 11, where we consider the effects of economic change and fluctuation on individual behavior. The world contains many economies which are struggling toward the level of industrialization and sophistication of the traditionally "developed" nations. How does this process of development affect individual behavior? The developed economies are also still subject to quite violent changes in the level of activity within them. What psychological effects, if any, do these have? Here again we have an opportunity to discover the key factors in the economic causation of individual behavior.

However controversial the idea of such causation might be, there is one group of psychologists who have embraced it wholeheartedly, namely the proponents of the "token economy." Here the whole idea is that, by changing the economic system within an institution, you make it possible to change the behavior of individuals in the most radical ways. The success or failure of this enterprise, and the precise nature of its effects, is perhaps the strongest evidence on the question with which we are concerned in this part of the book.

Because the level of the material in this part is variable, the chapters do not follow a common style. But there is one device that we have used wherever possible, and that is to review the kinds of individual economic behavior that were the subject of Part II, and see how they are affected by the particular economic factor currently under consideration. We should expect economic causes to have their most obvious effects on economic behavior. The different patterns revealed in these review sections, therefore, are an important test of the point of view we are taking here, that the economy is an important factor in the life of individuals.

11

TAXATION

In the mixed economy of the United Kingdom, some 42% of the GNP is collected in taxes. The figure is somewhat lower (around 33%) in the more rigorously free-enterprise economy of the United States and is somewhat higher in countries such as Sweden, which have a more social-ist orientation. But in any modern economy, a large proportion of eco-nomic resources ends up in the form of tax. Clearly, economic psycholo-gists must take an interest in taxation.

Taxation is one of the ways in which properties of the economy as a whole have an effect on individuals, so the reason for considering it in this part is clear. Two other points may not be so obvious, however. First, the effects of taxation on individual behavior are more various and more extensive than may at first be realized. Second, individual behavior also has an effect on the tax system, both because the imposition of a tax may alter behavior so much that its yield is greatly reduced and because people may conspire to avoid tax so successfully that tax policies have to be modified.

Taxation affects the economic behavior of individuals both directly and indirectly. The direct effect of taxes is to alter either the relative prices of goods or an individual's income (or usually, both). For instance, the imposition of a tax on cigarettes increases their price and should lead to a reduction in the number of cigarettes smoked (a result that may or may not be welcome to the authorities, depending on whether the aim of the tax is to raise revenue or to improve the health of the community). A cigarette tax also reduces the real income of smokers, since smokers require more money than they did before the tax imposition to maintain the same level of consumption.

The indirect effects of taxes are more subtle but may be more far reaching. Taxation may alter the functioning of the economy as a whole. Consider once again a cigarette tax. If its imposition raises the total yield from taxes to an amount exceeding what the government needs to finance its own expenditure, then the economy will deflate. As we shall see in Chapter 16, this will have a variety of effects on individuals' economic behavior and general psychological state. One thing that will certainly happen is that average incomes will fall, one consequence of which is that fewer cigarettes will be bought.

However, taxation does not affect only expenditure; at least in theory, it also affects the supply of labor and even the way people vote at general elections. Given the economic importance of all these effects, the sheer amount of tax collected, and the existence of strong personal reactions to taxation, it is not surprising that taxes have received a good deal of attention from economic psychologists. Up to now, the areas that have been studied in most detail are tax avoidance and attitudes to taxation; a social psychological approach has predominated in these areas. We shall review this work in some detail in this chapter, but we also want to take a more broadly interdisciplinary view. Therefore, in addition to looking at attitudes to taxation, we shall consider whether taxation is fair as well as its effects on various kinds of economic behavior. To put these questions in context we will begin by describing the form and function of modern taxation.

THE NEED FOR TAXATION

Chapter 2 explained how the price system functions to allocate resources. Given that this self-regulating system is claimed to solve the problems of production, distribution, and exchange, it is reasonable to ask why we have taxation at all. The answer comes in three parts.

First, taxation, and the subsequent provision of goods and services by government, helps overcome some of the inefficiencies of the price system. For example, the system may be inefficient in the case of public goods and those goods involving external costs and benefits. Public goods are those goods that, if supplied to one person, can be made available to others at no extra cost, and that others cannot be excluded from consuming, even if they do not pay for them. It is never in any individual's interest to provide such goods, but society may benefit if these goods are provided. Lighthouses are a classic example. Such goods can be provided by the government out of revenue raised by taxation. Similarly, where the production of a good has an external cost (i.e., a cost borne not by the producer but by others), the private sector will tend to produce too much of it because it does not take this cost into account. One solution to this inefficiency is to tax the producers of the good.

Second, taxation can help overcome some of the inequities of the price system. In a pure market economy, individuals' incomes would be determined by their output (plus any contribution from their assets). This would leave some individuals destitute and others very poor. If a society feels that such a distribution of income is unfair or otherwise undesirable, it may redistribute resources by taxing the more affluent and giving cash or some other benefit to the less affluent.

Finally, the government may use taxation to influence the functioning of the economy as a whole, for instance, to smooth out the peaks and troughs of the business cycle (see Chapter 3).

THE NATURE OF TAXES

Taxation can take a surprising variety of forms. We are all familiar with income tax and taxes on sales, such as value added tax (VAT) and purchase tax. But many British people probably do not consider the National Insurance contributions they pay as a tax. But because these payments are compulsory and do not take into account factors which a genuine insurance scheme would include (e.g., risk factors), it is more realistic to see them as a poll tax, that is, a tax levied at so many pounds sterling per head of the population. Describing them as insurance payments is probably a (successful) attempt to relieve them from some of the unpopularity attached to taxes generally.

Some idea of the range of taxes levied in a modern economy can be gained from Figure 11.1, which summarizes the taxes collected by central government in Britain (the situation would be much more complicated in the United States, because of the interacting effects of federal, state, city, and even commuter taxes). Taxes clearly differ in a number of important ways. Some are collected *directly* from the taxpayer (income tax, capital gains tax), while others are collected *indirectly*. Buyers, for instance, pay VAT indirectly through being charged a higher price for goods and services; businesses, in effect, act as collecting agencies for this tax. Taxes also differ in their rate. In Britain, VAT is currently 15%, income tax varies from zero to 60%, and excise duty on wine is 90p per liter.

As we explained in Chapter 3, the rate structure of a tax is usually described as progressive, proportional (or neutral), or regressive. These are mathematical and not evaluative terms. Taxes that take an increasing proportion of income as it rises are described as progressive, those that take a constant proportion of income are called proportional, and those that take a decreasing proportion of income as it rises are called regressive. The application of this distinction to income tax is obvious, but it is relevant to all taxes. A purchase tax on goods that tend to be bought by those with higher incomes would be progressive. By contrast, local government rates (property tax) in Britain are probably regressive. The effect of a tax is not always predictable. There is some evidence (Kay & King 1980) that the tax on tobacco in the U.K. is regressive, whereas the tax on alcohol, which is usually associated with the tobacco tax in public and media discussion, turns out to be progressive.

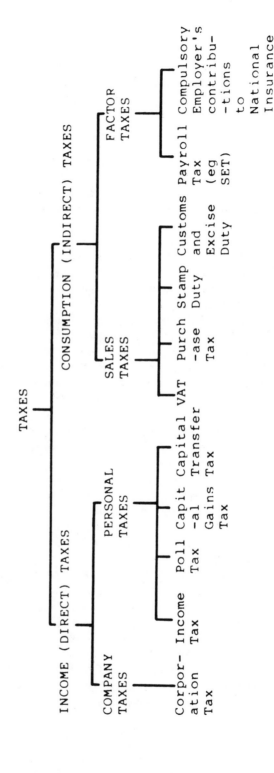

11.1. A classification of some taxes. (After Allan 1971.)

TAXATION AND SOCIETY

Is taxation efficient?

This question "sometimes appears to be the overriding concern of economists" (Lewis 1982). There are three senses in which a tax may be held to be inefficient. It may distort consumer choice and or labor supply, it may cost too much to administer, or it may cost too much to comply with.

The first is often advanced with strong ideological overtones. Taxation inevitably reallocates resources from the distribution they would have reached in a taxless economy, and some economic theorists would argue that this necessarily is less efficient and leads to a lower level of general welfare than the "unfettered" operation of the market. Such an argument depends, however, on rather special assumptions about the definition of both welfare and efficiency. The influence of this position in the domain of public policy in recent years probably depends more on the general (and, perhaps, unthinking) unpopularity of taxation than on any intellectual coherence or empirical support.

While the argument for the general inefficiency of taxation is therefore not of immediate interest here, specific cases of it certainly are. A particular tax, or a particular structure of taxation, may distort the labor supply and consumer choice. For example, a tax on cars that rises according to engine capacity may clutter the roads with large underpowered vehicles that use fuel very inefficiently. A combined system of taxes and means-tested social security benefits may cause a poor unemployed person to lose money by taking work. An even more bizarre example of economic inefficiency can be seen in the British window tax of the eighteenth century. This provoked many houseowners to brick up their windows, a practice that was clearly a cost to the houseowners and of no benefit to the government. But the question of whether a tax is inefficient in this way needs to be settled empirically, for each individual case, although theory may well be able to suggest which cases are most likely to produce problems.

There is not much economic psychology in the administration costs of taxes. Inefficiencies of this kind usually derive from some combination of historical accident and voter susceptibilities. The classic example is the British dog licence, fixed at seven shillings and sixpence in 1878, and remaining at its decimal equivalent, 37 and a half-pence, 107 years, and 2,000% of inflation later. This tax now costs roughly three times as much to administer as it yields, but it seems politically impossible either to increase it or to abolish it.

Curious as the political psychology of a nation of self-proclaimed dog lovers may be, the psychology of the compliance costs of taxation has been studied in substantially more detail. In countries such as the United States, where income tax is collected after self-assessment, the costs to individuals of complying with this most basic tax can be considerable. In Britain, businesses have to analyze their transactions to determine the appropriate payment of VAT, and for small businesses at least, the costs of doing so are very considerable and a frequent cause of complaint. Complaint as such is not, of course, evidence of inefficiency, but it does suggest that the costs of compliance may be large relative to the yield of the tax, or larger than they would be if the tax were collected in some other way; both would be grounds for condemning the tax as inefficient.

Economic psychologists have concerned themselves directly with some of the inefficiencies resulting from compliance costs, particularly through the application of research to the psychology of written communication. These costs are not insignificant. Sandford reports that in 1971–2, U.K. direct taxes had gross compliance costs of 3.8–5.8% of revenue. The compliance costs of VAT have been estimated at approximately 400 million pounds per year and administration costs at 85 million (Sanford, Godwin, Hardwick, & Butterworth 1981), about 11% of the annual yield. Such costs could be reduced by simplifying the tax structure, but any move in that direction is likely to have political and economic implications which may not be acceptable. A less contentious proposal is to make explanatory tax literature simpler and more comprehensible, and to redesign tax forms. Such changes are also likely to reduce administrative inefficiencies if they reduce either internal errors in the tax service or the number of queries that tax officials have to answer from the public.

The "readability" of tax literature from a variety of countries has been assessed in the last decade using reading measures such as FOG (a measure that determines a reading age for prose based on such measures as the length of sentences and the average number of syllables per word). In general, tax literature has been found to be reasonably accessible. The British Inland Revenue's standard tax guide, for example, has a reading age of 13.0, and the U.S. 1974 federal income tax form one of 12.5. But we need to bear in mind that there are approximately 2 million adults in Britain with a reading age of less than 9, and that if one is Australian the tax literature is not so inviting. Their standard tax guides have a reading age of 17, higher than that of a "quality" newspaper (James, Lewis, & Wallschutzky 1981).

Some tax literature has been improved recently. In an attempt to reduce the compliance costs for VAT, the British Customs and Excise department has simplified its forms, reducing the reading age of the VAT account from 14 to 10 (Sandford et al. 1981). Some of the recommendations of researchers interested in the design of official forms must seem obvious. It should not take an economic psychologist to point out that print should be readable and that subheadings should be used. What is interesting, as well as surprising, is how often the recommendations are ignored. For example, Morris (1975) notes that the 300,000 pensioners over 80 years of age who receive supplementary benefit forms by mail probably do not have good enough eyesight to read the small print.

As we shall see in more detail later, people's understanding of the tax system is generally rather poor. For example, taxpayers are very inaccurate in estimating their own and other's tax rates (Lewis 1978). Improvements in tax literature should improve understanding and, in turn, reduce compliance costs and inefficiency.

How does taxation affect expenditures?

As we explained above, taxation can affect expenditure in two ways: by reducing real income and by altering the relative price of goods and services. In this section we will consider only whether indirect taxes always lead to increased prices and who, in fact, pays the tax. Is it the consumer or the producer, the buyer or the seller, the employer or the employee? We will use a flat-rate customs duty on wine as an example because the analysis is similar, whether the tax is VAT, customs and excise duty, or a payroll tax.

The simple microeconomic theory of taxation is set out in Figure 11.2. In the absence of a customs duty a vineyard might have a supply schedule as shown in Figure 11.2a. If a duty of, say, $1 per liter is levied, every point on the supply curve will be shifted to the right by the amount of the tax. This ensures that the vineyard receives the same amount per liter as it was receiving before the imposition of the duty. This does not mean, however, that the price of wine increases by $1 per liter, although that may happen. What happens to price depends on demand as well as supply.

If the demand for wine is perfectly inelastic, the price of wine will indeed increase by $1 per liter; if it is perfectly elastic, the price will not increase at all (Fig. 11.2b, c). This suggests that taxes on goods with relatively elastic demand will have relatively little effect on prices and that, in this case, the burden of the tax falls mainly on the producer. Conversely, taxes on goods with relatively inelastic demand, such as alcohol and tobacco, will have a large effect on prices and will be mainly borne by the consumer. With an intermediate elasticity of demand, the effect on price will be intermediate between these extremes.

The elasticity of supply is also important. If supply is very elastic, the effect on price and/or quantity may be substantial (Fig. 11.2d), while with a more inelastic supply, the effects on both will be less (Fig. 11.2e). Again, with an intermediate elasticity of supply, the effect on price and quantity will be somewhere between these extremes.

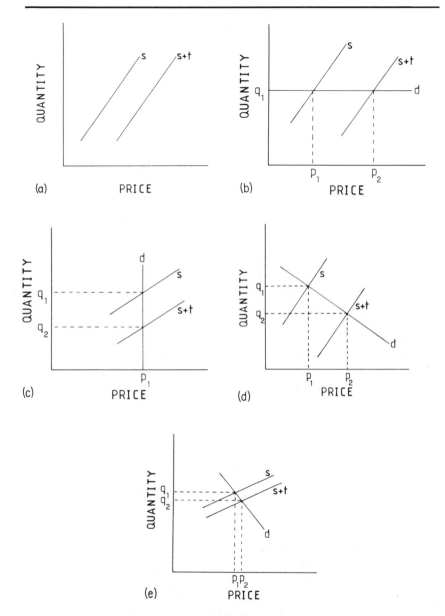

11.2. Effects of a tax on supply and demand. (a) Supply curve. (b) Effect on price with perfectly inelastic demand. (c) Effect on price with perfectly elastic demand. (d) Effect with elastic supply. (e) With inelastic supply.

All these analyses assume that the goods and services involved are being exchanged in a more-or-less competitive market. In many instances this may be a very unrealistic assumption. Nonetheless, it is worth examining some empirical evidence on these simple predictions.

In 1965 changes in the U.S. tax system provided researchers with the opportunity to investigate the impact on prices of reductions in federal excise taxes. The excise tax of 10% had been levied on a variety of "luxury" goods and was now completely abolished. Brownlee and Perry (1967), for example, examined price statistics for a variety of the goods affected, some which they expected to have relatively elastic supply (e.g., face powder, earrings) and some whose supply could be expected to be inelastic (cinema and race track seats). They believed demand elasticities for all these goods to be generally low and therefore predicted that the price changes would be approximately the same as the value of the tax changes for the goods with relatively elastic supply, and close to zero for goods with inelastic supply. This proved the case. The tax changes led to a 10.3% reduction in the price of face powder and a 8.8% reduction in the price of earrings. For cinema admissions, in contrast, there was a mean increase in price of 4% over the three-month period over which the tax was abolished.

These results are consistent with the predictions of elementary price theory but are concerned only with price changes. Hamovitch (1966) investigated the effect on quantity sold of changes in sales tax rates. He demonstrated that increases in sales tax rates in New York City (surrounded during the relevant period by tax-free shopping areas) reduced retail sales, whereas corresponding increases in Alabama, where there was no access to tax-free areas, had no significant effect on retail sales. The demand for goods sold in New York City would be relatively elastic because goods sold in New Jersey and New York State would be very close substitutes. We would therefore predict that an increase in the tax rate would lead to a large reduction in sales (as in Fig. 11.2c).

These examples illustrate that very elementary economic analysis can give us some insight into the functioning of the tax system. In the future economic psychologists may add to our understanding of the effects of taxation on expenditure through a consideration of the moderating role of tax perceptions. For example, does an increase in a tax on cigarettes have the same effect if it is presented as a health tax?

IS TAXATION FAIR?

At first glance, this may seem to be an ethical question, beyond the scope of this book. In fact, it takes us to the heart of the economic psychology of taxation, for two reasons.

In the first place, the fairness of taxation is obviously a question of considerable practical importance. When tax systems are seen as unfair, there may be resistance by taxpayers; even if the most dramatic forms of taxpayer resistance, such as the American revolution, are relatively rare, less dramatic forms (such as tax evasion and tax avoidance) are still important.

Second, we have to ask what the question means, and one possible answer is that fairness is always in the eye of the beholder. Taxation is fair if and only if it is perceived to be fair, and that is clearly a question in economic psychology. This is not the only possible answer, however, so we now consider the criteria for fairness of taxation in more detail.

The objective fairness of taxation

Apart from the subjective criterion we have suggested, economists have identified two criteria of objective equity – one uncontentious, the other more problematic. The uncontentious kind is horizontal equity. This principle asserts that taxpayers with similar taxable capacities should be treated equally. The problematic kind is vertical equity. This concept encompasses a range of principles which assert that people in different circumstances should be treated differently. The principle enunciated by Marx (1875/1962), "From each according to his abilities: to each according to his needs" is a classic attempt to resolve the vertical equity problem, but it is not the only possibility. For instance, other principles claiming to produce vertical equity are parity (the idea that everybody should have an equal share of scarce resources), the "investment principle" (which asserts that resources should be distributed according to the amount invested by an individual in time, money, effort, skill, and so forth) and the deliberate use of progressive taxation (which takes a larger proportion of income from those with most resources).

There are at least some documented cases of failure of horizontal equity. For example, Sandford's (1973) survey of the compliance costs of almost 3,000 taxpayers led him to conclude that such costs are inequitably high for the self-employed, the elderly, those on low incomes, and the least well educated.

Before we can decide whether current taxation is equitable in the vertical sense, we have to decide what the appropriate criterion of vertical equity is, and that is a hard task. It is unlikely that the three present authors could agree on a detailed criterion. But there does seem likely to be broad agreement on two general principles: The net effect of taxation should be progressive, so that incomes after tax have a more equal distri-

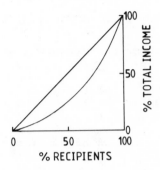

11.3. A Lorenz curve showing distribution of posttax income in Britain in 1982. (From Central Statistical Office, 1985, *Social Trends*, No. 15, Table 5.21.)

bution than incomes before tax, and the effect should not be totally redistributive; that is, there must be some residual reward for greater talent or effort. In other words, most of us would want to take from the rich to give to the poor rather than vice versa (Robin Hood may be misguided, but his converse would be intolerable), but we do not want to render the talented poor in the process.

As we mentioned briefly in Chapter 3, there are standard techniques for assessing the degree of inequality of income in an economy. For example, we can assess the proportion of total income that is received by the top 5% of recipients, the proportion received by the next 5%, and so on. If this information is plotted cumulatively the result is called a Lorenz curve (shown in Fig. 11.3). This particular curve reveals that in 1982, the lowest 60% of the British population received 37.4% of total income and the top 20% of the population received 38.6% of total income. The extent of inequality in the distribution of income is assessed by the Gini coefficient, which basically measures the area between the straight line of equal distribution and the Lorenz curve.

Gini coefficients can be used to compare the distribution of income in different years (to see if the distribution is becoming more or less equal) and of pretax income with posttax income (which examines whether the tax system is effectively redistributing income). Several surveys have been carried out in Britain that have made these comparisons (e.g., Paish 1957; Lydall 1959; Nicholson 1973; Diamond Commission 1976). These surveys show that between 1938 and 1957, the distribution of income moved toward equality and that the concentration of income in the top 5% of income earners was being reduced at an accelerating rate over this period. For the next decade there was little change and from the mid-1960s onward there was a gradual movement toward equality of pretax in-

Table 11.1. *The distribution of income in Britain between 1964 and 1973–4.*

	1964	1967	1972/3	1973/4
Pretax income of top 10%	29.1	28	26.9	26.8
Posttax income of top 10%	25.9	24.3	23.6	23.6
Pretax Gini coefficient	39.9	38.2	37.4	37
Posttax Gini coefficient	36.6	33.5	33.1	32.8

Source: Diamond Commission, 1976.

Table 11.2. *The redistribution of income in Britain in 1982.*

Original income	Original income and cash benefits	Income after all taxes and benefits
200	2,830	3,220
2,900	4,580	4,130
6,430	7,580	5,790
9,590	10,720	7,670
16,540	17,920	12,260

Source: Central Statistical Office (1985), *Social Trends no. 15,* Table 5.19.

comes, which was then accentuated by the effects of taxation (Table 11.1). However, the 1982 edition of *Social Trends* points out that since 1949 succesive reductions in the share received by the top 1% appear to have been largely retained in the top half of the distribution. For example, in 1949 the top 1% received 6.4% of all incomes and the top 50% received 74% of all incomes. By 1978, the share of the top 1% had been reduced to 3.9% of incomes, but the top 50% still received 74%. And between 1976 and 1982 the share of the bottom 40% actually dropped slightly, from 20.1% to 18.9% (Central Statistical Office 1985). Even if the tax system does seem to be operating to redistribute income reasonably effectively (Table 11.2), it nevertheless seems to be very unfair at the lowest income levels (Field, Meacher, & Pond 1977). There are a number of people in this position who face marginal rates of taxation of over 100% because of the way in which the tax system and the benefit system interact. It was estimated that in 1981 2% of all working families (330,000) would gain less than 50p from a 1-pound increase in gross earnings. Ten thousand families would receive no increase at all (Central Statistical Office 1985). This cannot, by any criterion, be considered equitable.

The perceived fairness of taxation

The abstract principles of horizontal and vertical equity are enunciated by economists at best on a priori grounds and at worst on the basis of mathematical convenience. The task of the economic psychologist is therefore clear: We have to discover what people actually experience as fair. Because of the difficulty of arriving at objective criteria of vertical equity, we shall pay particular attention to the perceived fairness of the redistributive effects of taxation.

A considerable body of research in social psychology suggests that people believe that resources should be distributed unequally according to the amount contributed by an individual (Walster, Bersheid, & Walster 1976) and therefore that the investment principle of vertical equity should be experienced as fair. For example, both less and more skilled people believe it is "right" for the more skilled to receive more pay and more prestige. Far from being a universal social psychological law, it has been claimed that this common observation merely reflects Western capitalist society (Moscovici 1972). The fact that developmental evidence suggests a shift from judgments based on parity toward those based on investment (Eiser & Eiser 1976; Moessinger 1975) could be taken to support this view (see Chapter 14).

If this "investment" theory of fairness is correct, we might expect the current tax systems in Western capitalist countries to be seen as generally fair, since they are only very mildly redistributive in effect. However, this prediction is not confirmed. Only 33% of a Swedish sample felt that the tax burden was distributed fairly (Vogel 1974) and studies carried out in Scotland reveal considerable discontent (Dean, Keenan, & Keeney 1980). Approximately 70% of a sample of more than 400 taxpayers believed they were paying too much tax compared with other people in general (vertical equity) and approximately 60% believed they were paying too much tax compared to people with incomes similar to their own (horizontal equity). There is some evidence, at least in the United States, that antitax sentiment has been growing over the past decade. A 1957 Gallup poll revealed that 61% of respondents felt the amount they paid in taxes was too high. By 1976, a Harris poll found that 72% held this view. More dramatically, in 1969, 54% felt that they had reached the breaking point with respect to their taxes, and this figure had risen to 66% by 1878.

To summarize, the economic and psychological evidence we have considered seems to reflect two historical trends. First, the distribution of income is very gradually becoming more equal, partly as a result of taxation. Second, the perceived inequity of the tax system is increasing as is resistance to it. There is a growing feeling that the tax burden is excessive and a growing desire to shift welfare services from the state to the private sector (Harris & Seldon 1979) at least in the United Kingdom. This may occur, in part, because the public has negative attitudes toward the bureaucracy needed to administer a welfare system. There is certainly evidence to suggest that people think it is possible to cut taxes without cutting services (see Citrin's 1979 analysis of the opinion patterns associated with California's Proposition 13) presumably through making administration more efficient.

These two trends can be illustrated quite dramatically by the example of Spain. Until 1977, the Spanish tax system had a predominance of indirect taxes, was generally regressive, and suffered a considerable amount of fraud. Not surprisingly, people saw the system as unfair. After the reform of 1977, which brought in a progressive system with far more revenue being collected in the form of income tax, we might have expected this feeling of inequity to have dissipated. However, the belief that the tax system is unfair persists. This seems to be because more Spaniards are aware of paying tax (since it is now collected directly) and because the government is seen as squandering their revenue (Martin & Lopez 1984).

What needs to be kept in mind, though, is that current attitudes toward taxation and the welfare system are based on very limited knowledge. The public is fiscally ignorant. In a recent Canadian study, only 20% of respondents had even an approximate idea of the size of the budget and how it was apportioned between health and social welfare (Auld 1978). Perhaps more important, few people make the fiscal connection between the price of government spending in terms of taxation and the benefits they enjoy as government services. This shows up very well in the differences between answers to survey questions in which the link between tax and expenditure is made explicit and those in which it is not. Stated simply, if the link is made explicit people express much more favorable attitudes toward taxation (see Lewis 1982, Chapter 4, for a summary of studies illustrating this). This suggests that providing people with more information about taxation and the welfare system may, in itself, help alter the feeling that taxation is unfair and perhaps reduce tax resistance, although given other evidence on changing public opinions (see Chapter 13) it would be naive to hope for a strong effect.

So, to return to the question that began this section, "Is taxation fair?", we have found that, in general, people seem to think that it is not. This is reflected in their tax attitudes. But do these results reflect anything more than ritualistic grumbles? To see whether perceptions of the tax system as being unfair actually influence people's behavior, we shall now consider investigations of tax avoidance and evasion.

INDIVIDUAL BEHAVIOR AND TAXATION

Tax evasion and avoidance

One possible response to perceived unfairness of taxation is an attempt to reduce the amount of tax paid. There are at least four distinct ways in which people can try to do this; any of them may also be engaged in for reasons that have nothing to do with perceived fairness. The least dramatic is the purely passive step of reducing one's consumption so as to pay less tax. For example, some peace campaigners in the United Kingdom deliberately pay to tax-exempt charities a proportion of their income which equals the proportion of government revenue used for military expenditure, so that they can feel that they are not contributing to an activity of which they do not approve. At the other extreme is open defiance of the tax laws, in the form of "tax strikes" or other such measures. For present purposes, however, the interesting cases are the intermediate ones, tax evasion and tax avoidance.

Let us begin with a few definitions. Tax avoidance is legal; it involves arranging one's affairs to pay the minimum amount of tax, in a way which is contrary to the spirit of the law, but not actually illegal. Tax evasion, on the other hand, is illegal. It may involve evasion by commission (i.e., some action by the taxpayer such as a false statement about the amount of interest earned on an investment) or by omission (the taxpayer simply fails to tell the Revenue department about certain assets). However, van de Braak (1983) pointed out that this conventional distinction between evasion and avoidance misses the point. Both activities are contrary to the intentions of the government, and both may bring about an unintended redistribution of income – or prevent an intended one.

It is understandably difficult to find out how prevalent tax evasion is. The chairman of the board of the Inland Revenue in Britain has estimated that about 7.5% of Britain's gross domestic product (GDP) evades being taxed; in the United States, estimates range from 3.4 to 5% of GNP (Tanzi, cited in Maital 1982) to 25 to 33% of GNP (Feige 1979). But these are "guesstimates" based on economic variables (such as the percentage of bank notes issued that are of large denominations and the divergence between income and expenditure estimates of gross domestic product) and they are clearly not very reliable. Other evidence, such as that from social surveys, suggests that tax evasion is not as prevalent as these economic estimates imply. Brown, Levin, Rosa, and Ulph (1984), for instance, looked solely at the earned income of workers and concluded that there was little evidence of evasion on their main jobs. Some income earned on second jobs probably did evade the tax system, but it represented at most 0.5% of the income earned in their main jobs. These conclusions require the assumption that respondents were honest, which they may not have been.

Economic models of tax evasion (e.g., Allingham & Sandmo 1972) assume that taxpayers are rational optimizers and will declare as little of their income as possible. They will be influenced by the chances of detection, by the tax authorities and the penalties for evasion. Feelings of inequity are irrelevant; inequity will be accepted if it maximizes an individual's estimated net benefits.

Allingham and Sandmo's model has been tested using simulation techniques. Friedland, Maital, and Rutenberg (1978), for example, conducted a small-scale experiment in which subjects were given tax tables and a monthly "income" which they then had to declare so as to maximize net income. The experiment had a 2 × 2 design with tax rates (25% and 50%) and frequency of auditing/severity of fine as independent variables. Friedland et al. found that large fines (with a small probability of detection) were a more effective deterrent than mathematically equivalent small fines (with a high probability of detection). In a follow-up study, Friedland (1982) found that vague information about the probability of audits enhanced the deterrent power of low-probability audits and small fines. In both studies, the basic economic model was generally supported. However, given that these experiments were set up as economic games in which the aim was to maximize net income (i.e., gross income, less tax, less fines), this is perhaps not all that surprising.

Spicer and Thomas's (1982) study of audit probabilities and tax evasion, similar in design to the study by Friedland et al., suffers from the same problem. Subjects were told that "a small money prize would be distributed to each participant based on his/her total salary minus taxes and fines paid." This strong biasing toward the economic model makes it all the more interesting that their results were not consistent with the model. Changing audit probabilities seemed to change an individual's propensity to cheat but not the amount of taxes he or she evaded.

However, neither this result nor that of Friedland et al. were confirmed by Webley and Halstead (1985) who implemented their simulations on a microcomputer. Webley and Halstead suggested that the situation facing an individual participating in a tax simulation is ambiguous. It can be interpreted in at least three different ways: as a game, as an optimizing problem, or as a tax situation. People's behavior will depend upon how the situation is perceived. Thus changing the instructions slightly (to alter how the simulation is perceived) was shown to alter evasion considerably. These results suggest that one should be extremely cautious about generalizing the results of simulation studies.

The equity variable has also been investigated using simulation techniques. Spicer and Becker (1980) used a procedure very similar to that of Friedland et al. They looked at two variables: equity and a measure of an individual's tax resistance (a Likert scale, which assessed propensity to evade taxes). All subjects used tax tables based on a rate of 40%, but one-third believed this was the average rate, another one-third that the average rate was 65%, and the final third that the average rate was 15%. This manipulation was devised to induce feelings of advantageous and disadvantageous inequity. The results demonstrated that while individual differences in "tax resistance" did not produce any clear result, feelings of inequity had a strong effect. The disadvantaged inequity group evaded the highest percentage of tax and the advantaged inequity group the lowest. However, this result was not confirmed by Webley, Morris, and Amstutz (1985), although they did use a more restricted range of tax rates. All their subjects were taxed at a rate of 30%, but one-third believed this was the average rate, another third that the average rate was 45%, and the final third that the average rate was 15%.

Spicer and Becker's results are, nonetheless, consistent with some of the survey research in this area. Spicer and Lundstedt's (1976) survey of 130 households (mainly from middle- and higher- income groups) in Ohio is a case in point. They investigated the relationship between a number of independent variables such as perceived probability of detection of evasion, perceived severity of sanctions, inequity, and so forth, and two dependent measures, the tax-resistance scale and a tax-evasion index. They found that perceived severity of sanctions did not correlate significantly with either of the dependent measures but that those taxpayers who considered their exchange (tax paid and benefits received) with the government inequitable did show more tax resistance and scored higher on the tax evasion index.

Although the feeling that taxation is unfair may lead to tax evasion, it is worth pointing out that other variables are probably more important and there may well be different types of tax evasion (Groenland & van Zon 1984). Warneryd and Walerud (1982) described five factors that have been used to explain tax evasion: financial strain, feelings of inequity, opportunity, group influence, and personality characteristics. They point out, however, that the evidence for the importance of some of these is weak and in one case (financial strain) nonexistent. They carried out a telephone survey of more than 400 Swedish male adults to investigate these factors (since more than 95% of all households in Sweden have a telephone, the sample was probably fairly representative). More than 18% of their respondents admitted to evading taxes, answering "yes" to the question "did you ever make an (income tax) deduction for an expense you had not had, or fail to report an income?" Multivariate analyses revealed that greater opportunity for tax evasion, younger age, and a lenient attitude to tax crimes were all significant factors related to tax evasion. A simpler chi-square analysis showed that feelings of inequity were also associated with evading taxes. Financial strain was not important. In fact, those men who admitted to tax evasion judged their economic situation more favorably than did the rest of the sample.

What is particularly interesting in this and in similar surveys (e.g., Song & Yarbrough 1978; Vogel 1974; Lewis 1979; Groenland & van Veldhoven 1983) is that tax evasion is not seen as a very serious crime. Vogel's Swedish respondents believed that housebreakers, drunken drivers, car thieves, and embezzlers should all be punished more severely than tax evaders. Song and Yarbrough's American respondents considered tax evasion slightly more serious than stealing a bicycle, and almost 40% of Lewis's British sample agreed with the statement that "people who illegally evade small amounts of tax should be treated leniently by the law." Moreover, the feeling that tax evasion is not a very serious crime seems to have grown during the past decade. Aitken and Bonneville (1980) compared the results of their large-scale interview survey with one carried out in 1966 by the Internal Revenue Service. These investigators asked respondents what penalties they felt were appropriate for people who cheat on their tax forms. Almost one-half felt that this small-scale tax evasion should involve no penalty at all; only about one-third of the 1966 sample had expressed this view.

Tax evasion is clearly a growing problem and is an area in which economic psychology can complement the more traditional economic approach. Social surveys can identify groups of likely tax evaders, changes in tax resistance, and possibly the extent of tax evasion, using such methods as the locked box technique or the randomized response technique (see McCrohan 1982). Simulation studies may also help identify the effect of key variables. As Lewis (1982, p. 160) points out, at the very least psychological investigations of tax evasion "indicate that a taxpayer's decision to evade tax is a function of his perceived chances of detection and so forth rather than his actual chances of detection."

Taxation and the incentive to work

Since we have already considered the relationship between tax rates and the number of hours worked in Chapter 6, we shall deal with this question only briefly here. Remember that elementary economic theory recognizes two ways in which taxes may affect the incentive to work: the income effect and the substitution effect.

The income effect is that a higher tax rate would encourage people to work more since they have a reduced real income. The substitution effect is that a higher tax rate would encourage people to work less since leisure becomes less expensive (the cost of leisure is the income forgone through not working). Elementary economic theory then is unable to predict what the overall effect of a change in tax rates would be because the income and substitution usually work in opposite directions. But what does the evidence suggest? There are three sources of evidence: econometric studies of the supply of labor, experimental evidence (the negative tax experiments described in Chapter 6, and not reconsidered here) and evidence from surveys. In general the econometric studies have revealed backward-bending supply curves (as in Fig. 6.2), for example, Owen's (1971) study of the nonagricultural sector in the United States, and Metcalfe, Nickell, and Richardson's (1976) study of hours of work and hourly earnings of manufacturing industry in the United Kingdom. One general finding is that the effects of different wage rates are very different for married women than married men. Aschenfelter and Heckman (1974) report, for example, that an increase in a wife's wage will encourage her to work more, but an increase in her husband's wage encourages her to work less. Correspondingly, there is evidence that men increase and women decrease work effort for increases in the marginal tax rate and that wives do more home production (housework, child care) and husbands less (Leuthold 1983).

What these studies suggest is that an increase in tax rates should actually increase the number of hours worked. Although Brown (1980) concludes that the most recent and most sophisticated econometric studies show the reverse, survey evidence seems to support the view that marginal tax rates are not a disincentive to work. For instance Barlow, Brazer, and Morgan (1966) interviewed almost 1,000 affluent Americans about their economic behavior and found that only one-eighth reported that they had reduced their work effort because of high marginal tax rates. As they conclude (1966, p. 7):

It is clear that there are many more powerful motives affecting the working behavior of high income people than the marginal income tax rates. People are aware of taxes and do not enjoy paying them, but other considerations are far more important to them in deciding how long to work.

The results from other surveys (e.g., Break 1957; Sanders 1951; Fields & Stanbury 1970) are very similar. People generally say that tax has little or no effect on the number of hours they work. The surveys mentioned so far have all relied on middle-class respondents. One study that cast its net a little wider was that of Brown and Levin (1974), who investigated 2,000 British weekly-paid workers. Their results were nonetheless comparable to those of other studies: 74% of the sample said that tax had no effect on work effort, 15% that it had an incentive effect, and 11% that it had a disincentive effect. Teachers in higher education are no different. They too consider income tax unrelated to work effort (Iles 1973). The picture for those paid more than average is thus clear cut: High marginal tax rates are not considered a disincentive to work and may not be. There is less evidence about people with low incomes, but the experimental work reviewed in Chapter 6 again suggests that disincentive effects would be modest, except perhaps for those facing effectively 100% marginal tax rates.

Taxation and choice between kinds of work

Does tax affect other aspects of work? Grubel and Edwards (1964) investigated whether taxation might influence the choice of occupation. None of the students asked about what factors influenced choice of profession spontaneously mentioned taxation. When asked directly, 80% said it was not an important consideration. Lindquist and Warneryd (1982) examined whether the willingness to be promoted among Swedish middle management is affected by the income tax system. The progressive nature of the Swedish system means that the net salary change is less noticeable than the nominal change and may not be seen as sufficient to compensate for the increased responsibility. However, they report finding no support for their hypothesis; age was the best predictor of willingness to be promoted, followed by the size of the expected net raise. A similar study of Dutch marketing men also found that taxes have no real effect on the desire to seek promotion (von Grumbkow & Warneryd 1984).

Given the remarkably consistent result, that high tax rates are not an important disincentive to work, it is worth asking why the contrary belief is so widespread, at least among conservatives. One possible answer can be derived from research into attribution theory (see Chapter 1). Recall that attribution theory is concerned with how people interpret the causes of behavior. One bias in such interpretations that has attracted a great deal of attention is the so-called actor-observer difference. Jones and Nisbett (1971) claim that actors tend to attribute their actions to situational requirements, whereas observers tend to attribute the same actions to personal dispositions. In other words, "I" evade taxes because the tax form is too difficult to understand and because tax rates are too high; "he" evades taxes because "he" is a dishonest character.

Attribution theory implies that the explanations that people give for the incentive/disincentive effects of taxation will be different when they are explaining their own behavior than when referring to the behavior of others. Unfortunately, as is often the case when deriving predictions from attribution theory, it is not clear how they will be different. On the one hand, actors may attribute an enduring personal disposition to others (he or she acts in self-interest) and infer that others will find high tax rates a disincentive to work. For themselves, actors may believe that a variety of situational factors affect their inclination to work, tax rates being merely one of the less important of these. According to this argument, people will regard high income tax as a disincentive to others but as not affecting themselves. This is actually what has been found. About three-quarters of one sample studied thought that income tax was a deterrent to work effort (Royal Commission on the Taxation of Profits and Incomes 1954) although, in the surveys reviewed earlier, few believed that it influenced them. But the argument could have been: "I am working less because of situational factors, including high marginal tax rates, while he is working less because he has a lazy disposition." So although attribution theory provides an explanatory framework for the actual finding, it does not predict it, as Lewis (1982, pp. 203-4) seems to claim.

According to the available evidence, then, the answer to the question

"Does taxation affect the incentive to work?" seems to be "no." But high marginal rates of tax may have other effects that are equally undesirable from the point of view of a national government. Pop groups, authors, even world-famous economists may emigrate to other countries where they can keep a greater proportion of their income. According to Lipsey (1979, p. 440) "emigration of successful people of this type from the United Kingdom to the United States and various even lower tax countries has been significant." Whether the British Conservative government's reduction of the top rate of tax from 83% to 60% has altered this transatlantic flow of talent is not known. The Swedish government has also recently (1982) reduced its high marginal tax rates, so that for 90% of Swedish taxpayers the maximum rate will be 50%. The effects of this change are being monitored by Swedish economic psychologists (Warneryd 1983; Wahlund 1983). Preliminary results suggest that a significant number of their all-male sample would work more in the future if overtime were tax-free and had refrained in the past from overtime work because of the taxes. This provides some support for the Swedish government's hope that the lower tax rates will encourage work. On average, however, people believed that the tax change would not affect their personal financial position, although it was better for the country than the previous system.

Voting and taxation

In Chapter 3, we briefly introduced the idea that voting behavior might tend to maximize the individual's economic advantage. Voters can only act on what they understand of the economic situation. For any voter, it is particularly interesting to consider the evidence that governments manipulate the tax system and its consequences for expenditure policy to enhance their electoral popularity. Such manipulation obviously depends on the fiscal ignorance of the public we described earlier. If people were aware of the connection between taxes and government expenditure, they would presumably be less impressed by highly visible tax cuts, which they would know would have to be "paid for" by cuts in services.

Some researchers have suggested that there is a relationship between the Phillips curve and electoral choice. Phillips (1958) observed that there was an inverse relationship between the rate of change of money wage rates and the unemployment rate in the United Kingdom between 1861 and 1957. This was interpreted to mean that there is a tradeoff between the rates of wage inflation and the level of unemployment: Inflation can be reduced, but only at the cost of higher unemployment, and unemployment can be reduced but only at the cost of higher inflation. As we saw in Chapter 3, this interpretation is now disputed, but it is still influential. Nordhaus (1975) proposed that a political business cycle is related to the

Phillips curve. After winning an election, governments, will raise unemployment to combat inflation and then, when the next election approaches, will reduce unemployment, but at the cost of producing inflation that will become visible only after the election. This argument is quite appealing, but the evidence Nordhaus presents is very scanty.

Much more impressive evidence has been gathered by Tufte (1978), on the more general issue of an electoral economic cycle. By examining the economic data from 27 countries, Tufte shows that in the decade after 1961 real disposable income grew in 64% of all election years, compared with 49% of nonelection years. This suggests definite efforts by governments to enhance their electoral chances. Mikesell's (1978) study of state governments in the United States also supports this view. His data suggest that state governments rely on voters having short memories; increases in tax rates are introduced only when they are politically expedient. Governments prefer to increase revenue through fiscal drag (Goetz 1977). Fiscal drag refers to the effect of inflation on effective tax rates. Through inflation, people are pushed into income brackets where higher marginal rates of tax apply. The current British government, pledged to reduce direct taxation, has used fiscal drag (by not adjusting income tax allowances in line with inflation) to increase tax revenues.

These economic studies, although demonstrating that governments do tend to manipulate the tax system to their electoral advantage, do not consider whether electors actually attend to such changes. Gilbert and Pommerehne (1984) looked at the relationship between the popularity of the Liberal government and various tax variables (e.g., total taxes, the percentage of tax raised indirectly) in Australia during the period 1971–7. They conclude that tax variables do play an important role; in particular, the percentage of revenue raised through direct taxation is significantly negatively correlated with government popularity (see Figure 11.4). However, this study also demonstrated that the observed tax data are not what one would predict if the government were simply maximizing its chances of being reelected. Instead, the data are as expected given the Liberal party's conservative ideological position.

British and American evidence (e.g., Butler & Stokes 1971; Campbell, Converse, Miller, & Stokes 1960) suggests that uncommitted voters in particular are influenced by economic variables. Partisan votes are not really influenced by them, at least as far as actual voting goes. It is not that uncommitted voters are more fiscally aware, just that they are more responsive to economic changes. But given the general ignorance of tax matters we noted earlier, the strength of the effect of economic variables is rather surprising. It is hard to believe that the average Australian would have been able to estimate correctly the percentage of total revenue raised through income tax in December 1977 or June 1978 or even to estimate correctly the tax they owed to the government.

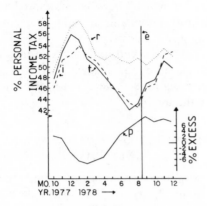

11.4. Ex-ante prediction of personal income taxes as a proportion of all taxation over the period Oct. 1977 to Dec. 1978 in Australia. Personal income taxes include deductions at source (PAYE), taxes on reported income, and deductions from dividends and interest payments. Legend: r= estimates of personal income taxes from the "re-election" model; i= estimates of personal income taxes from the "ideological" model; t= observed personal income taxes; p= excess of popularity of the Liberal-Country party over the Labour party (in percent, six-month moving average); e= general election. (From Gilbert & Pommerehne 1984.)

What then accounts for the effect of economic variables? Mosley (1982) has suggested that the mass media play a major role. He examined the economic coverage of the three most popular British daily newspapers (the *Daily Mirror, Daily Express,* and the *Sun*) over the period 1960–1980. The coverage they provide is extremely selective in two main ways. First, the *Mirror,* a traditionally pro-Labour party paper, gives more detail on unemployment whereas the *Sun* and *Express,* traditionally pro-Conservative party, give more detail on inflation. Second, information about any particular economic variable is most frequent during periods when it is suffering from accelerating deterioration. The economic information presented by the popular press is a much better predictor of government popularity than the official statistics. Inflation, for instance, which is only barely significantly related to government popularity if official statistics are used, becomes highly significant if the figures given in the *Daily Mirror's* "shopping clock" are considered. What this implies is that the party in government, in this imperfect market where the "product" may be less important than its presentation, may be able to act like one of Galbraith's (1967) modern corporations (see Chapters 13 and 18). Galbraith argues that, through advertising, modern corporations are able to educate people to buy the products it wishes to produce. Similarly the government may be able, through the media, to persuade the public to like the policies it has already decided on. This may be particularly true in countries in which there is some degree of political control of the media (e.g., in France) or in which there is substantial overlap of interests between newspaper proprietors and the ruling party, as in most democracies under right-wing governments.

The evidence we have reviewed in this section thus suggests that voting is not directly manipulated by tax changes, but that these do nonetheless exert an influence, through their effect on the economy and the presentation of the latter by the media.

THE ECONOMIC PSYCHOLOGY OF TAXATION: POSITIVE OR NORMATIVE?

Research into the economic psychology of taxation confronts us with an issue that is present in all areas of the discipline but that is especially relevant to the topics in Part III. The issue is this: Should economic psychology be a "positive" or a "normative" science? A positive science is one that is value-free, descriptive, and objective; a normative science is value-laden and prescriptive.

It is instructive to compare the comments of the authors of two recent books on taxation. First, from James and Nobes (1983, p. 83):

> Economists are trained from an early age to steer clear of normative arguments, and consequently are inclined to leave the definition of equity to others. In practice, decisions about the redistribution of income . . . are based on widely held notions that this is equitable. We will try to get as far as we can in examining the reasonableness of these feelings within the limitations of our knowledge . . . and the desire to remain "positive."

Psychologists, too, are trained to be positive, to investigate "what is" and not "what should be." They will advise what the appropriate means to particular ends are, but not what ends should be aimed for. There is no general interdisciplinary difference here. Nonetheless, the leading British authority on the economic psychology of taxation has something rather different to say:

> It seems to me that the findings in fiscal psychological research could be used and abused by a number of different sources and therefore it is best for psychologists to be aware of this and not abdicate responsibility; an action which may require a psychologist as researcher to take a "normative" stance from the very beginning. (Lewis 1982, p. 8)

It seems to us that the distinction between positive and normative science has been overdrawn. A positive science is not value-free; it is one that values objectivity, criticism, integrity, and "good" theories. That being the case, a researcher should not (a normative prescription) change results to establish agreement with his or her biases. But he or she will still have biases, conscious or unconscious. The responsible positive scientist must be aware of those biases and make his or her audience aware of them too, so that those who want to interpret the findings can draw their own conclusions about their objectivity (this, too, is a normative prescription). As a final normative constraint on positive science, researchers must, as Lewis says, take responsibility for their findings. This involves being aware of how they may be used or abused (at least in the short term), and making users aware of their fallibility. To take on oneself the cloak of science is to admit that one's conclusions are always provisional; they are good only until contradictory data are found. Anyone who claims to have produced eternal truth forfeits any claim to be a positive scientist.

It would seem that the research we have described in this chapter has unavoidable normative implications. Indeed, the literature contains a vast range of proposals for tax reform (e.g., Prest 1977). We will deal with just one problem: how tax evasion could be reduced. It should be noted that tax evasion is not neccesarily a bad thing, at least economically speaking. Bracewell-Milnes (1977) points out that the loss to the tax authorities may be more apparent than real if the alternative to tax evasion is not payment but a shift in activity which leads to a reduction in revenue. Thus suppression of evasion may lead to a loss to all parties. Economic models, which stress the importance of the chances of detection and the penalties for evasion, imply that increasing these will deter evasion. But more effective policing of the system and introducing stiffer penalties may be counterproductive. The actions of zealous tax authorities may worsen taxpayers' attitudes toward the tax authorities and produce more effective resistance. A more attractive policy for reformers would seem to be to aim for an improvement in tax attitudes and fiscal knowledge, to increase voluntary tax compliance. A program of fiscal education, through schools and the media, might go some way toward achieving this. This is certainly the view of researchers in the OECD: "There is room here for a vast effort in civic education and the rudiments of public finance" (quoted in Lewis 1982, p. 187).

Kelman's (1958) distinction among compliance, identification, and internalization is particularly interesting in the context of conforming to tax laws. Compliance is conforming outwardly to what an authority requires. You pay your taxes not because you believe it is right to do so, but because you suffer if you do not. Internalization involves a genuine change in beliefs in which new ideas are integrated into a person's existing value system. Having read this chapter, you are now more aware of the "fiscal connection" and will be more scrupulous in filling in tax forms in the future. Identification involves a change in beliefs in order to be like a group or person you admire. Thus, if your friends disapprove of evading taxes, you will tend not to evade taxes.

Governments should clearly concentrate on encouraging internalization and identification rather than simply compliance, although this is more easily said than done. Advertising campaigns that stress social disapproval may work through identification, but internalization is another matter.

The notion that tax evasion can be reduced through fiscal education and advertising campaigns is well intentioned but speculative. There is, however, at least one piece of empirical work on alternative ways of reducing evasion. Schwartz and Orleans (1967) investigated the comparative effectiveness of the threat of legal sanctions and appeals to conscience. They obtained tax compliance figures for three groups of taxpayers, an appeals to conscience group, a threat group, and a control group. A month before they filled in their tax return, all taxpayers were interviewed about political and tax issues. The questions they were asked were themselves the experimental manipulation, as they stressed either sanctions or responsibility. The tax records for the sample indicated a mean change in income declaration of $181 in the sanction group, $804 in the conscience group, and $87 in the control group. The sanctions group also increased their claims for tax-deductible allowances, suggesting that the threat of sanctions may actually increase tax avoidance. This study does not imply that appeals to conscience are necessarily superior to threats, but it certainly gives food for thought. Governments and tax authorities may be happy to adapt psychological strategies to reduce tax evasion. What they may be less happy with (and this raises the positive-normative distinction again) is a general increase in fiscal awareness, since a more knowledgeable public may be a less deferential public. Increasing fiscal awareness, however, may be just the kind of task for which the economic psychology of taxation is best suited.

12

MONEY

As we found with taxation, there are two ways in which we can consider the psychology of money. First, money has an important economic influence on individual behavior; central governments create and manipulate it partly for that reason. This is why the topic of money belongs in this part of the book. But it is also true that money is part of the economic behavior of individuals, being the medium through which much economic behavior is expressed. "Money," wrote George Bernard Shaw, "is the most important thing in the world." He was exaggerating, no doubt, but not all that much.

Money's importance is reflected in the amount of theorizing and research that economists have devoted to it. The economic literature is so extensive and well surveyed (e.g., Crockett 1979; Boughton & Wicker 1975) that we make no apology for referring to it relatively briefly. Psychologists, however, have paid surprisingly little attention to the topic, so our intention is to give a fairly detailed treatment of the psychological theories and research that are available. We wish to begin to create an economic psychology of money and shall first provide a context by briefly describing the economics of money. Then we shall consider current psychological approaches and sources of data before a tentative new theory is described.

THE ECONOMIC APPROACH TO MONEY

Economists have traditionally defined money as "any generally accepted medium of exchange – anything that will be accepted by virtually anyone in exchange for goods and services" (Lipsey 1978, p. 578). And they have a long-standing tripartite classification of the functions that money performs. It is a medium of exchange, a store of value, and a standard of value or unit of account.

Money's most obvious function is that of a medium of exchange; by being generally acceptable it overcomes some of the cumbersomeness of barter and it permits specialization. To be an efficient medium of exchange, however, money should have a number of characteristics. Ideally it must have a high value per unit weight, must be easily divisible, and should be hard to counterfeit. Gold is thus an ideal money substance, since it meets all three criteria. Cattle, despite their extensive use as money in many cultures, are not as efficient a money substance, since they meet only the last criterion. The second function of money is straightforward: Money is a convenient way of storing purchasing power. In barter one exchanges goods immediately, but with money one can store the proceeds of sale until they are needed to make a purchase later on. To perform this function well, money must have a stable value as well as being physically stable. Finally, the notion of money as a standard of value reflects money's function as a yardstick or measuring tool. Note that money need not be physically present to be used to place a value on things.

Economists have devised a wide range of theories about money at both the macro and micro levels. We introduced in Chapter 3 the classical quantity theory of money. This held that the amount of money in an economy does not affect the relative prices of goods but only the overall price level. This idea was formalized in the equation

$$MV = PT \tag{12.1}$$

where M is the quantity of money, V is the velocity of circulation (i.e., average number of times money is exchanged during a period), P is the average value of each transaction, and T is the number of transactions. Given the assumption that V and T are independant of changes in M, it is clear that changes in M would directly affect P, the average value of a transaction. So in this theory, money is important purely as the determinant of the price level; it has no effect on the size or distribution of real income.

Although the quantity theory in its classical form is now only of historical interest, the theories of the modern monetarist school resemble it. They are, of course, more sophisticated. Friedman (1956), for instance, assumed that there is a diminishing marginal rate of substitution (see Chapter 2) between money and goods. So the more money an individual has, given a fixed bundle of goods, the more the person will exchange money for goods. This implies that an increase in the amount of money will have a direct impact on the aggregate demand for goods (for a brief account of monetarist theories see Chapter 3; see also Pearce 1981; or Eatwell 1982).

A more micro level approach treats money as an asset with various characteristics such as liquidity, divisibility and predictability (e.g., Tobin 1965). Different forms of assets have different combinations of characteristics; cash is more liquid than a bank deposit account, for instance. Individuals (and institutions) must decide how to allocate their wealth among the various types of assets; that is, they must make up a portfolio of money. If the relative rate of return on a particular asset increases (e.g., bank interest rates go up), then some people will alter the composition of their portfolios. This kind of model can give an explanation of, for example, the structure of interest rates and it is the basis of many different macro theories.

These economic theories of money share some important properties. They are abstractions; they stem from a stylized, rational model of humankind and they are mainly concerned with money at a macroeconomic level. Much psychological data about money, on the other hand, have been concerned with pointing out the peculiarities of human behavior toward money, in effect with discovering irrationalities. In money as in many other areas of economic behavior, the economists' view is that individuals' deviations from the simplifying assumptions they make are very unlikely to be quantitatively significant. Even if psychologists can demonstrate that people generally do not behave in the simple way the theories require, such irrationalities are unlikely to be of economic importance.

We do not think that economic psychologists should be concerned merely with irrational aspects of money behavior. As Rachlin (1980) has argued (see Chapter 5) *any* behavior that is consistent is capable of being described as rational; explanations of irrationalities would thus be incorporated into mainstream economics. We contend that a more fruitful approach would be to explore the psychological, and ultimately economic, consequences of something having the properties that money has (or is supposed to have). The ultimate prize for this endeavor would be a psychological theory of money that explained some of the complexities of individual behavior toward money and, at the same time, made interesting predictions at the economic level.

PSYCHOLOGICAL THEORIES OF MONEY

We shall begin our search for an acceptable theory by discussing the existing psychological theories of money. We shall quickly find that none of them is very much help as it stands. Among the major psychological theories, we find only two that have concerned themselves directly with the question of money. These are psychoanalysis and the operant behaviorism of B. F. Skinner. But in addition, Foa (1971) has developed a resource theory of social exchange that is relevant and psychologists working within the Piagetian tradition have investigated how children come to understand and use money. These four theoretical positions will be considered in turn.

Psychoanalysis

In Chapter 1, we briefly described the characteristic psychoanalytic approach. Freud formulated a theory of money in a short paper in 1908 that was later developed by other psychoanalysts notably Ferenczi (1914/1976;

for a collection of psychoanalytic writings on money see Bornemann 1976). The crux of the psychoanalytic theory is that feces are the first property of the young child. With them the child gains power over the parents; appropriate defecation pleases them, inappropriate defecation provokes anger. In addition, feces are also one of the childs first "toys." Children tend to mold and press them although parents try to prevent this. These two aspects of anal behavior are transformed during maturation, through sublimation and reaction formation, into financial behavior. Thus, thrift is derived from the pleasure of retaining feces (the child's first savings) and profligate spending stems from the pleasure of releasing them.

The psychoanalytic theory also explains the nature of things which are chosen to serve as money, since attraction to money stems from attraction to feces. The child finds that playing with feces is forbidden and so developes a dislike of their smell. The child therefore begins to play with mud until this too becomes objectionable (it is sticky and dirty), and sand becomes preferred. From sand the child progresses to small stones, to artificial products like marbles and buttons, and finally to money. Pleasure in feces turns into an enjoyment of money, which is thus "nothing other than odourless dehydrated filth that has been made to shine" (Ferenczi 1914/1976). In a modern civilization even paper money can be explained in terms of an anal theory.

Finally, the anal theory of money also sheds some light on the attitude toward money revealed in our everyday language. Expressions such as "filthy lucre," "palm grease," and "tight arsed," and the phrase used by children "to do one's business," take on a new meaning. These kinds of expressions are not confined to English or to modern language. One of the most famous quotations about money is Bacon's "money is like muck, not good except it be spread."

On the face of it, the anal theory has little to offer economics. The theory claims to identify the motives underlying certain forms of economic behavior (e.g. saving, spending). This is interesting and may be useful clinically – but does it have wider significance? Perhaps not, but we should remember that for psychoanalysis, money is always symbolic. It is a *symbol* of feces that may help explain some of the irrationalities in our behavior toward money, that is, some of the ways in which modern money does not fulfill the definition of ideal general purpose money. It is not hard to think of transactions for which a recognized feces symbol would be an acceptable medium of exchange.

Operant behaviorism

In Chapter 1, we singled out basic learning theory as one of the major areas of psychology which are important to economic behavior. The learning theory account of money is a good instance. We described how initially neutral stimuli can acquire meaning through their association with a meaningful stimulus. According to learning theorists, any arbitrary stimulus can be established as a conditioned reinforcer as long as one presents at the same time (or preferably a brief instant later) an established reinforcer such as food. In most experiments such conditioned reinforcers are brief flashes of light, tones, or similar transient events, but it is also possible to use tokens. For example, Cowles (1937) used poker chips in experiments with chimpanzees, and ball bearings have been used in more recent experiments with rats (Boakes, Poli, Lockwood, & Goodall 1978; Malagodi 1967; Midgley 1984).

At a superficial level, there is an obvious similarity between an animal that has been trained to respond for token reinforcers and a person who works for money, which is then spent on food. But according to Skinner, the similarity is fundamental rather than superficial: Money is nothing more than a generalized conditioned reinforcer, by which he means a token that has been associated not only with food, but also with a myriad of consumable goods that serve as unconditioned reinforcers.

This theory has many attractions. It is grounded in well-established scientific psychology, and a therapeutic system based on it, the "token economy," has had considerable success in a variety of institutions since its introduction by Ayllon and Azrin (1963, 1968; see also Chapter 17). But a closer look demonstrates that Skinner's theory remains untested. As Bolles (1967) noted, there are hardly any experiments with animals where tokens (or for that matter other conditioned reinforcers) have served as *generalized* conditioned reinforcers. We do not really know how animals would behave toward such stimuli. And although the token economies testify to the fertility of Skinner's ideas, they tell us nothing about their accuracy. As we shall discuss in Chapter 17, it is quite possible that token economies are effective because their subjects already understand money. This objection would not apply to an animal token economy, but no one has studied one of these, with the possible exception of Markowitz (1975), who refers briefly to a project with Diana monkeys without telling us much about the results.

Unlike the psychoanalytic theory, it would seem that the behavioristic approach should have relatively direct economic implications, since much economic behavior is probably mediated by habits which are established through reinforcement. But if money really is a generalized conditioned reinforcer, we should expect it to be treated just as if it were the economists' generalized medium of exchange. A reinforcement account of money might be a suitable framework within which to explain the alleged "money illusion" (according to which people react to changes in values specified in money terms rather than real terms). In general, a reinforcement account of money would predict that the response to it would trail, rather than precede, changes in its real value. More surprising predictions

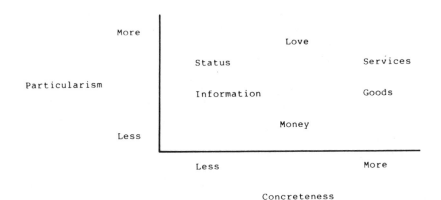

12.1. Foa's analysis of resource classes.

might follow, however, if we suppose that it is not particularly easy to create truly general conditioned reinforcers, as some recent evidence suggests. In this case, we would once again predict that the circuit of exchange even of modern money might be less general than strict economic theory requires.

Resource exchange theory

As we discussed in Chapter 2, one of the ways in which the economic approach to behavior has been applied to social interaction is through the work of exchange theorists such as Homans (1961). Exchange theory has been extended by Foa (Foa 1971; Foa & Foa 1980), who maintains that we need to take into account the fact that people can reward each other with a wide variety of resources. He proposed that there are six major resource classes (love, status, information, money, goods and services) and that two dimensions underlie these categories, particularism and concreteness. When the classes are plotted on a graph using these two dimensions as axes, they lie in a circle (see Fig. 12.1). A resource high in particularism is one whose value depends to a large extent on the particular people involved in the exchange. So love is highly particularistic, since it matters who we receive it from. By contrast, money is low on this dimension. A resource that is high in concreteness is something tangible, like groceries or mending a roof; one that is low in concreteness is more abstract and exchanged more symbolically (money is midway on this dimension).

Foa (1971) believes that this analysis helps explain what exchanges are seen as appropriate. The more similar two actions are in terms of concreteness and particularism, the more appropriate is an exchange between them. So to return love for money is unacceptable, but to exchange money for goods or services is reasonable.

There is a certain amount of evidence which supports Foa's analysis. Turner, Foa, and Foa (1971) found that people look on proximal resource classes as similar. Given one resource class as a standard, subjects had to judge which of the remaining categories was most similar. These judgments fitted the circular structure of resource classes suggested in Figure 12.1.

Brinberg and Castell (1982) investigated this structure in a rather more sophisticated manner using multidimensional scaling. College students had to rate the similarity of behaviors like "fix a car," "hug," and "spend money on" and rate the likelihood of one behavior given that a specified other had acted in a particular way. Although the predicted two dimensions were found to underlie the similarity judgments, the resource categories were not located quite where expected in the resulting space. In particular, money was seen as rather similar to love. Their subjects seemed to consider money a particularistic resource, perhaps because it was relatively infrequently exchanged and in many cases came originally from their parents. There was also some asymmetry in the exchange of resources. The students reported that they were likely to "hug" or "give respect" in exchange for a wide variety of behaviors, perhaps because these are resources which are readily available to students, unlike, say, money or the skill required to fix a car.

Foa's analysis suggests that money is one resource among many. In this way it complements the portfolio approach to money described above, which makes it clear that money is itself a set of distinct resources. The two theories provide interestingly contrasting resolutions of the apparent limitations of exchange of modern money: According to Foa, such limitations arise because some resources do not match up well with money as a resource class; according to portfolio theory, they arise because there is a better match for those resources elsewhere within the money class. Like portfolio theory, however, Foa does suggest dimensions along which assets may vary, though they are psychological rather than economic. But as it stands, this analysis is rather coarse grained, and thus we need to take a closer look at psychological dimensions relevant to money.

Piagetian psychology

Piaget himself did not investigate how children develop economic concepts and economic behavior, but a number of researchers have applied his theoretical approach to this issue (Berti & Bombi 1981; Burris 1981, 1983; Danziger 1958; Fox 1978; Furth 1978, 1980; Hong Kwang & Stacey 1981; Jahoda 1979; Strauss 1952; Sutton 1962). Since these researchers have adopted similar strategies and have asked similar questions, it is not surprising that they have come to similar conclusions about economic socialization. All report a series of stages through which a child passes in becoming competent in the world of money. The number of stages ranges from three to nine, but the processes proposed are the same in each case. All authors find a first stage in which the child does not understand the role of money in transactions; the child knows that money must be used for the transaction to be possible, but sees this necessity simply as a rite or moral imperative. There is no concept of exchange. At an intermediate stage, the child understands immediate exchanges, but neither the network of exchanges that constitute the economic system nor the divisibility of money. For instance, Strauss noted that if a piece of candy cost 5 cents and the child had only a dime (10 cents), then the child believed that the candy couldn't be purchased. The final stage, all authors agree, involves the understanding of all types of exchanges with money, including the concepts of profit, investment, and so on.

This approach is obviously tightly bound to the general Piagetian system of developmental psychology, introduced briefly in Chapter 1. Evidently, understanding the divisibility of money involves certain logico-mathematical structures. Moreover, the development of the understanding of money (and other economic concepts such as value and property) show parallels with general cognitive development, as Burris (1983) and Fox (1978) have documented (see Chapter 14). For example, according to Piaget, a preoperational child's thought is characterized by a number of "a-dualisms," one of which is the confusion of sign with signified. Names, for instance, are seen as part of an object in itself. Similarly, money is regarded at this stage as having an intrinsic rather than conventional meaning. To date, however, Piagetian psychologists have taken the economists' conception of money for granted. In essence, they have attempted to describe how children come to understand the current view of an economic concept (Webley 1983), but they have failed to recognize that money has a wide range of other connotations and that children will construct many different meanings of money from their dealings with others. If developmental studies are to have economic implications beyond that of identifying oddities in children's economic behavior, they will need to go beyond the received meaning of money.

SOURCES OF DATA ABOUT MONEY

The psychological theories described above provide a possible framework for understanding our behavior with and toward money. Three of them share the idea that money is a symbol. For psychoanalysts, money symbolizes feces; for Skinnerians, reinforcement; and for Piagetians money symbolizes different things at different stages. To determine whether this is a useful way of looking at money, we shall examine some of the data about individual behavior toward money. Evidence from anthropology, psychometrics, experimental psychology, and social psychology will be considered in turn.

Anthropological research on money

A consideration of the anthropological literature immediately calls the economists' ideal view of money into question. Most obviously, the literature contains numerous examples of money that fulfill only one of the economists' alleged functions of money. Bark cloth on the Polynesian island of Tikopia, for example, is used as a medium of exchange but is unsuitable as a store of value because of the effect of mold and pests. A more dramatic example is the stone money of the Pacific island of Yap (large millstones of aragonite, up to twice the size of a person). These seem admirably suited to function as a store of value, but they are of limited use as a medium of exchange. The anthropological literature also supplies data for a wide range of theories about the origins of money, and helps give an historical perspective on our behavior toward money. Moreover, anthropological studies give us an idea of the great variety of forms that money takes in different cultures.

The anthropological literature is extensive and by necessity our account of it will be highly selective. A useful starting point is Polanyi's (1957) assertion that modern societies have impersonal all-purpose money (essentially the economists' view), whereas primitive economies have limited or special purpose money. Limited money has been defined in two ways. Polanyi (1968) says that we have special purpose money when "different objects are as a rule employed in different monetary uses," and also "when money is confined to a particular circuit of exchange." Some kinds of money are special purpose in both senses. For example, on Rossel island in the Pacific, there are two forms of money, *ndap,* which consists of individual pieces of the shell Spondylus, and *nko,* which consists of ten pieces of shell. Einzig (1966, p. 62) notes that ndap is regarded as men's money, while nko is the women's. The two forms are thus at least partially confined to circuits of exchange defined by sex. Furthermore, different pieces of ndap have special uses. A number 18 must be given for bridewealth and for paying for a dog feast. Two number 17's will not do. Here different objects have different monetary uses.

Melitz (1970) has argued that, although the separation of functions is not so dramatic, current Western money is also special purpose money. Coins, paper money, and bank checking (current) accounts all serve as mediums of exchange, but are they really used as stores of value? Since any asset can act as a store of value (old masters, nineteenth-century bottles, even some old comic books), reference to a store of value function of money implies something over and above this, presumably that money is a particularly good store of value and is valued as such. Coin, paper currency, and bank checking accounts are, however, rather bad stores of value if either crime or inflation is at all rife. Different forms of Western money also have different exchange uses. Coins are used to pay petty sums, paper currency for moderate payments, and checks for large amounts. Some breach of etiquette is involved in paying a bill for $100 in coins, or a 50-cent one by a check. It is also the case that checks are not always accepted, especially from strangers, and there may be limits on the amounts of cash that will be accepted. For example, in Britain, bronze coins in amounts exceeding 20 pence are not compulsory legal tender. From this we can conclude that in Western society we too have not attained the idealized form of money; we too have special purpose money. Douglas (1967) argues that primitive money functions like "coupons" in a modern economy. It may be more appropriate to turn this argument on its head and to point out that in a modern economy there are many money forms, or near-moneys, which function like primitive money.

These facts are of some psychological and economic significance. They suggest that we are not dealing with a generalized medium of exchange but a set of partial mediums of exchange with the appearance of generality. We may not have a yardstick that can measure everything in exchange terms. At the economic level, this tends to support the portfolio theory of the functions of money. At the psychological level, it suggests that money should probably not be conceived of as a unitary symbol, but as involving multiple symbolizations, an idea we shall discuss in more detail below.

We mentioned earlier that the anthropological literature contains a wide range of theories about the origins of money. Such "origin theories" are important to economic psychology because the original use of money in a society may well be reflected in contemporary behavior; in addition, they give us an historical perspective on the economic psychology of money. Origin theories fall roughly into three categories: commercial theories and noncommercial theories, both concerned with money as a medium of exchange, and a rather miscellaneous group concerned with origin via the store or standard of value function.

Economists, understandably enough, tend to favor commercial theories that stress the idea that the origins of money lie in reducing the costs of trading by barter. Some theories emphasize the origins of money through internal trade, others through external trade. Internally, as trade expands and a greater variety of goods is available, it becomes more and more difficult, say, for a man wanting to barter a donkey for a wife to find someone who wants to swap a wife for a donkey. This is the so-called problem of the "double coincidence of wants." Money overcomes this problem, although it is easy to exaggerate the inconvenience of barter, since credit (delivering goods in return for future deliveries of other goods) makes the system work reasonably well. Other commercial theorists assume that ignorance of the availability of goods, their terms of trade, and attributes will all inspire efforts to reduce that ignorance (Alchian 1977). And one way of doing this is through the use of a common standard, that is, money.

Anthropologists generally prefer the idea that the origins of money lie in a good's use for noncommercial payments, such as bride payments, sacrificial and other religious payments, status symbols, payment of fines, and taxes. In many societies young men who wanted to marry had to save up in order to purchase a bride, or borrow the objects used for bride money and pay them back later (which is not unlike taking out a mortgage). Either way, this would contribute to the development of a primitive monetary system, since the young men would have to accumulate the bride price objects and would therefore prefer to accept them in payment for goods and services. Anybody who owned bride price objects would know that they could be exchanged for just about anything. So in internal trade the object used as bride money (frequently cattle) could readily become a medium of exchange.

Money may have had many different origins, so all parties to this discussion may have some truth on their side. However, the evidence, such as it is, tends to support noncommercial exchange theories. Pryor (1977), for instance, examined the relationship between the level of economic development and the use of money in a wide range of societies. He found that money used for noncommercial payments appears more often in societies at a lower stage of development than money used only for commercial payments. If this were true historically, a noncommercial payment origin is more likely.

Examples of the influence of origins and origin myths are readily found in "primitive" and modern economies. For instance, on Rossel Island, the ndap money is thought to have been created by the chief god and so certain of the high-valued units of the shell currency can only be handled in a kneeling position. On Pelew, in Micronesia, the highest-valued types of bead money are also thought to be of divine origin, and a premium has to be paid when exchanging the higher-valued types (as if one had to pay a $1 note plus 10 cents, rather than two 50-cent coins). Einzig (1966, p. 374) refers to one anthropologist's suggestion that this premium is paid to reconcile the hurt feelings of the high-value money. Similarly, it may be that acceptance of modern money depends upon its having previously been convertible into gold or some similar substance with intrinsic value. Historical events may produce strange consequences. Taussig (1977) describes the bizarre behavior among some Colombian peasants as a response to the intrusion of capitalism and Christianity into a primitive money system. They baptize the money given by godparents instead of baptizing the child. Baptism is thought to confer supernatural powers on the money; it will enable it to "make money," a prime feature of capitalism.

A final use of the anthropological literature is as evidence bearing on the psychological theories described earlier. For example, in the light of the wide range of forms that money takes in different cultures, from the wood-pecker scalps of some Californian Indians to the brass rods of the Tiv of Nigeria, it appears as if the anal theory could apply only to Western coin-based economies. However some psychoanalysts have extended Freud's theory and have applied it to other cultures. Posinsky (1956/1976), for instance, considered the shell money of the Yurok, a tribe of Californian Indians, to be symbolic of "the breast-penis equation." One of the most recent writers within the psychoanalytic tradition has broadened the theory still further, asserting that "the behavior of money is related not to any one body function, but to the sum total, to the whole body economy" (Wiseman 1974, p. 261). In other words, money does not symbolize only excrement but also oral eroticism and so forth.

There has been much less direct contact between other psychological theories of money and the anthropological evidence. With regard to the learning theory account of money, the anthropologists' stress on the existence of partial money suggests that learning theory might do better to consider money as a limited conditioned reinforcement. This is interesting in that it was precisely the lack of evidence about generalized tokens for which we criticized the learning theory approach. Foa's categorization of resource classes has been used by at least one economic anthropologist (Schneider 1974), who used it to refine the distinction between the social and material spheres in an economy and found it to be a useful and reasonably exhaustive classification system. Finally, the evidence from anthropology of the sheer variety of money and money behavior reinforces our feeling that developmentalists have been unwise to take for granted the economists' concept of modern money as the standard toward which children's understanding should develop. By doing this, they may have neglected important aspects of the development of the concept of money.

Psychometric studies of money attitudes and usage

A number of recent studies have looked at the relationship between personality and behavior with money and patterns of money usage. The results have some bearing on the anal theory. Rim (1982), for instance, found that stable extroverts were more carefree about their money than unstable extroverts. This fairly obvious finding is not of much theoretical import. More interestingly, Yamauchi and Templer (1982) developed a psychometrically satisfactory money-attitude scale. They administered this to 125 Californians and found that, as psychoanalytic theory would predict, money retention (a factor concerned with preparation for the future and security) was related to obsessionality. Furnham (1984) also constructed a money beliefs and behavior scale, and administered it to a British sample. A factor analysis of the responses revealed six factors, including power, obsession with money, and money retention. The existence of a money retention factor again gives at least limited support to the psychoanalytical approach. However, a number of demographic variables were related to these factors, and this would not be predicted by the anal theory.

Experimental psychology of money

Although experimental psychologists have generally neglected the study of money, there are a few useful data from this literature. We will comment on two areas: the size-value phenomenon in perception and studies of money as a reinforcement or incentive.

In a size-estimation experiment, Bruner and Goodman (1947) found that children seemed to perceive coins as being larger than they really are; the effect was strongest for the more valuable coins and with poor children. This result has been the subject of considerable dispute (for reviews see Saugstad & Schioldberg 1966; Tajfel 1957). Eiser (1980), for instance, claims that the size-value phenomenon tells us less about money than about general processes of social judgment. If one has learned that size and value are predictably related to each other in coins, then the value of a coin is an additional piece of information that can be taken into account in judging its size.

Nonetheless, the size-value effect seems well supported and new demonstrations and extensions are still appearing (Ginsburg & Courtis 1974; Smith, Fuller, & Forrest 1975). Lea (1981), for example, reasoned that since inflation has greatly reduced the value of British coins in recent years, according to Bruner and Goodman's argument the coins should now be perceived as smaller than they were formerly. This reasoning was experimentally supported in that people who estimated the size of British coins under their current names (ten and five pence) gave smaller estimates than others who did the same task using the predecimalization names (two and one shillings). Furnham (1983) demonstrated a similar effect. Subjects overestimated the size of the old pound note (which was withdrawn in 1979) and underestimated the size of the new one. The size-value phenomenon suggests that as a physical stimulus, money is not like other things; its appearance does not depend only on its physical dimensions but on additional social properties. Its appearance depends on what it symbolizes.

A similar issue is involved in studies of money as a reinforcer. Here the question is whether money is like other reinforcements or incentives or whether it has special properties. We do not have enough evidence to say for sure that money is different from all other reinforcers, but studies of the "overjustification effect" (see Chapter 6) make it clear that not all reinforcers have the same properties and that money may well be anomalous. Recall that the overjustification effect is said to occur when extrinsic rewards appear to reduce intrinsic motivation. Thus students who were paid for solving jigsaw puzzles of pictures from *Playboy* magazine subsequently rated the task as less enjoyable than those who were not paid (Calder & Staw 1975). A variety of explanations have been offered for the overjustification effect, but for our purposes we can simply note the connection between money (and to a lesser extent the other extrinsic rewards used in this kind of research) and the idea of payment. Payment implies an exact numerical assessment of the value of a behavior. Money is ideal for such assessments, but its association with the payment structure may give it meanings which affect people's behavior and attitudes to it in other contexts, perhaps making it less useful for some purposes. This argument is clearly close to Foa's ideas about the compatibility of resource classes in an exchange.

Social psychology of money

Despite the theoretical proposals of Foa, little empirical work has been directed at exploring the social psychology of money. Nonetheless, the literature does contain a considerable amount of information about money. We shall discuss a few examples.

Consider the question of gifts. Casual observation suggests that it is quite unusual for money to be used as a gift, at least with some donors and recipients, and that its use in these cases would not be acceptable (Lea & Webley 1981). If a neighbor helps us with an odd job , we may give him a small present by way of thanks, but money would be an insult. Webley, Lea, and Portalska (1983) investigated this question empirically. In one of their studies, students were asked how much they would spend on a birthday present for their mothers under one of three conditions. In the first condition, they were asked to imagine selecting and buying a present in the usual way. In the second and third, they were asked to imagine sending a gift token of some sort, or a check, respectively. Those who were asked how much they would spend when sending a check suggested amounts that averaged twice the amounts suggested by the other two groups. When asked whether they would be happier with a selected gift, a token, or a check, all subjects indicated that a selected gift would be more suitable than a check; the gift token was seen as intermediate. Similar results were obtained with a nonstudent sample of young adults.

These data indicate a very strong social convention, and one that seems irrational, at least at a superficial level. On average, a sum of money is of more use to the recipient than a present bought for the same price, since the present may fail to please, or may even be utterly useless. Money can always be used to buy what the recipient prefers, and yet the data show that money is preceived to be an inappropriate gift. This apparent irrationality may be due to a clash between the symbolism of money and that of affectionate family giving, perhaps because money symbolizes the exact reckoning of value. However, when students (and in another study their mothers) were asked what features were important in gifts, their answers suggested that gifts are valuable in proportion to the time and effort shown by the giver. Money involves no cost of this kind, so it should not be surprising if it has little value as a present. How many times have we heard someone say: "It is not the cost of a gift but the 'thought' that is important"? Students also believe that money might be spent on useful things rather than on something special or exceptional.

Hussein (1984) believed these results might be culture specific and so replicated two of Webley, Lea, and Portalska's studies in the Turkish part of Cyprus where it is conventional to use money as a gift on some occasions, notably weddings. Nonetheless, the Cypriot results were comparable to the British ones except in one interesting way. All subjects said that they would prefer either to give or to receive an individually selected gift rather than money, but their reasons differed from those given by the British sample. In fact, there was little consensus about why money was unacceptable. This suggests that the reasons given for money being unacceptable as a gift may be rationalizations. Either way, that money is an unacceptable gift again suggests that modern Western money is like primitive money in that there are restrictions on its use.

A second example involves the behavior technically called "hypothecation," the earmarking of money from a particular source for a particular expenditure. For example, the income that one of the present authors derives from teaching an extra night course is allocated to holidays. Even governments reason in this fashion. In Britain an ex-chancellor of the Exchequer argued that income from North Sea Oil should be used for special purposes; similar arguments have been put forward in the United States about the income from Alaskan oil and from state gambling revenues. This behavior is again apparently irrational. As we mentioned in Chapter 8, econometric studies (e.g., Bodkin 1960; Jones 1960) have shown that the marginal propensity to consume is much higher for windfall income than for permanent income. In other words, a higher proportion of a windfall is spent rather than saved than of an individual's expected average income. This result could well be caused by earmarking the windfall income. Perhaps windfall money symbolizes its source and so exceptional income implies, psychologically, exceptional spending (recall the proverb, so often applied to financial behavior: "easy come, easy go"). By contrast, hypothecation may simply be a kind of budgeting heuristic, facilitating sensible if not optimal planning of individual and national expenditure.

A third example involves people's reactions to new forms of money. In general the reaction is negative among the older members of society, who may well continue to use the old form if they can. There are a number of examples of this in the anthropological literature (e.g., Bohannan 1959) and a well-documented instance in Britain recently. The new 1-pound coin introduced in April 1983 was not well received, and cash register operators reported that they did not give old people 1-pound coins in change because of their extreme negative reaction (Hussein, 1985). One British daily newspaper even had a main front page headline in June 1983: "THE POUND BRITAIN DOESN'T WANT" (*Daily Mail* 24 June 1983). Similarly, it is not unusual in Britain for older people to think in the predecimal currency, which disappeared officially in 1971, or in France in terms of "old francs," which were superceded in 1960. This may be an instance of a more general conservatism and not specific to money (for instance, the British government was forced to abandon metrication of weights and measures by public hostility), but it may still reflect an important constraint on economic behavior. In an abstract idealized system it should make no difference what yardstick is used; real prices are, after all, relative. But people's behavior clearly falls far short of this ideal. This phenomenon may partly explain the "money illusion" (Fisher 1929) in which people react to changes specified in monetary rather than real terms. Unfortunately, although there are a few econometric studies of the money illusion (e.g., Cebula 1981; Katsimbris & Miller 1982), we know little about the psychological processes involved.

A fourth example concerns an issue we have already mentioned in the previous section, namely whether money is special or just another physical stimulus, incentive, or whatever. In this case the question is whether money is a special kind of scarce resource. Two studies are relevant here. Darley and Latane (1970), in investigating how costs affect helping, observed the responses of passersby to requests from strangers for help of one kind or another. Requests for information (simple street directions, the time) were granted much more readily than requests for minimal amounts of money (10 cents), although if a reason for the request was given people were much more helpful. Since there were clear costs in giving information (the time it would take to explain directions) and the amount of money was so small, this does suggest that money may be special.

Foa and Shay's (1982) results support this conclusion too. They investigated businessmen's preferences for distributive justice. The respondents had to indicate their preferences for distributing scarce resources – money, goods, services, love, status, and information – according to the principle of merit or equality. Various situations were used. On average, the respondents overwhelmingly preferred money to be distributed to those who deserved it, whereas for the other resources, the aggregate preference was for equal distribution. Similar findings were reported by Foa and Stein (1980).

Obviously, there are many possible explanations for this assortment of social psychological phenomena, but they are all consistent with the idea that money is in some way special. But is it qualitatively or quantitatively special? One possible explanation is that the drive to acquire and keep money is simply stronger than drives related to other resources. Alternatively, it might be a different kind of drive. Obviously, it must be an acquired motivation in contrast to the needs for society, love, self-esteem, and so forth, which would appear to be innate. Within social psychology, the usual way of explaining acquired drives is in terms of Allport's (1937) concept of "functional autonomy." We shall discuss this in more detail in Chapter 18, but it can be said at this point that Allport's theory does not immediately account for the various peculiarities of money which we have identified in this section.

TOWARD A NEW PSYCHOLOGICAL THEORY OF MONEY

Evidently, none of the psychological theories described earlier in this chapter can account for all or even most of the data we have considered. One consistent theme is that the theories attempt to account for the economists' idealized general purpose medium of exchange, whereas the data show that actual money does not function in quite this way. On the one hand, it is a limited medium of exchange; on the other, it has special properties not shared by other objects of comparable value. Psychological (and anthropological) theory and data do, however, agree on a second common theme: Money carries meanings; it involves multiple symbolization. As Firth (1963, p. 124) wrote: "Money is a symbol. It represents in some measurable way some command over goods and services." We shall now explore some of the consequences of regarding money as both more and less than an abstract generalized medium of exchange.

The multiple symbolism of money

Melitz (1970) made the useful point that when people interpret money-stuff as symbols, the symbolism may not be what theorists generally suppose. For instance, money represents not only the goods it can purchase, but also its source and how it was obtained. Since the latter is necessarily specific, there are limits to how far money can function as an abstract medium of exchange. A Spanish friend reported that she spent money from her father (she called it "sacred money") very differently from money she earned herself. Hussein (1981) demonstrated a similar effect empirically. Seven-year-old children were asked how they would spend money acquired through a gift or through theft. As many as 70% reported that they would save money that was given, whereas only 30% reported that they would save stolen money. There are other possible explanations of this finding (perhaps stolen money should be exchanged as soon as possible to reduce the risk of discovery), but it does agree with the view presented here.

Part of money's meaning stems from its form (something that both economists and anthropologists have largely ignored). Larger coins tend to be seen as more valuable, and so do bigger and more decorative bank notes. Bruce, Gilmore, Mason, and Mayhew (1983) examined some of the factors affecting the perceived value of coins. They found that copper-colored coins were seen as the least valuable but silver-colored and gold-colored coins were equally often assigned to intermediate and high values. The shape and thickness of a coin also affected its perceived value. Seven-sided coins were seen as more valuable than 12-sided and circular coins, and thicker coins as more valuable than thinner ones. Checkbooks approach the abstract ideal, but even here the necessity of signing the check (with its connotations of a bond or obligation) may influence the meaning attached, and particular signatures may also alter meaning. The decorative style in which checks are traditionally printed is also suggestive of special meaning.

Measurement and the meaning of money

The obvious meaning that any form of money conveys is the value relations between other objects. But unlike other ways of expressing value, such as verbal labels of moral worth, money is precise and numerical. This has some important implications, as we will see, but it is notable that the numerical feature of money as a symbol is not the same in all societies. Following Codere's (1968) anthropological analysis, we suggest that money's function of expressing value can be carried out at various levels of measurement and that we may find examples of this both historically and developmentally. Four levels of measurement are commonly distinguished: nominal, ordinal, interval, and ratio (Stevens 1946). Money, in one society or another, has operated at three of these levels.

1. *Nominal.* The only relationship involved in a nominal scale is that of equivalence. Money operating at this level would have various forms, noted by Ma, Mb, etc., each of which could be exchanged only for a particular good or category of goods. With Ma you could buy only good a, with Mb only good b, and so forth. There would be no relationship between Ma and Mb.

An anthropological example that comes close to this is the Trobriand kula valuables. These consist of mwali (armbands of shell) and soulava (necklaces of shell). The two types are exchanged solely for one another by hereditary partners. There is no exchange of, say, an especially valuable mwali for three or four soulava.

2. *Ordinal.* An ordinal scale involves the relations of equivalence and "greater or less than." Money operating at this level would have various forms (i.e., M1, M2), which could be placed in rank order. Although M2 would be more valuable than M1 and M3 than both of them, the difference in value between any two forms would not be the same. We have already come across one example of this kind of money, the ndap currency of Rossel Island (see the section on anthropological research on money).

3. *Interval and ratio.* In an interval scale we know the size of the differences between numbers and, for a ratio scale, we also have a true zero point. The difference between \$1 and \$2 is the same as that between \$2 and \$3, and the ratio between 100 pounds and 200 pounds is the same as that between 1,000 pounds and 2,000 pounds. This is the kind of money that exists in most money-using societies, including our own.

Using this analysis, we can see that hypothecation, for example, is the intrusion of a nominal heuristic in an interval system: The special allocation suggests that money from a different source belongs to a psychologically different "category," even though economically both belong to a more general interval money system. In learning to use Western money, children appear to go through a nominal stage when they consider that a 5-cent piece can only be used to purchase a 5-cent bar of chocolate.

The interweaving of the numerical system and the money system is also relevant to the size–value phenomenon in perception. Simmel (1900/1978) pointed out that people have "an inclination to base the equivalence of values on a direct external quality" and that, in the development of monetary systems, this tendency has only gradually been overcome. The earliest known bank note, for instance, was 46 cm long and 12 cm wide, and the largest coins are found in the least developed economies (Hitchcock, Munroe, & Munroe 1976). This interweaving (in Piagetian terms, a feature of concrete thinking) is still with us. Reducing the size of bank notes lessens their perceived value and substituting a coin for a note (as with the British pound in April 1983) turns it into "small change" (Webley, Lea, & Hussein 1983). Conversely, if the value of a coin drops then so does its perceived size (Lea 1981).

The precision and relativistic evaluation of the money system has usually been seen by economists as facilitating exchange. But precision can be a disadvantage. In contrast to the nonverbal system of communication, which is especially suited to expressing interpersonal attitudes because of its relative vagueness and ambiguity, money communicates too precise a message. In giving your neighbor money for help, you are being inappropriately precise: "Your help is worth × dollars; no more, no less." Similarly, the relativistic evaluation implicit in money probably helps to limit its generality. Informally (and sometimes formally, as for example by Simmel and Marx), money is often held to have a dehumanizing effect. An example of this perception is seen in the history of life insurance in America. Its initial lack of success was, it is thought, due to a value system within which a monetary assessment of death was unacceptable (Zelizer 1978). Life insurance was legitimized by assimilating it to concepts within the accepted moral and sacred code, so that it was seen not as unacceptable compensation for an immeasurable tragedy, but a proper and dutiful provision for dependants. "Far from 'profaning' life and death, money became ritualized by its association with them. Life insurance took on symbolic values quite distinct from its utilitarian function, emerging as a new form of ritual with which to face death" (Zelizer 1978, p. 594).

In other cases people continue to resist the spread of monetary evaluation, and this resistance may result in legal or conventional restrictions on the use of money. Selling a child, for instance, is both illegal and unacceptable in Western society.

Specifying the meaning of money

Merely demonstrating that money has multiple meanings is clearly inadequate: We need to go on to specify what those meanings are. Of course, they may vary between individuals.

Wernimont and Fitzpatrick (1972) investigated the meaning of money for various groups of people (salesmen, students, engineers, etc.) using a semantic differential technique (see Chapter 1). The respondents rated the concept of money along 40 scales such as good–bad, degrading–uplifting. A factor analysis then revealed seven dimensions of meaning. These were, in order of importance: money as a source of embarrassment and degradation, money as an okay thing, money as nothing very important, money as a moral evil, money as a source of economic security, money as socially unacceptable, and money as something secretive.

Wernimont and Fitzpatrick's results confirm the multiplicity of the meanings of money as a global construct. Hussein (1985) took a slightly different approach. She considered the rather disparate set of objects which function as money in a modern economy, and investigated whether people agreed about which of them are most typical, and whether the most typical items would be categorized fastest, as is true for concrete categories like "furniture" (Rosch 1975) and abstract ones like "justice"

(Hampton 1981). Hussein found that the money category was generally similar to these other fuzzy sets, although perhaps with less intersubject agreement about typicality.

A synthesis of our psychological understanding of money, therefore, might run as follows: Money is a complex concept carrying a plexus of meanings by means of a plexus of exemplars. Our behavior toward and with money will therefore only be fully understood through an historical and developmental perspective. Principally, money represents an exchange evaluation, but the subsidiary meanings embodied in every aspect of money (its source, form, and message) will affect how it is used and may well limit its general applicability.

AN ECONOMIC PSYCHOLOGY OF MONEY

Our remaining task is to integrate this improved psychological account of money with our economic knowledge. In our view, this can best be done by adapting Lancaster's characteristics theory of consumer demand (see Chapters 2 and 7). Recall that Lancaster built his approach on the straightforward idea that people do not demand goods per se, but rather the characteristics that goods possess. In developing this idea, Lancaster made the interesting distinction between "primitive" and "sophisticated" consumption technologies. In a primitive consumption technology, the consumer may have to accept more of one characteristic than desired in order to get enough of another, because not enough combinations of characteristics are on sale. Over a period of time, a market will become increasingly sophisticated and additional combinations of characteristics will become available.

Just as people demand characteristics of goods rather than goods per se, so too do they demand characteristics of money rather than money per se. As Fisher (1978, p. 28) stated: "The examination of 'characteristic space' for the money problem is at least as important as it is for any commodity." The problem then becomes what characteristics does money possess? This is the point, we think, at which the psychology of money links with the economics of money. Fisher's hypothetical example uses economic characteristics, such as "pays interest," and clearly this feature plus liquidity, reversibility, predictability, and other features used in the portfolio approach, are important. But so too are the kind of characteristics that psychology and anthropology have identified. Physical form, source, a limited sphere of exchange, even cleanliness in the Freudian sense as being far removed from feces, may all be significant characteristics. The relative importance of economic and noneconomic characteristics is open to question. For large institutions considering investment decisions, noneconomic characteristics may be totally irrelevant, but for individuals this is less likely to be true.

Psychological characteristics

The characteristics approach helps to structure the idea of money as a complex symbol. It also has the merit of recognizing the historical dimension, and of suggesting the most appropriate task for an economic psychology of money, which is to identify the characteristics of money and how they affect behavior. This is in line with Hussein's (1985) results on the money concept, since it closely resembles Rosch's (1975) approach to other complex categories. But it leads to a difficulty. Lancaster regards characteristics as objective, as residing in the goods. Symbols, be they simple or complex, reside in the mind, and are not the same in all minds. For psychological purposes at least, Lancaster's approach is too restrictive. As with our other uses of characteristics theory (e.g., Chapter 18), if we are to make progress we shall have to accept subjective characteristics. It is, after all, part of the business of psychologists to cope with the problem of subjective phenomena.

One obvious implication of a characteristics approach to money is that its historical development should not be from primitive to modern but from primitive to sophisticated. That is, instead of a single abstract money emerging, a wide range of monies, all consisting of different combinations of characteristics, should develop. A superficial consideration of recent monetary history confirms this view. There is now a proliferation of credit cards, accounts (bank and shop), and so on. Gift tokens, which (in the form of book tokens) were first put on the market in Britain by the National Book council in 1932, are distinguished by being limited, that is, exchangeable only for certain goods. This is clearly a desirable characteristic in some contexts; for example, Webley et al. (1983) found that, unlike ordinary money, gift tokens were not regarded as unacceptable as gifts.

This historical trend would partly account for the difficulty economists have in finding suitable definitions of money, and it perhaps suggests that the search is misguided. It would not be the money supply that was important, but the supply of certain characteristics. The historical approach also warns us against taking current conceptions for granted. A consideration of the range of possible characteristics of money may suggest desirable combinations that do not yet exist.

Another implication of the characteristics approach is that developmental psychologists may well have neglected some important characteristics of money. A developmental trend toward the differentiation of concepts has been noted by many (e.g., Scarlett, Press, & Crockett 1971); this would suggest that older children would be more able to deal with the multiple characteristics of money. Such an approach might also allow the developmental psychology of money to avoid the restrictive linear approach of Piagetian stages.

To get some idea of what the important characteristics are, Hussein (1985) asked people to rate pairs of money items (e.g., coins, credit cards, luncheon vouchers) as to how similar they were and also along various dimensions she thought might be important characteristics. The similarity ratings were then cluster analyzed. The results showed marked individual differences in how people perceived these money items, and few consistent clusters emerged apart from "coins" and "bank money" (e.g., checks, credit cards).

This is disappointing, and suggests that we should move on from the question, "What characteristics does money possess?" to the potentially more fruitful question, "How do those characteristics affect behavior with and toward money?". The changeover from the 1-pound note to the 1-pound coin in the United Kingdom in April 1983 provided the opportunity to partly answer this second question. What are the consequences for behavior of a change in a single characteristic of money, its physical form.

Webley, Lea, and Hussein (1983) predicted that the 1-pound coin would be spent before a 1-pound note, because people generally regard coins as less valuable than notes and therefore feel more at ease in parting with them. They tested this proposition by carrying out a "dwell-time" experiment, in which the average life expectancy of each coin and note was determined. Subjects had to provide their purses, pockets, or wallets every day (excluding weekends) for a month. Each coin and note that passed through was marked with invisible ink, which enabled the mean dwell time for each denomination to be calculated. Unfortunately, the number of 1-pound coins in circulation was so small that they were unable to draw firm conclusions. But for each subject who had received 1-pound coins, their dwell time was less than for 1-pound notes. Hussein (1985) subsequently overcame this problem by paying subjects for their participation in an unrelated experiment with either a 1-pound note or a 1-pound coin and then checking their purses the following day. This revealed that, indeed, 1-pound coins were spent much quicker than 1-pound notes. This seems, though, to be a result of a general dislike of the coin rather then an effect of it being a coin per se. In terms of our earlier discussion, the 1-pound unit has not just changed one objective characteristic; rather, it has changed a number of subjective ones.

Economic implications of the characteristics approach to money

We conclude this chapter by briefly considering three possible economic implications of the approach to money we have now adopted.

First, altering the form that represents purchasing power may be one of the cheapest ways for a government to influence economic behavior. For instance, substituting coins for notes should have the effect of stimulating small transactions. Hussein (1985) demonstrated that before the British pound coin was introduced, people expected it to have this effect. Conversely, paying all wages and salaries directly into bank accounts rather than wage packets should encourage a more abstract approach to money, discourage expenditure, and thus foster saving and investment.

The second point is closely related. Given any substantial level of inflation, governments must take active decisions about the forms money is allowed to take. Payne and Morgan (1981) have shown that the point at which a money system changes from coins to notes is closely related, across countries, to the typical day's pay. A note seems to be needed to represent roughly between one-twentieth and one-fiftieth of a day's pay. It should be possible to investigate what facts about economic behavior and attitudes toward money correspond to this striking regularity.

Finally, if money is a symbol for many things that, in a sense, it is not really "worth," perhaps people will pursue money even when they claim to be economically contented. From a characteristics viewpoint, such behavior may be entirely rational. Our modern money may be less sophisticated than we think. Perhaps people have to obtain more of one characteristic of money (say, liquidity) than they want in order to get enough of another (say, status), given the state of our money technology.

According to conventional economic theory, money measures the value of everything but is itself of no value. From virtually any psychological perspective, this combination of characteristics is impossible, or at any rate inherently unstable. Economic psychologists should therefore not be surprised that behavior toward money appears to involve many "irrationalities." But, as in other branches of economic psychology, we shall make no progress if we concentrate merely on demonstrating that irrationalities exist. The important issue is to discover the characteristics of our money institutions that make them possible.

13

ADVERTISING

Nobody knows how advertising works. Some of us know some of it. And some who do aren't telling. But the fundamental fact about this business is ignorance of its mechanism. (Bernstein 1972)

This chapter brings together some of the vast amount of research into advertising in an attempt to dispel some of the ignorance that Bernstein commented on. There are problems in accomplishing this task however. Much of the research on commercial advertising is confidential ("some who do aren't telling") and the results from research into noncommercial advertising, being mainly concerned with the effectiveness of Public Information Campaigns, are not all that helpful. Laboratory studies of the effect of advertising on individuals often suffer from lack of external validity, and studies in the "real world" often lack the proper controls. The research literature is very fragmented by disciplines and covers a large range of topics with a variety of methods, from experimental studies of the role of visual communication in persuasion to content analyses of the linguistic devices used in advertisements. In light of these difficulties, this chapter we will be very selective, paying particular attention to those areas which bear on the theme of this section of the book. Advertising is manifestly a process in which it is intended that economic forces will affect individual behavior. Whether (and how) this purpose is achieved, and whether the effects are confined to the self-evident, are questions we discuss in some detail.

AIMS AND CLAIMS OF ADVERTISERS

What is an advertisement?

We all think we know what an advertisement is. It is the thirty-second television commercial for soap powder, the newspaper advertisement imploring us to visit sunny Florida, or the billboard asking "Are you getting enough?" But advertising in our culture encompasses a far broader range of techniques. There are advertisements on television, radio, billboards, and towed behind airplanes; in newspapers, magazines, programs, yellow pages, and sports stadiums; and at the point of sale and on the backs of tickets. On a typical morning one might hear a radio commercial for a shop sale, read a publisher's blurb recommending more books by David Lodge, see posters urging attendance at a conference, and read private postcards selling second-hand books. In short, we are surrounded by advertising, and because we take much of it for granted, we probably underestimate the amount and variety that there is. Will (1982) estimates that the average American is exposed to 1,500 messages daily from national advertisers alone. Krugman (1975) points out that we "screen out" most advertising; about half of all print advertisements are noticed, a third of these to the point of brand identification. Bauer and Greyser (1968) found that when people were asked to count the number of advertisements seen in half a day, the modal response was between 11 and 20. This indicates a very effective screening indeed, although such self-reports probably underestimate the number of advertisements attended to and the extent of forgetting.

The amount spent on advertising varies considerably between different types of economy. There is relatively little advertising in socialist countries and less emphasis on press advertising in countries with high illiteracy rates. Even within "Western" economies, there is some variation: In the United States and United Kingdom, 1.38% and 1.34% of national income was spent on advertising in 1981, 31% and 28%, respectively, for television advertising. In Sweden, where there is no television advertising, the figure was less than 0.5% of national income (The Advertising Association 1984). The amount spent on advertising also varies between different product types. In 1970 advertising costs as a proportion of sales income were over 20% for firms like Colgate-Palmolive, but less than 1% for Ford (Reynaud 1981).

Aims of advertising

Despite the variety of expenditure and media used, all advertisements have one thing in common – their aims. Advertisers usually recognize two aims: to inform and to persuade. "Informing" might involve telling people about the existence and location of a product or service; "persuading" might involve influencing the nature of the consumer's preferences to the benefit of the advertiser. This need not involve persuading people to buy a particular product; prestige advertising and the sponsorship of sports events aim to produce a favorable impression of a firm (which may later increase sales of their products). A good example of this is the recent British Telecom "Power behind the button" campaign. This has steadily improved BT's image, which had been static for the previous two years. Many more people now believe that the firm is up to date and trying to be efficient (Brooks 1984). This is particularly interesting because the ultimate aim of this campaign was to sell shares in BT (as part of the British government's privatization program).

The distinction between informing and persuading, although commonly made, is not clear cut. As Mishan (1969) has argued, the persuasive potential of an advertisement may increase as it gets more informative. And it is hard to see how one could persuade at all without imparting some information (albeit perhaps of an unusual kind).

Claims of advertising

Some alarming claims about the effects of advertising have been made by both its practitioners and its opponents. That advertising agencies should exaggerate their influence is not surprising; after all, this is part of advertising themselves. But opponents of advertising may also exaggerate their influence. Galbraith (1967), for example, has argued that partially through advertising, the modern corporation has wrested sovereignty from the consumer. Instead of meeting the needs of consumers as expressed by demand in the free marketplace, firms are seen by Galbraith as manipulating the needs of consumers (see Chapter 18 for an extended discussion of this issue). Others who are worried about advertisers have written in almost hysterical terms. Blum, for instance, writes

The influence of advertising on the consumer is immeasurable. For example, it can create product and service expectations beyond reality . . . Among other things, advertising has a major influence on our health and safety. Just looking at the variety of products advertised . . . can make one aware of the power and potential of advertising. The influence of advertising on children is horrendous. (Blum 1977, p. 259)

Both advocates and critics probably overestimate the general level of effectiveness of advertisements. Since we live in a sea of mutually contradictory advertisements, most of them must be largely ineffective, at least regarding their specific attempts to change the details of our behavior. On the other hand, academic commentators such as Ehrenberg (1974) or Scitovsky (1976), who reckon that advertising is minimally effective, are probably too unconcerned about advertising; among other things, even competing advertisements may combine to make our entire society more consumption oriented than it might otherwise be. We clearly need to ignore the hyperbole and consider the evidence.

How effective is advertising?

The effectiveness of advertising can be examined in a number of ways. One can evaluate a campaign by looking at the awareness of a product, attitudes to a product, or sales of a product. This can be done using surveys, experiments, or econometric methods. We can take cognitive measurements such as recall or recognition, affective ones like attitudes, physiological ones such as GSR, or commercial ones such as sales. In the commercial field, advertising agencies, more often than not, use "soft" data such as group discussion. The usual method of "testing" advertisements in London today (according to Tuck 1976) is to set up group discussions of early versions of possible advertisements. This is to discover what impressions the consumers have of the advertising and the product. Normally, all group discussions are handled and reported by one individual, whose personal interpretations can obviously distort the information. This kind of research gives rise to enthusiastic descriptions like the following:

The "Wall's Money Mint" demonstrates how . . . a cash refund offer can be made more interesting simply by exploiting the ability of sales promotion to deal in real objects. Ice cream packets were printed with carefully drawn pictures of 5p coins and 10p coins . . . and the housewife invited to turn these coin pictures into real coins . . . For every picture of a coin she cut out and sent in she received back a real coin . . . The dramatisation of the offer by simply presenting it in terms of the real coins the housewife could obtain . . . rather than in arithmetical sums of money – aroused the housewife's much above average interest. (Toop 1978, p. 81)

We doubt whether such enthusiasm can be justified on the basis of group discussion research. In a personal communication, Toop (January 13, 1982) admits that a judgment of whether the promotion produced greater sales than would have been the case with a more conventional offer is "made difficult by the absence of any comparative data."

Another common way of assessing the effectiveness of advertisements is to test the consumer's recall of them. This has its pitfalls, as this newspaper extract reveals:

Discovery of the year: to determine the effectiveness of the sportsground advertising that occasionally strays into shot at televised events, the Nationwide Building Society [Savings and Loan organization] carried out a survey of the viewing public. It was gratified to find that it came second among building societies in recall of advertisements – particularly as Nationwide has never used this form of advertising. (*Sunday Times,* London, "Inside Track," 27 Dec., 1981)

On the face of it, this kind of report might make one wonder about the effectiveness of sportsground advertising. But the imagined recall of Nationwide sportsground advertisements probably depends on the fact that Nationwide advertises a great deal using other methods; the viewing public may well not remember where they saw an advertisement and the designer of the advertisement would presumably not care whether they did or not. Coming second among building societies in recall is, therefore, a tribute to their overall advertising effort. More importantly, we should probably not be asking the question, "Does sportsground advertising work?" or even, "Does advertising work?" Instead, we need to ask what type of advertisement, realized in what type of way, is most effective for which sort of individual with what set of beliefs in which set of circumstances. We need to evaluate a particular advertisement or campaign. Even small variations can have a dramatic effect. According to the Health Education Council's researchers, the famous pregnant nude advertisement (which featured an expectant mother smoking) significantly reduced smoking among pregnant women but was offensive in its original form (where the model's abdomen was bigger) and unsuccessful in the variant used the following year (when the model wore a nightie).

Memory is not the only cognitive measure relevant to the success of an advertisement. A great deal of advertising attempts to establish the factors that should be taken into account when buying one of a class of products. In other words, it aims to "frame the problem" for first-time buyers. Wright and Rip (1980) demonstrated that if a series of brochures for different colleges focused on a limited set of attributes, these were the ones then used to make preference judgments.

As we shall see when we come to consider the various models of the response to advertising, it is not logically necessary that advertisements should affect consumers' cognitions in order to affect their buying behavior, or that a cognitive change will be reflected in behavior. The surest yardstick for the effectiveness of an advertisement, therefore, is its effect on sales, if only that can be measured. Published accounts of good evaluation studies of the sales effect of advertising are rare, but they do exist. For example, Buzzell (1964) reports how duPont investigated the effect of advertising expenditure on sales of their paint. Fifty-six sales territories were divided into high, average, and low market share areas. Within each group of areas, duPont spent the normal amount of money on advertising in one-third of them, in another one-third more than double the normal amount, and in the remaining third four times the normal amount. Unsurprisingly they found that higher levels of advertising produced increased sales at a diminishing rate. Haley (1978) describes the results of nine such studies of the relationship between advertising expenditure and sales. Eight of the nine studies found a positive relationship.

At a more micro level, McDonald (1970) collected data on advertising exposure and individual purchases. Two hundred fifty London housewives kept a diary for 13 weeks in which they recorded what products they had bought, the newspapers they had seen, and the television they had watched. This study revealed that when the housewives switched between brands, they were 5% more likely to switch into a brand if, between the two purchases, they saw two or more advertisements for that brand.

The advent of cable television has meant that highly controlled, long-term field experiments are now possible (McGuire 1977). Raj's (1982) study of the effects of advertising on consumers of varying brand loyalty is an excellent example. He used consumer panel diary data from a split cable TV system, located in a city demographically representative of the United States. The consumers keep a weekly diary of their purchases, noting brand and price. They were connected to one of two cables, which meant that the effect of increased advertising on one cable could be compared with those of the control level received on the other. Raj's experiment lasted four years; it consisted of a one-year pretest, two years of increased advertising for one group, and a one-year posttest. Consumers' purchase behavior in the pretest era was used to classify them according to their degree of brand loyalty. The results revealed that while increased advertising of brand A increased the quantity of brand A bought by those loyal to it, there was no equivalent decrease in purchases of other brands. Conversely, the increased advertising of brand A reduced purchasing of brand B among those loyal to brand B, but there was no increase in their purchases of other brands (including brand A). The major effect of advertising, then, seemed to be on the amount of the product bought, rather than on the amount of switching between brands – at least, for the particular product under study.

Although sales are crucial in commercial advertising, there may be a wider range of target behaviors in public information campaigns. The aims in such campaigns may range from persuading people to wear seatbelts to persuading them not to use drugs. The best controlled study of public information advertising to date is the Stanford Heart Disease Study (Maccoby & Alexander 1980). The researchers selected three towns in California, each with a population of between 12,000 and 15,000. Random samples of 500 people, aged 35 to 59 years, were interviewed and medically examined before the project began and again at the end of each year of the three-year project. Additional samples of people were not given the initial testing (this ruled out changes caused by presensitization). In one town (Gilroy), a conventional media campaign, using TV, radio, newspapers, and direct mail communication, was mounted; in another town (Watsonville), the same sort of approach was supplemented by a behavior-modification program for a randomly selected group of high-risk people; and in another town (Tracy), the townspeople received no advertising except what occurred normally in the media. Over a two-year period, the population of Tracy became slightly more coronary prone, whereas in both the experimental towns, peoples' cholesterol levels, smoking, and other factors were reduced. Interestingly, there was no significant difference between the two experimental towns after two years, although after one year the Watsonville treatment was the more effective.

The demonstrated success of this campaign and of other public information campaigns has led to a mood of cautious optimism among advertisers. It would appear that advertising can be effective provided that one is modest in one's aims, that one diagnoses the beliefs, attitudes, and habitual actions of the target group accurately, and that one sets up support systems (Mendelsohn 1973; McGuire 1980).

ADVERTISING AND THE INDIVIDUAL

If we accept that some advertisements and some campaigns can be effective, we are forced to ask, "How do they work?" We shall now take up this question in some detail. First, we consider some of the general models that have been proposed as descriptions of the response to advertising. Subsequently, we shall move on to a more detailed psychological analysis of the processes of persuasion and information.

Models of advertising

Theorists who have devised models of how advertising works seem to be especially fond of acronyms. So we find DAGMAR (defining advertising goals for measuring advertising results), according to which the steps are awareness, comprehension, conviction, action; ATR (awareness, trial, reinforcement); AIDA (attention, interest, desire, action), and our favorite, the tongue-in-cheek GOTTERDAMMERUNG. Joyce (1967) pointed out that DAGMAR and AIDA are commonsense models and are based on no evidence. They assume that there is a sequential hierarchy of events from awareness through knowledge, thinking, preference, and conviction and that the object of advertising is to get consumers to learn something and thereby convince them to buy the product. Ehrenberg's (1974) ATR model and Krugman's (1965, 1975) "learning without involvement" model should be treated more seriously.

Ehrenberg's (1974) model stems from his earlier work on repeat buying behavior, with its behavioristic approach to attitudes (see Chapter 7). He sees advertising as essentially defensive and its main role as reinforcing satisfaction for brands already being used. Attitudes are not important; there is little for them to explain since they do not differentiate between brand users and nonusers. Advertising's task is simply to inform the consumer that brand X is as good as the others. This model may fit the advertising of inexpensive, frequently purchased, branded products but it says nothing about the advertising of goods for which we might expect the consumer to take a more rational approach. Also, like the repeat buying model, it is based on aggregate results, and it is debatable how much we learn about an individual by knowing how to predict mathematically at the aggregate level.

Krugman's "learning without involvement" model starts from the assumption that advertising usually operates in situations of low involvement. He draws an analogy between the learning of nonsense syllables (which show greater effects of order of presentation than meaningful material) and the learning of advertisements. The spontaneous recall of TV commercials presented four in a row forms a distinct U curve, for example, like the serial position curve found in many laboratory experiments on memory. Krugman argues that much of the impact of TV advertising depends on learning at a low level of involvement. As the trivial messages in the advertisements are repeatedly learned, forgotten, and relearned, they affect the perceptual salience of various attributes of a product. Then the purchase situation acts as "the catalyst that reassembles or brings out all the potentials for shifts of salience that have accumulated up to that point" (1965, p. 354). Krugman concludes, like Ehrenberg, that changes in attitudes, if they occur at all, will follow the purchase rather than precede it. This kind of "do-think-feel" model (Ramond 1976) has the merit of challenging traditional assumptions that advertising changes attitudes and thus behavior, but it probably applies only to a limited set of situations.

Vaughn (1980) makes this latter point clearly in his "planning" model of advertising (he calls this the FCB model but, to save acronymophobes further discomfort, we will ignore this label). Vaughn assumes that advertising works in different ways for different kinds of products and so categorizes these according to two dimensions: consumer involvement (cognitive) and consumer reaction (affective). With major purchases (house, car, furnishings), involvement will be high and people will respond to advertisements cognitively. They are being "thinkers" and so a learn–feel–do model is appropriate. With products that are involving but where feelings about them are also crucial (jewelry, cosmetics), the model is feel–learn–do. Low involvement products may be bought habitually (in this context we should perhaps call it do–learn–feel). Other low-involvement products (candies, films) are bought reactively, in which case the consumer is seen as a reactor whose interest will be hard to hold and short-lived: do–feel–learn.

These models help frame the problem and suggest methods of investigation, but none of them really gives us much insight into how advertisements change the behavior and attitudes of individuals. For a more detailed examination of some of the processes involved, we must turn to social psychology.

The social psychology of persuasive communication

Pioneering work on persuasion was carried out by C. I. Hovland and colleagues at Yale during the 1950s. Their pragmatic research approach may be summarized by the question, "Who says what to whom in what context?" They recognized four groups of factors which could affect the success of a persuasion attempt: source, message, target or audience, and context. The implicit model of the persuasion process was message learning; attention and comprehension were thought to determine whether the audience learned from a message, and other factors would then determine whether they accepted and acted on what they had learned (note the similarity to the hierarchy of effects model described above). There are a vast number of studies into the effects of source, message, target, and context variables (see Petty & Cacioppo 1981, or Aronson 1984, for a summary). We will comment on just one variable of each type.

We have already mentioned that credible and attractive sources are more persuasive than uncredible and unattractive ones (see Chapter 1). This is not surprising. More interestingly, if an audience thinks the source is putting across a message that represents a genuine feeling, they are more persuaded than if the message is seen as self-serving. For example, in a study by Walster, Aronson, and Abrahams (1966), each advocate was more persuasive when putting forward an unexpected position, such as a district attorney arguing for a reduction in police powers. Eagly and Chaiken (1975) extended this idea by suggesting that likeable people are normally expected to advocate likeable positions and disliked people disliked positions. If this is true then the most effective persuaders would be likeable people arguing for undesirable positions and disliked people arguing for desirable positions. In fact, Eagley and Chaiken found that likeable people were virtually equally persuasive, whatever kind of argument they were putting forward, although the disliked source was more effective with the desirable positions than the undesirable ones.

Perhaps the most thoroughly researched message variable has been the arousal of fear. The earliest research (Janis & Feshbach 1953) found that the least frightening film was the most effective in improving dental care. Most studies since have shown the reverse (studies showing an effect of fear outnumber those that do not by 4 to 1). For example, Dabbs and Leventhal (1966) found that the most frightening messages about the symptoms of tetanus not only had the most effect on intentions to get inoculated, they were also the most effective in bringing people forward for vaccination. The efficacy of fear appeals almost certainly interacts with other message variables, however. Rogers and Mewborn's (1976) study of antismoking communications suggests that fear appeals may only be effective if the recommended preventative measures are also seen by the recipient as effective.

One myth worth dispelling concerns a rather unusual message variable: whether a message is presented subliminally or not. A subliminal message is one that the recipient is not consciously aware of, because it is presented below his or her sensory threshold. During the 1950s there was considerable disquiet about the use of subliminal advertising. There were claims that sales of popcorn and ice cream increased when cinema audiences "saw" subliminal messages such as "Eat more ice cream" on or near the screen. Dixon (1971) debunks these claims, pointing out that there is no published evidence to substantiate them, but there are many reasons to doubt them. However, more recent experiments (e.g., Marcel 1983) have shown that subliminal material can at least affect the response to subsequent ambiguous stimuli. It would not be impossible for an advertisement to exploit this effect, but we are not aware of any attempts to do so.

Target variables (intelligence, self-esteem) have received rather less attention, perhaps because the initial rather simple research gave contradictory results. McGuire (1968) proposed that these discrepancies could be resolved if the persuasive process were considered as a series of stages, and the effects of personality variables examined at the different stages. For example, intelligent people may be persuaded by some messages that the less intelligent simply do not understand. Conversely, intelligent people may be less likely to yield to persuasion because of greater confidence in their own judgment. Eagly and Warren (1979) examined the effects of intelligence and found, as expected, that when a message was more complex it was more effective with the more intelligent. Simpler messages were more persuasive with the less intelligent.

Research into context has found less obvious results. It might seem that any distraction would necessarily reduce the effectiveness of a persuasive communication, but this is not true. Distraction inhibits the thoughts we have while listening and so reduces the effectiveness of a message we are in favor of but enhances that of one we disagree with (Petty, Wells, & Brock 1976).

The problem with much of this work, especially that of the Yale group, is that it gives rise simply to low-level generalizations rather than any useful theory. Brown (1965, p. 549) summed up the early phase of this research very neatly: "The work has been well done, but it lacks something of intellectual interest because the results do not fit into any generally compelling pattern. They summarize a set of elaborately contingent, but not very general, generalizations." More recent social psychological research has been more firmly grounded in theory, especially attitude theory, and it is to this that we now turn.

Advertising, attitudes, beliefs, and buying behavior

The study of attitudes has been social psychology's main concern during much of its history. As Murphy, Murphy, and Newcomb (1937, p. 889) said, "perhaps no single concept in the whole realm of social psychology occupies a more nearly central position than that of attitudes." The relationship between attitudes and behavior has therefore been a longstanding issue of particular importance (see Chapter 1). The accumulated evidence from many studies (through the late 1960s) suggested that there was very little relationship. This posed a grave problem for social psychologists; they responded in three ways. One was to deny the importance of these studies and claim that attitudes were an important part of a person's inner life even if they were not reflected in overt behavior. Another was to downgrade the importance of attitudes and to search for other variables that would be better predictors of behavior, such as abilities, motives, and situational factors. The most constructive response, however, was to develop a theory of social behavior that would incorporate attitudes into a structure involving other variables and thus actually predict behavior.

By far the most significant attempt using this latter approach was that of Fishbein and Ajzen (1975). Their theory revived interest in attitude studies among consumer researchers, who normally refer to the theory as the "extended Fishbein model." During the past few years, it has accounted for more published research in consumer behavior than any other theory (Kassarjian 1982). It "solves" the attitude–behavior problem.

Fishbein first proposed that instead of predicting behavior we can only hope to predict "behavioral intention." Intention can change over time, and the more closely in time to the actual behavior intention is measured, the better it will predict behavior. Behavioral intention is seen as a function of two, and only two, variables: the person's attitude to the behavior and the subjective norm. An intention to buy a gift, for example, depends upon attitude (does the person overall evaluate the buying of the gift positively?) and upon subjective norm (do people important in the person's life think that a gift should be purchased?). This commonsense idea is expressed mathematically as

$$BI = A_{\text{act}} \cdot w_1 + SN \cdot w_2 \tag{13.1}$$

where BI is the behavioral intention, A_{act} is the attitude toward the act, SN is the subjective norm, and w_1 and w_2 are empirically derived weights. To reiterate, this equation states that someone's intention to do something is made up of two components: the attitude toward the act and what the person thinks other people believe should be done. The empirically derived weights indicate that the relative importance of the attitude and subjective norm will depend on the situation. For example, in buying a replacement exhaust the attitudinal component may be most important, whereas in buying drinks in a bar the subjective norm may be more important. The two halves of the equation can be further separated into the following two equations:

$$A_{\text{act}} = \Sigma b_i e_i \tag{13.2}$$

where b_i are the beliefs about outcomes of the act (expressed as probabilities) and e_i are the evaluations of the outcomes. This means that a person's attitude to an act is the sum of his evaluations of the outcomes of an act, each evaluation being weighted according to how likely each outcome is. And:

$$SN = \Sigma NB_j MC_j \qquad (13.3)$$

where NB_j is the belief that individual j thinks that the person should perform the act, and MC_j is the motivation to comply with individual j. This means that a person's subjective norm is the sum of his beliefs about what others think he should do, each such belief being weighted according to his motivation to comply with the particular other.

There is a considerable amount of evidence in support of this theory for a wide variety of behaviors, both commercial (intentions to buy soft drinks and beer: Beardon & Woodside 1977; gift buying: Warshaw 1980) and noncommercial (voting: Ajzen & Fishbein 1980; infant feeding: Manstead, Profitt, & Smart 1983). Most reseachers working in consumer behavior have been concerned with the model's undoubted predictive power. Unfortunately, there are some problems with both the predictive and the descriptive aspects of the model.

As far as prediction is concerned, two factors have been examined in detail, the role of normative influences and the role of past behavior. Miniard and Cohen (1981) have pointed out that the distinctions made between the A_{act} and SN components are muddled. "My child thinks I should buy Sugar Puffs" is considered to be a normative belief, whereas "buying Sugar Puffs will please my child" is a belief about the outcome of an act (attitudinal). Although these are superficially different statements, it is clear that they may both reflect an underlying concern with the child's reactions. Using a role play involving the purchase of a dress, Miniard and Cohen showed that changing an important other's influence potential altered attitudinal as well as normative responses. This led the authors to conclude that "it [is] doubtful that this model will be useful in separating personal and normative reasons for engaging in a behavior" (Miniard & Cohen 1981, p. 330). Related to this, in a study of adolescents' drinking, Biddle, Bank, and Marlin (1980) argued that norms affect behavior through attitudes rather than norms and attitudes separately affecting behavior.

Other researchers have expressed dissatisfaction with the concept of "motivation to comply." Schlegel, Crawford, and Sandborn (1977), Budd, North, and Spencer (1984), and Kristiansen (1984) have all found that including this variable actually reduces the model's ability to predict behavioral intentions. Kristiansen found that a truncated measure (ΣNBj) was a better predictor.

As noted above, one crucial aspect of Fishbein and Azjen's theory is that *all* variables affect behavior only through their effects on A_{act} and SN. Bentler and Speckart (1979, 1981) report that past behavior affects attitudes *and* has a direct effect on behavior that is not mediated by behavioral intentions. College students' use of alcohol, marijuana, and hard drugs at one time helped to predict similar behavior two weeks later, even after behavioral intention had been taken into account. Ajzen (in press) argues that this was because the students lacked control over the behavior, and that, according to the theory of planned behavior (a recent refinement of the Fishbein and Ajzen model), past behavior should have no independent effect on current behavior when a person has complete control. But Kristiansen (1984) and Fredricks and Dossett (1983) obtained results similar to those of Bentler and Speckart (1981), even though the behaviors that they studied were obviously under individuals' control (teeth brushing and attending class, respectively).

In addition to worries about the predictive aspects of the Fishbein and Ajzen model, there has been some concern about its descriptive validity. It is, after all, very similar to *SEU* models and, as we saw in Chapter 5, *SEU* models are not good descriptions of the way people make decisions. As van der Plight and Eiser (1984, p. 165) neatly express it: "combining enormous quantities of information in one's head exceeds the computational capacity of anyone but an idiot savant." It is likely, then, that Fishbein and Ajzen's model is an overintellectualized view of the way people form attitudes.

Nonetheless, the model is useful in some ways. In particular, it suggests the following classification of the ways in which advertising can affect an individual's behavior. Advertising might change

1. Which beliefs are salient
2. The evaluations of the beliefs
3. The probability levels of the beliefs
4. Which others are used as referents
5. What a person thinks others think that person should do
6. Motivation to comply with what others think
7. The relative importance of attitudes and norms

This classification implies that if we stopped a person in the "purchase situation" we might find that advertising had not changed attitudes toward the product itself, but only the attitude or subjective norm to the act of purchase. Attitudes toward the product might change subsequently. It also implies that a persuasive message has a direct effect on beliefs, evaluations, and so forth so that the causal flow is

Advertising → attitude/subjective norm → *BI* → behavior

The postulated causal flow of effects, from changes in beliefs, evaluations, and so on, to changes in behavior has been tested in a consumer context by Lutz (1977). Lutz set up two experiments in which he tried to alter subjects' beliefs and evaluations of a particular detergent. One experiment attempted to manipulate beliefs about two important product characteristics; the other attempted to manipulate evaluations.

In the first experiment, subjects read a *Consumers' Report* article which gave information about nine different attributes of the fictitious detergent. Then after a few minutes, they received a communication which aimed to change one of the beliefs they had formed. The subjects' beliefs, evalutions of beliefs, attitudes toward purchase and intention to purchase were all measured separately. After the data were analyzed using a recursive, regression framework, Lutz concluded that a change in one belief induced by a communication had, indeed, led, via changes in attitude to purchase, to changes in behavioral intention. Unfortunately, these conclusions have been challenged by Dickson and Miniard (1977) and the Carnegie-Mellon University Marketing Seminar (1977), who have pointed out various flaws in analysis and design. The Seminar maintained that Lutz had investigated attitude formation rather than attitude change. They argued that his subjects had never formed attitudes based on the original information, and so when asked to express an attitude after the new information had been given, based this new attitude on the information alone. This view seems to be derived from the notion that a good deal of cognitive effort is necessary to form an attitude, and that there must be a reason for an individual to integrate stored information into an attitude (Fishbein and Azjen maintain that attitude formation is virtually automatic). Despite the criticisms, it appears that Lutz has demonstrated that the Fishbein model works in a dynamic setting.

Olson, Toy, and Dover (1982) have combined Greenwald's (1968) cognitive response model with Fishbein and Azjen's model to provide a more satisfactory account of the process by which an advertisement causes belief formation and changes in attitudes. In their model, the thoughts produced in response to a communication mediate the formation and change of beliefs. For example, counterarguing a claim made in an advertisement, (e.g., that Wizzo washes whiter) will reduce the strength of the belief in that claim, whereas a supportive argument will increase its strength. Their study of the formation of attitudes about brands of ballpoint pens supported this view, but the magnitude of the mediating effects were rather small.

For more empirical support for the idea that changes in attitude lead to changes in behavior we can turn to studies using a cross-lagged panel design. The basic idea in such studies is to measure attitudes and behaviors at various points in time and then examine the lagged correlations, that is, those between attitudes at time 1 and behavior at time 2 and behavior at time 1 and attitudes at time 2. If attitudes determine behavior rather than the reverse, then the correlation between attitude (time 1) and behavior (time 2) should be greater than that between behavior (time 1) and attitude (time 2). The fundamental purpose of cross-lagged panel designs is to make causal statements based on correlational evidence, something that every social science student is warned never to do. But a cross-lagged design can do just that, provided that two key assumptions (synchronicity and stationarity) are made in order to rule out the possibility that some third variable is responsible for the correlation (see Rogosa 1980, for a detailed discussion of this design). Synchronicity means that the processes represented in the synchronous correlations did actually occur at the same time, and stationarity means that the causal structure of the variables did not change over time.

Cross-lagged panel studies completed to date (Kahle & Berman 1979; Kahle, Klingel, & Kulka 1981; Andrews & Kandel 1979) have consistently shown that attitudes lead to behavior and not the reverse. This seems to imply that advertisers should revert to a think–feel–do model and that our concern about the overintellectualized nature of recent attitude models is misplaced. However, recent research suggests that there are two main routes to attitude change, a central route that involves comprehension, learning, and thinking, and a peripheral route where change is brought about if an attitude object is associated with pleasant or unpleasant cues (cf. Vaughn 1980). If this is the case, then advertising could produce its effects through either route. What conditions would favor one route or the other? Most current research focuses on involvement. This has been defined in various ways (see Burnkrant & Sawyer 1983), but all definitions agree that a decision with which a person is highly involved is of greater personal relevance and has potentially more significant consequences.

There are three main views about how involvement affects attitude change. Sherif, Sherif, and Nebergall (1965) claim that highly involved people should show more negative evaluations of communications, since high involvement is associated with an extended lattitude of rejection. Krugman (1965) proposed that involvement shifts the sequence of attitude change: under low involvement, communications influence behavior and later attitudes shift; under high involvement, the sequence is reversed. Petty and Cacioppo's (1981) elaboration likelihod model (ELM) was specifically developed with the distinction between central and peripheral routes in mind. Elaboration likelihood refers to the probability of an issue-relevant thought occurring during a persuasive attempt. If that probability is high, then the central route will be more effective; if it is low, the peripheral route will be. If involvement is high, people will be prepared to make a cognitive effort, and so advertisements that require such effort will be effective. If involvement is low, people will make little or no effort and so other factors (e.g., attractive blondes) will make for more effective advertisements.

The distinction between Krugman's approach and that of Petty and Cacioppo is as follows. Krugman would argue that, under high involvement, attitude change precedes behavior change, whereas Petty and Cacioppo make no such claim. In their model there is greater correspondence between attitudes and behavior under conditions of high involvement, but they make no statement about the sequence of attitude and behavior change.

Petty and Cacioppo have carried out a large number of studies into this model, some of them in a consumer context. In general, the results are congruent with their model. For example, Petty and Cacioppo (1980) investigated the effectiveness of shampoo advertisements and manipulated three variables: involvement, quality of arguments, and attractiveness of endorser. The quality of arguments had the most impact when the product was relevant to the individuals, but the attractiveness of the endorser was equally effective in all conditions. Petty and Cacioppo reasoned that this might have been because attractiveness was relevant to the product (in that it produced good-looking hair); they followed this study with one using a peripheral cue that could not be seen as a product-relevant argument (Petty, Cacioppo, & Schumann 1983). Participants saw advertisements for a fictitious product, the "Edge disposable razor." Two aspects of the advertisements were manipulated: the quality of the arguments in support of Edge and the status of the endorsers of Edge (celebrities or average man in the street). The participants were in either a high-involvement (the product would soon be on trial in their home town) or low-involvement condition. The results were consistent with the model. Increased involvement led to a significant improvement in brand name recall, but to a worsening of attitude if the arguments were weak. This suggests that recall may be a poor measure of an advertisement's effectiveness.

According to the ELM model, it is possible for a source variable to induce attitude change through a central route, or for a message variable to induce change through a peripheral route. For example, under low involvement, the mere number of arguments presented (a message variable) may be responded to peripherally, using the simple decision rule "the more the better." Under high involvement, however, the quality of the arguments would be more significant (Petty & Cacioppo 1984). Similarly, under high-involvement conditions a source variable such as the use of surreal visual material might engage a central route. The model also suggests what individual differences might be relevant to attitude change. Individuals high on a need for cognition scale (which distinguishes between those who enjoy and indulge in analytic activity and those who do not) were more affected by better quality arguments than those low on this scale (Cacioppo, Petty, & Morris 1983).

Even this very selective sample of the mass of data on communication and attitude change clearly shows that the data contain many contradictions. Petty and Cacioppo are right to emphasize that advertisements can work in different ways, and we still know very little about what processes are involved. Critics of Fishbein and Azjen are right to complain about the descriptive inadequacy of that model, but it is unlikely to fall out of use until an alternative theory makes its appearance. But we must not forget that advertising is only one aspect of product selection and use. Ginter (1974) introduced two new products toward which attitudes were unstable. He then provided advertising that aimed to influence attitudes, and measured behavior (purchasing the products on a simulated shopping trip) before and after the attitude change. He also measured attitudes before and after advertising, as well as before and after the simulated shopping trip. Ginter found that attitude change occurred both before and after a behavioral change but that the postchoice attitude change was the biggest. This suggests that the various models of the effects of advertising are actually dealing with different stages in an overall dynamic process.

Attitudes toward advertising

What of attitudes toward advertisements themselves, as opposed to attitudes toward the products or toward buying the products? Reynaud (1981, pp. 148–9) claims that people have a favorable general attitude toward advertising and believe that it performs a useful function. But if asked more specifically about advertisements in the newspapers they read or on television that they watch, their attitudes would be found to be rather less favorable.

The American public are ambivalent over television advertising (Bower 1973). Three-quarters of a nationwide sample agreed that there are too many commercials but about the same proportion agreed that "commercials are a fair price to pay for the entertainment you get." About 43% thought commercials were annoying and in bad taste but 54% agreed that some commercials are helpful and informative. Thirty-five percent even maintained that they frequently welcomed a commercial break, but the people did not report whether they valued the advertisements themselves or rather as an opportunity to make tea or visit the toilet. It is perhaps telling that the U.S. Public Broadcasting System includes "noncommercial breaks" in its programming. Newspaper advertising is preferred to television advertising, at least if one believes an American newspaper trade publication (*Newspapers are* 1975). Nearly 70% of respondents rated newspaper advertising as "mostly" or "completely favorable," while only 40% gave television advertising comparable ratings. Much the same results have been found in Britain, in a survey by The Advertising Association (1972). About 43% of the public liked or quite liked television commercials, whereas 50% liked or quite liked press advertisements.

Over the past forty years attitudes toward advertising have changed considerably. A compilation of American surveys (Zanot 1984) shows that they were initially neutral during the 1930s, became more positive during the 1950s, and then dropped throughout the 1960s, with a slight rise at the beginning of the 1970s.

As yet we have no idea how these general attitudes mediate the effect of advertising. There is some evidence, however, that attitudes toward particular advertisements have a significant role. Mitchell and Olson (1981) showed subjects advertisements for hypothetical face tissue brands and tried to explain differences in attitudes toward the brands using the Fishbein model. The model failed to provide a complete account of the observed differences in attitudes toward the brands. But when attitudes toward the advertisements were added as covariates, all significant differences were eliminated. Greyser (1973) reports that advertisements for some heavily advertised products (e.g., detergents, toothpastes, deodorants) are particularly disliked. If Mitchell and Olson are correct, this should affect people's attitudes toward the brands advertised, and presumably also their intentions to buy them. It is unlikely, however, that this is the whole story. The firms concerned are no doubt aware of the public attitude to their advertisements and also of the state of their sales; it is unlikely that they would persist with a seriously deleterious marketing strategy for very long. Presumably the situation is more complex than a simple comparison of Mitchell and Olson's results with Greyser's suggests.

Attributional processes and advertisements

As we saw in Chapter 1, attribution theory dominated social psychology in the 1970s, so it is not surprising that it has been applied to the effects of advertising on the individual. It was first applied to the advertising context by Settle and Golden (1974), who hypothesized that readers of advertisements would attribute the claims made in them either to the characteristics of the product or to the desire of the advertiser to sell the product. If they did the latter, they would be less confident of the claims and would form less favorable attitudes.

To examine this idea, Settle and Golden carried out an experiment using business students. The experimental manipulation consisted of two different versions of advertisements for five different products. One version (nonvaried product claims) promoted the product as superior in five characteristics (three important and two unimportant). The other version (varied product claims) promoted the product as superior on the three important characteristics, but not superior on the two unimportant characteristics. Advertisements for all five products were combined in a booklet that subjects read. All possible combinations of varied and nonvaried product claims were used. Settle and Golden concluded that varied product claims gave rise to higher confidence ratings, and so advertisers should be willing to disclaim superiority on an unimportant characteristic in order to increase credibility.

Two major criticisms have been leveled at this intriguing study. The first is that Settle and Golden did not directly measure attributions, nor did they carry out a manipulation check to ensure that the two versions of the advertisements were actually altering attributions (Burnkrant 1974). The second is that Settle and Golden had misinterpreted attribution theory and had applied Kelley's ideas on situations involving many observations to one involving just one observation (Hansen & Scott 1976). The appropriate causal inference process would be Kelley's (1967, 1971) discounting and augmentation principles (see Chapter 1).

Smith and Hunt (1978) argue that Jones and Davis' (1965) correspondent inference theory may be more appropriate for a product claim attribution model (see Chapter 1). In the advertising situation, the advertised message is the observed behavior, and readers may attribute dispositions to the sponsor, depending on content. Nonvaried product claims would be unlikely to give rise to correspondent inferences because they are so common. Consumers would not be able to infer much except that, like most advertisers, the sponsor wanted to sell the product. By contrast, varied product claims are unusual and seem at odds with the aim of increasing sales. Here the observed claim is more likely to be attributed to a disposition of the sponsor, such as truthfulness; this would increase credibility and confidence in the claims.

Smith and Hunt carried out a test of this product claim attribution model, and also checked that the advertising was evoking attributions. The design of their experiment was similar to Settle and Golden's but simpler: a two-way factorial design with type of claim and type of product (television or paint) as the factors. After looking at the advertisement, subjects filled in a questionnaire that used indirect questions to ascertain whether any attributions had been made, as well as direct questions on how common varied product claims were and how truthful the advertiser was. Thirty-eight percent of all subjects gave attributional responses (e.g., "a typical ad, trying to convince the public to buy a product by exaggerating its benefits"), although the varied product claims advertisements were a much more potent elicitor of attributions (66% of the subjects reading these advertisements made attributions). Varied products claims were seen as unusual and the advertisers of these products as more truthful, all of which supports this product claim attribution model.

Should advertisers, then, start to vary the claims they make for their products? Recent research on the effectiveness of comparative advertising, which has incorporated type of claim as a variable, suggests that advertisers should be cautious. Belch (1981), for instance, carried out a laboratory experiment using television commercials for a fictitious brand of toothpaste, and varied type of message (comparative or noncomparative), type of claim (varied or nonvaried), and number of repetitions. There was no effect of type of claim on attitudes, purchase intentions, or perceptions of the advertiser as truthful. Belch suggests that this may be because the varied commercials only claimed one attribute was "average" and that this manipulation was too subtle.

A study by Swinyard (1981) is more encouraging and more realistic. He carried out a field experiment in which different leaflets advertising a shop were distributed around a neighborhood. The leaflets made either varied or nonvaried claims about the shop and either made explicit comparisons with other shops or did not mention them. Varied claims were seen as more truthful and the key claim (that prices were the lowest) was accepted more often with these leaflets. But these beliefs did not translate into behavioral intentions or actual behavior (measured by the number of coupons printed on the leaflets that were redeemed). Nonetheless, it may be worthwhile for advertisers to make varied claims, because there might be a general positive effect in that all advertising might be seen as more credible, and consumers might come to have more faith in the business world. But this would require a degree of altruism unlikely to be found among advertisers.

Recently, Kelley's theory has been used as the framework for an experiment investigating the effects of advertising context on the perception of advertisements. Sparkman and Lockander (1980) examined how attributions to a product were affected by consensus, consistency, and distinctiveness by presenting shoppers with a car advertisement and one of sixteen scenarios which set the context for the advertisement. These were modeled on those used by McArthur (1972); for example, the low consensus, high consistency over time, and high distinctiveness scenario was as follows:

Ralph Jones . . . has recently agreed to appear in adverts for a mid-size car, Car X. Several other men and women will also appear in adverts for this car. Ralph has agreed to advertise Car X for the next three years . . . Ralph has never done an ad before and will not advertise any other products.

Shoppers were then asked to rate how likely it was that Ralph agreed to do the ad because of the good characteristics of car X. Only the consensus dimension significantly affected product attribution. This is contrary to the findings of McArthur (1972), and other studies in nonconsumer contexts (Nisbett & Borgida 1975; Nisbett, Borgida, Crandall, & Reed 1976), which have suggested that consensus information is systematically underused. Azjen (1977), however, has argued that this only happens when consensus has no apparent causal relationship to what is being judged; in Sparkman and Locander's experiment the causal link was clear cut.

In recent years, attribution theory has been criticized a great deal (Antaki 1981). Ironically, some of these criticisms, directed against the likely validity of attribution theory as an account of what goes on during social interaction, actually encourage us to feel that the theory has a useful role to play in explaining the individual's reaction to some advertisements. Three criticisms in particular have this reverse encouragement effect. Harre (1981, p. 141) said "The most prominent . . . feature for which one must be on the lookout, . . . [is] the question of whether the work was done by asking people to deal with, and produce, documents, or whether it was concerned with actions and speech in the real world." Since many advertisements are "documents," the fact that most attribution research involves documents would seem to be a positive point. Langer (1978) has contended that much social behavior is "mindless" and that in these situations people do not devote cognitive effort to making attributions. But on these grounds, for at least some advertisements (those for products with which people are involved), individuals are likely to make attributions. Finally, attribution research and theory has been criticized for being ethnocentric, merely a model of how middle-class Americans think. Since advertising is quintessentially American, other cultures that have been exposed to this particular form of transatlantic enculturization may also be attribution minded.

Advertisements as an indicator of quality

Gabor and Granger (1966), among others, have pointed out that buyers often use price as an indicator of quality, especially for products that are not easy to evaluate, or where other information is missing. The highest-priced aspirin in the United States, Bayer aspirin, continues to outsell lower-priced brands, probably because of this effect. The same kind of argument can be applied to certain advertisements. It may be that advertising per se, regardless of its content, is used in the same way. Consumers may attribute qualities such as efficiency and dynamism to the firm that chooses to advertise compared to one which does not.

In at least some cases, such attributions may be reasonable. For running shoes, for example, Archibald, Haulman, and Moody (1983) found that the amount of advertising is significantly correlated with quality ratings published by the leading running magazine. This is not just the result of manufacturers capitalizing on good publicity, since there is a significant correlation before the ratings are published.

A final word on the social psychology of advertising

We have sampled the psychological literature on advertising fairly selectively in this section, but it should be clear that every successive school of psychology has had something to say on the subject. As with all psychological questions, it is sometimes difficult to discern any consistent answers among the different analyses offered by the various schools. The selection of approaches we have considered seems to have merit beyond merely stating what a particular social psychological theory looks like when applied to advertising. There is no single, simple message, but it is at least clear that different advertisements will function in different ways in different circumstances and that some kinds of analysis are available that will make some sense of this diversity.

There is an additional reason why we should expect diversity in the effects of advertising. Advertising depends very heavily on factors that are intrinsically transitory. Advertisements need to be both novel and fashionable, and neither novelty nor fashion is an inherent property of any message, or even of any medium. The advertisement or approach to advertising that was effective last year may be absolutely useless today. The psychology of advertising will always consist of attempts to detect an unchanging deep structure under a rapidly changing surface.

In our survey of literature on advertising and the individual, we have concentrated on the use of systematic theories derived from social psychology or consumer behavior. However, there have been many less formal approaches to the effects of advertising on the individual. Galbraith (1958), for example, argues that advertising "creates wants"; that is, it alters individual preference structures. It is possible to translate such hypotheses into the language of, say, the extended Fishbein model ("creation of wants" would be interpreted as the raising of either attitude or subjective norm factors from a zero level), and that is a useful way of trying to submit ideas like Galbraith's to empirical test. But it is in a way artificial. The criticism of advertising for "creating wants" is embedded in a more general critique of the effects of advertising on society, and the consequent effects on individual behavior. We must now turn to the evaluation of those effects.

ADVERTISING AND SOCIETY

At the micro level, advertising aims to inform and persuade individuals. This is intended to produce various effects, most obviously to increase demand for a particular firm's products so that sales and profits are greater than they would otherwise have been. A less obvious aim is one that takes effect at a higher level of aggregation. This is to increase the costs of production for potential competitors, even if that means increasing the firm's own costs. An industry in which economics of scale are exhausted at a comparatively low level of output is easy to enter. Heavy advertising expenditure can forestall competition, because of the high fixed costs necessary to establish a new brand.

Although advertising thus has intended effects, both on individuals and competing firms, it also has some less obvious, and in some cases unintended, consequences. These can be loosely categorized as economic or social.

The economic consequences of advertising

There has been controversy for many years over the economic effects of advertising. Galbraith (1958), for example, argues that because advertising creates wants artificially, it does not just change allocations of existing expenditure (which all advertisers would acknowledge as their aim), but actually increases the propensity to consume in an economy. Other critics (e.g., Mishan 1969) have argued that advertising leads to inefficient use of resources, both in terms of the provision of information and in terms of resource allocation. Let us look at these two criticisms in a little more detail.

If providing information to the public is a good thing, then surely it is better for the information to be impartial rather than partial. Advertisers only tell us some of the truth; impartial agencies such as the Consumer's Association try to provide all relevant information and, although this information is necessarily incomplete and sometimes inaccurate, it is, at least, unbiased. As Mishan (1969, p. 117) says: "There does not appear to be much one can say in favour of continuing to use the present methods of advertising rather than directing the same amount of resources into the provision of consumer research organizations."

Mishan's second point concerns the allocation of resources in society. Because firms that advertise must cover both production costs and selling costs, the price of their products must include both of these costs. But the price of the media which carry advertisements is less than their production costs; the difference is covered by their advertising revenue. In effect, this means that the buyers of advertised products are subsidizing the media customers (e.g., people who buy newspapers). This study has a "distributional" and an "allocation" effect. The distributional effect involves a shift of real income from buyers of advertised products to media users. The first group pay more than the real costs of the products they buy; the second group pay less. The allocation effects involves a shift of the resources of society. Because of the distorted prices, more resources are allocated to the media than would otherwise be the case, and fewer are allocated to the products. This can be seen quite neatly with free newspapers. Free newspapers are free to the individual recipients; they are not "free" to society, and the resources used in their production could be employed elsewhere.

Certainly, Galbraith and Mishan are distinguished economists who express their objections to advertising with special pungency. But the belief that advertising increases the prices of goods, and enables a few firms to dominate a market, is widespread. Is it in fact justified? There are excellent published reviews of empirical work bearing on this aspect of the advertising controversy (Albion & Farris 1981; Reekie 1981), so here we will deal with just three questions: Does advertising increase (1) demand for a product class, (2) overall propensity to consume, and (3) the prices of advertised products?

Borden (1942) reports that advertising did increase primary demand for refrigerators, but not for sugar, walnuts, or shoes. More recent studies fit this pattern, with some products showing advertising effects and others not (Albion & Farris, 1981, chapter 4). McGuiness and Cowling (1975), for example, showed that advertising did increase the aggregate demand for cigarette characteristics in the United Kingdom during the 1960s. A general rule is that the product classes for which advertising most clearly increases overall demand are those in the early stages of their "life cycle," where the underlying conditions favor expansion (the U.K. cigarette example is obviously an exception). It looks as if advertising can accelerate the growth of new markets but has little effect on the ultimate size of a market.

The evidence that advertising increases total consumption, and thus the propensity to consume, is rather less clear cut. In fact, it is extremely difficult to disentangle the effects of advertising from those of a number of other factors. Rothschild (cited in Simon 1970) thought it hopeless to try to give a quantitative estimate of the effect of advertising on total consumption, but other economists have made the attempt. For example, Simon (1970, chapter 8) summarizes data collected during newspaper strikes, data on the distribution of advertising expenditures and consumption expenditures, and data on the effects of advertising designed to increase saving. Overall, he found that the evidence suggested no very great effect of advertising, although spending does apparently decrease during newspaper strikes.

Our final question, about the effects of advertising on the prices of advertised products, is perhaps the most controversial (Reekie 1979). There are two opposing schools of thought. One maintains that advertising is a business cost that is more significant than any savings that might be made because of increased production. Furthermore, it creates an oligopoly, where a few firms sell heavily advertised brands, and prices are higher than they would otherwise be under more competitive circumstances. This is the market power view. The alternative ("competitive") view is that advertising lowers prices through economies of scale, stimulates product innovation, and increases competition. A Price Commission report quoted by Reekie (1979, p. 41) expresses this view well:

In the first quarter of 1977, advertising and promotion probably added about 20p to the retail selling price of a litre of gloss paint and 15p for emulsion paint. Even so, the average retail prices of heavily promoted brands differed little from those of other leading brands. Advertising appears to create a level of sales which enables the manufacturer to lower his unit product costs and encourages the retailer to accept lower gross margins.

Reekie (1979, 1981) is certain that advertising generally leads to lower prices. To clinch his argument, he asserts that historical data show that advertised brands do not rise so rapidly in price as other products. There are some dramatic examples to support this view. Toy advertising was not permitted in France until 1975. The limited lifting of the ban that year led to a rapid drop in the price of toys that were allowed to advertise (Steiner, cited by Albion & Farris 1981). Benham (1972), Maurizi (1972), and Cady (1976) all studied situations in which one market area had advertising and another did not. In all three cases (involving gasoline, spectacles, and prescription drugs), prices were lower in the areas that had advertising.

Albion and Farris (1981) point out, however, that all three of these instances involve retail advertising. They describe new economic models that distinguish between the position of the retailer and the manufacturer. Manufacturers are generally in a position of market power (the evidence that Albion and Farris review suggests that high relative advertising expenditure is correlated with high relative factory prices), whereas retailers are in a competitive situation (the evidence suggests that high advertising is correlated with low brand prices at retail). Thus both the critics and the defenders of advertising probably have some truth on their side. It is interesting that public hostility to advertising, where it exists, seems to be directed at precisely those goods for which manufacturers probably do have oligopoly-derived market power, such as washing powder (see the discussion of attitudes to advertising above). In this case at least, the consumer may well have a good intuitive grasp on economic reality.

The social consequences of advertising

Advertisements aim to inform and persuade us about a product or service. But in informing and persuading us about a product, they are also informing and persuading us in other ways, and this can have both commercial and noncommercial side effects. These effects may be of two sorts.

First, specific advertisements may produce specific side effects. Nationwide, a British daily television magazine program, reported an interesting example on January 14, 1982. The Old English Sheepdog Association is apparently very disturbed by the increasing number of abandoned Old English Sheepdogs. They put this down to the use of the dog in the widely disseminated Dulux paint advertisements, which they claim sell the dog as much as the paint. Unfortunately, while Dulux paintwork may well be easy to care for and to keep looking attractive, Old English Sheepdogs certainly are not; when dream does not match reality, the result is abandoned sheepdogs. Of course, it is difficult to assess this claim, but it makes the point that if advertisements work at all, then at least some advertisements will produce unintended consequences.

Second, the fact that society is permeated with advertising may well have general effects. Williamson (1978) has argued that, through advertising, capitalism obscures the real distinctions between people in our society. The real distinctions, from her Marxist perspective, are created by peoples' roles in the process of production, which give rise to class differences. Advertising makes people identify with what they consume rather than with what they produce. This means that members of the working class are made to feel that they can rise in society by buying appropriate products.

According to Williamson (1978), advertising works by providing a structure that is able to transform the language of objects to the language of people, and vice versa. This is seen most clearly when objects in advertisements behave like people (peas talk, sausages ask you to eat them, and so forth), and when people are identified with objects. But, obvious or not, Williamson sees the process of transformation underlying all advertisements. Oxo, for example, may be advertised in such a way that it comes to symbolize motherly love, and diamonds so that they symbolize eternal love. Once this symbolic connection is made, we can treat the sign (Oxo) for what it symbolizes (motherly love); in using Oxo, a mother is loving her children; in giving one's fiancee a diamond ring, one is loving her. This kind of analysis led Williamson to write: "Advertisements are selling us something else besides consumer goods: in providing us with a structure in which we, and these goods are interchangeable, they are selling us ourselves" (Williamson 1978, p. 13). In other words, advertisements equate human meanings with products; in purchasing the products we purchase the meanings and are defined by the product or meaning.

This kind of argument seems to us to attribute far too much power to advertisements, and being based on an intensive personal analysis of selected advertisements, it lacks a sound empirical basis. Such empirical studies as exist, however, do tend to confirm that advertisements are helping to define us.

Consider, for example, the portrayal of men and women in advertisements. In a large number of studies in Britain and America, it has consistently been found that women are presented as conforming to the female stereotype (e.g., Courtney & Whipple 1974; Manstead & McCulloch 1981). Typically, women are shown in dependent roles, as housewives rather than workers, and as uninformed users of domestic products. How then does this stereotyped portrayal of men and women in advertisements influence the learning of stereotyped perceptions and behaviors by children and the maintenance of these things in adults? Unfortunately there is little evidence bearing on this question, probably because of the difficulty of finding a control group which has not been exposed to stereotyped advertising but is otherwise comparable to an experimental group that has.

Jennings, Geis, and Brown (1980) tried to overcome this difficulty by testing a contrast hypothesis, namely that advertisements that break sex-role stereotyping raise women's self-confidence and independence of judgment. Women college students saw either a series of four stereotyped television commercials (replicas of current commercials) or a series of four commercials identical to the first series, except that all the roles were acted by a person of the opposite sex. Women who saw the reversed-role advertisements were more independent (deviated further from false majority judgments) and were more self-confident when making an extemporaneous speech. This led Jennings et al. (1980, p. 209) to conclude: "This research strongly implies that even if women do not buy the advertised products, they buy the implicit image of femininity conveyed by the commercials, whether they know it or not."

A very common suggestion is that advertisements influence society through their effects on children. Growing up in a world permeated by advertisements, especially by advertisements on television, to which children are especially attracted, could well bias a person toward excessive consumption and materialism. This argument, however, is best considered within the context of a more general discussion of the economic socialization of children, so it is deferred until Chapter 14.

Insignificance of advertisements

Advertisements are only part of the media, however. It is hard to believe that they are as important as other aspects. If four reversed-role advertisements can have such an effect, what would a reversed-role television series do (of which there have now been several)? One thing it would almost certainly do is to suggest the commercial use of reversed-role advertising, especially given the need for advertisements to be both novel and fashionable. Indeed, it is possible to argue that advertising does not create stereotypes, it only reflects whatever exists already in society. And while that amplified reflection may well strengthen current tendencies, the very evanescence of advertising trends probably reduces the inertial effect of advertising on social change.

We have suggested that advertisements can produce effects that are intended and consequences that are not. But as Scitovsky (1976) has argued, the effects of advertisements probably pale into insignificance compared to the effects of other factors. He feels that the Puritan ethic, for example, strongly influences our economic behavior and that we favor comfort over pleasure unduly as a result. Regardless of the merit of this argument, it is clear that advertisements are only one factor influencing our behavior and others may be more important. In several countries, a succession of advertising campaigns failed to have much effect on seatbelt-wearing habits, but in several cases, when the wearing of seatbelts was made compulsory, major changes in behavior were produced (Fhaner & Hane 1979; Geller, Casali, & Johnson 1980).

CONCLUSIONS: ADVERTISING AND THE INDIVIDUAL IN THE ECONOMY

Despite the large amount of research carried out into advertising, we are still a long way from understanding how and why it works, and what exactly it does. Particular advertising campaigns can be effective, provided certain guidelines are followed. Advertising can have unfortunate unforeseen consequences, but those probably do not compare with the consequences from other aspects of the media, (such as television violence (e.g., see Andison 1977). Perhaps the British public have got it about right: Most agree that advertising makes people buy things they won't want, and that it puts prices up, but they also accept that advertising helps people choose between products and it can be entertaining (The Advertising Association 1972).

14

GROWING UP IN THE ECONOMY

What is it like to be a child in today's economy? How does adult economic behavior develop out of children's behavior? How do children learn about money, saving, giving, and the functioning of the economy? Until very recently, these questions had been largely ignored by economists and economic psychologists. Economists have generally favored a static form of analysis; this has meant that, in Maital's (1982, p. 24) phrase, "Economic man is an obstetric marvel. From the pages of economic journals he springs to life full blown." But to understand economic behavior fully, we need to address these questions concerning the development of economic behavior; and they are obviously relevant to this part of the book. In the first place, if the economy has any effect on individual behavior, we might expect to see it displayed most strongly in the formation of the economic behavior of children. Second, it is a commonplace of developmental psychology that children construct their own social world, which is, to some extent, independent of the world of grownups. Perhaps there is a "children's economy" within this "children's society," allowing us yet another comparative perspective on the different behaviors engendered by different economies.

In this chapter we draw on the work of market researchers, developmental psychologists, and sociologists, and attempt to point the way toward a developmental economic psychology. In the first section we consider what such a discipline might look like, then move on to review some relevant theoretical perspectives and the growing empirical work in this area.

A POSSIBLE DEVELOPMENTAL ECONOMIC PSYCHOLOGY

With very few exceptions (e.g., Maital 1982) economists have totally ignored children and the role they may play in the economy. This stems from the fact that in microeconomic theory the basic element is not the individual but the household. As Lipsey (1979, p. 69) puts it: "We assume that each household takes consistent decisions as if it were composed of a single individual. Thus we ignore many interesting problems of how the household reaches its decisions . . . [these] are dealt with by other social sciences."

Following this dubious lead, economic psychologists have ignored children, as children, almost completely. For instance, there is no mention of children or child development in Reynaud's (1981) *Economic Psychology* or Katona's (1975) *Psychological Economics*. At the most recent International Colloquium on Economic Psychology, in Tilburg, 1984, there were no papers on children's economic behavior. What is the reason for this neglect? It is probably the result of the handmaiden role that economic psychology has played vis-à-vis economics; there is, after all, little point in carrying out research that is irrelevant to your mistress's needs.

An infant is clearly not *Homo economicus*. Perhaps economics therefore requires an account of the development of rationality. It would be possible to provide such an account based on Piagetian psychology. As we explained in Chapter 1, Piaget (1970) described how an adult's ability to think logically develops out of a child's qualitatively different form of reasoning, which itself derives from behavior such as infant sucking and kicking. Piaget's theory is extremely complicated but we can identify two main propositions. First, thinking grows out of behavior. It involves a set of structures which are continually reconstructed in interaction between the child and the outside world. During the first two years of life, the child does not truly think, but nonetheless behaves intelligently. Thought, then, is considered interiorized action. Second, thinking proceeds from being global and action centered to being differentiated, hierarchically organized, and detached from actions.

The ramifications of this theory are many but here we need mention only three of its most important features. These are a concern with the structural characteristics of behavior and cognition, a consistent emphasis on the interactive nature of development, and commitment to a constructionist epistemology.

Superficially, it may appear that an outstanding feature of Piaget's theory is that it is a stage theory; in much of his work there are descriptions of developments of modes of thinking which can be said to be typical of a particular stage. Four stages are normally identified: the sensorimotor (birth to two years), the preoperational (approximately two to seven years), the concretely operational (roughly seven to eleven years), and the formally operational (eleven onward).

In the sensorimotor stage, infants develop a notion of permanence, understanding that people and objects continue to exist even when they cannot be seen. In the preoperational stage, children rely heavily on their perceptions and tend to see the world from their own perspective. One feature of preoperational thought is that children center on a certain attribute of a situation, often a perceptual attribute, and are unable to integrate two or more factors in arriving at a conclusion. Fox (1978) reports that when preoperational children are asked how they know that things belong to them, they center on visual cues, for example, "because it would say my name." "I look around and I see that it's mine." In the stage of concrete operations, children acquire the capacity to do in their heads what they previously had to do literally. Nonetheless they tend to solve problems by trial and error, rather than by thinking systematically. When they have attained the stage of formal operations, they are able to do just this, to think logically.

Most researchers interested in children's thinking about economic aspects of life have used the notion of stages, and have typically divided children's conceptions of debt, money, exchange, property, and so forth into three or four categories that comprise an ascending sequence (see Chapter 12 for a discussion of children's concept of money). Ward, Wackman, and Wartella (1977, p. 44), for instance, write that "highly organized and integrated structures of cognition characterize the thought processes of the child at distinct, age-related stages of intellectual development." Fox (1978) notes that

The literature . . . reveals age-related, qualitative changes in children's economic notions, which in several instances meet Piaget's criteria for cognitive-developmental stages . . . at each stage children's responses are qualitatively different, the stages are sequential, they are hierarchically integrated and each stage forms a structured whole (p. 480).

But Piaget's concept of stage is secondary, deriving from the notion of structure. The latter is essential in understanding that developmental changes occur as a result of an interaction between external pressure and internal imbalance, and not external pressure alone. The stage is merely a description of an ideal type; the important point is that later, mature forms of thought logically presuppose earlier ones.

Thus Piagetian psychology could be used to chart a personal history for the fully rational Economic Man. The adolescent in the stage of formal operations certainly seems capable of making rational decisions in the way economic theory describes. Unfortunately there are three problems with this approach. First, not everyone attains the stage of formal operations. Only about 25% of American college freshmen can solve the standard Piagetian logical reasoning tasks (McKinnon & Renner 1971). Since these subjects are selected for intelligence, this finding implies that people in general cannot reason formally. Second, Wason (1977) showed that mature intelligence is influenced by content and meaning to a greater extent than the theory of formal operations would allow: "Reasoning is radically affected by content in a systematic way and this is incompatible with the Piagetian view that in formal operational thought content of a problem has at last been subordinated to the form of relations in it" (p.

132). Similar results were reported by Jahoda (1970). Third, there is more to cognitive development than the ability to think logically.

All this suggests that developmental economic psychology should be more than just an account of the development of rationality. It should consider the processes underlying changes in children's economic thinking and the relationship between collective representations of the economic world and individual cognitive development. Research to date has been concentrated in areas of immediate concern, such as the influence of advertising on children and how children affect the purchasing decisions of their parents. What is needed now is a greater commitment to theorizing.

THEORETICAL PERSPECTIVES ON THE DEVELOPMENT OF ECONOMIC BEHAVIOR

Cognitive socialization and its limitations

Piaget's original concern was to describe and explain the way in which the individual represents the physical world, but his approach has been extended to cover social and economic reality. This has given rise to a particular type of approach to "cognitive socialization." Social psychology has always been concerned with the influence of the social environment on the individual's construction of reality. While this often involved examining social class variations in functioning, it was seldom conceived of as a transactional process. The child is seen as being molded by the environment via the rearing practices of the parents who, through reward and punishment, reinforce certain attitudes and behaviors. In more sophisticated models, the parents themselves are seen as reflecting social assumptions about personal control and efficacy (e.g., Bernstein 1971). By contrast, Piaget's theory suggests that "the reproduction of social knowledge involves not only the transmission of meanings by socializing adults, but equally the construction by children themselves of successive stages of meaning out of the interaction between their own social experience and their developing cognitive abilities" (Burris 1981, p. 3).

What Piagetian theory implies, and what researchers such as Burris (1981, 1983), Fox (1978), Jahoda (1979), Hong Kwang and Stacey (1981), and Furth (1978a, 1978b, 1980a) have found, is that the same stages will be found in the child's economic thinking as in other areas. Burris's work provides a good example.

Burris (1981, 1983) focused on children from three age groups: 4–5, 7–8, and 10–12 years. Burris examined their understanding of basic economic concepts, such as the commodity, value, exchange, work, class, and property. We have seen in previous chapters how the commodity is one of the fundamental economic concepts; it is the basic unit that is bought, sold, or exchanged in the marketplace. To investigate the child's understanding of commodity each child was asked to name things that might be bought and sold and then to name things that could not be bought and sold. A list of items was then presented, and the child was asked to classify each into these two categories.

The answers to these and follow-up questions provide some insights into children's economic thinking. Young children have a restricted notion of what constitutes a commodity; they also include some noncommodities on the list (e.g., babies). For them, a commodity is defined in terms of physical characteristics. A four-year-old will maintain that a cow cannot be bought and sold "because it is too big to put in the car" or a tree "because it stays in the ground." Buying and selling are thus understood as physical acts whereby objects are physically possessed or released. By contrast, older children attend to social norms and other aspects of the object rather than its physical attributes. You cannot buy a baby because "they wouldn't let you . . . it's against the law," explains a seven-year-old.

This growth in understanding mirrors that originally reported by Piaget concerning the child's representation of the physical world, where young children fail to differentiate between the physical and the social. A similar developmental trend was found in children's concept of economic value. This was explored by asking a range of questions about the prices of objects and by presenting children with pairs of objects and asking them to indicate which would cost more and why.

Among the youngest age group the dominant response is to explain the value of an object by referring to its physical size. Thus a diamond does not cost much "because it is so tiny" and a book costs more than a wristwatch because "it's bigger." Value is then a material attribute of the object itself; it is intrinsic. Seven- and eight-year-old children mainly represent value from the consumption point of view. Value is explained by the object's usefulness or function. A wristwatch costs more than a book because "you can tell time on a watch, but a book you can just read." A range of criteria are used to order into a hierarchy the different functions that objects serve; for some children, things have the most value because they are the most fun; for others because they are the most durable. The oldest children shift to understanding value from the point of view of production. Value is put into the object during production, and its magnitude depends on the type or cost of the inputs. A wristwatch is more expensive than a book "because it has glass and motors in it, and it comes with a band and that's leather, and it usually has silver or gold framing and . . . it's just got more." In a sense, then, children of this age are implicit believers of the labor theory of value espoused by Smith (1776/1908) and Marx (1867/1974) (cf. Chapter 18).

These findings, together with similar ones for other economic concepts, such as money (see Chapter 12), led Burris to conclude that there were general trends in the development of children's economic thinking. These include a shift from confusing social and natural phenomena to differentiating them, from seeing economic norms and institutions as objectively real to seeing them as conventional, and from conceiving the economic world in individualistic terms to apprehending the complex system of relationships involved in economic life. These trends reflect general cognitive development and are very similar to those reported by other investigators concerned with these "basic concepts."

Burris's results are typical; indeed, what is most striking about them is how consistent they are with those of other researchers. For instance, Waines (1983) obtained results with Egyptian children essentially the same as Danziger's (1958) with Australian children. Jahoda and Woerdenbagch (1982) showed that the development of ideas about the bank is the same in Scottish and Dutch children, and Hong Kwang and Stacey (1981) found that the development of economic concepts among Malaysian Chinese children was very similar to that reported for Western children.

Although comforting, this consistency is no cause for celebration. It is probably the result of investigators adopting similar strategies and asking similar questions (Webley 1983), although it is only fair to point out that Stacey (1983) disagrees with this interpretation of the literature. We would suggest that by looking at economic cognition as another instance of a general process of cognitive development, we may be paying inadequate attention to the variations in thought that are brought about by content. Since we learn about some aspects of the economic world primarily by engaging in the behavior and not, as with the physical world, directly and didactically via the mediation of others, the nature of the construction may be different. This is suggested by Signel's (1966) comparison of the development of concepts of people and of nations, which showed that experiential and didactic learning seem to produce different structures.

A useful theory in this context may be Harris and Heelas's (1979) "local constructivism." Borrowing a metaphor from Waddington (1957), they "envisage the child as working simultaneously in a number of relatively autonomous cognitive valleys." His progress in any one of these intellectual valleys has a constructive stage-like character, but there is little communication between valleys" (1979, p. 219). In some valleys (domains) there will be no constructive development, perhaps because innate mechanisms constrain the mode of information processing; the infant's perception of depth and motion, for example, may be fundamentally identical to an adult's. In those domains in which constructive development does occur, Harris and Heelas maintain that collective representations will develop chronologically in the same sequence as that present in children (again, because mature forms of thought logically presuppose less mature forms). Thus the stages found in the child's understanding of money will be the same as stages found historically in Western culture's collective representation of money. In cultures in which the money is "primitive," children will not move through the stages as Western children do, not because they are incapable of formal thinking, but because the collective representation in that domain is unsophisticated (presumably because there are no functional reasons for its elaboration).

Harris and Heelas's theory provides one possible answer to those who have questioned Piaget's concentration on the structure of thought and who have emphasized the importance of content and context. But given that researchers interested in children's economic thinking report so many similarities between this and other aspects of the child's thought, do we need a theory about how variations in the structure of thought relate to its content? We think the answer to this question is "yes." Researchers have found these similarities because that is what they were looking for. In the more advanced field of social cognitive development, it took a decade before attention switched from demonstrating that social cognition was equivalent to impersonal cognition to trying to find content areas where such parallelism did not hold. This latter approach appears to have been more fruitful, in terms of the theories and empirical studies it has spawned (see, e.g., Light 1979).

This suggests that, having established broad parallels between economic cognition and general cognitive development, we should now be posing the question, "What is nonetheless distinct about economic concepts?" Two possible lines of investigation suggest themselves immediately. First, economic factors in many cases form the basis for power, both in the wider society and in interpersonal relationships. Thus in coming to understand notions of property, ownership, work, exchange, and so on, the child is confronting the power base of society. The concepts the child develops are therefore of great concern to the powerful (e.g., in that a collectivist notion of property may be threatening). We can see that this aspect has been neglected if we look again at children's understanding of money. As was pointed out in Chapter 12, "the third stage on which all authors agree, involves the understanding of all types of exchanges with money, and therefore the acquisition of the concepts of profit, investment, and so on." If children at this stage were asked why their parents give them pocket money or why husbands give wives housekeeping money or even why money is unacceptable as a gift, they might not demonstrate such total understanding or, if they did, might extend the researcher's ideas about what money is.

The second aspect that seems to make economic concepts special is that they can form a way of apprehending the social world. All aspects of life can be conceived of in exchange terms, for instance (Becker 1976). It is no exaggeration to say that a person's economic concepts can constitute an ideology. Under these circumstances, it would not be surprising to find that the acquisition of economic concepts followed different laws from the acquisition of concepts about the physical world.

The current approach to cognitive socialization also has some more obvious limitations. It is static; it attempts to describe how children come to understand the current collective representation of an economic concept. But a Piagetian framework alerts us to the transient nature of such collective representations and the need to locate the factors that produce change. Individuals do not just come to understand a concept like "ownership," "money," or "debt;" through understanding, they change it. For example, a child must construct all the different meanings of money from dealings with others, and it is through the tensions engendered by these overlapping constructions of money that different meanings and use of money will emerge in the future (Webley 1983). As Furth (1980b, p. 8) put it: "Since knowing means constructing, and constructing constantly creates new perspectives, these perspectives lead to a dialectical conflict with previous views and thereby instigate a new compensating synthesis. In simpler terms . . . the processes of any knowing . . . are the occasions for further development."

Second, the current literature in cognitive socialization is not concerned with individual differences, although group differences (e.g., social class effects, the role of political affiliation) have been investigated. Individual differences may be important; it is through the creative leaps of individuals that collective representations are modified. Finally, apart from social class distinctions, cognitive socialization has not attempted to produce a characterization of the environment which might explain variations in the development of economic thought.

Alternative theoretical perspectives I: distancing

One common feature of cognitive developmental approaches to child life is that they do not attempt to describe or analyze significant aspects of the child's environment. This may be, as Kuhn (1974) points out, because it is an extremely difficult task. But it is more probably due to the tendency of cognitive developmental theory to be biologically deterministic and individualistic. One attempt to extend Piaget's theory to deal with features of the environment may be useful in understanding the development of economic thought. This is Sigel and Cocking's (1977) distancing approach.

Sigel and Cocking's model is based on three main constructs: distancing behaviors, discrepancy, and dialectics. Distancing behaviors are those that create psychological, temporal, or spatial distance between self and object. "The behaviors or events in question require the child to attend to or react in terms of the non-present (future or past) or the non-palpable" (p. 209). Distancing behaviors can come from social and physical events, but all share the characteristic of inducing a cognitive separation between the individual and the immediate present. For instance, saving would be distancing and induce discrepancy and thus cognitive development. Certain forms of spending would be less distancing. This may have some bearing on Marshall and Magruder's (1960) finding that children who saved had more knowledge about money. The type of distancing behavior that is used is assumed to be influenced by sociocultural differences, personal characteristics and situational demands. Thus social class differences in saving [see Ward, Wackman, & Wartella (1977) in America, and Hussein (1981), in Britain, both of whom report that middle-class children save more than do working-class children] may be one factor that helps produce the class differences in children's economic thinking that Burris (1981) describes. Burris reports that at each age level, working-class children are more likely to explain exchange relationships and property rights in terms of restraint and coercion than are middle-class children. For example, asked why we give money when we buy things from a shop, they will explain this in terms of moral or legal imperatives: "If you didn't, you'd get put in jail." This is an example of what is called heteronomous reasoning – representing social order as the result of external constraint, rather than the result of mutual agreement.

One important factor that can be incorporated within this distancing framework is how economic information is communicated. Goody (1977) advances the view that some of the differences in intellectual processes found in cross-cultural research can be related to differences in the form of communication, particularly the use of writing. He argues that, historically, writing encouraged the kind of scrutiny that made possible the increase in the scope of critical activity and therefore rationality, logic, and skepticism. His formulation is easy to integrate with both Piaget's theory and the idea of distancing behaviors. "When an utterance is put into writing it can be inspected in much greater detail . . . out of context as well as in its setting. Speech is no longer tied to an 'occasion', it becomes timeless. Nor is it attached to a person; on paper it becomes more abstract, more depersonalized" (Goody 1977, p. 234).

In other words, literacy encourages a person to attend to the nonpresent; therefore it is a form of distancing. Since it externalizes the thought process, the use of literacy enables the individual to transcend limitations of personal experience and of cognitive storage capacity. Literacy may indeed be important in conveying economic information, but surely the social institution of money is more crucial in this regard. Money encourages a person to attend to the nonpresent; it also transcends the limitations described above. By rendering economic information timeless and impersonal, money may shift the baseline from which development in our economic thinking spirals.

Alternative theoretical perspectives II: Holmes's theory

Distancing is a fairly simple way of characterizing a child's environment. A more complicated description is that of Holmes (1976) who has attempted to produce a theory of the relationship between the individual and society that can deal with the problem of values.

Holmes's theory is built on the twin concepts of constructivism (from genetic epistemology) and self-centered manifest desires (from psychoanalysis). With respect to the former concept, during development, equilibration enables a child to see different experiences as somehow the same thing. So the infant who achieves an early stage in object constancy is able to see all the distinct images of a cup that have impinged on the eyes as a cup. Similarly, in attaining the ability to conserve, a child comes to understand that despite transformations, certain properties of objects remain unchanged. Consider a discussion that ends in agreement. This can be seen as a thing – the consensus – that subsumes the images that different individuals have contributed. In social life we reach equilibrium with those like ourselves and agree on what constitutes reality. As Holmes (1976, p. 180) states, "what is a group . . . but an agreement to accept the same self-created fictions." Equilibration involves disciplined interaction with the world (whether physical or social) but nonetheless the attainments of equilibrium (objects, things, "facts") need not be veridical. Holmes pertinently comments that "agreement between observers cannot by itself take the social sciences out of mythology." The consequence of the assumption of constructivism is to identify one source of instability in our social worlds (disagreement) and point to the relevance of the distribution of power within groups as a factor in defining social reality.

According to Holmes, society is made up of two strands, one economics, the other values. The economic strand is simply an extension of the principle of a person operating according to self-centered manifest desires in order to maximize rewards and minimize cost. By contrast, values are assumptions people hold of what ought to be. Thus "rights" are demands that values allow us to make. Values and economics are interwoven in society; even the marketplace is not an open arena for economic forces, as can be seen in the concepts of a fair wage, a minimum wage, and differentials. The same interweaving is found in interpersonal relationships. The employee obeys the boss because the employer has economic power but also because the employer is the boss.

The assumptions that are values are asserted on the basis of authority, authority being values that those more powerful than ourselves believe in. The authority could be God, the Common Good, or even the Gold Standard. The maintenance of these values depends on the continued existence of a powerful elite who believe in authority. If the elite assert themselves simply by virtue of being an elite, they will be revered only as long as they are present, and the values will wither away. Societies differ in the degree to which they are based on notions of value or notions of economics. A society based on the concept of value would be conservative and orthodox and behavior valued because it conformed to traditional norms. By contrast, a society of economics would be dynamic and radical because its members would continually be asserting their own interests and desires.

The point of this analysis is that by characterizing the nature of society in this way, it is possible to see how a society might affect individuals and their development. In a society of value, it is best for the individual if he or she obeys and values the old, established rules. To be well adapted and in equilibrium with such a society, a person would have to become an adept rule follower, but rather inflexible. In a society of economics (one more like our own), cognitive flexibility and originality are encouraged.

Holmes's speculations are not based on empirical data; they indicate the importance of the concepts of power and values. They point to the need to consider the nature of the social and economic reality within which the individual develops.

The theories reviewed in this section may all be wrong, but without a theoretical framework the research on growing up in the modern economy becomes no more than a catalog of unrelated findings, and we will only accumulate bits of knowledge rather than make progress in understanding. It is to this catalog that we now turn, hoping to understand some of its contents in terms of the theories we have described.

STUDIES OF CHILDREN IN THE ECONOMY

Studies of children in the economy fall into three rather disparate categories. There are investigations into children's concepts of economic reality, mainly carried out by developmental psychologists; into children's economic behavior, carried out by marketing academics, sociologists, and psychologists; and into children and advertising (again carried out by a range of social scientists). This variety of approaches offers a variety of perspectives on the economic life of children.

Children's concepts of economic reality

Until fairly recently there was little research in this area. Furth (1978b) believes that this partly reflects the split between academia and the real world of business, but it may also be because the idea that children need to be socialized to accept and understand the existing economic order is rather alien (Cummings & Taebel 1978). Whatever the reason, the past five years have seen a marked increase in interest in this problem and there are now a large number of studies describing children's concepts of a range of economic phenomena, from the bank to unemployment. (For a recent review, see Stacey 1982, with further comments by Webley 1983 and by Stacey 1983.)

Much of the research has been Piagetian and essentially descriptive. We read how children's concepts change with age, progressing from one stage to another. More enterprising researchers have looked at the processes that bring about changes in (e.g., Ng 1983) and influences on children's economic thinking (e.g., Jahoda 1983; Jundin 1983), as well as distinctive economic concepts such as social inequality (Connell 1977; Cummings & Taebel 1978; Siegal 1981; Leahy 1981, 1983a; Emler & Dickinson, 1985).

We have already discussed two examples of descriptive Piagetian research (Burris 1981, and the work described in Chapter 12), so here we will only briefly describe two further typical studies. Berti and Bombi (1979) interviewed children aged 3–8 about two topics: how people obtain money and the nature of work. The children's answers fell neatly into categories that formed an ascending sequence. For example, at level two (most 4-year-olds), children did not see work as the origin of money whereas at level four (some 4-year-olds, some 5-year-olds), parents were thought to obtain money by working but other people were not rewarded for working. The idea of payment for work seemed to emerge from a hinterland of spontaneous and erroneous beliefs about the origin of money.

Berti, Bombi, and Lis (1982) also investigated children's conceptions about means of production (factories, farms, and transport) and their owners. Again they identified a series of stages that children pass through in understanding these concepts. At level 1, children identify the owner as the person found in spatial contact with the means of production (e.g., the passenger is seen as owning the bus). At level 2, the owner is the one who exercises direct control, for example, the bus driver, factory worker, or farm laborer. Similar progressions in thinking are achieved up to level 5, at which point adult understanding is reached.

Nearly all these Piagetian studies have looked at children under the age of 12 and have asked about concrete economic concepts such as money and work. More ambiguous and abstract concepts, like wealth and poverty, are likely to develop in adolescence. Studies that have investigated economic thinking in teenagers (e.g., Furnham 1982), however, have generally not been developmental studies. Two exceptions to this rule suggest that age is still a potent factor in adolescence.

Despierre and Sorel (1979) studied adolescents' ideas about unemployment by interviewing 51 French children of two age groups (11–12 years and 15–16 years) and of two social classes. The subjects were presented with five photographs evocative of various degrees of unemployment and their interpretations were collected through semistructured interviews. Most 11-year-olds held an imagery level concept of unemployment, attributing it to the moral or physical characteristics of the worker, whereas the older group defined unemployment in more global terms. The adolescent group could distinguish among holidays, retirement, and unemployment, whereas many of the younger children confused these concepts. The children's ideas about unemployment differed by age but not social class. The 11-year-olds said things like: "They made a blunder at work"; "They don't want to work because it tires them." When economic reasons were given, they were very succinct: "There is no work"; "Factories aren't working." The older children were not so certain. Laziness, a frequent theme, appears less of a cause and more of an effect for this age group.

A similar study by Webley and Wrigley (1983) confirms this picture. Forty British children from the same two age groups were asked to define unemployment, to indicate if and how unemployed people differed from those with a job, and asked if they would like to be unemployed. The results showed that, with age, understanding of unemployment became more abstract and global. Compared with the younger children, adolescents offered more societal and fatalistic explanations for unemployment and saw the unemployed as fundamentally similar to the employed. They regarded the principal undesirable effects of unemployment as social-psychological rather than as economic, identifying the lack of time structure as its worst feature.

Descriptions of how children's economic concepts change with age may be interesting, but age subsumes a number of factors. What processes are actually involved in initiating changes in economic thinking? Piagetian psychologists place most weight on *equilibration* (Furth 1978a; Jahoda 1984). Equilibration is the working out of a balance between the world children observe and their understanding of it. This understanding depends partly on past experience and partly on an adaptive response to a new event. Such a response could be playful, a denial, or a search for logical coherence. If the latter, children pay more attention to what actually occurs and become more conscious of the theories that guide their understanding. Sometimes one can almost see equilibration at work. As Furth (1980, p. 91) states:

They express discontent about their own opinions and correct themselves or hesitate in an otherwise fluent conversation; they expressly volunteer their gap in understanding and subsequently get excited as they discover a new insight.

The only area of children's economic thinking in which equilibration has been investigated is in children's ideas about banks (Jahoda 1981, 1984; Ng 1983). These develop in a fairly coherent way. Initially, children become aware that banks pay interest on deposits; that they also charge interest on loans is a more difficult concept to grasp. Bank loans are seen in the same light as borrowing from friends. When children first realize that interest is payable on both deposits and loans they believe that interest on deposits is higher. Later they are seen as equal and still later it is realized that loan interest is higher than deposit interest. At first, they do not explain this in terms of profit, but later they do attain a more complete understanding.

Jahoda (1981) induced cognitive conflict (imbalance) by asking children to explain how banks managed to pay their employees. For a child who believed that loan interest was equal to deposit interest, being reminded that banks had to obtain income would pose a potential conflict with their initial views. This induced conflict generally had a marked effect on children's understanding, as in this child (Jahoda 1981, p. 69):

"How does the bank get its money?" [hesitation] "From other people's money." "What happens when the other person wants his money . . . ?"
"Perhaps they take it from someone else." [frowns and shrugs, clearly not happy with own reply]
"Paying back to bank?"
"You would have to pay back the same because . . . if you had to pay the bank more the bank would be gaining money you did not borrow."
"How does the bank get its money?" [considers for a while] "If we gave back more than we owed them, they could pay people who work there with the extra money!" [pleased]

Ng (1983) followed this up in a more systematic way. He created cognitive contrasts in Hong Kong children by posing parallel questions about saving and borrowing and induced conflict in a way similar to Jahoda's approach (1981). Cognitive conflict significantly enhanced understanding of banks whereas contrasts did not.

One interesting finding of Ng's (1983) study is that the development of ideas about the bank in Hong Kong children is comparable to that found in Scottish children. This is a fairly common result. Cross-cultural studies suggest that the stages in economic thinking that have been identified do apply in a range of cultures. Interestingly, it appears that children in Malaysia (Hong Kwang & Stacey 1981), Zimbabwe (Jahoda 1983), and Egypt (Waines 1983) are all more advanced than their Western counterparts, primarily because they have had greater direct experience with work, buying, and selling.

Children's notions of economic reality clearly change with age and there are some differences associated with social class and amount of direct experience. Jundin (1983) has looked at two further factors: the influence of social interaction and the media. She studied 230 Swedish children and found that those children who watched television the most and read more newspapers had the most extensive economic knowledge. The effect of social interaction was not so clear cut.

We suggested earlier that investigations of children's understanding of distinctively economic concepts were likely to be particularly valuable. A number of such studies have looked at aspects of socioeconomic inequality. Siegal (1981), for example, examined children's perceptions of adult economic needs. Children in four age groups from six to thirteen years were asked to indicate how much money men in four different occupational roles (doctor, shopkeeper, bus driver, and waiter) needed to take care of their families, and how much they actually earned. Then they were asked about whether the inequalities were fair. The youngest children generally did not think that adults had unmet needs, which is consistent with a belief in the omnipotence of the adult world. Older children recognized that unmet needs exist and were divided on the issue of whether inequality was fair. Twelve-year-olds who claimed that inequality was fair gave justifications like, "The doctor has more important jobs and abilities" and, "It is the waiter's own fault . . . that is what he chose to do," whereas those who claimed that inequality was unfair pointed out that "Everyone is good at their own job" or, "It's unfair but happens because the waiter and shopkeeper have hard jobs." This division of opinion cannot be explained in cognitive developmental terms and it does not appear to be related to parent's occupational status. Siegel suggests that perhaps those children for whom work efforts are rewarded will see inequality as fair, whereas those for whom the relationship between effort and reward is loose will see it as unfair. With no evidence, however, this is an open question.

Connell (1977) also looked at children's concepts of economic inequality by asking a sample of 119 Australian children whether they thought the difference between the wealthy and the poor was right. Young children saw the inequalities as unfair whereas teenagers generally saw them as justified and therefore fair. The normal justification was that reward should be proportional to effort, the implication being that it is and the existing economic system is fair. Connell also found no consistent class differences in these children's reactions to inequality.

Using a rather different method, Leahy (1981, 1983a, 1983b) investigated conceptions of economic inequality, by asking a large sample of American children to describe rich people and poor people and say how they were the same or different. He found that with age there is an increasing tendency to conceive of rich and poor people as not only differing in their observable characteristics, but also as being different kinds of people. This is similar to a developmental trend found in person perception; for example, Livesley and Bromley (1973) found that young children describe others in terms of observable characteristics whereas older children describe others in psychological terms. Adolescents used more societal conceptions, such as life chances, power, and prestige, in describing both rich and poor people.

What is particularly interesting about all three of these studies, however, is that they provide evidence relevant to two models of socialization. Sociological *functionalist* models (e.g., Parsons 1960) stress that socialization produces considerable uniformity among classes as to the nature of stratification in their society. This serves the function of making social institutions stable by providing a justification for the unequal distribution of resources. By contrast, a dialectical model of socialization would predict that children from the middle and working classes would have different concepts. A child must construct the meaning of being rich and poor from his dealings with the social environment. Since the latter differs between the social classes, children should not develop identical concepts. All these studies show that they do. Leahy reports that there were no class differences in mentions of class consciousness, and class consciousness was used in describing the rich more than in describing the poor. A less detached way of describing functionalist models is to claim that economic socialization is primarily concerned with legitimating corporate capitalism and existing inequality. Cummings and Taebel (1978) make this claim and back it up with data from a survey of 370 young Americans. This shows a progressive development of beliefs, values, and attitudes appropriate to American capitalism, for example, poverty being blamed on the poor themselves. However, their study is flawed in a number of ways; for example, they mention the existence of alternative ideas without analyzing them in any way.

Recent British research provides a rather different perspective on these models of socialization. Emler and Dickinson (1985) showed that children from different social classes hold different beliefs about the scale of economic inequality. Middle-class children believe inequalities in income are greater than do working-class children and they appear more committed to the justice of these inequalities. The effects of social class in their study were frequently greater than the effects of age. Dickinson's (1983) study of Scottish adolescents confirms this picture. Those adolescents whose fathers had manual jobs were significantly more likely than nonmanual respondents to consider income inequalities unfair. In line with functionalist models, Emler and Dickinson (1985) propose, that there is one dominant representation of economic inequality in our society but assert that it is unequally distributed. Children will assimilate those representations that are most important in their community; for the middle class, representations of inequality are more detailed and salient, whereas the same representations are less significant in working-class life.

The studies reviewed in this section have shown how children's verbal reports, which at the youngest ages fall strangely on adult ears, gradually come to conform to the everyday understanding of the economy. Clearly a process of socialization is going on. However, the data cannot tell us whether that would best be described in terms of an extended Piagetian theory, a distancing model, or a psychoanalytic constructivism like that of Holmes. Nor can they tell us whether the developmental process is one in which children increasingly come to be able to describe the economy in which they live or increasingly come to live in the same economy as that of adults. But it is reasonably clear how we could now proceed to investigate these questions, which we regard as more fundamental than those that have been posed so far.

THE ECONOMIC BEHAVIOR OF CHILDREN

The previous section was concerned with how children describe economic affairs. But we have repeatedly seen that actually behavior often deviates sharply from verbal descriptions of it. In this section, therefore, we consider the major economic behaviors of individuals, as we did in Part II, and ask what is known about children's participation in work, buying, saving, gambling, and giving. There is comparatively little research in this area, presumably because children are assumed to be economically unimportant. As we discuss below, however, this assumption cannot really be justified.

Work

Children, students, the retired, and the unemployed lie largely outside the network of social, financial, and motivational relationships that work establishes (see Chapter 6). Of course, they are not completely excluded. Members of all these groups may have part-time work, which can be important both economically and psychologically. Greenberger, Steinberg, and Vaux (1981), for instance, report that in the United States close to half of all 16-year-old students are employed during the school year. Nonetheless, legal restrictions on children's employment (in the United Kingdom children under 13 can only be employed in special circumstances and 13- to 15-year-olds for only two hours on schooldays), and conventions about what jobs are suitable, do restrict their contact with the world of work. Although children may not be part of this world, they are prepared for it (or for the lack of it) in a number of ways.

For instance, many studies have indicated that *occupational foreclosure*, that is, restricting one's range of occupational aspiration, begins when children are quite young. Clark (1967) found that two-thirds of 10- to 13-year-old girls wanted to be either teachers or nurses and similar occupational preferences are commonly found in preschool children. These preferences reflect widely held stereotypes about which jobs are appropriate for which sex and may be encouraged within the home (Thrall 1978; White & Brinkerhoff 1981a, 1981b) and outside it, for example by media portrayal of work. Since women in advertisements are generally portrayed as conforming to the female stereotype (see Chapter 13), O'Bryant and Corder-Bolz (1978) reasoned that this may be an important factor in children's learning of sex-appropriate work roles. They examined the effect of women featured in advertisements as having traditional roles (telephonist, model) or reversed roles (welder, pharmacist) on 7-year-old children's occupational knowledge, stereotypes, and preferences. Over a fortnight, the children viewed nine half-hour cartoons interspersed with commercials. One group saw genuine ads plus some artificial traditional role ads, while the other group received genuine ads plus artificial ads portraying reversed roles. The experience of reversed role ads had no effect on the stereotypes held, but it did alter girls' preferences: They expressed greater liking for nontraditional jobs after seeing those advertisements. This suggests that occupational foreclosure may be relatively easy to modify; socialization for work within the family may be more important, however, and this is less easy to change.

Thrall (1978) reports that some work within the home is stereotyped as "children's work" (e.g., setting the table, clearing the table, shoveling snow), and that parents indicate that sex of the child is a very important criterion in choosing other work for him or her. Household chores are seen as a good way of teaching sex-appropriate behavior. The best single predictor for the pattern of division of labor in any family is not social class, area of residence, or similar variables, but rather the pattern in the adults' own families. In other words, there is considerable continuity across generations. White and Brinkerhoff (1981a) and Goldstein and Oldham (1979) report a similar sex differentiation in children's chores. Boys tend to do outdoor work, while girls do housework and work in the kitchen; older girls also work for more hours than boys. Paid jobs outside the home are even more sex segregated than jobs at home: boys mow lawns and shovel pavements; girls babysit. White and Brinkerhoff (1981a) conclude, like Thrall, that sex typing in children's work is a ubiquitous feature of family life and that parental values, social class, and so on have a minimal influence on it. This is not encouraging for those who desire change. Neither are the results of a large-scale study of Goldstein and Oldham (1979). These workers interviewed 905 children aged 6 to 13 years about a variety of aspects of work and found age to be the most important independant variable. Social class had very small effects and then only among older children.

Although the family may be important in work socialization it is not the only factor. The ethos and organization of the schools they attend has been shown to have a striking and persistent effect on people (for a brief review see Geber and Webley 1980). West and Newton's (1984) longitudinal study of British school-leavers illustrates this nicely. Adolescents who attended a streamed school (Woodbank) had more negative attitudes toward their teachers and the school than did those who attended a school that used predominantly mixed ability teaching (Brookvale). These attitudes seemed to carry over to work; the ex-Woodbank pupils secured jobs of a lower status than they had hoped and found their jobs less interesting. They also found their co-workers less easy to get along with and were less favorable to their supervisors. As West and Newton admit there is no single or simple explanation for their results, but the similarity of the school's catchment areas and the jobs their ex-pupils attained suggests that some aspect of the schools themselves is responsible. At Woodbank, academic values and the rewards of hard work were stressed; this may have raised expectations, which when unmet, may have led to dissatisfaction. The effect of the "official" school culture is only half the story, however. In answering the question, "How do working-class children get working-class jobs?" Willis (1977) throws some light on the other half. The answer, derived from interviews and participant observation, is that what prepared them for the inferior rewards and increasing intrinsic meaninglessness of manual work was the working-class counterschool culture. Its most obvious dimension is opposition to authority:

The lads' specialize in a caged resentment which always stops just short of out-right confrontation. Settled in a class . . . there is a continuous scraping of chairs, a bad-tempered 'tut-tutting' at the simplest request, and a continuous fidget-ing . . . There is an aimless air of insubordination ready with spurious justification and impossible to nail down. (Willis 1977, p. 12)

The "ear'oles," on the other hand, conform to the school and this makes them a target for the "lads." Crucially the "lads" feel superior to the "ear'oles." As one "lad" said:

What will they remember of their school life? What will they have to look back on? Sitting in a classroom, sweating their bollocks off, you know, while we've been . . . I mean look at the things we can look back on, fightin the Pakis . . . some of the things we've done on teachers. It'll be a laff when we look back on it.

"Having a laff" is one of the most important parts of the lads' life; it is how time wrested from authority is used.

The meaning of work, as shaped by the counterculture, is carried over to "real" work. The school builds up a resistance to mental work; it demands too much and encroaches on the lads' private areas. So they incline toward manual work. Satisfaction is not expected, and every job is the same – just a way of earning money. For the "ear'oles," though, work can become a passion and is used as a means of enhancement and self-expression. This has some implications in an era of high youth unemployment. "Lads" who expect little and who emphasize the satisfaction from membership of an informal group will "adapt" better than "ear'oles," who may become bit-terly disillusioned.

Buying

One of the ways in which children participate in the economy directly is by spending money and by influencing their parents' spending. In certain areas children's direct purchases are quite substantial. During 1984, for example, children aged 5–16 in Britain received approximately 540 million pounds in pocket money. Although average pocket money per week is generous, it fell by 14% from 1983 to 1984 presumably because of the deepening recession. Five- to 7-year-olds receive 42p, 8- to 10-year-olds 73p, and 11- to 13-year-olds 113p (Walls 1984). With money from gifts and odd jobs, the total spending power of British children is a thousand million pounds per annum. Most of this is spent on sweets, chocolates, and ice cream, with comics and magazines the next most important category (Tysoe 1983). This concentration on confectionary was also found in a small-scale study by Hussein (1981) and by Ward, Wackman, and Wartella (1977).

Little is known about children's buying, however, apart from the amount of money involved. Guest (1955) interviewed a group of children 12 years after he had first interviewed them and found a strong degree of "brand loyalty" in sixteen different product categories; about one-third of his respondents still preferred the earlier named brands. But only 20% of the original children were located, so this is inconclusive. Moschis and Moore (1979) found that brand names and reduced prices were the two most important factors influencing adolescents' buying decisions. Brand preference was related to media exposure, especially newspapers, even though that medium was lacking in credibility. Peer influence, rather surprisingly, was not all that important.

More research has been carried out on children's influence on household purchases. An NOP poll in 1967 revealed that children were important in suggesting buying of a limited range of products – breakfast cereals, ice cream, cookies, and canned baked beans – although only groceries were included in the questionnaire. Berey and Pollay (1968) examined the nature of these influence attempts. They looked at how 8- to 11-year-old children influenced breakfast cereal purchases, reasoning that the more child centered the mother, the more likely she would be to purchase the child's favorite brand. They actually found the reverse. Mothers with a high degree of concern for their children bought "good" cereals (puffed wheat, perhaps) rather than those their children preferred (Sugar Puffs). Berey and Pollay comment that "a lot of advertising would be well directed at the mother, even if the mother is not a consumer of the product." The sample in this study was rather limited, and child centeredness is not easy to measure, and so this research needs careful interpretation.

Ward and Wackman (1972) and Ward, Wackman, and Wartella (1977) report studies based on much larger samples. Ward and Wackman asked mothers to indicate the frequency of their child's attempts to influence purchases in a range of categories (e.g., relevant foods, less relevant foods, durables for child's use, toiletries). The mothers reported that children often did attempt to influence food purchases but that these attempts decreased with age, as did influence attempts generally. Parents' yielding to a child's request increased with the child's age, presumably because parents trust older children's judgment more. However, using a much bigger sample (N = 615), Ward and co-workers did not confirm that influence attempts changed with age. The only age-related effect was that requests for child-relevant products increased with age. Interestingly, asking for particular brands increases as children grow older but brand preferences decrease with age. This is because older children are more likely to ask for several different brands of a product (see Chapter 7 for a discussion of brand loyalty).

Given that children's direct and indirect buying behavior is quite substantial, it is worth posing a variant of the central question raised in our discussion of buying: "Why do children buy (or influence others to buy) what they do?" We suggested in Chapter 7 that for people in general the answer was that goods contain characteristics that correspond to human needs. Children may thus buy goods different from those chosen by adults either because they have different needs or because their cognitive processing capacities are limited or different from those of adults.

The Gene Reilly Group (1973) presents some evidence on the first possibility. An American national sample of 6- to 12-year-olds was asked a series of paired comparison questions about product characteristics: "Would you like a product more if it was nutritious or tasted good?" Good taste was the most highly valued characteristic for all children but the relative importance of other characteristics varied with age. For 6-year-old children, a "prize" in the box was second in importance; for 12-year-olds, sweetness is the second most important factor. Older children show no greater emphasis on the nutritional value of food than younger children. Since prizes in boxes are probably aimed at the younger age group this implies no great age-related change in needs.

Ward, Wartella, and Wackman (1977) present some evidence on the second possibility that children and adults differ in their cognitive capabilities. Kindergarten children use fewer dimensions to compare brands, and these dimensions are generally perceptual attributes. Older children, on the other hand, use perceptual and functional attributes (e.g., "this toothpaste stops you from getting cavities") about equally often. Capon and Kuhn's (1980) study confirms this picture. They investigated children's preferences for notebooks which varied on four dimensions. The youngest children (kindergarten) made fairly random judgments, whereas older children focused consistently on one dimension. Taking more than one dimension into account began in adolescence.

Saving

Saving involves planning and deferred gratification. In light of laboratory studies by Mischel and collaborators (e.g., Mischel & Metzner 1962), we would expect saving to increase with age. We might also, on the basis of research into related areas, expect marked class differences in this behavior, with middle-class children saving more (Reid 1981). The first of these expectations is confirmed by the few studies that have been carried out; the second is not.

In as investigation of American rural white children, Dickins and Ferguson (1957) found that 60% of the 7-year-olds and 76% of the 11-year-olds claimed to have tried to save money (44% of the younger children and 62% of the older children successfully saved). Three-fifths in each age group said they were saving for a special purpose, Christmas presents being the most important category. Similar findings are reported by Ward, Wackman, and Wartella (1977). Unfortunately, neither of these studies took into account the well-known tendency (cf. Chapter 8) for the propensity to save to increase with income; as we have already seen, children's income also increases with age. However, in a recent British study, Furnham and Thomas (1984a) found that older children not only saved more than younger children, but also saved for different reasons and in a different way. They tended to use savings accounts because they anticipated needing the money in the future.

The picture that emerges from studies of social class differences is not so clear cut. Newson and Newson's (1976) exploration into the world of 7-year-olds revealed the expected difference. Middle-class children received less pocket money (18p versus 30p) but saved a greater percentage of it (90 versus 48 percent). Goldstein and Oldham (1979), on the other hand, found no social class differences in saving, and Ward et al. (1977) state that the only social class differences they found were for 13-year-olds' long-term savings behavior. This may be related to their finding that mention of long-term saving as a norm increases with age and was more frequent in the higher social classes. Hussein (1981, p. 21) describes how powerful this norm is for 7- and 8-year-old Exeter (England) middle-class children:

Seven [middle class children] gave this as their priority in disposing of their money while a further eight insisted that they saved at least some . . . if they were to be believed these children simply handled their pocket money for the brief space of time it took to put it in a money box, post office account or, in one case, a building society . . . the giving of pocket money is, in these cases little more than a ritualized lesson in saving, an activity which it was clear from the tone of the answers was held in high esteem.

Hussein also presented children with scenarios in which the source of money varied to see whether these class differences were maintained.

Even when the money was hypothetically stolen from their mother's purse, 50% of the middle-class children said they would save it, whereas most of the working-class children said they would rush out and spend it.

Two recent studies carried out in London, however, found no class differences in saving (Tysoe 1983; Furnham & Thomas 1984a). Tysoe was surprised at the number of children with savings accounts (60% of her 10-year-old subjects) and feels that "we are already breeding a new generation of economic sophisticates" (1983, p. 434). Furnham and Thomas claim that class differences are more apparent as children get older, perhaps because their study (Furnham & Thomas 1984b) of adults' views about how much pocket money children should get did reveal the expected class differences.

These studies have some obvious macroeconomic implications. If saving is simply a function of social class, the propensity to consume will only change as a result of slow changes in class structure (cf. Chapter 8). If, on the other hand, class differences in saving are disappearing (as claimed by Tysoe 1983) patterns of saving may be more volatile in the future.

Giving

Most studies of children's giving involve experimental studies of donating, where the amount donated is the dependent variable and other factors in the situation are manipulated. The pattern of results is very similar to that found for adults. For example, seeing another person giving generously increases the amount donated, often dramatically (Rushton 1975). Donating also increases with age, at least over the range of 6–11 years (Rushton 1980), although whether this is the result of moral development or social learning is not clear. There is evidence for consistent individual differences in altruism in children (Rushton 1980), despite Hartshorne and May's (1928) contrary conclusions from their large and intensive study.

Gifts to relatives and friends are a very important aspect of children's economic behavior. Unfortunately, we have traced only one study on gifts in the everyday life of children (Stanjek 1978), and this is concerned with very young children giving objects to other children and strange adults during social interaction. This behavior decreases between ages 1 and 6, but it seems to have little relevance to the psychology of normal gift giving in older children.

Gambling

In Chapter 9 we described gambling as a form of risk taking with special qualities, the most notable of which is that outcomes are determined by chance and the risk is an unnecessary one. In children's behavior, the factors of chance and risk seem to be separated. Many popular children's games, especially proprietary ones, depend on chance alone. While children certainly like such games and play them quite a lot, the very existence of these depends on the adult world. Looking at the games which are maintained in children's own independent culture, Sutton-Smith (1972) discovered that games that depend on chance are rare, although chance factors do enter into many games, especially those played by girls. The highest proportion of chance games is found among games of young children (ages 6–9), which involve guessing.

None of these games of chance, however, really involves gambling, since nothing is at risk except the possibility of losing the game itself. The same applies to the children's versions of adult gambling games (e.g., Lotto, roulette) which are to be found on the market. Apparently a range of true gambling games were played by New Zealand children during 1870–1920, but these were frowned upon by the school authorities, and only one of them survives today. Even that one (How many eggs in a basket?) is played very infrequently (Sutton-Smith 1972).

It is probable that the precursors of adult gambling are to be found elsewhere in the child's world. Daring games, such as "chicken," involve the element of risk, though without any very sophisticated chance element. Opie and Opie (1969) claim that such games help children to understand the nature of risk taking. They also enable a child to build a reputation through demonstrating a willingness to take risk s. These kinds of social rewards are likely to be important in getting children started in gambling, as they are in encouraging adolescents to acquire the smoking habit (Evans 1980). Although we have found no survey data on this point, our informal observation suggests that, by the age of about 12, large numbers of children are playing games such as pontoon which are capable of being used for gambling, and that money stakes make their appearance not long afterward.

The significance of children's economic behavior

The evidence in this section suggests that although children may be of relatively little importance economically, the prototype economic behavior they develop may have economic implications later on. Attitudes toward work, buying, and saving and toward the advertisers of products all develop during childhood in an interactive fashion; the child, the economy of children's subculture, and the adult economy all act on one another. These interactions may be a force for change. For example, disillusionment with the claims of advertisers might lead to a distrust of branded products and a preference for generics. This brings us to the final main topic of this chapter.

CHILDREN AND TELEVISION ADVERTISING

Throughout this chapter, we have noted that only recently has there been much research interest in most areas of children's economic psychology. The question of the effects on children of advertising, especially television advertising, has been investigated extensively, and there is now a substantial literature; a recent bibliography lists more than 500 references (Meringoff 1980).

Children see a large number of television commercials, in the United States around 20,000 a year – or the equivalent of three hours per week (Adler 1977). Not surprisingly, this has caused some concern. Parents and critics fear that commercials may create family conflict, a sense of dissatisfaction, and materialistic orientation toward life; this concern has given rise to pressure groups (e.g., Action for Children's Television), self-regulatory codes, legislation, and research into these issues. Three types of outcomes have been investigated: children's attention to commercials, their attitudes toward and understanding of commercials, and the impact of commercials on their behavior.

Several studies have looked at children's attention to commercials (e.g., Ward 1972; Ward, Levinson, & Wackman 1972), and all agree that attention is negatively correlated with age. Ward, Levinson, and Wackman, for example, found that 6-year-olds paid full attention to commercials around 50% of the time, whereas 12-year-olds did so 33% of the time. Younger children attended more to "irrelevant" commercials (e.g., for cosmetics), which may indicate that they are being used as a source of knowledge. Ward (1974) states that attention is related to cognitive development; the attention of younger children varies little between commercials, whereas that for older children is more differentiated.

As children grow older, they understand the purpose and content of commercials better; they also learn to distrust them. A number of studies (e.g., Blatt, Spencer, & Ward 1972; Robertson & Rossiter 1974) found that distrust of commercials is positively related to age: Specific advertisements are distrusted by the age of 8 and 9; by the time children are age 13, they have "global distrust" (Ward 1972). Blatt, Spencer, and Ward (1972) carried out interviews with 6-, 8-, 10-, and 12-year-old children and found the youngest group to have almost no understanding of the purpose of advertisements. Eight-year-olds know that advertisements are intended to sell products, and older children comment on the selling techniques involved. However, very young children can differentiate between commercials and programs (Levin, Petros, & Petrella 1982), even if they do not understand the purpose of advertisements.

A few studies have looked at whether children understand the disclaimers that often accompany advertisements, e.g., "Batteries not supplied" or, "Some assembly required." Liebert, Sprafkin, Leibert and Rubinstein (1977) found that "Some assembly required" (the commonest disclaimer used when advertising toys) was understood by less than 25% of 6- and 8-year-olds who saw a test commercial. If the disclaimer was expressed in more appropriate language, e.g., "You have to put it together," comprehension climbed dramatically. This has some implications for advertising standards.

Advertisers intend to alter children's preferences for products and thus the amount they purchase or that they ask their parents to purchase. Atkin (1980) reviews research into these intended effects and concludes that "There is ample evidence that television advertising plays a dominant role in shaping children's product preferences . . . both experiments and surveys show how exposure to advertising increases desire for, requests for, and consumption of televised products." We will describe just some of this evidence.

Atkin's 1975a study (cited in Atkin 1980) surveyed 10- to 14-year-old children and found that those who watched the most breakfast cereal advertising reported eating advertised cereals more often; a similar relationship was found for candy. In fact, general level of television viewing was positively related to consumption of snack foods like potato chips and hot dogs. Other surveys have found that amount of viewing of relevant advertisements is related to between-meal eating and to the use of deodorants, mouthwash, and acne cream (Dussere, cited in Atkin 1980).

We should not leap to conclusions about causality from such essentially correlational results. Despite the claim that children who buy a product do not subsequently look at advertisements for it (Ehrlich, Guttman, Schonbach, & Mills 1957), children with a stronger interest in food or appearance are likely to use relevant products more and to watch advertisements for them. However, experimental studies give much the same results as these surveys. Galst and White (1975) measured how much 3- to 11-year-old children attended to commercials in the laboratory and subsequently accompanied mother–child pairs to a supermarket. Children who paid more attention to advertisements tried to influence their mothers more often. Goldberg and Gorn (1974) showed boys aged 8–11 an episode of the Flintstones cartoon that contained either no commercial, one commercial, or three commercials. The commercials advertised a new toy. After viewing, the boys were given the opportunity to win the advertised toy by solving an insoluble problem. Boys who saw the commercials liked the advertised toy more than an unadvertised toy, and they persisted longer in attempting to solve the puzzle than boys who had not seen the commercials.

There are obviously problems with these studies. The laboratory experiments tend to be artificial and the surveys lack control. [Goldberg and Gorn (1983) discuss these problems in detail.] Gorn and Goldberg

(1982) overcame some of these problems by carrying out an experiment over a long period of time in a natural setting (two weeks in a summer camp). Children saw a different half-hour television program each day before their afternoon snack. The experimental manipulation was the nature of the messages shown during the program. These were either candy commercials, fruit commercials, messages on the value of moderating one's intake of sugar, or no messages at all. Children who saw candy commercials chose proportionately more candy than fruit for their afternoon snack. All the children indicated that they knew that the camp doctor wanted them to eat fruit. But whether they acted on this awareness seemed to depend on what commercials they had been shown.

Taken together, these studies indicate that some children's advertisements at least are getting the effects intended by their sponsors. Do they also have any unintended effects? The answer would seem to be "yes." As indicated above, watching more television advertisements makes children more likely to attempt to influence what their parents buy; this in turn may produce more parent-child conflict. Atkin (1975b, cited in Atkin 1980) found that heavy viewers of Saturday morning television argued more with their parents than light viewers. Ward and Wackman (1972) report a slight positive correlation between child product requests and the level of general parent-child conflict. Once again, we have a problem here in disentangling correlation and causality.

A more serious problem is that advertisements may produce dissatisfaction and a materialistic orientation toward life. Robertson and Rossiter (1976), in a survey of children's disappointment with Christmas presents, found that 24% of the heavy television viewers were dissatisfied with their gifts as compared with 8% of the light television viewers. Donohue, Meyer, and Henke (1978) showed children a commercial depicting a happy middle-class family enjoying lunch at a restaurant; three-quarters of the low-income black respondents saw the commercial family as happier than their own family. From their panel study of adolescents, Moschis and Moore (1982) concluded that increased exposure to advertising does contribute to the development of materialistic values (measured using a Likert scale including such items as, "It is really true that money can buy happiness") among those who have not yet developed such predispositions. Television seemed to affect the development of materialism in families in which parents did not discuss consumption matters with their children.

Experimental studies are equally depressing. Goldberg and Gorn (1978) showed 4- and 5-year-olds either a 10-minute program with no advertisements, the same program with two commercials for a new version of a familiar toy, or the latter on two successive days. Children were then asked if they would rather play with friends in the sandbox or with the advertised toy. Almost twice as many children who saw the program without advertisements chose to play with friends. Similarly, given the choice between playing with a "nice" boy without the toy or a "not so nice" boy with the toy, fewer than 35% of those children who saw the commercials chose the toyless nice boy compared with 70% of the other group.

This research demonstrates that advertisments can have significant effects on children, both intended and unintended. Here we have a clear example of the influence of the economy on the behavior of individuals, and we assume that influences that take place during the formative years will be especially important and long lasting. But to date there has been no research on how advertisements aimed at children influence lifelong consumption practices. Some obvious places to look for such effects would be food preferences, use of strongly advertised drugs such as alcohol and nicotine, and general orientation toward consumption.

TOWARD A DEVELOPMENTAL ECONOMIC PSYCHOLOGY

The theories and empirical studies reviewed in this chapter suggest a number of ways in which a developmental approach can contribute to our understanding of economic behavior. It can identify the antecedents of important individual and social differences and what factors contribute to their maintenance. It also directs our attention to socialization, and the importance of family, peers, the media, and ideology. Socialization does not stop at 18 or 21; it continues throughout our lives. Maital (1982, p. 49) says, "We march along the milestones of our economic lives carrying mental baggage dating back to childhood"; a developmental approach helps identify the contents of that baggage.

But a truly developmental economic psychology seems to us to require empirical and theoretical progress in two additional directions. The first is already beginning. This involves relating the economic structure of a society to the economic ideas and behavior that its younger members develop. Leahy's (1981) research and Holmes's (1976) speculations bear on this issue. The second direction can only be sketched out, although it is implicit in many recent writings on social cognitive development. Furth (1978, p. 103), for example, wrote that

We should recognize that children's peer relations are bound to be more real and their relations to the adult world more playful. Sitting quietly next to dad on a bus is for the 4 year old girl a play that she chooses to enact . . . In contrast, the girl's interactions with a friend, such as sharing an apple, helping the friend set up a toy, or pushing the friend to do something against her or his will, are for real: Here the two children are literally constructing their social life and fashioning themselves into socialized persons.

This suggests we should examine the economic world that children are constructing themselves. Bartering, swapping, allocating roles (e.g., in games) and rewards, giving presents to teachers and friends, betting, and daring, are all activities that deserve our attention. We do not pretend to know where these two directions will take us (since superficially they appear to be in opposition), but we are confident that they are paths worth treading. The more we learn about the autonomous economic world of childhood, the more developmental economic psychology will be able to inform us about the influence of the economy on the individuals who live within it and the way in which those individuals in turn shape economic structure.

15

PRIMITIVE ECONOMIES

Economic anthropology is concerned with socioeconomic systems that differ from industrial economies. In particular, it focuses on how primitive societies decide on what kinds of goods to produce and how to distribute them and, more generally, how the economic and social aspects of the society relate. These issues clearly bear upon the main question in this part of the book, namely the problem of how the economy influences individual behavior.

Economic anthropology is interesting for a variety of reasons. For one thing, it is probably the most developed area in which economics and another social science have been brought together. The field therefore provides us with a model for some of the ways in which economic psychology might develop as a discipline. For example, the model might possibly draw our attention to areas of the subject that we might otherwise neglect, and in doing so, may shed some light on the way in which an interdisciplinary approach can draw upon and feed back to its parent disciplines.

Second, we have already seen earlier that economic anthropology is one of the major sources of data for an economic psychologist. It provides the basis for a truly empirical, comparative microeconomics (with data on giving, work, saving, and so forth), and insight into the different ways in which entire economies may function. In earlier chapters, we used such data wherever they could shed light on the particular questions being discussed. Here, we shall look at them in a different way, asking to what extent the behavior of the individual in the economy is universal and to what extent we may be misled into thinking that the particular properties of our own industrialized economy reflect the only, or only appropriate, economic system.

THE IDEAL CROSS-CULTURAL APPROACH

Ideally, economic anthropology would provide some direct answers to our questions about the effects of the economy on individual behavior. For instance, it should be possible to gather information on individual economic behavior from a range of economies which differ systematically in their modes of organization of production and distribution. We would then be able to compare economies of type A with economies of type B, and identify the factors which led to differences in, say, saving. Lewis (1976), for example, discussed three different types of economy (hunter-gatherer, pastoral nomadic, and agricultural), and claimed that each had direct, although not universally applicable, implications for the life-style and social organization of the people in the society. Hunter-gatherers such as the !Kung bushmen tend to have a looseknit society consisting of small bands related by marriage; there are typically few or no positions of leadership, and the maintenance of order depends upon kinship. People have plenty of leisure (the Hazda derive a balanced and sufficient diet from two hours' work per day) and live well by their own simple standards. Pastoral nomads also have fairly fluid societies and are generally similar to hunter-gatherers, but they have more complex patterns of organization. Agriculturalists differ widely (cultivation seems to open the door to variety), but there is often a strong emphasis on territoriality.

Lewis's approach is quite plausible (and we shall discuss others like it later in this chapter), but it is hard to develop it much beyond the descriptive level. We cannot, for example, separate "economy" from "society" or from the individuals who make it up. Nor is there any way of determining the direction of causality, except perhaps from "natural experiments" such as when capitalism is introduced. Furthermore, current economic anthropology does not really answer the questions that we, as economic psychologists, want to pose to it. It has been predominantly descriptive (much more strongly influenced by anthropology than by economics at the methodological level) and concerned with relating the economic and social aspects of culture rather than disentangling them. The ideal cross-cultural investigation of the effects of the economy on the individual will have to remain a textbook ideal.

THE CONTRIBUTIONS OF ECONOMIC ANTHROPOLOGY

Nonetheless, economic anthropology does have a great deal to offer to economic psychology. First, it has its own distinct theoretical approaches, and these should be examined to see whether they help us. Second, a cross-cultural approach can greatly widen our view of economic behavior, especially with regard to the fundamental question of what kinds of behavior are and are not economic. Finally it provides comparative data on all kinds of economic behaviors of individuals. We shall consider the first two of these contributions briefly here; the third constitutes the final, and largest, section of this chapter.

Theoretical approaches to economic anthropology

The past twenty years have seen two major theoretical upheavals within economic anthropology. The 1960s saw a clash between the *substantivists* (Polanyi 1957; Dalton 1961) and the *formalists* (LeClair 1962; Cook 1966), while the 1970s saw the emergence of a self-styled new economic anthropology, influenced by Marxism and structuralism (Clammer 1978; Seddon 1978).

The argument between the substantivists and the formalists was, essentially, about whether economic theory could be applied to the economic processes of primitive economies. The substantivists claimed that it could not, since people in primitive economies were not profit motivated; the formal methods of economic analysis, developed for Western society, were simply irrelevant. These theorists believed that the material dimension was of secondary interest, and that the focus should be on people, how they relate, and how they are supported. The formalists, on the other hand, were willing to apply conventional economic theory to this problem and see whether the theory worked. A good example is Cook's (1970) analysis of a metate market in Mexico, which demonstrated how the production of these stone handmills correlated with demand and price conditions.

At first sight, the structuralist-formalist argument looks to be of great interest to an economic psychologist. It ought, surely, to tell us whether well-known economic processes are human universals, and thus provide a clue as to the direction we should look for their causation. But the actual discussion, as it reverberated around the anthropological journals of the 1960s, seems to an outsider to be curiously empty. Was it an unrecognized philosophical difference, with the formalists interested in the activities of the individual within the society, while the substantivists were more concerned with the structure of society – or was the argument really an empirical question? If so, no general answers were ever produced. Disappointingly, there is nothing here for economic psychology, except perhaps a warning against the destructive consequences of losing sight of the interdependence of individual behavior and economic structure.

The "new" economic anthropology, whatever one's beliefs about the importance of Marx and structuralism as general influences in social science, turns out to offer a little more. This point can best be illustrated by comparing the new economic anthropology with the more traditional approach. First, the latter was concerned with the relationships between the parent disciplines. It asked what anthropology had to say to economics, and vice versa. By contrast, the new approach attempts to ask questions about the nature of the problems to be examined, regardless of disciplinary boundaries. (At this level, at least, it is obviously thoroughly compatible with the approach to economic psychology taken in this book.) Second, traditional economic anthropology recognized that economics is embedded in other forms of social life, but it did not examine the nature of this embedding. For the new approach, this question is crucial because it leads to analyses using concepts such as dependency, inequality, and exploitation. The third and perhaps most obvious difference between the old and new approaches, however, is that whereas traditional economic anthropology focused on distribution (as we can see in the long-standing interest in giftlike transactions, and the central role given to the market), the new approach focuses on production (as one might expect from its Marxist background).

Is there any payoff for economic psychology from this new approach to economic anthropology? Certainly, throughout this book we have emphasized the Marxian (if not Marxist) point that economic structure influences the individual, and there are psychologists who study economic behavior within a Marxist framework (e.g., Garai et al. 1979). We started our discussion of individual economic behavior by focusing on the productive side (work), before proceeding to consider distributional questions, and if the latter have received more consideration that is because the psychology of productive activity is already relatively well developed. In a sense, economic psychology is ahead of economic anthropology and does not need a new approach. But there is an important moral to be drawn from the development of the new economic anthropology. We must learn not to take anything for granted, neither the theories of the parent disciplines nor the topics to be investigated. An interdisciplinary approach must set its own agenda.

We have suggested that the major theoretical debates within economic anthropology have been relatively unfruitful. At a slightly lower level of theorizing, however, economic anthropologists have devised and tested a range of hypotheses about economic behavior, some of which are highly relevant to economic psychology. For example, we have already encountered Codere's (1968) analysis of money (Chapter 12), and Douglas's (1982) approach to consumption (Chapter 7). The latter example provides a good illustration of some of the ways in which economic anthropology is useful to economic psychologists, so we shall discuss it in some more detail here.

Douglas (1982, p. 23) argues that people "need goods to involve others as fellow-consumers in . . . consumption rituals. Goods are for mobilizing other people. The fact that in the course of these rituals food gets consumed, flags waved and clothes worn is incidental. Subsistence is a fortunate by-product." In other words, the aim of consumption activity is to enter a social universe in which goods are matched to social situations. Goods are ritually presented and shared and are themselves graded in the process. The individual's purpose in all this activity is to help create a social universe and to assure a reasonable place in it. To achieve this one needs others to grade social occasions and the associated goods. Goods, then, are a system of communication. When a guest brings an already-opened bottle of wine to a dinner party, that marks the occasion as an informal one – or the guest as socially inept. Wedgwood china and silver cutlery on the table would mark it in rather a different way, though exactly what it would signify would depend on the social status of the participants and on current fashions.

Developing the idea of the communicative function of goods, Douglas and Isherwood (1979) put forward the interesting idea of consumption periodicities, referring to the frequency with which different goods are consumed. Periodicity in consumption marks rank and status and creates quality goods. Necessities are consumed in low-ranking, high-frequency events, while luxuries are used in high-ranking, low-frequency events. If society is stratified, then the luxuries of the common person may become the necessities of the higher classes. Thus it is not simply that goods are social and communicative objects; it is also possible to make predictions about the particular goods that will serve particular social and communicative functions.

Economic anthropology has thus provided economic psychology with a ready-made theory, since, as Douglas and Isherwood make clear, their *social* theory of consumption has its origins in anthropological data but is directly applicable to our own society. Their theory relates closely to economic theory (for example, Douglas and Isherwood draw on Lancaster's, 1966, characteristics approach to the demand for goods), as well as to sociological and psychological approaches such as those of Veblen (1899/1979) and Solomon (1983). It also has practical implications. As Douglas (1982, p. 31) writes:

Advocates of egalitarian policies should not be ignorant about the uses of goods. The prophets of anti-growth depend implicitly on the idea that goods are primarily needed for food and shelter. If that were all, we could cut them down to a healthy level. But as they are for communicating messages, highly discriminated ones, their use is like a balloon: press it down here and it will billow out there, new goods and new names will be invented.

There is no reason why such a theory could not have been developed without reference to cross-cultural data; indeed, Hirsch (1977) expresses some of the same ideas but, because of the wider data base and longer history of economic anthropology, it is no surprise that we find nothing of comparable weight in the literature devoted to Western economies.

Economic anthropology of modern society

It is arguable, in fact, that the crucial factor is the wider data base that a cross-cultural perspective allows. In a modern economy, the instrumental approach to goods is stressed so strongly that it masks other possibilities. For example, among the Tolai of New Britain studied by Epstein (1968), the social function of goods is blatant: Goods seem to be used only for display; they do not have the instrumentality usually associated with goods in Western economies. One of economic anthropology's most valuable contribution to economic psychology therefore is to alert us to different possibilities, and in particular to widen our view of what constitutes economic behavior. From an anthropological perspective, there is a great deal of economic activity in our own society which is not recognized as such, not least because it is ignored by economics. The most striking examples of such activity are the domestic economy and the hidden economy. Neither of these involves the market, so neither is included in national economic statistics, and yet both are of substantial importance. We shall look at each of them here, in anthropological perspective.

The importance of household work in modern society has recently come to public attention through some remarkable claims about its economic value. Oakley (1980) reckons that it accounts for 40% of all British production. Anthropological evidence suggests that we should concentrate less on sheer quantity than on the nature of household work and on the division of labor within households. As Sahlins (1974, chapter 2) points out, division of labor by sex is the dominant form of economic specialization in primitive societies. Douglas and Isherwood explain this using their notion of periodicities, which is as applicable to production as it is to consumption: Since the division of labor facilitates economies of scale (Smith 1776/1908, book 1, chapter 1), it makes sense for there to be a category of people who carry out high-frequency tasks. If you have to feed a baby whenever it needs food or comfort, you may as well also prepare meals three times a day, gather firewood every morning, collect water whenever it is needed, and so on. If you are free from the responsibilities of nursing, you can plan to spend several days at a time on a single absorbing task. Thus there is a tendency for tasks to cluster into complementary work roles, a low-status role constrained by high-frequency tasks, and a high-status role that is not. Although the precise tasks allocated to it vary, it is men, the world over, who occupy the high-status role within primitive economies (Burton, Brudner, & White 1977).

The same is true in our own society. Most often, women, especially those with young children, tend to do the high-frequency, low-status tasks that occur within the home, while men do the low-frequency, high-status task of going out to work. This simple household division of labor has direct effects on the wider economy. For example, an increase in a wife's wage will encourage her to do more paid work, but an increase in her husband's wage will encourage her to do less (Aschenfelter & Heckman 1974). Although this fact is consistent with the microeconomic theory of the labor–leisure choice and is certainly obvious to common sense, it is overlooked and liable to be disruptive, given the conventional macroeconomic practice of considering households as indivisible.

Even within the domestic economy, however, our society shows a marked division of labor along sex lines which is entirely consistent with Douglas and Isherwood's periodicity theory. Traditionally male tasks such as decorating and car maintenance are lower in frequency and higher in status than traditionally female tasks such as cleaning and child care. When both husband and wife have paid jobs, the contribution to housework by most men is minimal (Oakley 1974), and it tends to involve the most rewarding jobs such as putting the children to bed rather than doing the ironing. Young and Willmott (1973) concluded that these practices are declining, and that families are becoming more "symmetrical" with a more equitable distribution of chores. But this conclusion has been challenged (e.g., Webb 1982); declining or not, the inequalities are still evident. A good illustration of this inequity is found in Elston's (1980) study of 400 couples who were both doctors. In 80% of cases it was the woman who did the shopping, cleaned, and looked after children when they were ill. For those couples where major purchases were the responsibility of one member (a low-frequency, high-status task), they were made by the man in 67% of the cases.

In many primitive economies, the household is the basic production unit of the economy; everything that is produced within the household, even what is produced for exchange, could in principle be used within it. Such production is discontinuous, irregular, and unintensive (Sahlins 1974, chapter 2). In effect, it operates according to an anti-surplus principle: Households have economic aims, but once these are met, they stop producing. This helps to explain economic behavior which is inconsistent with conventional microeconomic theory or data. For example, Bardhan (1969, 1970) observed the extremely rare Giffen case – demand for a commodity increasing with price – in an Indian community where high prices led to increased producer income, leading in turn to consumption of grains that at other times would have been offered for sale. East African cattle-marketing boards found a similar effect, but for different reasons: The pastoralists had target sums of money, which they aimed to realize by selling cattle; once they had achieved these, they stopped selling (Lewis 1976). In effect, their indifference spaces contained "bliss points" (cf. Chapter 5).

A related feature of the domestic mode of production is referred to as Chayanov's rule (Sahlins 1974, chapter 2). Chayanov claimed that the intensity of labor in a system of domestic production varies inversely with the relative working capacity of the producing unit; the more able-bodied members a household has, the less work each of them does. One consequence is that the least effective households, especially those that do not produce enough to meet their own needs, are in a perilous situation, since the more effective households do not produce a surplus that could be used to help the less productive households.

An interesting parallel to Chayanov's rule in our own society can be found in some of the experimental research on working groups. Latane, Williams, and Harkin (1979) demonstrated that the larger a group, the less effect each individual exerts, especially when they are all performing the same task. These data also suggest that such "social loafing" may only occur when the group product is for immediate "use," not when production is organized by and for exchange value. This is consistent with the anthropological data, although it casts doubt on Maital's (1982, pp. 125 ff.) use of social loafing as a partial explanation for recent decreases in productivity growth in industrialized economies.

But Chayanov's rule, as well as other properties of the domestic mode of production as discovered by the anthropologists, may have much more relevance to the so-called "hidden economy" of barter, perks, permitted theft, and gift exchange. Contrary to our intuitions, Gershuny and Pahl (1981) showed that there is not a simple development from a primitive economy, with its economic relationships based on custom, to modern industrial society, where more and more social relationships are monetized. Rather, there are a series of transfers of production in all possible directions among the formal economy, the hidden economy, and the household economy. For example, a change from using a laundry to owning a washing machine constitutes a (partial) shift from the formal to the domestic economy. It is entirely in accord with microeconomic theory. With more efficient production (in this case, of clean linen), the price of productive capital (the washing machine) falls relative to the price of labor; it makes more sense to buy the machine and do the washing yourself than to pay the laundry to employ an expensive worker. Similarly, home alterations seem to be shifting from the formal economy to that part of the hidden economy in which work is paid for in cash, and receipts, even if requested, are unlikely to be forthcoming.

Gershuny and Pahl's analysis has two important implications. First, if the production of services is gradually shifting from the formal to the domestic economy, conventional macroeconomic statistics (see Chapter 3) will become progressively less adequate indicators of levels of production. Second, our ideas of what constitutes work will need to change in order to embrace all three economies (see Chapter 6).

Henry (1978) has approached the hidden economy in a more explicitly anthropological fashion. From his study of the amateur trade in stolen goods, Henry concluded that such trading is not really about making money at all, but is concerned with social relationships. People dealing in stolen goods often make no money on exchanges; they will buy things they do not really need in order to "do friends a favor." Henry (1978, p. 84) argues that "exchanges are managed so that the accounts are kept unbalanced, with one party always in credit and the other always in debt. In this way there is always a need to continue with the relationship."

The hidden economy is thus an economy in its own right, with its own rules and conventions, rather than part of the market economy of conventional crime. Its participants enjoy the obligations of relationships and also the competitive, play aspect. There is always some chance of getting caught, and there is competition for status between traders. Like the participants in the "potlatch" rituals of primitive economies (e.g., that of the Kwakiutl of the American Northwest coast; see Benedict 1935, chapter 6), traders in the hidden economy are keen to be known as the most generous.

Henry's account of the hidden economy may seem implausible since it is mainly derived from the traders' own descriptions of their behavior and they might well want to portray their illegal activities in a favorable light. But in fact economic language (e.g., bargains and deliveries) is commonplace in their descriptions. The distinctive nature of the hidden economy is revealed more in what actually happens than in what the partipants say about it. Pricing is a case in point. The price charged in amateur trading networks reflects the degree of the purchaser's involvement with the network and how friendly the person is with the seller. Frequently goods are sold for the same price they were bought for. As Ferman and Berndt (1981) also suggest, pricing in the hidden economy is idiosyncratic and particularistic.

If money is not the prime motive for participants in the hidden economy, what is? Henry suggests that the attraction of trading in stolen goods lies in the social rewards it offers. Thus, to go with the social theory of buying, economic anthropology now offers us a social theory of trading to set alongside a social theory of work motivation (see Chapter 6).

The domestic and hidden economies have been neglected by economic psychologists, yet they are clearly important in both economic and psychological terms. Moreover, the cross-cultural perspective shows us that their separation from the formal economy of our society is largely conventional. We see here a good example of the way in which economic anthropology can draw our attention to important questions in economic psychology.

CROSS-CULTURAL PERSPECTIVES ON THE ECONOMIC BEHAVIOR OF INDIVIDUALS

We have already used comparative data in previous chapters, most notably in our discussion of money (see Chapter 12). Here we shall consider the central questions of each of the chapters in Part II and examine how anthropological research helps answer them.

Work

Our earlier discussion of the domestic mode of production and its analogs in the modern economy reflect one very important contribution that anthropological study has made to the economic psychology of work. But there are a great many other strands of anthropological investigation in this area (Wallman 1979). Much of it is concerned with the concept of work and how work relates to identity, authority systems, and value. Work means different things to different people. The Yir Yiront aborigines of Australia made no distinction between work and play (Sharp 1952), while the Maenge of New Britain cannot say whether they are working though they do know whether they are toiling (Schwimmer 1979). Within societies, too, the boundaries between work and nonwork, and between subcategories of work, have been found to shift (Parkin 1979). Thus the meaning of work currently accepted in Western society is by no means the only possible one, and it may well be atypical. Indeed, Wadel (1979) argues that our view of work is heavily biased toward paid labor and ignores informal activities.

In Chapter 6, we devoted considerable time to the related questions of the motivations for work and to the determinants of the hours spent working. We identified four main classes of motivations for work: external reward, intrinsic enjoyment, self-fulfillment, and the satisfaction of various social needs. Evidence for all four of these can be found in other cultures, although their relative importance varies. Anthropologists have traditionally emphasized the importance of social factors, such as the person's obligations to kin and community, the possibilities of gaining prestige and building a reputation, and the influence of religious and magical systems. As Firth (1952/1968, p. 79) stated, "powerful incentives to work lie in the individual's membership of a social group. He dare not relax least he lose many of the benefits of membership."

Moral factors are also crucial because they often determine what work a "good" person should do. Particularly interesting in this context are the differences between production for use and production for exchange. Among the Orokavia of Papua New Guinea, growing taro, the subsistence crop, is considered pleasurable, while growing coffee, a cash crop, is not (Schwimmer 1979). Even the smell of coffee is considered dreadful. Such alienation from production for exchange is not unusual. Rather curiously, though, among the Giriami of the Kenyan coast, wage labor is valued above fishing, even though the latter is financially more rewarding (Parkin 1979).

We must remember that in many cases the incentive to work is based primarily on the need to satisfy material wants, that is, the need for food, shelter, and so on. And work can be very hard. Ploughing a paddy field in the hot sun, stooping for hours to transplant rice seedlings, and cutting and clearing a forest are all tiring and joyless activities. Not surprisingly, Halpern (1962) reports that Laotian peasants did not value these activities for their own sake; they worked simply to maintain themselves. As in many other primitive economies, production was geared to a limited target. If there was any surplus after subsistence had been assured, the first priority was the allocation of resources for religious purposes such as making contributions to the Buddhist monks and improving the local pagoda.

Even this kind of society, however, provides little evidence for the one integrated theory of work motivation we considered earlier, that of Maslow (1970). On the contrary, the anthropological data suggest that basic needs do not have to be satisfied before social needs begin to affect behavior. Social needs, whether for status or for self-identity, influence working behavior at all levels of subsistence, although the particular society one lives in may affect their importance relative to one another and to material needs.

Anthropological data on hours of work are frequently quite striking, for example the comparatively short working day of hunter-gatherers noted in Chapter 6. In any primitive economy based on production for use, in fact, a short working day is the norm. Sahlins (1974, chapter 2) gives a number of examples, among them the Brazilian Kuikuru, who spend an average of two hours a day on horticulture and less than that on fishing, and the Bemba tribe of Zambia, where men do no work at all on three days out of seven and between four and seven hours on the remaining days. Sahlins argues that this short working day occurs because economic decisions are primarily domestic decisions; they are taken with a view toward domestic contentment. When domestic groups become mere consumption units, and labor is employed externally, this is no longer possible.

But there is more to hours of work than this. The time spent working is much greater in some primitive economies than others, apparently as a result of differences in social and political organization. Douglas's (1962/1982) comparison of the Lele and Bushong economies provides a very clear example. Both tribes live in the area of forest park that borders on the Congo rain forest. They are separated only by a river, and they recognize a common origin, speak related languages, and have similar houses, clothes, and crafts. Yet the Bushong are affluent, while the Lele are poor. There are some differences in their natural resources, but they do not seem sufficient to account for the large disparity in wealth; the principal reason seems to be simply that the Lele do less work.

Douglas explains this fact in terms of the social organization of the Lele. In particular, the Lele form of marriage, which was essentially polygyny for the old men and extended bachelorhood for the young, led to attitudes and behavior that inhibited economic growth. For the Lele seniority led to status and a satisfying life, while for the Bushong work was the route to wealth and wealth the means to status. A young unmarried Lele man had little responsibility and could be fairly idle until his middle thirties; and he was encouraged to focus his sexual attentions on young women from other villages (i.e., away from the young wives of his own village elders). This led to a pattern of abduction and intervillage feuding which contributed to low levels of production. There was also a general lack of authority among the Lele; this exacerbated their economic inefficiencies. The crucial role of societal factors in inhibiting economic development was demonstrated during the 1950s, when the young Lele men broke away from the restraints of the social environment by becoming Christians, marrying young Christian women, and seeking outside employment (although Douglas does not record whether hours of work then increased).

These data support our earlier conclusion that hours of work are strongly influenced by social convention, both directly and indirectly. Work is not a simple phenomenon that can be encapsulated as one half of a simple labor–leisure choice. This sort of microeconomic analysis has its place, however. For instance, Alden (1981) points out that the standardization of the work week means that some workers may be underemployed and unable to achieve their desired tradeoff between income and leisure, even if the standard week corresponds to what most people prefer. Moonlighting is two to three times more common among those working a four-day week than among those working a five-day week (Poor 1970; American Department of Labor 1974). Most moonlighters are extremely energetic individuals and many work overtime on their main job. Their motivation for holding two paid jobs is directly financial, although a significant minority stresses social or intrinsic motivations (Alden 1977).

To summarize, the kind of society we live in and the kind of economy it embodies have a powerful influence both on why we work and on how much time we spend working, although within those constraints the different needs of individuals find expression in every society.

Buying

Buying is not something we associate with primitive economies, especially those that operate at a subsistence level or lack a general-purpose money. Nonetheless, a cross-cultural perspective can shed considerable light on two of the questions we considered in Chapter 7: the usefulness of microeconomic demand theory, and the relationship between needs and purchasing behavior. It also suggests an entirely new question: What determines what products can be bought?

Within our own culture, children have to learn what can be bought and sold. As they get older, the children come to attend to the relevant social norms; they learn that one cannot buy babies, for example. But what determines these norms? They certainly have changed considerably during recent history; for example, you cannot now purchase a commission in the army, whereas you can now buy land. They also differ from one society to another.

Where such constraints are particularly striking in a society, economic anthropologists describe it as having a multicentric economy, in which goods fall into two or more mutually exclusive spheres of exchange. Each sphere is organized differently, and each has a different moral value. Bohannan (1959) described the system that used to operate among the Tiv of Nigeria as follows: There were three spheres of exchange. The first was associated with subsistence (food, household utensils, tools), and exchange took place through barter or by gift giving. The second consisted of prestige goods (slaves, cattle, medicines and magic, metal rods) that were exchanged at ceremonies and ritualized wealth displays. The third and supreme sphere of exchange contained one item, rights in women. The only price of one woman was another woman. Exchanges within a sphere were morally neutral, but exchanges between spheres, when they occurred, occasioned moral comment: It was good to trade up and bad to trade down.

A similar system operates within New Guinea Siane society (Salisbury 1962). Here there are three different classes of goods: valuables (pigs), luxuries (palm oil, pandanus nuts), and things of no account (mainly vegetable food). Goods from different classes cannot be equated and therefore cannot be exchanged. When the Siane started doing wage labor they acquired cash in the form of pound notes, shillings, and coppers. But these different forms of money were not seen as just money; instead, pound notes were identified as valuables, shillings as luxuries, and coppers as of no account. This meant that you could not exchange shillings for notes or coppers for shillings.

Salisbury maintains that the different sets of commodities express different types of social relationships, so that to exchange commodities from more than one set would confuse the nature of the relationship. Alternative accounts of spheres of exchange are possible, however. Douglas (1967) claims that in societies where people of high status have prerogatives over certain goods, they will impose restrictions on the exchange of these goods with freely available commodities, so that their privileges should not be undermined. And Riches (1975) argues that, in some economies, the origin of distinct spheres of exchange lies in the strategies people use to sustain and control limited supplies of special commodities.

We have encountered restrictions on exchange in our own society, for example, in the taboo on the use of money for certain kinds of gift (cf. Chapters 9 and 12), which we explained in terms similar to those used by

Salisbury. In Western society, things that cannot be purchased have a greater moral value than those that can. We are slightly shocked to read of societies such as the Kapauku Papuans of West Guinea, where the services of a foster father and wives, and the grief expressed by strangers over the death of a relative can all be bought (Pospisil 1963). What seems to be crucial is that things that can be bought can all be expressed in terms of one another: one hour of grief equals five pigs, which equals five hundredweight of potatoes, amounting to $75, and so on. By defining some things as unbuyable, society protects what it regards as sacred from becoming mundane.

Even within a restricted sphere of exchange, however, no one can buy everything that is offered for sale. Therefore, we consider why people in primitive economies buy what they do. In Chapter 7, we argued that goods contain characteristics that in turn correspond to human needs. The goods exchanged in primitive economies are superficially very different from those marketed in the West. Does this reflect differences in technology or differences in underlying needs?

One area that provides information relevant to this question is research on the value of children to parents. In most cultures, for most people, the decision about having children is at least in part economic (we are not concerned here with the buying of children). Hoffman and Hoffman (1973) proposed that the satisfactions provided by children could be categorized into clusters corresponding to basic psychological needs, such as economic utility (help with household chores, security in old age), social comparison, and expansion of the self (self-fulfillment, giving purpose to life). The satisfaction derived from children would depend on the intensity of each kind of need, the relevance of children to it, and the availability of alternative sources of need satisfaction. Thus in economically developed countries, the economic utility of children is insignificant, but children may well satisfy the need to expand the self. Hoffman, Thornton, and Manis (1978) report the results of research carried out in seven countries using the Hoffman and Hoffman scheme. Married women, and in some cases their husbands, were asked about the advantages and disadvantages of having children. Their replies were categorized, falling easily into the classification scheme, regardless of nationality, which tends to confirm the universality of the proposed list of major needs. Data from the American sample also supported the idea that the availability of alternatives is important. Groups that were less well off gave more importance to economic utility values; unemployed women laid more stress on stimulation and urban residents on purpose in life.

Assessing needs through questionnaires is not very satisfactory, however. Ideally, we should like to investigate the characteristics of the goods exchanged in a primitive economy directly, and, with fewer goods in circulation, that should be considerably easier than it is in a modern economy. As far as we know, however, it has not yet been attempted.

At a simpler level than the characteristics theory of buying behavior, we can also ask whether microeconomic demand theory works within primitive economies. This question was at the center of the substantivist-formalist debate in the economic anthropology of the 1960s, but it was never properly resolved. Some useful data were gathered, however, such as Cook's (1970) analysis of the metate market in Oaxaca, Mexico, and Gray's (1960) reinterpretation of African wife-purchase.

Cook's paper illustrates how a market in a "primitive" economy can be analyzed in terms of elementary supply and demand theory, despite its superficial exotic appearance. He gathered data on the prices and output of metates (a kind of stone handmill) over a two-year period and also recorded a number of exogenous variables such as seasonal variations and cultural factors. This enabled him to solve, at least in part, the *identification problem* (Chapter 2) and to determine whether supply and/ or demand curves had shifted. For example, most metate producers regard metate making as a secondary occupation, farming being their primary concern. So during the planting season (April to July, approximately), the production and hence the supply of metates declines. Conversely, after the harvest is in (around December) production increases, and if the harvest is poor more people will start producing metates. On the demand side, it is only during and after harvest that people have large amounts of cash available. It is also during that period that marriages take place, and it is the custom to give the bride a richly decorated metate. Thus both supply and demand are expected to peak during the dry, postharvest season, and the quantity exchanged should then be greater than average, while both supply and demand should drop off during the growing season, and the volume of transactions should be correspondingly less. No predictions can be made, therefore, about price changes. Cook's data support the predicted relationship between the seasons and the quantity exchanged.

Cook's study is extremely unusual in that the data are quantitative and quite extensive. Most economic analyses of anthropological data are much more schematic. Gray's (1960) discussion of African wife purchase is a case in point. He argues that the doctrine that African marriage must not be regarded as an economic transaction has retarded anthropologists' understanding of it. He describes the marriage system of the Sonjo of Tanzania in detail, and those of four other tribes briefly, to support his claim that wives are transferred according to the same basic rules as other property.

Sonjo girls are normally betrothed in childhood and nearly all the bride price is paid at that time by the future husband's father. The price varies considerably (from 60 to 300 goats in 1955) and depends mainly on the social status of the girl's family. Since there is a long interval between betrothal and marriage, there are some risks involved; for example, if a man's fiancee should die, he will lose all the goats he has paid. If a man dies, before or after marriage, his wife rights are inherited by his brother, who may sell them; but the price for such a wife is fixed at 30 goats. On the face of it this seems a bit odd, especially for the case of a bereaved fiancee. Gray explains it, however, by reference to Sonjo beliefs. A bereaved wife or fiancee will join her original or intended husband in the spirit world after death, so a second husband is not purchasing full wife rights, only a life interest. Men can also sell or exchange their wives, and in this case a husband will try to get the full bride price he originally paid, though "how well he succeeds in this depends on conditions of supply and demand at the time" (Gray 1960, p. 42). Older women are worth much less than younger ones; one 40-year-old was apparently sold for as little as ten goats. The discrepancy between the price for a bereaved fiancee (fixed by custom) and a wife being sold (determined by supply and demand) suggests that the price for the former is "too low." The value of microeconomic theory here is that it suggests what data should be looked for; we would expect evidence of additional benefits to the sellers of bereaved fiancees or else some form of rationing.

The details among other tribes are rather different. Among the Gusii of Kenya, for instance, a seller remains permanently responsible for the quality and survival of what has been sold (cattle or wives), so if a fiancee dies, her bride price must be refunded. But the economic nature of the transaction is clear enough. The Gusii themselves "can only explain the fluctuations [in bride price] in terms of what the European might call the price mechanism" (Mayer 1950, as quoted by Gray 1960).

A reasonable conclusion is that the scope of demand theory is greater than might have been supposed; it can explain some superficially noneconomic transactions in primitive economies. This strengthens the suggestion (Becker 1976) that it may be applicable to some of the less obviously economic transactions of our own society. It also suggests that, although the objects traded and the manner of trading may differ greatly across cultures, the mechanisms underlying buying are probably much more uniform.

Saving

We noted earlier that saving is an area where economists have appealed to psychology for explanations of people's behavior. It is also an area where economists have taken an interest in the work of anthropologists. Perhaps the best example of this is Duesenberry's (1949) well-known relative income theory of household spending and saving.

Duesenberry rejected economic models on the grounds that they were excessively individualistic. He particularly objected to the assumption that a person's economic behavior is independent of other people's. Using Dubois's (1944) description of Alor as a model, he described a society in which there is continual pressure for the consumer to spend more. An individual who is relatively well off will be able to spend what is socially required and still have some income left to save. A person who is relatively poor will always be spending and never able to save.

Duesenberry's theory uses four basic ideas: the pressure to consume, the cultural boundary of a population, social emulation, and saving as feasible nonconsumption. The theory can be illustrated through his comparison of black and white Americans. At each income level, blacks save more than whites. Why? Duesenberry treats each group as a separate community (the idea of a cultural boundary), the black group, on the whole, being poorer than the white group. When incomes are equal, the position of a black relative to the black group is therefore higher than the position of a white relative to the white group. It follows that the black, who is relatively better off, should save more. Similarly, the fact that 11% of professional people identify socially with the upper class, but only 5% regard themselves as economically upper class, accounts for their tendency to be dissatisfied with their incomes. They are unable to meet culturally standardized expenditures – the idea of social emulation.

This is an extremely neat theory, but Duesenberry has been criticized by both economists and anthropologists. Economists claim that Friedman's permanent income hypothesis (see Chapter 8) can account for all Duesenberry's data, in addition to making other important predictions. Anthropologists (e.g., Douglas 1982) have pointed out how limited Duesenberry's ethnographic base is; social emulation is less significant in many cultures than in Alor or America. Furthermore, saving need not be a residual activity; in some cultures, saving is a culturally standardized priority, such as among the Basseri tribe of Iran (Barth 1964).

Douglas and Isherwood (1978) believe that both Friedman and Duesenberry use just one concept of society and an individual's place in it, and fail to take into account the range of possible societies and subcultures. This means that there are situations which neither can explain. Duesenberry would not predict the ruinous spending of the Bordeaux nobility in the Hundred Years War, and Friedman would not predict the thriftlessness of the intermittently employed laborer.

Other economic anthropologists (e.g., Firth 1964) give a different perspective on saving. Apparently, in some communities, the earner of the income is not the one who decides how much of it to save. In coastal Kelantan (Malaya), the husband earns the major income and his wife makes the decisions about saving and spending. This may seem a commonplace point, but it does have some economic implications. For example, a wife's consumption program for her life is likely to be somewhat different from a husband's program for his (for one thing, their life expectancies will be different). Descriptions of how people save in other cultures also reinforce the discussion in Chapter 8 of the problems involved in deciding what counts as saving. Swift (1964) describes the ownership of cattle among Malay peasants as a form of saving (since keeping cattle requires a great deal of work for little return), whereas owning goats and sheep is a form of production. The peasants in fact recognize that the extra time spent looking after cows could be spent more profitably in other activities, such as tapping rubber trees, but they believe that any extra income gained would simply be spent immediately. Essentially, then, a cow is what Douglas (1967) calls a coupon (cf. Chapter 12).

One observation pertinent to saving in peasant economies has given rise to some comment (Yamey 1964). This is the apparent long-term stability in the rate of interest in such societies. The rate of interest, being simply the price of money, should vary according to changes in supply and demand conditions. But a stable interest rate does not invalidate supply and demand analysis. Rather, the economist would look for evidence of indirect price reductions or increases, of rationing, and of secret price changes. There is no anthropological evidence on this point, but no one has seriously looked for it.

What an economic anthropological approach adds to our earlier discussion of saving is principally another factor that affects it. To our list of income, wealth, the state of the economy, and personal characteristics, we must now add cultural and subcultural factors. They are obviously related to income and wealth, but not in any simple fashion. This is a clear example of the way in which the wider economy affects individual behavior.

Gambling

Despite the importance of gambling in some primitive cultures, it has rarely been treated as a significant economic behavior by anthropologists. Although it is often mentioned in ethnographies, there is hardly any literature that gives an overall view. Two exceptions are the summary provided by Kroeber (1948) and the survey of gambling in Asia by Price (1971).

Kroeber expresses puzzlement at the distribution of gambling in cultures throughout the world. If we ignore people who belong to one of the organized world religions, there are about as many cultures in which gambling occurs as there are in which it does not. Nongamblers include the Australian aborigines, the Papuo-Melanesians, and most Polynesians. Of these, aborigines are fairly indifferent to property, while Melanesians are acquisitive. In Africa, nongambling cultures are found in the east, whereas gambling cultures are found in the west. And in pre-Columbian America, most of the northern continent gambled, while most of the southern continent did not. Kroeber sums up (1948, p. 553): "No consistent world-wide correlation of gambling with subsistence economy, wealth system or type of religion works out."

Price's (1971) survey of the material on gambling in the Human Relations Area Files for Asia leads to a more forceful conclusion. He claims that intensive gambling is associated with intensive agriculture; Asian pastoral societies, for instance, had little gambling. And in state societies, the form of gambling differed according to social class. The upper classes of traditional Asia gambled more (in terms of value of stakes) than the lower, but their games were longer, less decisive, and required more skill. Dicing, for example, was almost universally associated with the lower classes. A similar pattern is found in contemporary Jamaica (Stone 1976), which confirms our description of the role of sociological factors in gambling (see Chapter 10).

Anthropological descriptions add two things to our earlier discussion of gambling. First, it is clear that we have focused on gambling where there is a rake-off (e.g., betting on horses, entering lotteries). Although people in some primitive economies devote a great deal of time to gambling – for example, during the long dry season, Hazda men spend the greater part of days on end in gambling (Sahlins 1974, chapter 1) – the games are zero-sum for the participants. This suggests that we should give more attention to the economic psychology of informal gambling in our own culture. Second, we have ignored the social benefits of gambling. Topley (1964) points out that in Hong Kong's New Territories, gambling is an important social activity, and associated with all festivals. A farmer who never gambled would suffer social disapproval. Similarly, Riches (1975) describes gambling in the small Eskimo community he studied as a basic social event. In this community, which lacked compulsory working or ritual groups, participation in gambling seemed to be a manifestation of community integration. And Price (1971) points out that, although the Chinese were inveterate gamblers, they looked on gambling as a means of recreation among friends.

More generally, we see that differences between cultures cannot necessarily be interpreted as evidence of influences of the economy on individual behavior. In Kroeber's broad survey, it is clear that the important determinant of whether or not a culture has gambling is the part of the world in which it is found; gambling simply was not a possible behavior in pre-Columbian South America, for instance. It is only when we get to the finer scale of Price's analysis that we find the economic mode having a determining influence.

Giving

Gift giving has long been of interest to economic anthropologists, and phenomena such as the potlatch or Kula ring have frequently been described and reinterpreted (Codere 1950; Schneider 1974; Malinowski 1922; Rosman & Rubel 1978).

Mauss (1923–4) provided what are still the most important economic anthropological insights into the nature of gift giving (Panoff 1970). He argued that a gift is not simply a transfer of property, but a statement about the relationship between giver and receiver. Furthermore, the gift implies reciprocity; it is part of a network of indebtedness. From an individual's point of view, most gifts are partial repayments of debt. If a debt is completely settled than the relationship will cease. The relationship between giver and receiver may be symmetrical, between equals, or asymmetrical, with a giver who is dominant and who asserts superior status through giving. In this case the receiver is obliged to reciprocate with services or tribute.

Following Mauss's approach, economic anthropologists see few gift exchanges in terms of altruism or sentiment. Rather, they are concerned with alliances, power, reputation, and debt. But there are clearly different kinds of gift. Malinowski (1922) provides a classification based on the reciprocity commitments entailed. At one end of the continuum we have the pure gift (an offering for which nothing is given in return), and at the other pure barter (where the relative value of goods is adjusted by haggling). Taking an anthropological look at modern society, Moles (1972) identifies four common types of gift within it: disguised payments for services rendered, business gifts, spontaneous gifts, and ritual payments. Gifts may therefore signify duty, sympathy, affection, and so on, and may be a matter of obligation, choice, or a mixture of the two.

Pressures to give, to receive, and to reciprocate are extremely powerful in many societies. Cook (1973) describes the reciprocity system, which operates among the Zapotec of Central America. Here certain relatives and friends are obliged to give things if asked, and will suffer social disapproval if they refuse. This obligation to give is also associated with an obligation to receive, to accept a donation when it is offered. A refusal would lead to a breakdown in social relations. The recipient of a gift is also obliged to reciprocate in kind when asked by the original giver. And usually any donation is reciprocated with "interest" (ten dozen eggs are reciprocated with twenty dozen eggs and four kilograms of chocolate), which extends the donor/recipient/donor relationship indefinitely, as well as providing a form of saving.

It might be thought that these "economic" aspects of gift giving would only be important in primities economies that do not possess more efficient ways of distributing goods. But Shurmer (1971), Lowes, Turner, and Wills (1971), Davis (1972), and Sherry (1983) have argued that economic anthropology's analysis of gift giving applies just as much in Western as in primitive societies. Davis, for example, notes that the proportion of GNP spent on gifts in the United Kingdom (5%) is similar to that found in primitive economies. Although outwardly we give gifts to express love or friendship, and in most contexts claim that the monetary value of a gift is unimportant (Webley, Lea, & Portalska, 1983), there is likely to be an element of self-presentation or self-deception in the expression of such views. Lowes and co-workers report that the results of Gallup Poll surveys carried out in Bradford, England, in 1964–7 show a subtle mix of social factors influencing gift giving. As well as the selfish pleasure involved in choosing a gift and the selfless expression of love, there is the sheer force of social coercion. Reciprocity is clearly important within some contexts: More than one-third of households maintained lists of Christmas cards sent and received as a basis for the following year's mailings. Status and prestige is important in others, for example in holiday gifts and wedding presents. "Showing off" was the third most important reason reported for bringing gifts home from holiday.

Gift giving is only one aspect of giving, as we indicated in Chapter 9. Nonetheless, the anthropology of gifts reinforces many of the points we made there: the importance of norms in prescribing appropriate behavior, the influence of social factors, and the rather one-dimensional picture of giving provided by conventional microeconomics. Economic anthropology suggests that the economic influence on giving behavior is more pervasive than we are accustomed to think. It does not, however, provide strong evidence for the influence of the economy on individual behavior. Rather, it suggests that the form of economic behavior may be strongly influenced by noneconomic social norms. Within those norms, however, recognizably consistent economic principles can be found to be operating.

ECONOMIC ANTHROPOLOGY AND ECONOMIC PSYCHOLOGY

Although the material in this chapter has been rather disparate, and some of it may appear either speculative or, at the other extreme, obvious, there seems to be little doubt that economic psychology has much to gain from looking at economic behavior in other cultures. In this respect economic psychology is in much the same position as general psychology, which has (with a few honorable exceptions) ignored this source of data (Jahoda 1983). But there is also a specific lesson, indeed a warning, for economic psychology. Douglas (1982) describes how economic anthropology got off to a brilliant start with Mauss's work on the gift, but then languished on the fringes of anthropology. According to Douglas (1982, p. 174),

It should have been a thriving interdisciplinary enterprise, but therein lies its weakness. All subjects grow strongest when they are most autonomous. The centre of an intellectual discipline is defined by its capacity to settle its own theoretical problems on its own terms. Around this centre the most forceful exponents find it most worthwhile to cluster. The fringes are for the fringy.

Economic anthropology, like economic psychology, constantly had to be on the fringe, because it needed the collaboration of economics. Such a collaboration at a high theoretical level takes a huge amount of effort, and economic anthropologists, in general, have not made this effort. Even the most committed formalists, such as Cook and Schneider, have used only the simplest economic theories. As economic psychologists, we are probably equally guilty. But economic psychology is at an earlier stage of its development, and it need not stay on the fringe. The growth of behavioral economics contains within it a promise to fuse with economic psychology to create a firm interdisciplinary enterprise. Anthropological economics never got past the starting post, leaving economic anthropology waiting at the finish line for a horse that never arrived.

16

ECONOMIC GROWTH AND DEVELOPMENT

The fundamental question of this part of the book, the influence of the economy on the individual, can easily be oversimplified. There is not one economic system in the world, but many. And while each kind of "primitive economy" influences in a variety of ways the individuals who live within it, even within the "standard, modern" economy, there are variations. Most obviously, different political ideologies enforce different economic organizations; for example, economists might well see the difference between a "market" capitalist economy and a "command" socialist economy as overwhelming, although we should do well to remember that most real economies contain elements of both systems.

This chapter is concerned with two other variations or differences between modern economies. The two are linked but not identical. The first is the difference between prosperity (usually linked to expansion) and depression (usually linked to stagnation or slow growth) in developed economies. The second is the difference between more and less developed economies; this issue is usually studied in terms of differences between more and less developed countries or continents, but it is also important for the study of regional variations within nations.

The study of economic growth and development is an area in which it is even more important than usual to distinguish between empirical discussion, theoretical argument, and value judgment. We should emphasize that in discussing the factors that favor economic growth or development of the economies of Third World countries to the kind of sophistication seen in North America and Europe (East as well as West), we are not meaning to imply that this kind of development is necessarily desirable. As we shall discuss further in Chapter 19, there are defensible arguments that economic growth and development do not constitute progress at the human level. But whatever view one takes on this question, it is still important to understand how psychology enters into these economic processes and how it is affected by them.

PSYCHOLOGICAL CORRELATES OF EXPANSION AND
DEPRESSION IN ADVANCED ECONOMIES

We deal first with the psychology of variations within developed economies, since an obvious question to ask about the transition from underdevelopment to developed status is whether it involves the same mechanisms as these smaller-scale changes.

The language of discussions of economic dynamics is replete with
psychological content and overtones. One hears of the importance of
business confidence or of its collapse, of the growth mentality or of its
absence, of inflationary expectations. But there are few data to justify
these psychological terms. In accordance with our general approach to
economic psychology, we shall review what material we can find under
main two headings: Studies of the way in which individuals' psychology
may affect the progress of the economy and studies of the converse
process.

Economic variations due to individual producers

The idea that individual attitudes and aspirations are a factor in economic
growth is by no means new. Most well known, it was espoused by Weber
(1904/1976), who argued that the kind of attitudes nurtured by Protestantism encourage capitalistic entrepreneurship, and that, since the Ref-
ormation, this fact has contributed to the growth of northwest European
and North American economies relative to the generally Catholic Medit-
erranean area. Weber's ideas about the Protestant ethic have been taken
up by many social scientists (e.g., Tawney 1926), but it remains a historical argument open to criticism (e.g., Samuelsson 1961). Many of those
who have opposed Weber have in fact been resisting the more general
idea that individuals' attitudes are the dominant influence on economic
progress (e.g., Rhodes 1968), or even rejecting the idea that individuals
can have any effect at all.

A simple, although essentially negative, argument for the importance
of individual factors in economic growth is advanced by Reynaud (1981,
chapter 4). Reynaud starts from the conventional econometric formula
for predicting economic productivity, which expresses growth in production as a linear function of growth in the labor force, growth in the
quantity of capital engaged, and a residual factor usually written as *e*,
which represents the amount of variance in growth not explained by
either labor or capital growth.

Reynaud points out that more than 60% of the variance in observed
growth typically has to be assigned to the residual factor, and argues from

this that noneconomic factors must have a dominant influence on growth. He therefore replaces the error term e by an expression involving a new variable R, held to correspond to a set of complementary factors (some quantitative, some qualitative), which together explain the unexplained variance. Next he rewrites the expression involving R as the product Nrk, in which N represents the economic drive or dynamism of the individuals in the economy or sector of the economy under study, k the susceptibility of the economy or sector to such dynamism, and r is a scaling factor for relating the two, in effect a kind of residual of the residual. Finally, N itself is broken down according to the formula; $N = IJK$, where I, J, and K stand for intelligence, judgment, and knowledge.

The trouble with Reynaud's approach is that there are very few data to support his analysis. At every point, he shows that the approach is highly plausible, but he supports his argument merely by noting that quantitative factors at the economic level leave much of the variance in production unexplained. Unfortunately, there is really nothing else of substance that proves the importance of psychosocial factors, let alone that intelligence, judgment, and knowledge are the relevant psychosocial dimensions. Indeed, there is really only one area in which a psychological factor in growth can be identified more directly. Denison (1974, chapter 8) was able to estimate that improvements in the educational level of the workforce contributed around 0.5% to annual U.S. economic growth throughout the period 1929–69, during which total growth varied between 2.5% and 4% per annum. Reynaud uses the effect of education as an example to support his more general theme of the importance of qualitative psychosocial variables, but the argument is neither a strong nor a compelling one.

At least at a journalistic level, the psychosocial properties of producers have often been invoked in a rather different way to explain the difference in growth rates (and strike frequencies) between different countries. Comparisons are made among the attitudes to work found in, say, Japan, West Germany, Britain, and the United States. Most of these comparisons are not supported by any serious psychological data, although there have been some interesting case studies of differences in management style, particularly between Japanese and Western businesses (e.g., Pascale & Athos 1982). Psychologists would probably be wary of comparative data on the attitudes of Japanese and Western workers because of the great cultural differences involved, but that problem in itself suggests that there may be a phenomenon worth investigating here. A culture, after all, is (among other things) a collection of attitudes. It is to be hoped that some serious cross-cultural industrial psychology will one day be attempted. Reynaud (1981) mentions a number of relevant case studies, but his descriptions are not systematic enough to be of much use.

Economic variations due to individual consumers

So far, we have concentrated on the psychological properties of the producers within the economy. But Reynaud argues that consumers, too, vary in dynamism, and that this is a function of the same factors, and can be measured in the same way, as the dynamism of producers. As Le Pas (1968) notes, even education as measured by Denison will affect consumption habits as well as producers' competence. In the case of consumption, however, we can find more direct and more positive evidence of the effect of individual variables on economic processes. The notion that individuals' attitudes, expectations, and intentions can lead to variations in the overall performance of the economy is the cornerstone of the thinking of George Katona, and his work is most certainly empirically based.

Katona's views on the role of psychological processes in the economy find their most thorough expression in his 1960 book *The Powerful Consumer,* but the views are involved in both discussion and in the use of the index of consumer sentiment. As we noted in Chapter 7, the index is controversial. Katona and his followers (e.g., Juster 1981) argue that it provides information which cannot be captured by more conventional, economic predictors of the future behavior of the economy. While this may have been true during the late 1940s, when Katona's surveys of consumer attitudes were begun, increasing sophistication in the collection of purely economic data means that the index can now be outperformed by objective measures (e.g., Vanden Abeele 1983). Juster, however, suggests that components of the index may still give unique information. It also may be that the index gives different predictions from modern economic data only under exceptional conditions (which are the most important ones), and that, because governments and financial institutions nowadays heed the index, its most extreme predictions are likely to be preempted.

This controversy is less relevant to the present chapter than it might appear. Our interest is not in predicting economic changes but in understanding them. Even if economic indicators are correlated with the index of consumer sentiment to the extent that the indicators outpredict the index, it does not mean that consumer attitudes are irrelevant to the performance of the economy. It would more correctly suggest that attitudes themselves are not random phenomena; they are affected by economic factors too. This is what we should expect given the dual causation of economic phenomena. None of the detractors of the index has denied that it is well correlated with the behavior of the economy a few months later. The important question is whether that correlation implies that attitudes are a link in the causal chain or merely that the attitudes and economic performance are independent consequences of the economic factors that Vanden Abeele and others have identified. That question cannot really be answered from the data available.

Individual differences in the economy

So far, we have discussed the approaches taken by Reynaud and Katona in terms of the general psychological properties of the entire population of an economy. In practice, of course, people differ greatly in their economic drive and in their attitudes; as Katona (e.g., 1975, pp. 71–2) stressed, we cannot assume (as economics typically has) that these individual variations will average to zero. Much discussion of psychological effects on economic growth has focused on the psychology of key groups within the economy, most often entrepreneurs.

When we come to discuss the psychology of economic development, we shall see that the role and psychological properties of entrepreneurs come to the center of the stage, partly because of their importance in the influential work of McClelland (1961). Even in the advanced mixed economies of Western Europe, governments have established conditions that will encourage an entrepreneurial spirit. Part of the motivation for the building of the Berlin wall was to prevent the "leakage" of highly trained and ambitious individuals from the socialist DDR to West Germany; the same argument has been put forward as an objection to Jewish emigration from the Soviet Union to Israel. This theme, of the migration of the economically dynamic, is also relevant to the psychology of underdevelopment (e.g., Galbraith 1980, chapter 8), but for now, let us note that these political actions imply at least a widespread belief that a few individuals can have a dramatic influence on the health of the economy. This influence need not be positive. A few pathological individuals might have a thoroughly disruptive effect on economic processes. The use of the death penalty against economic saboteurs in some communist countries shows that this belief is held in some quarters.

Belief is one thing and evidence is another. Unfortunately, there are little or no systematic data to support the notion that attitudes among a few entrepreneurs have a measurable effect on economic growth within advanced economies. There are a few suggestive observations. For example, after the building of the Berlin wall, the economy of the DDR did indeed grow much faster, to the point at which its GDP per head approached that of the United Kingdom if not that of West Germany. Here we find ourselves forced back onto historical argument, which we rejected at the beginning of this section in finding Weber's theories an inadequate demonstration of the effects of individual behavior on economic growth. We are bound to conclude that the empirical evidence in support of such effects is generally weak, although more because relevant data have not been collected than because the hypothesis has been tested and found to be wrong.

Effects of economic change on mental disorder

When we turn to the opposite side of the coin – the effects of economic growth or depression on the behavior of individuals – we find no shortage of data in support of at least one proposition. It is generally found that times of economic depression are associated with an increase of every kind of social pathology, and, in particular, with an increase in recorded mental illness.

Some of the literature arguing this point of view is every bit as speculative as anything on the entrepreneurial spirit. There are some hysterical papers from the 1930s, condemning large numbers of the children of the great depression to a life of mental disorder because of the effects financial anxiety was having on their parents (Schumacher 1934) and school teachers (Myers 1934). In a slightly less speculative vein, Courtois (1934) examined the admissions to a Paris mental hospital for the years immediately before and after the stock market collapse and concluded that the depression actually had no psychopathogenic influence (if one discounted the suicides of ruined individuals!), except possibly to precipitate a few cases of depression in individuals who were already strongly disposed to it, and that it had some minor beneficial effects, such as reducing the incidence of acute alcoholism.

Even fifty years ago, there were quantitative studies demonstrating that the rate of first admissions to mental hospitals rises sharply during business crises (e.g., Gaudet & Curry 1933). There are now a number of such longitudinal surveys. Brenner (1973) devotes a book to the subject, and Dooley and Catalano (1980) provide a thorough analytic review of the literature and of the various methodological problems it poses. The conclusion is beyond reasonable doubt: Mental illness rises during economic depressions (as do various other kinds of social pathology such as alcoholism, petty crime, and suicide).

The issue is complex, however. First, the usual measure of mental illness is mental hospital admissions, and the capacity of mental hospitals may vary as a function of economic conditions. Marshall and Funch (1979) noted that Brenner had not taken this factor into account. However, when they reanalyzed a subset of Brenner's data, they confirmed his finding of a strong effect of the state of the economy on mental disorder, at least in the working-age population, even allowing for capacity effects.

The second complication is that economic growth may have some undesirable psychological effects, though these are masked in aggregated longitudinal studies by the larger ill effects of depressions. For example, Brenner (1973) found a positive relationship between economic conditions and admissions to mental hospitals for some social groups, and Murdock and Schriner (1979), in a study of nine rural communities in the western United States, found that both new and long-term residents of developing communities were less satisfied with community services during the development phase than was typical in communities that had never undergone rapid growth, or were in relative decline after the loss of a key industry. On the other hand, Burvill and Kidd (1975) found that, of two Australian mining towns of very similar levels of prosperity, the one that was currently expanding had less psychological illness, at least among women, than the one that was essentially stable.

We shall find that both these complications come into the foreground when we consider the more drastic economic changes that can occur in developing countries. But they are important even in this stage of the argument, for they bear on the theories that have been advanced to explain the effects of economic conditions on mental health.

Two classes of theory suggest themselves immediately. Most obviously, difficult economic conditions for a nation or a region imply difficult economic conditions for individuals within it. Poverty, unemployment, or the fear of either might well induce psychopathology. Most explanatory models of the effects of the economy on mental health follow this route. Dooley and Catalano (1980) formulated a model based on Rahe's concept of "stressful life events." Rahe, Meyer, Smith, Kjaer, and Holmes (1964) and Holmes and Rahe (1967) developed a list of events which are statistically linked to the onset of physical illness and pregnancy, and their scale has subsequently been shown to be related to the onset of mental pathology. Dohrenwend (1979) reviews the available data and discusses some of the problems in interpreting them. High on the Holmes and Rahe list are several events such as change or loss of a job that seem particularly likely to occur during an economic depression. Using data from a large-scale longitudinal study of the psychological state of residents of the Kansas City metropolitan area, Catalano and Dooley (1979) claimed to confirm the increased incidence of stressful life events in economically difficult times; however, their data are actually quite weak, as life events were only well predicted by a complex function of lagged measures of local and regional unemployment figures. Pearlin and Lieberman (1979) provide rather stronger data, showing that economic life events were among those most strongly associated with psychological distress, and also that the distressing effect of both economic and noneconomic life events was sharply accentuated by persistent economic hardship.

An approach based on Rahe's work has two obvious virtues. First, it can explain the occasional ill effects of economic growth (e.g., expansion can also lead to job change). Second, it allows an integration of the longitudinal studies cited above with the many cross-sectional studies that show that, at any given time within any given economy, economically disadvantaged individuals are, for a variety of reasons, most vulnerable to all kinds of ill health including mental disorder (e.g., Dohrenwend & Dohrenwend 1969; Hollingshead & Redlich 1958). Colledge (1982), like

Dooley and Catalano, argues that the effect of economic depression on mental health is mediated by stress. He points out that recessions have a selective effect, affecting the poorest members of a society disproportionately. Economic data suggest that middle- and upper-income groups may profit during a recession. For example, the real price of food in the United Kingdom fell steadily throughout the "bad" years of the 1920s and 1930s (Stone & Rowe 1966, chapter 11). However, Elder and Liker (1982) showed that, among women who did actually suffer financial hardship during the great depression of the 1930s, middle-class women seem to have derived some kind of psychological benefit, since their emotional health in 1979 was substantially better than that of their contemporaries who escaped hardship. Among working-class women, the more predictable adverse effect of hardship on emotional health fifty years later was observed. Thus, even if the objective effect of economic recession is the same in all strata of society, the poorest are likely to suffer most, presumably because of the cumulative effects of stressful life events.

There is a second possible class of explanation for the correlation between economic depression and psychiatric disorder. It could be that difficult conditions in the economy have a general effect, regardless of whether an individual personally suffers reduced prosperity. For example, Epstein and Babad (1982) regard inflation as a "psychological stressor." Some clinical psychologists recognize a class of "ideological depression," due to individuals' feelings of powerlessness in the face of what they regard as undesirable developments in the general state of the world.

There are a number of mechanisms by which such a general effect might be brought about. For instance, the material broadcast in the mass media might change. News items will almost inevitably reflect good or bad economic conditions unless the media are under total government control (and probably even then). Mosley (1982) showed that journalistic reporting of economic phenomena is often quite distorted, so the link between objective economic conditions and public attitudes may well be indirect. However, it may still be important; in fact, journalistic distortion makes it more likely that we shall be able to demonstrate the correlation, since distortions will reduce the correspondence between economic and psychological measures of the state of the economy.

Quite apart from their role in reporting economic news, the media may respond in more generalized ways to the state of the economy. Jorgenson (1975) examined the television programs shown in Los Angeles during the first week in October for every year from 1950 to 1974, and found that they were more authoritarian in content in years when there were actual or perceived economic problems. Padgett and Jorgenson (1982) showed that the frequency of articles on topics related to superstition (astrology and mysticism) in German magazines in the period 1918–40 showed a positive correlation with economic threat. On a much longer time scale, Kavolis (1964a) argued that predominant artistic style is correlated with economic conditions, revolutionary changes in human mastery over nature being associated with abstract art, more pragmatic periods with naturalism. Kavolis argues that the causal factor here is psychological congruity between style and attitudes to economic action or economic conditions, and speculates that art style may serve to modify such attitudes through the same congruity process.

Clearly, the way in which people respond to changes in general economic conditions is likely to be a function of individual personality or other noneconomic variables. Bronzaft and Dobrow (1976) found that students' essays on their reactions to the mild recession occurring in the mid-1970s could be classified into three groups. Some students claimed that it made them more motivated to do well, others that it increased their anxiety about finding jobs and so forth, while others reported that the recession did not affect them. These differences were confirmed by the two groups' performance on an achievement/anxiety test.

In conclusion, we should not maintain that hard times lead to increased mental illness only because of direct effects on individuals. No doubt that is part of the story, perhaps even the major part. But there also seem to be more general effects, and some individuals will be more vulnerable effects than others.

Economic change and individual behavior

Although data on the interaction of economic conditions and mental health make up a large majority of the literature on the effects of economic change on the individual within developed economies, other phenomena have been investigated. We need to distinguish between effects of economic change that are direct in the sense that they are due to particular individuals who are especially affected (e.g., by becoming unemployed) and more general effects. Once again, there is some dissociation between actual and perceived economic conditions.

There is good evidence that people's perceptions of general economic conditions can affect their behavior, both economic and noneconomic. Survey data have repeatedly shown that people who believe that the general condition of the economy has improved and is going to improve further are more likely to make major consumer purchases than those who believe that the economy is standing still or declining (e.g., Katona 1975, pp. 192–5). Since general economic conditions are actually the same for everyone, within as well as between years, Katona's finding must be due to attitudes rather than simply to the objective conditions that help to form them. Similarly, Epstein and Babad (1982) reported that consumers' (self-reported) buying and leisure behaviors were more strongly related to the perceived threat from inflation than to individual income, both in the United States, which has relatively little inflation, and in Israel, with inflation ten times higher. Such general responses to economic conditions are substantial enough for marketing experts to take them seriously (e.g., Kelley & Scheewe 1975).

Although there can certainly be a dissociation between perceived and actual economic circumstances at the individual as well as at the general level, objective personal circumstances have an additional power to force themselves on people's attention. Adjustments to economic behavior may be essential following a change in income, especially if it is a change for the worse. Strumpel (1976, chapter 11) summarized some of the ways in which individuals adjust their economic behavior to accommodate changes in their economic conditions and the psychological mechanisms involved (particularly changes in aspirations and values).

Economic conditions, both personal and general, may also affect non-economic behaviors. One example can be found in a careful study by Sales (1972), which demonstrated that conversions to authoritarian religious denominations became substantially more frequent in years of economic threat, while conversions to liberal denominations were more frequent in more prosperous years. This was true of the United States as a whole, and also, in particular, of the city of Seattle, which has a relatively isolated economy by virtue of its dependence on the Boeing aerospace concern.

Economic conditions and individuals' attitudes

In addition to affecting behavior, economic conditions (and changes in them) affect people's attitudes. The attitude changes may or may not be caused by the same causal agents that affect behavior. As noted in Chapter 1, this is one of the most controversial points in the psychology of attitudes. With the exception of the material relating to the Index of Consumer Sentiment, the point has not been investigated very thoroughly in connection with economic behavior. But three kinds of attitude measurement have been carried out extensively. The first is measurement of people's own assessments of their economic and general well-being or happiness; the second is measurement of satisfaction with the economic and social system; and the third is investigation of people's own explanations of economic conditions.

Assessment of people's subjective happiness or, in economic terms, their perceived welfare, has quite a long history. Easterlin (1974) was able to use data from Gallop polls in the United States going back to 1949. Some of the investigations have been extremely extensive (e.g., Andrews & Withey 1976). The measures used are reasonably reliable: test-retest correlations of 0.39 to 0.41 for individual questions, 0.53 for a combined quality of life index in a Canadian sample (Atkinson 1982);

Simon (1974) argues strongly that the measures are good estimates of welfare in the technical, economic sense.

Two results stand out consistently in such investigations. First, in any one country, at any one time, rated happiness is strongly correlated with income. Second, and apparently in contradiction, individuals' average ratings of their overall happiness were almost unchanged during the 62% rise in real incomes in the United States over the period 1946–70, and are almost unrelated to gross national product in international comparisons (Easterlin 1974). Scitovsky (1976, chapter 7) draws the obvious conclusion that social status (indicated by or correlated with income) is more important for happiness than income as such, though he also points to other factors, such as work satisfaction, enjoyment of novelty, and addiction to income or its uses.

But it is surely not status as such which is important here. Simon (1974) argues that the important factor is relative income, not social power. By comparing two Israeli kibbutzim organized on different ideological lines, Morawetz et al. (1977) showed that, at a given income level, people were happier in the community with the more egalitarian income distribution. In a sample of male family heads in the United States, Yuchtman (Yaar) (1976) also found that individuals' satisfaction with their standard of living was more strongly affected by the perceived equity of their economic situation, and the extent to which they attributed it to internal factors, than by objective income. Apel and Strumpel (1976) reached a similar conclusion on the basis of a comparison of satisfaction levels in Greece and Bulgaria in 1972–3. At that time, both countries had authoritarian regimes at the political level. Greece had a largely free market economy, while Bulgaria had a socialist economy with a more equal distribution of direct and indirect income.

An obvious response to difficult economic conditions, either personal or general, is disaffection either with the government of the day or the economic system of the country. This is the second kind of attitude whose relation to economic conditions, general and personal, has been investigated in detail. Geiger (1932/1967, pp. 109–22) suggested that the Nazi movement had its roots in the economic decline of the self-employed middle class. Gurr (1970) made a similar point about the origins of more recent protest movements. Strumpel (1976, chapter 9) has made a systematic study of survey data on satisfaction with the government, its policies, and the state of the economy in the United States. While such surveys have been criticized (e.g., Turner & Krauss 1978), Strumpel's major results are plausible, and they are also consistent with data we have already cited. It is not individuals' economic well-being as such that affects their attitude toward the government and the economic system, as much as it is the extent to which personal economic aspirations have been either fulfilled or frustrated.

The third kind of attitudinal investigation which we should mention is the study of individuals' explanations for economic conditions. Feagin (1972), Feather (1974), and Furnham (1982), working in the United States, Australia, and the United Kingdom, respectively, have studied the reasons people give for inequities in income within a society. All the studies agree that there are three classes of explanation: individualistic, structural, and fatalistic. Both Feagin and Feather found that poorer people tended to give more "structural" explanations, that is, to attribute poverty to properties of the economy and society, while wealthier people tended to attribute economic fortunes to properties of individuals. This was not true, however, in a study of attitudes in EEC countries (*The Perception of Poverty in Europe*, 1977 p. 73).

Closely related to such lay explanations of general economic phenomena are people's explanations of their own wealth or poverty, an economic form of what psychologists call "locus of control" (Rotter 1966). Strumpel (1976) found that the poorer an individual is, the more likely he or she is to attribute personal (relative) prosperity or poverty to external forces (e.g., the state or management of the economy) rather than to internal ones (e.g., motivation or ability). He also found that poorer people were more likely to have consistent explanations for their own economic situation and the economic situation of the country as a whole; that is, they attributed both national and personal economic difficulties to structural rather than individualistic causes. According to Gurin and Gurin (1976), however, the relationship between economic status and locus of control variables becomes more complex on closer examination.

The attitudinal data reviewed in this section are highly relevant to the question raised at the beginning of this chapter: Is economic growth necessarily to be interpreted as human progress? This question is considered in more detail in Chapter 19, but it is also discussed below because it bears directly on the psychological causes and effects of the transition from underdeveloped to developed status.

PSYCHOLOGY AND DEVELOPMENT ECONOMICS

When we consider the psychology of economic development outside of the familiar highly developed North American and Western European economies, questions of value force themselves to the forefront. Even our terminology becomes value laden. The original term, "underdeveloped countries," can be seen as incorporating a value judgment, implying that countries of lower GNP somehow morally ought to be seeking development in order to rival the United States, West Germany, or Japan. Among development experts, what were once called "underdeveloped countries" have successively become known as "less developed" and now "developing." While it is only proper to be sensitive to the susceptibilities and reasonable pride of those who may be seen as less economically fortunate, these terminological shifts do not solve the underlying problem. The very word "development" carries unambiguous and inevitable connotations of progress; to use it is to imply that the way of life of less wealthy countries is in some way lower or less desirable than that of the "developed world." Even the less obviously evaluative term, the Third World, can be criticized because it implicitly places most of those who use it into the First World.

There is no real escape from this dilemma, and it is compounded by the fact that the governments of most developing countries, most of the time, actively seek development. The usual title of the area of economics which deals with such problems is development economics. But, quite apart from our desire to avoid a patronizing approach to the people whose problems we are now considering, as economic psychologists we must be very careful to avoid the traps set by an inescapably evaluative terminology. We cannot afford to assume, explicitly or implicitly, that economic development is a desirable goal which every progressive person must strive toward. Economic psychologists are precisely those who should be most alert to the possibility that the process of development is destructive at the individual level. Economists may point out that development is leading to increasing impoverishment of the poorest members of a society; anthropologists may point to the toll it takes on indigenous cultures; but it is for the psychologists to discover the psychological costs (and benefits) of development to the individual.

With that caveat in mind, we shall use the currently accepted terminology developing countries. But the reader must remember that development is not necessarily progress, and that some of the countries referred to can scarcely be said to be developing at all at present. We begin, as in the first part of this chapter, by considering the effects individuals can have on economic development.

Psychological causation and development

Development is one of the fields of economic behavior in which psychologists have taken a strong interest and in which nonpsychologists have explicitly appealed to psychological explanations of economic phenomena. Perhaps the most ambitious program of this type is Benitah's (1980) attempt to construe economic development by means of an analogy to the Freudian theory of individual psychosexual development, but a number of sociological or economic authors have advanced what are recognizably psychological theories. Weber (1904/1930) should be considered the first of these psychological theorists insofar as his ideas about the Protestant ethic refer to individuals' attitudes. Weber, however, also recognized the social determinants of individual psychology (see Rhodes 1968).

Explicit psychological theorizing concerning development is also found in the writings on development of the sociologist Talcott Parsons, Weber's translator. Parsons (1951, pp. 59 ff.) maintained that there is a strictly limited and defined set of alternative patterns of value orientation. For example, he contrasted "cognitive" and the "cathectic" motivational orientations. The cognitive mode implies a universalistic standard of role expectation, according to which a person might be selected for a role on grounds of technical competence. The cathectic mode implies a particularistic standard, according to which a person might be selected on the basis of friendship or family membership. Economic development depends on a shift in these patterns of value orientations. In the example given here, obviously the cognitive, universalistic mode is more compatible with economic modernization than the cathectic, particularistic standard. It is true that Parsons, as a sociologist, sees these pattern variables as properties of roles more than of individuals, and as molded by social pressures. Parsons (1951, pp. 243 ff.) makes this explicit in his discussion of the profit motive. But at any one time, it is individuals who fill roles, and Parsons is clearly among those who see individuals' psychology as effecting social change, of which economic development is a part.

Another influential development theorist who has propounded a clearly psychological theory is Hagen (e.g., 1962, 1975). He argues that "social change will not occur without changes in personality" (1962, p. 86). Hagen draws a distinction between authoritarian and innovative personality types, arguing that they are characteristic of traditional and modern societies, respectively. Economic development therefore requires some impetus that will cause innovative personalities to develop within traditional societies. Hagen finds this cause in loss of status respect, particularly in minority religious or ethnic groups. He is thus able to account for the preponderance of nonconformists among English innovators of the eighteenth century or of samurai among Japanese innovators of the nineteenth without having to identify special features of these particular belief systems.

The distinction between traditional and modern personalities is made by many other social theorists. Lerner (1958) argued that the essential difference was one of mobility or empathy. To be modern is to be able to conceive of oneself in many different roles – to see that society could be different from the way it is or that economic ends might be achieved by different means than those in current use. Inkeles and Smith (1974) tried to construct a scale of overall modernity of personality, the OM scale; they tested it on samples of a thousand people in each of six developing countries. Rogers (1969, chapter 13) constructed a scale of innovativeness that measured the degree to which an individual adopts new ideas relatively earlier than others in his social system, and argued that it provided the best single indicator of an individual's degree of modernization. It is an empirical question as to whether any such single dimension can account for a significant proportion of the variation among people. Triandis (1973) claimed that it cannot, and Von Fleckenstein (1974) found very low intercorrelations between different measures of innovativeness in a sample of Thai farmers.

Even if we accept innovativeness or the OM scale as useful, in order to turn the distinction between traditional and modern personalities into a theory of economic development rather than simply of comparative economics, we once again need to supply an account of the transition between traditional and modern. Lerner (1958) and Rogers (1969) have sought such an account in the processes of communication, particularly via the mass media. Lerner talks of the media multiplier, Rogers, more colorfully, of the magic multiplier, which is applied to modernizing influences. Like new products (see Chapter 6), new economic ideas spread in predictable ways through a society. They are advertised, directly and indirectly; and the economic mood of a developing country is just as likely to be reflected in and affected by its mass media as that of an advanced economy (recall the media effects discussed earlier in this chapter).

One problem with all these approaches is that they tend to view economic development as the crossing of a single threshold between traditional and modern ways. Of course, what is currently modern might in time become traditional, but it is not clear how Lerner's mobile personality, or Hagen's innovator, could ever allow this to happen. History suggests that economic development is a continuing process. Countries that are relatively advanced in one era decay and need a new process of development at a later time. From a psychological point of view, therefore, this continuous approach to development implies that at any time there will be some people in a society whose personalities favor development. The question is how many there are, and whether circumstances allow them to have a major influence. It is this view that underlies one of the best-known psychological theories of economic development, D. C. McClelland's theory of achievement motivation. Because it is a particularly well worked out example of a psychological approach to an economic phenomenon, we shall consider McClelland's work in some detail, even though recent research suggests that its empirical support is by no means as strong as was once claimed.

Achievement motivation, entrepreneurship, and development

McClelland (1961) advanced the hypothesis that cultures differ in the extent to which they encourage a personality variable which he called "achievement motivation" or n Ach. He argued that n Ach was an essential component in the personality of the successful businessman, and that the transition from an underdeveloped to a developed economy depended crucially on the dynamism of a relatively small group of entrepreneurs. He also claimed that n Ach could be measured in individuals, ideally by "projective" methods such as Morgan and Murray's (1935) Thematic Apperception Test (TAT), that the extent to which a culture nurtured n Ach could be assessed (for example by examining a cross section of children's stories), that n Ach varied between cultures and between individuals within a culture as a function of child-rearing practices, and that, while n Ach was a relatively enduring property of a person, training designed to raise n Ach levels in suitable individuals could be accomplished and would be a relatively cheap way of encouraging economic development.

This is a formidable array of propositions in what we would now recognize as economic psychology, and they are all testable at least to some extent. Furthermore, McClelland and his followers have shown great persistence and ingenuity in finding empirical data which bear on them. The following brief account illustrates some of the more important results relevant to each of the major points of McClelland's argument.

1. *The measurement of n Ach:* McClelland, Clark, Roby, and Atkinson (1949) claimed a reliability coefficient of 0.95 for measurements of n Ach from the TAT. However, much of McClelland's work on economic questions has depended on less direct measures of n Ach, such as the rating of children's stories or other "products of imagination." McClelland (1961, p. 74) claims interrater reliability coefficients between 0.92 and 0.98 for the story ratings. Across the various measures of needs and values used by McClelland, n Ach consistently emerges as the factor that is most reliably assessed.

2. *The relationship between child-rearing practices and n Ach:* Child, Storm, and Veroff (1958) showed that, across a sample of 110 cultures, those whose folktales indicated that n Ach was important in their society tended to have child-rearing practices that encouraged self-mastery. Within the United States, Winterbottom (1958) found differences in the attitudes and behavior which mothers had toward sons who were classified as high or low in n Ach. McClelland (1961, p. 356) summarized the parental attitudes that favored high n Ach as "reasonably high standards of excellence imposed at a time when the sons can attain them, a willingness to let him [sic] attain them without interference, and real emotional pleasure in his achievements."

3. *Correlation between n Ach and entrepreneurial behavior:* McClelland (1961) showed that students' interest in business careers was correlated with their n Ach level, at least among students from a middle-class or lower-middle-class family background in the United States and possibly in Japan, but not in Brazil, West Germany, or India. Crockett (1962) showed that, in the United States, high levels of n Ach were

correlated with upward movements in social status, but again only in children from lower-class backgrounds. To explain this pattern of results, McClelland argues that business is only the path to achievement for certain people in certain types of society. Those who are already members of the elite, or whose society assigns no prestige to business occupations, seek achievement in other types of career. McClelland (1961, chapter 7) argues this point in great detail. Recent empirical support comes, for example, in a study by McClelland (1977) of the effects of educational background on the careers of Ethiopian students, and also from a study by Koo (1976) of petty entrepreneurs (stallholders, street traders, and the like) in a rapidly developing city in South Korea (although Koo found that such occupations only made possible rather limited social mobility).

4. *The dependence of economic growth on entrepreneurial behavior:* This is perhaps the weakest point in McClelland's argument because it demands purely economic rather than psychological evidence. Even in the economic literature on development, we have been unable to find direct evidence for the crucial role of the entrepreneurial individual. Historical argument for it, of course, is easy to find, from Weber to McClelland to the most recent writers on entrepreneurship such as Casson (1984).

5. *The possibility of training n Ach:* In a series of projects in India, McClelland and Winter (1969) showed that relatively brief periods of training, designed to increase businessmen's level of n Ach, led to increased levels of entrepreneurial activity for at least some years afterward.

6. *The relationship between n Ach and economic growth at the national level:* If every step in McClelland's argument is accurate, then it follows that countries whose culture inculcates a high level of n Ach should experience high rates of economic growth. McClelland (1961, chapter 3) collected samples of stories from children's school readers from the period 1920–9 for 23 countries, and from the period 1946–55 for 40 countries. He showed that, across countries, the level of achievement motivation revealed in the stories from the 1925 period was well correlated with economic growth as measured by the increase in electricity consumption from 1929 to 1959, provided that allowance was made for the fact that countries that were already advanced at the beginning of the period tended to grow faster. McClelland (1961, chapter 4) supported this result with some ingenious attempts to measure the achievement motivation of past societies (including measurements of the style of decoration used on vases from ancient Greece and pre-Columbian Peru), which, in almost all cases, were found to be correlated with the level of economic activity some decades afterward. Further analysis of the story material suggested that other motiva-

tional variables, in particular other-directedness, were also correlated with economic growth (McClelland 1961, chapter 5), but it is the correlation with n Ach that is perhaps McClelland's best-known result.

The current status of McClelland's theory

Some recent studies have supported McClelland's position. For example, in a comparison of three Nigerian tribes, LeVine (1966) found that n Ach, as measured from dream reports, and from mention of self-development in an opinion survey, varied between the three major ethnic groups in Nigeria in the same way as their observed status mobility and reputed entrepreneurship. Rogers (1969, chapter 11) reports correlations between n Ach and a variety of measures of farming success among Colombian peasants. Matter (1977) obtained autobiographies from a sample of high school graduates from a small town in Kansas and showed that those high in n Ach tended to stay in the town during the 1907–24 period when it was progressing economically, but tended to leave during the 1950–67 period when the town was in economic decline. This is a weak study, however, because of the many other differences between these time periods. Sinha and Chaubey (1972) found similar effects when comparing two relatively developed villages in India with two less developed but otherwise similar villages.

Although McClelland (1961) himself also argues each of his points in considerable theoretical and empirical detail, it is now obvious that some of his statistical analysis is not very compelling and that too much is made of correlations which, even if significant, were frequently very low (below 0.20 in many instances). McClelland's impressive structure (to which the highly selective summary above scarcely does justice) has not withstood the test of time. For example, Singh (1978) studied 51 pairs of farming brothers in Panjab, India, in each of which one brother's farm output was growing quickly while the other's was growing slowly. He found no significant differences in n Ach between the two groups. Hamer (1978) measured n Ach in a small sample of boys from the generally entrepreneurial and achievement-oriented Sadama people in southern Ethiopia in 1965, and repeated the measurement on the same individuals in 1973. The correlation between the two sets of measurements was essentially zero, and the changes could be interpreted fairly readily in terms of intervening economic events. This suggests that n Ach may be a result of economic progress, rather than a predictor of it. Within the developed economy of the United States, Cover and Johnson (1976) found that, over the period 1923–70, the general level of n Ach varied with the business cycle. They measured n Ach from the proportion of individuals featured in the cover pictures on the magazine *Time* whose social roles corresponded to "external" needs of the community (businessmen, politicians, scientists, military men and so forth, as opposed to entertainers, sportsmen, and educational or religious leaders). Cover and Johnson argue that their data contradicts McClelland's claim that n Ach is a relatively enduring property of a culture. If n Ach is, on the contrary, a product of the economic situation, rather than one of its causes, it would be expected to fluctuate with the immediate economic circumstances, which is what Cover and Johnson in fact observed.

The most direct attack on McClelland's position comes from a series of reports which have challenged the idea (McClelland 1961, p. 203) that those countries that show high levels of n Ach (and also "other-directedness," a second motivational variable that McClelland had found to be correlated with economic growth) would be the ones that would continue to grow more rapidly between 1960 and 1970. Note that McClelland had already shown at least a weak relation between n Ach as measured in 1950 and growth up to 1960. More recent studies have used McClelland's story data to provide n Ach levels for 1950, and UN statistics for growth since those data. Following McClelland's statistical procedures closely, Finison (1976) and Beit-Hallahmi (1980) obtained insignificant correlations of −0.02 and 0.11 between n Ach in 1950 and growth in electricity production from 1952 to 1970 and 1976, respectively. Even more damaging is a paper by Mazur and Rosa (1977). They note that, by present standards, McClelland's way of allowing for the fact that economies that are already advanced grow fastest is very unconventional. It would currently be normal to use a multiple regression approach in which both n Ach and electricity production at the beginning of the period of interest appear as independent variables. Doing the analysis this way (and also including other-directedness as an independent variable), Mazur and Rosa come to the same conclusion as Finison and Beit-Hallahmi: They find no relationship between motivational variables and economic growth. They then proceed to apply their multiple regression technique to McClelland's original data, and, despite using several variants of the regression, again find essentially no relationship between n Ach in 1925 and growth from 1925 to 1950. This raises a strong possibility that McClelland's original and much-discussed result is really an artifact of his unusual statistical approach. It is interesting that Hagen (1975, chapter 11) dismissed McClelland's evidence on just such statistical grounds, apparently before the adverse results of using more conventional methods were known. It could be that McClelland's account of the role of n Ach in entrepreneurship, hence in development, is essentially correct but that the causal chain is too long and the changes in n Ach over a twenty-five-year period too many for successful longitudinal predictions to be made, but at present the evidence in support of McClelland's position is weak at best.

A different kind of attack on McClelland's theories, and also on related ideas such as those of Hagen (1962), has been mounted by Inkeles (1983, chapter 7). Using the individual modernity (IM) scale, a modification of the overall modernity scale of Inkeles and Smith (1974), to allow for cross-national comparisons, he investigated whether subgroups within a society do in fact tend to have different IM scores, as all theories deriving from Weber (1904/1976) would tend to suggest. Inkeles found that any such differences are slight compared with the differences between countries.

Given the present state of evidence, we must clearly view McClelland's theories with some caution. It is hard to doubt that there is some correlation between some kinds of economic behavior and n Ach. But considerable doubt remains as to whether n Ach is the crucial variable in economic growth or merely a correlate of some other social or psychological process. Furthermore, with the critical longitudinal studies undermined, it is impossible to be clear about the direction of causality between the economic and psychological phenomena concerned. McClelland has been justly criticized (e.g., Rhodes 1968) for ignoring the historical dimension in economic development, and the extent of economic determination of individual behavior. As we have already seen, it may be that high levels of n Ach are a product rather than a cause of economic growth.

Culture and development

McClelland is by no means alone in arguing for an effect of individual psychology on economic development. The problem about direction of causality, however, is common to most accounts that attribute development to traits that individuals acquire from their culture. Many of the competing analyses have points in common with McClelland's but are either less thoroughly worked out or less securely based in empirical work. We have already mentioned the influential ideas of Weber about the connection between Protestantism and the transition to capitalism and industrialization in Western Europe. McClelland (1961, chapter 9) discusses this theme in considerable detail, summarizing empirical studies of current child-rearing practices and attitudes among Protestants, Catholics, and Jews in the United States and also among Protestants and Catholics in West Germany where denominational differences are much less confounded with ethnic and class differences. McClelland concludes that the psychological differences noted by Weber and others do exist but that their strength within any one country is hardly great enough to account for the massive social changes attributed to them by social historians. Furthermore, Weber's use of historical documents has been criticized as being biased (Samuelsson 1961).

In recent history, the economic development of Western Europe and its former colonies is paralleled only by the emergence of Japan as a major economic power from about 1850 onward to the first half of the twentieth century, and the more recent emergence of a number of East Asian states, especially those with strong ethnic Chinese elements in their population. Ayal (1963) offers a detailed comparison of Japanese and Thai societies in the latter half of the nineteenth century. He argues that they were superficially very similar but that the value system prevalent in Japan, with its emphasis on the subordination of the individual to collective effort and on active loyalty to the central state, provided both the goals and the means for development. Thai culture, on the other hand, emphasized a much more passive kind of loyalty, and a detached pursuit of individual merit to which economic achievement was simply irrelevant. Galbraith (1980) develops this theme in more detail. The cause of the mass poverty associated with underdevelopment, he argues, is the equilibrium permitted by people's accommodation to poverty. Where a culture sets up expectations of a higher standard of living, people who find themselves impoverished will strive to restore that standard. It is in these expectations, and not in any ethnic factor, that Galbraith finds the explanation of the rapid development of ethnically Chinese nations in Asia, of the rapid escape from poverty of German refugees after World War II, of the rapid economic development of north and east India relative to the south and west, and of the economic dynamism of North European immigrants to North America.

Similarly, Reynaud (1981, chapter 8) argues that economic development depends on the crossing of psychosocial thresholds. While these are more likely to be crossed by individuals of higher mental energy, hence economic drive, Reynaud also suggests that once a threshold has been crossed, the mental energy of the entire community is likely to be enhanced by increased access to education, information, and the products characteristic of a more advanced economy. In other words, although drive is a characteristic of individuals, it is not immutable and is affected by the expectations prevalent in a society.

Our reevaluation of McClelland's work led to the idea that the need for achievement, and consequent entrepreneurial activity, might be as much a product of economic development as its cause. Even McClelland's own ideas stress how much economically relevant personality variables depend on the general economic development of a society. The less systematic studies that we have just reviewed lead to the same conclusion. But all these analyses concentrate on the antecedent effects of economy or society on individuals. An alternative has been offered by Kunkel (1963), who advocates an operant analysis of the rewards offered by different societies to entrepreneurial individuals. He supports his theoretical approach by reinterpreting Hagen's (1962) account of the transition from a "traditional" to "modern" society in terms of the contingencies of reinforcement and punishment offered by each. It is not necessary to be a committed Skinnerian to see that such a prospective approach to entrepreneurial behavior might have some advantages, especially for an integration with economic theory; but at present Kunkel's is a lone voice, at least among psychologists.

We have identified society and its values – in a word, culture – as the likely cause of different rates of development in different countries. Of course, culture can either promote or hinder development. Hagen (1963, chapter 12) comments at length on how "traditional attitudes" can disrupt otherwise good development plans. In a later work (1975) he refers to the need to "break the crust of custom" if development is to be achieved. McClelland (1961, chapter 5) attempts to identify the attitudes likely to favor or discourage development. Among the latter we find, for example, religious advocacy of a passive acceptance of fate. Galbraith (1980) stresses the ill effects of accommodation to an impoverished environment. More specific cultural problems have also been identified. For example, Oommen (1961) suggests that the culturally enforced practices of buying prestige jewelry and paying for elaborate religious ceremonies reduce the extent to which Indians' savings are held in forms where they could be invested and so encourage economic growth. Oommen, however, notes that savings in the form of jewelry may be a highly practical measure in a country with an underdeveloped banking system. But not all cultural hindrances to development are "backward." Uribe Villegas (1962), for instance, argues that irrational attempts to copy the way of life of the United States are a negative influence on development in Mexico.

Everything we have said so far about individuals' effect on economic development has had to do with the affective and conative aspects of human nature. It is worth recalling that, in connection with economic growth in developed economies, Reynaud (1981) identified intelligence, judgment, and knowledge as the key personal qualities; all three are cognitive. The tremendous efforts that have been devoted to the problem of education in Third World countries indicate that at least policymakers believe that cognitive properties of individuals can influence development. There is a correlation between level of development and educational achievement in a country but, as with almost everything else we have mentioned so far, the direction of causality is uncertain.

Mental health and the transition to development

When we look at the psychological effects of the transition from underdeveloped to developed status, we find that one effect dominates the literature. It is the same effect as the one we found when considering fluctuations in economic success of developed societies (development appears to lead to various kinds of social pathology, including major increases in the incidence of mental disorder) but in reverse of most findings in developed economies: Times of economic depression and stagnation lead to increases in psychiatric problems in developed countries, but in societies undergoing the major changes that accompany industrialization, we find that material progress seems to cause, or be associated with, psychological distress.

Regarding national statistics, the literature is largely qualitative and impressionistic. Both formal provision for the mentally ill and record-keeping are likely to improve so much during the transition to developed status that longitudinal statistics are unlikely to mean much. It is worth remembering, though, that the well-established correlation between mental disorder and economic conditions in the United States was first investigated because of the "contentions of hospital superintendents and clinicians" (Gaudet & Curry 1933); impressions, therefore, cannot be ignored.

At the level of gross social pathology, however, reasonable national statistical data are available. Using data from the 1953–60 period and a cross section of 48 countries varying in industrialization and urbanization, Quinney (1965) showed that mental disorders and economic conditions were correlated with a decrease in the homicide rate but an increase in suicide. Hartnagel (1982) showed that economic development was correlated with an increase in female theft and fraud, but that there was no effect on female homicide. Papers arguing for a more general effect of economic development on mental disorder are not hard to find, but usually lack hard data (e.g., Binitie 1976). Better data on more strictly psychological questions are more readily obtained from smaller-scale studies of particular communities. Special attention has been focused on alcohol use, which frequently rises drastically as communities are drawn into the cash economy, for example, among the Naskapi Indians of Quebec, studied by Robbins (1973) or the native Alaskans studied by Foulks & Katz (1973); Guntern (1978) describes how the same process happened within the developed world, as the traditional Swiss village of Saas-Fee changed from an agricultural to a tourist economy. Other development-induced changes in psychopathology have also been documented. For example, Eastwell (1974) attributed an excess of psychiatric illness among the polygynously married members of the Murngin aborigine population of East Arnhem Land, northern Australia, to contact with the cash economy.

In contrast to the general weakness of the data, there has been no shortage of theory to account for the effects of development on social pathology. Many explanations focus on the disruption of traditional roles, which means that attitudes and expectations are discordant between individuals and out of tune with behavior (Christensen 1975; Eastwell 1974). Statistical evidence for this role-disruption account of development-induced social pathology is not easy to find, however. In the study of female crime mentioned above, Hartnagel (1982) looked at a number of measures of role change and concluded that none of them explained the effects of modernization; the best account he could give was that a more urbanized and industrialized society simply increased the opportunity for "economic" crime for both men and women.

Other explanations of the effects of development on mental health focus on the direct effects of economic change as such. Economic development may be seen as a source of stress (e.g., Sanvictores 1976), just as economic change within advanced economies may be. Another obvious suggestion is that, during the course of economic development, economic concerns tend to replace interpersonal relationships as primary values. Burt (1975) has claimed to document this process during the industrialization of the United States, by content analysis of a sample of front-page reports from the *New York Times* over the period 1877–1972. He found that the percentage of articles concerned with corporate entities rose by 0.24 per year, while the percentage concerned with individuals fell by the same amount. Binitie (1976) sees economic development as causing an increase in disruptive behavior by reducing the available legitimate means of impulse discharge, for example by the formation of shanty towns that lack both physical facilities and social coherence. Robbins (1973) suggests that development increases the incidence of interpersonal conflict, partly because the availability of consumer goods offers new ways of establishing and maintaining possibly conflicting ego identities and partly because the availability of cash employment shakes up established status relationships. The general theme that emerges is one of economic change as causing discontent and frustration.

Again, we have to be careful about the direction of causality. If the analysis offered by McClelland, Galbraith, Hagen, and others is even partly right, it is precisely the discontented, frustrated individuals who are likely to be the entrepreneurial engines of economic development. It is not surprising that many of them are to be found in societies that are undergoing transition; they are likely to be attracted to them and to be prominent within them. Discussing the "hidden agenda" for their book on modernization, Inkeles and Smith (1974) emphasize their desire to eliminate the myth that modernization is psychically harmful, and their results do go some way toward doing this. But at the same time, if Holmes and Rahe's (1967) schedule of stressful life events applies to developing as well as developed communities, it is clear that rapid development is indeed likely to be a time of great stress, and to lead to a relatively high incidence of stress-related physical and mental disorder for at least some people. The crucial question is whether the overall gains justify the damage incurred by some individuals.

Other effects of economic development on individuals

Despite the dominance of the question about mental health and economic development, there are a few reports of other effects of economic development on individuals.

Most obviously, development affects individuals' economic behavior.

Bardhan (1969, 1970) showed that, in the subsistence economy of an Indian village, the Giffen case of increasing demand for food grains with increasing price (and a corresponding falling supply with increasing price) may occur because the producers of the grains are also major consumers of them; this phenomenon is effectively unknown in developed economies. Koo (1976) has pointed out how the extensive migration into towns, which is seen as one of the major problems of rapidly developing countries, leads to huge increases in petty entrepreneurship, self-employment in stall-holding, minor service trades, and so forth.

At a more psychological level, the concept of "locus of control" (Rotter 1966) has been used to study the effects of economic development. Reitz and Groff (1974) compared factory workers' perceptions of the locus of control of the factors of leadership and success, respect, politics, and belief in luck and fate, between four countries, two of them developed (Japan and the United States), two of them less developed (Mexico and Thailand). A more internal locus of control for leadership and success was recorded in the two developed countries, while the other factors showed other kinds of intercountry differences. Similar effects have been reported within developing countries. For example, Singh and Vasudeva (1977) found that, in a sample from the Indian city of Amritsar, those of lower educational attainment and income were more likely to suggest that poverty had socioeconomic causes, while better-off individuals were more likely to advance explanations based on personal responsibility or misfortune. These data are obviously relevant to the studies of entrepreneurship discussed above, and given the popularity of locus of control and attribution measurements among social psychologists, future research in this area is likely to be pursued. But how useful new data are likely to be is another question, since locus of control scales have come under severe technical criticism from psychometricians.

Some of the suggested psychological effects of development are not at all obvious or conventional. For example, working within the theoretical framework of Parsons and McClelland, Kavolis (1964b) proposes that artistic creativity will be at elevated levels to a small extent just before, and to a large extent at the completion of, periods of rapid socioeconomic change. Others, however, take up themes that we have already found to be important elsewhere in this book. Nishio (1972) argues that as nations achieve developed status, leisure comes to be seen as an end in itself, not merely as an opportunity for the refreshment needed for continued work. Nishio goes on to ask whether leisure, inherently individualistic rather than social, can serve as the basis for a culture. Although he sees some continuity in Japanese attitudes through the "leisure revolution," Nishio is raising a question which, in another guise, was also considered by McClelland (1961). Could it be that the effects of successful economic development include the destruction of the conditions that produced it?

Neither Nishio nor McClelland has any serious data to support this contention, but the idea that economic development might be psychologically self-terminating is certainly an interesting one.

Basic needs and development

The last topic considers the psychological effects of economic development from a quite different standpoint. Instead of seeing psychological change as a complication to be reckoned with, this view proposes to use psychological data as a measure of the success of development policies. Development theorists are particularly anxious to find some yardstick of human welfare that can be used across wide variations in economic conditions and political arrangements and that can replace the familiar economic indicators such as GNP (Morris 1979). Two phases of the search for a scale can be distinguished.

The first is the attempt to create a scale of quality of life, using wholly objective indicators, which could be used to make comparisons between countries that are at different stages of development and that have different economic and social conditions. The most widely used indicators are life expectancy at birth (or infant mortality and life expectancy at age one take separately) and adult literacy (which is taken as a measure of capacity to participate in society). These measures are suitable because they seem to reflect fairly efficiently the resources which a society puts at the disposal of individuals, whether or not the resources are distributed through the money economy and thus appear in the GNP. Although these measures are purely objective (Morris 1979, refers to his scale as measuring "physical quality of life"), they clearly have some psychological content in that they are likely to be directly related to perceived welfare. But the psychology of these scales is purely informal. There is no attempt to measure the relative importance of these various factors, either objectively or by obtaining attitude reports from the people affected; the weightings are assigned according to the investigator's intuition. Therefore, although studies that have used such scales do give us some information about the psychological effects of development, the information is not very precise.

A similar but more precise approach to the problem of measuring the effects of development is used in the "basic needs" approach. Ghai, Khan, Lee, and Alfthan (1977) demonstrate how a number of development theorists simultaneously recognized the need to quantify the provision for the most basic human requirements, that is, satisfactory diet, shelter, health, and education. They also discuss the principles by which such a provision can be measured. It is striking how close theorists in this area come to Maslow's (1970) theory of needs, which we have referred to repeatedly in this book (see especially Chapters 1 and 18). Indeed, the success or failure of the basic needs approach to measuring the psychological effects of economic development is an important test bed for the application of Maslovian theory in economic psychology. At present, collection of data on basic needs is in full swing within development economics and attempts to systematize the data have not yet appeared, although Garcia-Bouza (1980) provides a useful bibliography.

It is possible to draw some tentative conclusions, however. Wheeler (1980) argues that current data do not support the fashionable distinction between welfare and output as objectives for development. Using World Bank data on provision for basic needs, he suggests that improving the health and nutrition of the poorest members of poor countries does, in fact, lead directly to an improvement in economic output. If this result is supported by further data, it will be of the utmost importance. It is also easy to see possible psychological mechanisms by which it might come about, but we must regard any such result with caution.

Wheeler's data raise the question of whether the basic needs approach should be considered as illustrating the psychological effects of development or its psychological causes. A correlation between basic needs provision and economic development tells us nothing about the direction of causation; either seems equally likely. We do not have to choose between alternatives here. In fact, the case of economic growth and development in general illustrates exceptionally well the major theme of this book: The individual and the economy are interdependent, and they act and react on each other in multiple and interacting ways. While the task of economic psychology is to disentangle the threads of causality which make up this complex system, this will not be achieved by premature concentration on one direction rather than another.

GROWTH AND DEVELOPMENT: ONE PROCESS OR TWO?

We have divided this chapter into two major sections, one dealing with economic growth in advanced economies and one with development in much poorer countries. An obvious question to ask is whether these are two quite distinct processes or whether the second is simply the first on a larger scale. At the psychological level, the processes that have been invoked, both as causes and consequences of economic progress, are decidedly similar in the two cases. That is what we should expect given the very general psychological principle that people respond more to changes in conditions than to their absolute levels. We see that principle at work in the most elementary (or fundamental, depending how you look at it) perceptual phenomena. We also see it at work in the success of Katona's scaling methods, which concentrate on asking subjects whether they anticipate an improvement or a decline in their economic fortunes, in the different norms of poverty adopted in countries of different wealth

(Taira 1969; see Scitovsky, p. 117), and in the correlation of rated happiness with income which exists within one time and economic system, but not across times.

Insofar as economic progress depends on the efforts of individuals, we should expect similar forces to operate on similar individuals to produce similar economic effects, regardless of whether the general level of wealth of a country is high or low. That is not to say that economic development is as easy (or difficult) for a poor country as for a rich one. Living in a poor country may mean that the efforts of a budding entrepreneur are constantly frustrated by economic colonialism, or it may mean that there are immense opportunities for introducing new products or methods that are already known in more developed economies. These are economic questions, not psychological ones. But there are differences at the psychological level, too. Economic progress has further to go and is capable of going faster when it starts from a low level; therefore, it is not surprising that the negative effects of economic growth on mental health are more obvious in developing countries than in advanced ones. We have not found any psychological mechanism that is active during economic growth in developed countries and not in developing ones. The data are sparse, and such differences may yet be discovered. On the basis of the work summarized in this chapter, however, we shall be surprised if they are.

17

TOKEN ECONOMIES

In Chapter 4, we introduced the concept of a token economy as a system, usually implemented in a mental hospital or some other total-care institution, where any behavior an inmate emits is likely to be rewarded by the presentation of a token. These tokens are valueless in themselves but may be exchanged, at fixed prices, for a variety of backup reinforcers. The backup reinforcers are commodities that, if presented directly after a subject had performed the response, would have increased the frequency with which that response would be emitted in the future. The aim of the system is nearly always therapeutic, that is, to increase the frequency with which the inmates emit "normal" or "healthy" behaviors that would enable them to live undisturbed lives in the outside community. In Part II, which focused on the economic behaviors of individuals, we made considerable use of data drawn from token economies. Now we consider them as an example of the way in which the economy may affect an individual's behavior.

In the previous chapters of this part of the book, we considered how economic forces act to modify individual behavior. By and large, these economic forces can be seen as unwilled and uncontrolled. Although politicians attempt to influence the economy and occasionally try to influence the individuals within it quite drastically (an example is the Bolsheviks' hope of creating a "socialist man" to replace *Homo economicus* after the Russian revolution), such measures have quite haphazard outcomes. Moreover, they are neither aimed at identified individuals nor monitored at the individual level. Often, in fact, any effect an economic policy has on an individual, especially an effect as drastic as a change in personality or general behavior, would be seen as an unfortunate by-product, to be avoided if possible and denied if not.

By contrast, in token economies, the aim of the economic system is to produce changes in individual behavior that will be as far reaching as possible. The token contingencies are aimed at specific, often highly detailed behavior patterns. However, it has frequently been claimed, and is obviously the most desirable outcome, that the whole style of behavior may be changed, so that, for example, a person previously diagnosed as schizophrenic no longer would be diagnosed as such.

The literature on token economies is so large that we could not attempt to review it all here. A number of authoratative reviews have appeared (Kazdin & Bootzin 1972; O'Leary & Drabman 1971; Gripp & Magaro 1974; Kazdin 1977, 1982), which we refer to when needed. For the most part, these reviews are concerned with token economies as practical systems for the modification of behavior. Our standpoint, however, is obviously different; it is with the economic aspects of token economies. These have also been reviewed by Fisher et al. (1977a, 1977b) and Winkler (1980), who have concentrated on the deliberately economic uses of token systems. Our aim in this chapter is to provide an economic psychological survey of the entire token literature.

The major question to be investigated is the claim that token economies are potential instruments of social change (Winett 1974). If manipulations within token economies can indeed affect the general pattern and style of an individual's behavior, an investigation of token systems may help us to disentangle the chains of causality that link individuals' behavior to the behavior of the economy as a whole. Such an examination should focus on therapeutic success of token economies, since the success may suggest the influence that economic conditions have on the individual in the economy.

A second reason for wanting to look at token economies in detail is their role, or potential role, as economics laboratories in which an entire working economic system can be manipulated without losing sight of individual behavior. This approach yields the kind of data about individual economic behavior that we have already discussed in Part II and makes a new kind of experimental comparative economics possible (Winett 1974).

ORIGINS AND TYPES OF TOKEN ECONOMIES

This section reviews the historical trends that led to the introduction of token economies, as well as the different types of programs that have been used. This intellectual and institutional background has had an important influence on the ways in which economics has and has not been integrated into the existing token economy systems.

Behaviorism, behavior therapy, and behavior modification

Token economies sprang from the behaviorist school of psychology. From its earliest days, behaviorism was applied to problems in abnormal psychology. J. B. Watson considered that neuroses and other abnormal behavior patterns must result from abnormal learning experiences in the sufferers' past lives hence that they could be open to correction by new learning experiences. According to this view, it should not be necessary to enquire into deep-lying unconscious motivations in order to explain abnormal behavior or psychological distress; the right approach would be to act on the disordered behavior directly, using techniques derived from systematic work on behavior and learning in other animals.

Several schools of behavior therapy soon developed, using different approaches to learning, all derived from different emphases within the broadly behavioristic orientation that characterized learning psychology in the first three decades of this century. Token economies emerged from one of the most recent of these approaches, known as "behavior modification." It had its roots in the radical behaviorism advocated by Skinner (e.g., 1974, pp. 22 ff.), which was more thoroughgoing in its rejection of mentalism than other trends that dominated both learning theory and behavior therapy. Skinner popularized "schedules" of reinforcement that were powerful new techniques for controlling the rates at which learned instrumental responses were performed (Ferster & Skinner 1957) as well as "shaping," a technique for establishing complex new responses by reinforcing successive approximations to them (see Chapter 1 discussion). These concepts proved crucial to token economy programs.

Both Skinner's philosophy and methods called for close attention to the observable details of behavior, with rewards given for responses that might, at first, be quite different from the ultimate target. This is what Skinner described as "shaping." It was soon realized that this approach had considerable potential in clinical practice. Shaping, for example, has obvious uses in contexts where patients have almost no functional behavior, and are quite inaccessible to verbal communication, on which earlier behavior therapies as well as more conventional psychotherapies depend. Similarly, the systematic approach to schedules of reinforcement has potential for adjusting the rates at which desirable or undesirable behaviors were shown in, for example, school rooms or prisons (both contexts in which the use of rewards and punishments was already well established).

From behavior modification to token economy

When Ayllon and Azrin (1965, 1968) first invented the token economy, they were simply trying to apply behavior modification on a grand scale, to an entire ward at once. Their approach featured two important additions to the basic behavior modification recipe.

First, they made use of the recent insights of Premack (1959, 1965) into the nature of reinforcement. Premack showed that there is no fixed list of reinforcers that is good for all members of a species and all conditions. Rather, any action might serve as a reinforcer, depending on the circumstances. The only way to find the reinforcers for any given organism is to allow free access to all the activities available in the environment and observe which ones the subject engages in for the longest time. Using this technique, Ayllon and Azrin were able to devise a long list of potential reinforcers for their subjects, all of whom were patients in a mental hospital ward. Examples of reinforcers included a room of one's own, an appointment with the doctor, a pass to walk on the grounds or to visit the nearby town, even an extra religious service.

Ayllon and Azrin's second innovation stemmed from an obvious property of the reinforcers on this list: Most are not suitable for administering either quickly or repeatedly. Yet it is well-established within learning theory that delayed rewards are much less effective than immediate rewards. The solution to the problem was found in another phenomenon that is also well established within learning theory. The effects of a delay can be negated if a distinctive stimulus is provided to bridge the gap between response and reward (Tarpy & Sawabini 1974). It was shown in early experiments with chimpanzees that an effective stimulus in this regard is a tangible token (e.g., Wolfe 1936). What Ayllon and Azrin did, therefore, was to give tokens rather than "primary" rewards during their behavior modifications procedures; these tokens could then be exchanged for any one of a long list of "backup" reinforcers.

The genesis of Ayllon and Azrin's program therefore lay within reinforcement theory, but the analogy to economics must have forced itself on their attention from the beginning, hence the title of their system and book, *The Token Economy*.

Fields of application of token economies

The first token economies were developed for mental institutions and for classrooms, which have continued to be the major uses of the system. But the range of uses within those contexts has expanded considerably such that token systems are now found in many other kinds of institution, in industry, in the community, and even in the home (Kazdin 1977, chapters 4, 5, and 9).

On the clinical side, many of the early token programs were instituted in the back wards of state mental hospitals. Whether by accident or design (for a good account of the social processes involved, see Goffman 1961), most large mental hospitals have one or two wards which contain patients who have been more or less abandoned therapeutically; they are looked after (not always very well) but there is no serious hope of "curing" or discharging them. These patients will have been in hospital for a long time, sometimes all their adult lives, and they are very likely to be officially diagnosed as schizophrenic. Whatever their formal diagnosis, they are likely to be suffering from severe, chronic institutionalization; some of them will be incapable of even the most basic self-care.

The early token economies claimed substantial success and, as a consequence, the systems are no longer confined to the backward, or to the restoration of basic self-care and social functioning. They have been applied to a wide variety of clinical problems, from the control of acute psychopathological symptoms (e.g., Crowley 1975; Reisinger 1972) to the regulation of excretion (e.g., Connell, Ryback, & La Fehr 1979; Nilsson 1976; Ortiz & Garzon 1978). Clinical use of token economies extends to many different countries, with very different economic and social systems, such as Ghana (Johnson & Majodina 1979), Poland (Czuma & Kedzierski 1983), and Latin America (e.g., Ortiz & Garzon 1978). Beyond the hospital context, token systems have been used in work with the mentally handicapped (e.g., Henderson & Scoles 1971; Knapczyk & Yoppi 1975), in prisons (e.g., Bassett, Blanchard, & Koshland 1975), and in related institutions such as hostels for delinquent boys (e.g., Phillips 1968).

Educational use has also expanded (see the review by O'Leary & Drabman 1971). In ordinary schools, token systems have typically been used either for behavioral control (e.g., Koch & Breyer 1974) or to encourage educational achievement (e.g., McLaughlin & Malaby 1975). An interesting variant is a project to teach economic principles (Krasner & Ullman 1973, pp. 385–7). There are even reports of the use of tokens in music lessons (Saltzberg & Greenwald 1977) and in a religious Sunday School (Ratcliff 1982). Token economy principles have also been applied to individual children within school classes (e.g., Walker & Buckley 1972), and in the home (e.g., Holland 1977), but these applications are less interesting for our present purposes because the analogy to the real economy is lost.

In industry, token systems have been used both to encourage the use of safety equipment (e.g., Zohar 1980) and to improve work quality (e.g., Anderson et al. 1982). Here it is difficult to distinguish token systems from the normal use of financial incentives in the work context.

Token systems have also been extended into the community, for example to discourage smoking (Barmann, Burnett, Malde, & Zinik 1980), or to encourage the reshelving of library books (Meyers, Nathan, & Kopel 1974), the use of campus buses (Everett, Hayward, & Meyers 1974), or the formation and use of car pools (Jacobs, Fairbanks, Poche, & Bailey 1982). Again, some of these applications may be confused with the more familiar uses of incentives in consumer and marketing psychology. A more radical development, however, is the use of token systems to facilitate the sharing of chores among groups of students living together (Feallock & Miller 1976; Masterton & Vaux 1982).

Finally, because of ethical problems in tampering with token systems that are implemented for the benefit of their inmates, there have been one or two attempts recently to set up purely experimental token economies, inhabited by paid volunteers (e.g., Miles, Congreve, Gibbins et al. 1974). These are very expensive programs, however, and there have been very few of them.

Different methods of implementing token economies

All token economies involve behavior modification using token reinforcers that can be exchanged at a later time for a range of backup
reinforcers. The specific method of implementing the system, however,
varies along a number of dimensions (Kazdin, 1977, chapter 3). Here we
shall concentrate on those with the most obvious economic content.

A prime question concerns the form of the token used. There are many
different possibilities. Wolff and Gray (1973) compare six, and their list is
not exhaustive. The most obvious choice is a metal or plastic chip. These
are cheap and durable, and they allow considerable variation of size,
shape, and color to indicate different denominations or functions. This
kind of token has been used in mental hospitals by, for example, Atthowe
and Krasner (1968), and in schools by Wolf, Giles, and Hall (1968).
Tokens of this sort are obviously good analogs of money, likely to induce
many money-related behaviors in those inmates with experience of the
real economy. Unfortunately, some of these sorts of tokens induce behaviors that are undesirable from the point of view of the administration,
such as theft (see Gates 1972). This has led to the introduction of personalized tokens that can only be cashed in by the person who earned them.
Often personalized tokens take the form of stamps or other symbols stuck
on to individuals' record cards. In an unusual variation on this theme,
Abrams, Hines, Pollack, Ross, Stubbs, & Polyot (1974) sought to encourage social interactions by using tokens that could be cashed in by anyone
except the person who earned them.

Another variant which allows but does not require individualization is
to use printed paper tokens. This facilitates a further variation from normal economic conditions in that tokens may be dated, and their value
allowed to change as a function of time between earning and spending
(e.g., Atthowe & Krasner 1968). Computer-readable tokens such as
punched cards (e.g., Tanner, Parrino, & Daniels 1975) offer the same
possibilities and some additional advantages in terms of record keeping,
both economic and therapeutic.

The logical continuation of this trend leads to the abandonment of the
physical token altogether, and its replacement by the award of points that
are recorded either on special record cards (e.g., McLaughlin & Malaby
1975; Phillips 1968) or in a central recording system (e.g., Milby et al.
1973; Lehrer, Schiff, & Kris 1970). Obviously this last kind of system is
only practicable when the inmates have a fair level of functioning intelligence. In effect, it is a money system that is more abstract than any that
has yet been made to work in society at large.

A second dimension along which token economies vary is the universality with which the system is applied. Normally, the minimum basic goods
and services are provided for ethical or legal reasons, so the token system

is not used for all backup reinforcers. Often, different inmates get their token rewards for different behaviors, or different individuals receive different numbers of tokens for the same behaviors. Thus, in the terms used by Kazdin (1977), individualized rather than standardized contingencies are used, a fact that could cause discontent if the inmates perceive tokens as pay for work.

Finally, in some cases the "prices" of backup reinforcers (i.e., the number of tokens that must be given for each one) may also vary with the individual (e.g., Winkler 1971). This practice seems to be a clumsy procedure, although Elder, Liberman, Rapport, and Rust (1982) report that staff and patients prefer it. Its advantage is that it exploits the undoubted fact that different objects are effective as backup reinforcers for different people; in economic parlance, consumers' tastes and the prices they are prepared to pay for commodities differ. Firms in the real economy would dearly like to be able to set their prices separately for each buyer, and a few retailers even succeed in doing so (Gabor 1977, pp. 115 ff., 136–7). Sometimes, not all individuals in the ward or other institutional setting are part of the token system, and in fact the ultimate "reward" for improved behavior under a token regime may be to graduate out of it. Kazdin and Mascitelli (1980) report a successful use of this procedure and suggest that it might offer a general solution to the difficult problem of transferring patients back to the real world from the protective sphere of the institution (this problem is discussed in more detail below).

Although individual contingencies are central to behavior modification approachs, some token economies also involve contingencies applied at the group level; that is, all the inmates are rewarded (or fined) for the appropriate (or inappropriate) behavior of each individual. Several investigators have found such group contingencies to be very effective (e.g., Bedell & Archer 1980; Salend & Kovalich 1981), and in some cases more effective than individual contingencies (e.g., Liebson, Cohen, & Faillace 1972). These procedures form an interesting parallel to the common industrial practice of awarding bonuses to an entire working group based on its common output, and to the practice, attempted by Ford in their U.K. car plants (see Beynon 1973, chapter 10), of penalizing groups for the actions of individual workers. But in the token economy, they are often accompanied by another innovation, less often found in industry: The inmates as a group may judge when behavior meets the criteria for reward (e.g., Heckel, Hursh, & Hiers 1977; Smith & Fowler 1984). Again, some investigators have found such procedures to be more successful than a more directive approach (see Greenberg & Meagher 1977). Participation of this sort may also be used, of course, with individual contingencies (e.g., Janzen & Love 1977).

One final dimension of variation of token economies is especially interesting for an economic analysis. In some token systems, it may be possible to exchange tokens for money. In the project designed by Phillips and co-workers, pocket money could be bought for tokens (points), although at a fairly punitive rate, since most of the things the boys were likely to buy could be obtained more cheaply, directly for points, in the internal shop. Kagel, Battalio, Winkler, Fisher, Miles, Basmann, and Krasner (1975) studied a cannabis economy, a short-stay institution in which tokens could be exchanged for money when the client left. Substantial numbers of tokens were accumulated under these conditions. In many long-stay institutions, there is no provision for exchanging tokens for money, since money is of little use to the inmates – at least in the eyes of the administrators. We know of no token economy that has allowed inmates to purchase tokens for money, and the effects of allowing this would seem likely to be very destructive. In fact, we suspect that even allowing the conversion of tokens into money tends to destroy the autonomy of the token system, by providing an external frame of reference against which the worth of tokens will almost inevitably be assessed. This external scale of values may be quite inappropriate in terms of the exchange values in force within the token economy, and may well tend to subvert them.

Ethical problems of token economies

Token economies have received a fair amount of criticism on ethical and broader, moral grounds (e.g., Gagnon & Davison 1976; Herşen 1976). Part of this criticism no doubt arises from the substantial claims that have been made for the effectiveness of token economies. People are justifiably more concerned about the rules for using a system if it seems to be able to modify behavior dramatically. Partly, too, concern results from token economies gaining attention when there has been increasing public concern about the welfare and rights of people in mental hospitals and like institutions. Less creditably, there is also a politically based mistrust of anything derived from either free-market economics or learning theory, let alone both at once, and this has sometimes been harnessed to a rather frivolous opposition to token economy programs.

With all due allowance for these factors, there remains considerable room for ethical concern about token economies, over and above the concern that should be shown about all psychological procedures used with involuntary or vulnerable subjects (Wexler 1973). These concerns have led to the formulation of various ethical codes governing token economies, such as the Florida guidelines (see Wexler 1975). Kazdin (1977, chapter 10) reviews the issues and some of the legal decisions that now constrain what may and may not be done within a token economy. Serious ethical problems are most likely to arise if token economies work well for the administrators and psychologists concerned, but not for the patients. In this respect, they would be no different from the existing ward system. But economic psychologists still need to beware, lest their enthusiasm for token economies as experimental systems leads them to support something that is doing its inmates no good.

Thus the ethical question, like the question about the relevance of token economies to the influence of the economic system on individual behavior, turns on the effectiveness of token economies. This forms the subject of the next section of this chapter.

OUTCOME STUDIES IN TOKEN ECONOMIES

Although the outcome question is crucially important, we cannot simply ask "Do token economies work?" In the first place, there are many different kinds of token systems; we need to know which systems work best under what circumstances (Kazdin 1982). Second, the outcome of a token economy program can be evaluated in a variety of ways. We need to ask whether the target behaviors of inmates change when token rewards are given for them; whether other behaviors also change, and if so whether for better or worse; whether the behavior of staff is changed; and whether any improvements in behavior can be maintained when the token system is withdrawn, either within the institution or after discharge into the community. We also should consider what kinds of experimental control are needed in studies of token economies and whether the effects of the systems can be attributed to the reinforcing effect of the tokens or by other changes in the environment that tend to go along with the introduction of tokens.

All these questions are complicated by a methodological difficulty, namely that the studies available have been carried out within single token systems. Although there may be some attempt at experimental control within that context, in general our information is of a clinical or historical, rather than a scientific, type (no one has attempted to look at random samples of token and nontoken institutions). This difficulty cannot be overcome by simply combining the published studies because they are biased. In particular, most reports come from token systems that worked well; the occasional article (e.g., Lachenmeyer 1969; Liberman, Ferris, Salgado, & Salgado 1975; Shedletsky & Voineskos 1976; Zeldow 1976) about less successful systems cannot tell us whether those systems failed because token economies inevitably fail on occasion or because the psychologists or administrators concerned were incompetent, half-hearted, or underfunded.

This difficulty applies to almost everything discussed in this section of the chapter. It applies with equal or greater force to all the other ways we have of investigating the effects of the economy on individual behavior. Only in the most recent cross-cultural work (e.g., Burton, Brudner, & White 1977) can we find any scientific attempt to relate variations in otherwise similar or randomly selected economic situations to variations in behavior. We stress the point here because the scientific, experimental spirit that pervades work on token economies may well obscure the fact that our information on them is, in one important sense, nonscientific.

Effects on target behavior of inmates

Reports from a wide range of environments claim that behavior changes when a token economy is introduced. Furthermore, there is overwhelming evidence that specific target behaviors change. At the lowest level, therefore, token economies can and frequently do work; when token rewards for specified target behaviors are introduced, the rates of those behaviors usually increase.

Formal demonstrations of the effects of tokens exist for a wide range of target behaviors. Of most interest to economic psychologists are experiments in which the reinforced behaviors look very much like jobs for which people are paid in the real economy. These were a feature of Ayllon and Azrin's program; they also figured largely in Phillips' Achievement Place, where different schemes of assignment and payment for such work were studied (Phillips, Phillips, Wolf, & Fixsen 1973). Other economically relevant behaviors that have been shown to respond to token rewards include saving. For instance, Phillips, Phillips, Fixsen, and Wolf (1971) showed that their boys would only save pocket money if reinforced by token points, which amounted to interest.

Experimental control is essential if the effects of token reinforcement on target behaviors are to be assessed properly. If precautions are absent, we may mistakenly conclude that the tokens are causing behavioral effects when, in fact, changes are really caused by other agents. For example, token economies necessarily involve new work opportunities for inmates. But some of the work undertaken may be done because it is suddenly available, not because token payments are made.

The usual way of combating this problem is to use an "ABA" experimental design. Here, baseline rates of the behavior are recorded during an initial phase (condition A); token rewards are introduced, while behavior rates are still being monitored (condition B); finally, tokens are removed and rates are again recorded. Everything except the contingent presentation of tokens following emission of the target behavior is kept as constant as possible. The usual result is an increase above baseline during the token reward phase, followed by a gradual decrease toward baseline when tokens are eliminated. Ayllon and Azrin (1968) used this experimental design in their pioneer token economy to demonstrate that token rewards would increase rates of self-care behaviors, attendance, and eating of meals, and many other responses. This kind of experiment has been repeated many times, with many different target behaviors.

Unfortunately, the ABA design involves an obvious contradiction. The aim of the behavior modifier is to produce lasting improvements in behavior. Insofar as this is achieved, we would not expect the behavior to return to baseline upon removing the tokens. There are experimental designs that can cope with manipulations that produce irreversible changes. For example, the manipulation may be applied to different subjects, or different behaviors, at different times (see Hersen & Barlow 1976). In another study, Agathon and Saillon (1976) attempted to introduce a token system gradually to three wards, but were forced to introduce it to the control wards by the demands of the patients who objected to being left out. Unfortunately, these procedures are not often used in token economy experiments, and they may not be practicable in the inherently systemwide context of token economy (see also Kistner et al. 1982).

Some experimental studies have found that tokens do not change target behaviors, or are less effective than other procedures. For example, Rickard and Hart (1973) found breakfast a more potent reinforcer than tokens for 9- to 11-year-old boys; Barkley, Hastings, Tousel, and Tousel (1976) found that tokens reinforced chores and discouraged littering in delinquent teenagers but had no effect on school performance; and Poirier and Jones (1977) reported a wholesale failure of a token economy program for drug-dependent soldiers. Kazdin (1982) suggests that a small proportion of inmates fail to respond in most successful token economies. But these reported failures are few in number, and in some cases the explanation is obvious. (Poirier and Jones, for example, report that official policy changes left them with no effective control over contingencies.) In a systematic investigation, Westphal (1975) found that the effectiveness of a token system for handicapped young men varied predictably with such parameters as the consistency and immediacy of reinforcement. These parameters obviously vary between programs. Overall, however, there seems no grounds for doubt that a well-run token system will normally lead to improvements in specific target behaviors while the token contingencies are maintained.

Effects on nontarget behaviors of inmates

The claim that token systems produce changes in nontarget behaviors is more controversial than any claim about changes in target behaviors. This claim is important for our present theme because, if it were true, we would have powerful evidence that the nature of the economic system under which an individual lives can have a general effect on his or her behavior and perhaps even on personality.

Many of the reported effects on nontarget behaviors involve social interactions. Maley, Feldman, and Ruskin (1973), used an especially rigorous evaluation procedure and showed that patients from a token economy ward had markedly better social skills than control patients who had received only standard custodial treatment. Anstey (1982) claimed that a token program targeting study behaviors in a group of teenage boys led to a reduction of the group's scapegoating of one member. Grzesiak and Locke (1975) suggested that changes in cognitive and internal psychological functioning could be detected eight months after the introduction of a token economy. Certain token economy procedures may particularly encourage this kind of nontarget effect. For example, Liebson et al. (1972) argue that nontargeted social behaviors were responsible for the success of group contingencies in their token economy for skid row alcoholics, and the use of transferable tokens by Abrams et al. (1974) was specifically intended to increase social interaction.

Even more impressive than these effects on social behavior, and perhaps more surprising, are reports that the introduction of a token economy leads to a general improvement in inmates' morale and well-being (e.g., Boegli & Wasik 1978; Wilkinson & Repucci 1973). Or it may lead to a decline or disappearance of schizophrenic or other psychopathological symptoms (e.g., see Atthowe & Krasner 1968, who report that, "for the entire ward, the lessening of apathy was dramatic").

Some well-controlled studies of token economies have looked for changes in nontarget behaviors and found none (e.g., Baker, Hall, & Hutchinson 1974). Steinglass and Wolin (1974) reported that, although a token program applied to a group of alcoholic patients successfully simulated much of the alcohol-related behavior of a drinking gang, the pattern of social interactions involved was impoverished. The number of cases in which nontarget effects have been reported is noticeably less than the number of reports of improvements in target behaviors. Kazdin (1977) puts little or no stress on this aspect of the token economy's success, despite his explicit position as an enthusiast for the system.

There is also the possibility that introducing tokens will have an adverse effect on nontarget behaviors. Indeed, this is predicted by both Skinnerian and economic theory: Whether the target behaviors are seen as operant responses or jobs, those positions expect people to make responses that are reinforced or take jobs that are paid, at the expense of other behaviors. A second problem is that token systems may have unfortunate effects on inmates not included in the program. Rickard and Melvin (1973) reported that, in an experiment on the effects of tokens on the classroom productivity of disturbed children, the performance of a control group who received no tokens deteriorated so much that tokens had to be introduced for them as well.

Perhaps the reports of beneficial effects on nontarget behaviors, especially social interactions, reveal less about the token systems than about the environments in which they have been imposed. In other words, when token economies affect nontarget behaviors, the cause may not be the token reinforcements per se, but rather something else that had not been done before, mediated perhaps by changes in staff behavior. We shall discuss the means by which token economies have their effects in more detail later. But even if nontarget effects are, in a sense, by-products of some other process, the results have some implications for the effects of the economic system on the individual. They imply that a pure Garden of Eden economy, where everything is available for no work, and neither effort nor ambition is meaningful, may not be psychologically healthy. This could be taken as a conservative political view, but it is really just another way of stressing the nonpecuniary motivations for working which are acceptable across a much broader political spectrum.

As with the effects on target behavior, conclusions about the data on nontarget behaviors must be cautious because of methodological problems. Nontarget effects of token economies are only likely to be observed in cases where data are collected on a fairly broad spectrum of the possible responses. Such studies usually extend the common ABA design with the use of multiple baselines. Here, one observes the rates of several different responses before, during, and after a period in which token reinforcements are available for only some of them. We judge that the token system had worked if we observe an increase in rate for only the reinforced behaviors during only the reinforcement period. A permanent, generalized effect of the token system, however, would require that all behaviors increase in rate during the reinforcement phase and remain at enhanced levels even after reinforcement was withdrawn. How could this be distinguished from abject failure of the entire token system? The answer is that it could not, unless there were some independent way of being sure that the token system was basically affecting individual behaviors. We do not know how many instances of generalized effects of token systems may have been lost to the literature because their authors thought they were looking at failure rather than success.

The verdict on the effects of token economies on nontarget behaviors must be "not proven." There is no reason to doubt that such effects have occurred, but we do not yet know either how to interpret them, or the conditions under which they are most likely to be found.

Effects of token economies on staff

Reports of the effects on staff of the introduction of token systems are strikingly inconsistent. Some studies (e.g., Fullerton, Cayner, & McLaughlin-Reidel 1978) report great improvements in staff morale, with corresponding decreases in staff turnover, absenteeism, and sick leave. Others (e.g., Lachenmayer 1969) report widespread disaffection, with staff seeking transfers out of token units, failing to implement token systems correctly, and even explicitly sabotaging the contingencies the system sets out to create.

There are sound reasons to expect both these phenomena. A token program makes substantial demands on staff at all levels. Everyone who works on a token economy ward needs to be aware of the system, and very possibly of each individual inmate's position within it. All must cooperate to see that contingencies are implemented as prescribed and that behavior, token delivery, and token spending are correctly recorded. A token system also involves a major shift of emphasis away from a purely caring or containing environment. Successful token economies are often found to have profound effects on staff-patient interactions (e.g., Trudel, Boisvert, Maruca, & Leroux 1974). All these changes may be seen in either a positive or a negative light by the staff concerned, depending on the circumstances and on individual attitudes.

Since token economies have usually been introduced by behavior theorists, it is not surprising that there have been several attempts to influence staff behavior by direct behavioral means rather than relying on information, instruction, and exhortation. The obvious procedure is to include the staff in the token system in some way. This would be of particular interest to economic psychologists because it makes a token economy more like a real economy; the contingencies are more likely to emerge through interpersonal interactions within the system, rather than being imposed from outside.

In practice, however, where staff have been given incentives, these have lain outside the inmates' token system. Pommer and Streedbeck (1974) and Hollander and Plutchik (1972) involved staff in separate token schemes, in the latter case using the trading stamps which were then at the height of their popularity. Katz, Johnson, and Gelfand (1972) gave seven psychiatric aides money payments contingent on the improvement of three patients in their care. The patients' functioning improved, and in two cases the improvement was lost when the staff incentive scheme was removed. A study by Wooley and Blackwell (1975) came closer to mimicking the conditions of the real economy. Those investigators allowed patients in a psychosomatic ward to give tokens to staff if they were pleased by their treatment. Different kinds of tokens were used for different behaviors; it was found that 70% of tokens given to staff were for caretaking and 22% for sociability. All these schemes have claimed some degree of success, but so far there are too few of them to justify any strong conclusions.

Maintenance, generalization, and discharge

Even if token reinforcement can be used to increase the frequency of desirable behaviors, that is by no means sufficient from a therapeutic point of view. The improvement in behavior needs to be maintained across an extended time period. And if there is to be any question of cure

464   HOW THE ECONOMY AFFECTS INDIVIDUAL BEHAVIOR

rather than mere palliation, behavior must generalize to situations in which token reward is not available and be sustained when the supportive environment of the institution is withdrawn. This is the most far-reaching issue of all concerning the influence of the economy on the individuals within it.

We have already discussed how the possibility of irreversible change conflicts with the basic theory of token economies. This conflict is absent only if the behaviors can be seen as skills. Adequate reinforcement exists in the ordinary world for skills if we can only give the patient the ability or confidence to perform them. Examples include feeding oneself instead of waiting to be spoon-fed (Berkowitz, Sherry, & Davis 1971), and basic social interaction (Baer & Wolf 1970).

But, as Gagnon and Davison (1976) have commented, society is sadly imperfect. Work does not, in general, earn a just reward. Even when behavior does have a skill-like nature, the patient's environment may not provide the reinforcements that the skill merits. The people with whom the patient lives may be too inadequate or ill disposed to respond normally to him or her; or the ex-patient's socioeconomic position may be so unfortunate that nothing he or she does will produce much good effect. If token economists accept that they cannot do much to change their patients' social or political environment, they must properly see themselves as equipping the patient to bear its inadequacies. Thus even when the behaviors induced in a token economy are, in effect, skills, it is still necessary that they should survive when token reinforcement and perhaps all reinforcement is withdrawn. According to the reinforcement account of token economies it is a near-impossible demand.

Even more pessimistic predictions for postprogram maintenance follow from alternative accounts of the token economy. For example, according to the intrinsic motivation theory (Deci 1975), the use of tokens should result in an overjustification effect (Lepper & Greene 1978; see also Chapter 6), so that when the tokens are withdrawn, behavior falls back below the original baseline, or below the level shown by a control group who have not experienced the token treatment. Greene, Sternberg, and Lepper (1976) reported an overjustification effect in a classroom token system, and there are a number of other experimental demonstrations of the effect, but evidence of it in functioning token programs is far from overwhelming (Vasta 1981). For example, Fisher (1979) could find no evidence for it with chronic psychiatric patients' toothbrushing behavior, and Davidson and Bucher (1978) found no overjustification effect when they rewarded preschool children with tokens for performance on game-like teaching machines. The clearest report of a decline of target behavior below baseline following withdrawal of tokens is in a study by Goldberg, Katz, and Yekutiel (1973), in which tokens were given to moderately retarded young adults for performance in a sheltered workshop.

The overjustification effect would be seen as an instance of successive behavioral contrast by a reinforcement account. Successive behavioral contrast is a general phenomenon in which a change in the schedule of reinforcement causes the individual to overreact as compared with individuals already receiving the new schedule. A similar phenomenon occurs with concurrently available schedules, and Walker, Hops, and Johnson (1975) suggest that this simultaneous behavioral contrast may account for a problem they found in a token economy that successfully eliminated behavior problems in the classroom; that is, the children started to show problems at home. Similarly, Kistner et al. (1982) found that when token economies were introduced in two out of three classes taken by children with reading difficulties, the popularity of the third teacher dropped catastrophically until she did the same. Finally, Simon, Ayllon, and Milan (1982) found that when tokens were given for performance at three learning stations in a classroom for disruptive and low-achieving teenagers, performance at another station declined.

In addition to these problems predicted by theory, there are practical difficulties in detecting the effects of token economies. Given that many token systems operate in "back wards" there are often many stages between discharge from the token system and discharge into the outside world. These stages will add much noise to the data for a token system, making the successes of these systems all the more impressive, although not exonerating the failures.

Despite all these problems, long-run success has been claimed for some token systems. Ratcliff (1982) noted that improved discipline in a Sunday school was maintained after a token program was removed; Woods et al. (1984) found that three chronic psychiatric patients out of six they studied showed permanent improvements in behavior after passing through a token ward, although for three other patients the effects were prosthetic at best; and Hollingsworth and Foreyt (1975), investigating the first 98 graduates of a token program, found that they showed less recidivism and equal or better community adjustment than graduates from a control ward. Fullerton et al. (1978) provide a brief review of discharge rates from token economies in mental hospitals, ranging from 23% (McReynolds & Coleman 1972) to 68% (Heap, Boblitt, Moore, & Hord 1970).

Fullerton and co-workers found that their own program allowed patients to be discharged form the hospital if they completed it. Seventy percent of those accepted into the program (the only criterion for acceptance was physical fitness) were discharged in this way, and on follow-up, approximately three years later, 72% of these were still living in a community. This is substantially better than the discharge and readmission rates following more conventional psychiatric treatment (e.g., Christensen 1974; Fakhruddin, Manjoorran, & Nair 1972).

But as Fullerton and associates very properly note, there was no control group in their study; the satisfactory outcome, therefore, could have depended, to some degree, on their hospital's successful community follow-up treatment program (the follow-up team saw 58% of the token program's "graduates" during the three-year period following treatment). Some studies with careful controls have failed to demonstrate any great advantage of token programs. For example, Fernandez and Alston (1978) showed that the pattern of response in a token economy for psychiatric inpatients had no effect on vocational functioning two years later. Shedletsky and Voineskos (1976) found lower discharge rates and higher readmission rates from a token program than from an otherwise matched ward where generic psychiatric treatment was given in otherwise similar conditions (discharge rates were 24% in the token economy, with 75% readmission, compared with 75% and 48% in the generic program). This hospital seems to have had a poor follow-up program, however, and Shedletsky and Voineskos comment on the necessity of having a structured posthospital environment and a therapeutic program which is tailored to it.

Two ways of doing this seem especially appropriate to token economies. One is to include in the token program procedures designed to facilitate transfer out of the system. For example, after initial training of new behaviors, tokens may be given only for completing them repeatedly (Kazdin & Polster 1973) or for completing a linked series (Jarman, Iwata, & Lorentzson 1983). The logical conclusion of this process is to allow the client gradually to disengage him or herself from the token system (Kazdin & Mascitelli 1980). Alternatively, the token system may be supported by a more cognitive approach. For example, Novak and Hammond (1983) found that, while tokens alone would improve reading performance, the improvement was not maintained unless descriptive praise was included in the token stage. In a residential program for predelinquent youths, Wood and Flynn (1978) found that self-evaluation of the reinforced behaviors increased their persistence when tokens were removed. Reviewing psychiatric token programs that have tried to include systematic transfer to nontoken control of behavior, Milby (1976) concludes that the results are generally positive, but that the controls are frequently poor.

The second possibility is to extend contingency management into the community environment. Its most obvious application is with children. Home-based token reinforcement programs, for use by parents, have been described (Fox & Roseen 1977; Holland 1977). But there are problems. It has repeatedly been found that those who are accustomed to wielding authority do not find it easy to adjust to a patient, constructive, uncondemning approach nor to pay sufficiently close attention to the behaviors that are involved in behavior modification programs, including token systems (Bassett & Blanchard 1977; Ringer 1973).

In conclusion those implementing token systems must try, insofar as possible, to teach their clients behaviors appropriate for coping with even the worst conditions that the community environment might offer. It is not clear that therapists can do this, especially considering that their clients would probably not be clients if they were not abnormally vulnerable to the conditions found in the environment.

The data just presented suggest that the economy can have a powerful effect on individual behavior but that such effects may not be permanent. While that may be a depressing conclusion for a token economy administrator, it is an optimistic one from the point of view of political economy. The evidence is, to be sure, weak, but it implies that whereas our economic situation may influence our behavior quite generally, it is unlikely to corrupt us incorrigibly.

The origins of the effects of token economies

A token economy requires widespread changes in the administration of the ward, school, or whatever other environment it is imposed on. The frequency and nature of staff–inmate contact are likely to be radically changed. Quite possibly, more attention will be paid to the inmates than ever before. Clearly, then, whatever effects the token economy may have need not be caused by the tokens themselves. There are many possible confounding factors. The only way to discover the specific effects of tokens is to conduct a controlled experiment in which either some other ward, or the experimental ward at some other time, is exposed to some or all of the nontoken aspects of the token system. There have been relatively few such controlled studies, and they are mostly recent (see Carlson, Hersen, & Eisler 1972; and Gripp & Magaro 1974).

Several of the outcome studies discussed above (e.g., Birky, Chambliss, & Wasden 1971; Gershone, Errickson, Mitchell, & Paulson 1977; Milby, Pendergrass, & Clarke 1975; Shedletsky & Voineskos 1976) have used control groups that received some kind of treatment not involving tokens. But while such groups control for the Hawthorne effect (see Chapter 6), they tell us nothing about the particular aspects of a token system that produce its benefits. The data on the effects of token reward on target behaviors are unambiguous (tokens can influence the rates of specific responses), but the generalized effects of a token economy are rather more elusive. Something rather more sophisticated than a simple comparison with a totally different kind of therapy will be needed if we are to understand their genesis.

One study that illustrates the approach needed is that of Baker, Hall, and Hutchinson (1974). They introduced a token economy into a ward for male chronic schizophrenics, in a series of phases. In a control phase before token reinforcement was introduced, an almost identical program was used, with the one difference that tokens were never given contingently on the patients' behavior. In all other respects, the control phase and the conventional token phase that followed it were as similar as possible. For instance, the same tokens were given to patients in each, identical backup reinforcers were available for purchase with tokens, and staff–patient interactions were encouraged to the same degree. Praise and social contact were contingent on patients' behavior in both phases. Baker and co-workers were only able to demonstrate minimal differences in patients' behavior between the two phases. On what they regarded as the crucial dependent variable – the psychiatric classification of the patients – there was actually a deterioration during the token phase. They concluded therefore that contingent token delivery was not an important factor in producing the therapeutic effects of a token economy.

Insofar as such control studies retain some response-contingent stimulus, they pose no threat to the theory underlying token economies. Tokens have always been seen as a means to an end (the increase in frequency of desirable behaviors) rather than an end in themselves. As Krasner and Ullman (1973) put it, the token is only a gimmick. A token economy may be the most effective way of getting the required result, even if the tokens as such are not the operative factor. But these studies do warn against believing that there is something uniquely powerful about the token economy just because it emulates the incentive structure of the capitalist economic system.

If results like those of Baker and co-workers turn out to be the rule, it is not the economic aspect of the token economy that is the effective agent of behavior change. But we cannot really discuss this question until we have considered in more detail whether that economic aspect really exists. That question will take up the rest of this chapter.

TOKEN ECONOMICS

To what extent are token systems really economies? Is there a meaningful analogy? Or is there just a misleading similarity consisting of nothing but the superficial resemblance of tokens to money? Our answer to these questions will determine the extent to which economic psychologists can make use of the data from token economies.

There are two rather different ways of approaching this issue. From one point of view, we want to know about the behavior of the individuals within a token economy. Is it an environment within which recognizable economic behaviors are shown? From another, we want to know about the behavior of the token economy as a whole. Does it resemble a national economy, for example? In other words, token economics divides into token microeconomics and token macroeconomics, and token systems might be convincing microeconomically, but not macroeconomically. One of the most obvious ways in which a token economy differs from the real economy is that production is decoupled from consumption. This is a macroeconomic problem, and need not impair the analogy at the microeconomic level. It could be that a token system needs to be macroeconomically convincing in order to convince its inmates, but in practice this does not seem to be a problem.

The literature on token economics is rather confusing, since much of it is to be found in papers that overlap, somewhat but not completely, in both content and authorship. Most of it emanates from just two or three token economies, and the investigators who instigated these different projects have frequently collaborated in writing papers. Because of the long-term nature of such projects, different papers have described essentially the same research in a different state of completion. And because of its interdisciplinary interest, different papers have appeared describing essentially the same results for different audiences and with different degrees and kinds of technical sophistication. The most recent and thorough review, written by one of the chief participants, is by Winkler (1980); economists may find the approach of Kagel and Battalio (1980) more congenial, however.

Economic behavior in token economies: token microeconomics

If the token system uses simple, nonindividualized, undated tokens, most aspects of individual behavior within the ordinary economy can, in theory, be reflected within it. There may be spontaneous trade between inmates, and payment for services; there may also be "economic" crime such as theft and forgery (Hall & Baker, 1973, point out that token spending regularly exceeded earnings by around 20% in Ayllon & Azrin's original token economy). It was this kind of behavior that led those who studied the World War II prisoner-of-war camps to talk about a cigarette economy (Clarke 1946; Einzig 1945), even though these too had a decoupling between production and consumption.

More sophisticated arrangements of tokens may limit the kinds of economic behavior that can be shown (often that is their aim). But in any token economy, some kinds of economic behavior (working and buying, separated by a medium of exchange) must occur. Sometimes much more sophisticated economic behaviors arise, often in what seems a very natural manner. The institution of banks, for example, occurs in several reports (Atthowe & Krasner 1968; Krasner & Ullman 1973, pp. 385–7) and is an inevitable consequence of some ways of automating a token economy (e.g., Lehrer et al. 1970; Tanner et al. 1975). Of course, that is not to say that the inmates spontaneously reinvent such institutions; part of the behavior seen in a token economy is undoubtedly carried over from real economic behavior.

Systematic token microeconomics

Throughout Part II, we used data on individual economic behaviors within token economies wherever they were relevant. We shall briefly review some of those studies, emphasizing those that allow us to compare token economies with more normal economic systems.

1. *Work.* The analog of work in a token economy is the target behavior that the program is designed to induce. Our entire discussion of the success of token economies, which has taken up most of this chapter, is therefore relevant to the token microeconomics of work. There is effectively no doubt that token rewards lead to increased rates of specific target behaviors. In economic terms, the rewards increase the supply of labor to the jobs for which they are paid. Higher rates of pay for some jobs than for others leads to more labor being supplied to the high-paid jobs (Kagel, Battalio, Winkler, & Fisher 1977), but raising real income by raising all token pay rates together may lead to a reduction in total labor supply (Milby, Clarke, Charles, & Willicutt 1977).

Kagel and co-workers showed that individuals with different token incomes respond in different ways, thus the aggregate effect is unpredictable. Furthermore, if there is a substantial sector of behavior outside the token system, a general increase in token wages may lead to a decrease in nontoken earning behaviors relative to token-earning ones (Boggs, Rozynko, & Flint 1976). Replacing token payments by a volunteer principle leads to immediate redistribution of work (Masterton & Vaux 1982). These results seem wholly consonant with other data on work reviewed in Chapter 6. In those studies that have used token economies in industrial contexts, it is difficult to know whether we are dealing with a token economy or a real economy, but these too confirm that tokens can enhance the performance of specific tasks (e.g., Anderson et al. 1982; Zohar 1980). The use of tokens to reward ward staff (e.g., Pommer & Streedbeck 1974) falls into this class of studies and leads to the same conclusion.

We should note, however, that some token economies reward work that seems quite different from those most often encountered in the outside world. Self-assessment of behavior (e.g., Wood & Flynn 1978) and group contingencies (e.g., Bedell & Archer 1980) have been found to be as effective as external evaluation and individualistic reward systems. It would be interesting to know how far these results can be generalized.

Several reports mention that some kinds of behavior are more easily strengthened in a token system than others. From the point of view of comparisons with the real economy, it is particularly interesting that Milby (1976) lists in-hospital work as one of the most readily reinforced. Studying the effects of tokens on retarded individuals' performance in a sheltered workshop, Close (1973) found that most aspects of work behavior could be improved by tokens, including attendance, punctuality, and the quality and quantity of work produced (although social responsiveness was the most easily reinforced of all).

Other properties of work in token economies seem to resemble those seen in the wider economy. Holidays seem to have a beneficial effect (Elliott 1977). The overjustification effect seems to be more of a theoretical than a real problem in token economies, although it is interesting that the one convincing report of it in a practical token system did come from a sheltered workshop situation (Goldberg et al. 1973). One other aspect of work behavior that is similar in token economies and real economies is the resultant distribution of incomes between individuals. This is discussed later in this chapter, since it is really a macroeconomic issue.

2. *Buying.* The effects of token prices on quantities of goods bought in token economies were discussed at length in Chapter 7. Broadly speaking, we concluded that prices of goods affect quantities purchased in a token economy in much the way we should expect from other sources of data (consumer behavior experiments, econometrics, animal studies). Similarly, the effects of token income on purchasing are consistent with econometric data and also with expectations based on economic theory (Winkler, 1980).

The total purchases made in a token economy is often a variable of interest, for it reflects the extent to which the clients are active within the token system. Obviously it is largely but not wholly determined by the total of token earnings. The proportion of token earnings that are spent (i.e., the propensity to consume tokens) does not, in fact, behave quite as we should expect from other data (this problem is discussed under the next heading, Saving). In some ways, the total of token purchases is affected by features of the buying situation. For example, a weekly auction of backup reinforcers enhanced total purchases, and the general effectiveness, of a psychiatric ward token economy (see Candler et al. 1982).

A common feature of successful token economies is the need to expand the range of backup reinforcers (i.e., commodities available for token purchase) over time. In particular, the proportion of tokens spent on edibles and cigarettes is often overwhelming at first but tends to fall (e.g., Ruskin & Maley 1972; Weisberg, Wilde, & Ballard 1975). Here we see, as in the wider economy, the pattern of purchases giving us information about consumers' needs.

3. *Saving.* Saving is one of the commonest kinds of behavior reported from token economies, sometimes to the surprise (and dismay) of their originators, who see token saving as hoarding – a common problem be-

havior in institutions (cf. Atthowe & Krasner 1968). The frequency of token saving presumably explains the recurrence of banks. Saving in token economies presents some usual and some unusual features (see discussion in Chapter 8). As in the wider economy, saving increases with income, and earning declines with accumulated savings (Winkler 1980). But in two respects the token economy behaves, in a sense, too perfectly. First, in Achievement Place, their elaborate point-token economy for predelinquent boys, Phillips et al. (1971) noted that token "interest" was necessary to encourage saving, while Bushell, Wrobel, and Michaelis (1968) observed preschool children lending tokens at interest. Although most economists have seen obtaining interest as a prime motive for saving, there is little evidence that interest rates affect the total amounts people save in the real economy. [Interestingly, Liberman et al. (1975) failed to obtain the same effect as Phillips et al. when they attempted to replicate Achievement Place.] Second, Winkler (1980) noted that the proportion of income saved (propensity to save) was constant across income levels in a token economy; in the real economy this is observed only in longitudinal studies, not in cross-sectional studies in which savers of different incomes are studied at a single point in time.

One other result may throw some light on the mechanisms underlying saving. The essence of a token system is that token reinforcements are given immediately, but the backup reinforcer (i.e., purchase) is often delayed. Deiker and Matson (1979) varied the availability of backups from immediate, to daily, to weekly, thus, in effect, enforcing saving. They found that in the enforced saving condition, clients scored higher on scales of internal locus of control and success orientation. In other words, personality variables often thought to explain saving behavior were found to result from it.

4. *Giving.* There seem to have been no systematic investigations of the extent to which token economy inmates give tokens to one another, although such behavior certainly occurs. In fact, the transferable tokens introduced by Abrams et al. (1974) were designed to encourage it. Steinglass (1975) notes how the drinking gang he simulated tolerated freeloaders who did not pay for their share of drinks. Ayllon and Azrin (1968) noted that tokens were occasionally placed in the collection plate at hospital chapel services and argued from this observation that the opportunity to give was an effective reinforcer.

Some token systems are in fact introduced to replace or supplement spontaneous altruistic behavior, where such behavior is too weak to ensure the common good. This is the situation, for example, when tokens are used to encourage car pool formation (Jacobs et al. 1982), or to organize housework in shared dwellings (e.g., Feallock & Miller 1976; Masterton & Vaux 1982).

5. *Gambling*. Surprisingly, we have found no systematic reports of gambling in token economies. Given its general frequency of occurrence in institutions, and in the cigarette economies of prisons and prisoner-of-war camps, we assume that it occurs fairly regularly, at least where tokens are not personalized. Atthowe and Krasner (1968) report that patients played cards for tokens and cite this as evidence in favor of the token economy's power to stimulate social interaction. No doubt the opportunity to gamble would be a powerful backup reinforcer, but ethical constraints prevent its being used.

In general, these data give a clear picture. The behavior of individuals within a token economy is largely what one would expect from a study of normal economic behavior. Token microeconomics is very much like any other kind of microeconomics (with the important exception that it lacks any firms). This is what we should expect, perhaps even including the too-perfect nature of some kinds of token economic behavior. The inmates of a token economy do face much the same kinds of contingencies as consumers (or "households") in the real economy.

Token macroeconomics: the token economy as a whole

In considering the token economy as an entire economic system, we first need to examine its basic structure. Clearly any token economy differs from a normal economy in one crucial respect: Most of the goods on sale are not produced within it, while most of the employment within it does not produce goods for sale. Consumption is decoupled from production. The relationship between labor supplied and goods available is therefore purely contrived rather than being a systematic function of the available capital and technology, as it is in a real economy. Consequently, prices and wages can be fixed by external authority, rather than emerging by equilibrium processes. The token economy is a command economy rather than a market economy, although it allows a far greater causal separation of production and consumption than the command economies of the socialist nations.

Given this fundamental deviation from the usual situation, we might expect that macroeconomic effects might be less readily studied in token economies than the smaller-scale microeconomic phenomena we have been discussing. But token macroeconomics is by no means empty. In particular, the scale of token economic activity is crucial to token economy administrators, because it is the index of the extent to which the clients are engaged with the therapeutic system. Thus, those running a token economy, like those running a national economy, find themselves trying to maintain economic growth (e.g., see Westphal 1975).

One problem that occurs in both situations concerns the relationship between the supply of money and the supply of goods. Because basic necessities tend to be provided token-free, almost all token income can be seen as discretionary income, (see Katona 1975, pp. 21 ff. and the discussion of this concept in Chapter 7). Token income is therefore available for the purchase of a wide variety of goods, and the amount of it held by all the consumers in the economy is likely to vary widely over quite a short time period. Such variations are characteristic of discretionary income in a real economy (and they are likely to be even more marked in a token economy) because the smaller number of consumers, and the fact that they are all in direct contact with one another, will reduce the stabilizing effect of averaging. In one extreme case (Steinglass 1975), there was no detectable correlation between tokens earned and tokens spent. It follows that those running a token economy will have problems keeping the supply of goods in balance with the tokens seeking to purchase them.

If token earnings expand, one of two steps must be taken. Either the administration may allow prices to rise, simulating wage-push inflation, which leads to discontent in the token economy (Lachenmeyer 1969), just as it does in the wider world (Katona & Strumpel 1978, pp. 38 ff.), or the quantity and range of goods on sale must be increased (as we saw above, the clients' tastes may change as a token economy develops, enforcing this kind of step for other reasons). Failure to take either of these steps leads to a rapid decline in token earning, which undermines the therapeutic aims of the system.

A second macroeconomic question that has been studied in token economies is that of income distribution. As we discussed in Chapter 3, the distribution of incomes across workers in most national economies is approximately lognormal, and the degree of inequality within an economy can be described by either the Gini coefficient or the slope of the Pareto function. Battalio, Kagel, and Reynolds (1977) present a range of estimates for the Gini coefficient of the modern U.S. economy, ranging from 0.26 to 0.46, where perfect income equality would lead to a coefficient of 0, and the maximum possible inequality to a coefficient of 1. In two token systems, the Central Islip token economy (Battalio, Kagel, Winkler, Fisher, Basmann, & Krasner 1973; Kagel et al. 1975) and the cannabis economy (Kagel et al. 1975), researchers found Gini coefficients that lay comfortably within this range. The slope of the Pareto function fitted national economy data well for the Central Islip token economy, although not for the cannabis economy (but this was a somewhat less natural arrangement in that tokens could be exchanged for money at the end of the inmates' relatively short stay).

Battalio et al. (1977) showed that several other typical properties of income distribution in national economies were reproduced in these two token economies. For example, female earnings averaged 70% of male earnings, only slightly more than the typical value in a developed Western economy (Phelps Brown 1977, pp. 148 ff.).

Both at the macro and at the micro level, an interesting feature of token economies is the way they extend the range of different economic systems we have available for comparative study. This is useful both for determining the kind of system that has the desired therapeutic or other effect, and for exploring kinds of economy which may not exist on a larger scale. The various kinds of group contingency, or group or individual assessment of token-earning performance, are examples of such unusual economic structures. The evidence is that some of these are at least as effective in maintaining performance as more conventional systems, although it is an open question as to whether they could ever be implemented on a wider scale.

THE LESSONS OF THE TOKEN ECONOMY

From our brief review of token economics, we conclude that it is indeed sensible to describe some of the behavior that occurs in token economies as economic behavior, and even to talk about the behavior of token economies as a whole in the same terms as we use for real, full-scale economies. What are the implications of this fact?

Token economics and reinforcement theory

We consider first the implications for the original account of token economies, which saw the economies as a special kind of behavior modification program, to be described and understood in terms of reinforcement theory. Many have disagreed with this position. Early skeptics considered token economies to be economic systems, in the belief that such an approach would improve on the view evident in reinforcement theory (Gripp & Magaro 1974; Hall & Baker 1973). More recently, as noted in Chapter 5, Rachlin (1980, pp. 225–6) has contrasted an economic view of behavior with an account based on the law of effect. And economists such as Cross (1980) and Stafford (1980) have been critical of the use of token economy data to address economic problems, on the grounds that the basis of token economies in reinforcement theory created an irreconcilable theoretical opposition.

But to take this view requires us to ignore all the evidence, reviewed in this and previous chapters, for the general compatibility between normal economic behavior exhibited in token economies, and behavior predicted by reinforcement theory. We might draw two very different conclusions from this general compatability. The first is that Skinnerian thought may have been strongly, if unconsciously, influenced by an intellectual environment in which free-market economics is part of the common currency of ideas, and perhaps by a social environment organized according to free-market principles. One need not be a vulgar Marxist to concede at least some plausibility to that analysis. The second implication is more controversial. It is that much economic behavior is very probably induced by reinforcement-like processes. That is, in the real economy as in the token economy, reinforced behavior patterns contribute substantially to our economic behavior.

Token economies and individual behavior

The major theme of this part of the book is the influence of the economic system on individual behavior. This chapter has made it very clear that token economies can be powerful agents of behavioral change. A change in the economic system, from a conventional ward to a token economy, can change an individual's behavior pattern from that of an institutionalized schizophrenic to approximately normal functioning. For the purposes of our general argument, it is not important whether this change is brought about by the reinforcing effect of tokens or the social interaction the token system involves. What matters is the dramatic evidence that the economic system can affect individual behavior.

We have seen in this chapter that this evidence is strongest for the individual behaviors that are subjected to token contingencies. This fact is important when considering how economic systems affect the individual; it means that the proportion and kind of exchange that is affected by the market is highly relevant. And real national economies vary greatly in this respect, both between countries and across time. This fact also agrees with the views of many economic thinkers: Whether, like Marx (1844/1975), we see payment as alienating the worker or, like many liberal economists, we see it as putting sovereignty into the hands of the consumer, the extent of the market has been seen as a crucial property of an economy. The effect of the token economy on target behaviors is evidence for that view.

In some ways, however, it is the evidence that token economies affect nontarget behaviors, which is the most important. The evidence for this effect is less overwhelming than for target behaviors, partly because of the methodological difficulties in demonstrating it, but it is reasonably solid. Here we see that an economic system can affect its inhabitants' entire psychology. We have been pressing toward that conclusion throughout this part of this book. With the token economy it is brought beyond serious question.

IV

IMPLICATIONS

There is no such thing as neutral data language. Nonetheless, we have thus far tried to let the data, or at least the authors we have cited, speak for themselves. Our aim has been to give various readers an idea of what has already been established in economic psychology, as well as what resources there are, in economics, psychology, and other academic disciplines, for extending our knowledge.

In this final part, we attempt to assess the implications of what we have learned. There are three chapters. In a sense they can be thought of as giving the implications for psychologists, for economists, and for economic psychologists. Chapter 18 reviews what we have learned about the ends people pursue in their economic behavior and the means by which they are pursued. Chapter 19 considers what a more psychological approach to economics might have to say about some important issues in economic policy. Finally, Chapter 20 attempts to bring the whole book together by looking at the ways in which economic psychology might make progress in the future.

Structurally, this part of the book is thus closely parallel to Part I. Chapter 18 looks at psychology after our study of economic psychology, just as Chapter 1 looked at it beforehand. Similarly, Chapter 19 looks again at topics raised in Chapters 2 and 3, and Chapter 20 is our closing statement about economic psychology just as Chapters 3 and 4 introduced it. But we are aiming at something rather more than an end-of-term review here. Several recent investigators have put forward general ideas about the relationship between economics and psychology. Where possible, we have brought them into earlier parts of the book. It is in this part, however, that we are able to deal with them in a little more detail and, most important, to assess them in the light of the evidence we have accumulated.

We suspect that readers (and reviewers) will find this the least satisfactory part of the book. That is as it should be. As far as possible, we have let the nature of the existing literature dictate the content of previous chapters, although the selection of topics reflects our own views and priorities. Conclusions are more subjective. If we have done our job properly in the rest of the book, the reader should now be as well equipped as we to draw conclusions. If your conclusions differ from ours, so be it. Disagreement is the stuff of scientific progress.

18

THE MEANS AND ENDS OF
ECONOMIC BEHAVIOR

Economic psychology is an interdisciplinary enterprise. It is neither part of economics nor part of psychology (Reynaud 1981, pp. 4–5). When we approach it as psychologists, we treat it like any other kind of applied psychology. That is, we take concepts and empirical principles that have been derived in abstract laboratory conditions and try to use them in the real-world context of economic behavior.

Taken too far, that approach will lead to a lifeless, sterile, obsolete psychology of economic behavior, since what is applied will almost inevitably be outdated psychology. The intellectual vigor of any applied science depends on the extent to which its results can be used to complement and correct the pure science on which it is based. Therefore, if economic psychology is to be intellectually interesting, it must produce results that are important for general psychology and general economics, not just for economic psychology. We shall look at the implications of economic psychology for psychology as a whole.

In this book we have applied many different kinds of psychology, and the success or failure of each of those applications provides a commentary on the original theories and experimental results. We cannot survey or even list them all here. Instead, we consider three general areas of psychology which have arisen over and over again: the theory of choice, the relationship between what people say and what they do, and the theory of motivation. The first two are concerned with the means by which we carry out our economic behavior and the last with the ends to which it is directed. This chapter asks what we can now say about the means and ends of economic behavior having studied economic psychology.

THE PSYCHOLOGY OF CHOICE

"Choice," wrote Herrnstein (1970, p. 255), "is nothing but behavior set into the context of other behavior . . . and not a psychological process or a special kind of behavior in its own right" (p. 255). That is a starkly behaviorist view, but you do not have to be a committed behaviorist to recognize it as an important clarification. It makes clear that a psychological theory of choice must specify the kinds of behavior that emerge when more than one physical possibility exists. It may also describe the mental processes by which the chosen behavior emerges (although radical behaviorists will choose not to do so).

If choice theory has to describe what behavior emerges from among the range of physical possibilities, it would seem as though it would have to encompass the whole of psychology. In practice, when we theorize about choice, we assume that a whole range of other psychological processes has occurred. For example, we presuppose a background of motivation and values, and we take for granted a history of previous choices that have brought the person to the current point of choice. The ultimate solution of any particular problem in choice theory may involve breaking out of that structure of assumptions but, in general, the choice problem we consider will be a highly constrained one, with a limited and well-defined set of behaviors available.

Rationality as a description of choice

Given such a well-specified set of possible behaviors, the theory of rational choice, the cornerstone of economic theory, provides one way of specifying what choices will be made. At the end of Chapter 5, we argued that a study of economic psychology precisely should not consist of an extended examination of the "rationality assumption." Nonetheless, the question finally must be faced: Do people, in their economic choices, act in ways that maximize their utility?

Recall that in Chapter 5 we distinguished two forms of the rationality question: the description of behavior and its mechanism. The minimalist approach to choice, exemplified by the quotation from Herrnstein given above, asks questions only about description. It is clearly at this level that we are now posing the rationality question. To state the question more boldly, we are asking whether economic theory successfully describes economic behavior.

In chapter after chapter, we have suggested that it can. For every kind of economic behavior we have considered, we have been able to find a description in terms of rationality, even in the face of apparently gross irrationality. For example, observed gambling, giving and saving behavior all involve substantial deviations from a rationality account, at least a superficial one, yet for each of them an "economic" theory exists that identifies sources of utility which the observed behavior would maximize. Similarly, the apparently aberrant economic behavior of people in primitive economies, or very young children, can be brought within a utility-maximizing description.

But while descriptive rationality has consistently been compatible with the data, it has also consistently failed to make interesting predictions.

Utility-maximizing theory is reactive rather than predictive. It accommodates the facts as they emerge rather than telling us what to expect in advance. Some of those accommodations are interesting, since they inform us about the background of needs and values that must be assumed if the choice set is to be specified accurately. Some of them (e.g., the life-cycle hypothesis of saving behavior) constitute stronger, though less general, theories constructed within the framework of utility-maximizing theory, and such lower-level theories do make predictions that are open to test. But utility maximization as such is not a theory which we can carry back to general psychology as a way of predicting what choices will be made.

Rational forethought as the mechanism of choice

What about the processes that lead to one choice rather than another? Two kinds of process theory of choice have been involved in our discussions of economic behavior, and neither of them emerges from our study in a very satisfactory state.

The first is the dominant information-processing, or cognitive, approach. People are seen as information-processing creatures who strive toward rational decisions, sometimes failing to reach them because of limitations in our own makeup, that is, limitations of memory, attention, or limitations in the kinds of problems we have been constructed or programmed to consider. This approach has been most widely applied in the study of buying, and recall that in Chapter 7 we were sharply critical of the kind of model it has led to in that context (e.g., Howard & Sheth, 1969; Engel, Kollat, & Blackwell 1972). But the same approach recurs in many other economic contexts. For example, when discussing gambling behavior (Chapter 10), we considered the problems that would be induced by the "choice heuristics" proposed by Tversky and Kahnemann (1974), while in Chapter 14, we saw how the study of children's economic behavior has been constrained by the common assumption that it is a straightforward function of cognitive development.

The information-processing approach to psychology is a wide-ranging system of thought. As applied to the choice process, however, it tends to reduce to the natural complement of the assumption of descriptive rationality; if people are active information processors, presumably the means by which they choose is some kind of rational forethought. As noted in Chapter 5, the fact that people are capable of rational forethought lends plausibility to the idea that our economic choices will maximize utility, but the two ideas are logically independent. Careful forethought can lead to bad decisions, and utility-maximizing choices can be made as a result of habit or instinct.

Information-processing choice theory has all the attractions of the currently fashionable. We have not found much clear evidence which is incompatible with this kind of approach. Our objections to it, in the light of our study of economic psychology, are negative rather than positive (e.g., the details of human information processing seem to contribute little to our understanding of economic behavior). We do not emerge from Parts II and III of the book with a strong sense of the particular cognitive capacities which are crucial to successful adaptation to the economy, or with a strong sense that economic behavior would be very different if people processed information differently. It is certainly possible to talk about economic behavior in information-processing terms, but it is not clear what that adds to the discussion. We do not doubt that problem solving is an accurate description of some kinds of economic decision making, but we have not seen the psychological theory of problem solving making a large contribution to our understanding of those decisions.

Habitual choice

The other process of choice to which we have made constant reference is habit. The idea of habit can be used in a purely negative way, to cover all behavior not governed by rational forethought. Technically, however, it refers to something more precise, namely to behavior that (however it originated) is now being repeated essentially because it has occurred before in the same context, and perhaps because it is followed by a particular kind of event called reinforcement. To describe behavior as habitual is thus to appeal to what psychologists call learning theory and perhaps more specifically to reinforcement theory.

The few basic ideas about learning and reinforcement introduced in Chapter 1 throw a useful alternative light onto the problems of economic behavior. But we have consistently been hampered in our use of such ideas by the absence of basic psychological knowledge about human habit. Basic learning theory has largely been developed by animal psychologists. Their results seem relevant to us in many instances, but we suspect that many readers will be puzzled, or even offended, to have their economic behavior compared with that of a rat, pigeon, or golden hamster.

For the past forty years at least, the thrust of the psychological study of human learning has been away from the kinds of process studied in animals, and toward the information-processing approach. Even the psychology of animal learning is moving away from ideas about reinforcement and habit formation (e.g., see Dickinson 1980; Tarpy 1982) – in itself, an important fact about human learning. It tells us that human problem solving is not to be understood in terms of simple processes of reinforcement and the strengthening of individual responses. It also tells us that it is very difficult to construct, in the laboratory, situations in which the human problem-solving capacity will not be brought into play.

There are, however, experimental conditions in which humans do behave like rats or pigeons, and there are very similar situations in which they do not (Lowe, Harzem, & Bagshaw 1978). Furthermore, social psychologists are increasingly interested in mindless behavior (e.g., Langer, Blank, & Chanowitz 1978) and in routines of social interaction dictated by prelearned scripts (e.g., Abelson 1981). The study of economic behavior tells us that in life outside the laboratory, habitual and mindless behavior is more common than it is in current experiments on human learning. We need a theory of human habit. It may be that the (now vast) corpus of knowledge on animal habits will provide us with one, ready made, and it is on that assumption that we have quoted animal data. But it is still no better than an assumption. The animal model is certainly not the only possible one; script theory, or, for example, the idea of motor programming used in the study of skilled performance are interesting alternatives. We do not know which would be the most profitable model to pursue. So much effort has gone into demonstrating that humans do not just behave like rats, by showing that our learning and problem solving transcend the habitual, that we do not know what human habitual behavior is like. Economic psychology provides some data on this point, but above all it shows that the question is one of considerable importance.

SAYING AND DOING

A second important question about the mechanism of behavior is the interpretation to be given to several different kinds of verbal expressions. Economic psychologists have traditionally made substantial use of data on individuals' attitudes. In addition, however, we have referred in this book to expressions of belief, behavioral intentions, and lay explanations. What role, if any, do these different kinds of utterances (or the mental states they reflect) have in the causation of economic behavior? This question is obviously important for the methodology of economic psychology; if what people say has little or no relationship to what they do, many kinds of empirical investigation (e.g., questionnaire surveys) are presumably useless. Because of the extent to which attitudes and other verbal data have been used in economic psychology, we can also hope to contribute to the continuing debate within general psychology about the status of people's utterances about their own behavior.

The problem is not independent of the argument about the rationality of economic choices. If rational forethought is the mechanism of behavior, then people will probably be able to give an accurate account of what they are doing and why they are doing it. The capacity to give an account does not imply that rational forethought has occurred, however. People may be astute observers of their own behavior, as Bem's (1967) theory of attitudes requires, or they may rationalize what is essentially habitual or irrational (cf. Nisbett & Wilson 1977).

Attitudes and attitude change

We have looked at the relationship between attitudes and behavior in several contexts. Many of the studies suggest that attitudes do not play a simple causal role in economic behavior. For example, in the study of work (Chapter 6), the factors that unquestionably led to variations in people's attitude toward their work did not necessarily lead to variations in productivity. Although consumer attitudes were correlated with the performance of the economy, in connection with buying behavior the attitudes could in turn be predicted by macroeconomic indicators. Moreover, changes in expressed intention to purchase particular branded goods usually followed, rather than preceding, changes in buying behavior (see Chapter 7). As noted in Chapter 8, most people have a favorable attitude toward saving, but few save as much as they wished and planned to. In Chapter 13, we discussed how the attitude-change approach to the effectiveness of advertising had not been very fruitful despite a very large body of relevant empirical work, although the Fishbein behavioral intention model did seem to describe some of the data on advertising quite well. Finally, though, in token economies, that is, systems designed to act directly on economic behavior, the model seemed to bring about a transformation of the apparent personality of an institutionalized individual, at least in some favorable cases (Chapter 17).

In other areas, attitudes did seem to play a useful explanatory role. For example, in economic development (Chapter 16) and in cross-cultural studies (Chapter 15), different kinds of economic system seemed to be sustained by the culturally determined values of the individuals within them.

It is clear from the evidence we have reviewed that the relation of attitudes to economic behavior is complex. Some attitudinal constructs seem to play at least a mediating role in determining economic behavior, but other constructs are a response to behavior that is occurring for other reasons. This weak conclusion seems unavoidable.

Social cognition and economic behavior

Perhaps the most fashionable current approach to the social psychology of economic behavior is to use the linked concepts of attribution (Kelley 1967) locus of control (Rotter, 1966), and lay explanation (Antaki 1981). According to this view, economic behavior may be understood in terms of the attributions people make about the causation of events, which in turn can be accounted for by the locus of control they normally perceive, and can be studied by asking them for their explanations of what has happened.

We have studied this kind of process in several contexts, for example, in connection with unemployment (Chapter 6) and with the variations in economic conditions that occur between times and between people (Chapter 16). Fashionable though it is, we find the approach unconvincing, or at least unproven, at present. In no case does it provide a revealing new analysis of economic phenomena. Although it is interesting to learn what explanations economic agents give of economic conditions, no causal role has yet been established for such explanations. Nor does the study of economic behavior seem to have implications for the study of social cognition in general; the published investigations of lay explanations of economic phenomena have generally been straightforwardly derivative from more typical social psychological studies.

The study of attribution is not the only way in which social cognition enters into the explanation of economic behavior, however. The entire cognitive developmentalist approach to the economic behavior of children (Chapter 14), for example, depends on the assumption that behavior and understanding are causally linked. In Chapter 14, we finally criticized that approach, though we must acknowledge that it has been fruitful in stimulating research. Furthermore, the results of that research have been consistent, interesting, and occasionally surprising. In fact, the study of the economic understanding of children provides rather a good example of both the strengths and limitations of the broadly Piagetian approach.

In social psychology as in psychology generally, the Zeitgeist is cognitive, and the kinds of social psychological theory that have been applied to economic behavior have reflected that tendency. Cognitive social psychology is certainly important, but, judging from the economic data, it is incomplete. Social behavior is at least partly about emotion, and even passion, and some of that is involved in economic behavior too.

THE NATURE OF HUMAN MOTIVATION

From the means that bring about economic behavior, we now turn to consider the ends it subserves, that is, to the study of motivation. Here we are faced with a considerable variety of material. Not only are there many different psychological accounts of motivation, there are, in effect, theories about the motivations underlying economic behavior. In this chapter, we review some new theories as well as summarizing our conclusions about ideas introduced earlier in the book.

Any theory of motivation must deal with three problems. First, there is a conceptual question: How should we describe motivation? What are the best words to use in any particular context (in our case, in connection with economic behavior)? Does it make better sense to use statements like "I need food" rather than the parallel, but at least superficially different, "I tend to eat?" Second, there is an empirical question: What are the things that motivate economic behavior? How can they best be classified or structured? Finally, there is the problem of the origin of motivation: Is there a fixed, immutable set of human motivations that we can recognize at work in any human situation, and therefore in any economy, however sophisticated or primitive its technology for production or consumption? Or is motivation created in and by particular economic situations, either by the inevitable working of historical, economic, or social processes, or by the deliberate manipulation of some economic actors?

Discussion of what things will motivate behavior cannot proceed until we are clear about what we mean by motivation. We therefore start by attempting to clarify some elementary motivational concepts.

Biological need

Perhaps the simplest account of motivation is the idea that behavior is directed by some fixed set of biological essentials, without which life is impossible. This biological need concept of motivation leads to an easy if drastic empirical test: Withhold the putatively needed object and see whether the organism in question dies. If it does, the object was needed. Unfortunately this concept is plainly much too restrictive. For example, it rules out sexual and parental motivations, even though casual observation shows that they are among the most powerful forces behind economic behavior. Nor can we improve the situation by attempting to redraw the idea of "biologically essential" to involve the survival of the species rather than the individual. For one thing, the idea that animals, in general, could behave in a manner that favors the survival of the species is biologically incoherent (Wilson 1975), at least in the absence of a culture and almost certainly also in its presence (Dawkins 1976, chapter 11; Pulliam & Dunford 1980). For another, such behaviors as seeking out addictive drugs cannot possibly be seen as favoring the survival of the species or even of the individual's genes, which is what investigators such as Wilson and Dawkins believe to be the true driving force behind evolutionary selection. Yet these behaviors are of immense economic significance; in many countries, economic life pivots around the production of alcohol, nicotine, or caffeine. Biological need, although conceptually straightforward, is, therefore, an inadequate account of the motivation of economic behavior.

Needs and wants

Ordinary language is rich in subtle distinctions among motivational constructs. One of the most pervasive is that between need and want:

"I don't really need a second helping, but it would be nice."
"No, you don't need an electric train set, you just want one."
"Social security payments should be sufficient for the necessities of life, not for luxuries like cigarettes and television sets."

Are such statements logically coherent? Their social manipulativeness is obvious: I need but you only want, especially if I am in a position of power over you. But does this social function exhaust their meaning? It is hard to believe that it does.

One attempt to give need more formal status can be found in microeconomic theory. Economists draw a distinction between necessities and luxuries, based on the relation between amounts consumed and income (the Engel curve, see Chaper 7). Goods which take up a higher proportion of income as income rises are called luxuries; those for which the reverse is true are called necessities. This is a purely formal distinction that says nothing about the basic nature of the goods concerned. In the population at large, econometric studies indicate that goods such as tobacco (e.g., Koutsoyiannis 1963) and beer (e.g., Walsh 1982) are necessities in this sense in all Western countries. In the United States, even color television sets, except of the most modern types, are nearly considered to be so (Tsurumi & Tsurumi 1980). Furthermore, there is no rigid distinction between necessities and luxuries. If we determine Engel curves for individuals (as we can, for example, in token economies, see Schroeder & Barrera 1976; Winkler 1980), we may find that one person's luxury is another's necessity. There may even be a shading from luxury to necessity across a range of similar goods, or a single good may change from one to the other as income rises or prices change. We saw in Chapter 7 how this has happened to meals outside the home in the United States during the past three decades.

Psychologists have attempted to draw comparable distinctions. Shettleworth (1972), for example, suggested that reinforcers for animal behavior might be divided into two classes (for the analogy between goods and reinforcers, see Chapter 7 and Lea 1978). She proposed that some reinfocers would be "homeostatic," so that as the response requirement to obtain one unit increased, the reinforcer intake would be held constant at the expense of increased responding. Others would be nonhomeostatic, so that an increased response requirement would result in constant response output and lowered reinforcer intake. Lea (1978) pointed out that this argument is readily rephrased in terms of own-price elasticities of demand (see Chapter 7); homeostatic reinforcers would be those for which demand was inelastic. Shettleworth's argument therefore fails to make an absolute distinction. Own-price elasticity varies with circumstances, income, price, and the prices of other gods (for further demonstration of this in the field from which Shettleworth drew her data, see Hogan & Roper 1978). Furthermore, the whole concept of homeostasis, which does indeed seem to capture something of what we mean by "need" as against "want," is now under attack. Bolles (1980) argues vigorously that it is no more coherent than the everyday conceptions it originally supplanted.

The failure of these two attempted distinctions between necessities and luxuries is instructive. It suggests that any simple dichotomy of motivations into needs and wants is doomed to failure. It is hard to break away from the idea that there are degrees of needing, but some more elaborate conceptual structure will be required to capture the reality underlying this common perception.

Drives and instincts

On their home ground, psychologists tend to avoid words like "want" and "need" but use such concepts as "drives," "instincts," or "states of tension" instead. A similar approach has been taken by ethologists (see Hinde 1970; Lea 1984). Is this type of solution of the motivational problem any help in understanding economic behavior?

To use a drive theory is to accept that there is no biological warrant for an a priori list of motivations and no way of distinguishing what is really needed from what is merely wanted. Rather we are faced with a series of different motivational forces, possibly of very various origin. All they have in common is their effect, which is to energize behavior. Thus far, the drive concept is in agreement with what we know about economic behavior.

There are many differences between drive theories, as one would expect given the great variety of authors who have proposed them (e.g., Hull 1943; Lorenz 1950; Freud 1932/1973, chapter 31). They have in common the view of drive as a kind of psychological "energy." This energy is essential for the performance of any behavior, and only available in limited amounts. The idea of psychological energy crops up in many ordinary language expressions, and has been used quite extensively in economic psychology. Reynaud (1981) made it the core of his theory of economic behavior, and it is a key concept in McClelland's motivational account of differences in economic growth (cf. Chapter 16). As Hinde (1960) showed, its plausibility fades on closer analysis. A concept of economic motivation based on drive theory, taking as needed anything for which people will strive energetically, is an exceedingly shaky notion, although there is one recent theory of specifically economic motivation worth considering.

Drive reduction or drive induction?

One of the issues which has divided psychologists interested in drive is the way in that drive is related to satisfaction. The most obvious approach is to suppose that "pleasure" or behavioral consequences held to be equivalent to pleasure follow when drive is reduced by providing an object deprivation of which was the source of the drive. In different ways, this is the view taken by Freud and Hull, but it is not the only possibility. Hebb (1955) pointed out that in many circumstances pleasure seems to be associated with the *arousal* of drives. Aperitifs and titillation, two obvious examples, are both of considerable economic importance. Berlyne (1960) applied this type of arousal theory to a great many fields of psychology, including exploratory behavior, humor, aesthetics, and intellectual curiosity. We have referred many times in this book to the work of Scitovsky (1976), who takes the kind of analysis used by Hebb and Berlyne, and applies it first to a thorough attack on traditional economic conceptions of need, and then to a comprehensive account of motivation in the modern economy.

Scitovsky takes from Berlyne the notion that there is a continuum of levels of arousal and that somewhere on this continuum lies an optimum. If the organism is more aroused than this optimum level, it seeks reductions in arousal; if it is less aroused, it seeks increases. Thus extremes of hunger or thirst lead to high arousal, and reduction is sought through finding food or water; monotony and safety lead to low arousal, and increases are sought through play, dangerous sports, or new artistic experiences. Scitovsky then argues for a distinction between comfort and pleasure. Comfort consists in being at the optimum arousal level; pleasure consists in moving toward it. The two are incompatible. A resourceful person, with access to sufficient external resources, may well be able to maintain continuous perfect comfort but will thus be paying the price of total absence of pleasure. Scitovsky's approach can be applied to individual economic behaviors such as work or buying. Scitovsky himself applies it on a grander scale. He sees modern economies as providing too much comfort and too little pleasure for most people, while in less wealthy societies comfort is unattainable except for the few. From these twin imbalances flow many of the problems of our time.

We shall return to this argument in the next chapter but wish to note here that Scitovsky's theoretical structure is endangered by its foundation in Berlyne's arousal theory. Berlyne's approach shares the conceptual problems of all drive theories. In addition, despite its fertility, it is of questionable empirical status. The idea of a nonmonotonic relationship between arousal level and external arousing factors is hard enough to test, although it can be done, since under some conditions the data are inconsistent with it (see Broadbent 1971, chapter 9). Perhaps economic psychology has something specific to contribute to general psychology here. Scitovsky (1976) makes a number of concrete predictions about economic behavior, which he argues are consistent with the data currently available; if these predictions continue to be supported by later research, that would strengthen the position of an arousal theory.

Reinforcement

Drive theories conceive motivation as involving states within the organism that push the organism into action, as it were. The alternative is to view external goals of the behavior as pulling or enticing the organism into pursuing it. As noted in Chapters 1 and 6, there are essentially two kinds of conceptual basis within psychology for this kind of analysis: the reinforcement account and the incentive account. We consider reinforcement first, since it is closer to the drive concept.

A reinforcement analysis concentrates attention on the objects or events that provide the end points of behavior. It is the presentation of food, not the hunger of the rat, which explains why the rat runs through the maze. That behavior, of course, depends also on a history of deprivation through which food has been established as a reinforcer, and a history of learning through which the running response has been reinforced.

We have seen (e.g., Chapters 7 and 17) that a reinforcement analysis of economic behavior can be quite powerful, although it is always controversial. Its importance for us here is the way in which reinforcers are defined. Skinner (e.g., 1953, chapter 5) specifically abandoned any attempt to root the reinforcement phenomenon in any prior biological fact. Rather, any stimulus that, presented after a response, leads to a subsequent increase in the rate of that response, is by definition a reinforcer. Thus the primary motivational construct of Skinnerian psychology must, by common consent, be determined from behavior.

Incentive and value

An alternative means of focusing on the motivating effect of the goals of behavior is to take a more cognitive approach. This leads to what are called incentive theories in psychology and to the question, traditionally considered within economics, of what gives external goals their value. Insofar as economists see rationality as the mechanism as well as a description of behavior, they are predisposed to this type of account of economic motivation; rational forethought implies a pull from the anticipated future rather than a push from the past.

Within psychology, even dedicated drive theorists like Hull were eventually forced to include incentive motivation among their theoretical constructs (e.g., Hull 1952). Explicit incentive theories, like those of Tolman (1938, 1955) or of Logan (1960, 1965a, 1965b), can generally be construed as versions of expected utility theory (see Chapters 5 and 10). They posit some subjective variable, called incentive or utility, that is related on an objective continuum of value in much the same way as the subjective perceptual variable like brightness is related to the corresponding physical dimension such as luminous intensity. Like the expected utility theory, the prognosis for simple incentive theories of economic motivation is not promising.

In any case, there is a more basic question, which has more often been considered by economists than by psychologists: What, if anything, confers objective value? Unless we can answer this question, the idea of incentive as the subjective correlate of objective value is clearly vacuous.

Several of the theories of value that have been important in economic thought would say that objective values can be determined. Historically, the most significant is the labor theory, which asserts that the value of an object is given by the labor time required to produce it (required rather than taken since an object is not made more valuable, according to this theory, by being made inefficiently). In different forms this was held by Adam Smith (1776/1908, book 1, chapter 5), Ricardo (at least in his early writings, e.g., 1817/1912, chapter 1), and Marx (e.g., 1898/1965). In Western economics it was largely displaced by the Scarcity Theory, which holds that value is in no way intrinsic; it depends only on forces of supply and demand. What is highly demanded but in short supply is highly valuable, and so forth. This was adopted as a virtual manifesto by such nineteenth and early twentieth century economists as Marshall (1920/1949), although they were not wholly loyal to its principles (see Robinson, 1964, chapter 3). Cutting across these grand theories almost at right angles are Adam Smith's distinction between value in use and value in exchange. For example, water has high value in use but little value in exchange, at least in the British climate.

Only a benevolent providence more implausible even than Adam Smith's "hidden hand" could keep objective value, as assessed by the labor theory, in line with people's needs. All attempts to run an economy according to the pure labor theory have failed (Reynaud 1981, pp. 133–4). On the other hand, the scarcity theory tells us nothing about motivation at all. It says only that when people want more of something than is available, value is conferred. Smith's "value in use" corresponds roughly to the concept of "economic motivation" we have used in this chapter. These theories of objective value seem to offer no help in interpreting the data about economic behavior surveyed in Parts II and III.

Utility

Perhaps we could get further by considering subjective value, or utility, without reference to any measure of objective value. This is the dominant approach of modern Western economic theory. It is essential to the utility-maximizing account of choice, which is useful as a framework if not as a theory in itself. Furthermore, it may actually be easier to compare utilities than values, just as it may be easier to compare the subjective loudness of two complex sounds than to decide which of several possible physical quantities should be taken as measuring their objective intensities. If someone prefers one orange to three apples, one orange has more utility (for that person) than three apples, regardless of how much labor was taken to produce each or how scarce each happens to be.

As an account of economic motivation, however, utility has obvious deficiencies. As Joan Robinson (1964, p. 48) remarks: "Utility is a metaphysical construct of impregnable circularity; utility is the quality in commodities that makes individuals want to buy them, and the fact that individuals want to buy commodities shows that they have utility." This circularity throws us back on the idea of assessing motivation from behavior, precisely the point we reached in our discussion of biological need and drive theories. The equivalence of the modern utility theory of demand (Hicks & Allen 1934; Debreu 1971) to Samuelson's (1938) "revealed preference" theory (Samuelson 1948; Houthakker 1950) gives the game away. Utility is nothing but a restatement of whatever motivations economic behavior reveals to us.

If the idea of utility does not solve our problem, it is neither useless nor empty. Under plausible restrictions, it is possible to ask whether a utility function exists and perhaps even to measure utility. Unfortunately, empirical evidence suggests that consistent utility functions will not be found (see Chapters 5 and 10). Moreover, the concept of utility is intrinsic in almost all economic analysis. At least some such analyses are successful. This preeminence of the utility concept thus reemphasizes the message that we cannot look for a theory of economic motivation anywhere but in economic behavior. The next section of this chapter takes this for granted and begins to formulate an account of human motivation based wholly on what things people actually strive for.

THE CONTENT OF ECONOMIC MOTIVATION

In this section, we shall consider a number of theories about the content of human motivation, that is, the set of objects, motives, or goals that seem to be the effective ends of human behavior. Our aim to see whether these theories are consistent with what we know about economic behavior.

Reliable basic motives

A common approach to the problem of describing motivation is to produce a list of human needs. This type of approach might be particularly useful in the application of motivation theory to other aspects of social science, since it aims to avoid the contentious and perhaps introvertedly psychological issues and to concentrate on what is definitely observable.

Table 18.1. *Innate propensities of the human species.*

1. To seek (and perhaps to store) food
2. To reject and avoid certain noxious substances
3. To court and to mate
4. To flee to cover in response to violent impressions that inflict or threaten pain or injury
5. To explore strange places or things
6. To feed, protect, and shelter the young
7. To remain in company with fellows and, if isolated, to seek that company
8. To domineer, to lead, to assert oneself over, or to display oneself before one's fellows
9. To defer, to obey, to follow, to submit in the presence of others who display superior powers
10. To resent and forcibly to break down any thwarting or resistance offered to the free exercise of any other tendency
11. To cry aloud for assistance when our efforts are utterly baffled
12. To construct shelters and implements
13. To acquire, possess, and defend whatever is found useful or otherwise attractive
14. To laugh at the defects and failures of our fellow-creatures
15. To remove, or to remove oneself from, whatever produces discomfort, as by scratching or by change of position and location
16. To lie down, rest, and sleep when tired
17. To wander to new scenes
18. A group of very simple propensities subserving bodily needs such as coughing, sneezing, breathing, evacuation

Source: McDougall (1932).

The problem of producing an applicable theory of motivation (applicable, that is, in other social sciences and in social life generally) was a particular concern of William McDougall (e.g., 1932). He is also the lister of motivations par excellence. His list of 18 innate propensities or instincts (Table 18.1) is perhaps his best-known contribution to psychology. Unfortunately, it has never received the serious attention it deserves from psychologists. It is a good list. The great majority of its items have obvious economic relevance, and almost every major kind of economic behavior can be presented in terms of one or another of them (the major exception is gambling). Here is a clear first approximation to a statement of what people need, and a consideration of economic behavior suggests that such simple statements can be useful.

Conflict of motivations

But a list of needs, however thorough, is not an adequate theory of motivation for understanding economic behavior. The essence of economics is to deal with scarcity, inevitably involving conflict between different motivations. The need to remain within a budget conflicts with the motivation to consume all the commodities available on the market. The need for income to spend on commodities conflicts with the need for time in which to enjoy them (see Chapter 6). The motivation to spend conflicts with the motivation to save (see Chapter 8). In Scitovsky's (1976) view, the need for pleasure conflicts with the need for comfort. In short, a list of needs, with no mechanism specified for resolving conflicts between them, could only give a very limited account of the motivation of economic behavior.

Psychologists have carried out many investigations of motivational conflict, both within the context of an incentive approach to motivation, and in the tradition of drive theory. Because preference testing is the basic operation in measuring utility, incentive theories tend to presuppose conflict. Modern procedures for utility measurement (e.g., Luce & Tukey 1964) revolve around the way in which difficult choices turn out. Although drive theories tend to treat conflict as an afterthought, and somewhat clumsily at that, they have generated some interesting theoretical and empirical results. Miller (1959) developed a neo-Hullian treatment of conflict which led to exactly the same defense of motivational intervening variables (in his case, drives) as is furnished by procedures like Luce and Tukey's for measuring utility. Miller's approach has been adapted by Alhadeff (1982) in an ambitious attempt to reformulate microeconomic theory on the basis of data and concepts from animal psychology.

Like most incentive theories of motivational conflict, Alhadeff's approach involves assessing the strengths of all current motivations, and letting behavior come under the control of the strongest. Some of the ideas and observations that have come out of drive conflict studies show that this is much too simple. A striking example is Lorenz's concept of the displacement response, examples of which are readily observed in many animal species and, with reasonable plausibility, in humans (Hinde 1970, pp. 406–18; Lea 1984, pp. 32–3). Animals in conflict betwen two motivations tend to come under the control of a third, less powerful than either. The commonest displacement activities are various kinds of preening or grooming. They can be observed in the conflict between approach and avoidance generated by a novel or costly source of food, in aggressive situations, where there is a conflict between fight and flight, and in courtship, where for many animals there is again a conflict between approach and avoidance.

It is possible to argue about the rationality, or adaptiveness, of displacement activities. What they do make clear, though, is that the kind of idealized analysis of conflict produced by Luce and Tukey, Miller, and Alhadeff, has no roots in reality.

A second important observation from studies of conflict is that motivations are clustered into groups of greater or less incompatibility. For example, Sevenster (1973) showed that it was useless to reward a male stickleback for biting a glass rod by presenting a ripe female, even if the male was in prime sexual condition; the prior activity of aggression preempted effective courtship and so eliminated any reinforcing effect. Yet aggression and courtship must belong to a single cluster at some higher level, since male sticklebacks will neither bite rods nor court females except in the breeding season. Thus many investigators who have worked on motivational conflicts have been led to the idea of a hierarchy of motivations, with the interactions between different motivations not depending on their strengths alone but on their relative positions in the hierarchy as well. It is the necessity for this kind of structure that dooms mere lists of needs, even if, like Kleinberg's, they are qualified by statements of their differing effectiveness.

Economic data strongly support the idea that motivations are somehow structured. The conflict between the incentive values of different commodities is expressed quantitatively in the cross-price elasticity of demand, the extent to which variations in the price of one commodity affect demand for another. There are several different ways in which cross-price elasticities can be organized into hierarchies, reflecting common functions (i.e., presumably, common motivations) for the consumer (see Chapter 7).

Biological versus social motivation

A different attack on the notion of a fixed list of needs is that, in humans at least, even the most basic motives are so greatly affected by social pressure and interpretation that they are no longer reliable, basic, or even very motivating. Thus Schachter and Singer (1962), interested in the role of humoral factors in motivation, argued that the effect of hormones such as adrenaline depended on the social labeling provided by the environment and the subject's expectations; there has been argument about this since, for example, Maslach (1979), but this is not the point for the moment. Leiss (1978, p. 65), for whom the modern economy is a near-disaster ecologically, psychologically, and politically, asserts that, "What really differentiates human beings . . . is the rich complexity of the human experience of needing, the fascinating diversity in the actual cultural expressions of need." Douglas and Isherwood (1979), full of contempt for the assaults of such "moralists," nonetheless claim that "Goods . . . are ritual adjuncts: consumption is a ritual process whose primary function is to make sense of the inchoate flux of events . . . Goods, then, are the visible basis of culture." Thus even the simplest goods, and the motivations for them, have cultural and hence variable aspects.

Katona (1975) takes a similar but rather more specific approach. He argues that needs are in effect inexhaustible; as people fulfill one need, so

they will see themselves as being in position to fulfill another. Their level
of aspiration will rise. Once again, this is a view in which social determinants of motivation override anything intrinsic or biological. Whatever
society and its technology make available, people will come to need once
higher-priority needs have been satisfied. That is not to say that anything
will be wanted if only it is produced; an innovation may be assigned such
low priority that no one will feel he or she needs it for the time being.

In part, this is really a theory about the origin of economic motivation.
As a theory of the content of motivation, the rising aspirations approach
is inadequate, since it gives no account of which motivations will have
high priority at any given stage. Yet in many kinds of economic behavior,
we find an orderly pattern of emergence of distinct motivations (e.g., in
acquisition patterns for durable goods, see Chapter 7; in the lifetime
variations in the motivations for saving, see Chapter 8; in the emergence
of economic behavior in children, see Chapter 14; and in the changes in
individual behavior during economic development, see Chapter 16). The
same criticism could be made of many other social theories of motivation.
They explain why human priorities might be hard to explain on biological
grounds, but all too often the theories do not come to grips with the
problem of conflict between different motivations and therefore cannot
account for the order that exists in economic behavior. In our view, the
problem is that they lack structure.

STRUCTURED MOTIVATION THEORIES

Clearly, an adequate account of economic motivation will have to say
something about the structure through which different motivations are
related. Here we consider two theories that meet this requirement. Both
have been influential within economic psychology, and both have already
been discussed in various places in this book.

The characteristics approach

The first approach is Lancaster's (1966a, 1966b, 1971) new theory of
consumer demand, which comes out of economics. At first glance, it is
not obvious why this should be considered as a theory of motivation. It
purports to deal only with buying behavior and Lancaster spurns against
any psychological content. In practice, however, Lancaster's approach
seems unlikely to be bettered by any attempt to produce an analytic
theory of motivation.

In Chapter 7, we discussed how Lancaster proposed that goods are
demanded not for their own sake, but for a limited set of characteristics
that they embody. In Chapter 12, we saw how a similar approach might
cope with the different and overlapping forms that are taken on by money

in a sophisticated modern economy. The characteristics approach is potentially much wider than those two examples suggest. For example, Chapters 6 and 8 described many possible motivations for work and for saving; it did not make sense to treat them as mutually exclusive. A characteristics approach might help explain how people choose one particular compromise job or one particular portfolio of savings assets out of the many that are available.

In the most general terms, the merit of Lancaster's theory is that it allows us to reduce demand for a virtually infinite and ever-changing range of objects to a relatively restricted set of more fundamental entities. In the original application of the theory, the objects in question were goods, but the principle is applicable in many contexts.

But what is the nature of the fundamental entities – the characteristics? Clearly, they must be motivational constructs. We could describe a characteristic as a source of utility. Characteristics are properties of goods. To any source of utility in goods, there must correspond some psychological, motivational quality of people. Some of these qualities might well be socially defined; not all of them need endure over long periods of time, although some of them would be expected to (McDougall's 18 propensities might well be a first approximation of a comprehensive set of characteristics). We concluded from our review of the conceptual basis of motivational constructs that motivation must be deduced from behavior. Lancaster's theory offers a way of deducing a coherent motivational structure from the chaotic totality of economic behavior.

Lancaster (1971, p. 113) warned against simple-minded empirical tests of his theory. It has nonetheless attracted considerable interest among empirically minded economists and consumer scientists. Some of the evidence relates to organizational rather than to consumer buying behavior (e.g., Hensher 1981; Morgan, Metzen, & Johnson 1979–80). But some of the data bear more directly on individual motivations, such as the data of Agarwhal and Ratchford (1980–1), who succeeded in predicting some of the behavior in the automobile market by using a characteristics approach.

Unfortunately, the list of characteristics obtained by Agarwhal and Ratchford, using repertory grid analysis, is far from McDougall's list of propensities. It includes engine capacity, luggage capacity, rear leg room, passing time, handling, and ride. The two lists seem to contain very different sorts of elements. The characteristics on one list are relatively objective small-scale properties of perhaps transitory importance, whereas McDougall's characteristics attempt to state universal properties of people. This is the gulf that we are most interested in bridging. In Agarwhal and Ratchford's version of the theory, the effects of the objective characteristics on each individual are mediated by a set of personal characteristics such as income, education, occupation, amount of do-it-yourself maintenance proposed, kind of use intended for the car, and so forth, but these are far from having a directly motivational character. The idea of making extended use of the characteristics approach within the psychology of economic motivation must therefore be regarded as so far unproven.

Maslow's hierarchy of needs

The other structured theory of motivation we shall consider comes out of psychology: Maslow's hierarchical theory of needs (see Chapter 6). Recall that Maslow (1954/1970) proposed five levels of need, arranged in a hierarchy, and argued that needs at each level would only become active when those at all lower levels were satisfied. Table 18.2 attempts to summarize the needs represented in each level of Maslow's hierarchy. Clearly, the actual list of needs is not all that different from McDougall's (compare Tables 18.1 and 18.2), but Maslow's theory adds an important structural component. In particular, it makes strong and subtle assertions about the relative strengths of different motivations. In one sense, low-level needs are the most powerful, for they must be satisfied first. In another, however, it is the higher-level needs that are dominant, because, once under their control, the person may decide to set lower-level needs aside. Maslow's theory also incorporates other features that our discussion so far has shown to be essential. Thus the biological aspect of motivation is given its due, but the social aspect is allowed to override it. Individual differences are expected, and the lay distinction between necessity and luxury is replaced by the much more sophisticated concept of successive levels of need.

In Chapter 6, we discussed the evidence relating to Maslow's theory as it has been applied to work motivation and noted that despite evidence for a hierarchy of different needs, some of the details of the theory were not well supported. There was, for example, no convincing evidence for more than two levels in the hierarchy, and needs at the different levels seemed to co-occur more than the theory suggests.

However, the theory does have some advantages that we did not consider. One is the way it allows apparently opposing points of view and bodies of evidence to be reconciled. The studies discussed in Chapter 6 were mainly carried out within single societies, often within fairly restricted social strata. When we take the wider perspective enforced on us by data on primitive economies (Chapter 15) or economic development (Chapter 16), the evidence for a need hierarchy becomes stronger, at least at an impressionistic level. The dominance of social over biological motivations seems obvious when we consider work motivation within developed economies, especially among the professional and managerial classses; striving for social status and the need for achievement (McClelland 1961) are plausibly invoked within this context. But something quite

Table 18.2 *The hierarchy of human needs.*

1. Physiological needs
   General hunger, thirst
   Appetites for specific nutrients (salt, sugar, protein, fat, calcium, minerals, vitamins, etc.)
   Appetites related to general humoral condition (oxygen content, acidity, hormone levels, etc.)
   Sexual desire, sleepiness, sheer activity and exercise, maternal behavior
   Sensory pleasure (tastes, smells, tickling, stroking)
2. Safety needs
   Security, stability, protection
   Freedom from fear, anxiety, chaos
   Need for structure, order, law, limits
   Strength in the protector
   Need for some undisputed routine or rhythm
   Preference for familiar rather than unfamiliar things, for the known over the unknown
   Religion, science, philosophy (in part)
3. Belongingness and love needs
   Friends, sweetheart, spouse, children
   Neighborhood, territory, clan, class, gang, colleagues
   Groupiness, contact, togetherness
   Tenderness and love
4. Esteem needs
   Stable, firmly based, usually high evaluation of oneself
   Self-respect or self-esteem
   The esteem of others
   Strength, achievement, adequacy, mastery, competence
   Confidence in the face of the world
   Independence and freedom
   Reputation, prestige, status, fame and glory, dominance, recognition, attention, importance, dignity, appreciation
5. The need for self-actualization
   The need to do what one, as a unique individual, is best fitted for: to be true to one's own nature
   Cognitive impulses – the impulse to know and understand
   Aesthetic needs
   Note that, by definition, individual differences are expected to be maximal in these needs.

Source: Maslow (1954/1970).
Note: Maslow himself does not provide a table; he explicitly rejects any attempt to construct lists of needs. The above should simply be taken as illustrative examples of the needs he sees as being placed at each level of the hierarchy. All are taken as more-or-less direct quotations from his summary exposition of the theory.

different is required to account for peasant agriculture (e.g., Halpern 1964); here we seem to be dealing with dire biological necessity, under the conditions in which Maslow asserts that it should be predominant.

Nonetheless, the detailed analyses of Chapters 15 and 16 again failed to support Maslow's theory. Although some kinds of work are motivated by basic needs, there is no clear evidence that these are always satisfied before social needs become important. On the contrary, the different conceptions of social need emerge as an important determinant of the different kinds of economic society that exist in the world, even at subsistence levels.

At an impressionistic level, it is not hard to find support for Maslow's position vis-à-vis economic behaviors other than work. The differing patterns of purchase found at different income levels (reflected in the Engel curves) reflect different levels of need. Snob and bandwagon effects (see Chapter 7) clearly show the dominance of social motivations over more basic ones, though the evidence for these could be stronger. And the shift from spending to saving that occurs as a function of income level (Chapter 8) appears to reflect the emergence of safety needs. The apparent irrationalities that characterize both giving and gambling suggest the emergence of social motivations that dominate more basic considerations; what is irrational, after all, depends on the end in view.

The problem is to weave these different suggestive strands of evidence into a coherent pattern, with clear statements of what types of people, at what stages of economic development, at what levels of income, and so forth can be expected to be operating at what levels of need. Except within the context of work, no one has really attempted this task. The nearest approach is in Reynaud's (e.g., 1981) extensive use of the threshold concept, the success or failure of which is not a fair test of need hierarchy theory.

Status of structural theories of motivation

The two structural theories of motivation we have considered in this section seem to be at about the right level of articulation to permit a meaningful experimental test. They are neither so detailed that they are bound to fail in any thorough investigation nor so vague that no conceivable data could disprove them. To put it another way, the amount of discernible structure in the data is approximately the same as that in the theories. Furthermore, both theories seem to have many of the properties needed to account for economic behavior. They are neither incompatible nor even alternatives, since they focus on slightly different aspects of motivation. But how good is the evidence for either of them? Not very. In the case of characteristics theory, the potential for empirical investigation has not yet been realized. Within a few years, one hopes it will have become clear whether the theory is a useful framework for empirical research or whether there will remain a gulf between the kind of characteristics identified from economic data and any kind of psychological meaning (as found in the results of Agarwhal and Ratchford, 1980–1). In the case of need hierarchy theory, the empirical results that are available are somewhat discouraging. In summary, neither theory can be said to have strong empirical support, and in the long run both could well fail.

Nonetheless, it seems likely that something not dissimilar will emerge as an adequate description of economic motivation. The problems faced by simpler theories of motivation show that some kind of structured theory is needed. Other structured theories exist. For example, Fromm's (1979) question "To have or to be" implies a two-level hierarchy of motivation similar to Maslow's but with some different features. Reynaud (1981) makes some use of this within the context of economic psychology.

THE ORIGINS OF MOTIVATION

There are many ways of asking about the origin of motivation. We might ask, for example, about the roots of particular kinds of motivation in individual development, in cultural development, or in the development of the human species through evolution. In economic psychology, however, one question dominates all others in this area: Are economic motivations psychological "givens" to which the economic process must be adapted? Or can they be manipulated, even created or eliminated, by economic pressures, applied by accident of history or by the will of powerful individuals or organizations?

This is clearly a general question: What is the direction of causality between the behavior of individuals and the behavior of economies? In grappling with this question now, we are trying both to use and to sum up much of what was said in the previous two parts of the book. At the same time, we are trying to introduce some of the many other authors who have dealt with the specific question of the origin of economic motivation.

Structural motivational theory and the origins of motivation

There is a sense in which the question has already been decided. We cannot formulate a satisfactory static theory of individual economic motivation. The least we must have is a structured motivational theory that will allow different motivations to be dominant under different circumstances. This already allows for considerable influence of the economy on individual motivation.

Even the most rigid economic determinism must allow at least some role, if only a shadowy one, to a constant underlying human reality on which economic forces act to produce different motivations. Conversely, the failure of a static theory of motivation means that circumstances must play some role in the effective motivation of the individual. Thus the gap between the possible answers to the question of the origin of economic motivation is clearly not very wide. Sharp differences of opinion about real issues do remain, but it seems that the disagreement must be quantitative rather than qualitative. Just how malleable are human motivations? Exactly how much must the economy bend to accommodate their inflexible demands? These are perhaps more tractable questions, if somewhat less dramatic than the bald: Does the economy determine human motivations? We shall now survey some of the answers that have been offered.

Robust conservatism: Katona

It is simplest to start with the point of view that motivations are relatively inflexible and that it is the economy that must adapt. The most relevant exponent of this point of view is Katona (e.g., 1975, chapter 10). His argument is an answer to the economic determinists, but we consider it first because it has the strongest links with the earlier sections of this chapter. Katona's position, briefly stated, is that needs do not change as a function of economic circumstances but that the opportunity for fulfilling them does. Needs are not felt unless there is a reasonable chance of fulfilling them. Thus until the present century, the only economically relevant needs felt by the vast majority of people were what Maslow calls the basic needs. With the advent of the technological economy, however, most people have discretionary income, and the acquisition of durable goods comes within their grasp. Their level of aspiration rises; the need for the more basic durables is felt. With continuing prosperity, discretionary income continues to be available even when these new-felt needs are satisfied; thus needs for "luxury" durables, for a reserve of savings, and perhaps to make donations to charities are felt. If still more discretionary income becomes available, the process can continue, without limit, and without the intervention of malign social forces or the implication of malignant social consequences.

It is difficult to produce data to refute Katona's account. It is clearly compatible with a structured view of the content of motivation, of the kind we advocated earlier in this chapter. The only way to parry this kind of robust defense of simple economic expansionism is to produce concrete evidence for a more skeptical point of view. Such evidence is a little thinner than one might expect, given the number of skeptical investigators in the field.

Acquired drives and functional autonomy

There are basic psychological reasons for questioning Katona's position. From the earliest days of drive theory, psychologists considered whether new drives could be constructed as it were "on top of" unlearned, primary drives. This was a natural way to extend the stimulus substitution view of learning made popular by the research on Pavlovian conditioning (see Chapter 1). For instance, perhaps goal stimuli, like the stimuli that unleashed reflexes, could be substituted for each other. This would give a natural explanation for the strong human drive to acquire money, a drive that no one would wish to dignify with a direct biological origin, yet clearly a powerful motivational force.

Experiments with animals, mostly using pain avoidance as a primary drive while trying to establish secondary drives for avoidance of pain-associated stimuli, seem to indicate that learned drives can be established, and that they then have all the properties (except permanence) associated with the "normal" unlearned drives. There is still some dispute about these experiments (Bolles 1967, chapter 11), but they do not in themselves pose any problems for a position like Katona's. The notion of an acquired drive was developed further within social psychology, most notably by Allport (1937, chapter 7), who coined the term *functional autonomy* to describe the state reached by an acquired motivation when it became independent of the primary drive upon which it had been constructed. If drives can be acquired, there is no reason why they cannot be created by economic processes. Katona's position would seem untenable in this light.

Unfortunately, the evidence on functional autonomy is inconclusive. Not all Allport's examples are convincing from a modern perspective. In some cases (e.g., neurotic symptoms such as tics) the evidence that the drive is acquired consists of no more than the absence of any simple biological need for its object. This obviously involves an appeal to a concept of motivation that we have already dismissed as too restrictive. Although the concept of functional autonomy is incompatible with Katona's robust conservatism, it is not strongly enough supported to force us to abandon the idea of relatively fixed economic motivations.

Marx: commodity fetishism and wage slavery

Typically, Marx also took a robust line, but it led to a very different point of view. He argued that the capitalist economy necessarily involves continuous accumulation (e.g., Marx, 1867/1974, chapter 24), hence the production of a continuously increasing quantity of goods. But these goods acquire a life of their own: "All our inventions and progress seem to result in endowing material forces with intellectual life, and in stultifying human life into a material force" (Marx, in a speech in 1856, quoted by Wilson 1972, p. 295). The value of an object, which according to Marx results only from the labor time required to produce them (an inherently social property), comes to be seen as an independent, external property of the thing itself. Marx (1867/1974, chapter 1) calls this "the Fetishism that attaches itself to the products of labour, so soon as they are produced as commodities," that is, for sale rather than for use by the producer or a visible enslaver. The virtually inevitable result, according to Marx, is a state of society in which "the process of production has the mastery over man, instead of being controlled by him."

The problem for Marx was not to explain why people bought commodities they did not need, but how they were forced into working in the appalling conditions of early-nineteenth-century industry. His answer, like others we are considering here, is one that stresses the social aspects of economic motivation. Employment, according to Marx, is slavery disguised, and undisguised slavery is an unmistakably social phenomenon. The economic behavior of slaves consists of work, and it is carried out not to satisfy any biological motivation but because of the social situation. Marx argues that the same is true of employees.

The different conditions of modern employment do not make those Marx described any less real. Marx's prestige, the forcefulness of his arguments, and the vigor of his vocabulary, should not blind us to the fact that there is no more actual evidence than we had for Allport's position; if anything rather less. Volume 1 of *Capital* needs commodity fetishism primarily because the facts of exchange in the market are clearly inconsistent with the labor theory of value; if we start from a different theoretical perspective, the evidence is not compelling. Of course it is doing Marx something less than justice to abstract one small feature of his system and consider it in isolation. Those who accept Marxism as a system of thought will probably accept commodity fetishism without close inquiry; anti-Marxists would probably reject it just because of its source, regardless of the evidence. From our point of view it seems best to see it as yet another plausible account of economic determination of motivation, neither supported nor refuted by any evidence we have yet encountered. Very probably Marxist thought is the unrealized source of many more recent ideas about the economic creation of motivation. Insofar as we are able (or unable) to find evidence to support them, Marx's general approach gains (or loses) in acceptability.

Veblen: conspicuous consumption

Another major historical source for ideas about economic influence is Veblen (1899/1979). Veblen did not directly claim that basic human motivations could be altered by economic circumstances; he held that the basic drive was always social and always toward the achievements of social status. But according to Veblen, the means by which this is achieved vary sharply with social and economic conditions as well as with mere passage of time. Thus the actual commodities that are sought are subject to social and economic determination. Furthermore, there is something arbitrary, even whimsical, about the way in which this happens. Goods are likely to be sought as status symbols just because they are currently expensive – the "Veblen effect on demand, discussed in Chapter 7. Since this increased demand is likely to lead, in due course, to increased supply at lower prices, it is an inherently self-defeating process, likely to be followed by a switch of attention to some other previously insignificant commodity.

Veblen's ideas clearly lend themselves beautifully to the explanation of trends and fashions. They also throw a sharp light on processes like the diffusion of innovations, discussed in Chapters 7 and 16. With one additional concept, they add up to a powerful analysis. The addition we need is provided by Scitovsky (1976), who argues that possession of any commodity can be addictive, if the commodity serves to provide comfort rather than pleasure. If the temporary motivation for conspicuous consumption of new (and therefore expensive) commodities is followed by a permanent acquired motivation due simply to the habit of consuming or possessing that commodity, we can explain even the most bizarre kinds of motivation with no effort.

In itself, this capacity for effortless explanation is dangerous rather than productive because the combined theory risks losing all empirical content. Like so many other ideas that invoke positive feedback in one form or another, it can explain any data that might be found. What is needed, therefore, is solid evidence for its consituent parts, for the tendency to conspicuous consumption and for the addictiveness of commodities. Chapter 7 noted that the evidence for Veblen effects in demand is tenuous. Chapter 10 argued that there was no evidence that the majority of gambling behavior, or the majority of any other kind of individual economic behavior, was the outcome of addiction. In both cases there is no negative evidence. What we lack is the right kind of empirical investigation.

Galbraith: artificially created wants

The purchasing of new, expensive commodities that do not correspond to any biological need does not take place in a vacuum. There are powerful agents at work in the economy, in whose interest it is that people should make such purchases. Marx embodied the actions of these agents in personifications of the commodities they produce, but of course he never lost sight of the fact that there were real human economic exploiters and oppressors behind those commodities. The most articulate recent exponent of what might be called the paranoid theory of economic motivation is Galbraith (e.g., 1958, 1972).

Galbraith argues that the motivation to acquire some commodities is created by the marketing experts within what he calls the "technostructure," the set of interlocking committees and administrators who run "the industrial system," or the "planning sector" (Galbraith 1974). According to his theory, the industrial system is that part of the economy that, by means of high technology, monopoly power, influence over government, transnational organization, and marketing technique, has been able to set itself above the laws of supply and demand. The firms in the industrial system are run by salaried managers, not by entrepreneurial owners; their capital expenditures are financed by retained profits rather than by issues of shares. They are therefore run to fulfill the needs of the managers not the owners, and what the managers need is first stability and second growth. Profit, the aim of all business behavior in the classical economic theory of the firm, is unimportant as long as it is sufficient to prevent shareholders' revolts.

The overriding need of the technostructure for stability and growth creates a need for predictable markets. Firms in the industrial system therefore concentrate their efforts on managing their consumers. Rather than seeking to maximize profits, which according to conservative theorists such as Denner (1971) can only be done by producing the goods the consumers most need, they seek to maximize stability and growth by producing in the consumers motivations for the goods the firms most want to produce. Galbraith (1972, pp. 271–4) calls this process "the creation of wants."

Galbraith has been attacked vituperatively by conventional economists, such as Friedman (1977), who cites a number of other critics, and with a little more moderation by businessmen (see, e.g., Tillman & McLaughlin 1974) and social theorists (e.g., Gafgen 1974). The reaction has been strong enough to make one suspect that he has touched a raw nerve. Certainly his arguments have the plausibility that any skeptical analysis of social phenomena tends to have in the face of a rosy-glow establishment view. But the fact is that once again his evidence is scant and always clinical or historical rather than experimental. He leans on treatments of advertising (e.g., Packard 1960), which are now out of date (cf. Chapter 13). More objective studies of the effects of advertising (e.g., Wilder 1974) do not support his hypothesis, and there are notorious cases in which the industrial system has failed, abjectly, to manipulate consumer demand. Galbraith himself discusses the failure of the Ford Edsel car in 1957, although he tries to present it as an exceptional case confirming his general analysis.

In other areas, at least some of the data are consistent with Galbraith's ideas (e.g., Capon, Farley, & Hulbert 1975; Edwards & Heggestad 1973). On balance, however, the critics seem to have the best of the empirical argument, though Galbraith's wider social perspective and deeper social insight make the reader want to believe that he must be right after all. Furthermore, the advertising case is crucial to Galbraith's system. As discussed in Chapter 13, the case that advertisers can create wants remains doubtful, and the suggestion that marketing creates a consumerist atmosphere within society has not yet been subjected to adequate empirical investigation.

Social limits to the satisfaction of wants

There is a direct line of conceptual descent (if not of actual influence) from Marx through Veblen to Galbraith. But the last decade has contributed themes of its own to the general idea that the economy can determine people's motivation. One of these has been the awareness of the limits on economic growth imposed by the finite nature of our planet and its resources (Meadowes et al. 1972). This ecological argument has a bearing on the question of the origin of motivation. The point is made most originally by Hirsch (1977), although somewhat similar views have been put forward by others, such as Leiss (1978).

Hirsch (1977) argues that there are in essence two kinds of commodity. One kind can be enjoyed regardless of how many or how few other people are enjoying it at the same time; the pleasure one gets from eating fish and chips is quite unaffected by whether someone else is eating fish and chips too. But the other kind of commodity is "socially limited." One cannot enjoy solitude on a beach if other people are also trying to enjoy solitude on the same beach. If most people own cars, they can conveniently commute to work in them and use them to visit historic cities. When a majority of people own cars, car commuters cannot reach work quickly or park within comfortable distances of their places of work, while historic cities disappear underneath the weight of exhaust fumes, car parks, road-widening schemes, and car-borne tourists.

Socially limited commodities are not new; if one person is the leader of a tribe of hunter-gatherers, another person cannot lead it too. Leadership is thus socially limited. What is new, according to Hirsch, is that advancing technology, increasing population, and diminishing resources are taking more and more goods into the socially limited sector. This radically changes the motivation to acquire these goods. It is in the nature of social limitation that the motivation for socially limited commodities is insatiable. This lends a further twist to the vicious spiral, because it makes people seek as substitutes other commodities, which then become socially limited in their turn. The effect is that, in a modern economy, most commodities are socially limited.

Hirsch's argument brings the wheel full circle from Katona's. Both see the motivation to acquire commodities in the modern economy as inherently insatiable. For Katona, this is because technology is always able to produce new kinds of commodity, to titillate our aspirations to ever-higher levels. For Hirsch it is because no amount of technology can ever make available to all what can in principle only be enjoyed by a minority.

It is clear that we do not have the data to settle this dispute, or to give any final answers to the more general question about the origin of motivation. Nonetheless, some preliminary conclusions can be drawn. Those who believe that economic motivation is systematically manipulated have the better of the argument from the point of view of style, scholarship, articulateness, persuasiveness, and harmony with the Zeitgeist. What they lack are data. One of the most important tasks currently confronting economic psychology, therefore, is to get this dispute out of the hands of the essayists and into those of the experimenters. To clarify the origins of motivation would not only greatly strengthen the foundations of economic psychology, it would also demonstrate, once and for all, that economic behavior is an important field in which to test theories of the widest psychological generality.

WHAT HAS ECONOMIC PSYCHOLOGY TO SAY TO PSYCHOLOGY?

Here, then, are our conclusions for psychologists.

1. In the study of choice, the rational/utility-maximizing approach will always provide a framework within which behavior can be described. However, it is not a predictive theory in the sense in which theories can be useful within psychology.
2. Much more information is needed about human habitual behavior, since much important behavior seems to involve relatively low levels of cognitive or intellectual involvement.
3. People's accounts of their own behavior and motivations are always interesting data, but their causal status will vary greatly in different situations. Consequently, a purely cognitive approach to economic behavior is inadequate; it must be supplemented with a motivational theory.
4. No static theory of human motivation is adequate. Effective motivation will always vary with circumstances.
5. Any adequate motivational theory must deal with the question of the conditions under which one motivation dominates others.
6. It is not yet clear how far individual motivations can be created or distorted by external pressures of the sort the economy, and other economic agents, exert. The solution of this problem is an urgent problem that is not likely to be solved using economic data alone.

19

ECONOMICS, POLICY, AND PSYCHOLOGY

Throughout this book, we have tried to balance psychology and economics and to stress that economic psychology does not represent an attempt by psychologists to take over economics, or vice versa, but rather a new and interdisciplinary approach to problems which have both a psychological and an economic aspect. In attempting to be balanced, however, we have always labored under one disadvantage. All three authors are by training psychologists. As we explained in the preface, while this fact provides certain advantages, it makes it somewhat difficult to maintain total symmetry between the two parent disciplines of economic psychology. In Chapter 18, we could be reasonably confident in our conclusions for psychology because they are the conclusions which we as psychologists have drawn. In this chapter, however, our conclusions for economics must be offered rather more diffidently. Nonetheless, the attempt to draw economic conclusions must clearly be made. We divide our thoughts into three types of conclusions: for the methodology of economics, about particular substantive areas of economics, and about economic policy.

THE METHODOLOGY OF ECONOMICS

In offering conclusions for economic methodology, we are not presuming to tell economists how they should go about their own business. Every discipline has its accepted standards for how things should be done. However, any discipline that wishes to be taken seriously outside its own boundaries must also meet certain common standards of scientific method. In this book, we have frequently tried to apply results from economics to questions in economic psychology. Such attempted applications often reveal the extent to which the internal conventions of a discipline meet the common requirements of science. The following remarks reflect our experience with applying economics.

Rationality

It should by now be thoroughly clear that we are not arguing that theoretical economics should abandon its use of the assumption of rational utility maximization. We have steadfastly claimed that economic psychology is not about testing the assumption of rationality. The assumption is a framework for the construction of theory, not a hypothesis about individual behavior. Indeed, in Chapter 20, we shall suggest that there are positive reasons to expect that behavior may well be approximately rational in the sense of roughly maximizing a fairly elementary utility function, even when the mechanisms underlying it involve no rational forethought.

There is, however, a price to be paid for the acceptance of rationality as the framework of economic theory. The price is this: The mere fact that a behavior is consistent with the maximization of some utility function cannot be taken as an explanation of that behavior. It is certainly an account of the behavior, but it is an account that needs to be tested. For an economic psychologist, the relevant test will often be an investigation of whether the proposed sources of utility (the arguments of the utility function) are sources of utility in other, related situations. For an economist, it will perhaps take the form of seeing whether the same utility function has a more general usefulness. But if those tests fail, the account fails, because it will be seen as arbitrary or ad hoc.

These remarks apply especially to the attempts (e.g., Becker 1965) to extend economic explanation to kinds of behavior that are more usually the province of psychologists or sociologists. It is, to be sure, of interest if a utility-maximizing model can account for, say, the incidence of marriage (Becker 1975) or family size (Becker 1960). Such models are not be rejected because other unrelated experiments show that people do not choose transitively or cannot delay gratification. But the models are not in themselves explanations of behavior. They create the potential for explanation, but the explanation resides in more specific assertions within the models and demonstrations that they are justified.

To clarify this point, consider Becker's economic analysis of fertility. Most of his discussion revolves around the prediction that the number of children in a family will, all other things equal, increase with family income. This prediction does not follow from the use of the utility-maximizing approach. It follows from (1) a set of additional assumptions Becker makes about the properties of children as consumption goods (that there are no close substitutes for them, that they are not low-quality members of a set of closely similar goods, that they will yield benefits over an extended period of time) and (2) the empirical observation that goods of that type generally have low positive income elasticities. The contribution of the utility-maximizing framework to Becker's analysis is, in fact, rather slight; most of the work is done by economic general knowledge. The same could be said of other predictions made by Becker (e.g., that family size will be less responsive to economic fluctuations than the purchase of consumer durables, because children take longer to produce than, say, cars).

Neither the utility-maximizing framework nor Becker's general knowledge persuades us to accept his analysis. What is persuasive is the statistical and econometric evidence that he assembles in support of his predictions. The construction of a model, in other words, gives us no more than a hypothesis. It leaves most of the explanation still unfinished, in the form of finding ways of testing that hypothesis.

Multiple sources of utility

The rationality assumption is a way of making explicit and precise assertions about the sources of utility that are effective in a situation. We do not think that economists would disagree with this description; in some cases, it is glaringly obvious. The microeconomic theory of demand, for example, rests on a specification of the possible sources of utility, that is, on a list of the goods available for consumption.

There is no difficulty, within utility-maximization theory, in taking into account many different sources of utility. The theory of demand can accommodate any number of different goods. In practice, however, economics has been notably reluctant to consider a number of sources of utility that may be loosely summarized as nonpecuniary. Four examples will illustrate different aspects of this problem.

The most obvious example is work. In Chapter 6, we identified four major reasons for working, each of which could be further broken down into a number of factors that might cause people to take employment, contribute to their well-being through work, or influence their choice between different jobs. In the simplest economic models of the labor–leisure choice, however, the only factors that appear are the time available for consumption and the wage derived from employment. The most complex available economic models (e.g., Lucas 1977) are barely more subtle. If labor economics is to be truly useful, it must bring into account sources of utility such as the social contacts made at work, the fulfillment derived from the exercise of skill, and the stress induced by the loss or even voluntary change of a job. It is not enough to invoke such factors to explain why theory and life experience do not agree; their contributions to utility must be made explicit if the utility-maximization approach is to remain credible.

A rather similar situation exists in the economic literature on saving (cf. Chapter 8). When Modigliani and Brumberg (1954) originally formulated the life-cycle hypothesis, they recognized that the desire to bequeath might be an important source of utility. Later developments of the theory often dropped this assumption. Without it, we are apparently unable to explain why retired people do not dissave (Mirer, 1979; Menchik & David 1983; but see also Davies 1981). Furthermore, when the utility of bequeathing is restored to the model, its predictions change quite radically (e.g., Barro 1974; Evans 1983). It is mathematically convenient to develop the life-cycle hypothesis under a zero-bequest assumption, but their simplification takes the model unrealistically far from current economic behavior. That may be acceptable for the purposes of clarifying theory, but the use of such a model for making policy recommendations (e.g., Powell 1960) is clearly questionable, if not dangerous.

Multiple sources of utility are also involved in giving behavior. To explain giving at all, microeconomic theory must assume that each individual's utility can be a function of one or several other individuals' benefit (e.g., Alchian & Allen 1969). We can ask immediately why this source of utility is never included in economic analyses of any other kind of behavior (except for a few treatments of saving that discuss bequests or other kinds of gifts). Collard's (1978) "nonselfish economics" is original precisely because he is prepared to extend the idea of others' good as a source of utility to a wide range of economic phenomena. A second unconventional source of utility is revealed by giving behavior, however. The economic explanation of the unacceptability of money for certain kinds of gift (Webley, Lea, & Portalska 1983) is that the time taken to think about a gift contributes to its utility for the receiver. Again, we should like to see economic models that make this idea explicit and that test them outside the original context.

Finally, we can point to the economic model that we specifically commended to psychologists in the previous chapter. Lancaster's (1966a, 1966b) characteristics theory of demand makes explicit the idea that multiple sources of utility are needed to account for the demand for any commodity. To that extent it is wholly consistent with what we are saying in this section of the present chapter. But Lancaster rejected the idea of psychological characteristics. Current attempts to use Lancaster's model at a behavioral level remain some way from any truly psychological set of relevant characteristics. Most of what we have said in this section is a plea to recognize "psychological" sources of utility. Utility is inherently a psychological as well as an economic concept, for it is, by definition, a subjective property of people. A study of economic psychology convinces us that psychological quantities relevant to economic behavior can be studied scientifically. There can be no serious objection to using them within demand theory, or within any of the other areas of economic life to which, we believe, the characteristics approach can fruitfully be applied.

Data matter

There have been times, during the writing of this book, when we have felt that what we were doing was not so much trying to describe economic psychology, as trying to construct a new kind of economics (e.g., a study of economics as if the data mattered, to borrow and distort the subtitle of

E. F. Schumacher's most famous book). In both preceding sections, we touched upon this point. Accepting that data are important is partly a matter of being prepared to determine the weights to be given to different sources of utility, not just keeping them in a system of equations as undetermined quantities. But it is also a much more general matter.

There is a huge difference of approach between economists and psychologists that is evident the moment one reads an elementary textbook on either subject or, for that matter, the moment one compares our own introductions to them (Chapters 1 through 3). Economics starts from theory; in an elementary treatment the only data one meets are hypothetical. Psychology is much more empirically oriented; an elementary treatment will try to justify its assertions, at a very early stage, by appeals to everyday experience, direct demonstrations that the reader can try, and citation of specific experimental studies. As suggested in Chapter 3, this difference is at its most extreme in the study of microeconomics, but it is all-pervading.

This issue threatens to open up the rationality question yet again, for it is the existence of a single theoretical framework that allows economics to develop without constant reference to merely contingent facts of experiment or experience. The fact that something can be done does not imply that it should be done, however, and we want to ask whether the detachment of economic theory from data is justifiable. A number of arguments in its favor can be put forward.

One is that the facts of economics do not have to be discovered; they are matters of everyday observation. Early economists, from Smith (1776/1908) to Marshall (1920/1949) certainly appeal to such common experience, but these examples show the weakness of the case. In the first place, what "everyone knows" may be a matter of prejudice or selective perception rather than objective fact; macroeconomic facts, at least, are often the outcome of economic policy, and their interpretation is a matter of political dispute. Moreover, the common experience of such historical figures is no longer ours, so we have only their word for their evidence.

Second, it may be argued that the facts of economics are simply too complicated for the kind of simple relationship used in the introductory psychology text to be extracted and displayed for our instruction. To this is sometimes added the argument (e.g., Fleming 1969, p. 57) that experiments, which make it possible to isolate simple relationships within complex systems, are impossible in economics. This entire argument seems to us to be quite inadequate. If the economy is a complex entity, so too is the behavior and mental life of an individual person; yet it is possible to extract simple empirical demonstrations of supposed general tendencies at the psychological level. A few introductory economics texts (e.g., Dorfman 1978; Hirshleifer 1984; Lancaster 1974) do incorporate some simple empirical relationships from econometric work. Some economists, at least, vigorously reject the idea that economic experimentation is impossible (e.g., Naylor 1972; see also Chapter 4).

Finally, it may be claimed that, given an adequate theory, empirical demonstration is superfluous. The model here, perhaps, is the elementary physics text, which does not refer the reader to Newton's experiments, but instead describes idealized experiments, which could not, in fact, be performed or would not have the required results if they did. This argument, however, rests on the assumption that utility maximization is an adequate theory, and such an assumption is inconsistent with the facts as noted in Chapters 5 and 18. Psychologists have traditionally argued that it is inadequate; we have taken the only alternative position (i.e., that it is not a theory).

There is much more to this point, of course, than introductory textbooks. Introductions to psychology stress empirical results because psychologists see themselves as constrained by data. Introductions to economics stress theory because economists see themselves as constrained by utility maximization. In this book, we have repeatedly made use of economic data to constrain and illuminate our argument, although that has often forced us to go against the grain of the literature. We offer to economists the conclusion that empirically driven argument is possible in economics, and could be used much more generally.

The need for theory at a lower level

Our various methodological conclusions converge into the following point: Utility maximization, on its own, is not an adequate theory; we have to specify, and be specific about the contributions of, multiple sources of utility; and we need to take the data into account. Those three points can be met if we are willing to take seriously the idea that utility maximization is a framework for the construction of theories, and construct some theories within it.

The fruitfulness of such an approach can be seen in cases where it has already been used. The life-cycle hypothesis of saving behavior is a good example; that is, it does not follow axiomatically from utility maximization, but is a lower-level construct within it. Using it makes it possible to determine the importance to saving behavior of a range of sources of utility (future consumption, pure hoarding, bequest, provision for emergencies). The development of the theory has been strongly constrained by econometric data. Our chapter on saving was no less empirically based than any other in Part II of the book, and almost all the data came from the economic literature.

The life-cycle hypothesis is not the only example of such lower-level theorizing in economics. Others include the various demand systems used in econometric analyses of economywide buying behavior (cf. Chapter 7), macroeconomic hypotheses like the quantity theory of money (cf. Chapters 3 and 12), and Lancaster's characteristics theory of consumer demand. These examples are still the exception though. Chapter 7 described regularity in buying behavior not reflected in any economic theory; the same was true in most of Part II. Our experience of trying to use economics within economic psychology suggests that they ought to become the rule.

SUBSTANTIVE CONCLUSIONS FOR ECONOMICS

There are many empirically supported generalizations about economic behavior in this book, and we cannot list them all here. Instead, we want to take a small number of examples where a mixture of psychological and economic approaches seems to us to have yielded conclusions of interest to general economics. They are not the only examples that would meet that specification; they have been chosen to represent a spread of subject areas and types of underlying discussion. We shall not repeat here substantive conclusions that are implicit in the methodological conclusions we have already drawn, for example, the importance of multiple sources of utility in work or saving behavior.

The labor–supply curve, tax, and benefits

One of the currently most worrying empirical questions about economics is the effect of marginal tax rates on labor supply. It is troublesome partly because it has implications for policy in an area where established political views also have clear policy implications, and partly because the simple utility-maximizing theory of the labor–leisure curve quite clearly predicts that a rise in effective wages will lead to either an increase or a decrease in hours worked.

In Chapters 6 and 11, we considered several kinds of data, and a few preliminary answers emerged. They may be summarized as follows. Those who have a very high level of nonemployment income are relatively unlikely to work, but some individuals will work very hard. There is little evidence that those whose main income comes from employment are influenced by marginal tax rates (and hence by effective marginal wage rates), and in many cases hours worked have increased substantially when there is no piece rate or overtime element at all. In a modern economy, those whose incomes are very low, so that state benefits form a high proportion of them and effective marginal tax rates can approach or even exceed 100%, nonetheless commonly continue in work. The only group whose tendency to work is strongly affected by the availability of benefits consists of married women in intact families. However, extremely unpleasant and low-paid jobs will be rejected except under very harsh economic conditions, such as may be found in rapidly developing economies. It is not natural for people to have to work this hard to avoid starvation. Even in the marginal environments they now inhabit, the hunter-gatherer peoples who are the modern representatives of our ancestral economy work a twenty- to thirty-hour week.

Savings and durables purchase

A troublesome conceptual question within economics concerns the classification of consumers' purchases of durable goods. Are these acts of expenditure (which is how they are treated in the national accounts), or of saving (as Friedman 1957, p. 116, suggests)? Either view is defensible, and our study of economic psychology tells us that both express part of the truth (cf. Chapters 7 and 8).

Consumers do not spontaneously classify durables purchases as saving. Psychologically they have different properties than saving. People typically buy more durables than they predict in a year, and save less than they predict. Nonetheless, durables purchase and saving do have points in common. Both are likely to increase disproportionately in response to income windfalls. Both tend to have positive income elasticities. And when they expect bad economic conditions, people tend to reduce durables purchasing and increase saving. It is reasonable to see this as a process of moving savings into a more liquid form.

Money: not from primitive to modern, but from primitive to sophisticated

Most economic treatments of money regard modern money as an abstract ideal, in which three functions (medium of exchange, standard of value, and store of value) perfectly cohere and inhere. This is in contrast to primitive money in which these functions are imperfectly and separately realized.

The economic psychology of money (see Chapter 12), on the other hand, shows that this picture is unrealistic. In the first place, an entity with those functions would be psychologically unstable because of the multiple symbolizations it must attract. In the second place, our money is best described not as modern but as sophisticated, in the sense in which Lancaster (1966a) speaks of a sophisticated consumption technology. Our money exists in many forms and has many characteristics. Different forms serve different functions to different extents. Macroeconomics recognizes this with its distinction between different measures of the money supply; that is, there is no single boundary that can be drawn around the exemplars of money (a sure sign that it is a polymorphous concept or fuzzy set).

The independent economic life of children

Our study of economic psychology has revealed at least one area of economic life that has been almost totally ignored by economists, namely the behavior of children. Marketing scientists and advertising researchers have taken an interest in the development of economic behavior, and as psychologists it was natural for us to include a developmental perspective in this book. But economics tends to work in terms of households. Children rarely if ever constitute an independent household, although their presence may greatly change the economic behavior of a household's other members.

We are not suggesting that this emphasis on household is misplaced. For many economic purposes it is no doubt a useful or even essential first approximation. It is clear, however, that it ought not to be the only focus. Children engage in many kinds of economic behaviors, and when they do so, they are not acting as agents of their households. Furthermore, their economic behavior is in some ways different from that of adults (e.g., when comparing brands, young children tend to use only perceptual attributes). A comprehensive economics ought to be able to study this kind of economic behavior (just as it can study economic behavior in other cultures) and provide a utility-maximizing account of it.

ECONOMIC POLICY

The academic study of economics has traditionally been much more closely linked to public policy than has the study of psychology. Psychology does have policy implications (e.g., in education, and in the treatment of the disturbed and the deviant), but these are much less political issues than are those involving a government's economic strategy. Does economic psychology have any distinct policy implications?

Policy is only partly determined by the kinds of facts and theories that can be produced by a positive science (cf. Chapter 11, in which the distinction between positive and normative approaches is discussed in more detail). From a given set of objective facts, different policies follow from different sets of values and beliefs. We are not writing a political or moral tract, and so we shall try to separate our ideas about policy into their "positive" and "normative" components. It would be naive to suppose that this can ever be done completely, however.

The means of policy

We begin with questions at the lowest and most positive level, in which the aim of policy is not in dispute but the implementation is far less clear.

No modern economy can be run without taxation, and everyone can agree that taxes should be collected as cheaply and conveniently as possible. The work on the comprehensibility of tax literature illustrates the way in which economic psychology can contribute to policy at this detailed level. With rather less certainty, economic psychologists can also suggest ways in which tax avoidance and evasion might be reduced (see Chapter 11).

Another example concerns the effects of unemployment on individuals. Consideration of the latent functions of work, and the psychopathological consequences of the loss of a job (cf. Chapter 6; see also Brenner 1973; Jahoda 1979) should lead to suggestions about ways in which unemployed people can be helped to remain psychologically healthy, hence reemployable.

Perhaps the most obvious area for applying economic psychology to the implementation of policy, however, concerns influencing and monitoring the acceptability of policy. It is clear that peoples' actions, as consumers and perhaps as employees as well, are capable of influencing the course of the economy. It is also clear that those actions can be predicted from various kinds of attitude survey, although such predictions may not be perfect (Turner & Krauss 1978). Nor do the predictions necessarily contain unique information. Peoples' attitudes to the economy can be predicted by economic data, but these are not the only influences upon them. Mosley (1982) showed that perceived inflation depended more on the attitude taken by the media than on the underlying economic facts.

There is room for more research on the interplay on economic and more general social factors in determining people's view of the economy and their consequent economic behavior. Nonetheless, there are clear (if not very surprising) messages for governments in the data we have now. First, if policies are not having the expected effect, it may be possible to find out why by investigating how people are perceiving them and the economy on which they are supposed to act. Second, if, as is to be hoped, policy is a rational response to an objective assessment of economic facts, it is important that those facts should be communicated clearly and consistently to the public.

The agenda for policy

The policy that a party, or a government, adopts is often largely determined by the list of things that it believes to be important, that is, the areas seen as being matters for policy. The process of agenda-setting probably cannot be objective. Economic psychology has some fairly direct implications for the problems which ought to be on the agenda of the makers of economic policy.

In part, this matter of the agenda for policy is a matter of welfare economics, the branch of economics that deals with how people as a whole are affected by different kinds of economic change or economic process. We have had little to say about welfare economics in this book. In most cases, conclusions about economic welfare are based on the utility-maximizing model; that is, peoples' welfare is assumed to be monotonically related to the utility they obtain. It follows that some of our methodological and substantive dissatisfactions with economics, already expressed in this chapter, have welfare implications.

For example, we drew attention above to the needless neglect of "psychological" sources of utility (and disutility) in economic theory. Taking these into account may change the order of priorities of economic policy questions. If we take account, for example, of the various sources of stress caused by redundancy and unemployment, we might give reduction of unemployment more urgency. If we take account of the way others' benefit may add to an individual's utility, we may give a higher priority to reducing economic inequality as a goal of policy.

Another example is policy with respect to advertising. Purely economic considerations might suggest that governments do not need to intervene, or even to have a view, on the quantity and nature of advertising which circulates. Economic psychology, on the other hand, suggests that advertising may have effects on society as a whole, and on children, whose disutility ought to be included as an external cost in an economic analysis of advertising (cf. Chapter 13). It is generally true that, where there are externalities, government action is needed if the general welfare is not to suffer (cf. Chapters 11).

There are cases in which politicians seem to have had an intuitive grasp of economic psychology in areas where its conclusions have differed from those of economics. For example, Keynesian macroeconomists have tended to see inflation as relatively benign; survey data indicate, however, that people have always seen it as a sign of poor economic prospects (Katona 1975, pp. 134–7). The perception of that public mood by politicians (many of them, though not all, conservative) may have had a lot to do with their success in giving "the fight against inflation" a dominant place on the agenda for economic policy during the past decade. That in turn has led to the implementation of what were proclaimed (not always accurately) as monetarist economic policies in most Western economies.

Another way in which economic psychology might help set the agenda for policy is through a systematic approach to economic motivation. As noted in Chapter 16, the basic needs approach to economic development is closely similar to Maslow's hierarchical theory of needs. While we criticized that theory in Chapter 18, it is possible that, under given conditions, some motivations will be paramount. The basic survival needs, for food, clothing, shelter, and health care, must be the first goals of a developing country's economic policy. We certainly did not need economic psychology to tell us that, but we cannot rely on economic behavior to reflect that priority consistently. Social motivations of various sorts will readily come to dominate behavior even under conditions of dire physical need. This means that policy must take such social needs into account, both with a view to allowing them to be met as well as to make sure that they do not sabotage provision for basic needs.

The ends of policy

The agenda for economic policy lists the questions that need to be asked. Does economic psychology also have any answers to offer? Here we move clearly into the range of the normative rather than the positive aspects of our discipline.

No scientist should make sweeping policy recommendations. Nonetheless, there are several points at which fairly clear generalizations do emerge from what we have discussed in this book. Many of them follow from themes which have already been developed in this and the previous chapter, in connection with our view of the rationality assumption. Without rejecting utility maximization, it is clear that conclusions that assume that a simple, pecuniarily defined utility will be maximized by all economic agents are likely to be misguided. That is as true of policy conclusions as it is of scientific ones. Let us look first at some of the ways in which policy is likely to be led astray by such an oversimplified view of economic rationality.

Many policy implications could be drawn from the economic psychology of work. Perhaps the most important concerns the effect of the marginal income from working (Chapters 6 and 11). There seems to be little evidence that high (and in some cases, very high) effective marginal tax rates have much influence on people's motivation to work. This is true whether we are concerned with high rates of income tax as they affect highly paid employees or with the effects of the withdrawal of means-tested benefit when social security claimants find low-paid jobs. In the latter case, women in intact families may leave work if benefits rise, but that might well bring other social benefits if we assume that they are taking up child care instead. Thus proposals to ensure that the marginal tax rate never rises too high should be based on considerations of justice rather than incentive. These conclusions are not inconsistent with an account based on a purely instrumental view of work, but they follow much more directly when we recognize that there are other reasons for working as well.

In the behavior of buyers, we found substantial evidence for a habitual component (Chapter 7); in fact, if consumers in the modern economy had to take careful, considered decisions every time they made a purchase, the economic process would grind to a halt. Furthermore, advertising, although not as powerful as some critics have supposed, does influence people's choices in ways that are in the advertisers' interest but against the consumers' interests (Chapter 13). It follows that the simple doctrine of *caveat emptor* is an inadequate basis for a policy toward consumers. Government must take on some kind of regulatory role, so that buyers do not suffer the worst consequences of unconsidered choice, and so that the information needed to make good choices with little decision time is readily available. Consumer protection of this kind is, in fact, now an established part of commercial life in advanced economies.

Saving, too, is an area in which economic psychology leads to many policy conclusions. People will not spontaneously save as much as they need to ensure comfort in old age because of a general preference for present consumption that goes beyond what is predicted by simple rationality. Government action is needed if everyone is to have a reasonable pension.

It would be possible to argue that people's behavior shows that they do not choose to make adequate provision for old age and that it is no business of government to interfere in the results of that free choice. Moreover, the attempt to do so may disrupt the process of capital formation in the economy.

It is important to disentangle the ideological laissez faire argument from the practical one here. From a practical point of view, the best available data suggest that government action to ensure adequate pension provision can be taken without gross damage to capital formation. Nonfunded social security wealth may reduce private saving, but not in proportion to its value; compulsory saving in pension schemes will displace some other saving, but not in proportion to its value.

Ideology is more a question of personal values, about which agreement is never likely to be complete. The extreme laissez faire view is probably more popular among economists than it is among the population at large, but most people might well agree with a moderate version of it, that is, that governments should not intrude on individual choice without good cause. In the case of saving, however, there may be good reasons for government action. For example, it can be argued that intertemporal choices are never free, being constrained by unavoidable ignorance about the future. It can also be argued that decisions about pensions involve externalities, since large numbers of indigent old people in a society would create an intolerable burden on it. In that case, the state as the representative of the common interest would have legitimate reason to act.

A less controversial area of policy is the management of money, one of the traditional roles of government. The economic psychology of money (see Chapter 12) shows that this task is always likely to be difficult because money seems to be many faceted and because people's reactions to it may depend on a variety of symbolic systems that deviate from its ostensible functions. Both the U.S. and U.K. governments have reason to give rueful assent to this last generalization, as a result of their attempts to change the normal form of the dollar and pound sterling from notes to coins – in both cases an apparently timely step in terms of efficiency and economy.

Curiously, people's conservatism about money, maddening to policy-makers when new official forms of money are in question, does not seem to prevent the constant emergence of new unofficial forms of money – also an inconvenience from a policy point of view, since it makes controlling or even measuring the money supply extremely difficult. Here, from the same moderated laissez faire position as we used above, we would argue that the different forms of money reflect different needs, or rather different combinations of needs. Other things equal, the forms are to be encouraged rather than deplored, unless of course their emergence seems to result from exploitative marketing.

Some other policy conclusions are less clearly tied to the need for an extended concept of rationality. For example, in policy toward economic growth and development, modern economic psychology must offer one negative conclusion. McClelland's (1961) approach gave a dominant role to the entrepreneur in development, to the need for achievement in the behavior of entrepreneurs, and to family values and the immediate cultural context in fostering a need for achievement. Evidence for every step in this argument now seems weak, and for the total argument, absent (see Chapter 16). If politicians believe that economic development and recovery depend on the psychology of the entrepreneur, they must do so on faith alone. Although there are a number of psychological factors that might be involved in growth and development, either as causes or as effects, we have nothing to replace McClelland's comprehensive structure. This is clearly a major disappointment.

One very general conclusion about the aims of economic policy does emerge from our discussions. At least in the short term, people seem to be more concerned by relative income and wealth than absolute levels. In a kibbutz situation, even the relatively well off are happier with a more egalitarian income distribution (Morawetz et al. 1977). In time-series studies, people's assessment of their own happiness depends on their relative income within their own nation or community, not on the national standard of living (Easterlin 1974). This suggests that there may be some scope for policies which sacrifice economic progress for a more equal distribution of existing resources. Together with the other evidence cited above, that is, that high marginal tax rates are not a disincentive to managerial work, and that social security does not depress capital formation, people's preferences (and practicality) argue for a more "welfarist" approach to economic policy, rather against the trend of recent years.

Our most general conclusion about the ends of policy, however, follows from the entire structure we have adopted for the book: Individuals are affected by the kind of economy they live in. That is seen most forcibly in token economies (Chapter 17), but it is true of any economy. This means that those who frame economic policy are indirectly framing human psychology. Some politicians would recognize this fact, and relish it. Others would find it disturbing. Whatever one's attitude, however, the conclusion means that economic policy can never be seen as a merely technical matter of achieving an objectively specified end by the most efficient means; there will always be human consequences, and usually human costs, to be considered.

THE PROBLEMS OF OUR TIME

All policy questions involve some element of personal perspective. Even the agenda for policy is subjective. It would not be hard to gain agreement, however, on a list of the major Problems of Our Time. As much as 67% of the world's economic production goes to support the standard of living of 15% of its population; about one-fourth of the world's people lack even the basic necessities of life, and are condemned to live in constant peril of early death from starvation or avoidable disease. Two nation states command sufficient military hardware to kill every human on our planet many times over. Every year, unknown numbers of the animal and plant species that share our planet are pushed to extinction by the expansion of technologically based societies (a thousand warm-blooded animal species are currently recognized as endangered). In at least one-third of the world's states, individuals risk assassination, torture, or ill treatment in custody if they disagree with the government. The world's most technologically advanced and democratic countries are barely able to control the values of the currencies their citizens use; and in those countries, millions of able people who are anxious to work are condemned to idleness, low income, and lower status because the economic system can find nothing for them to do (figures from Kidron & Segal 1984, maps 8, 21, 25, 37, and 50).

Some of these problems are very clearly economic, and nearly all have an economic aspect. In this last section, we argue that they are, at least in part, problems in economic psychology. This may seem overly ambitious. Can our modest subdiscipline of economic psychology really hope to contribute anything at this ultimately important level? It is necessary to recognize that these are human problems and, as such, they have to be solved at a human level and on a human scale. However huge the problem of world hunger, it breaks down to individual hungry people. If one of them is fed, some contribution has been made to its solution. Even with this reminder, though, global problems are inevitably daunting. The task is, quite simply, to change the world. How is it to be done?

The technological solution

There was a time, not so very long ago, when it seemed obvious that if one really wanted to change the world, the thing to become was a scientist, or better still an engineer. Which has done more in the last hundred years to liberate women in the technologically advanced West: women's suffrage or cheap automatic washing machines? Which has done more to ensure that it is now relatively easy to visit the Soviet Union: East–West detente or the jumbo jet? But more recent developments have shaken such technological optimism. The arguments are familiar. Meadowes et al. (1972), and many others since, have pointed out that technological development involves severe external costs. The Green Revolution, which greatly increased food production in poorer countries by encouraging new varieties and heavy use of artificial fertilizers, has enriched moderately wealthy farmers and made the truly poor poorer than ever (Griffin 1979; Pearse 1980; Wharton 1969; for a contrary view, albeit based on only one region, see Blyn 1983). Illich (1974, pp. 30–1) mischievously calculates that the economic speed of the motor car is four miles per hour, if one takes into account the time required to earn the money to pay for it. And, as we discussed in Chapter 18, Hirsch argues that there are some goods that can never be made more available by technological progress because they are inherently socially limited; they are defined in terms of social position. The technological fix no longer looks like a satisfactory solution of deep-rooted social problems.

The political solution

To many people, the natural conclusion from the perceived failure of science and technology was that real change could only be brought about by political means. The problem is not one of producing, say, food; the average calories per head available on the world's food markets each day (2,617 in 1978–80: Food and Agriculture Organization 1983) already exceeds the average requirement for a person, even in the relatively harsh climate of the United Kingdom (2,480: Greaves & Hollingsworth 1966). The problem is to ensure the fair distribution of that food. Only changes in both national and international politics could do that. From this sort of argument (pursued about many other problems as well) flowed the radicalization of much of the intellectual world in the West during the late 1960s and early 1970s. But political change, too, has proved a false hope in many ways. Looking over a longer time scale, the most radical attempts to ensure fair distribution by political means have been the communist revolutions in Russia and China. Although these have indeed produced rather more equal societies than are found in the West (e.g., Phelps Brown 1977, chapter 2), they have involved heavy costs in terms of both technological backwardness and loss of individual liberty. Most Western readers would find those costs unacceptable.

The economic dimension

If the problems of our time are neither primarily technological, nor primarily political, what are they? Many of them appear to have an economic aspect. Underdevelopment, inflation, unemployment, and inequality are all economic phenomena. Most Western readers would accept that economic policy should try to prevent, eliminate, or at any rate mitigate them, and that academic economics should tell us how such ends can be achieved. The interventionist economic policies that are associated above all with the name of Keynes had precisely this intent. But Keynesian policy is no longer politically acceptable, and many current academic economists hold that it could not work. The alternative policies which have succeeded it have not done visibly better. Economics alone does not seem to have the answer to the Problems of Our Time.

The psychological context

With all due modesty, we should like to suggest that some of the most troublesome of these problems arise at the point where individuals affect and are affected by the economic process, in other words, that they are problems in economic psychology. Inflation, for example, has to do with the value individual people are prepared to set on the abstract symbols we use to mediate economic transactions (cf. Chapter 12). Fair distribution of the world's resources may involve some people giving up opportunities to monopolize them; it is a problem in the economic psychology of giving (cf. Chapter 9; see also Collard 1978, pp. 102–4). The human costs of unemployment are at least partly due to the social psychology of working and nonworking environments and life-styles (cf. Chapter 6).

Economic psychology is certainly not in a position to offer solutions to this kind of problem. What it can reasonably offer is a point of view and a style of approach. The economic problems of our time are, in part, psychological; individuals' behavior, at the level at which it can be studied by psychologists, contributes to them as well as being affected by them. To judge by their public pronouncements, policymakers intuitively respond to this dual aspect of economic problems. The aim of economic psychology is to recognize and use it systematically.

20

THE CAUSATION OF ECONOMIC BEHAVIOR

Chapters 18 and 19 have attempted to draw some conclusions from the study of economic psychology, for psychologists and economists respectively. Here, we offer a number of conclusions to economic psychologists.

The structure of this book has been dictated by a particular view of the causation of economic behavior. In Part II we discussed the economic behaviors of individuals, that is, the extent to which these behaviors determine the behavior of the economy as a whole. In Part III we discussed the ways in which the economic system affects individual behavior. Individuals, of course, are neither simply the sovereign causes of economic phenomena nor simply helpless puppets in the face of economic determiners. Instead, multiple pathways of causation, much intertwined, and complicated by feedback relations, bind the individual to the economy in which he or she lives.

Within that complexity, however, we believe that two clear themes emerge. They can be summarized by saying that economic behavior is subject to dual causation. This conclusion is fairly simple and obvious, but we think it has not had sufficient recognition within economic psychology.

Individuals display economic behaviors. In fact, most of us spend much of our waking life engaged in economic behavior. We work, buy, save, give, gamble, and so forth. Each of these kinds of behavior is a legitimate subject of study for psychologists. In principle, at least, psychologists ought to be able to predict quite a lot about the way people do all these things. And it is a standard doctrine of economics that the choices individuals make about these kinds of behavior collectively determine the entire course of economic affairs. Individuals act on the economy, and the influence of their actions is paramount. This is the doctrine of consumer sovereignty.

Individuals also live within the economy, and the economy (although it is a social, not a physical, fact) is external to them. It is part of our environment and is a very important influence on behavior. The strongest form of this statement is the Marxian doctrine of economic determinism, which asserts that each individual's way of apprehending reality will be a function of personal economic situation and status. We do not have to be

Marxists, however, to see the importance of the economy as a cause of individual behavior. To take an example, the tax system is a potent influence on people's economic behavior but also on the way they perceive society and their roles within it. Many other examples could be cited. Money, which enters into so many behaviors, economic and otherwise, is a creation of a particular economic system. Advertising is an all-pervading aspect of a free-enterprise economy; indeed, many (e.g., Williamson 1978) have claimed that it affects even our gender stereotypes. And in the token economy (Ayllon & Azrin 1968; Kazdin 1977), we actually construct an economic system with the deliberate aim of modifying disturbed or deviant behavior.

So far, all we have done is repeat arguments that have already been stated at length earlier in this book. In this final chapter, however, we take a further step, one that may prove more controversial. We argue, first, that economic psychology is in need of a new paradigm, in the sense of Kuhn (1970), that is, a framework of agreed assumptions within which research can be carried on. Second, we suggest that a recognition of the dual causation of economic behavior in fact provides us with that new paradigm. Before developing these arguments further, however, we briefly review the kind of evidence which makes us describe economic behavior as subject to dual causation.

EXAMPLES OF DUAL CAUSATION

Work

What are the causes of work behavior? It is impossible to ignore either the effects of the individual or the effects of the economy. Individuals come to the employment market with very different motivations, arising from very different needs. This gives them greater or less willingness to take different kinds of jobs at different rates of pay, and this in turn will affect the general state of the economy. The willingness of individuals to undertake hard entrepreneurial work for low current returns may even make the difference between stagnation and prosperity (see Chapter 16). Does this mean that work is a field in which causation runs wholly from households to the wider economy? Surely not. In an economic depression, many individuals who would willingly take jobs are unable to do so. This may have profound psychological effects on them, possibly to the extent of rendering them unfit for future employment if it should become available. In a primitive gatherer-hunter economy, no one need work more than four hours a day (cf. Chapter 15); in a modern economy, anyone with as few possessions as a gatherer-hunter would be under severe pressure to work all the hours available to add to personal wealth.

Yet, it is the fact that individuals bow to such pressures that allows our economy to function as it does. People who have been sufficiently acculturated in a more "primitive" economy may not respond to the pressures of the consumer/producer society.

Giving

The tendency to general selfishness but occasional altruism is an enduring human trait that probably has its origins in more or less inevitable evolutionary pressures (see Chapter 10; see also Barash 1982, chapters 5 and 6; and Collard 1978, chapter 5). It has extremely wide-ranging economic consequences. Collard shows how the extent of altruism has strong implications for such questions as collective bargaining in wage disputes, levels of social security benefits that will be democratically acceptable, and aid to less developed countries. Yet giving behavior is also strongly determined by the kind of economy we live in. There are some social rules that apply to gifts in our own culture, such as the taboo on young adults giving money to their mothers. Much more powerful effects can be seen if we contrast the Western economy with the so-called primitive economies where giving is an important mechanism of exchange (cf. Chapter 16; see also Sahlins 1974, chapter 5). Our account of the economic psychology of giving would be radically incomplete without either one of these emphases.

THE RATIONALITY QUESTION

New paradigms are needed when we realize that the old ones are defective. It may not be recognized that economic psychology has always had a paradigm, but we suggest that it has. Whatever the issue in economic psychology, we found that much of the published literature approached it by considering, directly or indirectly, whether behavior, at the psychological level, is rational.

There are good reasons why this should be so. Almost all economic theory uses the assumption of rational, utility-maximizing choice at some point; in many parts of economic theory, especially those best known to noneconomists, it is the principal assumption, the key proposition, which allows for theoretical progress. By contrast, within psychology almost all the major developments of the last hundred years have come about through denials of human rationality. Scientific psychology has been a progress away from the concept of the rational human being whose behavior can be understood in terms of his or her stated motives and intentions, toward the causal factors of human behavior that are not even accessible to the individual's consciousness, let alone the objects of rational thought. This is true no matter what school of psychology we examine. Freud directed our attention to the unconscious motivations of behavior. The behaviorists argue that behavior consists of habits, established by processes of conditioning, of which we can be aware only as passive observers. Developmentalists of the Piaget school demonstrate that our cognitive capacities are the end product of a long succession of accommodations and assimilations; at every stage, the individual's abilities to apprehend the world are limited. Social psychologists show us that our attitudes and our judgments are constrained by our social world and our need for internal consistency in ways that have nothing to do with the objective state of the world. Cognitive psychologists demonstrate that human memory, attention, and processing speed are limited resources, with their own laws that reflect an internal structure rather than the structure of external reality.

The observed irrationality of behavior

Given this context, it is not hard to see why psychologists with an interest in economic affairs should want to ask, empirically, whether economic behavior really is rational in any sense. There are easy gains to be made. More or less whatever aspect of rationality we consider, irrationality can be found. In Chapter 5, three classic examples were discussed: the theory of riskless choice underlying microeconomic demand theory, the theory of choice under risk, and the theory of intertemporal choice. In each case we noted that the axioms of rational behavior were inconsistent with observed data on individual behavior. Furthermore, when we considered the kinds of real economic behavior to which those kinds of rationality are relevant – buying (Chapter 7), gambling (Chapter 10), and saving (Chapter 8) – we found that rationality in itself was an inadequate theory of behavior.

Such classic demonstrations of irrationality are important; after all, the nearest psychology has to a Nobel prize winner is Herbert Simon, whose greatest contribution to economic thought has been to point out the boundedness of human rationality and the deficiencies of the rational choice model, in situations not much more complicated than these.

But irrationality can also be demonstrated in kinds of choice which have a more modern ring. Let us take two influential ideas that have come into economics during the past quarter-century, both from Chicago: the economics of information and the study of time allocation.

Stigler (1961) recognized that real decision makers could not be perfectly informed about the range of prices available in a market, and that costs were involved in gaining information. From this, he was able to show that the rational but imperfectly informed buyer would do more searching when prices were more dispersed, when he or she had to buy more of the commodity in question, and when the commodity in question was more expensive.

In Chapter 7, we considered whether these predictions were confirmed and found that prepurchase search can indeed lead to a lower price being paid (Carlson & Gieseke 1983). Furthermore, consumer scientists and economic psychologists (e.g., Katona 1975, p. 221) have frequently argued that people spend more time and effort before making major purchases than before minor ones, so that choice for items like large durables is more nearly rational than choice for small, consumable items. Support for the other predictions of the economics of information is weak. Goldman (1977–8) investigated Jerusalem housewives' purchasing of furniture, clothing, and shoes. There were certainly differences in the amount of prepurchase search they carried out, but these differences were related to subcultural norms and personal style, not to any of the factors Stigler would indicate. Goldman and Johansson (1977–8) considered gasoline purchases in an American city. Again, there were obvious differences in the amount of search, but they were unrelated to the mean size of purchase. It seems that the economics of information is not a major or direct influence on real consumer behavior.

A similar conclusion can be reached for the theory of the allocation of time. Becker (1965) sought to extend economic analysis to a wide range of human behavior by recognizing that time is the fundamental and irreplaceable human resource and that each individual's earning capacity sets a price on time used for nonwork activities. Thus those with a higher earning potential should be more willing to pay for time-saving goods and less willing to pay time (e.g., in searching for a lower price for other goods). Again, Chapter 7 recorded support for some of the predictions of this theory. Goldman (1972) found that Jerusalem housewives' knowledge of meat prices, and the extent to which they sampled alternative meat suppliers, varied inversely with household income. In general, however, the cost of time is a poor predictor of economic behavior. A number of studies have considered the use of time-saving goods by households in which both husband and wife are employed, so that time is both valuable and in short supply (e.g., Nickols & Fox 1983–4; cf. Chapter 7). The conclusion is consistent: Although such households do use more time-saving goods than the average, this is simply part of the higher standard of living their higher-than-average income makes possible. Households of the same income but having only the husband in employment use time-saving goods to just the same extent. Once again, a rational theory fails to predict observed behavior.

Objections to the rationality question

Real economic behavior clearly does contain irrationalities. Why, then, cannot economic psychology devote itself to using psychological methods for classifying and studying these irrationalities or to producing a more realistic description of human choice on which a more realistic economics could be based?

In one sense, that is what some economic psychologists have tried to do. George Katona (1951) started his first book on economic behavior with a brief account of the rationality idea and then proceeded to a more psychologically defensible analysis of choice. Herbert Simon, whom we should no doubt like to claim as an economic psychologist, succeeded in producing a new principle of choice, *satisficing* (Simon 1957), which is indeed capable of being included in axiomatic developments of economic theory. And some economists have called on psychology to provide an underlying theory. In trying to account for people's failure to delay gratification (as psychologists would put it), Fisher (1930) advanced an essentially psychological account of "impatience." The conventional theory of rational choice is recognizably incomplete in the area of time preference, although the incompleteness is slight (Koopmans 1960).

For most economists, however, the offer of an improved, psychologically based choice theory is one they can very easily refuse. Herein lies our first objection to the rationality question as an organizing principle for economic psychology. To ask the question, "Is behavior rational?" may, indeed, seem to go to the heart of economics, but in the process, it antagonizes economists. It dooms economic psychology to an adversarial mode of existence, in which psychologists try to undermine economic theory, economists try to explain why their claims are irrelevant to what they are doing. In the meantime, economic psychology as a new, interdisciplinary synthesis makes no progress at all. Anyone who finds it hard to believe this could happen should consult the book by Florence (1927), written in rebuttal of McDougall's attacks on *economic man*. It shows all too clearly that the idea of bringing psychology to bear on the irrationalities of economic behavior is not new, and that it has led to nothing.

Our second argument against attacks on rationality is that they misunderstand the nature and function of the rationality assumption. As Friedman (1953) argued, the axioms of decision theory are not advanced as descriptions of individual behavior; they are advanced as minimal postulates from which testable, and in fact true, propositions about the functioning of the economy can be derived. Rationality in economics is an "as if" assumption; we expect economic agents to behave "as if" they are rational decision makers, or the economy to behave "as if" its constituents were rational decision makers. Without this assumption, a positive theory of economic behavior would be very hard to develop. All we could have would be a historical account.

We do not have to agree completely with Friedman, especially when he asserts that the implausibility of the rationality assumptions constitutes their strength. We may see advantages in recognizing that economic events are embedded in history, and are not just the outworkings of a timeless axiom system. It may be better to collect empirical regularities before elaborating a theory to explain them. We must concede, however, that theories should be tested at the level of what they seek to explain. For economic theories, that means at the level of the real economic behavior of individuals and the behavior of the economy as a whole. If economic psychology is to question the rationality assumption, it must produce an alternative account of behavior at these levels. This is much harder than running laboratory experiments on artificial choices. Furthermore, the economy as a whole is such a large and complex entity, and the real economic behavior of individuals is embedded in such a mesh of different causalities, that it is extremely difficult even to describe either of them without making some use of the rationality assumption.

This is only the grossest way in which the rationality question approach misunderstands the rationality assumption. Take the example of giving which was mentioned pereviously as a possible objection to the axiom of greed. Perhaps 5% of the U.K. consumer economy is involved with gifts. Most of these are within families (and it must be remembered that much economic theory treats the members of a household as one individual). In the United States as much as 3% is given to charities, that is, to recipients completely outside any circle of reciprocity. Giving is thus a sizable economic fact. But is it an objection to economic rationality? Does it violate the axiom of greed? Not if we allow that another individual's benefit may add to a person's utility. Psychologists are apt to cry "foul" when rationality is "rescued" in this way, but this simply illustrates their misunderstanding of the function of the rationality assumption. Utility maximization is a framework within which to express economic facts. The way in which different economic events are said to contribute to utility is open to modification in the light of those facts. Thus nonpecuniary motivations for working can be absorbed into a rational account of the labor–leisure choice, just as giving can be incorporated into a rational account of buying. Rationality would fail only if the effort to include another's benefit, or the pleasure of working, in a person's utility rendered the whole concept of utility (or of its maximization) incoherent. But, since this does not happen, the rationality assumption escapes unscathed.

Our third objection to the rationality question as a paradigm for economic psychology is that it often rests on the confusion between rationality as description and rationality as process. The rationality assumption, as it is used in economics, has to do only with what a biologist would call the ultimate explanation of economic behavior, whereas most of the objections to it have focused on the proximate mechanisms of behavior. It is true that humans, unlike animals, have the option of subjecting their environment and behavior to verbal analysis, and that this makes an enormous difference to our behavior, even in the simplest situations (e.g., Lowe 1979). But there is no identity between rationality as mechanism and utility maximization as result. In a reasonably constant environment, habitual shopping behavior may produce the optimal result for a consumer; conversely, if a consumer has limited understanding, the best decision-making process he or she can muster may produce a very poor result.

In defense of rationality

At the time when scientific economics was being born, the fact of human reason provided what seemed to be good grounds for a presumption of rational behavior. What psychology has done is to remove those grounds. Can we nonetheless provide a final bulwark for economic utility maximization, by finding some alternative basis for a presumption of rationality in economic behavior? There are perhaps three grounds for doing so, although none of them is necessarily compelling.

The first concerns the behavior of firms. It has often been argued that, in a competitive economy, organizations will come to behave optimally whatever the quality of their internal decision making. The reason is that some firms will make optimal decisions; their competitors must either imitate them (and firms, unlike genes, can imitate), or go out of business. The parallel to Darwinian natural selection has been drawn explicitly, for example, by Hirshleifer (1977). Organizational behavior may seem irrelevant to the behavior of the individual in the economy, but it is worth remembering that a very high proportion of firms are one-person or one-household operations, and thus effectively identical to individuals. This proportion is higher in less developed economies (e.g., Koo 1976) and may become higher again in the postindustrial society, which is, some say, about to dawn on the developed economies.

A second ground for presuming rationality also depends on a well-informed minority. According to rational expectations theory (cf. Chapter 3), if a few individuals make rational deductions from current theory and data, and make their conclusions public through their roles as journalists, advisors, or spokespeople, it is not difficult for the majority to learn to take their advice. This is all that is required for rational models to work.

Our third ground for a presumption of rationality is more speculative. It rests on the parallel between ecology and economics that runs much deeper than mere etymology. Both ecology and economics are concerned with adaptation to scarce resources; in both kinds of adaptation, learning is likely to be crucial importance. We have suggested that much buying behavior is habitual, especially where small, recurrently bought items are concerned (these will constitute the bulk of purchases, in number if not in value terms). We know little of the laws of human habit, but it is reasonable to suppose that they will be similar to those that govern habitual behavior in animals, that is, to the laws of conditioning. It can be argued (e.g., Lea 1981, 1982; Maynard Smith 1984) that such laws would be expected to produce optimal behavior. Thus it may be that optimal behavior in the economic environment can be expected to exist as a phylogenetic legacy from a prelinguistic need for optimal adjustment to an ecological environment.

Finally, it must be recognized that the Darwinian principle of natural selection is much more general than its application to the origin of species. One of the most exciting developments in biology in recent years has been the attempt to apply evolutionary theory to human (and animal) culture. What is at issue here is not the crude application of biological evolutionism to mental and cultural phenomena, which became popular with such late-nineteenth-century writers as Herbert Spencer (e.g., 1870), but the recognition that cultural phenomena are also inherited through tradition and that they may be subject to selection pressures at that level. This is a revival of a long-standing movement within anthropology and sociology, which is at least as old as Alfred Wallace (1864) and has always retained some respectable following within anthropology (e.g., Service 1971; White 1959). The idea that social phenomena are subject to gradual change has always been essential to philology, for instance. What is new is the serious application to cultural phenomena of current, strict, evolutionary theory (e.g., Lumsden & Wilson 1981, 1983) rather than the misconceptions about fitness used by Spencer. The modern view is that replicators – which might be genes, or might be ideas – will increase if they produce behaviors that favor their replication. In the case of genes, these behaviors may be to the disadvantage of the individual carrying the genes; this is the sociobiological explanation of altruism (e.g., Dawkins 1976). Presumably something similar is true of ideas. In the main, selfish genes are expected to produce optimal behavior in their owners. What about selfish ideas? Can we not expect those ideas that cause their owners to engage in optimal economic behavior to gain extra opportunities to replicate? If we can, we have an additional reason to expect human economic behaviors, on the whole and on the average, to be describable in terms of rationality.

Two alternative paradigms

Attacks on economic rationality may not be simply unproductive; they may actually be wrong. How then are we to organize our thoughts about economic psychology?

One possibility is not to organize them at all, or at least try to avoid any theoretical structure. An important difference between economists (or ecologists) and psychologists is that economics starts from a theoretical framework, and takes it as far as it can before comparing the results with observation, while psychology tries to support its arguments with data at every step. It would be an interesting exercise to write an introduction to some branch of economics in the way that we introduce students to psychology, with observed regularities in behavior coming first and theory in the background.

The trouble is that this is what much of the consumer behavior literature does, or at least used to do and as we have noted, the results are not encouraging: too many data, too little theory, and theories that are only exhaustive webs of nonexplanatory boxes.

Another possibility is to draw on the ultimate/proximate distinction used in biology, and view economic psychology as describing proximate mechanisms, which in turn produce the ultimate effects described by economics. A good deal of progress could be made by this approach. It has the merits of accepting economics for what it can offer, and it avoids any clash with the rationality assumption. Some of the better recent work in consumer behavior can be fitted quite well into this paradigm. We can cite two examples.

The first is the study by Sheluga, Jaccard, and Jacoby (1979–80), in which subjects were found to select information about those attributes of a commodity which were most important to them (rational), use that information (rational), and thereby produce choices that were somewhat different from those they would have made if they had had full information available (irrational?). Here the mechanism by which information and choice interact is exposed, showing how an apparently irrational outcome can occur as a result of a series of rational choices.

A second example is Verhallen's (1982) investigation of the effects of scarcity on demand. In Chapter 7 we commented on the lack of data to support Veblen's (1899/1979) idea that social factors, particularly rarity and cost, affect demand for goods. Verhallen established a situation in which the extent and mechanism of scarcity effects could be measured. This approach should encourage empirical investigation of the mechanisms at the economic level.

The problem with a function/mechanism paradigm, however, is that it is not truly interdisciplinary. It causes economic psychologists to operate simply as psychologists with an interest in economic behavior, much in the way that a psychologist might have an interest in social, abnormal, or child behavior. It brings psychology to bear on economic questions, and recognizes the validity of economic analysis, but it does not give economics any role in psychology.

DUAL CAUSATION AS A PARADIGM

We are arguing that an economic psychology that restricts itself to finding the psychological mechanisms of economic behaviors is, in a word, not economic enough [just as social psychologists have recently been complaining since the early 1970s that current social psychology is not social enough (e.g., Semin & Manstead 1979; Taylor & Brown 1979)]. To become more economic, we have to allow economics to enter into psychology just as much as we allow psychology to enter into economics. We have to recognize that causality is not one way. The economy is one of the facts within the constraints of which individuals exist. It is, to be sure, a social fact, created by the behaviors of individuals. The economy does not have a mind of its own, but it does have laws and a history of its own. Those laws, and that history, are part of what determines individual behavior.

These statements are not theories, nor do they depend on a study of economic psychology. They are facts of obvious experience. The metascientific question is whether they are important facts and, in particular, whether they constitute a framework within which research in economic psychology can flourish. The test of a new paradigm is not whether it accounts for all the available data (Kuhn argues that, usually, it will not) but whether it can account for the data that are most awkward to handle under the existing paradigm, and whether it suggests obvious lines for new research. The theory should answer questions that, under the old paradigm, could not be answered and should ask the questions that are not being asked.

The biggest and most awkward fact under the old paradigm of the rationality question is that, despite all psychological demonstrations of the irrationality of human choice, economics continues to use the rationality assumption and continues to make progress. There is no difficulty in understanding this under dual causation. We can accept provisionally the arguments, given above, that the economy will work on individuals so as to produce descriptively rational behavior in the real economic context. Since we can also accept, unconditionally, the distinction between rational result and rational process, we can understand why behavior may appear irrational if taken out of its natural economic context. In that context, it may well be, in Katona's word, sane.

Research areas that were, essentially, conceived under the old paradigm of the rationality question, might have had a happier outcome under a dual causation paradigm. Let us consider three examples.

1. During the 1950s and 1960s, George Katona made the concept of economic psychology reasonably well known. Yet his approach failed to fire any enthusiasm within psychology, and economists remained skeptical. In our view, this is at least partly because Katona depended so heavily on the notion that attitudes make a contribution to economic growth independent of any economic process. With developing knowledge in economic forecasting and (ironically) economic psychology, the independent psychological contribution was whittled away

(e.g., Vanden Abeele 1983), leaving psychologists feeling unsure of their role and economists justified in their scepticism. A more broadly based approach would have acknowledged, indeed expected, that economic variables would themselves help to determine attitudes, and so perhaps would have developed more strongly the idea (present in Katona's earlier writings) of attitudes as intervening variables, which, however predictable from economic variables, may still be the effective cause and best locus of prediction of certain kinds of subsequent phenomena.

2. One kind of economic behavior has traditionally been given serious attention by large numbers of psychologists: work. Chapter 6 could not begin to summarize all the data that have been gathered by industrial, occupational, and organizational psychologists. Yet the psychology of work has had almost no influence whatever on mainstream psychology (it remains a low-prestige specialization, without a place in the conventional undergraduate curriculum) and has had no influence whatever on labor economics. The problem is that psychologists have wanted to apply existing psychological knowledge rather then uncover new kinds of causal influence which might, for example, have important implications for the psychology of motivation. Nor have they been ready to see how their findings might influence the traditional economic analysis of the labor–leisure choice; the study of nonpecuniary work motivations in economics has been pursued largely in isolation from existing knowledge in occupational psychology.

3. The very large data bases collected by econometricians and consumer scientists might well have formed the foundation of an interdisciplinary study of buying behavior. Instead they have been largely ignored by both economics and psychology. To psychologists they have seemed to involve a trivial and tedious application of general principles that are already well known. To economists, they seemed to involve studying processes whose general explanations were already well known. Yet, as noted in Chapter 7, empirical demand curves contain a number of surprises for both economists and psychologists. The problem has simply been a failure to perceive the wider implications of the phenomenon under study. This too we attribute to the failure to grasp all the interconnections between individual behavior and the behavior of the economy at large.

What of the new research that a new paradigm ought to stimulate? Here we must, of necessity, speculate. It seems to us that the dual causation paradigm immediately makes us supplement old questions with new ones. In the two central sections of this book, we divided the subject matter of economic psychology into two sections: questions about the economic behaviors of individuals and questions about the ways the economy affects individuals. This organization reflects such a dual causation paradigm. When we take the paradigm seriously, it also leads us to see that, although the division must be made, it must also be transcended. If economic behavior is dually caused, we must go further to ask new questions. How does the economy affect an individual's buying, saving, or working behavior? How do individuals affect the tax system, money, or advertising? How do the inmates of a token economy determine the behavior of its administrators? As soon as we pose these questions, we can see that they are interesting, unusual, and that various answers or part answers are already available. True to the Kuhnian analysis, those answers come from the parts of economic psychology that have not been well integrated under the current paradigm.

There is one final way in which the dual causation paradigm can guide research. To recognize that individuals influence the economy and that the economy influences individuals is to recognize that there is a closed loop of causative influence. In other words, the economy and the individuals within it constitute a system. It is characteristic of systems that the processes that make them up usually do not behave in the same way when isolated as they do when embedded in their natural context. To take a biochemical analogy, in vitro behavior is not always a good guide to in vivo behavior. Yet the isolable processes we study in vitro are the processes that make up the system in vivo. We should not be too discouraged if the economic behaviors we can study by psychological means do not always look like the economic behavior we see around us. What we have to do is to understand how these behaviors fit together to make up the economy. When we can do that, we shall have taken a major step both toward explaining individual behavior and toward explaining the behavior of the economy.

Implications of dual causation for economics and psychology

We have discussed the implications of economic psychology for its parent disciplines in the preceding two chapters. But does this paradigm shift also have implications of this sort? We believe that it does, for both economics and psychology both stand in constant danger of adopting an oversimplified model of the causation of economic behavior.

It is in psychology that this tendency is most obvious. The reductionist spirit of so much Anglo-Saxon psychology, born of a false analogy with nineteenth-century physical science, predisposes us to look to the smallest possible unit as the locus of causation. In economic questions, this creates a natural bias toward seeing the individual as the origin of all phenomena of interest. The sterility of this approach is sufficiently illustrated by the output of the consumer-science approach to buying behavior, as discussed above. Social psychology is much more inclined to admit the influence of society at large on individual behavior, and throughout this book we have struggled to conceive of economic psychology as a part of that kind of social psychology. The task, however, has not been easy, because among social theorists an interest in economic determination and an interest in social psychology seem almost to exclude each other.

Economics, with its classic distinction between micro and macro processes, offers at least a framework for considering both kinds of causality. Here too dogma interferes. Conventional economics must, to remain respectable, assert consumer sovereignty as the basis even for macro processes. Marxian economics sees them as resulting from impersonal forces of history and the struggle between classes, with very little autonomy for the individual consumer or worker (e.g., Desai 1979, p. 22). In practice the effects of the system disappear from serious consideration in microeconomics, and the individual largely disappears from macroeconomics. The resulting failures of both kinds of system are painfully obvious. Practical textbooks on management treat the pure microeconomic theory of pricing with near contempt (e.g., Dalrymple & Thompson 1969; Gabor 1977). In recent years, most individuals in the advanced Western countries have suffered from the inadequacies of naive macroeconomic theories naively applied to economic policy.

EXPLANATION AND CONTROL OF ECONOMIC BEHAVIOR

"It is all very well to interpret the world," wrote Marx (1845/1969), "the thing is to change it." Understanding the causes of natural phenomena, and being able to control them, are closely but not inevitably linked. Some psychologists have made "control over behavior" into a virtual slogan. Skinner (e.g., 1953, chapter 15) argues that the final test of our understanding of behavior is always our ability to mold it. It is obvious how an experimental approach to science leads to such a point of view. The essence of experimentation is that we should be able to set up not just a controlled situation in which we can predict what phenomena will occur, but a series of different controlled situations in which we can predict that different phenomena will occur. In a real sense this means that we have the phenomena under our control.

Yet there are natural and social phenomena that we feel we understand very well but cannot control at all. In the natural sciences, the obvious example is astronomy. We can give very good accounts of the behavior of planets, stars, and galaxies, but we cannot influence them in the slightest, if only because their behavior may already be millions of years old by the time we observe them. Even astronomy, however, is more nearly an experimental science than it used to be, now that rocketry makes it possible to add to the heavenly bodies, observe them from new points of view, even bring back material from them.

In social science, too, there are phenomena that we feel we understand but that we are powerless to influence. An obvious example is the occurrence of economic crimes. It can be predicted with confidence that an excise duty, tariff, import quota, or ban imposed on any commodity will lead to smuggling of that commodity. Using principles described by Ehrlich (1982) in his general analysis of the supply and demand for crime, it would not be hard to construct an econometric model that would predict the extent of smuggling as a function of the prices of the commodity inside and outside the frontier concerned (if only the extent of smuggling were more easily observed). But this degree of understanding gives us no power at all to inhibit smuggling, except by doing away with the tariff or control we are trying to implement. Another example is the occurrence of conflict between individuals within families. Recent developments in sociobiology have given us a highly plausible theory of why such conflicts are likely to occur (see Barash 1982, chapter 14), but that is no help at all in trying to resolve them.

Economic psychology is interesting because it concerns the real world. Seen as a branch of psychology, it stands alone in dealing with that part of our life that we spend in economically related behaviors (probably nearly half of the total lifetime of an adult). Seen as a branch of economics, it is almost alone in considering real individuals and the behaviors they actually engage in, rather than theoretical abstractions and the behaviors they ought rationally to engage in. The obvious role of economic psychologists is to provide interpretations of these vitally interesting behaviors of individuals, and the economic forces that contribute to them. To what extent, though, does our understanding of the causation of economic behavior allow us to control it?

The word "allow" was deliberately chosen to be ambiguous; it admits of either a practical or a moral interpretation. The next two sections of this chapter therefore pose two questions: If we understand the dual causation of economic behavior, can we control it? and should we control it?'

Applied economic psychology

From a practical point of view, we have drawn quite a lot of our data from unambiguously applied research projects. The marketing specialist investigating different methods of advertising, the consumer scientist investigating the effects of price differentials, the fiscal expert trying to devise a loophole-free tax system, the occupational psychologist trying to find the most appropriate job for an individual or the most appropriate individual for a job, the econometrician trying to model the effects on national output of a change in unemployment benefit – all are trying to use economic psychology to exert control over the economic behavior of individuals or the behavior of the economy as a whole. Do their efforts have any hope of success, or can they hope, at best, to stand by and interpret intelligently processes that will continue regardless of anything they may or may not do?

We cannot hope to answer this question in detail; all we can do here is to restate our belief that the practical applications of economic psychology are manifold. As stressed above, our data have often been drawn from the work of applied scientists. Although few of them would have called themselves economic psychologists, they belong to well-established professions that have proved their usefulness over decades. If we are saying anything new in asserting that economic psychology should be a useful applied discipline, it is that bringing together all these different approaches to economic behavior should result in a synthesis that would enrich each of them. The reader of this book, whatever constituent of economic psychology provides his or her own intellectual background, is probably in a better position than anyone else to decide whether that is true.

The moral use of economic psychology

We argued in the previous chapter that many of the outstanding problems of our time were, at least in part, problems in economic psychology. That clearly provides at least a partial justification for studying economic psychology; it also provides a prima facie case for applying it. In this century, however, we cannot leap to the conclusion that knowledge should always be applied or even that it should always be gained. It is said that, after Hiroshima, Einstein remarked, "If I had known, I should have been a locksmith." Economic psychology is unlikely to unleash a nuclear holocaust, but it is proper to ask who might benefit, and who might suffer, from its wider investigation and application.

Part of the point of economic psychology is that it is about important behaviors, both in terms of the proportion of our time they take up, and the central role they can play in our lives. Psychologically, it is a very different thing to live in the consumer capitalist society of twentieth-century Europe or North America, compared to living in the feudal society of medieval Europe, or the Stone Age economy of prehistoric Europe or the present-day New Guinea highlands. A good knowledge of economic psychology might allow us to move between such different psychologies at will, but do we actually want to be able to do so?

More important, do we want others to have this, or even a smaller, degree of psychological influence over us? Do we want our employers to be able to inculcate in us the sense of the social purpose of their business, and a consequent loyalty to them? At least one highly successful Japanese firm sees this as the key to its success (see Pascale & Athos 1982, chapter

2). Many other firms would like to be able to emulate this success, and they might well ask economic psychologists to help them do so. Do we want to be kept in a state of ever-rising aspirations for consumer-durable goods? Few people ask to be exposed to advertisements, yet none of us can escape the pressures toward consumption that they exert. Do we want our governments to be able to control with accuracy how much we will save, rather than spend, and how much of our tax bills we will pay rather than avoid or evade?

Those examples illustrate a general trend. Just because the behaviors studied by economic psychologists are of economic importance, they are particularly vulnerable to manipulation by interested others, who may not be benevolent. Does this not place a large moral question mark over the study of economic psychology? We would argue that, on the contrary, it provides it with its major moral justification. It establishes that, safe or not, the study of economic psychology is not only useful but necessary. The argument turns upon the essentially dual nature of the causation of economic behavior.

Einstein was wrong. The knowledge that led to the nuclear bomb would not have been prevented from emerging if he had used his ingenuity in some harmless technology. Its emergence was caused not by Einstein's genius, but by the political, social, and economic forces that created the structures of modern science, World War II, and the Allies' program of weapons research. Einstein was forgetting the dual causation of individual behavior – intellectual as well as economic. Einstein himself was not irrelevant to the process, but he does not have to bear all the moral responsibility for the consequences of his discoveries. They would have emerged in due course anyway. Similarly, whether or not we study economic psychology, the manipulation of our economic behavior by powerful others will go on, and often it will be quite sophisticated.

Our only defense against such manipulation is to understand it. As we have repeatedly said in earlier chapters, it is likely that much of the best empirical research into some aspects of economic psychology will never see the light of day, or even the half-light of the academic journals, because it is commercially valuable. Commercially valuable information is simply information that can be used for someone's profit, at someone else's expense. The object of the disinterested study of economic psychology should be to make a knowledge of the subject as widely available as possible, so that individuals can understand the pressures they come under, understand the effects their behavior will have on the economy, and act accordingly.

This is by no means a complete answer to the moral question. It comes close to the "all knowledge is good" argument, which supposes that the role of science is to produce knowledge without wondering what the wider community will do with it. Since the wider community will always include a number of malevolent individuals (and, on some theories, since all individuals are largely selfish), this may well be naive and irresponsible; knowledge is more likely to be used for bad purposes than for good purposes. But there is a difference between physical knowledge and social knowledge. In the case of social knowledge, it is individuals themselves who are the objects of knowledge. To spread social knowledge as widely as possible is to give people the only possible defense against its abuse, whereas spreading physical knowledge more widely merely allows more people to compete in abusing it.

Although this has been an academic textbook, we shall not judge its success or failure wholly by whether it becomes a useful ancillary to university or college teaching. That is of some importance, since there are few merits in books that are never read. What matters, however, is not whether this book helps its readers pass their examinations but whether it helps them understand their own economic behavior and interpret the economic world in which they live. If we have done that, we shall have begun, in a small way, the process of changing that world.

REFERENCES

Abelson, R. P. (1981). Psychological status of the script concept. *American Psychologist, 36,* 715–29.

Abrams, L., Hines, D., Pollack, D., Ross, M., Stubbs, D. A., & Polyot, C. J. (1974). Transferable tokens: Increasing social interaction in a token economy. *Psychological Reports, 35,* 447–52.

Adam, D. (1958). *Les reactions du consommateur devant le prix.* Paris: Sedes.

Adams, F. G. (1964). Consumer attitudes, buying plans, and purchases of durable goods: a principal components, time series approach. *Review of Economics and Statistics, 46,* 347–55.

Adams, J. S. (1963). Towards an understanding of inequity. *Journal of Abnormal and Social Psychology, 67,* 422–36.

Adams, J. S. (1965). Inequity in social exchange. In L. Berkowitz (Ed.), *Advances in experimental social psychology: Vol. 2* (pp. 267–99). New York: Academic Press.

Adams, J. S., & Jacobsen, P. R. (1964). Effects of wage inequities on work quality. *Journal of Abnormal and Social Psychology, 69,* 19–25.

Adams, J. S., & Freedman, S. (1976). Equity theory revisited: Comments and annotated bibliography. In L. Berkowitz & E. Walster (Eds.), *Advances in experimental social psychology: Vol. 9* (pp. 43–90). New York: Academic Press.

Adelman, I., & Griliches, Z. (1961). On an index of quality change. *Journal of the American Statistical Association, 56,* 535–48.

Adler, R. P., & Faber, R.J. (1980). Background: children's television viewing patterns. In R. P. Adler, G. S. Lesser, L. K. Meringoff, T. S. Robertson, J. R. Rossiter, & S. Ward (Eds.), *The effects of television advertising on children: review and recommendation.* Lexington, MA: Lexington Books.

Advertising Association. (1972). *Public attitudes to advertising.* London: Author.

Advertising Association. (1984). Trends in total advertising expenditure in 29 countries, 1970–1982. *International Journal of Advertising, 3,* 63–93.

Agarwhal, M. J., & Ratchford, B. T. (1980–1). Estimating demand functions for product characteristics: the case of automobiles. *Journal of Consumer Research, 7,* 249–62.

Agathon, M., & Saillon, A. (1976). [An attempt to establish a token economy in a psychiatric setting.] *Perspectives Psychiatriques, 58,* 275–79.

Ainslie, G. W. (1974). Impulse control in pigeons. *Journal of the Experimental Analysis of Behavior, 21,* 485–489.

Ainslie, G. W. (1975). Specious reward: A behavioral theory of impusiveness and impulse control. *Psychological Bulletin, 82,* 463–96.

Aitken, S., & Bonneville, E. (1980). *A general taxpayer opinion survey.* Washington, DC: CSR Incorporated.

Ajzen, I. (1977). Intuitive theories of events and the effects of base-rate information on prediction. *Journal of Personality and Social Psychology, 35,* 303–14.

Ajzen, I. (in press). From intentions to actions: A theory of planned behavior. In J. Kuhl & J. Beckman (Eds.), *Action-control: From cognition to behavior.* New York: Springer.

Ajzen, I., & Fishbein, M. (1973). Attitudinal and normative variables as predictors of specific behaviors. *Journal of Personality and Social Psychology, 27,* 41–57.

Ajzen, I., & Fishbein, M. (1977). Attitude-behavior relations: A theoretical analysis and a review of empirical research. *Psychological Bulletin, 84,* 888–918.

Ajzen, I., & Fishbein, M. (1980). *Understanding attitudes and predicting social behavior.* Englewood Cliffs, NJ: Prentice-Hall.

Albion, M. S., & Farris, P. W. (1981). *The advertising controversy.* Boston: Auburn House.

Albou, P. (1982). Pierre-Louis Reynaud (1908–81). *Journal of Economic Psychology, 2,* 33–8.

Alchian, A. A. (1977). Why Money? *Journal of Money, Credit and Banking, 9,* 133–40.

Alchian, A. A., & Allen W. R. (1969). *Exchange and production: Theory in use.* Belmont, CA: Wadsworth.

Alderfer, C.P. (1969). An empirical test of a new theory of human needs. *Organizational Behavior and Human Performance, 4,* 142–75.

Aldis, O. (1961). Of pigeons and men. *Harvard Business Review, 39*(4), 59–63.

Alhadeff, D. A. (1982). *Microeconomics and human behavior.* Berkeley, CA: University of California Press.

Allan, C. M. (1971). *The theory of taxation.* Harmondsworth: Penguin.

Allen, E. K., Hart, B. M., Buell, J. S., Harris, F. R., & Wolf, M. M. (1964). Effects of social reinforcement on isolate behavior of a nursery school child. *Child Development, 35,* 511–18.

Allingham, M. G., & Sandmo, A. (1972). Income tax evasion: A theoretical analysis. *Journal of Public Economics, 1,* 323–38.

Allison, J. (1976). Contrast, induction, facilitation, suppression, and conservation. *Journal of the Experimental Analysis of Behavior, 25,* 185–98.

Allison, J. (1979). Demand economics and experimental psychology. *Behavioral Science, 24,* 403–15.

Allison, J. (1981). Economics and operant conditioning. In P. Harzem & M. D. Zeiler (Eds.), *Advances in analysis of behavior, Vol. 2: Predictability, correlation and contiguity* (pp. 321–52). Chichester: Wiley.

Allison, J. (1983). Behavioral substitutes and complements. In R. L. Mellgren (Ed.), *Animal cognition and behavior* (pp. 1–30). Amsterdam: North-Holland.

Alloy, L. B., & Tabachnik, N. (1984). Assessment of covariation by animals and humans: The joint influence of prior expectations and current situational information. *Psychological Review, 91,* 112–49.

Allport, G. W. (1937). *Personality: A psychological interpretation.* New York: Holt, Reinhart and Winston.

Amato, P. R. (1983). Helping behavior in urban and rural environments: Field studies based on a taxonomic organization of helping episodes. *Journal of Personality and Social Psychology, 45,* 571–86.

Amsel, A. (1967). Partial reinforcement effects on vigor and persistence. In K. W. Spence & J. T. Spence (Eds.), *The psychology of learning and motivation* (pp. 2–65). New York: Academic Press.

Anderson, D. C., et al. (1982). Behavior management in the public accommodation industry: A three-project demonstration. *Journal of Organizational Behavior and Management, 4*, 33–66.

Anderson, G., & Brown, R. I. F. (1984). Real and laboratory gambling, sensation seeking and arousal: Towards a Pavlovian component in general theories of gambling and gambling addictions. *British Journal of Psychology, 75*, 401–10.

Anderson, N. H. (1971). Integration theory and attitude change. *Psychological Review, 78*, 171–206.

Anderson, N. H. (1976). Equity judgments as information integration. *Journal of Personality and Social Psychology, 33*, 291–99.

Anderson, N. H. (1980). Integration theory applied to cognitive responses and attitudes. In R. E. Petty, T. M. Ostrom, & T. C. Brock (Eds.), *Cognitive responses in persuasion*. New York: Lawrence Erlbaum.

Andison, F. S. (1977). TV violence and viewer aggression: a cumulation of study results, 1956–1976. *Public Opinion Quarterly, 41*(3), 314–31.

Andreasen, A. R. (1975). *The disadvantaged consumer*. New York: Free Press.

Andrews, F. M., & Withey, S. B. (1976). *Social indicators of well-being*. New York: Plenum.

Andrews, K. H., & Kandel, D. B. (1979). Attitudes and behavior: A specification of the contingent consistency hypothesis. *American Sociological Review, 44*, 298–310.

Anstey, M. (1982). Scapegoating in groups: Some theoretical perspectives and a case record of intervention. *Social Work in Groups, 5*, 51–63.

Antaki, C. (Ed.) (1981) *The psychology of ordinary explanations of social behaviour*. London: Academic Press.

Apel, H., & Strumpel, B. (1976). Economic well-being as a criterion for system performance: A survey in Bulgaria and Greece. In B. Strumpel (Ed.), *Economic means for human needs* (pp. 163–86). Ann Arbor, MI: Survey Research Center, Institute for Social Research, University of Michigan.

Archibald, R. B., Haulman, C. A., & Moody, C. E. (1983). Quality, price, advertising and published quarterly ratings. *Journal of Consumer Research, 9*, 347–56.

Argyle, M. (1972). *The social psychology of work*. Harmondsworth: Penguin.

Argyris, C. (1964). *Integrating the individual and the organization*. New York: Wiley.

Arkes, H. R., & Garske, J. P. (1977). *Psychological theories of motivation*. Monterey, CA: Brooks/Cole, 1977.

Aronson, E. (1984). *The social animal* (4th ed.). New York: Freeman.

Aronson, E., & Carlsmith, J. M. (1968). Experimentation in social psychology. In G. Lindzey and E. Aronson (Eds.), *Handbook of social psychology: Vol. 2* (2nd ed.) (pp. 1–79). Reading, MA: Addison-Wesley.

Alden, J. (1977). The extent and nature of double-jobbing in Britain. *Industrial Relations Journal, 8*, 1–33.

Alden, J. (1981). Holding two jobs: An examination of "moonlighting." In S. Henry (Ed.) *Can I have it in cash?* (pp. 43–57). London: Astragal Books.

American Department of Labor. (1974). *American Current Population Survey, May issue*. Washington: Department of Labor.

Aschenfelter, O., & Heckman, J. (1974). The estimation of income and substitution effects in a model of family labour supply. *Econometrica, 42*, 73–85.

Atkin, C. (1980). Effects of television advertising on children. In E.L. Palmer & A. Dorr (Eds.), *Children and the faces of television* (pp. 287–305). New York: Academic Press.

Atkinson, J. (1957). Motivational determinants of risk taking behavior. *Psychological Review, 64,* 359–72.

Atkinson, J., Bastioni, J., Earl, R., & Litwin, G. (1960). The achievement motive, goal setting, and probability preferences. *Journal of Abnormal and Social Psychology, 60,* 27–36.

Atkinson, T. (1982). The stability and validity of quality of life measures. *Social Indicators Research, 10,* 113–32.

Atthowe, J. M., & Krasner, L. (1968). Preliminary report on the application of contingent reinforcement procedures (token economy) on a "chronic" psychiatric ward. *Journal of Abnormal Psychology, 73,* 37–43.

Atwood, R. W., & Howell, R. J. (1971). Pupillometric and personality test score differences of female agressing pedophiliacs and normals. *Psychonomic Science, 22,* 115–6.

Auld, D. L. (1978). Public awareness and preferences in Ontario. Discussion paper cited in A. Lewis, *The psychology of taxation.* Oxford: Martin Robertson.

Autor, S. M. (1969). The strength of conditioned reinforcers as a function of frequency and probability of reinforcement. In D. P. Hendry (Ed.), *Conditioned reinforcement* (pp. 127–62). Homewood, IL: Dorsey.

Axelrod, R., & Hamilton, W.D. (1981). The evolution of cooperation. *Science, 211,* 1390–6.

Ayal, E. B. (1963). Value systems and economic development in Japan and Thailand. *Journal of Social Issues, 19*(1), 35–51.

Ayllon, T., & Azrin, N. H. (1965). The measurement and reinforcement of behavior of psychotics. *Journal of the Experimental Analysis of Behavior, 8,* 357–83.

Ayllon, T., & Azrin, N. H. (1968). *The token economy.* E. Norwalk, CT: Appleton-Century-Crofts.

Ayllon, T., & Houghton, E. (1962). Control of the behavior of schizophrenics by food. *Journal of the Experimental Analysis of Behavior, 5,* 343–52.

Ayllon, T., & Michael, J. (1959). The psychiatric nurse as a behavior engineer. *Journal of the Experimental Analysis of Behavior, 2,* 323–34.

Baer, D. M., & Wolf, M. M. (1970). The entry into natural communities of reinforcement. In R. Ulrich, T. Stachnik, & J. Mabry (Eds.), *Control of human behavior: Vol. 2.* Glenview, IL: Scott-Foresman.

Baker, R., Hall, J. N., & Hutchinson, K. (1974). A token economy project with chronic schizophrenic patients. *British Journal of Psychiatry, 124,* 367–84.

Bandura, A. (1971). *Psychological modeling.* Chicago: Aldine-Atherlin.

Bandura, A. (1972). *Social learning theory.* Morristown, NJ: General Learning Press.

Bandura, A. (1977). *Social learning theory.* Englewood Cliffs, NJ: Prentice-Hall.

Bandura, A., & Kupers, C. J. (1964). Transmission of patterns of self-reinforcement through modeling. *Journal of Abnormal and Social Psychology, 69,* 1–9.

Bandura, A., Ross, D., & Ross, S. A. (1963). A comparative test of the status envy, social power, and secondary-reinforcement theories of identificatory learning. *Journal of Abnormal and Social Psychology, 67,* 527–34.

Banks, A.S., DeWitt, R.P., Carlip, V., & Overstreet, W. (Eds). (1981). *Economic handbook of the world: 1981.* New York: McGraw-Hill.

Banister, D., & Fransella, F. (1983). *Inquiring man.* Melbourne, FL: R. E. Drieger Pub.

Barash, D. P. (1977). *Sociobiology and behavior.* New York: Elsevier.

Barash, D. P. (1982). *Sociobiology and behavior* (2nd ed.). London: Hodder and Stoughton.

Bar-Tal, D. (1976). *Prosocial behavior: Theory and research.* Washington, DC: Hemisphere, 1976.

Barber, T. X., & Silver, M.J. (1968). Fact, fiction, and the experimenter bias effect. *Psychological Bulletin Monograph, 70,* 1–29.

Bardhan, K. (1969). A note on price-elasticity of demand for food grain in a peasant economy. *Oxford Economic Papers* (New Series), *21,* 104–8.

Bardhan, K. (1970). Price and output response of marketed surplus of foodgrains: A cross-sectional analysis of some north Indian villages. *Journal of Farm Economics, 52,* 51–61.

Barkley, R. A., Hastings, J. E., Tousel, R. E., & Tousel, S. E. (1976). Evaluation of a token system for juvenile delinquents in a residential setting. *Journal of Behavior Therapy and Experimental Psychiatry, 7,* 227–30.

Barlow, R., Brazer, H. E., & Morgan, J. N. (1966). *Economic behavior of the affluent.* Washington, DC: Brookings Institution.

Barmann, B. C., Burnett, G. F., Malde, S. R., & Zinik, G. (1980). Token reinforcement procedures for reduction of cigarette smoking in a psychiatric outpatient clinic. *Psychological Reports, 47,* 1245–6.

Barro, R. J. (1974). Are government bonds new wealth? *Journal of Political Economy, 82,* 1095–117.

Barth, F. (1964). Capital, investment and the social structure of a pastoral nomad group in south Persia. In R. Firth & B. S. Yamey (Eds.), *Capital, saving and credit in peasant communities* (pp.69–81). London: Allen & Unwin.

Bassett, J. E., & Blanchard, E. B. (1977). The effect of the absence of close supervision on the use of response cost in a prison token economy. *Journal of Applied Behavior Analysis, 10,* 375–9.

Bassett, J. E., Blanchard, E. B., & Koshland, E. (1975). Applied behavior analysis in a penal setting: Targeting free world behaviors. *Behavior Therapy, 6,* 639–48.

Battalio, R. C., Kagel, J. H., & Green, L. (1979). Labor supply behavior of animal workers: Towards an experimental analysis. In V. L. Smith (Ed.), *Research in experimental economics: Vol. 1* (pp. 231–53). Greenwich, CT: JAI.

Battalio, R. C., Kagel, J. H., & Reynolds, M. O. (1977). Income distribution in two experimental economies. *Journal of Political Economy, 85,* 1259–71.

Battalio, R. C., Kagel, J. H., Winkler, R. C., Fisher, E. B., Basmann, R. L., & Krasner, L. (1973). A test of consumer demand theory using observations of individual consumer purchases. *Western Economic Journal, 11,* 411–28.

Bauer, R., & Greyser, S. A. (1968). *Advertising in America: the consumer view.* Boston: Harvard Business School.

Baum, W. M. (1974). On two types of deviation from the matching law: Bias and undermatching. *Journal of the Experimental Analysis of Behavior, 22,* 231–42.

Baum, W. M. (1979). Matching, undermatching, and overmatching in studies of choice. *Journal of the Experimental Analysis of Behavior, 32,* 269–81.

Bean, L. H. (1946). Relation of disposable income and the business cycle to expenditures. *Review of Economics and Statistics, 28,* 199–207.

Beardon, W. O., & Woodside, A. G. (1977). Testing variations of Fishbein's behavioral intention model within a consumer context. *Journal of Applied Psychology, 62,* 352–57.

Beck, R. C. (1978). *Motivation theories and principles.* Englewood Cliffs, NJ: Prentice-Hall.

Becker, G. S. (1960). An economic analysis of fertility. In *Demographic and economic change in advanced countries*. Princeton, NJ: Princeton University Press.

Becker, G. S. (1965). A theory of the allocation of time. *Economic Journal, 75,* 493–517.

Becker, G. S. (1975). A theory of marriage. In T. W. Schultz (Ed.), *Economics of the family*. Chicago: University of Chicago Press.

Becker, G. S. (1976a). *The economic approach to human behavior*. Chicago: University of Chicago Press.

Becker, G. S. (1976b). Altruism, egoism and genetic fitness: Economics and sociobiology. *Journal of Economic Literature, 14,* 817–26.

Bedell, J. R., & Archer, R. P. (1980). Peer managed token economies: Evaluation and description. *Journal of Clinical Psychology, 36,* 716–23.

Begg, D. K. H. (1982). *The rational expectations revolution in macroeconomics*. Oxford: Philip Allan.

Behling, O., & Starke, F. A. (1973). The postulates of expectancy theory. *Academy of Management Journal, 16,* 373–87.

Beit-Hallahmi, B. (1980). Achievement motivation and economic growth: A replication. *Personality and Social Psychology Bulletin, 6,* 210–5.

Belch, G. E. (1981). An examination of comparative and non-comparative television commercials – the effects of claim variation and repetition on cognitive response and message acceptance. *Journal of Marketing Research, 18,* 333–49.

Belk, R. W., Bahn, K. D., & Mayer, R. N. (1982–3). Developmental recognition of consumption symbolism. *Journal of Consumer Research, 9,* 4–17.

Bell, F. W. (1968). The Pope and the price of fish. *American Economic Review, 58,* 1346–50.

Bellante, D., & Jackson, M. (1979). *Labor economics*. New York: McGraw-Hill.

Bem, D. J. (1965). An experimental analysis of self-persuasion. *Journal of Experimental Social Psychology, 1,* 199–218.

Bem, D. J. (1967). Self-perception theory: an alternative interpretation of cognitive dissonance phenomena. *Psychological Review, 74,* 183–200.

Bem, D. J. (1970). *Beliefs, attitudes, and human affairs*. Belmont, CA.: Brooks/Cole.

Bem, D. J. (1972). Self-perception theory. In L. Berkowitz (Ed.), *Advances in Experimental Social Psychology: Vol. 6* (pp. 1–62). Hillsdale, NJ: Erlbaum.

Benedict, R. (1935). *Patterns of culture*. London: Routledge and Kegan Paul.

Benham, L. (1972). The effects of advertising on the price of eyeglasses. *Journal of Law and Economics, 15,* 337–52.

Benitah, M. (1980). *Besoins economiques et pouvoir*. Paris: Anthropos.

Bennett, S., & Wilkinson, J. B. (1974). Price-quantity relationships and price elasticity under in-store experimentation. *Journal of Business Research, 2,* 27–33.

Bennis, W. G. (1961). Revisionist theory of leadership. *Harvard Business Review, 39*(1), 26–36; 146–150.

Bentler, P. M., & Speckart, G. (1979). Models of attitude-behavior relations. *Psychological Review, 47,* 265–76.

Bentler, P. M., & Speckart, G. (1981). Attitudes 'cause' behaviors: A structured equation analysis. *Journal of Personality and Social Psychology, 40,* 226–38.

Berey, L. A., & Pollay, R. W. (1968). The influencing role of the child in family decision making. *Journal of Marketing Research, 5,* 70–1.

Bergler, E. (1958). The psychology of *gambling*. London: Hanison.

Berkowitz, L., & Daniels, L. R. (1963). Responsibility and dependency. *Journal of Abnormal and Social Psychology, 66,* 429–36.

Berkowitz, L., & Daniels, L. R. (1964). Affecting the salience of the social responsibility norm: Effects of past help on the response to dependency relationships. *Journal of Abnormal and Social Psychology, 68,* 275–81.

Berkowitz, S., Sherry, P. J., & Davis, B. A. (1971). Teaching self-feeding skills to profound retardates using reinforcement and fading procedures. *Behavior Therapy, 2,* 62–7.

Berlyne, D. E. (1960). *Conflict, arousal and curiosity.* New York: McGraw-Hill.

Bernoulli, D. (1954). Specimen theoriae novae de mensura sortis. *Economica, 22,* 23–36. (Trans. L. Sommer)

Bernstein, B. (1971). *Class codes and control. Vol. 1.* London: Routledge and Kegan Paul.

Bernstein, D. (1972). What advertising is. In M. Smelt (Ed.), *What advertising is* (pp. 11–38). London: Pelham Books.

Berti, A. E., & Bombi, A. S. (1979). Da dove vengono i soldi? La genesi del nesso tra denaro nel bambino. *Archivio di Psicologia, Neurologia e Psichiatria, 40,* 53–77.

Berti, A. E., & Bombi, A. S. (1981). The development of the concept of money and its value: A longitudinal study. *Child Development, 52,* 1179–82.

Berti, A. E., Bombi, A. S., & Lis, A. (1982). The child's conception about means of production and their owners. *European Journal of Social Psychology, 12,* 221–39.

Bettman, J. R., & Park, C. W. (1980–1). Effects of prior knowledge and experience and phase of the choice process on consumer decision processes: A protocol analysis. *Journal of Consumer Research, 7,* 234–48.

Beynon, H. (1973). *Working for Ford.* Harmondsworth: Penguin.

Biddle, B. J., Bank, B. J., & Marlin, M. M. (1980). What they think, what they do, and what I think and do: Social determinants of adolescent drinking. *Journal of Studies on Alcohol, 41,* 215–41.

Bijou, S. W. (1957). Patterns of reinforcement and resistance to extinction in young children. *Child Development, 28,* 47–54.

Bijou, S. W., & Baer, D. M. (1966). Operant methods in child behavior and development. In W. K. Honig (Ed.), *Operant behavior: Areas of research and application* (pp. 718–89). E. Norwalk, CT: Appleton-Century-Crofts.

Binitie, A. (1976). Mental health implications of economic growth in developing countries. *Mental Health and Society, 3,* 272–85.

Bird, R. C., & Bodkin, R. G. (1973). The national service life-insurance dividend of 1950 and consumption: A further test of the "strict" permanent income hypothesis. *Journal of Political Economy, 73,* 499–515.

Birky, H. J., Chambliss, J. E., & Wasden, R. (1971). A comparison of residents discharged from a token economy and two traditional psychiatric programs. *Behavior Therapy, 2,* 46–51.

Blascovich, J., Ginsburg, G., & Howe, R. (1976). Blackjack, choice shifts in this field. *Sociometry, 39,* 274–6.

Blatt, J., Spencer, L., & Ward, S. (1972). A cognitive developmental study of children's reactions to television advertising. In E. A. Rubinstein, G. A. Comstock, & J. P. Murray (Eds.), *Television and Social Behavior: Vol. 4* (pp. 452–67). Washington, DC: U.S. Dept of Health, Education and Welfare.

Blinder, A. S. (1975). Distribution effects and the aggregate consumption function. *Journal of Political Economy, 83,* 447–76.

Blum, M. L. (1977). *Psychology and consumer affairs.* New York: Harper & Row.

Boakes, R. A., Poli, M., Lockwood, M. J., & Goodall, G. (1978). A study of misbehaviour: Token reinforcement in the rat. *Journal of the Experimental Analysis of Behavior, 29,* 115–34.

Bodkin, R. (1959). Windfall income and consumption. *American Economic Review, 49,* 602–14.

Boegli, R. G., & Wasik, B. H. (1978). Use of the token economy system to intervene on a school-wide level. *Psychology in the Schools, 15,* 72–8.

Boehm-Bawerk, E. von (1891). *Capital and interests* (Trans. W. Smart). New York: Stechert.

Boggs, L. J., Rozynko, V., & Flint, G. A. (1976). Some effects of reduction in reinforcement magnitude in a monetary economy with hospitalized alcoholics. *Behaviour Research and Therapy, 14,* 455–61.

Bohannan, P. (1959). The impact of money on an African subsistence economy. *The Journal of Economic History, 19,* 491–503.

Bolles, R. C. (1967). *Theory of motivation.* New York: Harper & Row.

Bolles, R. C. (1975). *Theory of motivation* (2nd ed.). New York: Harper & Row.

Bolles, R. C. (1980). Some functionalist thoughts about regulation. In F. M. Toates & T. R. Halliday (Eds.), *Analysis of motivational processes* (pp. 63–75). London: Academic Press.

Borch, K. (1978). Consumption and saving: Models and reality. *Theory and Decision, 9,* 241–53.

Borden, N. H. (1942). *The economic effects of advertising.* Chicago: Richard D. Irwin.

Boring, E. G. (1957). *A history of experimental psychology.* E. Norwalk, CT: Appleton-Century-Crofts.

Bornemann, E. (1976). *The Psychoanalysis of money.* New York: Urizen.

Boskin, M. (1978). Taxation, saving and the rate of interest. *Journal of Political Economy, 86,* S3-S27.

Boughton, J. M., & Wicker, E. R. (1975). *The principles of monetary economics.* Homestead, IL: Richard D. Irwin.

Bower, R. T. (1973) *Television and the public.* New York: Holt, Rinehart and Winston.

Bowlby, J. (1981). *Attachment and loss: Vol 3. Loss.* Harmondsworth: Penguin.

Boyle, P., & Murray, J. (1979). Social security wealth and private saving in Canada. *Canadian Journal of Economics, 12,* 456–67.

Bracewell-Milnes, B. (1977). The fisc and the fugitive: Exploiting the quarry. In *The state of taxation* (pp. 81–8). London: Institute of Economic Affairs.

Brady, D. S., & Friedman, R. D. (1947). Savings and the income distribution. In *Studies in income and wealth: Vol. 10* (pp. 247–65). New York: National Bureau of Economic Research.

Branson, W. H., & Klevorick, A. K. (1969). Money illusion and the aggregate consumption function. *American Economic Review, 59,* 832–49.

Brayfield, A. H., & Crockett, W. A. (1955). Employee attitudes and employee performance. *Psychological Bulletin, 52,* 396–424.

Break, G. F. (1957). Income taxes and incentives to work: An empirical study. *American Economic Review, 47,* 529–49.

Breakwell, G. M., Collie, A., Harrison, B., & Propper, C. (1984). Attitudes towards the unemployed – effects of threatened identity. *British Journal of Social Psychology, 23,* 87–8.

Brehm, J. (1956). Postdecision changes in the desirability of alternatives. *Journal of Abnormal and Social Psychology, 52,* 348–89.

Brennan, T. (1948). *Midland city.* London: Dobson.

Brenner, M. H. (1973). *Mental illness and the economy*. Cambridge, MA: Harvard University Press.

Blyn, G. (1983). The green revolution revisited. *Economic Development and Cultural Change, 31,* 705–25.

Brinberg, D., & Castell, P. (1982). A resource exchange approach to interpersonal interactions: A test of Foa's theory. *Journal of Personality and Social Psychology, 43,* 260–9.

Broadbent, D. E. (1971). *Decision and stress*. London: Academic Press.

Broadbent, D. E., & Aston, B. (1978). Human control of a simulated economic system. *Ergonomics, 21,* 1035–43.

Bronzaft, A. L., & Dobrow, S. B. (1976). Test anxiety and the economic recession. *Psychological Reports, 38,* 1211–5.

Brooks, J. (1981). *Showing off in America*. Boston: Little, Brown.

Brooks, R. (1984, August 19). BT pushes in the final plug. *Sunday Times,* p. 45.

Brown, C. V. (1980). *Taxation and the incentive to work*. Oxford: Oxford University Press.

Brown, C. V., & Levin, E. (1974). The effects of income taxation on overtime: The results of a national survey. *Economic Journal, 84,* 833–48.

Brown, C. V., Levin, E. J., Rosa, P. J., & Ulph, D. T. (1984). Tax evasion and avoidance on earned income: Some survey evidence. *Fiscal Studies, 5,* 1–22.

Brown, F. E. (1971). Who perceives supermarket prices most validly? *Journal of Marketing Research, 8,* 110–3.

Brown, R. (1965). *Social Psychology*. New York: Free Press.

Brownlee, O., & Perry, G. L. (1967). The effects of the 1965 Federal excise tax reductions on prices. *National Tax Journal, 20,* 235–49.

Bruce, V. G., Gilmore, D., Mason, L., & Mayhew, P. (1983). Factors affecting the perceived value of coins. *Journal of Economic Psychology, 4,* 335–47.

Bruner, J. S., & Goodman, C. C. (1947). Value and need as organising factors in perception. *Journal of Abnormal and Social Psychology, 42,* 33–44.

Brunner, J. A., & J. L. Mason (1970). The influence of driving time upon shopping center preference. *Journal of Marketing, 34,* 12–7.

Bryan, J. H., & Test, M. A. (1967). Models and helping: Naturalistic studies in aiding behavior. *Journal of Personality and Social Psychology, 6,* 400–7.

Buchanan, J. M., & Tullock, G. (1962). *The calculus of consent*. Ann Arbor, MI: University of Michigan Press.

Budd, R. J., North, D., & Spencer, C. P. (1984). Understanding seat-belt use: A test of Bentler and Speckart's extension of the theory of reasoned action. *European Journal of Social Psychology, 14,* 69–78.

Burkhauser, R. V., & Turner, J. A. (1982). Social security, preretirement labor supply, and saving: A confirmation and critique. *Journal of Political Economy, 90,* 643–6.

Burnkrant, R. E. (1974). Attribution theory in marketing research: Problems and prospects. In M. J. Schlinger (Ed.), *Advances in Consumer Research: Vol 2.* Chicago: Association for Consumer Research.

Burnkrant, R. E., & Sawyer, A. G. (1983). Effects of involvement and message content on information-processing intensity. In R. J. Harris (Ed.), *Information processing research in advertising* (pp. 43–64). Hillsdale, NJ: Erlbaum.

Burris, V. (1981). *The child's conception of economic relations: A study of cognitive socialization*. Paper presented at the annual meeting of the American Sociological Association, Toronto.

Burris, V. (1983). Stages in the development of economic concepts. *Human Relations, 36,* 791–812.

Burt, R. S. (1975). Corporate society: A time series analysis of network structure. *Social Science Research, 4,* 271–328.

Burton, H. L., Brudner, L. A., & White, D. R. (1977). A model of the sexual division of labour. *American Ethnologist, 4,* 227–51.

Burvill, P. W., & Kidd, C. B. (1975). The two-town study: A comparison of two contrasting Western Australian mining towns. *Australian and New Zealand Journal of Psychiatry, 9,* 85–92.

Bushell, D., Wrobel, P. A., & Michaelis, M. L. (1968). Applying "group" contingencies to the classroom study behavior of preschool children. *Journal of Applied Behavior Analysis, 1,* 55–61.

Butler, D., & Stokes, D. (1971). *Political change in Britain.* Harmondsworth: Penguin.

Butler, R. A. (1953). Discrimination learning by rhesus monkeys to visual exploration motivation. *Journal of Comparative and Physiological Psychology, 46,* 95–8.

Buzzell, R. D. (1964). *Mathematical models and marketing management.* Boston: Harvard University.

Byrne, D. (1971). *The attraction paradigm.* New York: Academic Press.

Cacioppo, J. T., Petty, R. E., & Morris, K. J. (1983). The effects of need for cognition on message evaluation, recall and persuasion. *Journal of Personality and Social Psychology, 45,* 805–18.

Cady, J. (1976). Advertising restrictions and retail prices. *Journal of Advertising Research, 16,* 27–30.

Cagan, P. D. (1965). *The effect of pension plans on aggregate saving.* New York: Columbia University Press.

Cain, G. G., Nicholson, W., Mallar, C., & Wooldridge, J. (1977). Labor-supply response of wives. In H. W. Watts & A. Rees (Eds.), *The New Jersey income-maintenance experiment: Vol. 2. Labor-supply responses* (pp. 115–62). New York: Academic Press.

Cairncross, A. (1975). *Introduction to economics* (5th ed.). London: Butterworths.

Calder, B. J., & Staw, B. M. (1975). Self perception of intrinsic and extrinsic motivation. *Journal of Personality and Social Psychology, 31,* 599–605.

Cameron, B., & Myers, J. L. (1966). Some personality correlates of risk taking. *Journal of General Psychology, 74,* 51–60.

Campbell, A., Converse, P., Miller, W., & Stokes, D. (1960). *The American voter.* New York: Wiley.

Campbell, D. T. (1963). Social attitudes and other acquired behavioral dispositions. In: S. Koch (Ed.), *Psychology: A study of a science: Vol 6.* New York: McGraw-Hill.

Campbell, D. T., & Stanley, J. C. (1963). Experimental and quasi-experimental designs for research on teaching. In N. L. Gage (Ed.), *Handbook of research on teaching* (pp. 171–246). Chicago: Rand McNally.

Campbell, J., & Pritchard, R. D. (1976). Motivation theory in industrial and organizational psychology. In M. Dunnette (Ed.), *Handbook of industrial and organizational psychology* (pp. 63–130). Chicago: Rand McNally.

Candler, W. L., Rozendal, F. G., Rogers, N. W., & Reynolds, W. (1982). Use of an auction to increase the reinforcing properties of a token economy. *Behavioral Engineering, 8,* 35–42.

Cannon, W. B., & Washburn, A. L. (1912). An explanation of hunger. *American Journal of Physiology, 29,* 441–54.

Capaldi, E. J. (1966).Partial reinforcement: A hypothesis of sequential effects. *Psychological Review, 73,* 459–77.

Caplan, H. J., Karpicke, J., & Rilling, M. (1973). Effects of extended fixed-interval training on reversed scallops. *Animal Learning and Behavior, 1,* 293–6.

Caplovitz, D. (1967). *The poor pay more.* New York: Free Press.

Capon, N., & Kuhn, D. (1980). A developmental study of consumer information processing strategies. *Journal of Consumer Research, 7,* 225–33.

Capon, N., Farley, J. U., & Hulbert, J. (1975). Pricing and forecasting in an oligopoly firm. *Journal of Management Studies, 12,* 133–56.

Carlsmith, J. M., & Gross, A. E. (1969). Some effects of guilt on compliance. *Journal of Personality and Social Psychology, 11,* 232–40.

Carlson, C. G., Hersen, M., & Eisler, R. M. (1972). Token economy programs in the treatment of hospitalized adult psychiatric patients. *Journal of Nervous and Mental Diseases, 155,* 192–204.

Carlson, J. A., & Gieseke, R. J. (1983) Price search in a product market. *Journal of Consumer Research, 9,* 357–67.

Carman, J. M. (1970). Correlates of brand loyalty: Some positive results. *Journal of Marketing Research, 7,* 67–76.

Carnegie-Mellon University Marketing Seminar. (1978). Attitude change or attitude formation? An unanswered question. *Journal of Consumer Research, 4,* 271–6.

Casson, M. (1984). *The entrepreneur.* Oxford: Martin Robertson.

Catalano, R., & Dooley, C. D. (1977). Economic predictors of depressed mood and stressful life events in a metropolitan community. *Journal of Health and Social Behavior, 18,* 292–307.

Catania, A. C., & Reynolds, G. S. (1968). A quantitative analysis of the responding maintained by interval schedules of reinforcement. *Journal of the Experimental Analysis of Behavior, 11,* 327–33.

Cattell, R. B., & Horowitz, J. Z. (1952). Objective personality tests investigating the structure of altruism in relation to source traits A, H, and L. *Journal of Personality, 21,* 103–17.

Cebula, R. J. (1981). "Money illusion" and migration decisions: an international comparison of the U.S. and Canadian experiences. *Regional Studies, 15,* 241–46.

Centers, R. (1948). Motivational aspects of occupational stratification. *Journal of Social Psychology, 28,* 187–217.

Central Statistical Office (1982). *Social Trends no. 12.* London: Her Majesty's Stationery Office.

Central Statistical Office (1985). *Social Trends no. 15.* London: Her Majesty's Stationery Office.

Child, I. L., Storm, T., & Veroff, J. (1958). Achievement themes in folk tales related to socialization practice. In J. W. Atkinson (Ed.), *Motives in fantasy, action and society* (pp. 479–92). Princeton, NJ: Van Nostrand.

Christensen, C. W. (1975). The Puerto Rican woman: The challenge of a changing society. *Character Potential, 7,* 89–96.

Christensen, J. K. (1974). A five-year follow-up study of male schizophrenics. *Acta Psychiatrica Scandinavica, 50,* 60–72.

Christensen, L. R., Jorgenson, D. W., & Lau, L. J. (1975). Transcendental logarithmic utility functions. *American Economic Review, 65,* 367–83.

Church, R. M., Raymond, G. A., & Beauchamp, R. D. (1967). Response suppression as a function of intensity and duration of a punishment. *Journal of Comparative and Physiological Psychology, 63,* 39–44.

Cialdini, R. B., Darby, B. L., & Vincent, J. E. (1973). Transgression and altruism: A case for hedonism. *Journal of Experimental Social Psychology, 9,* 502–16.

Cialdini, R. B., Bickman, L., & Cacioppo, J. T. (1979). An example of consumeristic social psychology: Bargaining tough in the new car showroom. *Journal of Applied Social Psychology, 9,* 115–26.

Citrin, J. (1979). Do people want something for nothing?: Public opinion on taxes and government spending. *National Tax Journal, 32,* 113S–129S.

Clammer, J. (1978). *The New Economic Anthropology.* London: Macmillan.

Clark, E. T. (1967). Influence of sex and class on occupational preference and perception. *Personnel and Guidance Journal, 45,* 440–4.

Clark, R. D., & Word, L. E. (1972). Why don't bystanders help? Because of ambiguity? *Journal of Personality and Social Psychology, 24,* 392–400.

Clarke, G. B. (1946). The experiment. *Clare Market Review, 41,* 27–31.

Clarke, Y., & Soutar, G. N. (1981–2). Consumer acquisition patterns for durable goods: Australian evidence. *Journal of Consumer Research, 8,* 456–60.

Close, D. W. (1973). The use of token reinforcement with trainable mentally retarded in a work activity setting. *Vocational Evaluation and Work Adjustment Bulletin, 6,* 6–14.

Clower, R. W., & Johnson, M. B. (1968). Income, wealth and the theory of consumption. In N. Wolfe (Ed.), *Value, capital and growth* (pp. 45–96). Edinburgh: Edinburgh University Press.

Codere, H. (1950). *Fighting with property: a study of Kwakiutl potlatch and warfare 1792–1930.* New York: J. J. Augustin.

Codere, H. (1968). Money-exchange systems and a theory of money. *Man, 3,* 557–77.

Cohen, A. R. (1962). An experiment on small rewards for discrepant compliance and attitude change. In J. W. Brehm & A. R. Cohen (Eds.), *Explorations in cognitive dissonance* (pp. 73–8). New York: Wiley.

Cohen, J. (1964). *Behavior in uncertainty and its social implications.* London: Allen & Unwin.

Cohen, J. (1975). The psychology of gambling. *New Scientist, 68,* 266–9.

Coke, J. S., Batson, C. D., & McDavis, K. (1978). Empathic mediation of helping: a two stage model. *Journal of Personality and Social Psychology, 36,* 752–66.

Collard, D. (1978). *Altruism and economy.* Oxford: Martin Robertson.

Colledge, M. (1982). Economic cycles and health: towards a sociological understanding of the impact of the recession on health and illness. *Social Science and Medicine, 16,* 1919–27.

Collier, G., Hirsch, E., & Hamlin, P. E. (1972). The ecological determinants of reinforcement in the rat. *Physiology and Behavior, 9,* 705–16.

Collins, A. M., & Quillian, M. R. (1969). Retrieval time from semantic memory. *Journal of Verbal Learning and Verbal Behavior, 8,* 240–47.

Colonial study (1964, January). *Progressive Grocer,* pp. C91–C96.

Command Paper 6527 (1944). *Employment policy.* London: Her Majesty's Stationery Office.

Connell, R. (1977). *Ruling class, ruling culture.* Melbourne: Cambridge University Press.

Connell, R. H., Ryback, D., & La Fehr, S. (1979). Reduction of epileptic seizures by reinforcement of bladder continence. *British Journal of Psychology, 70,* 17–20.

Cook, S. (1966). The obsolete "anti-market" mentality: a critique of the substantive approach to economic anthropology. *American Anthropologist, 68,* 323–45.

Cook, S. (1970). Price and output variability in a peasant-artisan stoneworking industry in Oaxaca, Mexico: An analytical essay in economic anthropology. *American Antropologist, 72,* 776–881.

Cook, S. (1973). Economic Anthropology: Problems in theory, method and analysis. In J. J. Honigman (Ed.), *Handbook of Social and Cultural Anthropology* (pp. 795–860). Chicago: Rand McNally.

Coombs, C. H. (1964). *A theory of data.* New York: Wiley.

Coombs, C. H., & Pruitt, D. G. (1960). Components of risk in decision making: Probability and variance preferences. *Journal of Experimental Psychology, 60,* 265–77.

Cooper, J. B., & Pollock, D. (1959). The identification of prejudicial attitudes by the galvanic skin response. *Journal of Social Psychology, 50,* 241–5.

Cooper, J., Zanna, M. P., & Goethals, G. R. (1974). Mistreatment of an esteemed other as a consequence affecting dissonance reduction. *Journal of Experimental Social Psychology, 10,* 224–33.

Copeman, M. (1981). *The National Accounts: A short guide.* London: Her Majesty's Stationery Office.

Cornish, D. B. (1978). *Gambling: A review of the literature.* London: Home Office Research Study No. 42.

Courtney, A. E., & Whipple, T. W. (1974). Women in TV commercials. *Journal of Communication, 24,* 110–8.

Courtois, A. (1934). Crise economique et psychopathie. *Prophylaxie Mentale, 8,* 18–23.

Cover, J. D., & Johnson, N. R. (1976). Need achievement, phase movement and the business cycle. *Social Forces, 54,* 760–74.

Cowles, J. T. (1937). Food tokens as incentives for learning by chimpanzees. *Comparative Psychology Monographs, 14,* 1–96.

Cox, W. E., & Cooke, E. F. (1970). Other dimensions involved in shopping centre preference. *Journal of Marketing, 34,* 12–7.

Crafton, S. M., & Hoffer, G. E. (1980–1). Do consumers benefit from auto manufacturer rebates to dealers? *Journal of Consumer Research, 7,* 211–4.

Cramer, J. S. (1962). *The ownership of major consumer durables.* Cambridge: Cambridge University Press.

Cravens, R. W., & Renner, K. E. (1969). Conditioned hunger. *Journal of Experimental Psychology, 81,* 312–6.

Crockett, A. (1979). *Money: Theory, policy, institutions* (2nd ed.). Sunbury-on-Thames, Middlesex: Nelson.

Crockett, H. J. (1962). The achievement motive and differential occupational mobility in the United States. *American Sociological Review, 27,* 191–204.

Cross, J. G. (1980). Some comments on the papers by Kagel and Battalio and by Smith. In J. Kmenta & J. B. Ramsey (Eds.), *Evaluation of econometric models* (pp. 403–6). New York: Academic Press.

Crowley, T. J. (1975). Token programs in an acute psychiatric hospital. *American Journal of Psychiatry, 132,* 523–8.

Cummings, S., & Taebel, D. (1978). The economic socialization of children: A neo-marxist analysis. *Social Problems, 26,* 198–210.

Czuma, K., & Kedzierski, H. (1983). Wartosc systemu "token economy" w swielte efetow rehabilitacji chorych na schizofrenico wieloletnim okresie hospitalizacji. *Psychiatrica Polska, 17,* 131–5.

Dabbs, J. M., & Leventhal, H. (1966). Effects of varying the recommendations in a fear arousing communication. *Journal of Personality and Social Psychology, 4,* 525–31.

Dalrymple, D. J., & Thompson, D. L. (1969). *Retailing: An economic view.* New York: Free Press.

Dalton, G. (1961). Economic theory and primitive society. *American Anthropologist, 63,* 1–25.

Daly, H. B. (1970). Combined effects of fear and frustration on acquisition of a hurdle-jump response. *Journal of Experimental Psychology, 83,* 89–93.

Daly, M. J. (1983). Some microeconometric evidence concerning the effect of the Canada Pension Plan on personal saving. *Economica, 50,* 63–9.

D'Amato, M. R. (1974). Derived motives. *Annual Review of Psychology, 25,* 83–106.

Danziger, K. (1958). Children's earliest conceptions of economic relationships (Australia). *Journal of Social Psychology, 47,* 231–40.

Darby, M. R. (1974). The permanent income theory of consumption – a restatement. *Quarterly Journal of Economics, 88,* 228–50.

Darby, M. R. (1975). Postwar US consumption, consumer expenditures, and saving. *American Economic Review, 65*(2), 217–22.

Darley, J. M., & Latane, B. (1968). Bystander intervention in emergencies: Diffusion of responsibility. *Journal of Personality and Social Psychology, 8,* 377–83.

Darley, J., & Latane, B. (1970). Norms and normative behavior: Field studies of social interdependence. In J. Macaulay & L. Berkowitz (Eds.), *Altruism and helping behavior.* New York: Academic Press.

Davidson, D., Suppes, P., & Siegel, S. *Decision making: An experimental approach.* Stanford, CA: Stanford University Press.

Davidson, M. C. (1974). A functional analysis of chained fixed-interval schedule performance. *Journal of the Experimental Analysis of Behavior, 21,* 323–30.

Davidson, P., & Bucher, B. (1978). Intrinsic interest and extrinsic reward: The effects of a continuing token program on continuing nonconstrained preference. *Behavior Therapy, 9,* 222–34.

Davidson, R., & MacKinnon, J. G. (1983). Inflation and the savings rate. *Applied Economics, 15,* 731–43.

Davies, J. (1981). Uncertain lifetime, consumption, and dissaving in retirement. *Journal of Politica Economy, 89,* 561–77.

Davis, J. (1972). Gifts and the U.K. economy. *Man, 7,* 408–29.

Davis, J. M. (1958). The transitivity of preferences. *Behavioral Science, 3,* 26–33.

Dawes, R. M. (1972). *Fundamentals of attitude measurement.* New York: Wiley.

Dawkins, R. (1976). *The selfish gene.* Oxford: Oxford University Press.

De Groot, A. D. (1966). Perception and memory vs. thought: Some old ideas and recent findings. In B. Kleinmuntz (Ed.), *Problem solving: Research, method and theory* (pp. 19–50). New York: Wiley.

Deacon, R., & Shapiro, P. (1975). Private preference for collective goods revealed through voting on referenda. *American Economic Review, 65,* 943–55.

Dean, P., Keenan, T., & Keeney, F. (1980). Taxpayer's attitudes to income tax evasion: An empirical study. *British Tax Review,* 28–44.

Deaton, A. (1977). Involuntary saving through unanticipated inflation. *American Economic Review, 67,* 899–910.

Deaton, A., & Muellbauer, J. (1980a). An almost ideal demand system. *American Economic Review, 70,* 312–26.

Deaton, A., & Muellbauer, J. (1980b). *Economics and consumer behavior.* Cambridge: Cambridge University Press.

Debreu, G. (1965). *Theory of value.* New York: Wiley.

DeCasper, A. J., & Zeiler, M. D. (1972). Steady-state behavior in children: A method and some data. *Journal of Experimental Child Psychology, 13,* 231–9.

Deci, E. L. (1971). Effects of externally mediated rewards on intrinsic motivation. *Journal of Personality and Social Psychology, 18,* 105–15.

Deci, E. L. (1972). The effects of contingent and noncontingent rewards and controls on intrinsic motivation. *Organizational Behavior and Human Performance, 8,* 217–29.

Deci, E. L. (1975). *Intrinsic motivation.* New York: Plenum.

DeFleur, M. L., & Westie, F. R. (1958). Verbal attitudes and overt acts: An experiment on the salience of attitudes. *American Sociological Review, 23,* 667–73.

Deiker, T., & Matson, J. L. (1979). Internal control and success orientation in a token economy for emotionally disturbed adolescents. *Adolescence, 14,* 215–20.

Denison, E. F. (1974). *Accounting for United States economic growth 1929–1969.* Washington, DC: The Brookings Institution.

Denner, A. (1971). *Principes et pratique du marketing.* Paris: Delmas.

Desai, M. (1979). *Marxian economics.* Oxford: Blackwell.

Despierre, J., & Sorel, N. (1979). Approche de la representation du chomage chez les jeunes. *L'Orientation Scolaire et Professionnelle, 8,* 347–64.

Deutsch, M. Trust and suspicion. (1958). *Journal of Conflict Resolution, 2,* 265–79.

Devereaux, E. C. (1968). Gambling in psychological and sociological perspective. *International Encyclopedia of the Social Sciences, 6,* 53–62.

Dews, P. B. (1969). Studies on responding under fixed-interval schedules of reinforcement: The effects on the pattern of responding of changes in requirement at reinforcement. *Journal of the Experimental Analysis of Behavior, 12,* 191–9.

Diamond Commission. (1976). *The Royal commission on the distribution of income and wealth, report no. 4.* London: Her Majesty's Stationery Office.

Dickerson, M. G. (1979). FI schedules and persistence at gambling in the UK betting office. *Journal of Applied Behavior Analysis, 12,* 315–23.

Dickerson, M. G. (1984). *Compulsive gamblers.* London: Longman.

Dickins, D., & Ferguson, V. (1957). *Practices and attitudes of rural white children concerning money.* (Technical Report no 43). MS: Mississippi State College Agricultural Experiment Station.

Dickinson, A. (1980). *Contemporary animal learning theory.* Cambridge: Cambridge University Press.

Dickinson, J. (1983). *Economic socialization: learning to live with inequality.* Paper presented at the B. P. S. Postgraduate psychology conference, St. Andrews.

Dickinson, R. (1982–3). Search behavior: A note. *Journal of Consumer Research, 9,* 115–6.

Dickson, P. R., & Miniard, P. W. (1978). A further examination of two laboratory tests of the extended Fishbein attitude model. *Journal of Consumer Research, 4,* 261–6.

Dickson, P. R., Lusch, R. F., & Wilkie, W. L. (1982–83). Consumer acquisition priorities for home appliances: a replication and re-evaluation. *Journal of Consumer Research, 9,* 432–5.

Didow, N. M., Perreault, W. D., & Williamson, N. C. (1983). A cross-sectional optimal scaling analysis of the Index of Consumer Sentiment. *Journal of Consumer Research, 10,* 339–47.

Dillehay, R. C., & Jernigan, L. R. (1970). The biased questionnaire as an instrument of opinion change. *Journal of Personality and Social Psychology, 15,* 144–50.

Dixon, N. F. (1971). *Subliminal perception: The nature of a controversy.* London: McGraw-Hill.

Doenges, R. C. (1966). Transitory income size and savings. *Southern Economic Journal, 33,* 258–63.

Dohrenwend, B. P. (1979). Stressful life events and psychopathology: Some issues of theory and method. In J. E. Barrett (Ed.), *Stress and mental disorder,* pp. 1–15. New York: Raven.

Dole, G. E., & Carneiro, R. L. (1958). A mechanism for mobilizing labor among the Kuikuru of central Brazil. *Transactions of the New York Academy of Sciences, 21,* 58–60.

Donohue, T., Meyer, T., & Henke, L. (1978). Black and white children's perceptions of television commercials. *Journal of Marketing, 42,* 34–40.

Dooley, D., & Catalano, R. (1980). Economic change as a cause of behavioral disorder. *Psychological Bulletin, 87,* 450–68.

Dorfman, R. (1972). *Prices and markets* (2nd ed.). Englewood Cliffs, NJ: Prentice-Hall.

Dorfman, R. (1978). *Prices and markets* (3rd ed.). Englewood Cliffs, NJ: Prentice-Hall.

Dornoff, R. J., & Tatham, R. L. (1972). Congruence between personal image and store image. *Journal of the Market Research Society, 14*(1), 45–52.

Dorris, J. W. (1972). Reactions to unconditioned cooperation: A field study emphasizing variables neglected in laboratory research. *Journal of Personality and Social Psychology, 22,* 387–97.

Dostoevski, F. (1915). *The gambler.* London: J. M. Dent.

Douglas, M. (1967). Primitive rationing. In R. Firth (Ed.), *Themes in Economic Anthropology* (pp. 119–46). London: Tavistock.

Douglas, M. (1982). *In the active voice.* London: Routledge and Kegan Paul.

Douglas, M., & Isherwood, B. (1979). *The world of goods.* Harmondsworth: Penguin.

Douty, C. M. (1972). Disasters and charity: Some aspects of cooperative economic behavior. *American Economic Review, 62,* 580–90.

Doyle, P., & Gidengil, B. Z. (1977). A review of in-store experiments. *Journal of Retailing, 53*(2), 47–62.

Dubois, C. (1944). *People of Alor.* Minneapolis, MN: University of Minnesota Press.

Duesenberry, J. S. (1949). *Income, saving, and the theory of consumer behavior.* Cambridge, MA: Harvard University Press.

Dunn, L. F. (1978). An empirical indifference function for income and leisure. *Review of Economics and Statistics, 60,* 533–40.

Eagly, A. H. (1980). Recipient characteristics as determinants of responses to persuasion. In R. E. Petty, T. M. Ostrom, & T. C. Brock (Eds.), *Cognitive responses in persuasion.* New York: Erlbaum.

Eagly, A. H., & Chaiken, S. (1975). An attribution analysis of the effect of communicator characteristics on opinion change: the case of communicator attractiveness. *Journal of Personality and Social Psychology, 32, 136–44.*

Eagly, A. H., & Warren, R. (1979). Intelligence, comprehension and opinion change. *Journal of Personality, 44,* 226–42.

Eagly, A. H., Wood, W., & Chaiken, S. (1978). Causal inferences about communicators and their effect on opinion change. *Journal of Personality and Social Psychology, 36,* 424–35.

Easterlin, R. A. (1974). Does economic growth improve the human lot? In P. A. David & M. W. Reder (Eds.), *Nations and households in economic growth* (pp. 89–125). New York: Academic Press.

Eastwell, H. (1974). Dilemmas of Aboriginal marriage in East Arnhem Land,

North Australia. *Australian and New Zealand Journal of Psychiatry, 8,* 49–53.

Eatwell, J. (1982). *Whatever happened to Britain?* London: Duckworth.

Edwards, A. L. (1957). *The social desirability variable in personality research.* New York: Dryden.

Edwards, A. L. (1967). *The social desirability variable: a broad statement. In I. A. Berg (Ed.), Response set in personality assessment* (pp. 48–70). Chicago: Aldine.

Edwards, F. R., & Heggestad, A. A. (1973). Uncertainty, market structure, and performance: The Galbraith-Caves hypothesis and managerial motives in banking. *Quarterly Journal of Economics, 87,* 455–73.

Edwards, W. (1954). The theory of decision making. *Psychological Bulletin, 51,* 380–417.

Edwards, W. (1954). Variance preferences in gambling. *American Journal of Psychology, 67,* 441–52.

Edwards, W., Lindman, H., & Phillips, L. D. (1965). Emerging technologies for making decisions. *New directions in psychology II* (pp. 261–325). New York: Holt Rinehart & Winston.

Ehrenberg, A. S. C. (1966). Laws in marketing: A tail-piece. *Applied Statistics, 15,* 257–67.

Ehrenberg, A. S. C. (1972). *Repeat buying: Theory and application.* Amsterdam: North-Holland.

Ehrenberg, A. S. C. (1974). Repetitive advertising and the consumer. *Journal of Advertising Research, 14*(2), 25–34.

Ehrenberg, R. G., & Smith, R. S. (1982). *Modern labor economics.* Glenview, IL: Scott-Foresman.

Ehrlich, D., Guttman, I., Schonbach, P., & Mills, J. (1957). Post decision exposure to relevant information. *Journal of Personality and Social Psychology, 54,* 98–102.

Ehrlich, I. (1982). The market for offences and the public enforcement of laws: An equilibrium analysis. *British Journal of Social Psychology, 21,* 107–20.

Einzig, P. (1945). The cigarette standard. *The Banker, 75–6,* 148–50.

Einzig, P. (1966). *Primitive money* (2nd ed.). Oxford: Pergamon.

Eisenberger, R. (1972). Explanation of rewards that do not reduce tissue needs. *Psychological Bulletin, 77,* 319–39.

Eiser, C., & Eiser, J. R. (1976). Children's concepts of a fair exchange. *British Journal of Social and Clinical Psychology, 15,* 357–64.

Eiser, J. R. (1978). Cooperation and competition between individuals. In H. Tajfel & C. Fraser (Eds.), *Introducing social psychology* (pp. 151–75). Harmondsworth: Penguin.

Eiser, J. R. (1980). *Cognitive social psychology.* London: McGraw-Hill.

Elder, G. H., & Liker, J. K. (1982). Hard times in women's lives: historical influences across forty years. *American Journal of Sociology, 88,* 241–69.

Elder, J. P., Liberman, R. P., Rapport, S., & Rust, C. (1982). Staff and patient reactions to the modernization of a token economy. *Behavior Therapist, 5,* 19–20.

Elliott, P. A. (1977). The effect of holidays on a token economy regime. *British Journal of Psychiatry, 130,* 481–3.

Elston, M. A. (1980). Medicine: Half our future doctors? In R. Silverstone & A. Ward (Eds.), *Careers of Professional Women.* London: Croom Helm.

Emler, N., & Dickinson, J. (1985). Children's representation of economic inequality. *British Journal of Developmental Psychology, 3,* 191–8.

Engel, J. F., & Blackwell, R. D. (1982). *Consumer behavior* (4th ed.). New York: Dryden.

Engel, J. F., Kollat, D. T., & Blackwell, R. D. (1972). *Consumer behavior* (2nd ed.). Hinsdale, IL: Dryden.

Epstein, T. S. (1968). *Capitalism, primitive and modern; some aspects of Tolai economic growth.* Canberra: Australian National University Press.

Epstein, Y. M., & Babad, E. Y. (1982). Economic stress: notes on the psychology of inflation. *Journal of Applied Social Psychology, 12,* 85–99.

Etgar, M., & Malhotra, N. K. (1981–2). Determinants of price dependency: Personal and perceptual factors. *Journal of Consumer Research, 8,* 217–22.

Evans, O. J. (1983). Tax policy, the interest elasticity of saving, and capital accumulation: Numerical analysis of theoretical models. *American Economic Review, 73,* 398–410.

Everett, P. B., Hayward, S. C., & Meyers, A. W. (1974). The effect of a token reinforcement procedure on bus ridership. *Journal of Applied Behavior Analysis, 7,* 1–9.

Eysenck, H. J. (1977). Personality and factor analysis: A reply to Guilford. *Psychological Bulletin, 84,* 405–11.

Eysenck, H. J., & Eysenck, S. B. G. (1976). *Psychoticism as a dimension of personality.* London: Hodder and Stoughton.

Fair, R. (1974–6). *A model of macroeconomic activity: Vols. 1 and 2.* Cambridge, MA: Ballinger.

Fakhruddin, A. K. M., Manjooran, A., Nair, A. P. V., & Neufeldt, A. (1972). A five-year outcome of discharged chronic psychiatric patients. *Canadian Psychiatric Association Journal, 17,* 433–5.

Fantino, E. J. (1967). Preference for mixed- *versus* fixed-ratio schedules. *Journal of the Experimental Analysis of Behavior, 10,* 35–44.

Farley, J. U. (1964a). Why does brand loyalty vary over products? *Journal of Marketing Research, 1,* 9–14.

Farley, J. U. (1964b). Brand loyalty and the economics of information. *Journal of Business, 37,* 370–81.

Feagin, J. R. (1972). Poverty: We still believe God helps those who help themselves. *Psychology Today* (New York), *6*(November), 101–110, 129.

Feallock, R., & Miller, L. K. (1976). The design and evaluation of a worksharing system for experimental group living. *Journal of Applied Behavior Analysis, 9,* 277–88.

Feather, N. (1974). Explanation of poverty in Australian and American samples: The person, society, or fate? *Australian Journal of Psychology, 26,* 199–216.

Feather, N. (1982). Unemployment and its psychological correlates: A study of depressive symptoms of self-esteem, Protestant Ethic values, attributional style and apathy. *Australian Journal of Psychology, 34,* 309–23.

Feige, E. L. (1979). How big is the irregular economy? *Challenge,* Nov–Dec, 5–13.

Feingold, B. D., & Mahoney, M. J. (1975). Reinforcement effects on intrinsic interest: undermining the overjustification hypothesis. *Behavior Therapy, 6,* 367–77.

Feldstein, M. S. (1974). Social security, induced retirement, and aggregate capital accumulation. *Journal of Political Economy, 82,* 905–26.

Feldstein, M. S. (1974). Social security and private saving: Reply. *Journal of Political Economy, 90,* 630–42.

Felson, M. (1976). The differentiation of material life styles: 1925 to 1966. *Social Indicators Research, 3,* 397–421.

Felton, M., & Lyon, D. O. (1966). The postreinforcement pause. *Journal of the Experimental Analysis of Behavior, 9,* 131–4.

Ferenczi, S. (1976). The ontogenesis of the interest in money. In E. Bornemann (Ed.), *The psychoanalysis of money* (pp. 81–90). New York: Urizen.

Ferman, L. A., & Berndt, L. E. (1981). The irregular economy. In S. Henry (Ed.), *Can I have it in cash?* (pp. 26–42). London: Astragal Books.

Fernandez, R., & Alston, P. P. (1978). Effect of reinforcement response patterns on success in rehabilitation. *Rehabilitation and Counseling Bulletin, 22,* 66–9.

Ferster, C. B., & Skinner, B. F. (1957). *Schedules of reinforcement.* E. Norwalk, CT: Appleton-Century-Crofts.

Festinger, L. (1954) A theory of social comparison processes. *Human Relations, 7,* 117–40.

Festinger, L. (1957). *A theory of cognitive dissonance.* Evanston, IL: Row, Peterson.

Festinger, L., & Carlsmith, J. M. (1959). Cognitive consequences of forced compliance. *Journal of Abnormal and Social Psychology, 58,* 203–10.

Fhaner, G., & Hane, M. (1979). Seat belts: Opinion effects of law-induced use. *Journal of Applied Psychology, 64,* 205–12.

Field, F., Meacher, M., & Pond, C. (1977). *To him who hath: A study of poverty and taxation.* Harmondsworth: Penguin.

Fields, D. B., & Stanbury, W. T. (1970). Incentives, disincentives and the income tax: Further empirical evidence. *Public Finance, 25,* 381–415.

Finison, L. J. (1976). The application of McClelland's national development model to recent data. *Journal of Social Psychology, 98,* 55–59.

Firth, R. (1963). *Elements of social organisation* (3rd ed.). Boston: MIT Press.

Firth, R. (1964). Capital, saving and credit in peasant societies: A viewpoint from economic anthropology. In R. Firth & B. S. Yamey (Eds.), *Capital, saving and credit in peasant societies* (pp. 15–34). London: Allen & Unwin.

Firth, R. (1968). The social framework of economic organisation. In E. E. LeClair & H. K. Schneider (Eds.), *Economic Anthropology.* New York: Holt, Rinehart and Winston.

Fishbein, M., & Ajzen, I. (1972). Attitudes and opinions. *Annual Review of Psychology, 23,* 487–544.

Fishbein, M., & Ajzen, I. (1975). *Belief, attitude, intention and behavior: An introduction to theory and research.* Reading, MA: Addison-Wesley.

Fishbein, M., & Coombs, F. S. (1974). Basis for decision: An attitudinal analysis of voting behavior. *Journal of Applied Social Psychology, 4,* 95–124.

Fisher, D. (1978). *Monetary theory and the demand for money.* London: Martin Robertson.

Fisher, E. B. (1979). Overjustification effects in token economies. *Journal of Applied Behavior Analysis, 12,* 407–15.

Fisher, I. (1911). *The purchasing power of money.* New York: Macmillan.

Fisher, I. (1926). A statistical relation between unemployment and price changes. *International Labour Review, 13,* 785–92.

Fisher, I. (1929). *The money illusion.* London: Allen & Unwin.

Fisher, I. (1930). *The theory of interest.* New York: Macmillan.

Fisher, S., & Greenberg, R.P. (1977). *The scientific credibility of Freud's theories and therapy.* New York: Basic Books.

Fisher, W. F. (1963). Sharing in pre-school children as a function of amount and type of reinforcement. *Genetic Psychological Monographs, 68,* 215–45.

Fiske, D. W., & Maddi, S. R. (1961). *Functions of varied experience.* Homewood, IL: Dorsey Press.

Fitzgerald, R. D., & Teyler, T. J. (1970). Trace and delayed heart-rate conditioning in rats as a functon of US intensity. *Journal of Comparative and Physiological Psychology, 70,* 242–53.

Fjellman, S. M. (1976). Natural and unnatural decision making. *Ethos, 4,* 73–94.

Flanders, J. P. (1968). A review of research on imitative behavior. *Psychological Bulletin, 69,* 316–37.

Fleming, M. (1969). *Introduction to economic analysis.* London: Allen & Unwin.

Florence, P. S. (1927). *Economics and human behavior.* London: Kegan Paul, Trench, Trubner.

Foa, U. (1971). Interpersonal and economic resources. *Science, 171,* 345–52.

Foa, E. B., & Foa, U. G. (1980). Resource theory: Interpersonal behavior as exchange. In K. J. Gergen, M. S. Greenberg, & R. H. Willis (Eds.), *Social Exchange: Advances in theory and research.* New York: Plenum.

Foa, U. G., & Shay, S. A. (1982). The influence of business success on preference for distributive justice. Unpublished manuscript.

Foa, U. G., & Stein, G. (1980). Rules of distributive justice: Institution and resource influences. *Academic Psychology Bulletin, 2,* 89–94.

Folkes, V. S. (1983–4). Consumer reactions to product failure: An attributional approach. *Journal of Consumer Research, 10,* 398–409.

Food and Agriculture Organization of the United Nations (1983). *FAO production yearbook* (Vol. 36). Rome: Author.

Foulks, E. F., & Katz, S. (1973). The mental health of Alaskan natives. *Acta Psychiatrica Scandinavica, 49,* 91–6.

Fowler, H. Satiation and curiosity. (1967). In K. W. Spence & J. T. Spence (Eds.), *The psychology of learning and motivation: Vol. 1* (pp. 158–227). New York: Academic Press.

Fox, K. F. A. (1978). What children bring to school – the beginnings of economic education. *Social Education, 42,* 478–81.

Fox, R. A., & Roseen, D. L. (1977). A parent administered token program for dietary regulation of phenylketonuria. *Journal of Behavior Therapy and Experimental Psychiatry, 8,* 441–3.

Frank, R. E., & Massy, W. F. (1970). Shelf position and space effects on sales. *Journal of Marketing, 7*(February), 59–66.

Frank, R. E., Massy, W. F., & Lodahl, T. M. (1969). Purchasing behavior and personal attributes. *Journal of Advertising Research, 9,* 15–24.

Fraser, C., & Bradford, J. W. (1983–4). Competitive market structure analysis: Principal partitioning of revealed substitutabilities. *Journal of Consumer Research, 10,* 15–30.

Fredricks, A. J., & Dossett, D. L. (1983). Attitude-behavior relations: A comparison of the Fishbein-Ajzen and Bentler-Speckart models. *Journal of Personality and Social Psychology, 45,* 501–12.

Freedman, J. L. (1963). Attitudinal effects of inadequate justification. *Journal of Personality, 31,* 371–85.

Freedman, J. L., Wallington, S. A., & Bless, E. (1963). Compliance without pressure: The effects of guilt. *Journal of Personality and Social Psychology, 7,* 117–24.

Freire, E., Gorman, B., & Wessman, A. E. (1980). Temporal span, delay of gratification and children's socioeconomic status. *Journal of Genetic Psychology, 137,* 247–55.

Freud, S. (1959). Character and anal eroticism. In J. Strachey (Ed.), *The standard edition of the complete psychological works of Freud* (Vol. 9, pp. 169–175). London: Hogarth. (Original work published 1908.)

Freud, S. (1961). Dostoevsky and parricide. In J. Strachey (Ed.), *The standard edition of the complete psychological works of Freud* (Vol. 21, pp. 177–94). London: Hogarth Press.

Freud, S. (1973). *New introductory lectures on psychoanalysis*. Harmondsworth: Penguin. (Originally published, 1932.)

Frey, R. L., & Kohn, L. (1970). An economic interpretation of voting behaviour on public finance issues. *Kyklos, 23,* 792–805.

Friedland, N. (1982). A note on tax evasion as a function of the quality of information about the magnitude and credibility of threatened fines: some preliminary research. *Journal of Applied Social Psychology, 12,* 54–9.

Friedland, N., Maital, S., & Rutenberg, A. (1978). A simulation study of income tax evasion. *Journal of Public Economics, 10,* 107–16.

Friedlander, F. (1963). Underlying sources of job satisfaction. *Journal of Applied Psychology, 47,* 246–50.

Friedman, E. A., & Havighurst, R. (1954). *The meaning of work and retirement.* Chicago: University of Chicago Press.

Friedman, M. (1953). *Essays in positive economics.* Chicago: University of Chicago Press.

Friedman, M. (1956). The quantity theory of money – A restatement. In M. Friedman (Ed.), *Studies in the quantity theory of money* (pp. 3–21). Chicago: University of Chicago Press.

Friedman, M. (1957). *A theory of the consumption function.* Princeton, NJ: Princeton University Press.

Friedman, M. (1962). *Capitalism and freedom.* Chicago: University of Chicago Press.

Friedman, M. (1963). Windfalls, the "horizon," and related concepts in the permanent income hypothesis. In C. F. Christ and others, *Measurement in economics* (pp. 3–28). Stanford, CA: Stanford University Press.

Friedman, M. (1977). *Inflation and unemployment.* London: Institute of Economic Affairs.

Friedman, M. (1977). *From Galbraith to economic freedom.* London: Institute of Economic Affairs.

Friedman, M. (1982). Linguistic change in a consumption oriented society. Paper presented at the 7th international symposium on economic psychology, Edinburgh.

Friedman, M., & Savage, L. J. (1952). The expected-utility hypothesis and the measurability of utility. *Journal of Political Economy, 60,* 463–75.

Friend, I., & Hasbrouck, J. (1983). Saving and after-tax rates of return. *Review of Economics and Statistics, 65,* 537–43.

Fromm, E. (1979). *To have or to be.* London: Sphere.

Fullerton, D. T., Cayner, J. J., & McClaughlin-Reidel, T. (1978). Results of a token economy. *Archives of General Psychiatry, 35,* 1451–3.

Furnham, A. (1982a). Why are the poor always with us? Explanations for poverty in Britain. *British Journal of Social Psychology, 21,* 311–22.

Furnham, A. (1982b). The protestant work-ethic and attitudes towards unemployment. *Journal of Occupational Psychology, 55,* 277–85.

Furnham, A. (1982c). The perception of poverty among adolescents. *Journal of Adolescence, 5,* 135–47.

Furnham, A. (1982d). Explanations for unemployment in Britain. *European Journal of Social Psychology, 12,* 335–52.

Furnham, A. (1983a). Attitudes towards the unemployed receiving social security benefits. *Human Relations, 36,* 135–50.

Furnham, A. (1983b). Inflation and the estimated sizes of notes. *Journal of Economic Psychology, 4,* 349–52.

Furnham, A. (1984). Many sides of the coin: The psychology of money usage. *Personality and Individual Differences, 5,* 501–9.

Furnham, A. (1985). Attitudes to, and habits of, gambling in Britain. *Personality and Individual Differences, 6,* 493–502.

Furnham, A., & Lewis, A. (in press). *The economic mind: The social psychology of economic behavior.* Brighton: Harvester.

Furnham, A., & Thomas, P. (1984a). Pocket money: a study of economic education. *British Journal of Developmental Psychology, 2,* 205–12.

Furnham, A., & Thomas, P. (1984b). Adult's perceptions of the economic socialization of children. *Journal of Adolescence, 7,* 217–31.

Furse, D. H., Punj, G. N., & Stewart, D. W. (1983–4). A typology of individual search strategies among purchasers of new automobiles. *Journal of Consumer Research, 10,* 417–31.

Furth, H. G. (1978a). Children's societal understanding and the process of equilibration. In W. Damon (Ed.), *New Directions for Child Development: Vol. 1* (pp. 101–22). San Francisco: Jossey-Bass.

Furth, H. G. (1978b). Young children's understanding of society. In H. McGurk (Ed.), *Issues in childhood social development.* London: Methuen.

Furth, H. G. (1980a). *The world of grown-ups.* New York: Elsevier.

Furth, H. G. (1980b). Piaget's theory of knowledge. In H. J. Silverman (Ed.), *Piaget, philosophy and the human sciences* (pp. 1–10). Brighton: Harvester.

Gabor, A. (1977). *Pricing: principles and practice.* London: Heinemann Educational.

Gabor, A., & Granger, C. W. J. (1961). On the price consciousness of consumers. *Applied Statistics, 10,* 170–88.

Gabor, A., & Granger, C. W. J. (1966). Price as an indicator of quality: Report on an enquiry. *Economica, 33,* 43–70.

Gabor, A., Granger, C. W. J., & Sowter, A. P. (1970). Real and hypothetical shop situations in market research. *Journal of Marketing Research, 7,* 335–9.

Gafgen, G. (1974). On the methodology and political economy of Galbraithian economics. *Kyklos, 27,* 705–31.

Gagnon, J. H., & Davison, G. C. (1976). Asylums, the token economy, and the metrics of mental life. *Behavior Therapy, 7,* 528–34.

Galanter, E. H. (1962). The direct measurement of utility and subjective probability. *American Journal of Psychology, 75,* 208–20.

Galbraith, J. K. (1958). *The affluent society.* London: Hamilton.

Galbraith, J. K. (1967). *The new industrial state.* London: Hamilton.

Galbraith, J. K. (1972). *The new industrial state* (2nd ed.). London: Andre Deutsch.

Galbraith, J. K. (1974). *Economics and the public purpose.* London: Andre Deutsch.

Galbraith, J. K. (1975). *Economics and the public purpose.* Harmondsworth: Penguin.

Galbraith, J. K. (1980). *The nature of mass poverty.* Harmondsworth: Penguin.

Galbraith, J. K., & Cummings, L. (1967). An empirical investigation of the motivational determinants to task perfomance: Interactive effects between instrumentality-valence and motivation-ability. *Organizational Behavior and Human Performance, 2,* 237–57.

Galst, J., & White, M. (1976). The unhealthy persuader: the reinforcing value of television and children's purchase influence attempts at the supermarket. *Child Development, 47,* 1080–96.

Garai, L., Eros, F., Jaro, K., & Kocski, M. (1979). Towards a production-centred theory of personality. *Social Science Information, 18,* 137–66.

Garcia-Bouza, J. (1980). *A basic-needs analytical bibliography.* Paris: Organization for Economic Co-operation and Development.

Gates, J. J. (1972). Overspending (stealing) in a token economy. *Behavior Therapy, 3,* 152–3.

Gaudet, F. J., & Curry, M. A. (1933). The effects of business conditions upon the sanity of a population. *Journal of Applied Psychology, 17,* 130–5.

Geber, B. A., & Webley, P. (1980). Experience and society. In S. Modgil & C. Modgil (Eds.), *Towards a theory of psychological development* (pp. 201–32). Windsor: NFER.

Geiger, T. (1967). *Die soziale Schichtung des Deutsches Volkes.* Stuttgart: Enke. (Originally published, 1932).

Geller, E. S., Casali, J. G., & Johnson, R. P. (1980). Seat belt usage: A potential target for applied behavioral analysis. *Journal of Applied Behavioral Analysis, 13,* 669–75.

Gene Reilly Group. (1973). *The assumption of the child of the role of the consumer.* Darien, CT: Author.

Gershone, J. R., Errickson, E. A., Mitchell, J. E., & Paulson, D. A. (1977). Behavioral comparison of a token economy and a standard psychiatric treatment ward. *Journal of Behaviour Therapy and Experimental Psychiatry, 8,* 381–5.

Gershuny, J. I., & Pahl, R. E. (1981). Work outside employment: Some preliminary speculations. In S. Henry (Ed.), *Can I have it in cash?* (pp. 73–88). London: Astragal.

Ghai, D. P., Khan, A. R., Lee, E. L. H., & Alfthan, T. (1977). *The basic-needs approach to development.* Geneva: International Labour Organization.

Gilbert, G., & Pommerehne, W. W. (1984). Preferences fiscales et politique d'imposition. *Public Finance, 29,* 25–69.

Gilly, M. C., & Gelb, B. D. (1982–3). Post-purchase processes and the complaining consumer. *Journal of Consumer Research, 9,* 323–8.

Gilmer, B. van H., & Deci, E. L. (1977). *Industrial and organizational psychology* (4th ed.). New York: McGraw-Hill.

Gilovich, T. (1983). Biased evaluation and persistence in gambling. *Journal of Personality and Social Psychology, 44,* 1110–26.

Ginsburg, N., & Courtis, R. (1974). The effect of value on perceived numerosity. *American Journal of Psychology, 87,* 481–6.

Ginter, J. L. (1974). An experimental investigation of attitude change and choice of a new brand. *Journal of Marketing Research, 11,* 30–40.

Giovanni, A. (1983). The interest elasticity of savings in developing countries: The existing evidence. *World Development, 11,* 601–7.

Godley, W., & May, R. M. (1977). The macroeconomic implications of devaluation and import restriction. *Economic Policy Review, 7,* 32–42.

Goetz, C. J. (1977). Fiscal illusion in state and local finance. In T. Borcherding (Ed.), *Budgets and bureaucrats: The sources of government growth.* Durham, NC: Duke University Press.

Goffman, E. (1961). *Asylums.* Garden City, NY: Doubleday Anchor.

Goldberg, J., Katz, S., & Yekutiel, E. (1973). The effects of token reinforcement on the productivity of moderately retarded clients in a sheltered workshop. *British Journal of Mental Subnormality, 19,* 80–4.

Goldberg, M. E., & Gorn, G. J. (1974). Children's reactions to television advertising: an experimental approach. *Journal of Consumer Research, 1,* 69–75.

Goldberg, M. E., & Gorn, G. J. (1978). Some unintended consequences of television advertising to children. *Journal of Consumer Research, 5,* 22–9.

Goldberg, M. E., & Gorn, G. J. (1983). Researching the effects of television advertising on children: A methodological critique. In M. J. A. Howe (Ed.), *Learning from television* (pp. 125–51). London: Academic Press.

Goldman, A. (1977). Consumer knowledge of food prices as an indicator of shopping effectiveness. *Journal of Marketing, 41,* 67–75.

Goldman, A. (1977–8). The shopping style explanation for store loyalty. *Journal of Retailing, 53*(4), 33–46; 94.

Goldman, A., & Johansson, J. K. (1978–9). Determinants of search for lower prices: an empirical assessment of the economics of information theory. *Journal of Consumer Research, 5,* 176–86.

Goldsmith, R. W. (1955). *A study of saving in the United States:* Vol. 1. Princeton, NJ: Princeton University Press.

Golstein, B., & Oldham, J. (1979). *Children and work: A study of socialization.* New Brunswick: Transaction Books.

Goodman, P. S., & Friedman, A. (1971). An examination of Adams' theory of inequity. *Administrative Sciences Quarterly, 16,* 271–88.

Goody, J. (1977). Literacy, criticism and the growth of knowledge. In J. Ben-David & T. Clark (Eds.), *Culture and its creators* (pp. 226–43). Chicago: University of Chicago Press.

Goranson, R. E., & Berkowitz, L. (1966). Reciprocity and responsibility reactions to prior help. *Journal of Personality and Social Psychology, 3,* 227–32.

Gorin, M. (1985). *Argent—contes et comptes.* Unpublished doctoral thesis, Ecole des Hautes Etudes en Sciences Sociales, Paris.

Gorman, W. M. (1959). The empirical implications of a utility tree: A further comment. *Econometrica, 27,* 489.

Gorman, W. M. (1968). The structure of utility functions. *Review of Economic Studies, 35,* 367–90.

Gorn, G. J., & Goldberg, M. E. (1982). Behavioral evidence of the effects of televised food messages on children. *Journal of Consumer Research, 9,* 200–5.

Graen, G. (1969). Instrumentality theory of work motivation: Some experimental results and suggested modifications. *Journal of Applied Psychology Monographs, 53,* 1–25.

Graft, D. A., Lea, S. E. G., & Whitworth, T. L. (1977). The matching law in and within groups of rats. *Journal of the Experimental Analysis of Behavior, 27,* 183–94.

Gray, R. F. (1960). Sonjo bride-price and the question of African "wife purchase." *American Anthropologist, 62,* 34–57.

Greaves, J. P., & Hollingsworth, D. F. (1966). Trends in food consumption in the United Kingdom. *World Review of Nutrition and Dietetics, 6,* 34–89.

Green, G. F. (1981). The effect of occupational pension schemes on saving in the United Kingdom: A test of the life cycle hypothesis. *Economic Journal, 91,* 136–44.

Greenberg, D. J., & Meagher, R. B. (1977). The courts and the token economy: An empirical approach to the problem. *Behavior Therapy, 8,* 377–82.

Greenberg, M. E., & Weiner, B. (1966). Effects of reinforcement history upon risk-taking behavior. *Journal of Experimental Psychology, 71,* 587–92.

Greenberger, E., Steinberg, L. D., & Vaux, A. (1981). Adolescents who work: Health and behavioral consequences of job stress. *Developmental Psychology, 17,* 691–703.

Greene, D., Sternberg, B., & Lepper, M. R. (1976). Overjustification in a token economy. *Journal of Personality and Social Psychology, 34,* 1219–34.

Greenson, R. R. (1947). On gambling. *American Imago, 4,* 61–77.

Greenwald, A. G. (1968). Cognitive learning, cognitive responses to persuasion and attitude change. In A. G. Greenwald, T. C. Brock, & T. H. Ostrom (Eds.), *Psychological foundations of attitudes* (pp. 147–70). New York: Academic Press.

Grether, D. M., & Plott, C. H. (1979). Economic theory of choice and the preference reversal phenomenon. *American Economic Review, 69,* 623–38.

Greyser, S. A. (1973). Irritation in advertising. *Journal of Advertising Research, 13*(1), 3–10.

Grice, G. R. (1968). Stimulus intensity and response evocation. *Psychological Review, 75,* 359–73.

Griffin, K. (1979). *The political economy of agrarian change* (2nd ed.). London: Macmillan.

Gripp, R. F., & Magaro, P. A. (1974). The token economy program in the psychiatric hospital: A review and analysis. *Behaviour Research and Therapy, 12,* 205–28.

Groenland, E. A. G., & van Veldhoven, G. M. (1983). Tax evasion behavior: A psychological framework. *Journal of Economic Psychology, 3,* 129–44.

Groenland, E. A. G., & van Zon, I. (1984). *Tax evasion behaviour: An empirical exploration.* Paper presented at the 9th international symposium on economic psychology, Tilburg.

Gronhaug, K., & Zaltman, G. (1981). Complainers and noncomplainers revisited: Another look at the data. *Journal of Economic Psychology, 1,* 121–34.

Grubel, H. G., & Edwards, D. R. (1964). Personal income taxation and choice of professions. *Quarterly Journal of Economics, 78,* 158–63.

Grusec, J. E. (1971). Power and the internalization of self-denial. *Child Development, 42,* 93–105.

Grusec, J. E. (1972). Demand characteristics of the modeling experiment: Altruism as a function of age and aggression. *Journal of Personality and Social Psychology, 22,* 139–48.

Grusec, J. E., & Skubiski, S. L. (1970). Model nurturance, demand characteristics of the modeling experiment, and altruism. *Journal of Personality and Social Psychology, 14,* 352–9.

Grzesiak, R. C., & Locke, B. J. (1975). Cognitive and behavioral correlates to overt behavior change within a token economy. *Journal of Consulting and Clinical Psychology, 43,* 272.

Guest, L. P. (1955). Brand loyalty twelve years later. *Journal of Applied Psychology, 39,* 405–8.

Guntern, G. (1978). Alpendorf: Transactional processes in a human system. Report from the Laboratory for Clinical Stress Research, Karolinska Institute, Stockholm, Sweden.

Gurin, G., & Gurin, P. (1976). Personal efficacy and the ideology of individual responsibility. In B. Strumpel (Ed.), *Economic means for human needs* (pp. 131–57). Ann Arbor, MI: Survey Research Center, Institute for Social Research, University of Michigan.

Gurr, T. R. (1970). *Why men rebel.* Princeton, NJ: Princeton University Press.

Guthrie, H. W. (1963). An empirical evaluation of theories of saving. *Review of Economics and Statistics, 45,* 430–3.

Hagen, E. E. (1962). On the theory of *social change.* Homewood, IL: Dorsey.

Hagen, E. E. (1963). *Planning economic development.* Homewood, IL: Irwin.

Hagen, E. E. (1975). *The economics of development* (2nd ed). Homewood, IL: Irwin.

Hahn, F. H. (1970). Savings and uncertainty. *Review of Economic Studies, 37,* 21–4.

Haley, R. I. (1978). Sales effect of advertising weight. *Journal of Advertising Research, 14*(2), 25–34.

Hall, D. T., & Nougaim, K.E. (1968). An examination of Maslow's need hierarchy in an organizational setting. *Organizational Behavior and Human Performance, 3,* 12–35.

Hall, J., & Baker, R. (1973). Token economy systems: Breakdown and control. *Behaviour Research & Therapy, 11,* 253–63.

Halpern, J. M. (1964). Capital, saving and credit among Lao peasants. In R. Firth & B. S. Yamey (Eds.), *Capital, saving and credit in peasant societies* (pp. 82–103). London: Allen & Unwin.

Hamer, J. (1978). Goals, status, and the stability of n achievement: A small sample from southern Ethiopia. *Ethos, 6,* 42–62.

Hamner, W. C. (1974). Reinforcement theory and contingency management in organizational settings. In H. L. Tosi & W. C. Hamner (Eds.), *Organizational behavior and management: A contingency approach* (pp. 86–112). Chicago: St. Clair.

Hamovitch, W. (1966). Sales taxation: An analysis of the effects of rate increases in two contrasting cases. *National Tax Journal, 19,* 411–20.

Hampton, J. A. (1981). An investigation of the nature of abstract concepts. *Memory and Cognition, 9,* 149–56.

Hansen, R. A., & Scott, C. A. (1976). Comments on attribution theory and consumer credibility. *Journal of Marketing Research, 13,* 193–7.

Harre, R. (1981). Expressive aspects of descriptions of others. In C. Antaki (Ed.), *The psychology of ordinary explanations of social behaviour* (pp. 139–56). London: Academic Press.

Harris, P., & Heelas, P. (1979). Cognitive processes and collective representations. *Archives Europeenes de Sociologie, 20,* 211–41.

Harris, R., & Seldon, A. (1979). *Over-ruled on welfare.* London: IEA.

Harrod, R. F. (1948). *Towards a dynamic economics.* London: Macmillan.

Hart, B. M., Allen, K. E., Buell, J. S., Harris, F. R., & Wolf, M. M. (1964). Effects of social reinforcement on operant crying. *Journal of Experimental Child Psychology, 1,* 145–53.

Hartnagel, T. F. (1982). Modernization, female social roles, and female crime: A cross-national investigation. *Sociological Quarterly, 23,* 477–90.

Hartshorne, H., & May, M. A. (1928). *Studies in the nature of character: Vol. 1, Studies in deceit.* New York: Macmillan.

Hayashi, F. (1982). The permanent income hypothesis: Estimation and testing by instrumental variables. *Journal of Political Economy, 90,* 895–916.

Hayden, T., Osborne, A. E., Hall, S. M., & Hall, R. G. (1974). Behavioral effects of price changes in a token economy. *Journal of Abnormal Psychology, 83,* 432–9.

Hayes, J., & Nutman, P. (1981). *Understanding the unemployed.* London: Tavistock.

Heap, R. F., Boblitt, E. E., Moore, C. H., & Hord, J. E. (1970). Behavior-milieu therapy with chronic neuropsychiatric patients. *Journal of Abnormal Psychology, 76,* 349–54.

Hebb, D. O. (1955). Drives and the CNS (Conceptual Nervous System). *Psychological Review, 62,* 243–54.

Heckel, R. V., Hursh, L., & Hiers, J. M. (1977). Analysis of process data from token groups in a summer camp. *Journal of Clinical Psychology, 33,* 241–4.

Heider, F. (1958). *The psychology of interpersonal relations.* New York: Wiley.

Heinemann, K., Roehrig, P., & Stadie, R. (1980). *Arbeitslose Frauen im Spannungsfeld von Erwerbstaetigkeit Hausfrauenrolle.* Vols. 1 and 2. Melle: Knoll.

Helfgott, R. B. (1974). *Labor economics.* New York: Random House.

Hemming, R., & Harvey, R. (1983). Occupational pension scheme membership and retirement saving. *Economic Journal, 93,* 128–44.

Henderson, J. D., & Scoles, P. E. (1970). A community-based behavioral operant environment for psychotic men. *Behavior Therapy, 1,* 245–51.

Henry, S. (1978). *The hidden economy.* London: Martin Robertson.

Hensher, D. A. (1981). Towards a design of consumer durables. *Journal of Economic Psychology, 1,* 135–64.

Herman, R. D. (1976). *Gamblers and gambling.* Lexington, MA: Heath.

Herniter, J. D., & Magee, J. F. (1961). Customer behavior as a Markov process. *Operations Research, 9,* 105–22.

Herrnstein, R. J. (1961). Relative and absolute strength of response as a function of frequency of reinforcement. *Journal of the Experimental Analysis of Behavior, 4,* 267–72.

Herrnstein, R. J. (1970). On the law of effect. *Journal of the Experimental Analysis of Behavior, 13,* 243–66.

Herrnstein, R. J., & Vaughan, W. (1980). Melioration and behavioral allocation. In J. E. R. Staddon (Ed.), *Limits to action* (pp. 143–76). New York: Academic Press.

Hersen, M. (1976). Token economies in institutional settings. *Journal of Nervous and Mental Diseases, 162,* 206–11.

Hersen, M., & Barlow, D. H. (1976). Single-case experimental designs. Oxford: Pergamon.

Herzberg, F., Mausner, B., & Snyderman, B. B. (1959). *The motivation to work.* New York: Wiley.

Hess, E. H., Seltzer, A. L., & Shlien, J. M. (1965). Pupil response of hetero- and homosexual males to pictures of men and women: A pilot study. *Journal of Abnormal Psychology, 70,* 165–8.

Hess, H. F., & Diller, J. V. (1969). Motivation for gambling as revealed in the marketing methods of the legitimate gambling industry. *Psychological Reports, 25,* 19–27.

Hicks, J. R., & Allen, R. G. D. (1934). A reconsideration of the theory of value. *Economica* (New Series), *1,* 52–76; 196–219.

Hinde, R. A. (1960). Energy models of motivation. *Symposia of the Society for Experimental Biology, 14,* 199–213.

Hinde, R. A. (1970). *Animal behavior* (2nd ed.). New York: McGraw-Hill.

Hirsch, F. (1977). *Social limits to growth.* London: Routledge and Kegan Paul.

Hirshleifer, J. (1980). *Price theory and applications.* (2nd ed.). London: Prentice-Hall International.

Hirshleifer, J. (1984). *Price theory and applications* (3rd ed.). Englewood Cliffs, NJ: Prentice-Hall.

Hitchcock, J., Munroe, R., & Munroe, R. (1976). Coins and countries: the value-size hypothesis. *Journal of Social Psychology, 100,* 307–8.

Hodge, R. W., Treiman, D. J., & Rossi, P. M. (1967). A comparative study of occupational prestige. In R. Bendix & S. M. Lipset (Eds.), *Class, status and power* (2nd ed.) (pp. 309–21). London: Routledge and Kegan Paul.

Hoffman, L. W., & Hoffman, M. L. (1973). The value of children to parents. In

J. T. Fawcett (Ed.), *Psychological perspectives on population*. New York: Basic Books.

Hoffman, L. W., Thornton, A., & Manis, J. (1978). The value of children to parents in the United States. *Journal of Population, 1*, 91–131.

Hogan, J. A., & Roper, T. J. (1978). A comparison of the properties of different reinforcers. *Advances in the Study of Behavior, 8*, 155–255.

Holbrook, M. R., & Hirschman, E. C. (1982-3). The experiential aspect of consumption: consumer fantasies, feelings, and fun. *Journal of Consumer Research, 9*, 132–40.

Holbrook, R. S. (1967). The three-year horizon: An analysis of the evidence. *Journal of Political Economy, 75*, 750–4.

Holden, K., Peel, D. A., & Thompson, J. L. (1982). *Modelling the UK economy*. Oxford: Martin Robertson.

Holland, C. J. (1977). A token economy system for home-based behaviour modification. *Canada's Mental Health, 25*(4), 17–9.

Hollingshead, A. de B., & Redlich, F. C. (1958). *Social class and mental illness*. New York: Wiley.

Hollingsworth, R., & Foreyt, J. P. (1975). Community adjustment of released token economy patients. *Journal of Behavior Therapy and Experimental Psychiatry, 6*, 271–4.

Hollander, M. A., & Plutchik, R. (1972). A reinforcement program for psychiatric attendants. *Journal of Behavior Therapy and Experimental Psychiatry, 3*, 297–300.

Holmes, R. (1976). *Legitimacy and the politics of the knowable*. London: Routledge and Kegan Paul.

Holmes, T. H., & Rahe, R. H. (1967). The social readjustment rating scale. *Journal of Psychosomatic Research, 11*, 213–8.

Holmstrom, V. L., & Beach, L. R. (1973). Subjective expected utility and career preferences. *Organizational Behavior and Human Performance, 10*, 201–7.

Homans, G. C. (1961). *Social behavior: Its elementary forms*. New York: Harcourt Brace.

Hong Kwang, R. T., & Stacey, B. G. (1981). The understanding of socio-economic concepts in Malaysian chinese school children. *Child Study Journal, 11*, 33–49.

Horai, J., Naccari, N., & Fatoullah, E. (1974). The effects of expertise and physical attractiveness upon opinion agreement and liking. *Sociometry, 37*, 601–6.

Hovland, C. I., Harvey, O. J., & Sherif, M. (1957). Assimilation and contrast effects in reactions to communication and attitude change. *Journal of Abnormal and Social Psychology, 55*, 244–52.

Hovland, C. I., & Janis, I. L. (1959). *Personality and persuasability*. New Haven, CT: Yale University Press.

Hovland, C. I., Janis, I. L., & Kelley, H. H. (1953). *Communication and persuasion*. New Haven, CT: Yale University Press.

Hovland, C. I., Lumsdaine, A., & Sheffield, F. (1949). *Experiments on mass communication*. Princeton: Princeton University Press.

Houthakker, H. S. (1950). Revealed preference and the utility function. *Economica, 17*, 159–74.

Houthakker, H. S., & Taylor, L. D. (1970). *Consumer demand in the United States: analyses and projections* (2nd ed.). Cambridge, MA: Harvard University Press.

Howard, J. A., & Sheth, J. N. (1969). *The theory of buyer behavior*. New York: Wiley.

Howe, M. J. A. (1980). *The psychology of human learning.* New York: Harper & Row.

Hubbard, R. (1978–9). A review of selected factors conditioning consumer travel behavior. *Journal of Consumer Research, 5,* 1–21.

Huff, D. L. (1962). A probabilistic analysis of consumer spatial behavior. In W. S. Decker (Ed.), *Emerging concepts in marketing* (pp. 443–61). Chicago: American Marketing Association.

Hull, C. L. (1943). *Principles of behavior.* E. Norwalk, CT: Appleton-Century-Crofts.

Hull, C. L. (1952). *A behavior system.* New Haven, CT: Yale University Press.

Hursh, S. R. (1980). Economic concepts for the analysis of behavior. *Journal of the Experimental Analysis of Behavior, 34,* 219–38.

Hursh, S. R., & Natelson, B. H. (1981). Electrical brain stimulation and food reinforcement dissociated by demand elasticity. *Physiology and Behavior, 26,* 509–15.

Hussein, G. (1981). *Aspects of schoolchildren's understanding of money.* Unpublished undergraduate project, University of Exeter, Department of Psychology, Exeter.

Hussein, G. (1984). Is money an unacceptable gift in Cyprus? Unpublished manuscript.

Hussein, G. (1985). An examination of the psychological aspects of money. Unpublished M. Phil. thesis, University of Exeter.

Hymans, S. H. (1970). *Consumer durable spending.* Washington, DC: Brookings Institute.

Iles, D. J. (1973). The disincentive effects of income taxation on work effort. Unpublished MSc thesis, cited in A. Lewis, *The psychology of taxation.* Oxford: Martin Robertson.

Illich, I. D. (1974). *Energy and equity.* London: Calder and Boyars.

Inkeles, A. (1983). *Exploring individual modernity.* New York: Columbia University Press.

Inkeles, A., & Smith, D. H. (1974). *Becoming modern.* London: Heinemann.

International Labour Office (1983). *1983 Yearbook of labour statistics.* Geneva: Author.

Isen, A. M. (1970). Success, failure, attention and reaction to others: The warm glow of success. *Journal of Personality and Social Psychology, 15,* 294–301.

Isen, A. M., Clark, M., & Schwartz, M. (1976). Duration of the effect of good mood on helping: "Footprints in the sands of time." *Journal of Personality and Social Psychology, 34,* 385–93.

Isen, A. M., & Levin, P. F. (1972). Effect of feeling good on helping: Cookies and kindness. *Journal of Personality and Social Psychology, 21,* 384–88.

Jacobs, H. E., Fairbanks, D., Poche, C. E., & Bailey, J. S. (1982). Multiple incentives in encouraging car pool formation on a university campus. *Journal of Applied Behavior Analysis, 15,* 141–9.

Jacoby, J., Olson, J. C., & Haddock, R. A. (1971). Price, brand name, and product composition characteristics as determinants of perceived quality. *Journal of Applied Psychology, 55,* 570–80.

Jacoby, J., Szybillo, G. J., & Busato-Schach, J. (1976–7). Information acquisition in brand choice situations. *Journal of Consumer Research, 3,* 209–16.

Jahoda, G. (1970). Supernatural beliefs and changing cognitive structures among Ghanaian university students. *Journal of Cross-Cultural Psychology, 1,* 115–30.

Jahoda, G. (1979). The construction of economic reality by some Glaswegian children. *European Journal of Social Psychology, 9,* 115–27.

Jahoda, G. (1981). The development of thinking about economic institutions: The bank. *Cahiers de Psychologie Cognitive, 1,* 55–73.

Jahoda, G. (1983). European "lag" in the development of an economic concept: A study in Zimbabwe. *British Journal of Developmental Psychology, 1,* 113–20.

Jahoda, G. (1983). *Psychology and anthropology: A psychological perspective.* London: Academic Press.

Jahoda, G. (1984). The development of thinking about socio-economic systems. In H. Tajfel (Ed.), *The social dimension* (pp. 69–88). Cambridge: Cambridge University Press.

Jahoda, G., & Woerdenbagch, A. (1982). The development of ideas about an economic institution: A cross national replication. *British Journal of Social Psychology, 21,* 337–8.

Jahoda, M. (1979). The impact of unemployment in the 1930s and the 1980s. *Bulletin of the British Psychological Society, 32,* 309–14.

James, S. R., Lewis, A., & Wallschutzky, I. (1981). Fiscal fog: A comparison of the comprehensibility of tax literature in Australia and the U. K. *Australian Tax Review, 10,* 26–35.

James, S. R., & Nobes, C. (1983). *The economics of taxation* (2nd ed.). Oxford: Philip Allan.

Janis, I. L., & Feshbach, S. (1953). Effects of fear-arousing communications. *Journal of Abnormal and Social Psychology, 48,* 78–92.

Janis, I. L., & King, B. T. (1954). The influence of role playing on opinion change. *Journal of Abnormal and Social Psychology, 49,* 211–8.

Janis, I. L., & Mann, L. (1965). Effectiveness of emotional role-playing in modifying smoking habits and attitudes. *Journal of Experimental Research in Personality, 1,* 84–90.

Janzen, W. B., & Love, W. (1977). Involving adolescents as active participants in their own treatment plans. *Psychological Reports, 41,* 931–4.

Jarman, P. H., Iwata, B. A., & Lorentzson, A. M. (1983). Development of morning self-care routines in multiply handicapped persons. *Applied Research in Mental Retardation, 4,* 113–22.

Jaspers, J. M. F. (1978). The nature and measurement of attitudes. In H. Tajfel & C. Fraser (Eds.), *Introducing social psychology* (pp. 256–76). Harmondsworth: Penguin.

Jennings, J., Geis, F. L., & Brown, V. (1980). Influence of television commercials on women's self-confidence and independent judgement. *Journal of Personality and Social Psychology, 38,* 203–10.

Jevons, W. S. (1911). *The theory of political economy* (4th ed.). London: Macmillan. (Originally published, 1871.)

John, E. R., Chesler, P., Bartlett, F., & Victor, I. (1968). Observation learning in cats. *Science, 159,* 1489–91.

Johnson, D. B. (1982). The free-rider principle, the charity market and the economics of blood. *British Journal of Social Psychology, 21,* 93–106.

Johnson, F. A., & Majodina, M. Z. (1979). A token economy pogramme on a ward for chronic psychotic patients: A pilot study. *African Journal of Psychiatry, 5,* 81–5.

Johnson, M. B. (1971). *Household behaviour.* Harmondsworth: Penguin.

Johnston, J. (1972). *Econometric methods* (2nd ed.). Tokyo: McGraw-Hill Kogakusha.

Jones, E. E., & Davis, K. E. (1965). From acts to dispositions. *Advances in Experimental Social Psychology, 3,* 1–24.

Jones, E. E., & Nisbett, R. (1971). *The actor and the observer: divergent perceptions of the causes of behavior.* Morristown, NJ: General Learning Press.

Jones, R. C. (1960). Transitory income and expenditures on consumption categories. *American Economic Review, 50*(2), 584–92.

Jorgenson, D. O. (1975). Economic threat and authoritarianism in television programs: 1950–1974. *Psychological Reports, 37,* 1153–4.

Joyce, T. (1967). Advertising. In A. S. C. Ehrenberg & F. G. Pyatt (Eds.), *Consumer Behaviour* (pp. 151–78). Harmondsworth: Penguin.

Jump, G. V. (1980). Interest rates, inflation expectations, and spurious elements in measured real income and savings. *American Economic Review, 70,* 990–1004.

Jundin, S. (1983). *Children's economic socialization.* Paper presented at the eighth international symposium on economic psychology, Bologna.

Jung, C. G. (1971). Psychological types. In *Collected works: Vol. 6.* Princeton, NJ: Princeton University Press. (Originally published, 1921.)

Juster, F. T. (1964). *Anticipations and purchases: An analysis of consumer behavior.* Princeton, NJ: Princeton University Press.

Juster, F. T. (1981). An expectational view of consumer spending prospects. *Journal of Economic Psychology, 1,* 87–103.

Juster, F. T., & Taylor, R. D. (1975). Towards a theory of saving behavior. *American Economic Review, 65,* 203–9.

Kagel, J. H., & Battalio, R. C. (1980). Token economy and animal models for the experimental analysis of economic behavior. In J. Kmenta & J. B. Ramsey (Eds.), *Evaluation of econometric models* (pp. 379–401). New York: Academic Press.

Kagel, J. H., Battalio, R. C., Green, L., & Rachlin, H. (1980). Consumer demand theory applied to choice behavior of rats. In J. E. R. Staddon (Ed.), *Limits to action* (pp. 237–67). New York: Academic Press.

Kagel, J. H., Battalio, R. C., Rachlin, H., & Green, L. (1981). Demand curves for animal consumers. *Quarterly Journal of Economics, 96,* 1–15.

Kagel, J. H., Battalio, R. C., Rachlin, H., Green, L., Basmann, R. L., & Klemm, W. R. (1975). Experimental studies of consumer demand using laboratory animals. *Economic Inquiry, 13,* 22–38.

Kagel, J. H., Battalio, R. C., Winkler, R. C., & Fisher, E. B. (1977). Job choice and total labor supply: an experimental analysis. *Southern Economic Journal, 44,* 13–24.

Kagel, J. H., Battalio, R. C., Winkler, R. C., Fisher, E. B., Miles, C. G., Basmann, R. L., & Krasner, L. (1975). In C. G. Miles (Ed.), *Experimentation in controlled environment* (pp. 71–88). Toronto: Addiction Research Foundation.

Kagel, J. H., & Winkler, R. C. (1972). Behavioral economics: areas of cooperative research between economics and applied behavior analysis. *Journal of Applied Behavior Analysis, 5,* 335–42.

Kahle, L. R., & Berman, J. J. (1979). Attitudes cause behaviors: A cross-lagged panel analysis. *Journal of Personality and Social Psychology, 37,* 315–21.

Kahle, L. R., Klingel, D. M., & Kulka, R. A. (1981). A longitudinal study of adolescents attitude-behavior consistency. *Public Opinion Quarterly, 45,* 402–14.

Kalman, P. J. (1968). Theory of consumer behavior when prices enter the utility function. *Econometrica, 36,* 497–510.

Kamin, L. J. (1969). Predictability, surprise, attention, and conditioning. In B. A. Campbell & R. M. Church (Eds.), *Punishment and aversive behavior* (pp 279–96). E. Norwalk, CT: Appleton-Century-Crofts.

Kassarjian, H. H. (1982). Consumer psychology. *Annual Review of Psychology, 33,* 619–49.

Kasulis, J. J., Lusch, R. F., & Stafford, E. F. (1979–80). Consumer acquisition patterns for durable goods. *Journal of Consumer Research, 6,* 44–57.

Katona, G. (1942). *War without inflation.* New York: Columbia University Press.

Katona, G. (1953). Rational behavior and economic behavior. *Psychological Review, 60,* 307–18.

Katona, G. (1959). Repetitiousness and variability of consumer behavior. *Human Relations, 12,* 35–49.

Katona, G. (1960). *The powerful consumer.* New York: McGraw-Hill.

Katona, G. (1965). *Private pensions and individual saving.* Ann Arbor, MI: Institute for Social Research.

Katona, G. (1975). *Psychological Economics.* New York: Elsevier.

Katona, G., & Strumpel, B. (1978). *A new economic era.* New York: Elsevier North-Holland.

Katsimbris, G. M., & Miller, S. M. (1982). Money illusion, distribution effects and the household and business demands for money. *Journal of Banking and Finance, 6,* 215–31.

Katz, D., & Kahn, R. L. (1978). *The social psychology of organizations* (2nd ed.). New York: Wiley.

Katz, R. C., Johnson, C. A., & Gelfand, S. (1972). Modifying the dispensing of reinforcers: Some implications for behavior modification with hospitalized patients. *Behavior Therapy, 3,* 579–88.

Kavolis, V. (1964a). Economic conditions and art styles. *Journal of Aesthetics and Art Criticism, 22,* 437–41.

Kavolis, V. (1964b). Economic correlates of artistic creativity. *American Journal of Sociology, 70,* 332–41.

Kay, J. A., & King, M. A. (1980). *The British tax system.* Oxford: Oxford University Press.

Kazdin, A. E. (1977). *The token economy.* New York: Plenum.

Kazdin, A. E. (1982). The token economy: A decade later. *Journal of Applied Behavior Analysis, 15,* 431–45.

Kazdin, A. E., & Bootzin, R. R. (1972). The token economy: An evaluative review. *Journal of Applied Behavior Analysis, 5,* 343–72.

Kazdin, A. E., & Mascitelli, S. (1980). The opportunity to earn oneself off a token system as a reinforcer for attentive behavior. *Behavior Therapy, 11,* 68–78.

Kazdin, A. E., & Polster, R. (1973). Intermittent token reinforcement and response maintenance in extinction. *Behavior Therapy, 4,* 386–91.

Kelley, E. J., & Scheewe, L. R. (1975) Buyer behavior in a stagflation/shortages economy. *Journal of Marketing, 39,* 44–50.

Kelley, H. H. (1967). Attribution theory in social psychology. *Nebraska symposium on Motivation, 15,* 192–238.

Kelley, H. H. (1971). Causal schemata and the attribution process. In E. E. Jones, D. E. Kanouse, H. H. Kelley, R. E. Nisbett, S. Valins, & B. Weiner, *Attribution: perceiving the causes of behavior* (pp. 151–74). Morristown, NJ: General Learning Press.

Kelman, H. C. (1958). Compliance, identification and internalization: Three processes of attitude change. *Journal of Conflict Resolution, 2,* 51–60.

Kelman, H. C. (1965). Manipulation of human behavior: An ethical dilemma for the social scientist. *Journal of Social Issues, 21,* 31–46.

Kelvin, P. (1980). Social psychology 2001: The social psychological bases and implications of structural unemployment. In R. Gilmour and S. Duck (Eds.), *The development of social psychology* (pp. 293–316). London: Academic Press.

Kelvin, P. (1982). *Psychological response to economic change: reactions to unemployment as a function of economic environment.* Paper presented at the sixth international symposium on economic psychology, Edinburgh, July.

Kelvin, P., & Jarrett, J. (1985). *Social psychological consequences of unemployment.* Cambridge: Cambridge University Press.

Kendall, S. B. (1972). Some effects of response-dependent clock stimuli in a fixed-interval schedule. *Journal of the Experimental Analysis of Behavior, 17,* 161–8.

Keppel, G., Zavortink, B., & Shiff, B. B. (1967). Unlearning in the A-B, A-C paradigm as a function of percentage occurrence of response members. *Journal of Experimental Psychology, 74,* 172–77.

Kershaw, D., & Fair, J. (1976). *The New Jersey income-maintenance experiment: Vol. 1. Operation, surveys and administration.* New York: Academic Press.

Keynes, J. M. (1936). *The general theory of employment, interest and money.* London: Macmillan.

Kidron, M., & Segal, R. (1984). *The new state of the world atlas.* London: Pan.

Kiesler, C. A., & Munson, P. A. (1975). Attitudes and opinions. *Annual Review of Psychology, 26,* 415–57.

Kilby, P. (1965). Patterns of bread consumption in Nigeria. *Food Research Institute Studies, Stanford University, 5,* 3–18.

Kish, G. B. (1955). Learning when the onset of illumination is used as reinforcing stimulus. *Journal of Comparative and Physiological Psychology, 48,* 261–264.

Kish, G. B. (1966). Studies of sensory reinforcement. In W. K. Honig (Ed.), *Operant behavior: Areas of research and application* (pp. 109–159). E. Norwalk, CT: Appleton-Century-Crofts.

Kistner, J., Hammer, D., Wolfe, D., Rothblum, E., & Drabman, R. A. (1982). Teacher popularity and contrast effects in a classroom token economy. *Journal of Applied Behavior Analysis, 15,* 85–96.

Kline, P. (1967). An investigation into the Freudian concept of the anal character. Unpublished Ph.D. dissertation, University of Manchester.

Kline, P. (1975). *Psychology of vocational guidance.* London: Batsford.

Kline, P. (1979). *Psychometrics and psychology.* London: Academic Press.

Kline, P. (1981). *Fact and fantasy in Freudian theory* (2nd ed.). London: Methuen.

Knapczyk, D. R., & Yoppi, J. O. (1975). Development of cooperative and competitive play in developmentally disabled children. *American Journal of Mental Deficiency, 80,* 245–55.

Knox, R. E., & Safford, R. K. (1976). Group caution at the race track. *Journal of Experimental Social Psychology, 12,* 317–24.

Koch, J. V. (1972). Student choice of undergraduate major field of study and private internal rate of return. *Industrial and Labor Relations Review, 26,* 680–5.

Koch, L., & Breyer, N. L. (1974). A token economy for the teacher. *Psychology in the Schools, 11,* 195–200.

Koo, H. (1976). Small entrepreneurship in a developing society: Patterns of labor absorption and social mobility. *Social Forces, 54,* 775–87.

Koopmans, T. C. (1960). Stationary ordinal utility and impatience. *Econometrica, 28,* 287–309.

Korte, C. (1980). Urban-nonurban differences in social behavior. *Journal of Social Issues, 36,* 29–51.

Korte, C., & Kerr, N. (1975). Response to altruistic opportunities in urban and nonurban settings. *Journal of Social Psychology, 95,* 183–4.

Koskela, E., & Viren, M. (1983). Social security and household saving in an international cross-section. *American Economic Review, 73,* 212–7.

Koutsouyannis, A. P. (1963). Demand functions for tobacco. *The Manchester School, 31,* 1–20.

Krasner, L., & Ullman, L. P. (1973). *Behavior influence and personality.* New York: Holt, Rinehart and Winston.

Krebs, D. L. (1975). Empathy and altruism. *Journal of Personality and Social Psychology, 32,* 1134–46.

Kreinin, M. E. (1961). Windfall income and consumption – additional evidence. *American Economic Review, 51,* 388–90.

Kristiansen, C. M. (1984). *Preventive health behaviour: A social psychological analysis.* Unpublished doctoral dissertation, Exeter University, Exeter.

Kroeber, A. L. (1948). *Anthropology.* New York: Harcourt, Brace.

Krugman, H. E. (1965). The impact of television advertising: learning without involvement. *Public Opinion Quarterly, 29,* 349–56.

Krugman, H. E. (1975). What makes advertising effective? *Harvard Business Review, 53,* 96–103.

Kuehn, A. A. (1962). Consumer brand choice – a learning process? In R. E. Frank, A. A. Kuehn, & W. F. Massy (Eds.), *Quantitative techniques in marketing analysis* (pp. 390–403). Homewood, IL: Irwin.

Kuhn, D. (1974). Inducing development experimentally: comments on a research paradigm. *Developmental Psychology, 10,* 590–600.

Kuhn, T. S. (1970). *The logic of scientific revolutions* (2nd ed.). Chicago: University of Chicago Press.

Kunkel, J. H. (1963). Psychological factors in the analysis of economic development. *Journal of Social Issues, 19*(1), 68–87.

Kusyszyn, I., & Rutter, R. (1978). Personality characteristics of heavy, light, non-gamblers and lottery players. Paper presented at the fourth Annual Conference on Gambling, Nevada.

Kutner, B., Wilkins, C., & Yarrow, P. R. (1952). Verbal attitudes and overt behavior involving racial prejudice. *Journal of Abnormal and Social Psychology, 47,* 649–52.

Kuznets, S. (1942). *Uses of national income in peace and war.* New York: National Bureau of Economic Research.

Kuznets, S. (1946). *National product since 1869.* New York: National Bureau of Economic Research.

Kuznets, S. (1966). *Modern economic growth.* New Haven, CT: Yale University Press.

La Fontaine, J. de (1974). *Fables* (Livres 1 a VII). Paris: Gallimard. (Originally published 1668–79).

Lachenmeyer, C. W. (1969). Systematic socialization: observations on a programmed environment for the habilitation of social retardates. *Psychological Record, 19,* 247–57.

Ladd, G. W., & Zober, M. (1977–78). Model of consumer reactions to product characteristics. *Journal of Consumer Research, 4,* 89–101.

Laming, D. R. J. (1973). *Mathematical psychology.* London: Academic Press.

Lancaster, K. J. (1966a). A new approach to consumer theory. *Journal of Political Economy, 74,* 132–57.

Lancaster, K. J. (1966b). Change and innovation in the technology of consumption. *American Economic Review, 56*(2), 14–23.

Lancaster, K. J. (1971). *Consumer demand: A new approach.* New York: Columbia University Press.

Lancaster, K. J. (1974). *An introduction to modern microeconomics* (2nd ed.). Chicago: Rand-McNally.

Landsberger, M. (1966). Windfall income and consumption: Comment. *American Economic Review, 56,* 534–40.

Landy, F., & Trumbo, D. (1980). *Psychology of work behavior* (2nd ed.). Homewood, IL: Dorsey.

Langer, E. J. (1975). The illusion of control. *Journal of Personality and Social Psychology, 32,* 311–28.

Langer, E. (1978). Rethinking the role of thought in social interaction. In J. Harvey, W. J. Ickes, & R. F. Kidd, *New directions in attribution research* (Vol. 2, pp. 35–58). Hillsdale, NJ: Erlbaum.

Langer, E. J., Blank, A., & Chanowitz, B. (1978). The mindlessness of ostensibly thoughtful action: the role of "placebic" information in interpersonal interaction. *Journal of Personality and Social Psychology, 36,* 635–42.

Langer, E. J., & Roth, J. (1975). Heads I win, tails it's chance: The illusion of control as a function of the sequence of outcomes in a purely chance task. *Journal of Personality and Social Psychology, 32,* 951–5.

Lanier, D. L., Estep, D. Q., & Dewsbury, D. A. (1974). Food hoarding in muroid rodents. *Behavioral Biology, 11,* 177–87.

LaPiere, R. T. (1934). Attitudes versus actions. *Social Forces, 13,* 230–7.

Latane, B., & Darley, J. M. (1968). Group inhibition of bystander intervention. *Journal of Personality and Social Psychology, 10,* 215–21.

Latane, B., Nida, S. A., & Wilson, D. W. (1981). The effects of group size on helping behavior. In J. P. Rushton & R. M. Sorrentino (Eds.), *Altruism and helping behavior: Social, personality and developmental perspectives.* Hillsdale, NJ: Erlbaum.

Latane, B., Williams, K., & Harkin, S. (1979). Many hands make light the work: The causes and consequences of social loafing. *Journal of Personality and Social Psychology, 37,* 822–32.

Laties, V. G., & Weiss, B. (1963). Effects of a concurrent task on fixed-interval responding in humans. *Journal of the Experimental Analysis of Behavior, 6,* 431–6.

Laumas, P. S. (1969). A test of the permanent income hypothesis. *Journal of Political Economy, 77,* 857–61.

Laumas, P. S., & Mohabbat, K. A. (1972). The permanent-income hypothesis: Evidence from time-series data. *American Economic Review, 62,* 730–4.

Lawler, E. E. (1968a). Equity theory as a predictor of productivity and work quality. *Psychological Bulletin, 70,* 596–610.

Lawler, E. E. (1968b). Effects of hourly overpayment on productivity and work quality. *Journal of Personality and Social Psychology, 10,* 306–13.

Lawler, E. E. (1973). *Motivation in work organizations.* Belmont, CA: Brooks/Cole.

Lawler, E. E., & Suttle, J. L. (1972). A causal correlation test of the need hierarchy concept. *Organizational Behavior and Human Performance, 7,* 265–87.

Le Pas, J. (1968). *Dynamisme des structures et croissance economiques.* Paris: Genin.

Lea, S. E. G. (1978). The psychology and economics of demand. *Psychological Bulletin, 85,* 441–6.

Lea, S. E. G. (1980). Supply as a factor in motivation. In F. M. Toates & T. R.

Halliday (Eds.), *Analysis of motivational processes* (pp. 153–77). London: Academic Press.

Lea, S. E. G. (1981). Animal experiments in economic psychology. *Journal of Economic Psychology, 1,* 245–71.

Lea, S. E. G. (1981). Concurrent fixed-ratio schedules for different reinforcers: A general theory. In C. M. Bradshaw, E. Szabadi, & C. F. Lowe (Eds.), *Quantification of steady-state operant behaviour* (pp. 101–12). Amsterdam: Elsevier.

Lea, S. E. G. (1981). Inflation, decimalization and the estimated size of coins. *Journal of Economic Psychology, 1,* 79–81.

Lea, S. E. G. (1981). Correlation and contiguity in foraging theory. In P. Harzem & M. D. Zeiler (Eds.), *Advances in analysis of behavior, Vol. 2: Prediction, correlation and contiguity* (pp. 355–406). Chichester: Wiley.

Lea, S. E. G. (1982). The mechanism of optimality in foraging. In M. L. Commons, R. J. Herrnstein, & H. Rachlin (Eds.), *Quantitative analyses of behavior, Vol. 2: Matching and maximizing accounts* (pp. 169–88). Cambridge, MA: Ballinger.

Lea, S. E. G. (1983). The analysis of need. In R. L. Mellgren (Ed.), *Animal cognition and behavior* (pp. 31–63). Amsterdam: North-Holland.

Lea, S. E. G. (1984). *Instinct, environment and behaviour.* London: Methuen.

Lea, S. E. G., & Roper, T. J. (1977). Demand for food on fixed-ratio schedules as a function of the quality of concurrently available reinforcement. *Journal of the Experimental Analysis of Behavior, 27,* 371–80.

Lea, S. E. G., & Tarpy, R. M. (1986). Hamsters' demand for food to eat and hoard as a function of deprivation and cost. *Animal Behaviour 34,* 1759–68.

Lea, S. E. G., & Webley, P. (1981). Theorie psychologique de la monnaie. Paper presented at the sixth international symposium on economic psychology, Paris.

Leahy, R. L. (1981). The development of the conception of economic inequality. I. Descriptions and comparisons of rich and poor people. *Child Development, 52,* 523–32.

Leahy, R. L. (1983a). The development of the conception of economic inequality. II. Explanations, justifications and concepts of social mobility and change. *Developmental Psychology, 19,* 111–25.

Leahy, R. L. (1983b). The development of the concept of social class. In R. L. Leahy (Ed.), *The child's construction of social inequality* (pp. 79–107). New York: Academic Press.

Leander, J. D., Lippman, L. G., & Meyer, M. E. (1968). Fixed-interval performance as related to subject's verbalizations of the reinforcement contingency. *Psychological Record, 18,* 469–74.

Leavitt, H. J. (1954). A note on some experimental findings about the meaning of price. *Journal of Business, 27,* 205–10.

LeClair, E. E. (1962). Economic theory and economic anthropology. *American Anthropologist, 64,* 1179–203.

Lee, T. (1962). "Brennan's Law" of shopping behavior. *Psychological Reports, 11,* 662.

Lefkowitz, M., Blake, R. R., & Mouton, J. S. (1955). Status factors in pedestrian violation of traffic signals. *Journal of Abnormal and Social Psychology, 51,* 704–6.

Lehrer, P., Schiff, L., & Kris, A. (1970). The use of a credit card in a token economy. *Journal of Applied Behavior Analysis, 3,* 289–91.

Leibenstein, H. (1950). Bandwagon, snob and Veblen effects in the theory of consumers' demand. *Quarterly Journal of Economics, 64,* 183–207.

References 581

Leimer, D. R., & Lesnoy, S. D. (1982). Social security and private saving: New time series evidence. *Journal of Political Economy, 90,* 606–29.

Leiss, W. (1978). *The limits to satisfaction.* London: Marion Boyars.

Lepper, M. R., & Greene, D. (1978). *The hidden costs of reward.* Hillsdale, NJ: Erlbaum.

Lepper, M. R., Greene, D., & Nisbett, R. E. (1973). Undermining childrens' intrinsic interest with extrinsic rewards: A test of the overjustification hypothesis. *Journal of Personality and Social Psychology, 23,* 129–37.

Lerner, D. E. (1958). *The passing of traditional society.* New York: Free Press.

Lerner, M. J. (1970). The desire for justice and reactions to victims. In J. Macaulay & L. Berkowitz (Eds.), *Altruism and helping behavior* (pp. 205–29). New York: Academic Press.

Lerner, M. J. (1974). Social psychology of justice and interpersonal attraction. In T. Huston (Ed.), *Foundations of interpersonal attraction* (pp. 331–51). New York: Academic Press.

Leuthold, J. H. (1983). Home production and the tax system. *Journal of Economic Psychology, 3,* 145–57.

Leventhal, H. (1970). Findings and theory in the study of fear communications. In L. Berkowitz (Ed.), *Advances in experimental social psychology* (Vol. 5, pp. 119–186). New York: Academic Press.

Levi-Strauss, C. (1965). The principle of reciprocity. In L. A. Coser & B. Rosenberg (Eds.), *Sociological theory* (pp. 74–84). New York: Macmillan.

Levin, S. R., Petros, T. V., & Petrella, F. W. (1983). Preschoolers' awareness of television advertising. *Child Development, 53,* 933–7.

Levine, F. M., & Fasnacht, G. (1974). Token rewards may lead to token learning. *American Psychologist, 29,* 816–20.

LeVine, R. A. (1966). *Dreams and needs: Achievement motivation in Nigeria.* Chicago: University of Chicago Press.

Lewis, A. (1978). Perceptions of tax rates. *British Tax Review, 6,* 358–66.

Lewis, A. (1979). An empirical assessment of tax mentality. *Public Finance, 2,* 245–57.

Lewis, A. (1982). *The psychology of taxation.* Oxford: Martin Robertson.

Lewis, D. J., & Duncan, C. P. (1957). Expectation and resistance to extinction of a lever pulling response as functions of percentage of reinforcement and amount of reward. *Journal of Experimental Psychology, 54,* 115–20.

Lewis, D. J., & Duncan, C. P. (1958). Expectation and resistance to extinction of a lever pulling response as a function of percentage of reinforcement and number of acquisition trials. *Journal of Experimental Psychology, 55,* 121–8.

Lewis, I. M. (1976). *Social anthropology in perspective.* Harmondsworth: Penguin.

Liberman, R. P., Ferris, C., Salgado, P., & Salgado, J. (1975). Replication of the Achievement Place model in California. *Journal of Applied Behavior Analysis, 8,* 287–99.

Lichtenstein, S. (1965). Bases for preferences among three-outcome bets. *Journal of Experimental Psychology, 69,* 162–9.

Lichtenstein, S., & Slovic, P. (1971). Reversals of preference between bids and choices in gambling decisions. *Journal of Experimental Psychology, 89,* 46–55.

Lichtenstein, S., & Slovic, P. (1973). Response-induced reversals of preference in gambling: An extended replication in Las Vegas. *Journal of Experimental Psychology, 101,* 16–20.

Lichtenstein, S., Slovic, P., & Zink, D. (1969). Effect of instruction in expected value on optimality of gambling decisions. *Journal of Experimental Psychology, 79,* 236–40.

Liebert, R., Sprafkin, J., Leibert, R., & Rubinstein, E. (1977). Effects of television commercial disclaimers on the product expectations of children. *Journal of Communication, 27,* 118–24.

Liebson, I., Cohen, M., & Faillace, L. (1972). Group fines: Technique for behavioral control in a token economy. *Psychological Reports, 30,* 895–900.

Light, P. H. (1979). *The development of social sensitivity.* Cambridge: Cambridge University Press.

Likert, R. (1932). A technique for the measurement of attitudes. *Archives of Psychology, 140,* 44–53.

Lilien, G. L. (1973–4). A modified linear learning model of buyer behavior. *Management Science, 7,* 1027–36.

Linder, D. E., Cooper, J., & Jones, E. E. (1967). Decision freedom as a determinant of the role of incentive magnitude in attitude change. *Journal of Personality and Social Psychology, 6,* 245–54.

Lindner, R. M. (1950). The psychodynamics of gambling. *Annals of the American Academy of Political and Social Science, 268,* 93–107.

Lindquist, A., & Warneryd, K-E. (1982). *The income tax system and the willingness to be promoted among Swedish middle management.* Paper presented at the seventh international symposium on economic psychology, Edinburgh.

Lindqvist, A. (1981). A note on determinants of household saving behavior. *Journal of Economic Psychology, 1,* 39–57.

Lipsey, R. G. (1979). *An introduction to positive economics* (5th ed.). London: Weidenfeld and Nicolson.

Livesley, W. J., & Bromley, D. B. (1973). *Person perception in childhood and adolescence.* London: Wiley.

Lluch, C., Powell, A. A., & Williams, R. A. (1977). *Patterns in household demand and saving.* Oxford: Oxford University Press.

Locke, J. (1777). Some considerations of the consequences of the lowering of interest and raising the value of money. In *The works of John Locke* (8th ed., Vol. 2, pp. 1–84). London: W. Strahan and others. (Originally published 1691.)

Locke, J. (1961). *An essay concerning the human understanding.* Vol. 1. London: Dent. (Originally published, 1690).

Logan, F. A. (1960). *Incentive.* New Haven, CT: Yale University Press.

Logan, F. A. (1965a). Decision-making by rats: Delay versus amount of reward. *Journal of Comparative and Physiological Psychology, 59,* 1–12.

Logan, F. A. (1965b). Decision-making by rats: Uncertain outcome choices. *Journal of Comparative and Physiological Psychology, 59,* 246–51.

Lorenz, K. (1950). The comparative method of studying innate behavior patterns. *Symposia of the Society for Experimental Biology, 4,* 221–68.

Lowe, C. F. (1979). Determinants of human operant behavior. In M. D. Zeiler & P. Harzem (Eds.), *Reinforcement and the organization of behavior* (Vol. 1). New York: Wiley.

Lowe, C. F., Beasty, A., & Bentall, R. P. (1983). The role of verbal behavior in human learning: Infant performance on fixed-interval schedules. *Journal of the Experimental Analysis of Behavior, 39,* 157–64.

Lowe, C. F., Harzem, P., & Bagshaw, M. (1978). Species differences in temporal control of behavior: II. Human performance. *Journal of the Experimental Analysis of Behavior, 29,* 351–61.

Lowes, B., Turner, J., & Wills, G. (1971). Patterns of gift giving. In G. Wills (Ed.), *Explorations in marketing thought* (pp. 82–102). London: Bradford University Press.

Lucas, R. E. B. (1977). Hedonic wage equations and psychic wages in the returns to schooling. *American Economic Review, 67,* 549–58.

Luce, R. D. (1959). *Individual choice behavior.* New York: Wiley.

Luce, R. D., & Tukey, J. W. (1964). Simultaneous conjoint measurement: A new type of fundamental measurement. *Journal of Mathematical Psychology, 1,* 1–27.

Lumsden, C. J., & Wilson, E. O. (1981). *Genes, mind and culture.* Cambridge, MA: Harvard University Press.

Lumsden, C. J., & Wilson, E. O. (1983). *Promethean fire.* Cambridge, MA: Harvard University Press.

Luthans, F., & Davis, T. R. V. (1979). Behavioral self-management: The missing link in managerial effectiveness. *Organizational Dynamics, 8,* 42–60.

Luthans, F., & Kreitner, R. (1975). *Organizational behavior modification.* Glenview, IL: Scott Foresman.

Lutz, R. J. (1977). An experimental investigation of causal relations among cognitions, affect and behavioral intention. *Journal of Consumer Research, 3,* 197–208.

Lydall, H. F. (1959). The long term trend in the size distribution of income. *Journal of the Royal Statistical Society A, 122,* 1–37.

Lydall, H. F. (1968). *The structure of earnings.* Oxford: Clarendon.

Maccoby, N., & Alexander, J. (1980). Use of media in lifestyle programs. In P. O. Davidson & S. M. Davidson (Eds.), *Behavioral medicine; changing health lifestyles* (pp. 351–70). New York: Brunner/Mazel.

MacCrimmon, K. R., & Toda, M. (1969). The experimental determination of indifference curves. *Review of Economic Studies, 36,* 433–51.

MacKay, D. B., & Olshavsky, R. W. (1975–6). Cognitive maps of retail locations: An investigation of some basic issues. *Journal of Consumer Research, 2,* 197–205.

Maier, N. R. F. (1931). Reasoning in humans: II. The solution of a problem and its appearance in consciousness. *Journal of Comparative Psychology, 12,* 181–94.

Maier, N. R. F. (1970). *Psychology in industry* (3rd ed.). London: Harrap. (Original work published 1946).

Maital, S. (1982). *Minds, markets and money.* New York: Basic Books.

Maital, S. (1984). *The psychology of macroeconomic conflict.* Paper presented at the ninth international symposium on economic psychology, Tilburg, June.

Malagodi, E. F. (1967) Acquisition of the token reward habit in the rat. *Psychological Reports, 20,* 1335–42.

Maley, R. F., Feldman, G. L., & Ruskin, R. S. (1973). Evaluation of patient improvement in a token economy treatment program. *Journal of Abnormal Psychology, 82,* 141–4.

Malinowski, B. (1922). *Argonauts of the western pacific.* London: Routledge and Kegan Paul.

Mandeville, B. de (1924). *The fable of the bees.* Vols. 1 and 2. Oxford: Clarendon. (Originally published 1714–1729).

Mansfield, E. (1975). *Microeconomics: Theory and applications* (2nd ed.). New York: Norton.

Manstead, A. S. R., & McCulloch, C. (1981). Sex-role stereotyping in British television advertisements. *British Journal of Social Psychology, 20,* 171–180.

Manstead, A. S. R., Proffitt, C., & Smart, J. L. (1983). Predicting and understanding mother's infant feeding intentions and behavior: Testing the theory of reasoned action. *Journal of Personality and Social Psychology, 44,* 657–71.

Marcel, A. J. (1983). Conscious and unconscious perception: experiments on visual masking and word recognition. *Cognitive Psychology, 15,* 197–237.

Markowitz, H. (1975). Analysis and control of behavior in the zoo. In *Research in zoos and aquariums.* Washington, DC: National Academy of Sciences.

Marlatt, G. A. (1970). A comparison of vicarious and direct reinforcement control of verbal behavior in an interview setting. *Journal of Personality and Social Psychology, 16,* 695–703.

Marshall, A. (1949). *Principles of economics* (8th ed.). London: Macmillan. (Originally published 1920.)

Marshall, H., & Magruder, L. (1960). Relations between parent money education practices and children's knowledge and use of money. *Child Development, 31,* 253–84.

Marshall, J. R., & Funch, J. P. (1979). Mental illness and the economy: A critique and partial replication. *Journal of Health and Social Behavior, 20,* 282–9.

Martin, F. A., & Lopez, J. G. (1984). *Taxation and income distribution.* Paper presented at the ninth international symposium on economic psychology, Tilburg.

Martineau, P. (1958). Social classes and spending behavior. *Journal of Marketing, 23*(1), 121–30.

Marx, K. (1962). Critique of the Gotha programme. In K. Marx & F. Engels, *Selected works in two volumes.* (Vol 2, pp. 18–37). Moscow: Foreign Languages Publishing House. (Original work published 1875.)

Marx, K. (1965). *Wages, price and profit.* Beijing: Foreign Languages Press. (Original edition published 1898).

Marx, K. (1969). Thesen ueber Feuerbach. In K. Marx and F. Engels, *Werke* (Vol. 3). Berlin: Dietz. (Originally published 1845).

Marx, K. (1974). *Capital.* London: Lawrence and Wishart. (Original work published 1867.)

Marx, K. (1975). Economic and political manuscripts. In K. Marx, *Early writings* (pp. 279–400). Harmondsworth: Penguin. (Originally published 1844.)

Maslach, C. (1979). Negative emotional biasing of unexplained arousal. *Journal of Personality and Social Psychology, 12,* 158–63.

Maslow, A. H. (1943). A theory of human motivation. *Psychological Review, 50,* 370–96.

Maslow, A. H. (1970). *Motivation and personality.* New York: Harper & Row. (Originally published 1954).

Mason, R. S. (1981). *Conspicuous consumption.* Farnborough: Gower.

Massy, W. F., Montgomery, D. B., & Morrison, D. G. (1970). *Stochastic models of buying behavior.* Cambridge, MA: MIT Press.

Masterton, J. F., & Vaux, A. C. (1982). The use of a token economy to regulate household communities. *Behavioral Psychotherapy, 10,* 75–8

Matsui, T., Kagawa, M., Nagamatsu, J., & Ohtsuka, Y. (1977). Validity of expectancy theory as a within-person behavioral choice model for sales activities. *Journal of Applied Psychology, 62,* 764–7.

Matter, D. E. (1977). High-school graduates' achievement motivation and the prediction of the economic development of a small midwestern community from 1907 to 1977. *Psychological Reports, 41,* 167–72.

Matthews, B. A., Shimoff, E., & Catania, A. C. (1977). Uninstructed human responding: Sensitivity to ratio and interval contingencies. *Journal of the Experimental Analysis of Behavior, 27,* 453–67.

Maurice, R. (1968). *National accounts statistics: sources and methods*. London: Her Majesty's Stationery Office.

Maurizi, A. R. (1972). The effect of laws against price advertising: The case of retail gasoline. *Western Economic Journal, 10*, 321-9.

Mauss, M. (1954). *The gift: Forms and functions of exchange in archaic societies* (Ian Cunnison, Trans.). London: Routledge & Kegan Paul.

May, K. O. (1954). Intransitivity, utility, and the aggregation of preference patterns. *Econometrica, 22*, 1-13.

Maynard Smith, J. (1966). *The theory of evolution*. Harmondsworth: Penguin.

Maynard Smith, J. (1984). Game theory and the evolution of behaviour. *Behavioral and Brain Sciences, 7*, 95-125.

Mayo, E. (1933). *The human problems of an industrial civilization*. New York: Macmillan.

Mazur, A., & Rosa, E. (1977). An empirical test of McClelland's "achieving society" theory. *Social Forces, 55*, 769-74.

Mazur, J. E. (1975). The matching law and quantifications related to Premack's principle. *Journal of Experimental Psychology: Animal Behaviour Processes, 1*, 374-86.

McArthur, L. A. (1972). The how and what of why: Some determinants and consequences of causal attribution. *Journal of Personality and Social Psychology, 22*, 171-93.

McCauley, C., Stitt, C. L., Woods, K., & Lipton, D. (1973). Group shift to caution at the race track. *Journal of Experimental Social Psychology, 9*, 80-6.

McClelland, D. C. (1961). *The achieving society*. Princeton, NJ: Van Nostrand.

McClelland, D. C. (1977). The psychological causes and consequences of modernization: an Ethiopian case study. In M. Nash (Ed.), *Essays on economic development and cultural change in honor of Bert F. Hoselitz* (pp. 43-66). Chicago: University of Chicago Press.

McClelland, D. C., Clark, R. A., Roby, T. B., & Atkinson, J. W. (1949). The projective expression of needs. IV. The effect of the need for achievement on thematic apperception. *Journal of Experimental Psychology, 39*, 242-55.

McClelland, D. C., & Winter, D. G. (1969). *Motivating economic achievement*. New York: Free Press.

McCrohan, K. F. (1982). The use of survey research to estimate trends in non-compliance with federal income taxes. *Journal of Economic Psychology, 2*, 231-40.

McCullough, M. L. (1983). A testing time for the test of time. *Bulletin of the British Psychological Society, 36*, 1-5.

McDonald, C. (1970, November). What is the short-term effect of advertising? *Admap*, 350-6; 366.

McDougall, W. (1932). *The energies of men*. London: Methuen.

McEwen, W. J. (1977-8). Bridging the information gap. *Journal of Consumer Research, 4*, 247-51.

McGoldrick, P. J. (1982). The development and positioning of generic grocery ranges in Britain. Paper read at the ninth International Marketing Research Seminar, Aix-en-Provence, June.

McGuinness, T., & Cowling, K. (1975). Advertising and the aggregate demand for cigarettes. *European Economic Review, 6*, 311-28.

McGuire, T. W. (1977). Measuring and testing relative advertising effectiveness with split-cable TV panel data. *Journal of the American Statistical Association, 72*, 736-45.

McGuire, W. J. (1968). Personality and susceptibility to social influence. In E. F. Borgatta & W. W. Lambert (Eds.), *Handbook of Personality Theory and Research* (pp. 1130–87). Chicago: Rand McNally.

McGuire, W. J. (1969). The nature of attitudes and attitude change. In G. Lindzey & E. Aronson (Eds.), *Handbook of social psychology* (2nd ed., Vol. 3, pp. 136–314). New York: Addison-Wesley.

McGuire, W. J. (1972). Attitude change: The information-processing paradigm. In C. G. McClintock (Ed.), *Experimental social psychology*. New York: Holt, Rinehart & Winston.

McGuire, W. J. (1980). Communication and social influence processes. In M. Feldman & J. Orford (Eds.), *Psychological problems: The social context* (pp. 341–65). London: Wiley.

McKinnon, J. W., & Renner, J. W. (1971). Are colleges concerned with intellectual development? *American Journal of Physics, 39,* 1047–52.

McLaughlin, T. F., & Malaby, J. E. (1975). The effects of various token reinforcement contingencies on assignment completion and accuracy during variable and fixed token exchange schedules. *Canadian Journal of Behavioural Science, 7,* 411–9.

McNeil, J. (1974-5). Federal programs to measure consumer purchase expectations: A post-mortem. *Journal of Consumer Research, 1,* 1–10.

McReynolds, W. T., & Coleman, J. (1972). Token economy: Patient and staff changes. *Behaviour Research and Therapy, 10,* 29–34.

Meadowes, D. L., & others (1972). *The limits to growth.* New York: Universe.

Meichenbaum, D. (1977). *Cognitive behavior modification: An integrative approach.* New York: Plenum.

Meichenbaum, D. H. (1969). The effects of instructions and reinforcement on thinking and language behavior of schizophrenics. *Behavior Research and Therapy, 7,* 101–14.

Melitz, J. (1970). The Polanyi school of anthropology on money: An economist's view. *American Anthropologist, 72,* 1020–40.

Menchik, P. L., & David, M. (1983). Income distribution, lifetime savings, and bequests. *American Economic Review, 73,* 672–90.

Mendelsohn, H. (1973). Some reasons why information campaigns can succeed. *Public Opinion Quarterly, 37,* 50–61.

Meringoff, L. (1980). *Children and advertising: An annotated bibliography.* New York: Council of Better Business Bureaus Inc.

Merrens, M. R. (1973). Nonemergency helping behavior in various sized communities. *Journal of Social Psychology, 90,* 327–8.

Messick, S. J. (1967). The psychology of acquiescence: an interpretation of the research evidence. In I. A. Berg (Ed.), *Response set in personality assessment* (pp. 115–45). Chicago: Aldine.

Metcalfe, D., Nickell, S., & Richardson, R. (1976). The structure of hours and earnings in British manufacturing industry. *Oxford Economic Papers, 28,* 284–303.

Metzner, H., & Mann, F. (1953). Employee attitudes and attitudes. *Personnel Psychology, 6,* 467–85.

Meyers, H., Nathan, P. E., & Kopel, S. A. (1977). Effects of a token reinforcement system on journal reshelving. *Journal of Applied Behavior Analysis, 10,* 212–8.

Midgeley, D. F., & Dowling, G. R. (1977-8). Innovativeness: the concept and its measurement. *Journal of Consumer Research, 4,* 229–42.

Midgely, D. F. (1976–7). A simple mathematical model of innovative behavior. *Journal of Consumer Research, 3,* 31–41.

Midgley, M. (1984). Misbehaviour and autoshaping: The effects of varying the length of the intertrial interval and the type of reinforcement on misbehaviour. Paper presented at the Experimental Analysis of Behaviour Group, Sussex, England.

Midlarsky, E., Bryan, J. H., & Brickman, P. (1973). Aversive approval: Interactive effects of modeling and reinforcement on altruistic behavior. *Child Development, 44,* 321–8.

Mikesell, J. L. (1978). Election periods and state tax policy cycles. *Public Choice, 33,* 99–106.

Milby, J. B. (1976). A review of token economy treatment programs for psychiatric patients. *Hospital and Community Psychiatry, 26,* 651–8.

Milby, J. B., Clarke, C., Charles, E., & Willicutt, H. C. (1977). Token economy process variables: Effects of increasing and decreasing the critical range of savings. *Behavior Therapy, 8,* 137–45.

Milby, J. B., Pendergrass, P. E., & Clarke, C. J. (1975). Token economy versus control ward: A comparison of staff and patient attitudes toward ward environment. *Behavior Therapy, 6,* 22–9.

Milby, J. B., Willcutt, H. C., Hawk, J. W., MacDonald, M., & Whitfield, K. (1973). A system for recording individualized behavioral data in a token program. *Journal of Applied Behavior Analysis, 6,* 333–8.

Miles, C. G., Congreve, G. R. S., Gibbins, R. J., Marshman, J., Devenyi, P., & Hicks, R. C. (1974). An experimental study of the effects of daily cannabis smoking on behaviour patterns. *Acta Pharmacologica et Toxicologica, 34* (Supp. 1), 1–44.

Milgram, S. (1970). The experience of living in cities. *Science, 167,* 1461–68.

Milgram, S., Mann, L., & Horter, S. (1965). The lost-letter technique of social research. *Public Opinion Quarterly, 29,* 437–8.

Miller, C., & Crandall, R. (1980). Bargaining and negotiation. In P. B. Paulus (Ed.), *Psychology of group influence* (pp. 333–74). Hillsdale, NJ: Erlbaum.

Miller, D. T., & Smith, J. (1977). The effect of own deservingness and deservingness of others on children's helping behavior. *Child Development, 48,* 617–20.

Miller, D. T., Weinstein, S. M., & Karniol, R. (1978). Effects of age and self-verbalization on children's ability to delay gratification. *Developmental Psychology, 14,* 569–70.

Miller, N. E. (1959). Liberalisation of basic S-R concepts: Extension to conflict behavior, motivation, and social learning. In S. Koch (Ed.), *Psychology: A study of a science: Study 1* (Vol. 2, pp. 196–292). New York: McGraw-Hill.

Miller, N., Maruyama, G., Beaber, R. J., & Valone, K. (1976). Speed of speech and persuasion. *Journal of Personality and Social Psychology, 34,* 615–24.

Miller, N. E., & Dollard, J. (1941) *Social learning and imitation.* New Haven, CT: Yale University Press.

Miniard, P. W., & Cohen, J. B. (1981). An examination of the Fishbein-Azjen behavioral intentions model's concepts and measures. *Journal of Experimental Social Psychology, 17,* 309–39.

Mirels, H. L., & Garrett, J. B. (1971). The Protestant Ethic as a personality variable. *Journal of Consulting and Clinical Psychology, 36,* 40–4.

Mirer, T. W. (1979). The wealth-age relation among the aged. *American Economic Review, 69,* 435–43.

Mischel, H. N., & Mischel, W. (1983). The development of children's knowledge of self-control strategies. *Child Development, 54*, 603–19.

Mischel, W. (1958). Preference for delayed reinforcement: An experimental study of a cultural observation. *Journal of Abnormal and Social Psychology, 56*, 57–61.

Mischel, W. (1961a). Delay of gratification, need for achievement, and acquiescence in another culture. *Journal of Abnormal and Social Psychology, 62*, 1–7.

Mischel, W. (1961b). Father absence and delay of gratification: Cross-cultural comparisons. *Journal of Abnormal and Social Psychology, 63*, 116–24.

Mischel, W., & Ebbesen, E. B. (1970). Attention in delay of gratification. *Journal of Personality and Social Psychology, 16*, 329–37.

Mischel, W., Ebbesen, E. B., & Zeiss, A. (1972). Cognitive and attentional mechanisms in delay of gratification. *Journal of Personality and Social Psychology, 21*, 204–18.

Mischel, W., & Metzner, R. (1962). Preference for delayed reward as a function of age, intelligence, and length of delay interval. *Journal of Abnormal and Social Psychology, 64*, 425–31.

Mischel, W., & Moore, B. (1973). Effects of attention to symbolically presented rewards on self-control. *Journal of Personality and Social Psychology, 28*, 172–9.

Mischel, W., & Moore, B. (1980). The role of ideation in voluntary delay for symbolically presented rewards. *Cognitive Therapy and Research, 4*, 211–21.

Mishan, E. J. (1969). *21 popular economic fallacies*. London: Allen Lane.

Mishara, B. L., & Kastenbaum, R. (1974). Wine in the treatment of long-term geriatric patients in mental institutions. *Journal of the American Geriatrics Society, 22*, 88–94.

Mitchell, A. A., & Olson, J. C. (1981). Are product attribute beliefs the only mediator of advertising effects on brand attitude. *Journal of Marketing Research, 18*, 318–32.

Mitchell, T. R. (1974). Expectancy models of job satisfaction, occupational preference and effort: A theoretical, methodological, and empirical appraisal. *Psychological Bulletin, 84*, 1053–77.

Mitchell, V. F., & Moudgill, P. (1976). Measurement of Maslow's need hierarchy. *Organizational Behavior and Human Performance, 16*, 334–49.

Modigliani, F. (1970). The life-cycle hypothesis and inter-country differences. In W. Eltis (Ed.), *Inflation, growth and trade* (pp. 197–255). Oxford: Clarendon.

Modigliani, F., & Brumberg, R. (1954). Utility analysis and the consumption function: An interpretation of cross-sectional data. In K. K. Kurihara (Ed.), *Post-Keynesian economics* (pp. 388–438). New Brunswick, NJ: Rutgers University Press.

Moessinger, P. (1975). Developmental study of fair division and property. *European Journal of Social Psychology, 5*, 385–94.

Moles, A. A. (1972). *Theorie des objets*. Paris: Editions Universitaires.

Montgomery, K. C. (1954). The role of exploratory drive in learning. *Journal of Comparative and Physiological Psychology, 47*, 60–4.

Moore, B., Mischel, W., & Zeiss, A. (1976). Comparative effects of the reward stimulus and its cognitive representation in voluntary delay. *Journal of Personality and Social Psychology, 34*, 419–24.

Moore, W. L., & Lehmann, D. R. (1980–81). Individual differences in search behavior for a non-durable. *Journal of Consumer Research, 7*, 296–307.

Moran, E. (1970). Varieties of pathological gambling. *British Journal of Psychiatry, 116*, 593–7.

Morawetz, D., & others (1977). Income distribution and self-rated happiness: Some empirical evidence. *Economic Journal, 87,* 511–22.

Morehead, A. H. (1950). The professional gambler. *Annals of the American Academy of Political and Social Science, 269,* 81–92.

Morgan, C. D., & Murray, H. A. (1935). A method for investigating fantasies: The thematic apperception test. *Archives of Neurology and Psychiatry, 34,* 289–94.

Morgan, C. T., Stellar, E., & Johnson, O. (1943). Food-deprivation and hoarding in rats. *Journal of Comparative Psychology, 35,* 275–95.

Morgan, J. N. (1964). The achievement motive and economic behavior. *Economic Development and Cultural Change, 12,* 243–67.

Morgan, K. J., Metzen, E. J., & Johnson, S. R. (1979–80). An hedonic index for breakfast cereals. *Journal of Consumer Research, 6,* 67–75.

Morris, M. D. (1979). *Measuring the condition of the world's poor.* New York: Pergamon.

Morris, P. (1975). New forms for old. *Community Care* (January 22).

Morse, N.C., & Weiss, R.S. (1955). The function and meaning of work and the job. *American Sociological Review, 20,* 191–8.

Moschis, G. P., & Moore, R. L. (1979) Decision making among the young: A socialization perspective. *Journal of Consumer Research, 6,* 101–12.

Moschis, G. P., & Moore, R. L. (1982). A longitudinal study of television advertising effects. *Journal of Consumer Research, 9,* 279–86.

Mosley, P. (1982). *The economy as presented in the popular press.* Paper presented at the seventh international symposium on economic psychology, Edinburgh.

Moscovici, S. (1972). Society and theory in social psychology. In J. Israel & H. Tajfel (Eds.), *The context of social psychology* (pp. 17–68). New York: Academic Press.

Mosteller, F., & Nogee, P. (1951). An experimental measurement of utility. *Journal of Political Economy, 59,* 371–404.

Mueller, E., & Lean, J. A. (1967). The savings account as a source for financing large expenditures. *Journal of Finance, 22,* 375–93.

Mundell, R. (1963). Inflation and real interest. *Journal of Political Economy, 71,* 280–3.

Munnell, A. H. (1976). Private pensions and saving: New evidence. *Journal of Political Economy, 84,* 1013–32.

Munson, R. F. (1962). Decision-making in an actual gambling situation. *American Journal of Psychology, 75,* 640–3.

Muraz, R. (1977). *La parole aux francais: cinq ans de sondages, dossier publimetrique 1972–77.* Paris: Dunod.

Murdock, S. H., & Schriner, E. C. (1979). Community service satisfaction and stages of community development: An examination from impacted communities. *Journal of the Community Development Society, 10,* 109–24.

Murphy, G., Murphy, L. B., & Newcomb, T. M. (1937). *Experimental Social Psychology.* New York: Harper & Brothers.

Murray, H. A. (1938). *Explorations in personality.* New York: Oxford University Press.

Myers, G. C. (1934). The present crisis and the mental health of the school child. *Mental Hygiene, 18,* 294–8.

Nathanson, C. A. (1980). Social roles and health status among women: the significance of employment. *Social Science and Medicine, 14A,* 463–72.

Naumov, N. P., & Lobachev, V. S. (1975). Ecology of desert rodents of the U. S.

S. R. (jerboas and gerbils). In I. Prakash & P. K. Ghosh (Eds.), *Rodents in desert environments* (pp. 465–598). The Hague: Junk.

Navarick, D. J., & Fantino, E. (1972). Transitivity as a property of choice. *Journal of the Experimental Analysis of Behavior, 18,* 389–401.

Navarick, D. J., & Fantino, E. (1974). Stochastic transitivity and unidimensional behavior theories. *Psychological Review, 81,* 426–41.

Naylor, T. H. (1971). *Computer simulation experiments with models of economic systems.* New York: Wiley.

Naylor, T. H. (1972). Experimental economics revisited. *Journal of Political Economy, 80,* 347–52.

Newman, J. W. (1977). Consumer external search: Amount and determinants. In A. G. Woodside, J. N. Sheth, & P. D. Bennett (Eds.), *Consumer and industrial buying behavior* (pp. 79–94). New York: North-Holland.

Newman, J. W., & Lockeman, B. D. (1976–7). Measuring prepurchase information seeking. *Journal of Consumer Research, 2,* 216–27.

Newson, J., & Newson, E. (1976). *Seven years old in the home environment.* London: Allen & Unwin.

Newspapers are the public's favorite ad medium. (1975, March 29). *Editor and Publisher,* p. 12.

Ng, S. H. (1983). Children's ideas about the bank and shop profit: Developmental stages and the influence of cognitive contrasts and conflict. *Journal of Economic Psychology, 4,* 209–21.

Nicholson, R. J. (1973). The distribution of personal income. In A. B. Atkinson (Ed.), *Wealth, income and inequality* (pp. 99–110). Harmondsworth: Penguin.

Nickols, S. Y., & Fox, K. D. (1983–4). Buying time and saving time: Strategies for managing household production. *Journal of Consumer Research, 10,* 197–208.

Nicosia, F. M. (1966). *Consumer decision processes.* Englewood Cliffs, NJ: Prentice-Hall.

Nilsson, D. E. (1976). Treatment of encopresis: Token economy. *Journal of Pediatric Psychology, 4,* 42–6.

Nisan, M. (1974). Exposure to rewards and the delay of gratification. *Developmental Psychology, 10,* 376–80.

Nisbett, R. E., & Borgida, E. (1975). Attribution and the psychology of prediction. *Journal of Personality and Social Psychology, 32,* 932–43.

Nisbett, R. E., Borgida, E., Crandall, R., & Reed, H. (1976). Popular induction: Information is not always informative. In J. S. Carroll & J. W. Payne (Eds.), *Cognition and social behavior* (pp. 113–33). Hillsdale, NJ: Erlbaum.

Nisbett, R. E., & Wilson, T. D. (1977). Telling more than we can know. *Psychological Review, 84,* 231–59.

Nishio, H. K. (1972). The changing Japanese perspectives and attitudes towards leisure. *Humanitas, 8,* 367–88.

Noam, E. M. (1981). Public preferences for economic policies. *Journal of Economic Psychology, 1,* 273–81.

Noblin, C.D. (1962). Experimental analysis of psychoanalytic character types through the operant conditioning of verbal responses. Unpublished Ph.D. dissertation. Louisiana State University.

Nordhaus, W. (1975). The political business cycle. *Review of Economic Studies, 42,* 169–90.

Norman, R. (1975). Affective-cognitive consistency, attitudes, conformity and behavior. *Journal of Personality and Social Psychology, 32,* 83–91.

Norman, R. (1976). When what is said is important: A comparison of expert and attractive sources. *Journal of Experimental Social Psychology, 12,* 294–300.

Northrop, J. T. (1978). Money saving by children: The effects of interest and instructions. *Dissertations Abstracts International, 39,* 2479B.

Novak, G., & Hammond, J. M. (1983). Self-reinforcement and descriptive praise in maintaining token economy reading performance. *Journal of Educational Research, 76,* 186–9.

Nuttin, J. M. (1974). *The illusion of attitude change: Towards a response contagion theory of persuasion.* New York: Academic Press.

O'Bryant, S. L., & Corder-Bolz, C. R. (1978). Black children's learning of work roles from television commercials. *Psychological Reports, 42,* 227–30.

O'Leary, K. D., & Drabman, R. (1971). Token reinforcement programs in the classroom: A review. *Psychological Bulletin, 75,* 379–98.

Oakley, A. (1974). *The sociology of housework.* Oxford: Martin Robertson.

Oakley, A. (1980). For love or money: The unspoken deal. *New Society, 54,* 564–5 (iv–vi).

Olander, F., & Seipel, C. M. (1970). *Psychological approaches to the study of saving.* Urbana, IL: University of Illinois.

Oldman, D. J. (1974). Chance and skill: A study of roulette. *Sociology, 8,* 407–26.

Olshavsky, R. W. (1979–80). Time and the rate of adoption of innovations. *Journal of Consumer Research, 6,* 425–8.

Olshavsky, R. W., & Granbois, D. H. (1979–80). Consumer decision making – fact or fiction? *Journal of Consumer Research, 6,* 93–100.

Olson, J. C., Toy, D. R., & Dover, P. A. (1982). Do cognitive responses mediate the effects of advertising content on advertising structure. *Journal of Consumer Research, 9,* 245–62.

Oommen, T. T. (1961). Social factors in mobilizing small savings in India. *Indian Journal of Social Work, 22,* 193–5.

Opie, I., & Opie, P. (1969). *Children's games in street and playground.* Oxford: Oxford University Press.

Orlando, R., & Bijou, S. W. (1960). Single and multiple schedules of reinforcement in developmentally retarded children. *Journal of the Experimental Analysis of Behavior, 3,* 339–48.

Orne, M. T. (1962). On the social psychology of the psychological experiment. *American Psychologist, 17,* 776–83.

Ortiz, L., & Garzon, C. R. (1978). [Modification of urinating behavior of enuretic preadolescents using a token economy]. *Aprendizaja y Comportamiento, 1,* 75–86.

Osborne, S. R. (1977). The free food (contrafreeloading) phenomenon – a review and analysis. *Animal Learning and Behavior, 5,* 221–35.

Osborne, S. R. (1978). A quantitative analysis of the effects of amount of reinforcement on two response classes. *Journal of Experimental Psychology: Animal Behavior Processes, 4,* 297–317.

Osgood, C. E., Suci, G. I., & Tannenbaum, P. H. (1957). *The measurement of meaning.* Urbana, IL: University of Illinois Press.

Oskamp, S. (1971). Effects of programmed strategies on cooperation in the Prisoner's Dilemma and other mixed-motive games. *Journal of Conflict Resolution, 15,* 225–59.

Owen, J. D. (1971). The demand for leisure. *Journal of Political Economy, 79,* 56–76.

Packard, V. (1960). *The hidden persuaders.* Harmondsworth: Penguin.

Padgett, V. R., & Jorgenson, D. O. (1982). Superstition and economic threat: Germany 1918–1940. *Personality and Social Psychology Bulletin, 8,* 736–41.

Paish, F. W. (1957). The real incidence of personal taxation. *Lloyds Bank Review, 43,* 1–16.

Panoff, M. (1970). Marcel Mauss' "The Gift" revisited. *Man, 5,* 60–70.

Papandreou, A. G. (1957). A test of a stochastic theory of choice. *University of California Publications in Economics, 16,* 1–18.

Parker, S. (1980). *Older workers and retirement.* London: Her Majesty's Stationery Office.

Parker, S. (1982). *Work and retirement.* London: Allen & Unwin.

Parkin, D. (1979). The categorisation of work. In S. Wallman (Ed.), *The social anthropology of work* (pp. 317–35). London: Academic Press.

Parkin, M., & Bade, R. (1982). *Modern macroeconomics.* Oxford: Philip Allan.

Paroush, J. (1965). The order of acquisition of consumer durables. *Econometrica, 33,* 225–35.

Parsons, T. (1951). *The social system.* London: Routledge and Kegan Paul.

Parsons, T. (1960). *The social system.* Glencoe, IL: Free Press.

Pascale, R. T., & Athos, A. G. (1982). *The art of Japanese management.* Harmondsworth: Penguin.

Patterson, D. (1983). *The unemployed and their changing patterns of consumer behaviour.* Unpublished undergraduate project, University of Exeter, Department of Psychology, Exeter.

Payne, J. W. (1973). Alternative approaches to decision making under risk: Moments versus risk dimensions. *Psychological Bulletin, 80,* 493–53.

Payne, J. W., & Braunstein, M. L. (1971). Preferences among gambles with equal underlying distributions. *Journal of Experimental Psychology, 87,* 13–8.

Payne, L. C., & Morgan, H. M. (1981). UK currency needs in the 1980's. *The Banker,* April, 45–53.

Peak, H. (1955). Attitudes and motivation. In M. R. Jones (Ed.), *Nebraska symposium on motivation* (pp. 149–88). Lincoln, NE: University of Nebraska Press.

Pearce, D. W. (1981). *The Macmillan dictionary of modern economics.* London: Macmillan.

Pearlin, L. I., & Lieberman, M. A. (1979). Social sources of emotional distress. In R. Simmons (Ed.), *Research in community and mental health.* Greenwich, CT: JAI.

Pearse, A. (1980). *Seeds of plenty, seeds of want.* Oxford: Clarendon.

Pen, J. (1971). *Income distribution.* London: Allen Lane.

Pennington, A. L. (1968). Customer-salesman bargaining in retail transactions. *Journal of Marketing Research, 5,* 255–62.

Pettigrew, J. (1979). The ultimate attribution error: Extending Allport's cognitive analysis of prejudice. *Personality and Social Psychology Bulletin, 5,* 461–76.

Petty, R. E., & Cacioppo, J. T. (1980). Effects of issue involvement on attitudes in a marketing context. In G. G. Gorn & M. Goldberg (Eds.), *Proceedings of the Division 23 program* (pp. 75–9). Montreal: American Psychological Association.

Petty, R. E., & Cacioppo, J. T. (1981). *Attitudes and persuasion: classic and contemporary approaches.* Dubuque, IA: William C. Brown.

Petty, R. E., & Cacioppo, J. T. (1984). The effects of involvement on responses to argument quantity and quality: Central and peripheral routes to persuasion. *Journal of Personality and Social Psychology, 46,* 69–81.

Petty, R. E., Cacioppo, J. T., & Schumann, D. (1983). Central and peripheral routes to advertising effectiveness: the moderating role of involvement. *Journal of Consumer Research, 10,* 135–46.

Petty, R. E., Wells, G. L., & Brock, T. C. (1976). Distraction can enhance or reduce yielding to propaganda: Thought disruption versus effort disruption. *Journal of Personality and Social Psychology, 34,* 874–84.

Phelps Brown, H. (1977). *The inequality of pay.* Oxford: Oxford University Press.

Phillips, A. W. (1958). The relation between unemployment and the rate of change of money wage rates in the United Kingdom, 1861–1957. *Economica, 25,* 283–99.

Phillips, E. L. (1968). Achievement Place: Token reinforcement procedures in a home-style rehabilitation setting for "pre-delinquent" boys. *Journal of Applied Behavior Analysis, 1,* 213–23.

Phillips, E. L., Phillips, E. A., Fixsen, D. L., & Wolf, M. M. (1971). Achievement Place: Modification of the behavior of pre-delinquent boys within a token economy. *Journal of Applied Behavior Analysis, 4,* 45–59.

Phillips, E. L., Phillips, E. A., Wolf, M. M., & Fixsen, D. L. (1973). Achievement Place: Development of the elected manager system. *Journal of Applied Behavior Analysis, 6,* 541–61.

Phillips, R. (1972). Probability preferences of gamblers and non-gamblers. *Psychological Reports, 31,* 652–4.

Piaget, J. (1970). Piaget's theory. In P. Mussen (Ed.), *Carmichael's manual of child psychology* (Vol. 1, pp. 703–32). New York: John Wiley.

Pigou, A. C. (1933). *The theory of unemployment.* London: Macmillan.

Piliavin, I. M., Piliavin, J. A., & Rodin, J. (1975). Costs, diffusion and the stigmatized victim. *Journal of Personality and Social Psychology, 32,* 429–38.

Piliavin, J. A., & Piliavin, I. M. (1972). Effect of blood on reactions to a victim. *Journal of Personality and Social Psychology, 23,* 353–61.

Piliavin, I. M., Rodin, J., & Piliavin, J. A. (1969). Good samaritanism: An underground phenomenon? *Journal of Personality and Social Psychology, 13,* 289–99.

Pitts, R. E., Willenborg, J. F., & Sherrell, D. L. (1981–2). Consumer adaptation to gasoline price increases. *Journal of Consumer Research, 8,* 322–30.

Poirier, J. G., & Jones, F. D. (1977). A group operant approach to drug dependence in the military that failed: Retrospect. *Military Medicine, 142,* 366–9.

Polanyi, K. (1957). The economy as instituted process. In K. Polanyi, C. M. Arensberg, & H. W. Pearson (Eds.), *Trade and Market in the early empires* (pp. 243–70). New York: Free Press.

Polanyi, K. (1968). Appendix: notes on primitive money. In G. Dalton (Ed.), *Primitive, archaic and modern economies: essays of Karl Polanyi* (pp. 190–203). Garden City: Doubleday.

Pommer, D. A., & Streedbeck, D. (1974). Motivating staff performance in an operant learning program for children. *Journal of Applied Behavior Analysis, 7,* 217–21.

Poor, R. (1970). *4 days, 40 hours.* Cambridge, MA: Bursk and Poor.

Porter, L. W., & Lawler, E. E. (1968). *Managerial attitudes and performance.* Homewood, IL: Dorsey.

Posinsky, S. H. (1976). Yurok shell money and "pains." In E. Bornemannn (Ed.), *The psychoanalysis of money* (pp. 183–224). New York: Urizen.

Pospisil, L. (1963). *The Kapauku Papuans of West Guinea.* New York: Holt, Rinehart and Winston.

Powell, J. E. (1960). *Saving in a free society.* London: Hutchinson.

Premack, D. (1959). Towards empirical behavior laws: I. Positive reinforcement. *Psychological Review, 66,* 219–33.

Premack, D. (1965). Reinforcement theory. In D. Levine (Ed.), *Nebraska Symposium on Motivation, 1965* (pp. 123–88). Lincoln, NE: University of Nebraska Press.

Premack, D. (1971). Catching up with common sense or two sides of a generalization: reinforcement and punishment. In R. Glaser (Ed.), *The nature of reinforcement* (pp. 121–50). New York: Academic Press.

Prest, A. R. (1977). What is wrong with the UK tax system. In *The state of taxation* (pp. 3–12). London: Institute of Economic Affairs.

Preston, M. G., & Baratta, P. (1948). An experimental study of the auction-value of an uncertain outcome. *American Journal of Psychology, 61*, 183–93.

Price, J. A. (1971). Gambling in traditional Asia. *Anthropologica, 14*, 157–80.

Projector, D. S., & Weiss, G. S. (1966). *Survey of financial characteristics of consumers*. Washington, DC: Board of Governors of the Federal Reserve System.

Pruitt, D. G. (1962). Pattern and level of risk in gambling decisions. *Psychological Review, 69*, 187–201.

Pryor, F. (1977). The origins of money. *Journal of Money, Credit and Banking, 9*, 391–409.

Pryor, K. W., Haag, R., & O'Reilly, J. (1969). The creative porpoise: Training for novel behavior. *Journal of the Experimental Analysis of Behavior, 12*, 653–61.

Pulliam, H. R., & Dunford, C. (1980). *Programmed to learn*. New York: Columbia University Press.

Pyatt, F. G. (1964). *Priority patterns and the demands for household durable goods*. Cambridge: Cambridge University Press.

Quinney, R. (1965). Suicide, homicide, and economic development. *Social Forces, 43*, 401–6.

Rachlin, H. (1980). Economics and behavioral psychology. In J. E. R. Staddon (Ed.), *Limits to action* (pp. 205–36). New York: Academic Press.

Rachlin, H., & Green, L. (1972). Commitment, choice and self-control. *Journal of the Experimental Analysis of Behavior, 17*, 15–22.

Rachlin, H., Kagel, J. H., & Battalio, R. C. (1980). Substitutability in time allocation. *Psychological Review, 87*, 355–74.

Radke, M. (1972). *Manual of cost-reduction techniques*. London: McGraw-Hill.

Rahe, R. H., Meyer, M., Smith, M., Kjaer, G., & Holmes, T. H. (1964). Social stress and illness onset. *Journal of Psychosomatic Research, 8*, 35–44.

Raj, S. P. (1982). The effects of advertising on high and low loyalty consumer segments. *Journal of Consumer Research, 9*, 77–89.

Ramond, C. (1976). *Advertising research: the state of the art*. New York: Association of National Advertisers.

Ramsey, F. P. (1931). Truth and probability. In *The foundations of mathematics* (pp. 156–98). London: Routledge and Kegan Paul.

Rapaport, G.M. (1955). A study of the psychoanalytic theory of the anal character. Unpublished Ph.D. dissertation. Northwestern University.

Rapoport, A., & Wallsten, T. S. (1972). Individual decision behavior. *Annual Review of Psychology, 23*, 131–76.

Ratcliff, D. (1982). Behavioral discipline in Sunday school. *Journal of Psychology and Christianity, 1*, 26–9.

Ratliff, R. G., & Ratliff, A. R. (1971). Runway acquisition and extinction as a joint function of magnitude of reward and percentage of rewarded acquisition trials. *Learning and Motivation, 2*, 289–95.

Reekie, W. D. (1979). *Advertising and price*. London: The Advertising Association.

Reekie, W. D. (1981). *The economics of advertising*. London: Macmillan.

Reid, I. (1981). *Social class differences in Britain* (2nd ed.). London: Grant McIntyre.

Reid, M. G. (1962). Consumption, savings and windfall gains. *American Economic Review, 52,* 728–37.

Reisinger, J. J. (1972). The treatment of "anxiety-depression" via positive reinforcment and response cost. *Journal of Applied Behavior Analysis, 5,* 125–30.

Reitz, H. J., & Groff, G. K. (1974). Economic development and belief in locus of control among factory workers in four countries. *Journal of Cross-Cultural Psychology, 5,* 344–55.

Rescorla, R. A. (1967). Pavlovian conditioning and its proper control procedures. *Psychological Review, 74,* 71–80.

Rescorla, R. A. (1968). Probability of shock in the presence and absence of CS in fear conditioning. *Journal of Comparative and Physiological Psychology, 66,* 1–5.

Rescorla, R. A. (1973). Second-order conditioning: Implications for theories of learning. In F. J. McGuigan & D. B. Lumsden (Eds.), *Contemporary approaches to conditioning and learning* (pp. 127–50). Washington, DC: V. H. Winston & Sons.

Reynaud, P-L. (1954). *La psychologie economique.* Paris: Riviere.

Reynaud, P-L. (1981). *Economic psychology* (S. E. G. Lea, Trans.). New York: Praeger.

Rhodes, R. I. (1968). The disguised conservatism in evolutionary development theory. *Science and Society, 32,* 383–412.

Ricardo, D. (1912). *The principles of political economy and taxation* (3rd ed.). London: Dent. (First edition published 1817.)

Riches, D. (1975). Cash, credit and gambling in a modern Eskimo economy: Speculations on origins of spheres of economic exchange. *Man, 10,* 21–33.

Rickard, H. C., & Hart, J. L. (1973). Trial, error and the obvious: Control of "clean-up" behavior in a summer camp. *Journal of Community Psychology, 1,* 217–20.

Rickard, H. C., & Melvin, K. B. (1973). The effects of bonus tokens in a remedial classroom for behaviorally disturbed children. *Behavior Therapy, 4,* 378–85.

Rim, Y. (1982). Personality and attitudes concerning money. Paper presented at the seventh international symposium on economic psychology, Edinburgh.

Ringer, V. M. J. (1973). The use of a "token helper" in the management of classroom behavior patterns and in teacher training. *Journal of Applied Behavior Analysis, 6,* 671–7.

Robbins, R. H. (1973). Alcohol and the identity struggle: Some effects of economic change on interpersonal relations. *American Anthropologist, 75,* 99–122.

Roberts, W. A. (1969). Resistance to extinction following partial and consistent reinforcement with varying magnitudes of reward. *Journal of Comparative and Physiological Psychology, 67,* 395–400.

Robertson, T. S. (1971). *Innovative behavior and communication.* New York: Holt, Rinehart and Winston.

Robertson, T. S., & Rossiter, J. R. (1974). Children and commercial persuasion: an attribution theory analysis. *Journal of Consumer Research, 1,* 13–20.

Robertson, T. S., & Rossiter, J. R. (1976). Short-run advertising effects on children: A field study. *Journal of Marketing Research, 13,* 68–70.

Robinson, J. (1964). *Economic philosophy.* Harmondsworth: Penguin.

Roeder, J.-J., Chetcuti, Y., & Will, B. (1980). Behaviour and length of survival of populations of enriched and impoverished rats in the presence of a predator. *Biology of Behaviour, 5,* 361–9.

Rogers, E. M., & Shoemaker, F. (1971). *Communication of innovations.* New York: Free Press.

Rogers, E. M. (1969). *Modernization among peasants: the impact of communication.* New York: Holt, Rinehart and Winston.

Rogers, E. M. (1975–6). New product adoption and diffusion. *Journal of Consumer Research, 2,* 290–301.

Rogers, R. W., & Mewborn, R. (1976). Fear appeals and attitude change: Effects of a threat's noxiousness, probability of occurrence and the efficacy of coping responses. *Journal of Personality and Social Psychology, 34,* 54–61.

Rogosa, D. (1980). A critique of cross-lagged correlation. *Psychological Bulletin, 88,* 245–58.

Rosch, E. (1975). Cognitive representations of semantic categories. *Journal of Experimental Psychology: General, 104,* 192–223.

Rosch, E., & Mervis, C. B. (1975). Family resemblances: studies in the internal structure of categories. *Cognitive Psychology, 7,* 573–605.

Rosen, S. (1974). Hedonic prices and implicit markets: product differentiation in pure competition. *Journal of Political Economy, 82,* 34–55.

Rosenbaum, M. (1956). The effect of stimulus and background factors on the volunteering response. *Journal of Abnormal and Social Psychology, 53,* 118–21.

Rosenthal, A. M. (1964). *Thirty-eight witnesses.* New York: McGraw-Hill.

Rosenwald, G.C. (1972). Effectiveness of defenses against anal impulse control. *Journal of Consulting and Clinical Psychology, 39,* 292–8.

Rosman, A., & Rubel, P. G. (1978). Exchange as structure; or why doesn't everyone eat his own pigs. In G. Dalton (Ed.), *Research in Economic Anthropology* (Vol. 1, pp. 105–30). Greenwich, CT: JAI Press.

Ross, A. S., & Braband, J. (1973). Effect of increased responsibility on bystander intervention. II: The cue value of a blind person. *Journal of Personality and Social Psychology, 25,* 254–8.

Rotter, J. B. (1966). Generalized expectancies for internal versus external control of reinforcement. *Psychological Monographs, 80*(1) (Whole no. 609).

Royal Commission on the taxation of profits and income. (1954). London: Her Majesty's Stationery Office.

Rubner, A. (1966). *The economics of gambling.* London: Macmillan.

Rushton, J. P. (1975). Generosity in children: Immediate and long term effects of modeling, preaching, and moral judgment. *Journal of Personality and Social Psychology, 31,* 459–66.

Rushton, J. P. (1975). Generosity in children: immediate and long term effects of modeling, preaching and moral judgement. *Journal of Personality and Social Psychology, 31,* 459–66.

Rushton, J. P. (1980). *Altruism, socialization and society.* Englewood Cliffs, NJ: Prentice-Hall.

Rushton, J. P., & Sorrentino, R. M. (1981). *Altruism and helping behavior: Social, personality and developmental perspectives.* Hillsdale, NJ: Erlbaum.

Ruskin, R. S., & Maley, R. F. (1972). Item preference in a token economy ward store. *Journal of Applied Behavior Analysis, 5,* 373–8.

Sagi, A., & Hoffman, M. L. (1976). Empathic distress in the newborn. *Developmental Psychology, 12,* 175–6.

Sahlins, M. (1974). *Stone age economics.* London: Tavistock.

Salend, S. J., & Kovalich, B. (1981). A group response-cost system mediated by free tokens: An alternative to token reinforcement. *American Journal of Mental Deficiency, 86,* 184–7.

Sales, S. M. (1972). Economic threat as a determinant of conversion in authoritarian and non-authoritarian churches. *Journal of Personality and Social Psychology, 23,* 420–8.

Salisbury, R. F. (1962). *From stone to steel.* Melbourne: University of Melbourne Press.

Saltzberg, R. S., & Greenwald, M. A. (1977). Effects of a token system on attentiveness and punctuality in two string instrument classes. *Journal of Music Therapy, 14,* 27–38.

Samuelson, P. A. (1938). A note on the pure theory of consumer demand. *Economica, NS 5,* 61–71.

Samuelson, P. A. (1948). Consumption theory in terms of revealed preference. *Economica, 15,* 243–53.

Samuelson, P. A. (1958). An exact consumption-loan model of interest with or without the social contrivance of money. *Journal of Political Economy, 66,* 467–82.

Samuelson, P. A. (1976). *Economics* (10th ed.). New York: McGraw-Hill.

Samuelsson, K. (1961). *Religion and economic action* (E. G. French, Trans.)., Bonniers, Sweden: Svenska Bokforlaget.

Sanders, T. H. (1951). Effects of taxation on executives. Harvard University Graduate School of Business Administration.

Sandford, C. T. (1973). *Hidden costs of taxation.* London: Institute for Fiscal Studies.

Sandford, C. T. (1981). Economic aspects of compliance costs. In A. Peacock & F. Forte (Eds.), *The political economy of taxation* (pp. 163–73). Oxford: Basil Blackwell.

Sandford, C. T., Godwin, M., Hardwick, P., & Butterworth, I. (1981). *Costs and benefits of VAT.* London: Heinemann Educational Books.

Sanvictores, L. L. (1976). Mental health and economic growth. *Phillipine Journal of Mental Health, 7,* 18–21.

Saugstad, P., & Schioldberg, P. (1966). Value and size perception. *Scandinavian Journal of Psychology, 8,* 102–14.

Saunders, D. M. (1979). Aspects of schedule control within a gambling environment. Unpublished M.Sc. Thesis, Exeter University.

Sawyer, J. (1965). The altruism scale: A measure of cooperative, individualistic and competitive interpersonal orientation. *American Journal of Sociology, 71,* 407–16.

Scarlett, H., Press, A. N., & Crockett, W. H. (1971).Children's descriptions of peers: A Wernerian developmental analysis. *Child Development, 42,* 439–54.

Schachter, S., & Hall, R. (1952). Group-derived restraints and audience persuasion. *Human Relations, 5,* 397–406.

Schachter, S., & Singer, J. E. (1962). Cognitive, social and physiological determinants of emotional state. *Psychological Review, 69,* 379–99.

Schaffer, R. H. (1953). Job satisfaction as related to need satisfaction in work. *Psychological Monographs, 47* (Whole No. 364).

Schlegel, R. P., Crawford, C. A., & Sanborn, M. D. (1977). Correspondence and mediational properties of the Fishbein model: an application to adolescent alcohol use. *Journal of Experimental Social Psychology, 13,* 421–30.

Schmitt, D. R. (1974). Effects of reinforcement rate and reinforcer magnitude on choice behavior in humans. *Journal of the Experimental Analysis of Behavior, 21,* 409–19.

Schneider, H. K. (1974). *Economic man.* New York: Free Press.

Schneider, J. M. (1968). Skill versus chance activity preference and locus of control. *Journal of Consulting and Clinical Psychology, 32,* 333–7.

Schoenfeld, W. N. (1970). *Theory of reinforcement schedules.* E. Norwalk, CT: Appleton-Century-Crofts.

Schroeder, S. R., & Barrera, F. (1976) How token economy earnings are spent. *Mental Retardation, 14*(2), 20–4.

Schultz, D. (1976). *Theories of personality.* Monterey, CA: Brooks/Cole.

Schultz, H. (1938). *The theory and measurement of demand.* Chicago: Chicago University Press.

Schultz, T. W. (1961). Investment in human capital. *American Economic Review, 51*, 1–17.

Schumacher, H. C. (1934). The depression and its effect on the mental health of the child. *Mental Hygiene, 18*, 287–93.

Schumpeter, J. A. (1939). *Business cycles.* Vols. 1 & 2. New York: McGraw-Hill.

Schwartz, B. (1967). The social psychology of the gift. *American Journal of Sociology, 73*, 1–11.

Schwartz, B., Schuldenfrei, R., & Lacey, H. (1978). Operant psychology as factory psychology. *Behaviorism, 6*, 229–54.

Schwartz, R. A. (1970). Personal philanthropic contributions. *Journal of Political Economy, 78*, 1264–91.

Schwartz, R. D. & Orleans, S. (1967). On legal sanctions. *University of Chicago Law Review, 34*, 274–300.

Schwimmer, E. (1979). The self and the product: concepts of work in a comparative perspective. In S. Wallman (Ed.), *The social anthropology of work* (pp. 287–315). London: Academic Press.

Scitovsky, T. (1976). *The joyless economy.* Oxford: Oxford University Press.

Scitovsky, T. (1985). Psychologizing by economists. In H. Brandstaetter & E. Kirchler (Eds.), *Economic psychology* (pp. 17–20). Linz: Trauner.

Scodel, A., Minas, J. S., Ratoosh, P., & Lipetz, M. (1959). Some descriptive aspects of two-person non-zero-sum games. I. *Journal of Conflict Resolution, 3*, 114–9.

Scott, W. E. (1976). The effects of extrinsic reward on "intrinsic motivation." *Organizational Behavior and Human Performance, 15*, 117–29.

Seddon, D. (1978). *Relations of production.* London: Frank Cass.

Semin, G. R., & Manstead, A. S. R. (1979). Social psychology: Social or psychological? *British Journal of Social and Clinical Psychology, 18*, 191–202.

Service, E. R. (1971). *Cultural evolutionism.* New York: Holt, Rinehart and Winston.

Settle, R. B., & Golden, L. L. (1974). Attribution theory and advertiser credibility. *Journal of Marketing Research, 11*, 181–5.

Sevenster, P. (1973). Incompatibility of response and reward. In R. A. Hinde & J. Stevenson-Hinde (Eds.), *Constraints on learning* (pp. 265–83). London: Academic Press.

Sexauer, B. (1977). The role of habits and stocks in consumer expenditure. *Quarterly Journal of Economics, 91*, 127–42.

Shapiro, H. T. (1972). The index of consumer sentiment and economic forecasting: A reappraisal. In B. Strumpel, J. N. Morgan, & E. Zahn (Eds.), *Human behavior in economic affairs* (pp. 373–96). Amsterdam: North Holland.

Sharp, L. (1952). Steel axes for stone-age Australians. *Human Organisation, 11*, 17–22.

Shaw, G. K. (1984). *Rational expectations: an elementary exposition.* Brighton: Wheatsheaf Books.

Sheard, J. L. (1970). Intrasubject prediction of preferences for organizational types. *Journal of Applied Psychology, 54*, 248–52.

Shedletsky, R., & Voineskos, G. (1976). The rehabilitation of the chronic psychiatric patient: Beyond the hospital-based token economy system. *Social Psychiatry, 11,* 145–50.

Sheluga, D. A., Jaccard, J., & Jacoby, J. (1979–80). Preference, search, and choice: An integrative approach. *Journal of Consumer Research, 6,* 166–76.

Sherif, C. W., Sherif, M., & Nebergall, R. E. (1965). *Attitude and attitude change.* Philadelphia: Saunders.

Sherry, J. F. (1983). Gift-giving in anthropological perspective. *Journal of Consumer Research, 10,* 157–68.

Shettleworth, S. J. (1972). Constraints on learning. In D. S. Lehrman, R. A. Hinde, & E. Shaw (Eds.), *Advances in the study of behavior* (Vol. 4, pp. 1–68). New York: Academic Press.

Shettleworth, S. J., & Krebs, J. R. (1982). How marsh tits find their hoards: The role of site preference and spatial memory. *Journal of Experimental Psychology: Animal Behavior Processes, 8,* 354–75.

Shugan, S. M. (1980–1). The cost of thinking. *Journal of Consumer Research, 7,* 99–111.

Shurmer, P. (1971). The gift game. *New Society, 18,* 1242–4.

Shybut, J. (1968). Delay of gratification and severity of psychological disturbance among hospitalized psychiatric patients. *Journal of Consulting and Clinical Psychology, 32,* 462–8.

Siegal, M. (1981). Children's perceptions of adult economic needs. *Child Development, 52,* 379–2.

Siegel, J. J. (1979). Inflation-induced distortions in government and private savings statistics. *Review of Economics and Statistics, 61,* 83–90.

Sigel, I. E., & Cocking, R. R. (1977). Cognition and communication; a dialectic paradigm for development. In M. Lewis & L. Rosenblum (Eds.), *Interaction, conversation and the development of language* (pp. 207–26). New York: Wiley.

Signel, K. A. (1966). Cognitive complexity in person perception and nation perception: A developmental approach. *Journal of Personality, 34,* 517–37.

Simmel, G. (1978). *The philosophy of money* (T. Bottomore & D. Frisby, Trans.). London: Routledge and Kegan Paul. (Originally published 1900.)

Simmons, P. J. (1974). *Choice and demand.* London: Macmillan.

Simon, H. A. (1955). A behavioral theory of rational choice. *Quarterly Journal of Economics, 69,* 99–118.

Simon, H. A. (1957). *Models of man.* New York: Wiley.

Simon, J. L. (1970). *Issues in the economics of advertising.* Urbana, IL: University of Illinois Press.

Simon, J. L. (1974). Interpersonal welfare comparisons can be made – And used for redistributive decisions. *Kyklos, 27,* 63–98.

Simon, S. J., Ayllon, T., & Milan, M. A. (1982). Behavioral compensation: Contrastlike effects in the classroom. *Behavior Modification, 6,* 407–20.

Simpson, G. G. (1951). *The meaning of evolution.* New York: Mentor.

Sinclair, S. (1983). *The world car.* London: Euromonitor.

Sinden, J. A. (1974). A utility approach to the valuation of recreational and aesthetic experiences. *American Journal of Agricultural Economics, 56,* 61–72.

Singh, S. (1978). n Achievement, decision making, orientation, and work values of fast and slow progressing farmers in India. *Journal of Social Psychology, 106,* 153–60.

Singh, S., & Vasudeva, P. N. (1977). A factorial study of the perceived reasons for poverty. *Asian Journal of Psychology and Education, 2,* 51–6.

Sinha, D., & Chaubey, N. P. (1972). Achievement motive and rural economic development. *International Journal of Psychology, 7,* 267–72.

Skinner, B. F. (1938). *The behavior of organisms.* New York: Appleton-Century-Crofts.

Skinner, B. F. (1953). *Science and human behavior.* New York: Macmillan.

Skinner, B. F. (1962). Two "synthetic social relations." *Journal of the Experimental Analysis of Behavior, 5,* 531–33.

Skinner, B. F. (1969). *Contingencies of reinforcement: A theoretical analysis.* E. Norwalk, CT: Appleton-Century-Crofts.

Skinner, B. F. (1974). *About behaviorism.* New York: Knopf.

Slovic, P. (1964).The assessment of risk taking behavior. *Psychological Bulletin, 61,* 220–33.

Slovic, P., & Lichtenstein, S. (1968). Importance of variance preferences in gambling decisions. *Journal of Experimental Psychology, 78,* 646–54.

Slovic, P., & Lichtenstein, S. (1968). Relative importance of probabilities and payoffs in risk taking. *Journal of Experimental Psychology Monographs, 78*(3).

Smiles, S. (1875). *Thrift.* London: Murray.

Smith, A. (1908). *An enquiry into the nature and causes of the wealth of nations.* London: Bell. (Originally published 1776).

Smith, H. V., Fuller, R. G. C., & Forrest, D. W. (1975). Coin value and perceived size: a longitudinal study. *Perceptual and Motor Skills, 41,* 227–32.

Smith, L. C., & Fowler, S. A. (1984). Positive peer pressure: The effect of peer monitoring on children's disruptive behavior. *Journal of Applied Behavior Analysis, 17,* 213–27.

Smith, R. E., & Hunt, S. D. (1978). Attributional processes and effects in promotional situations. *Journal of Consumer Research, 5,* 149–58.

Smith, V. L. (1976). Experimental economics: induced value theory. *American Economic Review, 66*(2), 274–9.

Solomon, M. R. (1983). The role of products as social stimuli: A symbolic interactionist perspective. *Journal of Consumer Research, 10,* 319–29.

Sommer, R., & Aitkens, S. (1982–3). Mental maps of two supermarkets. *Journal of Consumer Research, 9,* 211–5.

Song, Y. D., & Yarbrough, T. E. (1978). Tax ethics and taxpayers' attitudes. *Public Administration Review, 38,* 442–52.

Sowter, A. P., Gabor, A., & Granger, C. W. J. (1971). The effect of price on choice: A theoretical and empirical investigation. *Applied Economics, 3,* 167–81.

Sparkman, R. M., & Lockander, W. B. (1980). Attribution theory and advertiser effectiveness. *Journal of Consumer Research, 7,* 219–24.

Spence, D. L. (1968). Patterns of retirement in San Francisco. In F. M. Carp (Ed.), *The retirement process.* Washington, DC: US Government Printing Office.

Spence, K. W. (1958). A theory of emotionally based drive (D) and its relation to performance in simple learning situations. *American Psychologist, 13,* 131–41.

Spencer, H. (1870). *Principles of psychology* (2nd ed.). London: Longman.

Spicer, M. W., & Becker, L. A. (1980). Fiscal inequity and tax evasion: An experimental approach. *National Tax Journal, 33,* 171–5.

Spicer, M. W., & Lundstedt, S. B. (1976). Understanding tax evasion. *Public Finance, 31*(2), 295–305.

Spicer, M. W., & Thomas, J. E. (1982). Audit probabilities and the tax evasion decision: An experimental approach. *Journal of Economic Psychology, 2,* 241–5.

Springer, W. L. (1968). Did the 1968 surcharge really work? *American Economic Review, 65,* 644–59.

Srinivasan, V., & Kesavan, R. (1976–7). An alternative interpretation of the linear learning model of brand choice. *Journal of Consumer Research, 3,* 76–83.

Staats, A. W., & Staats, C. K. (1958). Attitudes established by classical conditioning. *Journal of Abnormal and Social Psychology, 57,* 37–40.

Stacey, B. G. (1982). Economic socialization in the pre-adult years. *British Journal of Social Psychology, 21,* 159–73.

Stacey, B. G. (1983). Economic socialization. *British Journal of Social Psychology, 22,* 265–6.

Staddon, J. E. R. (1980). *Limits to action.* New York: Academic Press.

Stafford, F. P. (1980). Some comments on the papers by Kagel and Battalio and by Smith. In J. Kmenta & J. B. Ramsey (Eds.), *Evaluation of econometric models* (pp. 407–10). New York: Academic Press.

Stanjek, K. (1978). [The giving of gifts: its function and development in the early years.] *Zeitschrift fur Entwicklungspsychologie und Padagogische Psychologie, 10,* 103–13.

Starke, F. A., & Behling, O. (1975). A test of two postulates of expectancy theory. *Academy of Management Journal, 18,* 703–14.

Staw, B. M. (1976). Knee-deep in the Big Muddy: A study of escalating commitment to a chosen course of action. *Organizational Behavior and Human Performance, 16,* 27–44.

Steers, R. M. (1975). Effects of need for achievement on the job performance-job attitude relationship. *Journal of Applied Psychology, 60,* 678–82.

Steinberg, S. A., & Yalch, R. F. (1978). When eating begets buying: The effects of food samples on obese and nonobese shoppers. *Journal of Consumer Research, 4,* 243–6.

Steinglass, P. (1975). The simulated drinking gang: An experimental model for the study of a systems approach to alcoholism. II: Findings and replications. *Journal of Nervous and Mental Diseases, 161,* 110–22.

Steinglass, P., & Wolin, S. (1974). Explorations of a systems approach to alcoholism. *Archives of General Psychiatry, 31,* 527–32.

Stephenson, G. M. (1984). Intergroup and interpersonal dimensions of bargaining and negotiation. In H. Tajfel (Ed.), *The social dimension: European developments in social psychology* Vol. 2 (pp. 646–67). Cambridge: Cambridge University Press.

Steurle, E. (1983). Building new wealth by preserving old wealth: Savings and investment tax incentives in the postwar era. *National Tax Journal, 36,* 307–19.

Stevens, S. S. (1946). On the theory of scales of measurement. *Science, 103,* 677–80.

Stevens, S. S. (1957). On the psychophysical law. *Psychological Review, 64,* 153–81.

Stevens, S. S. (1959). Measurement, psychophysics, and utility. In C. W. Churchman & P. Ratoosh (Eds.), *Measurement: Definitions and theories* (pp. 18–63). New York: Wiley.

Stewart, I. M. T. (1979). *Reasoning and method in economics.* London: McGraw-Hill.

Stigler, G. J. (1961). The economics of information. *Journal of Political Economy, 69,* 213–25.

Stoetzel, J., Sauerwein, J., & Vulpian, A. de (1954). Sondages francais: Etudes sur la consommation. In P-L. Reynaud (Ed.), *La psychologie economiqe* (pp. 161–209). Paris: Riviere.

Stone, C. (1976). The political economy of gambling in a neocolonial economy. *Review of Black Political Economy, 6,* 189–99.

Stone, J. R. N. (1954). Linear expenditure systems and demand analysis: An application to the pattern of British demand. *Economic Journal, 64,* 511–27.

Stone, R. (1954). *The measurement of consumers' expenditure and behaviour in the United Kingdom 1920–1938* (Vol. 1). Cambridge: Cambridge University Press.

Stone, R., & Rowe, D. A. (1966). *The measurement of consumers' expenditure and behaviour in the United Kingdom 1920–1938* (Vol. 2). Cambridge: Cambridge University Press.

Stotland, E. (1969). Exploratory investigations of empathy. In L. Berkowitz (Ed.), *Advances in experimental social psychology* (Vol. 4, pp. 271–314). New York: Academic Press.

Strauss, A. L. (1952). The development and transformations of monetary meanings in the child. *American Sociological Review, 17,* 275–84.

Strickland, L. H., & Grote, F. W. (1967). Temporal presentation of winning symbols and slot maching playing. *Journal of Experimental Psychology, 74,* 10–3.

Strickland, L. H., Lewicki, R. J., & Katz, A. M. (1966). Temporal orientation and perceived control as determinants of risk-taking. *Journal of Experimental and Social Psychology, 2,* 143–51.

Strober, M. H., & Weinberg, C. B. (1977–8). Working wives and major family expenditures. *Journal of Consumer Research, 4,* 141–7.

Strotz, R. H. (1957). The empirical implications of a utility tree. *Econometrica, 25,* 269–80.

Strotz, R. H. (1959). The utility tree – a correction and further appraisal. *Econometrica, 27,* 482–8.

Strumpel, B. (1976). *Economic means for human needs.* Ann Arbor, MI: Survey Research Center, Institute for Social Research, University of Michigan.

Suits, D. B. (1970). *Principles of economics.* London: Harper & Row.

Suls, J. M., & Miller, R. L. (1977). *Social comparison processes: Theoretical and empirical perspectives.* Washington, DC: Hemisphere.

Summers, L. H. (1981). Capital taxation and accumulation in a life-cycle growth model. *American Economic Review, 71,* 533–44.

Surrey, M. J. C. (1974). *An introduction to econometrics.* Oxford: Clarendon.

Sutton, R. S. (1962). Behavior in the attainment of economic concepts. *Journal of Psychology, 53,* 37–46.

Sutton-Smith, B. (1972). *The folkgames of children.* Austin: University of Texas Press.

Swift, M. G. (1964). Capital, saving and credit in a Malay peasant economy. In R. Firth & B. S. Yamey (Eds.), *Capital, saving and credit in peasant societies* (pp. 133–56). London: Allen & Unwin.

Swinyard, W. R. (1981). The interaction between comparative advertising and copy claim variation. *Journal of Marketing Research, 18,* 175–86.

Taira, K. (1969). Consumer preferences, poverty norms and extent of poverty. *Quarterly Journal of Economics and Business, 9,* 31–44.

Tajfel, H. (1957). Value and the perceived judgement of magnitude. *Psychological Review, 64,* 192–204.

Takooshian, H., Haber, S., & Lucido, D. J. (1977, February) Who wouldn't help a lost child? You maybe. *Psychology Today,* 67.

Tanner, B. A., Parrino, J. J., & Daniels, A. C. (1975). A token economy with "automated" data collection. *Behavior Therapy, 6,* 111–8.

Tarpy, R. M. (1982). *Principles of animal learning and motivation.* Glenview, IL: Scott Foresman.

Tarpy, R. M., & Sawabini, F.L. (1974). Reinforcement delay: A selective review of the last decade. *Psychological Bulletin, 81,* 984–97.

Taussig, M. (1977). The genesis of capitalism among a South American Peasantry: Devil's labour and the baptism of money. *Comparative Studies of Society and History, 19,* 130–55.

Tawney, R. H. (1926). *Religion and the rise of capitalism.* London: Murray.

Taylor, D. M., & Brown, R. J. (1979). Towards a more social social psychology. *British Journal of Social and Clinical Psychology, 18,* 173–80.

Taylor, F. W. (1947). *Scientific management.* New York: Harper & Row. (Original work published 1912.)

Taylor, G. T. (1974). Stimulus change and complexity in exploratory behavior. *Animal Learning and Behavior, 2,* 115–8.

Teger, A. I. (1980). *Too much invested to quit.* New York: Pergamon.

Terkel, S. (1974). *Working.* Harmondsworth: Penguin.

The perception of poverty in Europe (1977). Brussels: Commission of the European Communities.

Theil, H. (1965). The information approach to demand analysis. *Econometrica, 33,* 67–87.

Thibaut, J. W., & Kelley, H. H. (1959). *The social psychology of groups.* New York: Wiley.

Thompson, R. F. (1972). Sensory preconditioning. In R. F. Thompson & J. S. Voss (Eds.), *Topics in learning and performance* (pp. 105–29). New York: Academic Press.

Thrall, C. A. (1978). Who does what? children's work in the household. *Human Relations, 31,* 249–65.

Thurstone, L. L. (1927). A law of comparative judgement. *Psychological Review, 34,* 273–86.

Thurstone, L. L. (1928). Attitudes can be measured. *American Journal of Sociology, 33,* 529–54.

Thurstone, L. L. (1931a). *The measurement of social attitudes.* Chicago: University of Chicago Press.

Thurstone, L. L. (1931b). The indifference function. *Journal of Social Psychology, 2,* 139–67.

Tillman, R., & McLaughlin, C. P. (1974). Six executives on Galbraith. *Harvard Business Review, 52*(3), 18–34; 155–60.

Titmuss, R. M. (1970). *The gift relationship.* London: Allen & Unwin.

Tobin, J. (1965). The theory of portfolio selection. In F. Hahn & F. Brechling (Eds.), *The theory of interest rates* (pp. 3–51). London: Macmillan.

Tolman, E. C. (1938). The determinants of behavior at a choice point. *Psychological Review, 45,* 1–41.

Tolman, E. C. (1955). Principles of performance. *Psychological Review, 62,* 315–26.

Toner, I. J., Holstein, R. B., & Hetherington, E. M. (1977). Age and overt vocalization in delay-maintenance behavior in children. *Journal of Experimental Child Psychology, 24,* 123–8.

Toop, A. (1978). *Only 3.95!.* London: The Sales Machine.

Topley, M. (1964). Capital, saving and credit among indigenous rice farmers and immigrant vegetable farmers in Hong Kong's New Territories. In R. Firth & B. S. Yamey (Eds.), *Capital, saving and credit in peasant societies* (pp. 157–86). London: Allen & Unwin.

Triandis, H. C. (1973). Subjective culture and economic development. *International Journal of Psychology, 8,* 163–80.

Trist, E. L., & Bamforth, K. W. (1951). Some social and psychological consequences of the longwall method of coal-getting. *Human Relations, 4,* 1–38.

Trivers, R. L. (1971). The evolution of reciprocal altruism. *Quarterly Review of Biology, 46,* 35–7.

Tsurumi, H., & Tsurumi, Y. (1980). A Bayesian test of the product life-cycle hypothesis as applied to the United-States demand for color-TV sets. *International Economic Review, 21,* 583–97.

Tuck, M. (1976). *How do we chose?* London: Methuen.

Tufte, E. R. (1978). *Political control of the economy.* Princeton: Princeton University Press.

Tullock, G. (1976). *The vote motive.* London: Institute of Economic Affairs.

Turchi, B. A. (1980). *Estimation of the subjective rate of time preference.* Paper presented at the fifth international symposium on economic psychology, Leuven, August.

Turner, C. F., & Krauss, E. (1978). Fallible indicators of the subjective state of the nation. *American Psychologist, 33,* 456–70.

Turner, J. L., Foa, E. B., & Foa, U. G. (1971). Interpersonal reinforcers: Classification, inter-relationships and some differential properties. *Journal of Personality and Social Psychology, 19,* 168–80.

Tversky, A. (1967). Additivity, utility and subjective probability. *Journal of Mathematical Psychology, 4,* 175–202.

Tversky, A. (1969). Intransitivity of preferences. *Psychological Review, 76,* 31–48.

Tversky, A. (1972). Elimination by aspects: A theory of choice. *Psychological Review, 79,* 281–299.

Tversky, A., & Kahnemen, D. (1974). Judgement under uncertainty: Heuristics and biases. *Science, 185,* 1124–31.

Tversky, A., & Russo, J. E. (1969). Substitutability and similarity in binary choices. *Journal of Mathematical Psychology, 6,* 1–12.

Tysoe, M. (1983). Children and money. *New Society, 66,* 433–4.

Underwood, B., Berenson, J. F., Berenson, R. J., Cheng, K. K., Wilson, D., Kulik, J., Moore, B. S., Wenzel, G., and Cobbleigh, T. (1977). Attention, negative affect & altruism: An ecological validation. *Personality and Social Psychology Bulletin, 3,* 51–3.

United Nations (1968). *A system of national accounts and supporting statistics* (Revision 3). New York: Author.

Uribe Villegas, O. (1962). El desarrollo economico-social y las actitudes psicosociales. *Revista Mexicana di Sociologia, 24,* 441–61.

Van de Braak, H. (1983). Taxation and tax resistance. *Journal of Economic Psychology, 3,* 95–111.

Van der Plight, J., & Eiser, J. R. (1984). Dimensional salience, judgment and attitudes. In J. R. Eiser (Ed.), *Attitudinal judgment* (pp. 161–78). New York: Springer.

Vanden Abeele, P. (1983). The index of consumer sentiment: predictability and predictive power in the EEC. *Journal of Economic Psychology, 3,* 1–17.

Van Duijn, J. J. (1983). *The long wave in economic life.* London: Allen & Unwin.

Vasta, R. (1981). On token rewards and real dangers: a look at the data. *Behavior Modification, 5,* 129–40.

Vaughn, R. (1980). How advertising works: A planning model. *Journal of Advertising Research, 20*(5), 27–33.

Veblen, T. (1979). *The theory of the leisure class.* Harmondsworth: Penguin. (Original work published 1899.)

Vera-Lapuz, L. (1974). The changing Filipino personality. *Philippine Journal of Mental Health, 5,* 97–9.

Verhallen, T. M. M. (1982). Scarcity and consumer choice behavior. *Journal of Economic Psychology, 2,* 299–322.

Vogel, J. (1974). Taxation and public opinion in Sweden: An interpretation of recent survey data. *National Tax Journal, 28,* 499–513.

Voissem, N. H., & Sistrunk, F. (1971). Communication schedule and cooperative game behavior. *Journal of Personality and Social Psychology, 19,* 160–7.

Von Fleckenstein, F. (1974). Are innovativeness scales useful? *Rural Sociology, 39,* 257–60.

Von Grumbkow, J., & Warneryd, K-E. (1984). *Does the tax system ruin the motivation to seek advancement?.* Paper presented at the ninth international symposium on economic psychology, Tilburg.

Vroom, V. H. (1964). *Work and motivation.* New York: Wiley.

Waddington, C. H. (1957). *The strategy of the genes.* London: Allen & Unwin.

Wadel, C. (1979). The hidden work of everyday life. In S. Wallman (Ed.), *The social anthropology of work* (pp. 365–84). London: Academic Press.

Wahba, M. A., & Bridwell, L.G. (1973). Maslow reconsidered: A review of research on the need hierarchy theory. *Proceedings of the thirty-third Annual Meeting of the Academy of Management,* 514–20.

Wahlund, R. (1983). *The income tax system and the will to be promoted.* Paper presented at the eighth international symposium on economic psychology, Bologna.

Waines, N. O. (1983). *Development of economic concepts in Egyptian children.* Unpublished manuscript.

Walker, H. M., & Buckley, N. K. (1972). Programming generalization and maintenance of treatment effects across time and across settings. *Journal of Applied Behavior Analysis, 5,* 209–24.

Walker, H. M., Hops, H., & Johnson, S. M. (1975). Generalization and maintenance of classroom treatment effects. *Behavior Therapy, 6,* 188–200.

Wallace, A. (1864). The origin of human races and the antiquity of man deduced from "the theory of natural selection." *Anthropological Review, 2,* 158–87.

Wallman, S. (1979). Introduction. In S. Wallman (Ed.), *The social anthropology of work* (pp. 1–24). London: Academic Press.

Walls (1984). *Pocket money monitor, 1984.* Surrey: Author.

Walsh, B. M. (1982). The demand for alcohol in the UK: A comment. *Journal of Industrial Economics, 30,* 439–66.

Walster, E., Aronson, E., & Abrahams, D. (1966). On increasing the persuasiveness of a low prestige communicator. *Journal of Experimental Social Psychology, 2,* 325–42.

Walster, E., Bersheid, E., & Walster, G. W. (1976). New directions in equity research. *Advances in Experimental Social Psychology, 9,* 1–42.

Wanous, J. P. (1972). Occupational preferences: Perceptions of valence and instrumentality and objective data. *Journal of Applied Psychology, 56,* 152–5.

Ward, S. (1972). Children's reactions to commercials. *Journal of Advertising Research, 12,* 37–45.

Ward, S. (1974). Consumer socialization. *Journal of Consumer Research, 1,* 1–14.

Ward, S., Levinson, D., & Wackman, D. B. (1972). Children's attention to television advertising. In E. A. Rubinstein, G. A. Comstock, & J. P. Murray

(Eds.), *Television and social behavior: Vol 4* (pp. 491–515). Washington, DC: US Dept of Health, Education and Welfare.

Ward, S., & Wackman, D. B. (1972). Children's purchase influence attempts and parental yielding. *Journal of Marketing Research, 9,* 316–9.

Ward, S., Wackman, D. B., & Wartella, E. (1977). *How children learn to buy.* London: Sage.

Ware, C. F. (1942). *The consumer goes to war.* New York: Funk and Wagnalls.

Warneryd, K-E. (1983). *Taxes and economic behaviour: the Swedish tax-payer facing a tax system change.* Paper presented at the eighth international symposium on economic psychology, Bologna.

Warneryd, K-E., & Walerud, B. (1982). Taxes and economic behaviour: Some interview data on tax evasion in Sweden. *Journal of Economic Psychology, 2,* 187–211.

Warr, P. (1983). Work, jobs and unemployment. *Bulletin of the British Psychological Society, 36,* 305–11.

Warshaw, P. R. (1980). Buying a gift: Product price moderation of social normative influences on gift purchase intentions. *Personality and Social Psychology Bulletin, 6,* 143–8.

Wason, P. (1977). The theory of formal operations – a critique. In B. A. Geber (Ed.), *Piaget and knowing: Studies in genetic epistemology.* London: Routledge and Kegan Paul.

Wason, P. C., & Shapiro, D. (1971). Natural and controlled experience in a reasoning problem. *Quarterly Journal of Experimental Psychology, 23,* 63–71.

Watts, H. W., & Horner, D. (1977). Labor-supply response of husbands. In H. W. Watts & A. Rees (Eds.), *The New Jersey income-maintenance experiment: Vol. 2.*

Watts, H. W., & Horner, D. (1977). Labor-supply response of husbands. In H. W. Watts & A. Rees (Eds.), *The New Jersey income-maintenance experiment: Vol. 2. Labor-supply responses* (pp. 57–114). New York: Academic Press.

Webb, M. (1982). The labour market. In I. Reid & E. Wormald (Eds.), *Sex differences in Britain* (pp. 114–74). London: Grant McIntyre.

Weber, M. (1976). *The Protestant ethic and the sprit of capitalism* (2nd ed., T. Parsons, Trans.). London: Allen & Unwin (Originally published, 1904.)

Weber, S. J., & Cook, T. D. (1972). Subject effects in laboratory research. *Psychological Bulletin, 77,* 273–95.

Weber, W. (1970). The effect of interest rates on aggregate consumption. *American Economic Review, 60,* 591–600.

Weber, W. (1975). Interest rates, inflation, and consumer expenditures. *American Economic Review, 65,* 843–58.

Webley, P. (1983). Economic socialization in the pre-adult years: a comment on Stacey. *British Journal of Social Psychology, 22,* 264–5.

Webley, P., & Halstead, S. (1985). Tax evasion on the micro: significant simulations or expedient experiments?. *Journal of Interdisciplinary Economics, 1,* 87–100.

Webley, P., Lea, S. E. G., & Hussein, G. (1983). *A characteristics approach to money and the changeover from 1 pound note to 1 pound coin.* Paper presented at the eighth international symposium on economic psychology, Bologna.

Webley, P., Lea, S. E. G., & Portalska, R. (1983). The unacceptability of money as a gift. *Journal of Economic Psychology, 4,* 223–38.

Webley, P., Morris, I., & Amstutz, F. (1985). Tax evasion during a small business simulation. In H. Brandstaetter & E. Kirchler (Eds.), *Economic Psychology* (pp. 233–42). Linz: Trauner.

Webley, P., & Wrigley, V. (1983). The development of conceptions of unemployment among adolescents. *Journal of Adolescence, 6,* 317–28.

Weigel, R. H., & Newman, L. S. (1976). Increasing attitude-behavior correspondence by broadening the scope of the behavioral measure. *Journal of Personality and Social Psychology, 33,* 793–802.

Weigel, R. H., Vernon, D. T. A., & Tognacci, L. N. (1974). Specificity of the attitude as a determinant of attitude-behavior congruence. *Journal of Personality and Social Psychology, 30,* 724–8.

Weinberg, C. B., & Winer, R. S. (1983–4). Working wives and major family expenditures: Replication and extension. *Journal of Consumer Research, 10,* 259–63.

Weiner, B. (1980). *Human motivation.* New York: Holt, Rinehart & Winston,

Weiner, H. (1962). Some effects of response cost upon human operant behavior. *Journal of the Experimental Analysis of Behavior, 5,* 201–8.

Weiner, H. (1969). Human behavioral persistence. *Psychological Record, 20,* 445–56.

Weiner, H. (1964). Conditioning history and human fixed-interval performance. *Journal of the Experimental Analysis of Behavior, 7,* 383–5.

Weinstein, M. (1969). Achievement motivation and risk preference. *Journal of Personality and Social Psychology, 12,* 153–72.

Weisberg, P., Wilde, C. A., & Ballard, K. J. (1975). Decreases in selection of edible rewards by disadvantaged preschool children. *Psychological Reports, 36,* 825–6.

Wernimont, P., & Fitzpatrick, S. (1972). The meaning of money. *Journal of Applied Psychology, 56,* 218–26.

West, M. A., & Newton, P. (1984). Social interaction in adolescent development: schools, sex roles and entry to work. In W. Doise & A. Palmonari (Eds.), *Social interaction in individual development* (pp. 249–60). Cambridge: Cambridge University Press.

Westphal, C. R. (1975). Variables affecting the efficacy of a token economy. *Mental Retardation, 13,* 32–4.

Wetzel, J., & Hoffer, G. (1982–83). Consumer demand for automobiles: A disaggregated market approach. *Journal of Consumer Research, 9,* 195–9.

Wexler, D. B. (1973). Token and taboo: Behavior modification, token economies, and the law. *California Law Review, 61,* 81–109.

Wexler, D. B. (1975). Behavior modification and other behavor change procedures: The emerging law and the proposed Florida guidelines. *Criminal Law Bulletin, 11,* 600–16.

Wharton, C. R. (1969). The green revolution: Cornucopia or Pandora's box? *Foreign Affairs, 47,* 68–9.

Wheeler, D. (1980). Basic needs fulfilment and economic growth. *Journal of Development Economics, 7,* 435–51.

White, L. A. (1959). *The evolution of culture.* New York: McGraw-Hill.

White, L. K., & Brinkerhoff, D. B. (1981a). The sexual division of labour: Evidence from childhood. *Social Forces, 60,* 170–81.

White, L. K., & Brinkerhoff, D. B. (1981b). Children's work in the family: Its significance and meaning. *Journal of Marriage and the Family, 43,* 789–98.

Whitman, R. H. (1942). Demand functions for merchandise at retail. In O. Lange, F. McIntyre, & T. O. Yntema (Eds.), *Studies in mathematical economics and econometrics* (pp. 208–21). Chicago: University of Chicago Press.

Wicker, A. W. (1969). Attitudes versus actions: The relationship of verbal and overt behavioral responses to attitude objects. *Journal of Social Issues, 25,* 41–78.

Wicklund, R. A., & Brehm, J. W. (1976). *Perspective on cognitive dissonance.* Hillsdale, NJ: Erlbaum.

Wilder, R. P. (1974). Advertising and inter-industry competition: Testing a Galbraithian hypothesis. *Journal of Industrial Economics, 22,* 215–24.

Wilkinson, G. S. (1984). Food sharing in the vampire bat. *Nature, 308,* 181.

Wilkinson, L., & Repucci, N. D. (1973). Perceptions of social climate among participants in token economy and non-token economy cottages in a juvenile correctional institution. *American Journal of Community Psychology, 1,* 36–43.

Will, G. F. (1982, May 10). But first a message from . . . . *Newsweek,* p. 98.

Williams, C. (1983). The work-ethic, non-work and leisure in an age of automation. *Australian and New Zealand Journal of Sociology, 19,* 216–37.

Williamson, J. (1978). *Decoding advertisements.* London: Marion Boyars.

Willis, P. (1977). *Learning to labour: How working class kids get working class jobs.* London: Saxon House.

Wilson, D. T. (1977). Dyadic interactions. In A. G. Woodside, J. N. Sheth, & P. D. Bennett (Eds.), *Consumer and industrial buying behavior* (pp. 355–65). New York: North-Holland.

Wilson, E. (1972). *To the Finland Station.* London: Collins. (Original edition published 1940.)

Wilson, E. O. (1975). *Sociobiology.* Cambridge, MA: Harvard University Press.

Wilson, E. O. (1978). *On human nature.* Cambridge: Harvard University Press.

Winett, R. A. (1974). Behavior modification and social change. *Professional Psychology, 5,* 244–50.

Wingate, J. H. (1958, October). Developments in the super market field. *New York Retailer,* p. 6.

Winkler, R. C. (1971a). The relevance of economic theory and technology to token reinforcement systems. *Behaviour Research and Therapy, 9,* 81–8.

Winkler, R. C. (1971b). Reinforcement schedules for individual patients in a token economy. *Behavior Therapy, 2,* 534–7.

Winkler, R. C. (1972). A theory of equilibrium in token economies. *Journal of Abnormal Psychology, 79,* 169–73.

Winkler, R. C. (1973). An experimental analysis of economic balance, savings and wages in a token economy. *Behavior Therapy, 4,* 22–40.

Winkler, R. C. (1980). Behavioral economics, token economies and applied behavioral analysis. In J. E. R. Staddon (Ed.), *Limits to Action* (pp. 269–97). New York: Academic Press.

Winterbottom, M. R. (1958). The relation of need for achievement to learning experiences in independence and mastery. In J. W. Atkinson (Ed.), *Motives in fantasy, action and society* (pp. 479–92). Princeton, NJ: Van Nostrand.

Wiseman, T. (1974). *The money motive.* London: Hutchinson.

Wolf, M. M., Giles, D. K., & Hall, V. R. (1968). Experiments with token reinforcement in a remedial classroom. *Behaviour Research and Therapy, 6,* 51–64.

Wolfe, J. B. (1936). Effectiveness of token-rewards for chimpanzees. *Comparative Psychology Monographs, 12*(5) (Whole no. 60).

Wolff, R., & Gray, J. J. (1973). Physical attributes of tokens: Comparison. *Psychological Reports, 32,* 675–8.

Wood, R., & Flynn, J. M. (1978). A self-evaluation token system versus an external evaluation token system alone in a residential setting with predelinquent youth. *Journal of Applied Behavior Analysis, 11,* 503–12.

Woodmansec, J. J. (1970). The pupil response as a measure of social attitudes. In G. F. Summers (Ed.), *Attitude measurement*. Chicago: Rand McNally.

Woods, P. A., Higson, P. J., & Tannahill, M. M. (1984). Token-economy programmes with chronic psychiatric patients: The importance of direct measurement and objective evaluation for long-term maintenance. *Behaviour Research and Therapy, 22,* 41–51.

Wooley, S. C., & Blackwell, B. (1975). A behavioral probe into social contingencies in a psychosomatic ward. *Journal of Applied Behavior Analysis, 8,* 337–9.

Working, E. J. (1927). What do statistical "demand curves" show? *Quarterly Journal of Economics, 41,* 212–35.

Wray, I., & Dickerson, M. G. (1981). Cessation of high-frequency gambling and "withdrawal" symptoms. *British Journal of Addiction, 76,* 401–5.

Wright, P., & Rip, P. D. (1980). Product class advertising effects on first-time buyers decision strategies. *Journal of Consumer Research, 7,* 176–88.

Wrightsman, L. S. (1969). Wallace supporters and adherence to "law and order." *Journal of Personality and Social Psychology, 13,* 17–22.

Wyer, R. S. (1974). *Cognitive organization and change: An information-processing approach.* Potomac, MD: Erlbaum.

Yaari, M. E. (1965). Uncertain lifetimes, life insurance, and the theory of the consumer. *Review of Economic Studies, 32,* 137–50.

Yamauchi, K. T., & Templer, D. I. (1982). The development of a money attitude scale. *Journal of Personality Assessment, 46,* 522–8.

Yamey, B. S. (1964). The study of peasant economic systems: some concluding comments and questions. In R. Firth & B. S. Yamey (Eds.), *Capital, saving and credit in peasant societies* (pp. 376–86). London: Allen & Unwin.

Yates, B. T., & Mischel, W. (1979). Young children's preferred attentional strategies for delaying gratification. *Journal of Personality and Social Psychology, 37,* 286–300.

Young, M., & Willmott, P. (1973). *The symmetrical family.* London: Routledge and Kegan Paul.

Yuchtman (Yaar), E. (1976). Effect of social-psychological factors on subjective economic welfare. In B. Strumpel (Ed.), *Economic means for human needs* (pp. 107–29). Ann Arbor, MI: Survey Research Center, Institute for Social Research, University of Michigan.

Yukl, G., Wexley, K. N., & Seymore, J. (1972). Effectiveness of pay incentives under variable ratio and continuous reinforcement schedules. *Journal of Applied Psychology, 56,* 10–3.

Zanot, E. J. (1984). Public attitudes towards advertising: The American experience. *International Journal of Advertising, 3,* 3–15.

Zeldow, P. B. (1976). Some antitherapeutic effects of the token economy: A case in point. *Psychiatry, 39,* 318–24.

Zelizer, V. A. (1978). Human values and the market: The case of life insurance and death in nineteenth century America. *American Journal of Sociology, 84,* 591–610.

Zohar, D. (1980). Promoting the use of personal protective equipment by behavior modification techniques. *Journal of Safety Research, 12,* 78–85.

AUTHOR INDEX

SUBJECT INDEX